Paula Byrne was born in Birkenhead and has a PhD from the University of Liverpool, where she is a Research Fellow in English Literature. Her first book, *Jane Austen and the Theatre*, was shortlisted for the Theatre Book Prize. A regular contributor to the *Times Literary Supplement*, she lives in Warwickshire with her two young children and her husband, the critic and biographer Jonathan Bate.

For automatic updates on Paula Byrne visit harperperennial.co.uk and register for AuthorTracker.

From the reviews of *Perdita*:

'Mary Robinson, scandalous darling of the 18th-century stage and letters, is given a welcome rebirth. A full-scale literary biography . . . a fitting tribute to her' *Observer*

'Enthralling and perceptive . . . A fine biographer has conjured up a dazzling personality and brought her, laughing, back to life' *Sunday Times*

'Robinson's is a life that bears the retelling. She cuts a figure in the history of celebrity culture and in literary history. Paula Byrne's full-scale biography is scholarly, lively and important' *Daily Telegraph*

'She was, many believed, the most beautiful woman in England. And one of the most fascinating . . . small wonder that Perdita has been dubbed the Madonna of the eighteenth century. A scholarly, entertaining and well-written book' ADAM SISMAN, *Literary Review*

'We seem to have an insatiable appetite for biographies of 18th-century women . . . a superbly researched and narrated life of a woman whose capacity for self-transformation, when combined with beauty, talent, wit and passion suggest that she may be the most interesting of them all' MIRANDA SEYMOUR, *Sunday Times*

'Engaging . . . Here was a woman who entertained Wordsworth, Coleridge, and William Godwin, and of whom Coleridge would write "her work was good, bad and indifferent . . . but full and overflowing"' *Sunday Telegraph*

'Robinson's story – particularly the early, dazzling part – makes highly enjoyable entertainment' *New Statesman*

Also by Paula Byrne

Jane Austen and the Theatre

Perdita

THE LIFE OF MARY ROBINSON

PAULA BYRNE

HARPER PERENNIAL

Harper Perennial
An imprint of HarperCollins*Publishers*
77–85 Fulham Palace Road,
Hammersmith,
London W6 8JB

www.harperperennial.co.uk

This edition published by Harper Perennial 2005

3

First published in Great Britain by HarperCollins*Publishers* 2004

A catalogue record for this book
is available from the British Library

ISBN 0-00-716459-9

Set in Postscript Linotype Minion by
Rowland Phototypesetting Ltd,
Bury St Edmunds, Suffolk

Printed and bound in Great Britain
by Clays Ltd, St Ives plc

In memory of my grandmother,
another Mary Robinson

CONTENTS

LIST OF ILLUSTRATIONS ix
ACKNOWLEDGEMENTS xi
PROLOGUE 1

PART ONE: ACTRESS

1. 'During a Tempestuous Night' 7
2. A Young Lady's Entrance into the World 22
3. Wales 32
4. Infidelity 46
5. Debtors' Prison 58
6. Drury Lane 73
7. A Woman in Demand 92

PART TWO: CELEBRITY

8. Florizel and Perdita 105
9. A Very Public Affair 127
10. The Rivals 143
11. Blackmail 158
12. Perdita and Marie Antoinette 171
13. A Meeting in the Studio 182
14. The Priestess of Taste 203
15. The Ride to Dover 227
16. Politics 236

PART THREE: WOMAN OF LETTERS

17. Exile 251
18. Laura Maria 262
19. Opium 283
20. Author 308
21. Nobody 325
22. Radical 342
23. Feminist 364
24. Lyrical Tales 377
25. 'A Small but Brilliant Circle' 395

EPILOGUE 419
APPENDIX: The Mystery of Mrs Robinson's Age 429
NOTES 431
BIBLIOGRAPHY 453
INDEX 463

ILLUSTRATIONS

COLOUR PICTURES

1. The Fleet Prison, by Thomas Rowlandson, from Ackermann's *Microcosm of London*, 1809
2. David Garrick, by Angelica Kauffmann
3. Interior of Theatre Royal, Drury Lane, viewed from the stage, altered and decorated by the Adam brothers, 1775
4. George IV as Prince of Wales, miniature by Jeremiah Meyer
5. Mary Robinson by George Romney, 1781
6. Mary Robinson by Thomas Gainsborough, 1782
7. Mary Robinson by Sir Joshua Reynolds, 1782
8. Marie Antoinette in white muslin dress by Madame Vigée-Lebrun, 1783
9. Colonel Banastre Tarleton by Sir Joshua Reynolds, 1782
10. 'The Thunderer': caricature of Tarleton by James Gillray, 1782
11. Charles James Fox, miniature by Thomas Day
12. 'Paridise Regain'd': caricature of Mrs Robinson, Fox, and the Prince by James Gillray, 1783
13. Mary Robinson by Sir Joshua Reynolds, second portrait, 1783
14. Thomas Rowlandson, 'Vaux-Hall', 1785
15. John Hoppner's later portrait of Mary, circa 1796

BLACK AND WHITE PICTURES

1. The Minster House, Bristol, where Mary was born
2. 'The Dramatic Enchantress and The Doating Lover': Mary Robinson and Lord Malden, from the *Town and Country Magazine*, June 1780
3. Mary Robinson cross-dressed, engraving by W. Ridley in *Picturesque Magazine*, 1793
4. Mary Robinson, engraved from the life by J. K. Sherwin, 1781
5. Mary Robinson having her portrait painted, watercolour by Thomas Rowlandson
6. Reverend Henry Bate, journalist, mezzotint after Gainsborough
7. 'Perdito and Perdita – or – the Man and Woman of the People': caricature of Fox and Mrs Robinson by T. Colley, 1782

8. 'The new Vis-à-vis, or Florizel driving Perdita': anonymous caricature of the Prince, Mrs Robinson, Fox, and North, from the *Rambler's Magazine*, August 1783
9. 'The Goats Canter to Windsor or the Cuckold's Comfort', caricature of Perdita and her lovers, March 1784
10. 'Perdita upon her last legs': caricature from the *Rambler's Magazine*, August 1784
11. Mrs Robinson's cottage at St Amand les Eaux, ink drawing, probably by her daughter Maria, in the original manuscript of *Memoirs of the Late Mrs Robinson, Written by Herself*
12. Mary Robinson by George Dance, 1793
13. Portrait of Mary Robinson late in life, by John Chubb
14. William Godwin by James Northcote
15. Mary Robinson's grave in Old Windsor

TEXT ILLUSTRATIONS

1. Playbill for Mary Robinson as Perdita on the night of the royal command performance
2. 'Florizel and Perdita': anonymous caricature of the Robinsons and the Prince, 1780
3. 'Florizel and Perdita': anonymous caricature of the Prince and Mrs Robinson, October 1783
4. 'The Adventure of Prince Pretty Man': caricature of Fox, the Prince, the Perdita, and the Armistead by J. Boyne, 1784
5. Colonel Banastre Tarleton, anonymous engraving
6. 'Scrub and Archer', caricature of Fox, North, and Perdita by J. Boyne, 1783
7. 'The Aerostatick Stage Balloon': caricature by 'Hanibal Scratch', December 1783
8. 'General Blackbeard Wounded at the Battle of Leadenhall', caricature of Fox and his followers, including Perdita, by J. Boyne, January 1784
9. Samuel Taylor Coleridge around the time he met Mary Robinson
10. A letter in Mary Robinson's hand, 1793
11. Title page of *Lyrical Tales*, 1800
12. Title page of *Memoirs*, 1801, with frontispiece engraved from portrait of Mary painted by James Crank in 1798

ACKNOWLEDGEMENTS

I gratefully acknowledge the support of the British Academy in the form of a generous research grant to help defray the cost of illustrations, permissions, microfilms, photocopies, and travel expenses.

I am very grateful to the following scholars, archivists, and librarians for assistance of various kinds: Irene Andrews, Matthew Bailey, Jennie Batchelor, Peter Beal, Jane Bradley, Siân Cooksey, Hilary Davies, Elizabeth Dunn, Julie Flanders, Amanda Foreman, Flora Fraser, Ted Gott, Katie Hickman, Alison Kenney, Jacqueline Labbe, Tom Mayberry, Judith Pascoe, Charlotte Payne, Matthew Percival, Linda Peterson, Maggie Powell, David Rhodes, Angela Rosenthal, Wendy Roworth, Diego Saglia, Helen Scott, Sharon Setzer, Stephen Tabor, Teresa Taylor, William St Clair, Judy Simons, Jessica Vale, Steve Wharton, Frances Wilson, Robert Woof, Georgianna Ziegler.

This biography could not have been written without the resources of the following institutions: Bodleian Library, Oxford; Central Library, Bristol; Bristol Record Office; British Library (special thanks to Matthew Shaw in the Manuscripts Room and all the helpful staff in the Newspaper Division at Colindale, which was my most important source); Department of Prints and Drawings, British Museum; Cambridge University Library; Chawton House Library; Folger Shakespeare Library, Washington DC; Garrick Club Library (special thanks to Marcus Risdell); Harvard Theatre Collection, Houghton Library, Harvard University (special thanks to Luke Dennis); Hertfordshire Archives and Local Studies, Hertford; Huntington Library, San Marino, California; Liverpool Record Office; the Pforzheimer Collection at the New York Public Library (Astor, Lenox, and Tilden Foundations; special thanks to Stephen Wagner); Royal Archives and Collection (special thanks to the Registrar, Miss Pamela Clark); Shakespeare Birthplace Trust, Stratford-upon-Avon; Shakespeare Institute, Stratford-upon-Avon; Surrey Records Office; Theatre Museum, London; Wallace Collection, London; Warwick

University Library; City of Westminster Archives Centre; Witt Library, London.

I am especially grateful to Rear Admiral Sir Peter and Dame Elizabeth Anson for their generosity in allowing me to see the correspondence between the Prince of Wales and Mary Hamilton and to quote from it here; also for their hospitality while I was in their home. Equal thanks are owed to the staff of the residence where the original manuscript of Mary Robinson's *Memoirs* is held and to the Trustees of the collection for permission to quote from it (special thanks to Rodney Melville). Thanks also to Rev. Nicholas Chubb for directing me to his ancestor John Chubb's portrait of Mary, to Hélène at the Tourist Office in Calais, and to Graham Dennis of Blacklock Books in Englefield Green for local knowledge when I was in search of Mary's cottage.

Thanks to my incomparable agents Andrew Wylie and Sarah Chalfant. Grateful thanks to my publishers Michael Fishwick and Kate Hyde at HarperCollins in London and Susanna Porter at Random House in New York, and Juliet Davis in the picture department at HarperCollins. Many thanks to Carol Anderson for her scrupulous copy editing.

A huge debt is owed to my friend and research assistant Héloïse Sénéchal. She has been indefatigable in her efforts and has provided assistance and companionship from the darkened rooms of the Colindale library, where we pored over eighteenth-century newspapers for days on end, to the London pubs where we shared lively discussions about Mary Robinson. Heartfelt thanks to Dr Chris Clark for her scrupulous research on rheumatic fever. Rachel Bolger has read the entire manuscript and I am extremely grateful for her most valuable suggestions and comments. Thanks to the mums at the Croft School, especially Tracey Rigby, Sally Manners, and Bev Clarke, who have helped in numerous ways.

Gratitude is due to my good friends who take a generous interest in my work, especially Phil and Jane Davis, Paul Edmondson, Kelvin and Faith Everest, Carol Rutter, and Stanley Wells. Thanks also to my siblings, Collette, Chris, David, Claire, Joe and Rachael, and my wonderful parents, Tim and Clare. My children Tom and Ellie have shown remarkable patience, especially when I was away on research trips – thanks and love to you both. My deepest gratitude belongs to my husband and dearest friend Jonathan Bate, who has endured the pleasures, pains, and privileges of being so long in the company of Mrs Robinson. I salute you, and thank you for your patience and wisdom. My grandmother (also called Mary Robinson, though no relation) has been an inspiration to me all of my life. Though she died a week before the book was completed, I feel sure she would have enjoyed Mary's story. This book is for her.

PERMISSIONS ACKNOWLEDGEMENTS

Illustrations are reproduced by kind permission of the following:

Blake Museum, Sedgemoor District Council (b/w 13)
Bristol Central Library (b/w 1, 3, 4, text illus. 10)
British Museum, Department of Prints and Drawings (b/w 7–10, text illus. 2–7)
Burghley House Collection, Lincolnshire / Bridgeman Art Library (colour 2)
Chawton House Library, photograph by Steve Shrimpton (text illus. 12)
Folger Shakespeare Library, Washington DC (b/w 2)
Her Majesty Queen Elizabeth II, the Royal Collection (colour 4, b/w 5)
Huntington Library, San Marino, California (b/w 2, text illus. 1)
Mary Evans Picture Library (text illus. 9)
National Gallery, London (colour 9)
National Gallery of Victoria, Melbourne (colour 15)
National Portrait Gallery, London (colour 10–12, b/w 6, 12, 14)
Private Collection, photograph by Albert Rigby ARPS (b/w 11)
Schlossmuseum, Darmstadt / akg-images (colour 8)
Stapleton Collection / Bridgeman Art Library (colour 3)
Victoria and Albert Museum / Bridgeman Art Library (colour 1)
Waddesdon, The Rothschild Collection, The National Trust (colour 7)
Wallace Collection (colour 5, 6, 13)
Yale Center for British Art: Paul Mellon Collection / Bridgeman Art Library (colour 14)

Longer quotations from unpublished manuscript sources are reproduced by kind permission of the following: Abinger Deposit, Bodleian Library, Oxford; Rear Admiral Sir Peter and Dame Elizabeth Anson; Bristol Central Library; Folger Shakespeare Library, Washington DC; Garrick Club

Library; Harvard Theatre Collection; Huntington Library, San Marino, California; Carl H. Pforzheimer Collection of Shelley and his Circle, New York Public Library (Astor, Lenox, and Tilden Foundations); Private Collections; Broadley Collection, Westminster Archives.

I was delighted at the Play last Night, and was extremely moved by two scenes in it, especially as I was particularly interested in the appearance of the most beautiful Woman, that ever I beheld, who acted with such delicacy that she drew tears from my eyes.

(George, Prince of Wales)

There is not a woman in England so much talked of and so little known as Mrs Robinson.

(*Morning Herald*, 23 April 1784)

I was well acquainted with the late ingenious Mary Robinson, once the beautiful *Perdita* . . . the most interesting woman of her age.

(Sir Richard Phillips, publisher)

She is a woman of undoubted Genius . . . I never knew a human Being with so *full* a mind – bad, good, and indifferent, I grant you, but full, and overflowing.

(Samuel Taylor Coleridge)

I am allowed the power of changing my form, as suits the observation of the moment.

(Mary Robinson, writing as 'The Sylphid')

PROLOGUE

In the middle of a summer night in 1783 a young woman set off from London along the Dover road in pursuit of her lover. She had waited for him all evening in her private box at the Opera House. When he failed to appear, she sent her footman to his favourite haunts: the notorious gaming clubs Brooks's and Weltje's; the homes of his friends, the Prince of Wales, Charles James Fox, and Lord Malden. At 2 a.m. she heard the news that he had left for the Continent to escape his debtors. In a moment of panic and desperation, she hired a post chaise and ordered it to be driven to Dover. This decision was to have the most profound consequences for the woman famous and infamous in London society as 'Perdita'.

In the course of the carriage ride she suffered a medical misadventure.* And she did not meet her lover at Dover: he had sailed from Southampton. Her life would never be the same again.

Born Mary Darby, she had been a teenage bride. As a young mother she was forced to live in debtors' prison. But then, under her married name of Mary Robinson, she had been taken up by David Garrick, the greatest actor of the age, and had herself become a celebrated actress at Drury Lane. Many regarded her as the most beautiful woman in England. The young Prince of Wales – who would later become Prince Regent and then King George IV – had seen her in the part of Perdita and started sending her love letters signed 'Florizel'. She held the dubious honour of being the first of his many mistresses.

In an age when most women were confined to the domestic sphere, Mary was a public face. She was gazed at on the stage and she gazed back from the walls of the Royal Academy and the studios of the men who painted her, including Sir Joshua Reynolds, who was to painting

* As with many incidents in her life, the circumstances are not absolutely clear, as will be seen in chapter 15.

what Garrick was to theatre. The royal love affair also brought her image to the eighteenth-century equivalent of the television screen: the caricatures displayed in print-shop windows. Her notoriety increased when she became a prominent political campaigner. In quick succession, she was the mistress of Charles James Fox, the most charismatic politician of the age, and Colonel Banastre Tarleton, known as 'Butcher' Tarleton because of his exploits in the American War of Independence. The prince, the politician, the action hero: it is no wonder that she was the embodiment of – the word was much used at the time, not least by Mary herself – 'celebrity'.

Her body was her greatest asset. When she came back from Paris with a new style of dress, everyone in the fashionable world wanted one like it. When she went shopping, she caused a traffic jam. What was she to do when that body was no longer admired and desired?

Fortunately, she had another asset: her voice. Whilst still a teenager, she had become a published poet. Because of her stage career, she had an intimate knowledge of Shakespeare's language – and the ability to speak it. So, as her health gradually improved, she remade herself as a professional author. Having transformed herself from actress to author, she went on to experiment with a huge range of written voices, as is apparent from the variety of pseudonyms under which she wrote: Horace Juvenal, Tabitha Bramble, Laura Maria, Sappho, Anne Frances Randall. She completed seven novels (the first of them a runaway bestseller), two political tracts, several essays, two plays and literally hundreds of poems.[1]

Actress, entertainer, author, provoker of scandal, fashion icon, sex object, darling of the gossip columns, self-promoter: one can see why she has been described as the Madonna of the eighteenth century.[2] But celebrity has its flipside: oblivion. Mary Robinson had the unique distinction of being painted in a single season by the four great society artists of the age – Sir Joshua Reynolds, Thomas Gainsborough, John Hoppner, and George Romney – and yet within a few years of her death the Gainsborough portrait was being catalogued under the anonymous title *Portrait of a Lady with a Dog*. In the twentieth century, despite the resurgence of the art of life-writing and the enormous interest in female authors, there was not a single biography of Robinson. Before the Second World War, she was considered suitable only for fictionalized treatments, historical romances and bodice-rippers with titles such as *The Exquisite*

Perdita and *The Lost One*. In the 1950s her life was subordinated to that of the lover she thought she was pursuing to France.* A book on George IV and the women in his life did not even mention Mary's name, despite the fact that she was his first love and he remained in touch with her for the rest of her life.[3] Finally in the 1990s, feminist scholars began a serious reassessment of Robinson's literary career. However, their work was aimed at a specialized audience of scholars and students of the Romantic period in literature.[4]

When Mary Robinson began writing her autobiography, near the end of her life, there were two conflicting impulses at work. On the one hand, she needed to revisit her own youthful notoriety. She had been the most wronged woman in England and she wanted to put on record her side of the story of her relationship with the Prince of Wales. But at the same time, she wanted to be remembered as a completely different character: the woman of letters. As she wrote, she had in her possession letters from some of the finest minds of her generation – Samuel Taylor Coleridge, William Godwin, Mary Wollstonecraft – assuring her that she was, in Coleridge's words, 'a woman of genius'. Royal sex scandal and the literary life do not usually cohabit between the same printed sheets, but in a biography of the woman who went from 'Mrs Robinson of Drury Lane' to 'the famous Perdita' to 'Mary Robinson, author', they must.

The research for this book took me from the minuscule type of the gossip columns of the *Morning Herald* in the newspaper division of the British Library at Colindale in north London to the Gothic cloister of Bristol Minster, where Mary Robinson was born. I stood below the incomparable portraits of her in the Wallace Collection tucked away off busy Oxford Street and in stately homes both vast (Waddesdon Manor) and intimate (Chawton House). In the Print Room of the British Museum I pored over graphic and sometimes obscene caricatures of her; via the worldwide web I downloaded long-forgotten political pamphlets in which she figured prominently; in the New York Public Library, within earshot

* Robert Bass, *The Green Dragoon: The Lives of Banastre Tarleton and Mary Robinson* (New York, 1957) – as the title reveals, the main emphasis is on Tarleton's military career. Though Bass undertook valuable archival research, his transcriptions were riddled with errors, he misdated key incidents, and he failed to notice many fascinating newspaper reports, references in memoirs, and other sources. It is no exaggeration to say that his inaccuracies outnumber his accuracies: if Bass says that an article appeared one November in the *Morning Post*, one may rest assured that it is to be found in December in the *Morning Herald*.

of the traffic on Fifth Avenue, I pieced together the letters in which Mary revealed her state of mind in the final months of her life, as she continued to write prolifically even as she struggled against illness and disability.

I found hitherto neglected letters and manuscripts scattered in the most unlikely places: in a private home in Surrey, I opened a cardboard folder and found the Prince of Wales's account of the night he saw 'Perdita' at Drury Lane, written the very next day, in the first flush of his infatuation with her; in the Garrick Club, among the portraits of the great men of the theatre who launched Mary's career, I discovered a letter in which she laid out her plan to rival the *Lyrical Ballads* of Wordsworth and Coleridge; and in one of the most securely guarded private houses in England – which I am prohibited from naming – I found the original manuscript of her *Memoirs*, which is subtly different from the published text. I became intimate with the perfectly proportioned face and the lively written voice of this remarkable woman. Yet as I was researching the book, people from many walks of life asked me who I was writing about: hardly any of them had heard of the eighteenth-century Mary Robinson. So I have sought to recreate her life, her world and her work, and to explain how it was that one of her contemporaries called her 'the most interesting woman of her age'.[5]

PART ONE

Actress

CHAPTER 1

'During a Tempestuous Night'

> The very finest powers of intellect, and the proudest specimens of mental labour, have frequently appeared in the more contracted circles of provincial society. Bristol and Bath have each sent forth their sons and daughters of genius.
>
> Mary Robinson, 'Present State of the Manners, Society, etc. etc. of the Metropolis of England'

Horace Walpole described the city of Bristol as 'the dirtiest great shop I ever saw'. Second only to London in size, it was renowned for the industry and commercial prowess of its people. 'The Bristolians,' it was said, 'seem to live only to get and save money.'[1] The streets and marketplaces were alive with crowds, prosperous gentlemen and ladies perambulated under the lime trees on College Green outside the minster, and seagulls circled in the air. A river cut through the centre, carrying the ships that made the city one of the world's leading centres of trade. Sugar was the chief import, but it was not unusual to find articles in the *Bristol Journal* announcing the arrival of slave ships en route from Africa to the New World. Sometimes slaves would be kept for domestic service: in the parish register of the church of St Augustine the Less one finds the baptism of a negro named 'Bristol'. Over the page is another entry: Polly – a variant of Mary – daughter of Nicholas and Hester Darby, baptized 19 July 1758.[2]

Nicholas Darby was a prominent member of the Society of Merchant

Venturers, based at the Merchants' Hall in King Street, an association of overseas traders that was at the heart of Bristol's commercial life. The merchant community supported a vibrant culture: a major theatre, concerts, assembly rooms, coffee houses, bookshops, and publishers. Bristol's most famous literary son was born just five years before Mary. Thomas Chatterton, the 'marvellous boy', was the wunderkind of English poetry. His verse became a posthumous sensation in the years following his suicide (or accidental self-poisoning) at the age of 17. For Keats and Shelley, he was a hero; Mary Robinson and Samuel Taylor Coleridge both wrote odes in his memory.

Coleridge himself also developed Bristol connections. His friend and fellow poet Robert Southey, the son of a failed linen merchant, came from the city. The two young poets married the Bristolian Fricker sisters and it was on College Green, a stone's throw from the house where Mary was born, that they hatched their 'pantisocratic' plan to establish a commune on the banks of the Susquehanna River.

Mary described her place of birth at the beginning of her *Memoirs*. She conjured up a hillside in Bristol, where a monastery belonging to the order of St Augustine had once stood beside the minster:

> On this spot was built a private house, partly of simple and partly of modern architecture. The front faced a small garden, the gates of which opened to the Minster-Green (now called the College-Green): the west side was bounded by the Cathedral, and the back was supported by the antient cloisters of St Augustine's monastery. A spot more calculated to inspire the soul with mournful meditation can scarcely be found amidst the monuments of antiquity.

She was born in a room that had been part of the original monastery. It was immediately over the cloisters, dark and Gothic with 'casement windows that shed a dim mid-day gloom'. The chamber was reached 'by a narrow winding staircase, at the foot of which an iron-spiked door led to the long gloomy path of cloistered solitude'. What better origin could there have been for a woman who grew up to write best-selling Gothic novels? If the *Memoirs* is to be believed, even the weather contributed to the atmosphere of foreboding on the night of her birth. 'I have often heard my mother say that a more stormy hour she never remembered.

The wind whistled round the dark pinnacles of the minster tower, and the rain beat in torrents against the casements of her chamber.' 'Through life,' Mary continued, 'the tempest has followed my footsteps.'[3]

The Minster House was destroyed when the nave of Bristol Minster was enlarged in the Victorian era, but it is still possible to stand in the courtyard in front of the Minster School and see the cloister that supported the house in which Mary was born. And next door, in what is now the public library, one can look at an old engraving which reveals that the house was indeed tucked beneath the great Gothic windows and the mighty tower of the cathedral itself.

The family had Irish roots. Mary's great-grandfather changed his name from MacDermott to Darby in order to inherit an Irish estate. Nicholas Darby was born in America and claimed kinship with Benjamin Franklin.[4] As a young man he was engaged in the Newfoundland fishing trade in St John's. His daughter described him as having a 'strong mind, high spirit, and great personal intrepidity', traits that could equally apply to herself.[5]

Mary was always touchy about issues of rank and gentility. In her *Memoirs* she took pains to emphasize the respectability of the merchant classes. Her father had some success in cultivating the acquaintance of the aristocracy: in an unpublished handwritten note, Mary remarked with pride that 'Lord Northington the Chancellor was my Godfather' and that at her christening 'the Hon Bertie Henley stood for him as proxy'.[6]

Mary's mother, Hester, née Vanacott, made a romantic match with Nicholas Darby when she married him on 4 July 1749 in the small Somerset village of Donyatt. Hester was a descendant of a well-to-do family, the Seys of Boverton Castle in Glamorganshire, and a distant relation (by marriage) of the philosopher John Locke. Vivacious and popular, she had many suitors and her parents would have expected her to marry into a landed family. They did not approve of her union with Darby.

In 1752, three years after their marriage, Nicholas and Hester had a son, whom they named John.[7] A daughter called Elizabeth followed in January 1755. She died of smallpox before she was 2 and was buried in October 1756. It was a great comfort to Nicholas and Hester when Mary was born just over a year later, on 27 November 1757.*

* See Appendix for the uncertainty over the year of Mary's birth.

In the days before vaccination, smallpox was a lethal threat to children. The disease took not only the infant Elizabeth, but probably also a younger brother, William, when he was 6. Another younger brother for Mary, named George, fared better: he and John both grew up to become 'respectable' merchants, trading at Leghorn (Livorno) in Italy.

Hester soon found that she had entered into an unhappy union. Nicholas spent much of his time in Newfoundland on business. By 1758, he was putting down roots there, joining with other merchants in an enterprise to build a new church. He returned to Bristol for the winter months, but he can only have been a shadowy presence in his daughter's early life.

The Darby boys were extremely handsome, with auburn hair and blue eyes. Mary took after her father; she described her own childhood looks as 'swarthy', with enormous eyes set in a small, delicate face. She was a dreamy, melancholy, and pensive child who revelled in the gloominess of her surroundings in the minster. The children's nursery was so close to the great aisle that the peal of the organ could be heard at morning and evening service. Mary would creep out of her nursery on her own and perch on the winding staircase to listen to the music: 'I can at this moment recall to memory the sensations I then experienced, the tones that seemed to thrill through my heart, the longing which I felt to unite my feeble voice to the full anthem, and the awful though sublime impression which the church service never failed to make upon my feelings.' Rather than playing on College Green with her brothers she would creep into the minster to sit beneath the lectern in the form of a great eagle that held up the huge Bible. The only person who could keep her away from her self-imposed exile there was the stern sexton and bell-ringer she named Black John, 'from the colour of his beard and complexion'.[8]

As soon as she learnt to read, she recited the epitaphs and inscriptions on the tombstones and monuments. Before she was 7 years old, she had memorized several elegiac poems that were typical of the verse of the eighteenth century. Her taste in music was as mournful as her taste in poetry.

Mary confessed that the events of her life had been 'more or less marked by the progressive evils of a too acute sensibility'. One thinks here of Jane Austen's first published novel, *Sense and Sensibility*, with its satirical portrait of the ultra-sensitive Marianne Dashwood: she bears more than a passing resemblance to the melancholy young Mary Darby, quoting morbid poetry and thoroughly enjoying the misery of playing sombre music and being left in solitary contemplation. As a writer, Mary was always acutely aware of her audience: her image of herself in the *Memoirs* as a child of sensibility was designed to appeal to the numerous readers of Gothic novels and sentimental fiction. At the same time, her self-image appealed to the romantic myth of the writer as a natural genius who begins as a precociously talented but lonely child escaping into the world of imagination.

Though Mary presented herself as a 'natural' genius, she was the beneficiary of improvements in education and the growth of printed literature aimed at a young audience. This was a period when private schools for girls of middling rank sprang up all over England. Bristol was the home of Hannah More, playwright, novelist, Evangelical reformer, and political writer. Though Hannah became famous for rectitude and Mary for scandal, their lives were curiously parallel: born and bred in Bristol, each of them had a theatrical career that began under the patronage of David Garrick and each then turned to the art of the novel. In the 1790s they both became associated with contentious debates about women's education.

Mary attended a school run by Hannah More and her sisters. An upmarket ladies' academy, it had opened in 1758 in Trinity Street, behind the minster, just a few hundred yards from Mary's birthplace. The curriculum concentrated on 'French, Reading, Writing, Arithmetic, and Needlework'. A recruitment advertisement added that 'A Dancing Master will properly attend.'[9] The school was immensely popular and four years later moved to 43 Park Street, halfway up the hill towards the genteel district of Clifton. When Mary Darby attended, the enrolment had risen to sixty pupils. Each of the More sisters took responsibility for a different 'department' of the curriculum, with – in Mary's words – 'zeal, good sense and ability'. The earnest and erudite Hannah 'divided her hours between the arduous task "of teaching the young ideas how to shoot," and exemplifying by works of taste and fancy the powers of a mind already so cultivated'.[10]

In the summer of 1764 Bristol was in the grip of theatre mania. The famous London star William Powell played King Lear with a force said to rival that of the great Garrick himself. Within two years Powell was combining management with performance at a new building in the city centre. The first theatre in England to be built with a semicircular auditorium, it had nine dress boxes and eight upper side boxes, all inscribed with the names of renowned dramatists and literary figures.

The highlight of the first season in this new Theatre Royal was another *King Lear*, with Powell in the lead once again and his wife Elizabeth playing Cordelia. Powell had become very friendly with Hannah More, and she wrote an uplifting prologue for the performance. The whole school turned out for the play. It was the 8-year-old Mary Darby's first visit to the theatre. She vividly remembered the 'great actor' of whom Chatterton said 'No single part is thine, thou'rt all in all.'[11] She was less taken by the performance of his wife who played Cordelia without 'sufficient éclat to render the profession an object for her future exertions'.[12] Among Mary's school friends were Powell's two daughters and the future actress Priscilla Hopkins, who would later become the wife of John Kemble and sister-in-law of Sarah Siddons, the most famous actress in Britain. The girls developed a passion for theatre together.

Hannah More continued to be fascinated by the theatre. She wrote a pastoral verse comedy called *The Search after Happiness*, which was acted by the schoolgirls. It advocates a doctrine of female modesty and submission that would be echoed in the anti-feminist tracts she wrote in later life. One of the characters is an ambitious girl who longs to 'burst those female bonds, which held my sex in awe' in order to pursue fame and fortune: 'I sigh'd for *fame*, I languished for renown, / I would be prais'd, caress'd, admir'd, and known.' It is tempting to see the young Mary Darby playing this part, and hearing her aspirations rebuked by another character: 'Would she the privilege of *Man* invade? . . . / For *Woman* shines but in her *proper* sphere.'[13]

By the end of the century Hannah More had turned herself into one of the most formidable conservative propagandists of the age. She deeply resented her connection with her old pupil, the infamous Perdita. That one of the most reviled women of the era was taught by one of the most revered was an irony not lost on the bluestocking Mrs Thrale: 'Of all Biographical Anecdotes none ever struck me more forcibly than the one saying how Hannah More *la Dévote* was the person who educated fair *Perdita la Pécheresse*.'[14] Mary, in turn, made it abundantly clear that her literary gifts owed little debt to Hannah and her sisters. She stressed that the education she received from the school was merely in feminine accomplishments of the sort that were required for the marriage market. Women were expected to be ornaments to society and, once married, to be modest and retiring creatures confined to the domestic sphere rather than competing with men in the public domain.

As the daughter of a prosperous merchant, Mary benefited from the privileges that could be bought by new money. The distinguished musician Edmund Broderip taught her music on an expensive Kirkman harpsichord bought by her father. The family moved to a larger, more elegant house as Nicholas Darby, keen to show off the fruits of his upward mobility, insisted upon living like a gentleman, buying expensive plate, sumptuous silk furniture, foreign wine, and luxurious food, displaying 'that warm hospitality which is often the characteristic of a British merchant'.[15] He ensured that his daughter lived in the best style. Her bed was of the richest crimson damask; her dresses, ordered from London, were of the finest cambric. The family spent the summer months on gentrified Clifton Hill in order to benefit from the clearer air. Darby's appetite for 'the good things of the world' would be inherited by his daughter.

Mrs Darby, meanwhile, provided emotional security. Unlike many of the other girls at the More sisters' school, Mary never boarded: she did not 'pass a night of separation from the fondest of mothers'. In retrospect, she considered herself overindulged, suggesting that her mother's only fault was 'a too tender care', a tendency to spoil and flatter her children: 'the darlings of her bosom were dressed, waited on, watched, and indulged with a degree of fondness bordering on folly'.[16] Given that Nicholas Darby was absent abroad for much of the time, it is not surprising that Hester threw so much into her children. Mary implies that an absent father and an indulgent mother proved a dangerous combination for a headstrong girl like herself.

The *Memoirs* paints a picture of Mary's early childhood as a fairy-tale existence, a paradise lost. Her life changed for ever, she says, when she was in her ninth year. Nicholas Darby had a lifelong history of travelling, fishing, and trading in the far north of Newfoundland. In the early 1760s he was acting as spokesman for the Society of Merchant Venturers, advising the Government on the defence of Newfoundland, which was a key strategic outpost fought over by the British and French during the

Seven Years War. Then in 1765 he became obsessed with what Mary describes as an 'eccentric' plan, a scheme 'as wild and romantic as it was perilous to hazard, which was no less than that of establishing a whale fishery on the coast of Labrador; and of civilizing the Esquimaux Indians, in order to employ them in the extensive undertaking'.[17]

This was dangerous territory. Not only was the weather extremely inclement, but the area in question – the Strait of Belle Isle – had only been held in British hands for a couple of years. But Darby had some powerful backers: Mary records that his scheme was given approval by the Governor of Newfoundland, Lord Chatham (William Pitt the Elder) and 'several equally distinguished personages'. The venture seemed 'full of promise'. Darby dreamed that the day might come when, thanks to him, British America could rival the whale industry of Greenland.

Having got permission from the Government, he told his family that the scheme would require his full-time residence in America for a minimum of two years. Hester was appalled by the idea. The northern wastes were no place for children, so accompanying her husband would have meant leaving her beloved sons and daughter to complete their education at boarding schools in England. She also had a phobia of the ocean. The decision to stay with her children would cost Hester her marriage. Nicholas duly sailed for America. The eldest boy John was placed in a mercantile house at Leghorn, whilst Mary, William, and George stayed with Hester in Bristol.

At first, Nicholas wrote regularly and affectionately. But his letters gradually became less frequent, and when they did arrive they began to seem dutiful and perfunctory. Then there was a long period of silence. And finally 'the dreadful secret was unfolded': Darby had acquired a mistress, Elenor, who, as Mary wryly testified, was only too happy to 'brave the stormy ocean' alongside him. She 'consented to remain two years with him in the frozen wilds of America'.[18]

Darby had sailed from England to Chateau Bay with 150 men. He was then given headquarters on Cape Charles, where he constructed lodgings, a workshop, and a landing stage. Fishing began well, but then the local Inuit burned his boats and destroyed his crucial supply of salt. His men fought with each other and refused to winter on the coast. He made a second attempt a year later, in partnership with a fellow merchant, returning with new men and more sophisticated equipment. But more fighting ensued and in the summer of 1767 ten men were arrested on murder charges. Then in November, around the time of Mary's tenth birthday, the Labrador project came to a violent end: another band of Inuit attacked a crew preparing for winter sealing, killed three men, burned Darby's settlement, and set his boats adrift. Thousands of pounds' worth of ships and equipment were destroyed. 'The island of promise' had turned into a 'scene of barbarous desolation' – though Mary's account characteristically exaggerates the slaughter, turning the three casualties into the murder of 'many of his people'.[19] Darby's patrons refused to honour their promise of financial protection and, with more losses incurred, he dissolved his partnership and set in train the sale of the family home.

Back in Bristol, Hester Darby faced a series of calamities: the shame that came with the news that her husband was residing in America with his mistress, the financial losses that would cost her everything, and the death – from smallpox or possibly measles – of Mary's 6-year-old brother William. On his return to London, Nicholas lived with his mistress Elenor, but the manuscript of Mary's *Memoirs* has an intriguing memorandum, excluded from the published text: 'Esquemaux Indians brought over by my father, a woman and a boy.'[20] Could this have been another mistress? And could it then be that Mary had an illegitimate half-Inuit half-brother?

Mary always felt torn between pride in her father's achievements and resentment at his abandonment of the family. Her ambivalence can be seen in the way that she emphasizes his dual nationality. When she speaks of his bold and restless spirit, and his love of sea life, she ascribes this to his status as an American seafarer, yet at other times he is that stalwart of the community, a 'British merchant'. Mary blamed her father's mistress for bewitching his senses at a time when he was isolated in America, away from his wife and family. She herself learnt a valuable lesson at a particularly vulnerable age: loss of fortune and position swiftly loses friends. Dropped by the people who had been happy to take advantage of their former prosperity, the family were left bereft.

A year later, Hester, Mary, and the surviving younger son, George, were summoned to London to their father's lodgings in fashionable Spring Gardens, near the famous Vauxhall pleasure gardens. Hester was unsure as to whether to expect 'the freezing scorn, or the contrite glances, of either an estranged or repentant husband'.[21] His 'coldly civil' letter had 'requested particularly' that she should bring the children with her: this ought to have been enough to make her realize that the meeting would be a farewell, not a reunion.

When they met, her father was in tears and could barely speak. The embrace he gave his wife was 'cold' – and it was the last she was to receive from him. Once the initial recriminations had blown over, Nicholas set out his plans. The children were to be placed at schools in London, while his wife was to board with a respectable clergyman's family. He would be returning across the Atlantic. And, indeed, the following year he launched a new and much more successful venture in Labrador, this time employing experienced Canadian fishermen.

The next stage of Mary's education was to be crucial to her vocation as a writer. She was sent to a school in Chelsea and came under the tuition of a brilliant and accomplished woman, Meribah Lorrington. Lorrington was highly unconventional in that she had been given a masculine education by her schoolteacher father, and was as well versed in the classics as she was in the modern languages, arithmetic, and astronomy. She was the living embodiment of a character type that Mary would fictionalize in several of her novels, the female who benefits from the education usually reserved for boys.

Mary worshipped her teacher, elevating her influence far above that of the More sisters: 'All that I ever learned I acquired from this extraordinary woman.'[22] The classical education she was given in Chelsea meant that in the long term her writings would demand a respect that was not often granted to female authors. There is an especially striking breadth of classical allusion in her feminist treatise *A Letter to the Women of England, on the Injustice of Mental Subordination.*

Pupil and teacher became close companions, even sharing the same bedroom. Mary dates her love for books from this relationship: 'I applied rigidly to study, and acquired a taste for books, which has never, from that time, deserted me.'[23] The women read to one another and Mary began composing verses, some of which were included in her first collection of poems, which she was to publish from debtors' prison. In Mary's narrative of her own life, her intellect first blossoms in an all-female community, with Meribah and half a dozen fellow pupils (among whom Mary is clearly singled out as the favourite). Far from aligning herself with the highly respectable Hannah More, she chooses to identify Lorrington as her mentor – and then goes on to reveal that she was an incorrigible drunkard.

Mary often complained of the contemptuous treatment that she received from her own sex, but she paid the utmost respect to the women who inspired and supported her, especially in her writing career. As Meribah Lorrington was credited for encouraging her juvenile writing, so Mary's first literary patron was another woman of dubious reputation, Georgiana Duchess of Devonshire. Mary adored both women, though Meribah was a hopeless alcoholic and Georgiana an equally addicted gambler.

Mary accepted the explanation that Meribah gave for her addiction to drink: she was grief-stricken by the death of her husband and was the victim of a bullying, disciplinarian father, a stern-speaking silver-bearded Anabaptist who wandered round the girls' schoolroom wearing nothing but a loose flowing robe which made him look like a necromancer. Mary noticed that the presence of the father always made the daughter reach for the bottle.

Meribah Lorrington's 'state of confirmed intoxication' even during teaching hours led to the demise of the Chelsea school. Some time later, Mary discovered a drunken beggar woman at dusk in the street. She gave her money, then, to her surprise, the woman said, 'Sweet girl, you are still the angel I ever knew you.' Their eyes met and Mary was horrified to discover that it was her old teacher. She took her home, gave her fresh clothes, and asked her where she lived. Meribah refused to say, but promised she would call again in a few days. She never did. Years later, Mary learned that her brilliant but flawed mentor had died a drunk in the Chelsea workhouse.

Mary describes herself in her *Memoirs* as well developed for her age, tall and slender. At the age of 10, she says, she looked 13. During her fourteen-month period boarding at the Lorrington Academy, she visited her mother every Sunday. One afternoon over tea she had a marriage proposal from a friend of her father's. Hester was a little surprised; she asked her visitor how old he thought her daughter was. 'About sixteen,' he replied. Hester informed him that Mary was still only 12. He found this hard to believe, given that she was such a well-developed girl both physically and intellectually, but he was prepared to wait – he was a captain in the Navy, just off on a two-year voyage. He had great prospects for the future and hoped that Mary might still be unattached on his return. Just a few months later he perished at sea.

In this version of Mary's first encounter with male desire, she is the innocent: a child, albeit with the body of a woman. The first 'biography' of her, published at the height of her public fame in 1784, tells a very different story. *The Memoirs of Perdita* is a source that must be treated with great caution, since – as will be seen – it was written with both a political and a pornographic agenda. Nevertheless, there is no doubt that the book's anonymous author had a very well-informed source. The 'editor' claimed in his introduction that 'the circumstances of her life were communicated by *one* who has for several years been her confidant, and to whose pen she has been indebted for much news paper panegyric' – a description that very much suggests Henry Bate of the *Morning Herald*, a key figure in Mary's story. According to the 'editor' of *The Memoirs of Perdita*, 'the following history may with propriety be said to be dictated *by herself*: many of the mere private transactions were indisputably furnished by her; nor could they possibly originate from any other source'.[24] In some instances this is true: *The Memoirs of Perdita* published personal information about Mary's life that was not previously in the public domain. In other instances, however, these supposed memoirs can safely be assumed to offer nothing more than malicious fantasy.

According to *The Memoirs of Perdita*, Mary's first love affair occurred soon after the Darbys moved to London. Her father supposedly brought home a handsome young midshipman called Henry, who was allowed 'private interviews' and 'little rambles' with Mary. They went boating together on the Thames. On one occasion, they stopped for refreshments at Richmond. The only room the landlord had available in which to serve them with a glass of wine and a biscuit happened to be a bedchamber – which had crimson curtains that matched the 'natural blush' to which Mary was excited by the sight of the bed. The young midshipman duly took her hand and sat her with him on the white counterpane. 'Perdita's blushes returned – and Henry kissed them away – She fell into his arms – then sunk down together on the bed. – The irresistible impulse of nature, in a moment carried them into those regions of ecstatic bliss, where sense and thought lie dissolved in the rapture of mutual enjoyment.'[25]

The affair supposedly lasted for some time, until the 'jovial tar' was summoned back to his ship, never to be seen again. In all probability, 'Henry' is pure invention, perhaps spun at second hand from some passing remark about the sailor's proposal. After all, given that Nicholas Darby was estranged from his family, he was not there to introduce a midshipman into the household. But it would be unwise to dismiss out of hand the possibility that the young Mary – steeped as she was in poetry and romance – might have had some kind of sexual awakening in her early teens.

Mary was moved to a more orthodox boarding school in Battersea, run by a less colourful but nevertheless 'lively, sensible and accomplished woman' named Mrs Leigh.[26] Nicholas Darby then stopped sending money for his children's education. The resolute Hester took matters into her own hands and set up her own dame school in Little Chelsea. The teenage Mary became a teacher of English language, responsible for prose and verse compositions during the week and the reading of 'sacred and moral lessons, on saints'-days and Sunday evenings'.[27] Readers of her *Memoirs* would have been at best amused at the idea of one of the most notorious women of the age presenting herself as a teacher of morals and religion. Mary also had responsibility for supervising the pupils' wardrobes, and making sure that they were properly dressed and undressed by the servants.

In 1770, Nicholas Darby ran into more problems. Just as he had a thousand pounds' worth of seal skins ready for market, a British military officer arrived at his Labrador fishery and confiscated all his produce and tackle on the grounds that he was illegally employing Frenchmen and using French rather than British equipment. He was left marooned. He eventually made it back to London and asked the Board of Trade for compensation, claiming that he did not know that his Canadian crew were actually French subjects. The Board of Trade passed the buck, saying it had no jurisdiction in the case. Nicholas had a moral victory when the Court of King's Bench awarded him £650 damages against the Lieutenant who had seized the goods, but the money was uncollectible. In the circumstances, one might have expected him to be grateful for his estranged wife's initiative in establishing a school. But he was a proud man: 'he considered his name as disgraced, his conjugal reputation tarnished, by the public mode which his wife had adopted for revealing to the world her unprotected situation'.[28] He lived openly with his mistress, but could not abide seeing his wife publicly revealed as someone akin to an impoverished widow or spinster. He demanded that the school be closed immediately. It had lasted for less than a year.

Hester and her children moved to Marylebone. Like Chelsea, this was an expanding village on the edge of London, but it had a less rural feel and was fast being recognized as an integral part of the metropolis. Mary reverted from teacher to pupil, finishing her education at Oxford House, situated near the top of Marylebone High Street, bordering on Marylebone Gardens. Nicholas Darby and his mistress Elenor settled in the more fashionable and gentrified Green Street, off Grosvenor Square in Mayfair, a district that was becoming increasingly popular with merchants and rich shopkeepers as well as the gentry.

Mary must have been acutely conscious of the differences in lifestyle between her mother and her father. She sometimes accompanied her father on walks in the fields nearby, where he confessed that he rather regretted his 'fatal attachment' to his mistress – they had now been together so long and been through so much that it was impossible to dissolve the relationship. On one of their walks, they called on the Earl of Northington, a handsome young rake and politician, whose father had been one of the sponsors of Darby's Labrador schemes. They were very well received, with Mary being presented as the goddaughter of the older Northington (now deceased). In later years, she did not deny rumours that she might have been the old Lord's illegitimate daughter. The young Lord, meanwhile, treated her with 'the most flattering and gratifying civility'.[29]

When Nicholas returned to America, Hester moved her children to Southampton Buildings in Chancery Lane. This was lawyers' territory, backing onto Lincoln's Inn. She had placed herself under the protection of Samuel Cox, a lawyer. Perhaps she had applied to him for legal help after the separation from Nicholas became final. Being 'under the protection' of a man was usually code for sexual involvement, so it may have been more than a professional relationship.

It was during her time at Oxford House that Mary was drawn towards the stage. The governess, Mrs Hervey, spotted her talent for 'dramatic exhibitions', and persuaded Hester to let her daughter try for the stage, despite the fact that it was not considered to be a respectable career. Hester was persuaded that there were actresses who 'preserved an unspotted fame'. Nicholas obviously had his doubts. Upon setting off on his new overseas adventure, he left his wife with a chilling injunction to 'Take care that no dishonour falls upon my daughter. If she is not safe at my return I will annihilate you.'[30]

The school's dancing master was also ballet master at the Theatre Royal Covent Garden. Through him, Mary was introduced to an actor called Thomas Hull, who was impressed by her recitation of lines from Nicholas Rowe's tragedy *Jane Shore* of 1714. But nothing came of the audition. Mary did not despair and she was rewarded with a much greater opportunity. Her mother's protector Samuel Cox knew Dr Samuel Johnson and that was enough to open the door of Johnson's old pupil and friend, David Garrick.

What was Mary Darby like at the time that she met Garrick? Though she may have been a plain child with dark swarthy looks, she had become a very beautiful teenager. She had curly, dark auburn hair and soft blue eyes that were to enchant men from the Prince of Wales to Samuel Taylor Coleridge. She had dimples in her cheeks. But there was always an elusive quality to her beauty. Sir Joshua Reynolds's pupil, James Northcote, remarked that even his master's portraits of her were failures because 'the extreme beauty' of her was 'quite beyond his power'.[31]

CHAPTER 2

A Young Lady's Entrance into the World

> As London is the great emporium of commerce, it is also the centre of attraction for the full exercise of talents, and the liberal display of all that can embellish the arts and sciences.
>
> Mary Robinson, 'Present State of the Manners, Society, etc. etc. of the Metropolis of England'

London was like nowhere else in the world. Bigger than any other city in Europe, with a population more than ten times that of Bristol, it was a place of extremes. Riches and squalor, grandeur and wretchedness, appeared cheek-by-jowl. This was an era of unprecedented consumerism: for companionship and entertainment there were coffee houses, taverns, brothels, parks, pleasure gardens, and theatres. Above all there were shops. Napoleon had good reason to dismiss the English as a nation of shopkeepers. By the time of Mary's arrival in the metropolis, London had one for every thirty residents. Oxford Street alone boasted over a hundred and fifty. Everything was on display, from plate laden in silversmiths' shops to fruits and spices piled high on street-barrows. Tea, coffee, sugar, pepper, tobacco, chocolate, and textiles – the 'fruits of empire' – were sold in vast quantities.[1] There were print shops, book shops, milliners, linen drapers, silk mercers, jewellery shops, shoe shops, toy shops, confectioners. London was the epicentre of fashion, a place to gaze and be gazed at. It was an urban stage, and few understood this as well as Mary.

For the young poet William Wordsworth, London's inherent theatricality was disturbing. His section on 'Residence in London' in his autobiographical poem *The Prelude* describes with unease 'the moving pageant', the 'shifting pantomimic scenes', the 'great stage', and the 'public shows'. For Wordsworth, the gaudy display and excessive showiness of the city signalled a lack of inner authenticity; 'the quick dance of colours, lights and forms' was an alarming 'Babel din'.[2] Mary Robinson also captured the cacophony of urban life in her poem 'London's Summer Morning', but she relished what Wordsworth abhorred:

> Who has not wak'd to list the busy sounds
> Of summer's morning, in the sultry smoke
> Of noisy London? On the pavement hot
> The sooty chimney-boy, with dingy face
> And tatter'd covering, shrilly bawls his trade,
> Rousing the sleepy housemaid. At the door
> The milk-pail rattles, and the tinkling bell
> Proclaims the dustman's office, while the street
> Is lost in clouds impervious. Now begins
> The din of hackney-coaches, wagons, carts;
> While tinmen's shops, and noisy trunk-makers,
> Knife-grinders, coopers, squeaking cork-cutters,
> Fruit-barrows, and the hunger-giving cries
> Of vegetable vendors, fill the air.
> Now ev'ry shop displays its varied trade,
> And the fresh-sprinkled pavement cools the feet
> Of early walkers.[3]

She finds poetry in everything from the dustman to the 'neat girl, / Tripping with bandbox lightly' to the street vendor of second-hand clothes.

Mary was to experience London in its entirety, from debtors' prison to parties given in her honour as the Prince's consort at St James's Palace. She became notorious for her self-promotion and her skill in anticipating the next new thing, be that in fashion or poetry. But she also grasped the very essence of urban culture in the late eighteenth century in a way that eluded Wordsworth. She knew that in order to survive and thrive in the new consumer society, she had to work to sell her wares. The literary marketplace was as crowded as the London streets and it took guts, brashness, and ostentation to make your voice heard – especially if you were a woman.

She must have felt some trepidation at meeting Garrick: 'King' David, the man who had single-handedly transformed the theatre world, acting on stage with unprecedented naturalism, producing behind the scenes with prodigious energy, and above all conferring on his profession a respectability it had never had before.

The 14-year-old girl was summoned to the actor's elegant and grand new house in Adelphi Terrace, designed by the fashionable Adam brothers and overlooking the Thames. The Garricks had recently moved there and had furnished it lavishly. Mary would have entered through the large hall, with its imposing pillars, and then been shown into the magnificent first-floor drawing room, with its elaborate plaster ceiling crowned by a central circular panel of Venus surrounded by nine medallion paintings of the Graces. Garrick would have soon put her at ease with his good humour and liveliness. His wife, Eva Maria Veigel, a former dancer, was usually at his side and was especially considerate to young girls, as the future dramatist and novelist Fanny Burney testified when she visited the Garricks at their new house the same year: 'Mrs Garrick received us with a politeness and sweetness of manners, inseparable from her.'[4]

Garrick, always susceptible to beauty, was captivated by Mary's loveliness. Her voice reminded him of Susannah Cibber, an actress and singer he had favoured in his youth. An added attraction came in the form of Mary's long, shapely legs, ideal for the highly popular 'breeches roles' that were required of actresses on the Georgian stage. In an age when women wore full-length dresses all the time, the actress who cross-dressed in boys' clothing – as Shakespeare's Rosalind and Viola, and in dozens of similar roles in eighteenth-century comedies – provided a unique spectacle: the public exhibition of the shape of a female leg.

Garrick's personal interest was in no sense salacious. His faith in this young unknown was typical of his unfailing support for women in the theatre. His patronage of female actresses and female playwrights was highly unusual in a society that discouraged women from the stage and still regarded actresses as little better than prostitutes. Garrick 'discovered' many a young actress and gave playwrights such as Hannah More and Hannah Cowley their first break. In return these young women adored him and his wife.

He offered to train Mary for the part of Cordelia to his own King Lear in the version of Shakespeare's tragedy that he had reworked from Nahum Tate's Restoration era adaptation, in which Cordelia is happily married off to Edgar instead of being hanged. Garrick was now in his fifties, beginning to suffer from gout and gallstones. He was conserving his energy, limiting the number of his appearances on stage. Lear, which he had been playing since he was 25, was not only one of his most celebrated but also one of his most demanding roles. This late in his career, it was an extraordinary gamble to entrust Cordelia to a complete unknown. He and Mary spent hours preparing for her debut in the role.

But it was not all work: in the *Memoirs*, she draws a charming picture of them dancing minuets (Garrick was an excellent dancer) and singing the favourite ballads of the day. Her memory remained vivid: 'Never shall I forget the enchanting hours which I passed in Mr Garrick's society: he appeared to me as one who possessed more power, both to awe and to attract, than any man I ever met with.'[5] She also noticed his dark side: 'His smile was fascinating; but he had at times a restless peevishness of tone which excessively affected his hearer; at least it affected me so that I never shall forget it.' His temper was renowned. Fanny Burney reported in her diary that Dr Johnson attributed Garrick's faults to 'the *fire* and hastiness of his temper'. Burney loved Garrick and was mesmerized by the lustre of his 'brilliant, piercing eyes', but she also noted that 'he is almost perpetually giving offence to some of his friends'.[6] Others could feel irritated by his attention-seeking behaviour. As his friend Oliver Goldsmith put it, he was always natural, simple and unaffected on stage – ''Twas only when he was off, he was acting.'[7]

Garrick had a genius for self-publicity and was astonishingly energetic: in the light of Mary's subsequent career, one might say that he was her perfect role model. Mary adored him and took his advice seriously. He advised her to frequent Drury Lane and familiarize herself with its practices before she made her debut. She quickly became known as Garrick's new protégée and drew a swarm of admirers. This was Mary's first taste of celebrity and she loved the 'buzz' (her term). While Hester fretted about her daughter's reputation, Mary was confident that she could tread the thin line between fame and infamy: 'my ardent fancy was busied in contemplating a thousand triumphs, in which my vanity would be publicly gratified, without the smallest sacrifice of my private character'.[8]

Hester worried that her daughter was making too much of a stir amongst the young rakes who frequented the theatre just to flirt with the latest ingénue. She kept her eye on one man in particular. In her *Memoirs* Mary described him as a graceful and handsome officer – a Captain – who was very well connected, though she declined to name him. After a brief courtship, and offers of marriage, Hester discovered that he was already married. Mary was informed of the deception, but brushed it off: 'I felt little regret in the loss of a husband, when I reflected that a matrimonial alliance would have compelled me to relinquish my theatrical profession.' Another rich suitor came forward at this time, but, to Mary's horror, he was old enough to be her grandfather. She had set her heart on being an actress: 'the drama, the delightful drama, seemed the very criterion of all human happiness'.[9]

She was naturally flirtatious and her beauty attracted a stream of admirers. One of her most persistent suitors was a young solicitor's clerk, who lived across the way from her lodgings. He would sit in the window staring at the fresh-faced Mary. He was languorous and sickly looking, which would have appealed to a girl of strong 'sensibility'. Mrs Darby's response to the flirtation was to keep the lower shutters of the windows permanently closed. Fancying 'every man a seducer, and every hour an hour of accumulating peril', she sighed for the day when her daughter would be 'well married'.[10]

The articled clerk was named Thomas Robinson. He was training with the firm of Vernon and Elderton in the buildings opposite. He persuaded a friend (a junior colleague of Samuel Cox) to invite Mary and her mother to a dinner party out in Greenwich, without disclosing that Robinson himself would be present. Mother and daughter opened the door of their carriage only to find him ready to hand them down. Hester was duly horrified while Mary professed herself only 'confused'. Fortunately, though, she had dressed very carefully for dinner, sensing that a conquest was afoot: 'it was then the fashion to wear silks. I remember that I wore a nightgown of pale blue lustring, with a chip hat, trimmed with ribbands of the same colour.'[11] The English nightgown was a simple, flowing shift dress that had been popular for many seasons. It was modest in comparison to the revolutionary 'Perdita' chemise that Mary herself would popularize in the 1780s. Lustring was a plain woven silk with a glossy finish that was very popular for summer wear, while the fashionable chip hat, made of finely shaved willow or poplar, was to be worn at a jaunty angle.

Mary's obsession with her outfits might be considered as shallow and frivolous, but this is to misunderstand the power of fashion: she was very attuned to the ways in which clothing could transform her image. Fashion was central to the consumer society of the late eighteenth century. A plethora of shops offered ready-to-wear collections, while there were second-hand clothes stalls for the less well off. Silks, linens, and cottons were more widely available than ever before. Journalism and fashion went hand in hand: new monthly publications such as the *Lady's Magazine* included plates and detailed descriptions of the latest styles. Ladies could even hand-colour the black and white engravings and send them off to a mantua-maker with instructions for making up.

Mary loved to remember the tiniest details of the clothes she was wearing on a particular occasion. On the day that she met her future husband in Greenwich she felt that she had never dressed so perfectly to her own satisfaction. Thomas Robinson spent most of the evening simply staring at her. The party dined early and then returned to London, where Robinson's friend expatiated upon the many good qualities of Mary's new suitor, speaking of 'his future expectations from a rich old uncle; of his probable advancement in his profession; and, more than all, of his enthusiastic admiration of me'.[12] Robinson was apparently the heir of a rich tailor called Thomas Harris, who had a large estate in Wales. Hester Darby sensed that the secure marriage she needed for her daughter was within grasp.

As the date set for Mary's stage debut approached, Robinson was assiduous in his courtship. He knew that it was crucial to win her mother's approval and did so by his constant attentions and a flow of presents calculated to impress. Hester was especially fond of 'graveyard' literature, and she was delighted when Robinson brought her an elegantly bound copy of James Hervey's lugubrious *Meditations among the Tombs* of 1746. She was 'beguiled' by these attentions and Robinson accordingly 'became so great a favourite, that he seemed to her the most perfect of existing beings'. He gained more credit when smallpox again threatened the family. This time it was George, Hester's favourite son, who was dangerously ill.

Mary postponed her stage appearance and Robinson was 'indefatigable in his attentions' to the sick boy and his anxious mother. Robinson's conduct convinced Hester that he was '"the kindest, the best of mortals!", the least addicted to worldly follies – and the man, of all others, who she should adore as a *son-in-law*'.[13]

Robinson might have convinced the mother, but he still had some way to go with the daughter. Luck was on his side. When George recovered from the smallpox, Mary fell sick herself. This was a test that would reveal the extent of the suitor's devotion: would he persist in his courtship despite the threat of death or at the very least disfigurement of her lovely features? He did not waver and duly exerted 'all his assiduity' to win Mary's affections, proving the 'disinterested' quality of his fondness. For Mary, the relationship was more fraternal than romantic: 'he attended with the zeal of a brother; and that zeal made an impression of gratitude upon my heart, which was the source of all my succeeding sorrows'.[14]

The combined forces of mother and lover were irresistible. Every kind of persuasion and emotional blackmail was employed to press the suit. Hester urged Mary to promise that if she survived the disease she would marry Robinson. She reiterated the threat made by Mary's father and even intimated that her daughter's refusal was proof that she retained affection for the 'libertine Captain'. Mary was cajoled and bullied, 'repeatedly urged and hourly reminded' of her father's vow. Hester's only hesitation was the thought of the inevitable separation between mother and daughter that marriage would bring. But the resolute lover overcame this obstacle with his promise of the ultimate sacrifice: he insisted that the bride's mother should live with them, overseeing the domestic duties. Could Mary really refuse him when he offered her abandoned mother a home?

This was how Mary recollected the courtship when she came to write her memoirs. By making her mother an accomplice in Robinson's scheme to force her hand, she gave the impression that it was not a marriage of affection on her part. But Hester's culpability is debatable. Her worries were genuine. Her daughter was headstrong, and Hester was doubtful about a stage career. She was worried about Nicholas and the threat he had issued. Robinson's motives seemed genuine enough. His was hardly a mercenary choice, as Mary brought no money or prospects. Few men would cherish the idea of living with their mother-in-law during the first years of marriage. It would appear that Robinson was genuinely in love with Mary. Neither was his devotion skin deep. He could well have withdrawn his suit when the ravages of smallpox threatened her beauty. At its worst, this horrific disease rendered its surviving victims disfigured and scarred beyond all recognition. Robinson risked his own health to nurse George and attend Mary. Considered in this light, his commitment could not be doubted.

Mary's timid acquiescence in the match seems uncharacteristic. She had inherited her father's intrepidity and her mother's determination. Every action of her eventful life suggests strength of will and force of personality that little could dampen. But she was weak and vulnerable with illness when she finally agreed to Robinson's proposal. While she lay on her sickbed, the banns were published during three successive Sunday morning services at the church of St Martin-in-the-Fields, in what is now Trafalgar Square.

An unflattering biographical account of the Robinsons, published in 1781, in which the writer claimed that he knew a great deal about the couple's affairs, claimed that, despite his humble position as a lawyer's clerk, Thomas presented himself to Mary and Hester as a gentleman of £30,000, sole heir to a Mr Harris of Carmarthenshire, who gave him an allowance of £500 per year and far greater expectations for the future. According to this early biographer, both Mary and her mother jumped at the match.[15]

Doubts may have crept in when Robinson urged mother and daughter to keep the engagement secret. He gave two reasons. One was that he still had three months' training to serve as an articled clerk and the second that there was another young lady who wished to marry him as soon as he came into independence. Mary had found a small window of opportunity for delay and urged him to postpone the marriage until he came of age. Robinson absolutely refused. Now that she had recovered, with no loss to her looks, Mary still harboured hopes of a stage career. Garrick, wholly unaware that he was in danger of losing his protégée, was agitating for a performance date. Robinson, appealing shrewdly to Hester's insecurities, invoked strong arguments against the theatre. Nicholas Darby would be horrified by the prospect. Mary's health would suffer from the 'fatigues and exertions of the profession'. He also voiced the anti-theatrical prejudice of the age's moralists when he suggested that

Mary would become an object of male desire whose reputation would be irrevocably damaged 'on a public stage, where all the attractions of the mimic scene would combine to render [her] a fascinating object'.[16]

Time was running out for Mary. She now had to decide whether to risk the social embarrassment of pulling out of the marriage even though the banns had been posted or to abandon her hopes of a stage career. With increasing pressure from all angles to choose between the professions of respectable marriage or disreputable acting, she relented: 'It was now that Mr Robinson and my mother united in persuading me to relinquish my project; and so perpetually, during three days, was I tormented on the subject – so ridiculed for having permitted the bans to be published, and afterwards hesitating to fulfil my contract, that I consented – and was married.'[17]

In the original manuscript of her *Memoirs*, Mary proceeded in the next paragraph to describe her feelings as she knelt at the altar on her wedding day. But she later returned to the manuscript and inserted an additional paragraph that creates a compelling picture of herself as little more than a schoolgirl, coerced into marriage out of gratitude and filial obedience. Up until her marriage, she claims, she dressed like a child (though this does not square with the description of her attire on the day she met Robinson for the first time). She insists that she looked 'so juvenile' in her appearance that even two years after her wedding shopkeepers would address her as Miss, assuming she was a daughter and not a wife. She even adds that she still retained the manners of a child, playing with her dolls only three months before she became a wife. One senses a certain overegging of the pudding here. The image of the child with her dolls does not equate with that of the young lady being trained by Garrick for the stage and pursued by the 'libertine Captain', who was still writing to Mary and following her around in public despite her discovery of the fact that he was already married.

The vicar officiating at the church, Dr Erasmus Saunders, remarked that he had never 'before performed the office for so young a bride'. The wedding took place on 12 April 1773: Mary Darby became Mary Robinson when she was just under 15½. In the *Memoirs* she presents herself as sexually innocent: 'the only circumstance which induced me to marry was that of being still permitted to reside with my mother, and to live separate, at least for some time, from my husband'.[18] She chose for her wedding attire the habit of a Quaker – 'a society to which, in early youth, I was particularly partial'.[19] But when the bride left the church for the wedding breakfast at a friend's house, she changed her plain dress for something altogether more glamorous. Her gown was muslin, with a matching white sarsenet scarf-cloak; she wore a chip hat with silk ribbons and satin slippers embroidered with silver thread. The change of costume is symbolic of Mary's struggle to reconcile the contrasting aspects of her character. On the one hand she wanted to be seen as a prudish Quaker, a sexual innocent almost forced into an arranged marriage, but on the other she wanted to be viewed as a beautiful and fashionable bride, decked out in white and silver.

Mary always insisted that her marriage was not a love match. She was deeply romantic and cherished hopes of a soul mate. Robinson was not the man. Of her feelings for her future husband, she wrote, 'I knew not the sensation of any sentiment beyond that of esteem; love was still a stranger to my bosom.'[20] But according to the *Memoirs*, it was not another, more dashing suitor that she thought of as she spoke her marriage vows kneeling at the altar of the church of St Martin-in-the-Fields. Her thoughts wandered instead to the theatrical career that she was sacrificing, to the glimmer of fame, and the lost opportunity of an independent livelihood.

CHAPTER 3

Wales

> There is nothing in life so difficult as to acquire the art of making time pass tolerably in the country.
>
> Mary Robinson, *The Widow*

The wedding party of four set out in a phaeton and a post chaise. They stopped for the night at an inn near Maidenhead. Robinson was accompanied by an old school friend, Hanway Balack, who kept the groom in good cheer whilst the young bride Mary walked in the gardens with her mother, weeping and describing herself as 'the most wretched of mortals'. She confessed to Hester that although she esteemed Mr Robinson she did not feel for him that 'warm and powerful union of soul' which she felt was indispensable for marriage.[1]

Mary was already beginning to regret the clandestine quality of the marriage. During the onward journey to Henley-on-Thames the following day, Hanway had quoted facetiously from Isaac Bickerstaff's comic opera *The Padlock* of 1768, then in 'high celebrity', which depicted the insecurities of an aged bachelor called Don Diego. His teasing made her painfully aware of the precariousness of her position: Robinson had not told even the friend who was accompanying them on the honeymoon that they were married. Ironically, though, Hanway was to remain a close and loyal friend to Mary throughout her life, long after Robinson had disappeared from it.*

* He later changed his name to Hanway Hanway. He was related to philanthropist Jonas Hanway, who campaigned against boy chimney sweeps and was one of the first men to carry an umbrella.

The honeymoon by the river at Henley lasted for ten days. Mary had the painful task of sending Garrick the news that she was married and was therefore relinquishing her stage career. When the couple returned to London, it was to separate residences. Robinson returned to his job in Chancery Lane, while Mary and her mother hired an elegant house in Great Queen Street in fashionable Lincoln's Inn Fields, backing onto Chancery Lane. Robinson stuck to his insistence that the marriage should be kept secret until he had come of age and finished his articles. Whilst he was busy in chambers, Mary grew bored and found herself a young female companion, who shared her romantic disposition. The girls spent hours wandering in Westminster Abbey, peering at its Gothic windows and listening to the echoes of their footsteps vibrating along the aisles. Mary felt transported back to her childhood in Bristol Minster.

Hester became anxious about her new son-in-law's continued desire for secrecy. She began to regret the part she had played in promoting the marriage. Then she learnt to her dismay that Robinson had been spinning a web of lies from the very start. He had claimed that his inheritance would fall due when he came of age, but in fact he was already 21. And he had much further to go in his training than he had pretended. Worst of all, Hester discovered the true story of Robinson's origins. He was not the legitimate heir of his uncle, Thomas Harris, and heir presumptive to a 'handsome fortune and an estate in South Wales'. He was actually Harris's illegitimate son – according to one source, the result of a fling with a laundress. Furthermore, with an industrious and ambitious older brother in the picture (whom Robinson had conveniently forgotten to mention), his financial prospects were dim. It was extremely unlikely that he would inherit anything at all from his father. He also owed a lot of money.

Mary, meanwhile, unexpectedly met Garrick walking in a London street. This was the first time she had seen him since informing him by letter of her marriage. She was highly sensible that he had not yielded any return on his protégée and that she had not told him of her defection face to face. After all, she had been trained by the greatest actor of the age and he was not accustomed to having his time wasted by fickle would-be-actresses who changed course at the final hurdle. To his infinite credit and to her utmost relief, he greeted her warmly and congratulated her on her marriage. Mary's charm and beauty had won him over again.

She does not record what she said to him at this meeting. Perhaps she intimated to him, as she did in her *Memoirs*, that she had been persuaded to marry against her will, and that she deeply regretted the sacrifice of her career. However she managed it – and David Garrick was not the easiest person in the world to sweet-talk – he continued to be a friend and supporter. Mary had a unique talent for maintaining loyal, protective friends, most of whom fell headlong in love with her wit and charm.

Garrick's knowledge of Mary's marriage put increasing pressure on Robinson to make the union public. Every day that passed with a disavowal from him put Hester under increasing strain, and Mary's reputation at greater risk. She could fall pregnant at any time, a plight that Garrick and George Colman the Elder had exploited in their popular comedy of 1766 *The Clandestine Marriage*. In this play, the lovely young heroine Fanny Sterling is persuaded by her new husband, against her better judgement, to keep her clandestine marriage secret, even though she is heavily pregnant. Despite her condition, she is pursued by many suitors, especially the lecherous aristocrat Lord Ogleby. Mary hints at a similar dilemma in her *Memoirs*, though it was her mother who was furious with Thomas: 'The reputation of a darling child, she alleged, was at stake; and though during a few weeks the world might have been kept in ignorance of my marriage, some circumstances that had transpired now rendered an immediate disclosure absolutely necessary.'[2] There is, however, no evidence that Mary was indeed pregnant at this time. Her daughter was born a full year later.

Perhaps this was an example of Mary's penchant in her *Memoirs* for conflating fact and fiction, drawing upon a literary cliché of secret unions and swollen stomachs. She was writing with the memory of having drawn attention from the press for playing the part of the pregnant Fanny Sterling in *The Clandestine Marriage* whilst she herself was heavily pregnant with her second child. Another possibility is, of course, that Mary and her mother used a feigned pregnancy as a final card to force Thomas's hand and frighten him into submission. If that was the trick, it seems to have worked: Hester confronted her son-in-law and demanded that he make the marriage public before Mary's reputation was irrevocably damaged.

Finding Hester inexorable, Robinson resolved to leave for South Wales to avow his marriage and present his young bride to his 'uncle' – he still stubbornly disputed the fact of his illegitimacy, though his secret was now out. Hester insisted on travelling with the couple as far as Bristol, ostensibly in order to visit her old friends in the city, but no doubt also to keep an eye on developments. In the absence of her husband, she was determined to protect her daughter's honour. The journey to Bristol was enlivened by a stopover in which they visited the Oxford colleges and took a guided tour of Blenheim Palace – 'with the hope of soothing my mother's resentment, and exhilarating my spirits, which were now perpetually dejected'.[3]

Robinson went on alone from Bristol to the family seat in Tregunter, Wales. He assured his wife that he would be smoothing the way for her eventual cordial reception at Tregunter House, but, in truth, neither was at all confident that Thomas Harris would sanction the union. On the surface, it seemed a very peculiar marriage. Thomas and Mary had now been married for six months without living together under the same roof. Now Mary was being left again so that Robinson could persuade his father, from whom he had been estranged for some time, to give his blessing to a marriage without prospects or money. It was an inauspicious start to domestic life. Still, they both wanted money and status, and wanted to live well. Mary was prepared to let him go to do his best to win round his father. She insists that although she did not feel overwhelmed with love, she was nevertheless attached 'to the interest as well as to the person of my husband'.[4] Though she later came to despise him, she was aware of his qualities, his easy-going temperament and affability.

Nor was she willing to sit and mope whilst their future hung in the balance. She was gratified by the homecoming she received at Bristol. News had spread that Mary Darby had made a good marriage 'to a young man of considerable expectations' and she was once again 'received as the daughter of Mr Darby'. Given her father's marital infidelity and her husband's true circumstances, she saw the irony in the way that she was deriving respectability from her status as a wife and a daughter. She was struck by the numerous invitations she now received, in stark contrast to the time when she and her mother had left Bristol in humiliation: 'I found that fortune was, to common minds, a never-failing passport.'[5] She was in a sense returning in triumph, restoring her mother and herself to the respectability that had been lost when Nicholas Darby walked out. Friends who now greeted Hester and Mary warmly had turned their backs when they had most needed friendship. They could turn again. Mary rarely forgot a social slight, and felt it keenly if someone wronged her – a reaction which perhaps stemmed from those Bristol years when the family had endured social ostracism.

Her return to the place of her birth affected her deeply. She took a solitary walk back to the scenes of her childhood: the schoolhouse, the green, the tombs of her ancestors. In the minster she once more crept under the wings of the huge brass eagle in the middle aisle, just as she had done as a child. 'Language cannot describe the sort of sensation' which she felt when she suddenly heard the peal of the organ ringing out as it had in her youth. But now the family home was a ruin: 'The nursery windows were dim, and shattered; the house was sinking to decay.' She remembered how she had walked in the cloisters that linked her old home to the minster: '"Here," said I, "did my infant feet pace to and fro" . . . On those dark and winding steps, did I sit and listen to the full-toned organ, the loud anthem, and the bell, which called the parishioners to prayer.'[6] As she re-entered the cathedral, she read and reread the monumental inscriptions, finding the grave of the actor William Powell, whose Lear had been her first experience of theatre. And she dropped a tear on the stone tablet that commemorated an old family friend. As so often in the *Memoirs*, this account is embellished with many a literary flourish, but there is no reason to doubt that when Mary returned to Bristol as Mrs Robinson she must have felt that her childhood was well and truly over, her innocence lost.

Her melancholy was no doubt exacerbated by the uncertainty over her future. Everything depended upon Thomas Harris's generosity. Perhaps she even feared that her husband would abscond. Hope returned when Robinson sent a letter from Tregunter relating that his '*uncle* seemed disposed to act handsomely'. Mary learned that at first Robinson was too frightened to tell his father that he was already married, but upon revealing the truth, Harris expressed the hope that she was neither too young nor too beautiful, since 'beauty, without money, is but a dangerous sort of portion'. Still, Harris had grudgingly accepted the inevitable: 'If the thing is done, it cannot be undone.'[7] He agreed to a visit. Robinson duly wrote with the news, instructing Mary to obtain funds for the journey by requesting a loan from one of his friends back in London – a man she had sometimes seen in his company.

'One or two letters passed on this subject,' she writes in the *Memoirs*. And then her husband returned in order to escort her to Wales. The man to whom she had written was the notorious John King, generally known as 'Jew' King, a young and ambitious money-broker. In the *Memoirs* Mary claims disingenuously that she was 'an entire stranger to the transaction which rendered him the temporary source of my husband's finances'.[8] She represents herself as the very picture of innocence and passivity. The emphasis on her melancholy mood and her recollections of childhood as she waited in Bristol draws the reader away from any thought of her possible implication in her new husband's messy financial affairs.

That phrase 'one or two letters' is, however, economical with the truth. To a greater extent than at any other point in the *Memoirs*, Mary was whitewashing her own past. The real story of her involvement with 'Jew' King reveals that she was by no means the naive newlywed she would have her readers believe in.

At the height of her fame, Mary was notorious not only for the love letters sent to her from the Prince of Wales under the signature 'Florizel', but also for a much sleazier correspondence with King. In 1781, as part of a concerted press campaign to blacken her name, there appeared a slim quarto volume, published at two shillings, which purported to contain copies of real letters that passed between Mrs Robinson and a 'certain Israelite' between 21 September and 30 November 1773. Her letters were all dated from Bristol and addressed to King in London. In one of them, dated 9 November, she says that on the previous Tuesday Mr Robinson had set out for Carmarthenshire, where he intended to stay a week, and that he would then send for her to join him. The circumstances fit precisely with the account in the *Memoirs* of how Mary waited at Bristol with her mother while Robinson went forward to pave the way for her reception in Wales. Many details in the published letters are so specific that it is impossible to suppose that the volume was merely a malicious fabrication. What is more, as will be seen in a later chapter, Mary and her then lover, Lord Malden, made strenuous efforts to recover the original letters. This attempt strongly suggests that in reality more than 'one or two letters' passed between Mary Robinson and John King in the first year of her marriage. Though in all probability King spiced up the text for the purposes of publication, *Letters from Perdita to a Certain Israelite, and his Answers to them* gives us the very voice of the young Mary with an immediacy that is altogether lacking in the carefully self-censored retrospective narrative of the *Memoirs*.[9]

The letters reveal an intimacy that would never have been guessed from the casual passing reference to King in the *Memoirs*. The first of them reads as follows:

> Bristol, 21st Sept. 1773
>
> Sir,
>
> I never deemed myself happier, than I found myself those few Days you accompanied us upon the Road; indeed your Company, from the first Moment of our Acquaintance, has been so agreeable, that I scarcely know how to spare you. Shall we expect you at *Bristol*? Write me soon; write the Style you know I like; let it be plaintive; sooth the Wanderings of my pensive Breast.
>
> *Your humble Servant*,
>
> M. R—

Just as the Robinsons were accompanied at the beginning of their honeymoon not only by Hester Darby but also by Hanway Balack, so they set off for Bristol with King as well as Mary's mother. The information that Mary has found King's company highly agreeable ever since their first acquaintance reveals that she must have spent considerable time in his company in the five months since her marriage. What is more, the preface explaining the circumstances of the correspondence includes the information that – on the basis of Thomas Robinson's prospects of inheriting an estate – King had already lent the couple a substantial sum of money.

The extent of their involvement is further exposed in Mary's second letter, in which we discover that King was with the Robinsons when they stopped for their sightseeing in Oxford:

> Bristol, 29th Sept. 1773
>
> With Pleasure I take this Opportunity of answering my worthy Friend's obliging Epistle. R— is not yet gone to *Wales*, but as he will go soon, it makes me uneasy; you know *how I love him*, therefore will excuse my mentioning him. The Weather is extremely fine, and nothing but your Company is wanted to

> enliven the Place. We hope by this Time you have seen dear little George, and that he is well. You cannot conceive with what Regret we parted with you at *Oxford*; the Three last Days were not spent half so agreeable as the first. I am quite ashamed of this intolerable Scroll, but I hope you will pardon it, for I am fatigued almost to Death. Mrs Darby begs her respects.
>
> *Your Friend.*

King, then, not only travelled with Thomas, Mary, and Hester as far as Oxford: he was also asked to keep an eye on George, Mary's younger brother left behind in London. King's response to this letter was flirtatious and literary. Mary wrote again a week later. She, too, flirts in one sentence and moralizes in the next. She was missing him and missing the buzz of London still more:

> I wish you were sincere in what you say, I do not think you are, but still I believe myself happy in your good Opinion; you treat me so much in a Style of Compliment, that I really do not know in what Manner to return it; you express so much Friendship, that the hardest Task, I ever undertook in my whole Life, is how to return Thanks suitable to the Favours I have received from you . . . I long to be in Town. Do not forget our intended Party to *Drury-Lane* Theatre; you know I am passionately fond of Plays, and I was going to say, I envy you, but Envy I detest.

But then she comes to the main point:

> not that I think Generosity consists in throwing Money away at Random, without Distinction or Judgment, but in bestowing it in proportion to the Merit and Condition of those who stand in need of our Assistance. I agree with my favourite Author, who says, in Trust, Intimacy and Confidence, be as particular as you can; in Humanity, Charity and Benevolence, universal. I shall depend on your Promise this Week for I am really distressed.

A plea for funds is dressed up as a moral duty and spiced with literary allusion. King's response begins in a similar high-minded tone: 'Morality is that great fundamental Tie that forms and preserves the Peace and Welfare of Society.' But it quickly turns to an admonition that Mary's 'immoderate' desire for material wellbeing is in danger of leading her to 'Indiscretion' and exposing her to 'the destructive Stratagems of some libidinous Profligate'. Having warned her against the seductions of fashionable society, King then lets his own emotions speak:

> That fair youthful Frame is such an Invitation to Love, as no moral or platonic Tenets can restrain. How I pant to be at *Bristol*, to accompany you through the verdant Meads to the Side of some Silver Stream, slow wandering its Meanders down the Glade, or to the cool Recess of a shady Grove, where every Gale whispers Pleasure, Contentment and Love! Your Breath will add new Fragrance to the Amaranth; the Rose will receive a deeper Hue from the Reflection of those florid Tincts that adorn thy blooming Cheeks, while you melt my Soul to all the soft Attainments of Love.

The expression of such sentiments was King's price for the payoff signalled by the end of the letter: '*Adieu! Be ever happy as you are good.* Inclosed £50.'

The next letter purportedly from Mary would severely damage her reputation when King published the correspondence eight years later:

> I wish you would not write, for while you endeavour to inculcate such good Doctrine, you know I am charmed by your Letters to a Sin. How call I love that stupid Thing R—! yet I am his, Fortune has made it so; but I cannot think I am bound to abide strictly by an Engagement that I was trepanned into, for you know he *deceived* me. Shall I ever write as well as you do? I am fond of Poetry, and you shall correct some Attempts in that Way, when I come to *London*. My Friend, you know I esteem you: is it a Crime to say I *love* you? I feel an Inclination to love Somebody; and how can I love him who is too stupid to return it? Why then, I will love you. Write again, write every Evening, or I shall be melancholy.

Despite his sordid profession as a moneylender, King had a reputation as a man of culture. John Taylor, an oculist who moved in the very best circles and who was himself a poet and a friend of Mary Robinson, recorded in his memoirs that he had known King for forty years and always found him honourable, hospitable, and attentive, and that he especially liked having men and women of talent at his table.[10]

Mary's letter accords with this image: King is presented as a companion for theatregoing and literary talk, associated with poetry and the language of sensibility. The reference to her own efforts at poetry suggests that, with her stage debut forestalled by her marriage, she is already thinking of a literary career. Robinson, meanwhile, is anything but a sensitive literary man: he is a 'stupid Thing' and Mary effectively admits that she only married him because of his supposed financial prospects. Because of his deception on this front, he has forfeited any right to strict conjugal loyalty.

For King, this was sufficient encouragement. His reply brings him to a pitch of excitement:

> I will not think you sincere, when you say you love; yet if you are not in earnest, you have given *too serious* a Testimony of it for one only *in Joke*; but it is almost Blasphemy to suspect one of such heavenly Form, so beautiful, such Symmetry of Features, such delicate welformed [sic] Limbs, such panting snowy Breasts, such – Oh! What *Raptures* ineffable seize my *delighted Imagination*, when I *recollect* the *delirious Transports* that throbbed to my very Soul, when that beauteous Form stood confessed in all the resistless Power of – *Nakedness*. I must stop till my *enraptured* Fancy returns from the *ecstatick* Thought.

Is this a ripe fantasy or had he really caught a glimpse of a naked Mary in Oxford or on some other occasion?

With the flirtation getting this far out of hand, Mary cooled the temperature in her following letter – though she still needed to keep King sweet, because she was, as she put it in a postscript, 'rather short'. The correspondence had by now lasted for a month. On 1 November, King wrote with further references to 'the *mystick* Meaning of thy *wanton* Love' and his '*melting Senses*' drowning in '*delicious* Transports', while at the same time delivering a rebuke: 'You little Prodigal, you have spent £200 in Six Weeks: I will not answer your Drafts.' King's refusal to forward any more funds, despite a further request, brought the correspondence to an abrupt end in the final week of November. Mary's last letter is in a very different tone from the preceding ones:

> I Find you have not yet answered my Draft. I do not wish an Acquaintance with any Man who professes so much Love, but who gives so little Proof of it. I wish I could recall those imprudent Moments when I suffered your *deluding* Promises, and *seductive* Tongue, to betray me into Sin; but unless you give me the Token of your Sincerity that I ask for, I will take care how I trust you again. I am astonished that you should scruple to lend me such a Sum as £100 when it was the last I should borrow, and should have repaid it faithfully. Now you have an Opportunity of shewing your Love, or I shall see that you have all along deceived me.

King responded with a long and vitriolic letter on the evils of ambition and avarice, and the correspondence ended. His failure to recover either his original loan or his subsequent advances, together with a not unjustifiable sense of having been taken for a ride by Mary's flirtatious manner, accounts for his action in publishing the letters in 1781. There is no evidence that King himself had any further dealings with Mary thereafter, though by a curious twist his daughter became a passionate fan of her poetry.*

Late in November, Robinson returned to Bristol to fetch his wife. They left Hester and headed across to Wales. They endured a hazardous crossing at Chepstow in an open boat in the midst of a fierce storm. In the *Memoirs*, Mary novelistically interprets this as an ill omen, akin to the storm that coincided with her birth. Throughout the journey Robinson tried to prepare his refined young wife for her first meeting with his family. Still denying that Harris was his father, he asked Mary to 'overlook anything harsh that might appear in the manners of his *uncle*'. But she was busy absorbing the beauties of the landscape as they drove into the remote Welsh countryside: 'We passed through a thick wood, the moun-

* Charlotte King (later Dacre) grew up to publish Robinson-influenced poetry in the *Morning Post* under the name 'Rosa Matilda'; she then wrote Gothic and sentimental novels, heavily influenced by Mary's.

tains at every brake meeting our eyes covered with thin clouds, and rising in a sublime altitude above the valley. A more romantic space of scenery never met the human eye!'[11]

With a shift of tone typical of Mary's mercurial nature, the narrative of her visit to the in-laws then turns from romantic novel to comedy of high and low life, with the sophisticated townies meeting the country bumpkins. Mary was fabulously dressed, as usual, in a dark claret riding habit and a white beaver hat trimmed with feathers. She looked askance at the odd couple that waited to greet her, her father-in-law, Thomas Harris, and his daughter, Elizabeth. Harris, evidently pleased with the elegant Mrs Robinson, kissed her 'with excessive cordiality', while his daughter led her into the house 'with cold formality'. 'She could not have taken my hand with a more frigid demeanour,' Mary adds, clearly relishing the memory.[12]

The young women sized one another up. Elizabeth was not a great beauty and must have felt threatened by her brother's fashionable wife. She was cold and haughty and took an instant dislike to her new sister-in-law. To Mary's sharp eyes, she looked a fright. Elizabeth seemed older than her twenty years, moved stiffly, without grace or elegance, and was short and clumsy looking. She had a rustic face with a snub, upturned nose, and cheeks 'somewhat more ruddy than was consistent with even good health'.[13] Her countenance, Mary thought, was 'peculiarly formed for the expression of sarcastic vulgarity'. The elegantly dressed Mrs Robinson was equally appalled by Elizabeth's vulgar attire; she wore a cheap gaudy chintz gown and a 'thrice-bordered cap' decked with a profusion of ribbons. Her initial impression of retired tailor Thomas Harris was just as dismaying: he wore an unfashionable brown fustian coat, a scarlet waistcoat trimmed with gold, a gold-laced hat, and – instead of the silk stockings that befitted a gentleman – a hideous pair of woollen 'spatter-dashes'. He cuts an engagingly comic figure, his manners coarse and boorish, but kind of heart – the very embodiment of Squire Western in Fielding's *Tom Jones* or Goldsmith's Mr Hardcastle in *She Stoops to Conquer*.

Harris was, in fact, an influential figure in Glamorganshire. He was the squire of two large estates, Tregunter and Trevecca, and was a Justice of the Peace. One of his brothers was Howel Harris, a well-known Methodist reformer. Possibly through his brother's influence, the religious reformer

Selina Hastings, Countess of Huntingdon, had established a seminary at Trevecca House for the training of ministers. Elizabeth Robinson was a convert to Lady Huntingdon's 'sect', and sometimes took Mary with her to Trevecca. Squire Harris preferred the local church where he could throw his weight around and fine the rustics for swearing, even though 'every third sentence he uttered was attended by an oath that made his hearers shudder'.[14] Harris spent most of the days on his estate, riding his small Welsh pony, only appearing at meal times.

Mary was thoroughly bored by her husband's family. She quickly discovered that the real ruler of the household was Molly Edwards, the housekeeper. She heartily disliked her: 'a more overbearing, vindictive spirit never inhabited the heart of mortal than that which pervaded the soul of the ill-natured Mrs Molly'.[15] Miss Betsy and Mrs Molly were jealous of Mary, who supped ale with the squire and soon became his favourite: 'They observed me with jealous eyes; they considered me as an interloper, whose manners attracted Mr Harris's esteem, and who was likely to diminish their divided influence in the family.'[16]

Mary often alienated other young women, who were left feeling dowdy and dull in her presence. She was naturally flirtatious and men were captivated by her charm, but she was perhaps less keen to cultivate the friendship of other women, if she did not think it worth her time. She noticed the 'side-long glances' of Miss Betsy and Mrs Molly when she entertained visitors who praised her 'good looks, or taste in the choice of my dresses'. The women taunted her for acting like a duchess with her fine clothes and her accomplishments – 'a good housewife had no occasion for harpsichords and books'.[17] They reminded her that she had no money to support her fancy ways. But Mary did not care. She had her beauty and her elegance and her humour to protect her. When she went riding with Miss Betsy, she laughed at her odd appearance: 'Miss Robinson rode on horseback in a camlet safe-guard, with a high-crowned bonnet. I wore a fashionable habit, and looked like something human.'[18]

More disturbingly, Harris seemed to have fallen in love with her even though in his sixties he was old enough to be her grandfather. When he declared that he should 'have liked me for a wife, had I not married *Tom*', she decided it would be prudent to leave. She feared that 'through the machinations of Miss Betsy and Mrs Molly I should lose the share I had gained in his affections'. Betsy and Molly were duly furious when the squire insisted upon accompanying Mary to Bristol: 'he swore that he would see me safe across the Channel, whatever might be the consequences of his journey'.[19]

In Bristol, meeting the charming Hester and getting a taste of her active social life, Harris decided to stay a while. Hester introduced him to her friends and he was invited to several dinner parties. Mary danced with him and, after he had supped his evening draught, she would sing to him. He was flattered by the attention and dropped hints to the effect that Tom would inherit the estate. He asked for advice on refurbishments for Tregunter House, and together they picked out smart marble chimney-pieces: 'Choose them as you like them, Mrs Robinson, for they are all for you and Tom when I am no more.'[20]

CHAPTER 4

Infidelity

> The town still full of alluring scenes, faro tables, assemblies, to say nothing of Ranelagh, the opening beauties of Kensington, and the morning lounge of St James's street.
>
> Mary Robinson, *The Widow*

> We are taught to cherish deceit, indifference, vanity, contempt, and scorn; we cannot bear neglect, because it awakens our self-love; we think not of the natural fickleness of man; but we tremble, lest the world should suppose, that a husband's infidelity proceeds from our own want of attractions to hold him faithful.
>
> Mary Robinson, *The False Friend*

As soon as Harris had left Bristol, the Robinsons set out for London. According to Mary, they adopted young George Darby and brought him up as their own, until he was old enough to be sent abroad to a merchant house, like his elder brother, John. Elated by the great expectations that Harris had held out for them, the Robinsons threw themselves into London life. The first step they took was to move to a newly built house in Hatton Garden, a location in the 'city' at the east end of London as opposed to the more fashionable 'town' (or *ton*) in the west end. Close to Smithfield Market and St Paul's, the Hatton Garden district was home to newly prosperous merchants and Jewish moneylenders, jewellers, and lawyers – it was conveniently placed for the Inns of Court.

The Robinsons furnished their new property lavishly and bought a phaeton, the modish open-top carriage that was the same kind of status symbol as a modern convertible. Thomas Robinson also got to know the local jewellers and silversmiths. He bought his wife an expensive watch, enamelled with musical trophies.

From where did they get the money? In her *Memoirs* Mary claimed ignorance about her husband's financial affairs and debts (which she always described as his debts rather than hers), but according to King she devised a scheme – played out by Robinson and a group of fellow swindlers – that involved raising 'immense Quantities of Goods on the Credit of foreign Letters, which they had transmitted them for the Purpose, from *Holland*, *Ostend* and France'.[1] Whatever the truth of this allegation, the handsome house in Hatton Garden would have been enough to persuade traders and lenders that the Robinsons' credit was good.

With a smart address, a flashy phaeton, and Mary's dazzling good looks, they burst upon the social scene, determined to get themselves noticed. Mary knew how to use her sex appeal: 'A new face, a young person dressed with peculiar but simple elegance, was sure to attract attention at places of public entertainment.'[2] She describes her entrance into society as making her debut 'in the broad hemisphere of fashionable folly'. She might have lost her chance to perform at Drury Lane, but she saw the metropolis as a great urban stage where she could still be a star.

Her first stop was the pleasure gardens at Ranelagh. Pleasure gardens ranked high in London's recreational activities, but the two most popular were those of Ranelagh in Chelsea and Vauxhall in Lambeth. Here, in the open air, people gathered to stroll, chat, and listen to music. By day they could walk amongst the grottoes, groves, and waterfalls, and by night look at the brilliant lights strewn in the trees, attend concerts, balls and masquerades, and see the fireworks. Ranelagh was the classier venue: at two shillings and sixpence, its entrance fee was more than twice that of raucous Vauxhall. It had Chinese buildings, temples, statues, a canal, and a bridge. It also boasted the rotunda, an enormous circular hall for concerts, ringed with fifty-two boxes. An orchestra played whilst the ladies and gentlemen strolled around the main floor. Regular concerts were held in the summer; the 8-year-old Mozart performed there in 1764. After the concert, one would sit and eat a light supper. It was a place to be noticed and to join the smart set. The royal princes were known to frequent the pleasure gardens with their aristocratic friends. Women of fashion promenaded the main walks to show off their latest gowns and hats, and to make a stir. Prostitutes, dressed in their finery, plied their trade in the wooded groves. In Fanny Burney's novel *Evelina*, the innocent heroine mistakes the Ranelagh prostitutes for ladies of fashion and is herself mistaken for a whore when she wanders onto a wrong path.

Mary chose her outfit carefully. She wore a simple Quaker-style, light brown silk dress, with close cuffs. Breaking with the convention of powdering her hair, she perched a plain round cap and a white chip hat on her tumbling auburn locks. She wore no other accessories – no jewellery and no ornaments. She was simplicity itself. Never one to follow fashion slavishly, she had confidence in her individual style and panache. Needless to say, she cut a figure: all eyes were fixed upon her.

The Robinsons' next outing was to the indoor equivalent of Ranelagh, the Pantheon in Oxford Street. It had only opened a couple of years before, when it was described by Charles Burney as the 'most elegant structure in Europe, if not on the globe'.[3] In the main it was a musical venue, housing concerts, balls, masquerades, and dances. It also had a central rotunda where visitors could play cards or take supper on ordinary evenings. Tickets for masquerades were expensive and exclusive: by subscription only, at two guineas (the equivalent of about a hundred pounds in today's money). Mary described it as 'the most fashionable assemblage of the gay and the distinguished'. As though at court, visitors dressed formally in large hoops and towering headdresses. The women's hair was raised high with padding and false hair, and then greased with pomade before being powdered. Mary spent hours preparing herself, wearing an exquisite gown of pink satin trimmed with sable, and arranging her suit of 'rich and valuable point lace', which was given by her mother. By this time, though, she really was pregnant: 'my *shape* at that period required some arrangements, owing to the visible *increase* of my domestic solicitudes'.[4]

Mary was overwhelmed by the Pantheon rotunda: 'I never shall forget the impression which my mind received: the splendour of the scene, the dome illuminated with variegated lamps, the music, and the beauty of the women, seemed to present a circle of enchantment.'[5] It was the women who made the strongest impact upon the impressionable young girl, four of them in particular: the celebrated beauty Lady Almeria Carpenter ('the admiration of the men, and the envy of the women'[6]), the actress and singer Sophia Baddeley, Frances Manners the first Countess of Tyrconnel, and Anne Montgomery Marchioness Townshend. Mary was thrilled to be so close to the rich and famous. With a boldness that belies her self-image as a wide-eyed innocent, she took a seat opposite Anne Montgomery, who was flanked by two fashionable admirers. They looked at Mary and one turned to the other and asked 'Who is she?'

'Their fixed stare disconcerted me,' wrote Mary in her *Memoirs*. 'I rose, and, leaning on my husband's arm, again mingled in the brilliant circle.' One cannot help thinking that this little promenade also had the effect of showing off her frock to its best advantage. The gentlemen set off in pursuit, despite the presence of her husband. As she mingled in the crowd, they asked, 'Who is that young lady in the pink dress trimmed with sable?' 'My manner and confusion plainly evinced that I was not accustomed to the gaze of impertinent high breeding,' Mary says in the *Memoirs*, with due propriety, but even in this account written so long after the event – and after the accident that crippled her – one can still sense her pleasure in the power of her looks.[7]

She noticed that the men were joined by a third party, whom she recognized as Robert Henley, the son of her godfather, the politician Lord Northington. The latter had died in 1772, so Henley now had the title Lord Northington himself. He approached her, 'Miss Darby, or I am mistaken?'[8] She informed him of her change in status and introduced him to her husband, and together they strolled round the rotunda and chatted. Northington asked after her father, and complimented her on her appearance, asking that he be permitted to call on her. A notorious rake and womanizer, he must have been surprised by the transformation of his late father's lowly godchild Miss Darby into the lovely Mrs Robinson.

Feeling faint with the heat of the rotunda, and fatigued with the promenading, Mary requested tea, but there was not a single seat available in the tearoom. She finally found a sofa near the door, but her husband refused to leave her for a moment, even to bring refreshments. Henley brought her a cup of tea and introduced his two friends, the gentlemen who had been flirting with the Marchioness Townshend before pursuing Mary around the room. They were cousins: Captain George Ayscough and Lord Lyttelton. Both had highly respected fathers: Ayscough senior had been Dean of Bristol Minster during the 1760s when Mary was growing up, while the elder Lyttelton was a distinguished politician and one of Mary's favourite poets. The sons were not so virtuous: they, like young Northington, were notorious rakes. Lyttelton junior was known as 'the wicked' Lord, in contrast to his father, 'the good'. Mary described him as 'perhaps the most accomplished libertine that any age or country has produced'.[9]

Robinson set off to find the carriage, giving Lyttelton another opportunity to ingratiate himself with Mary by offering the use of his own vehicle. She declined and returned home with her husband. The next morning, the three men called on Mary, whilst she was home alone (it was conventional once an introduction had been made at an evening party to call the next day to enquire after the lady's health).

Lyttelton was by far the most persistent of the three. In Mary's version of events, she was entirely the victim of his unwanted attentions: 'Lord Lyttelton was uniformly my aversion. His manners were overbearingly insolent, his language licentious, and his person slovenly even to a degree that was disgusting.'[10] But her abhorrence did not prevent her from being drawn into his lordship's circle. Lyttelton cultivated her husband's friendship in order to gain access to her. He gave her presents, which she accepted – contrary to the advice of the conduct books on such matters. Among the gifts was the latest volume of poetry by the 'bluestocking' Anna Laetitia Barbauld. Lyttelton knew how to flatter Mary's intellect as well as her beauty.

Mary was beginning to write poetry herself at this time. Barbauld's poems fired a spirit of emulation: 'I read them with rapture; I thought them the most beautiful Poems I had ever seen, and considered the woman who could invent such poetry, as the most to be envied of human creatures.' She added to her praise a wonderfully derogatory and deflating codicil: 'Lord Lyttelton had some taste for poetical compositions, and wrote verses with considerable facility.'[11]

Lyttelton introduced the couple to his wide acquaintance, cultivating Tom Robinson as a friend and companion. The Robinsons were beginning to rub shoulders with aristocrats, politicians, and actors. Mary met and was dazzled by the intelligent and cultivated Imperial Ambassador the Count de Belgeioso, but was less impressed by the rake Lord Valentia (who later eloped with a courtesan). One of the most controversial figures Mary met during this heady time was George Fitzgerald, an Irish libertine and duellist, known as 'Fighting Fitzgerald'. Other new acquaintances included an Irish gamester called Captain O'Byrne and the actor William Brereton. The latter would subsequently share the stage with Perdita and marry her childhood friend Priscilla Hopkins.

Lord Northington continued to call and some female friendships were also established – with Lady Julia Yea, a prominent figure in West Country society, and the talented and witty writer Catherine Parry. At a party hosted by Mrs Parry, Mary met the actress Fanny Abington and was captivated by her charm, beauty and exquisite dress sense. Mary began again to harbour dreams of acting.

In the midst of all this socializing, Lyttelton was always at the couple's side: Mary describes him as her *cavaliere servante*, a fashionable male companion, a sort of 'mere Platonic cicisbeo – what every London wife is entitled to', as Sheridan mockingly wrote in *The School for Scandal*. But Lyttelton wanted to be more than Mary's friend and companion. He expected a payoff for the investment he had made in the Robinsons. When he realized that flattery was not the way to her bed, he tried a more perverse route: he insulted her in public and 'affected great indifference' in a vain attempt to excite her interest. He mocked her for being young and insipid and when she lost her temper he would apologize for making the 'pretty child angry'. He would repeatedly call her 'the child' in public to humiliate her. He mocked her literary endeavours and her thwarted plans to play Cordelia at Drury Lane. His final resort was to get to her through her weak husband. He embarked upon a strategy of ruination and bankruptcy for Robinson, taking him to gaming houses and brothels, 'the haunts of profligate debasement'.[12] They were seen often at the races, at Ascot and Epsom.

Whilst Robinson led a riotous life, gambling, drinking, and womanizing with his aristocratic friends, his pregnant wife was left neglected and alone. She missed the counsel of her mother, who had repaired to Bristol with young George to help him recuperate from illness. Mary blamed Lyttelton for the change in her husband's behaviour. In her *Memoirs* she said that she reacted by devoting her time to poetry, but this picture of her confined existence devoted to literary pursuits is contradicted by her own claim that 'Dress, parties, adulation, occupied all my hours.'[13]

As her pregnancy advanced in the summer of 1774 she felt resentful that she was being left alone without protection or companionship. One of the most pernicious effects of her husband's neglect was the temptation opened up by her countless admirers. The 'most dangerous' rake was George Fitzgerald, whose 'manners towards women were interesting and attentive'. He sympathized with her plight of being left without her husband, then proclaimed his devotion. Though 'surrounded by temptation, and mortified by neglect', Mary did not waver.[14]

It was not long before the couple plunged into debt. For all her claims that she knew little about their financial affairs, Mary was quite aware that they were living beyond their means – though when she did make enquiries about their financial position, her husband assured her that they were well provided for. Lyttelton promised to procure advancement for his young friend, though Thomas was sceptical that he would do anything for them.

Lyttelton tried one last desperate attempt to win Mary away from her husband. With her usual aplomb for setting a scene, she describes the day when Lyttelton called upon her for a meeting, pleading important business. He told Mary that he had a secret to reveal about Robinson. Lyttelton then confessed to his part in alienating her husband's 'conjugal affections', revealing that Thomas Robinson had a mistress, 'a woman of abandoned character' who lived in Princes Street, Soho. He told Mary that Robinson spent money on his mistress, money that they should have been saving for the birth of the baby. He even named the other woman: she was called Harriet Wilmot. Robinson visited her every day.

Lyttelton made Mary promise not to tell her husband who was the source of the revelation. If she did, there would have to be a duel. Having reduced her to tears of sorrow and mortification, Lyttelton suggested that Mary should take revenge on her husband by placing herself under his protection: 'You cannot be a stranger to my motives for thus cultivating the friendship of your husband; my fortune is at your disposal. Robinson is a ruined man; his debts are considerable, and nothing but destruction can await you. Leave him! Command my powers to serve you.'[15]

Mary was mortified at the proposal, but she was also angry and determined enough to face her rival. Perhaps she was spurred by the memory that her mother had had to endure a similar revelation. The encounter in Soho is described in the *Memoirs* in the style of sentimental fiction.

Needless to say, the *virtuous young wife* vanquishes the profligate mistress. With her novelist's eye for detail, Mary recalled the dirty servant girl who let her into Miss Wilmot's apartment, the incriminating new white silk underwear spread out on the bed, her beating heart as she heard Miss Wilmot's footsteps approach the room.

Mary's rival was a handsome older woman who was visibly distressed by the presence of her lover's pregnant young wife. Her lips were 'as pale as ashes'. She did not deny the charges levelled against her, and as she drew off her gloves to cover her eyes, presumably from shame, Mary noticed Tom's ring on her finger. Harriet tried to return the ring, to no avail. Mary refused to take it. Harriet said, 'Had I known that Mr Robinson was the husband of such a woman —' As Mary rose to leave, Harriet spoke, 'I never will see him more – unworthy man – I never will again receive him.' Mary swept out of the room without a further word. As usual, Mary remembered her costume for the occasion, as though she were an actress playing her part: she wore a morning dress of white muslin, with a white lawn cloak and a straw bonnet. Her rival was dressed in a printed Irish muslin and wore a black gauze cloak and a chip hat trimmed with lilac ribbons.[16]

Devastated by the encounter as Mary claimed to be, she accompanied her husband to Drury Lane that evening with Lord Lyttelton. She concealed her true feelings and participated in the fun with her usual gusto. It was only in the morning that she confronted Robinson. He did not deny the charge. Mary learned that he had had another mistress at the time of their marriage, and that his infidelities were public knowledge. The extent of his debts also became clear to her. Robinson had got himself caught in the invidious position of borrowing money from loan sharks to pay off his creditors. He was deeply involved with King the moneylender. Indeed, 'the parlour of our house was almost as much frequented by Jews as though it had been their synagogue'.[17] Mary's protestations that she was a 'total stranger' to the business transactions were, of course, untrue – John King had the proof of that.

Despite Robinson's infidelity, he is not depicted in Mary's narrative as the outright villain of the piece. She presents her husband as weak and impressionable, rather than vicious. It was Lord Lyttelton she blamed. She despised him for the way he treated women, in particular for his contemptuous behaviour towards his estranged wife and his mistress, a

Miss Dawson. The press suggested that Mary and Lyttelton were having an affair, a claim that she vehemently denied: 'he was the very last man in the world for whom I ever could have entertained the smallest partiality; he was to [illegible] most hateful of existing beings'.[18]

Handsome George Fitzgerald was quite another matter: 'his manners *towards women* were beautifully interesting'. He tried to seduce Mary on a warm summer's evening at Vauxhall. The Robinsons stayed until the early hours of the morning and then while they were waiting for their carriage to take them home, Fitzgerald made his move. A late night quarrel broke out between two men and Robinson and Fitzgerald took off to view the commotion. Mary tried to follow but was soon lost in the throng of people. Later, only Fitzgerald returned. He took Mary towards the exit to wait for her husband. To her alarm, Fitzgerald's carriage appeared as if out of nowhere and he tried to bundle Mary in. As the door swung open, she noticed a pistol in the pocket of the door. His servants, who were clearly in on the attempted abduction, kept at a discreet distance, while Fitzgerald grabbed Mary around the waist. She struggled free and ran back towards the entrance to the pleasure gardens, where she found her husband. Fitzgerald acted as though nothing had happened: 'Here he comes!' he exclaimed with an easy nonchalance, 'we had found the wrong carriage, Mr Robinson, we have been looking after you, and Mrs Robinson is alarmed beyond expression.' 'I am indeed!' replied Mary.[19]

She decided to say nothing to Robinson for fear of repercussions: an advanced state of pregnancy was no time to lose one's husband in a duel. 'Fighting Fitzgerald' was a brilliant shot. He killed eighteen men in the course of his duelling career, before being hanged. From that point on, Mary avoided Fitzgerald's company despite – or because of – his charisma: 'he was too daring, and too fascinating a being to be allowed the smallest marks of confidence'.

As on so many occasions in the *Memoirs*, the veracity of this story cannot be taken for granted: the abduction and rape of young women at public places had been a standard twist in the romantic novel ever since the attempted abduction of Harriet Byron in Samuel Richardson's hugely influential *Sir Charles Grandison*. We cannot be sure that Mary was not indulging here in a novelist's licence with the truth.

As with the trip to Bristol and Wales, there is another version of the story of these months – which the *Memoirs* may indeed have been consciously attempting to erase. Again, it was the *Letters from Perdita to a Certain Israelite* that made the case for the prosecution. According to John King, Mary was no innocent that first night at the Pantheon. He claimed that she made a play for the three fashionable aristocrats:

> At every fashionable Place of Resort, [the Robinsons] appeared as brilliant as any in the Circle; the Extravagance of the Diversions was no Check to their Vanity. At a Masquerade one evening, she was noticed by Lord Lyttelton, Lord Valencia, and Lord Northington; her Pride was highly gratified to be distinguished by Three such fashionable Noblemen; and that an Acquaintance so fortunately begun should not be lost, she wrote the following Note to each Gentleman the next day. 'My Lord, a Lady in the Character of an Orange Girl that had the Honour of being distinguished by your Lordship last Night at the Masquerade, was a Mrs R—, of *Hatton-Garden*, who will esteem herself further honoured if your Lordship should condescend to favour her with a Visit.' – On this singular Invitation, the Gentlemen came, and paid their respective Addresses to her; but it was the *intrepid persevering* Lord Lyttelton that most succeeded, it was the Splendor of his Equipage that seduced her vain Heart, till at length his Familiarity with her became the Topic of the whole Town. They were continually together at every Place of Amusement; and the Husband trudged after them, as stupid and as tranquil as any Brute of the cornuted Creation.[20]

King left his readers in no doubt that Mary and Lyttelton had a full-scale affair. He told of how they would engage in amorous dalliance in a closed carriage, with Robinson riding 'a Mile or Two behind on Horseback'. Far from taking umbrage at the intimacy, the husband 'continually boasted among his Acquaintance, the Superiority of his Connections, and his Wife's Ascendancy over every fashionable Gallant'.[21] This was the kind of story that gave Robinson a reputation as little better than his wife's pimp.

A garbled and exaggerated version of this story about Mary making love in a moving coach with the full complaisance of her husband also found its way into the muckraking *Memoirs of Perdita* published in 1784. Here, though, her high-speed dalliance is with a well-endowed sailor who gives her 'a pleasure she never could experience in the arms of debilitated peers and nobles'. He takes her four times, with Thomas Robinson riding not on a horse somewhere behind, but on the roof of the very carriage.[22]

King also claimed that Lyttelton intervened to save Robinson from prosecution when his fraudulent financial dealings were on the point of being exposed. According to this account, Lord Lyttelton dropped Mary on discovering that she and her husband were mere swindlers out to fleece him for all they could get. The truth of the matter is probably somewhere in the middle between Mary's picture of aristocratic villainy and King's far from disinterested portrayal of sexual misconduct for financial ends. There can be no doubt that the Robinsons lived way beyond their means: was it only the Jewish moneylenders who gave them the capacity to do so? Or did Lyttelton dig deep into his pocket? And if he did, was it in expectation of sexual favours or as payment for delights already delivered?

Whatever the precise means, Mary's beauty, wit, and connections were taking her well on the way to the achievement of her ambition of fame: 'I was now known, by name, at every public place in and near the metropolis.'[23] At the same time, the Robinsons were becoming notorious for their debts. In the autumn of 1774, in the final weeks of her pregnancy, their creditors foreclosed on them and an execution was brought on Robinson. The couple were forced to flee Hatton Garden for a friend's house in Finchley, which was then a village on the outskirts of London. They were deserted by all of their staff with the exception of a single faithful black servant. Mary barely saw her husband, who spent most of his time in town.

In the meantime, Hester returned from Bristol with George and helped her daughter to prepare for her confinement. They sewed baby clothes, and Mary continued to read and write. Robinson acquired the habit of taking George with him on his 'business trips' to London, but George, who adored his sister, confessed that they called upon disreputable women. He also told her that her valuable watch, which Mary presumed had been taken by the bailiffs, had actually been given to one of Robinson's mistresses. When confronted, he did not bother to deny the infidelity.

Despite Robinson's indifference, which was particularly insensitive so close to the birth of his first child, Mary continued to blame others more than her husband for their predicament. Perhaps she felt guilty for contributing to his debts by her expensive taste. She blamed Lyttelton, their creditors and even Robinson's father: 'had Mr Harris generously assisted *his son, I am fully and confidently persuaded that he would have pursued a discreet and regular line of conduct*.'[24]

It was to Harris that Robinson turned in desperation. He decided to leave London and head for Tregunter, where he could plead for his father's help. Robinson insisted that Mary accompany him, despite the discomfort and danger of travelling all those miles in her condition. He no doubt anticipated that the presence of his favoured young wife heavy with a future grandchild would help to soften up old Harris. Mary, for her part, did not want to leave her mother when she needed her during the trials of labour. Childbirth was traumatic at the best of times for women in the eighteenth century: it was common for mothers to write their unborn children farewell letters to be read in the event of their death during labour or its aftermath. Mary feared that she might die in Wales and the baby be left amongst strangers. With her youthful pride, she also dreaded the sneers she would have to face from Elizabeth Robinson and Mrs Molly upon returning to Tregunter in debt and disgrace.

CHAPTER 5

Debtors' Prison

> 'Tis not the whip, the dungeon, or the chain that constitutes the slave; freedom lives in the mind, warms the intellectual soul, lifts it above the reach of human power, and renders it triumphant over sublunary evil.
>
> Mary Robinson, *Angelina*

News had reached Tregunter of Robinson's imminent arrest. Harris was away from home when they arrived, but on his return he lost no time in making his position clear: 'Well! So you have escaped from a prison, and now you are come here to do penance for your follies?'[1] Over the following days, he taunted the couple, though he did at least offer them refuge.

When Mary tried to amuse herself by playing an old spinet in one of the parlours, Harris mocked her for giving herself airs and graces: 'Tom had better married a good tradesman's daughter than the child of a ruined merchant who was not capable of earning a living.' She may have smarted from the insults, but her husband, knowing her temper, pleaded with her to ignore Harris's behaviour. She was furious, though, when he openly insulted her at a dinner party. A guest, remarking on her swollen stomach, expressed his pleasure that she was come to give Tregunter 'a little stranger' and joked (as Harris was renovating his house) that they should build a new nursery for the baby. 'No, no,' replied Mr Harris, laughing, 'they came here because *prison doors* were open to receive them.'[2]

The renovation of Tregunter meant that Mary could not be housed for her confinement – at least that was the excuse given by Harris. Only two weeks away from giving birth, Mary was told that she must go to Trevecca House, which was just under two miles away, at the foot of a mountain called Sugar Loaf. Away from Harris and his female cronies, she relaxed and communed with nature:

> Here I enjoyed the sweet repose of solitude: here I wandered about woods entangled by the wild luxuriance of nature, or roved upon the mountain's side, while the blue vapours floated round its summit. O, God of Nature! Sovereign of the universe of wonders! in those interesting moments how fervently did I adore thee![3]

The sentiments are typical of the age of sensibility. If she really wandered thus so late in her pregnancy, she must have been unusually healthy and energetic.

Though Mary writes here of the 'sweet repose of solitude', Trevecca House was actually more crowded than Tregunter. One part housed the Huntingdon seminary and another part of the building was converted into a flannel manufactory. Nevertheless, she was no longer forced to endure the jibes of her husband's vulgar family, for they seldom visited her. According to the *Memoirs*, she was indifferent to their ill-treatment of her. Her spiritual communion with the mountains made her all the more conscious that she had 'formed an union with a family who had neither sentiment nor sensibility'.

The child, named Maria Elizabeth Robinson,* was born on 18 October 1774, just a few weeks before Mary's seventeenth birthday. Delighted with her beautiful daughter, the young mother allowed her nurse to show Maria Elizabeth to the factory workers who clamoured to see the 'little *heiress* to Tregunter'. Mary was at first alarmed at the prospect of exposing the baby to the cold October air, but the nurse soothed her fears and cautioned her that the local people would consider Mary 'proud' if she refused to show the 'young squire's' baby. It was a happy day for Mary,

* Sometimes called Mary and sometimes Maria (both by her mother and herself) – I will call her Maria Elizabeth throughout, to distinguish her from her mother.

as the crowd heaped blessings on the baby, and the nurse, Mrs Jones, passed on every detail of their praises to the exhausted mother.

There is no mention of Robinson in the narrative, but later that evening Harris paid a visit. After asking after Mary's health he demanded to know what she was going to do with the child. When she made no answer he honoured her with his own recommendation: '"I will tell you," added he; "Tie it to your back and work for it."' For good measure he added, 'Prison doors are open . . . Tom will die in a gaol; and what is to become of you?' Mary was all the more humiliated by the impropriety of these taunts being spoken in front of the nurse. Maybe Harris would have been kinder if the baby had been a boy, but one senses that his own infatuation with Mary had now worn off and that he considered her expensive lifestyle to have been a major factor in Tom's improvidence. When his daughter Elizabeth made her visit, she suggested that it would be a mercy for the infant 'if it pleased God to take it'.[4]

Three weeks later, Robinson's creditors caught up with him. They had discovered that he had fled to Wales, and in order to avoid the spectacle of being arrested at Harris's house – which would have been the final nail in the coffin of his hoped-for inheritance – he left immediately. They were on the run once more. Though still weak from the delivery of her child, Mary refused to stay at Trevecca without her husband. She travelled against the advice of the capable Mrs Jones. They set off for Monmouth, where Mary's grandmother lived. Mrs Jones travelled in the post chaise as far as Abergavenny, cradling the baby on a pillow on her lap. The local people were sorry to see them go, but 'Neither Mr Harris nor the *enlightened females* of Tregunter expressed the smallest regret, or solicitude on the occasion.'[5]

Mary was worried about taking care of her baby after the departure of Mrs Jones. Her education had not prepared her for 'domestic occupations'. She was still only 17, and without her mother. But she trusted her maternal instincts and did the best she could. Lacking a wet nurse, she breastfed her own baby, which was still perceived as an unusual step for a woman of her class – though it was something that would be advocated by the feminist writers of the 1790s.

The next day they arrived at Monmouth, where Mary's grandmother Elizabeth lived. They received a warm welcome, though how much her grandmother knew about their state of affairs is not clear. Seventy-year-old Elizabeth, who had been a beauty in her day, was still an attractive woman; she dressed in neat, simple gowns of brown or black silk. She was a pious, well-respected figure, and mild of temper: Mary envied her grandmother's tranquillity and her fervent religious faith.

Here at Monmouth they received 'unfeigned hospitality'. There was a lively social scene. Once more Mary's contradictory nature is revealed. Her favourite amusements were wandering by the River Wye and exploring the castle ruins: thus the woman of sensibility who would become one of the most successful Gothic novelists of the age. But she also loved company and attended local balls and dances: thus the lady of fashion who would become a fixture on the London social scene.

Determined not to let breastfeeding interfere with the chance to dance at a local ball, she once took Maria Elizabeth with her, so that she could feed her at intervals. After a particularly strenuous bout of dancing, she fed her in an antechamber. But something went wrong and by the time they arrived home the baby was in convulsions. Mary was hysterical, with the result that her milk would not then come at all, which left the baby parched and continuing to fit. Mary was convinced that her vigorous dancing and the excessive heat of the ballroom had affected her milk and brought on the fit. She stayed awake with Maria Elizabeth all night. In the morning, friends and well-wishers called to enquire after the infant. One such man was the local clergyman, who was moved to see the frantic young mother in such despair. Mary refused to let the baby be taken from her lap, but the clergyman begged her to let him try a home remedy that had been successful with one of his own children suffering the same way. Mixing aniseed with spermaceti, he gave the medicine to the baby and almost instantaneously the convulsions abated and she fell peacefully asleep.

Shortly after this episode, Tom Robinson once more heard that his creditors were about to catch up with him. Yet again, they prepared to travel before Robinson was arrested. But this time they were too late. An execution for a 'considerable sum' was served on him and the local sheriff of Monmouth arrived to arrest him. In the event, the sheriff, who knew Mary's grandmother, took pity on them and offered to accompany the Robinsons back to London.

On returning to the metropolis, Mary hastened to her mother, who was now living in York Buildings just off the Strand. Hester was, of course, thrilled to see her new granddaughter. Robinson, in the meantime, discovered that the person responsible for alerting the sheriff was none other than his best friend Hanway. The latter's excuse was that the debt in question was relatively small and he had assumed that Robinson's father would have paid it. They came to an arrangement and patched up their friendship. The Robinsons then took lodgings in Berners Street, just north of Oxford Street.

Mary began to make arrangements to fulfil a secret ambition that she had been harbouring for many years. She now had ready for publication her first book of poems: she had been working on them even before her marriage. In her *Memoirs*, she spoke disparagingly of her first literary efforts as 'trifles'; she expressed the hope that no copies survived, except for the treasured one that her mother had preserved. Regardless of the quality, her determination in preparing the volume in such difficult circumstances is impressive. She was also unusual among upwardly mobile women in undertaking the everyday care of her own baby. She insisted on dressing and undressing her daughter. The baby was breastfed and always slept in her presence, by day in a basket, by night in her own bed. Mary had heard horror stories about the neglect of servants towards children who were too young to tell tales, and she resolved only to let herself and Hester tend to the child.

Her devotion as a mother and her plans to become a published poet did not stop her from socializing, and she began visiting her old haunts such as Ranelagh with her female friends, while Tom kept a low profile. Mary had renewed confidence in her personal appearance and her deportment. She had grown taller in the last year and felt more worldly and sophisticated than when she had first broken upon the social scene two years earlier. She felt confident, serene, and was a little harder edged. The special occasion of her reappearance in London society is marked in her *Memoirs* by a description of a new dress. This one was of lilac silk with a wreath of white flowers for a headdress. 'I was complimented on my looks by the whole party,' she recalled, before stressing that her first concern was to be a good mother: 'with little relish for public amusements, and a heart throbbing with domestic solicitude, I accompanied the party to Ranelagh'.[6]

As she entered the rotunda the first person she encountered was her old 'seducer' George Fitzgerald. He was startled to see her, but lost no time in greeting her, welcoming her re-entry into 'the world' and observing that she was without Robinson. He followed her for the remainder of the evening, and as she left she observed his carriage drawing up alongside hers. The next morning he arrived at the house to pay his respects, as she sat correcting proofs of her poetry, with her daughter sleeping in a basket at her feet. She was annoyed at the intrusion and her vanity was piqued by the fact that she was dressed in a matronly morning dress rather than 'elegant and tasteful *dishabille*'. Papers were strewn over the table, making the room look like a cross between 'a study and a nursery'.

She received him frostily. Undeterred, Fitzgerald complimented her on her youth and her child on her beauty. The attention to Maria Elizabeth led to a thaw. Fitzgerald then took a proof sheet from the table and read one of the pastoral lyrics, praising her efforts. 'I smile while I recollect how far the effrontery of flattery has power to belie the judgment,' Mary wryly notes in her *Memoirs*.[7] She asked him how he had discovered her place of residence and Fitzgerald confessed that he had followed her carriage from Ranelagh the previous evening.

The next evening he returned and took tea with the Robinsons, inviting them to a dinner party at Richmond. Mary declined, but she and Tom tentatively began to socialize with their old friends. Returning to Ranelagh a few days later they reacquainted themselves with Lord Northington, Captain O'Byrne, Captain Ayscough, and the wicked Lord Lyttelton, who had not changed one bit and was – as only to be expected – 'particularly importunate'.

For a few weeks it looked as if the Robinsons were embarking on their old life again, but then Tom was arrested on a debt of £1,200, consisting principally of 'the arrears of annuities, and other demands from Jew creditors'. Mary insisted that the debts were all his own: 'he did not at that time, *or at any period since*, owe fifty pounds for *me*, or to any tradesman on *my* account whatever'.[8] Robinson stayed in custody in the sheriff's office for three weeks. He felt too depressed even to go through the motions of trying to raise the money from his father or his friends. Prison was inevitable and he was duly committed to the Fleet on 3 May 1775. He would spend the next fifteen months there.

The Fleet housed about three hundred prisoners and their families. It was a profit-making enterprise: prisoners had to pay for food and lodging, pay the turnkey to let their families in and out, and even pay not to be kept shackled in irons. There were opportunities for work, though some inmates were reduced to begging from passers-by – a grille was built into the prison wall along Farringdon Street for this purpose.

It was not a requirement, but was nevertheless common, for wives to accompany their husbands to debtors' prisons such as the Fleet, the Marshalsea and the King's Bench. Mary did so – as her fellow novelist and poet Charlotte Smith would when her husband was confined a few years later. Often wives would come and go, bringing in food for their confined husband. Young children were, however, usually left with relatives. It is a mark of Mary's deep devotion to her baby that she took the 6-month-old Maria Elizabeth to prison with her rather than leaving her in the care of Hester. For that matter, she could presumably have stayed with Hester herself. Her loyalty to Tom Robinson is striking, especially in the light of his infidelities.

They were given quarters on the third floor of the towering prison block, overlooking the racquet ground, which the inmates were at leisure to use for exercise. Robinson – an 'expert in all exercises of strength' – played racquets daily while Mary tried her best to make a home in the squalid surroundings, and took care of her baby. She barely ventured outdoors during daylight hours for a period of nine months, though she did at least have a nurse to help her with the baby. The cells were small, dark, and sparsely furnished, but at least they were given a pair of rooms and not just one. This meant, however, that they paid extra for lodging, which meant that it would take longer to put aside the money to pay off the debt.

According to the memoirs of Laetitia Hawkins, a neighbour of Mary's during her years of fame, Robinson was sent a guinea a week subsistence money by his father. He was also offered some employment 'in writing' -- probably the copying of legal documents, an activity for which he was well trained – but he refused to do anything. Mary, by contrast, not only attended to her child but also 'did all the work of their apartments, she even scoured the stairs, and accepted the writing and the pay which he had refused'.[9]

Less welcome offers of assistance came from the rakish lords, Northington, Lyttelton, and Fitzgerald. She knew, though, from the 'language of gallantry' and 'profusions of *love*' in their letters what the offers really meant. It was above all her maternal devotion that kept her from exchanging a life of poverty for the temporary comforts afforded to a courtesan.

At night, she would walk on the racquet court. One beautiful moonlit evening, she went out with her baby and the nursemaid. Mary would later remember it as the night when her daughter 'first blessed my ears with the articulation of words'. They danced the child up and down, her eyes fixed on the moon, 'to which she pointed with her small fore-finger', whereupon a cloud suddenly passed over it and it disappeared. Little Maria Elizabeth dropped her hand slowly and, with what her mother perceived as a sigh, cried out 'all gone'. These were her first words – a repetition of the phrase used by her nurse when she wanted to withhold something from the baby. In retrospect, it seemed like the one joyful moment in the long months of captivity. They walked until midnight, watching the moon play hide and seek with the clouds as the 'little prattler repeated her observation'.[10]

Twenty years later, Mary's friend Samuel Taylor Coleridge would make one of his loveliest poems out of a similar experience. Coleridge writes of how his infant son Hartley could recognize the song of the nightingale before he could talk:

My dear babe,
Who, capable of no articulate sound,
Mars all things with his imitative lisp,
How he would place his hand beside his ear,
His little hand, the small forefinger up,
And bid us listen!

He then tells of how one night when baby Hartley awoke 'in most distressful mood', he scooped him up and hurried out into the orchard

And he beheld the moon, and, hushed at once,
Suspends his sobs, and laughs most silently,
While his fair eyes, that swam with undropped tears,
Did glitter in the yellow moon-beam.[11]

Coleridge's poem was written in April 1798, two years before Mary drafted this section of her *Memoirs*. It was published in *Lyrical Ballads*, a book she knew well (it would inspire the title of her final volume of poetry, *Lyrical Tales*). What is more, Coleridge visited her on several occasions in the early months of 1800, when she was writing the *Memoirs*.

They subsequently wrote poems inspired by each other's work. There can, then, be little doubt that the phrasing of her memory of Maria Elizabeth by moonlight – the idea of 'articulation', the baby's raised forefinger, the dancing yellow light – was shaped by a memory of Coleridge's poem for Hartley. Later in 1800, she paid a further compliment in the form of a lovely poem for Coleridge's third son, Derwent.

It was only as a result of the literary revolution of the 1790s, in which Coleridge and Robinson each played an important part, that intimate memories of this kind became the stuff of poetry and autobiography. Mary's early verse, published while she was in the Fleet, was stilted and artificial in comparison. *Poems* by Mrs Robinson, an octavo volume of 134 pages, was published in the summer of 1775, with a frontispiece engraved by Angelo Albanesi, a fellow prisoner who had been befriended by Tom. The volume garnered a mediocre notice in the *Monthly Review*: 'Though Mrs Robinson is by no means an Aiken or a More, she *sometimes* expresses herself decently enough on her subject' (Anna Aikin and Hannah More were the most admired 'bluestocking' poets of the age).[12]

The volume includes thirty-two ballads, odes, elegies, and epistles. For the most part, they consist of pastorals ('Ye Shepherds who sport on the plain, / Drop a tear at my sorrowful tale') and moral effusions (pious outbursts addressed to Wisdom, Charity, Virtue, and so forth) that are typical of later eighteenth-century poetry at its most routine. But a handful of the poems show signs of future promise: there are, for instance, some brief character sketches in which one may see the seeds of the future novelist's voice.

Several of the poems were modelled on the work of Anna Aikin (later Barbauld): 'The Linnet's Petition', for example, was an imitation of her 'The Mouse's Petition'. Women's poetry of the period was often written in the form of verse letters. Mary's 'Epistle to a Friend' is written with a lightness of touch and warmth of feeling:

> Permit me dearest girl to send
> The warmest wishes of a friend
>   Who scorns deceit, or art,
> Who dedicates her verse to you,
> And every praise so much your due,
>   Flows genuine from her heart.[13]

One is left wondering about the identity of the friend, especially as the following poem is an elegy 'On the Death of a Friend', which ends 'May you be number'd with the pure and blest, / And Emma's spirit be Maria's guard.' We know hardly anything about Mary's female companionship of these early years, beyond a passing reference in the *Memoirs* to her close friendship with a talented, witty, and literary-minded woman called Catherine Parry. In Mary's last years, by contrast, she was sustained by a large circle of intellectually accomplished women. The only one of these early poems with a clearly identifiable biographical subject is an elegy on the death of the 'generous' Lord Lyttelton, whose poems were among the first that Mary loved. Needless to say, it makes no mention of the younger Lord Lyttelton.

The one poem in the collection that has real merit, and that deserves to be anthologized, is a 'Letter to a Friend on leaving Town'. The virtue of a simple country life as against the vice of indulgence in the city was a common poetic theme in the period, but here there is a real sense of Mary writing from experience:

> Gladly I leave the town, and all its care,
> For sweet retirement, and fresh wholsome air,
> Leave op'ra, park, the masquerade, and play,
> In solitary groves to pass the day.
> Adieu, gay throng, luxurious vain parade,
> Sweet peace invites me to the rural shade,
> No more the Mall, can captivate my heart,
> No more can Ranelagh, one joy impart.
> Without regret I leave the splendid ball,
> And the inchanting shades of gay Vauxhall,
> Far from the giddy circle now I fly,
> Such joys no more, can please my sicken'd eye.

Although Mary adopts the conventional pose of condemning fashionable London life, all her poetic energy belongs to that life – her heart is still captivated by Ranelagh and Vauxhall. Yet she also has the maturity to see their dangers. At the centre of the poem is a telling portrait of the society belle who loses her looks, and thus the interest of the gentlemen of fashion, but remains addicted to the treadmill of the social calendar:

Beaux without number, daily round her swarm,
And each with fulsome flatt'ry try's to charm.
Till, like the rose, which blooms but for an hour,
Her face grown common, loses all its power.
Each idle coxcomb leaves the wretched fair,
Alone to languish, and alone despair,
To cards, and dice, the slighted maiden flies,
And every fashionable vice apply's,
Scandal and coffee, pass the morn away,
At night a rout, an opera, or a play;
Thus glide their life, partly through inclination,
Yet more, because it is the reigning fashion.
Thus giddy pleasures they alone pursue,
Merely because, they've nothing else to do;
Whatever can afford their hearts delight,
No matter if the thing be wrong, or right;
They will pursue it, tho' they be undone,
They see their ruin, – yet still they venture on.[14]

This poem – an accomplished piece of work for a 17-year-old girl – was almost certainly written when Mary was moving in the fashionable circles of London society. It is at one level an anxious imagining of her own future fate. But seeing it in print, she must have wished she was back gliding her life away in the world of 'scandal and coffee' rather than languishing in the Fleet surrounded by women whose good looks had been worn down by penury.

Mary knew that her own beauty was fragile. She wrote in the *Memoirs* of how during her 'captivity' in prison her health was 'considerably impaired'. She declined, however, to 'enter into a tedious detail of vulgar sorrows, of vulgar scenes'.[15] At this point in the original manuscript of the *Memoirs* several lines are heavily crossed out. It is impossible to decipher the words beneath the inking over, but there just might be a reference to pregnancy. It is therefore striking that the malicious but well-informed John King wrote in his *Letters from Perdita to a Certain Israelite*: 'the Husband took refuge in the Fleet, immured within whose gloomy Walls they pined out Fifteen Months in Abstemiousness and Contrition, where her *constrained Constancy* gave birth to a Female Babe, distorted and crippled from the tight contracted fantastic Dress of her conceited Mother'.[16] Since 'Fifteen Months' is an exactly correct detail, we cannot immediately dismiss King's other piece of information about this period: his startling claim that Mary had a baby while in prison. 'Distorted and crippled' is certainly not a description of the lovely little Maria Elizabeth. Could it then be that the deleted passage in the *Memoirs* referred to a miscarriage or an infant death?

Imprisonment for debt was known as 'captivity', and this gave Mary the title for a new poem, much her longest work to date. Written in an overblown style, it is a plea on behalf of the wives and children of imprisoned debtors:

> The greedy Creditor, whose flinty breast
> The iron hand of Avarice hath press'd,
> Who never own'd Humanity's soft claim,
> Self-interest and Revenge his only aim,
> Unmov'd, can hear the Parent's heart-felt sigh,
> Unmov'd, can hear the helpless Infant's cry.
> Nor age, nor sex, his rigid breast can melt,
> Unfeeling for the pangs, he never felt.[17]

'Captivity' was published in the autumn of 1777, just over a year after the Robinsons' release from the Fleet. It was accompanied by a poetic tale of marital infidelity called 'Celadon and Lydia', into which Mary presumably poured some of her anger over Robinson's philandering. This second volume of poetry was more handsomely produced than the first. Albanesi provided an elegantly engraved title page and the book bore a dedication guaranteed to grab attention: it was inscribed 'by Permission, to her Grace the Duchess of Devonshire'. The dedication described the Duchess as 'the friendly Patroness of the Unhappy' author and ended by 'repeating my Thanks to you, for the unmerited favors your Grace has bestowed upon, Madam, Your Grace's most obliged and most devoted servant, MARIA ROBINSON'.

Georgiana Spencer was Mary's exact contemporary in age, but came from a very different background: born into one of England's most illustrious aristocratic families in 1757, she became Duchess of Devonshire and mistress of Chatsworth – one of the greatest houses in England – in the summer of 1774, just before the Robinsons went on the run from their creditors. She was already cutting a spectacular figure in London society. Someone mentioned to Mary that Georgiana was an 'admirer and patroness of literature'. Mary arranged for her little brother George, an extremely handsome boy, to deliver to the Duchess a neatly bound copy of her first collection of poems. She also enclosed a note 'apologizing for their defects, and pleading my age as the only excuse for their inaccuracy'.[18] Georgiana admitted George and asked particulars about the author, as Mary no doubt expected. Georgiana was touched by the plight of the young mother sharing her husband's captivity. She invited Mary to Devonshire House, her magnificent town residence in Piccadilly, the very next day. Robinson urged her to accept the invitation and she duly went, dressed modestly in a plain brown satin gown.

Mary was mesmerized by the Duchess's look and manner: 'mildness and sensibility beamed in her eyes, and irradiated her countenance'. Georgiana listened to her story and expressed surprise at seeing such a young person experiencing 'such vicissitude of fortune'. With 'a tear of gentle sympathy', she gave her some money. She asked Mary to visit again, and to bring her daughter with her. Mary made many visits to her new friend – the two women both beautiful and cultivated, but in such contrasting circumstances. Mary described the Duchess as 'the best of women', 'my admired patroness, my liberal and affectionate friend'.[19] They would continue to be closely acquainted for many years. Georgiana loved to hear the particulars of Mary's sorrows: her father's desertion, her poverty, her unfaithful husband, her troubles as a young mother, her captivity. She shed tears of pity as she heard the story. Inspired by the Duchess's patronage, Mary finished the poem that put her reflections on prison life into heroic couplets.

Mary remained unwaveringly loyal to those who helped her. She loved the Duchess and years later paid tribute in verse to her great qualities. She was particularly gratified by her friendship at a time when numerous female companions of happier days had deserted her. It was with the latter in mind that she wrote in her *Memoirs* of how 'From that hour I have never felt the affection for my own sex which perhaps some women feel.' She added with uncharacteristic bitterness: 'Indeed I have almost uniformly found my own sex my most inveterate enemies . . . my bosom has often ached with the pang inflicted by their envy, slander, and malevolence.'[20] This outburst is, however, belied by the female friendships that she forged and sustained throughout her life.

As spouse of a debtor, she was free to come and go, but the visits to Georgiana were the only time she ever left the Fleet. While she was away from the prison being entertained in the splendour of Devonshire House, Robinson took the opportunity to do some entertaining of his own: Albanesi procured prostitutes for him and brought them into the prison. If the *Memoirs* are to be believed, after a while Mary was humiliated even further when her husband took to sleeping with prostitutes while she and little Maria Elizabeth were in the very next room. When she confronted him, he brazenly denied the charges.

Despite Albanesi's supposed responsibility for Tom's infidelities, the Italian engraver and his glamorous Roman wife became the Robinsons' closest friends among their fellow detainees. The wife, Angelina, was formerly mistress to a prince and subsequently the lover of the Imperial Ambassador, Count de Belgeioso. Unlike Mary, she chose not to share her husband's captivity, but she paid frequent visits, dressed to the nines and comporting herself like a duchess. She was a fascinating older woman, in her thirties, a 'striking sample of beauty and of profligacy' who gave Mary an insight into the life of a courtesan. She always insisted on visiting Mary when she came to see Albanesi, and she would ridicule the teenage bride for her 'romantic domestic attachment'. She told Mary that she was wasting her beauty and her youth; she 'pictured, in all the glow of fanciful scenery, the splendid life into which I might enter, if I would but know my own power, and break the fetters of matrimonial restriction'.[21] She suggested that Mary should place herself under the protection of rake and celebrated horseman, Henry Herbert, the Earl of Pembroke – she had already told him about Mary and his lordship was ready to offer his services.

Mary blamed Angelina for trying to persuade her into a life of dishonour. Both the Albanesis filled her young head with tales of 'the world of gallantry'. Despite the disapproval of the couple expressed years later in the *Memoirs*, Mary was obviously enthralled by the way in which they offered a window into another world – a world that she had briefly tasted and must have longed to return to. Albanesi sang and played various musical instruments with easy accomplishment. And he told good jokes: Mary would herself become a notable wit.

On 3 August 1776, Robinson was discharged from the Fleet. He had managed to set aside some of his debts and give fresh bonds and securities for others. Mary wrote to her 'lovely patroness' with the news – she was at Chatsworth – and received a congratulatory letter in return. At the first possible opportunity, Mary headed for Vauxhall: 'I had frequently found occasion to observe a mournful contrast when I had quitted the elegant apartment of Devonshire-house to enter the dark galleries of a prison; but the sensation which I felt on hearing the music and beholding the gay throng, during this first visit in public, after so long a seclusion, was indescribable.'[22]

CHAPTER 6

Drury Lane

> The invitation to meet the new actresses was whispered as though they were meditating to exhibit something monstrous and extraordinary . . . She had engaged in a profession which vulgar minds, though they are amused by its labours, frequently condemn with unpitying asperity. She was engaging, discreet, sensible, and accomplished: but she was an actress, and therefore deemed an unfit associate for the wives and daughters of the proud, the opulent, and the unenlightened.
>
> Mary Robinson, *The Natural Daughter*

Though Mary was thrilled to be back on the social scene at Vauxhall, the Robinsons had no means of sustaining their expensive lifestyle. Tom was still up to his ears in debt; he had failed to complete his legal apprenticeship and his father refused to aid him. Mary's poems were not going to make her serious money, so once again she turned her mind to the theatre. This time she was not going to let her husband or her mother stop her. Now that he needed the money, Tom's scruples about the profession swiftly evaporated.

The Robinsons took lodgings with a confectioner in Old Bond Street, near to London's main shopping thoroughfare. Walking one day in St James's Park with her husband, Mary met the actor William Brereton, who was soon to marry her school friend, the actress Priscilla

Hopkins.* He joined them for dinner. He had seen Mary's rehearsals with Garrick and was enthusiastic when she told him that she was thinking of reactivating her stage career. Some time later, when the Robinsons had moved to 'a more quiet situation' in the form of 'a very neat and comfortable suite of apartments in Newman-street',[1] Brereton appeared unexpectedly one morning with his friend, the playwright and theatre manager of Drury Lane, Richard Brinsley Sheridan.

Sheridan had been a schoolfellow with Tom Robinson at Harrow, but Tom encountered a very different man from the shy and shabby boy he had once known. Sheridan had taken over from Garrick on the great man's retirement in 1776 and looked set to shine even brighter. He had all the right credentials: a playwright, the son of an actor-manager and a writer, the son-in-law of a renowned musician; his wife was a musician of rare gifts, the beautiful Elizabeth Linley. Sheridan had caused a scandal when he had eloped with Miss Linley and fought two duels in her honour. Drawing on his celebrity, in 1775 he rocked London with a play based on his amorous adventures, *The Rivals*. Though not conventionally handsome, with his florid complexion and rugged features, he was clever and charming, renowned for his wit and talent.

When Sheridan called on Mary at her home, he was just months into his new role as manager of the most famous theatre in London and was scouting for talent. Mary found Sheridan's demeanour 'strikingly and bewitchingly attractive'. He in turn was entranced by her beauty and asked her to read for him. Looking back, she remembered that she was not dressed properly, a state in which she always felt insecure. She was several months into a further pregnancy and her health was poor – she attributed this to the combined influence of the pregnancy and her continuance in breastfeeding Maria Elizabeth even though the girl was nearly 2. But she agreed to read some passages from Shakespeare. Mary was gratified that the celebrated Sheridan proved so gentle and encouraging. They were to become great friends. He asked her to prepare for a public trial, and read with her himself.

Then Sheridan got Garrick on board. With extraordinary loyalty to the girl who had let him down three years before, he agreed – despite ill

* Brereton died in 1787 after a year's confinement in the Hoxton lunatic asylum. Later the same year Priscilla married another famous actor, John Philip Kemble (brother of Sarah Siddons).

health – to come out of retirement and tutor her once again. Garrick and Sheridan decided on Juliet for her debut role, in Garrick's own adaptation of the play. Brereton would be Romeo. Mary ran through Juliet's lines for the first time in the green room at Drury Lane. Garrick was 'indefatigable at the rehearsals; frequently going through the whole character of Romeo himself, until he was completely exhausted with the fatigue of recitation'.[2] Mary never forgot Garrick's kindness and his willingness to give her a second chance. When he died three years later, she wrote an elegy in his memory:

> Who can forget thy penetrating eye,
> The sweet bewitching smile, th' empassion'd look!
> The clear deep whisper, the persuasive sigh,
> The feeling tear that Nature's language spoke?[3]

Mary's stage debut was set for 10 December 1776. It was announced to the press some time in advance. Managers often paid newspapers to 'puff' their actors. Sheridan and Garrick both had reputations for their publicity skills: Sheridan had planted an article in the *Morning Chronicle* puffing *The Rivals* after its initial failure. Garrick owned shares in various newspapers and his friendship with the journalist Henry Bate ensured favourable reviews and publicity for his plays. So it was that a great deal was made of Mary's educated background and 'superior understanding'. Sheridan and Garrick's choice of role was astute: they knew that the press would be very forgiving towards a beautiful young woman playing Juliet for the first time. Mary, meanwhile, took the prudent step of writing to Chatsworth to inform Georgiana of her intentions. It was vital to get the patronage of the ladies, as many theatrical prologues of the period testify. The Duchess gave her approval to her young protégée and with 'zeal bordering on delight' Mary readied herself for her debut.[4]

What was the theatre like when Mary Robinson first stepped onto the boards of Drury Lane? The Licensing Act of 1737, which had been introduced in order to keep a check on plays satirizing the Government, confined legitimate theatrical performances to two patent playhouses in London, the Theatres Royal Drury Lane and Covent Garden. During the summer season when the two licensed theatres were closed, the 'Little Theatre' in the Haymarket had a summer patent. Drury Lane, London's oldest theatre, had at this time a seating capacity of about two thousand. In the late Georgian period theatre was an essential part of fashionable life. A vibrant cross-section of the London community came to sit in box, pit, and gallery. Liveried servants were sent to reserve seats when the doors opened at five o'clock in the afternoon. Critics and raffish young men paid three shillings each to squash onto a bench in the pit; the well-to-do sat in private boxes for five shillings; honest citizens and visitors to town crammed into two-shilling places in the first gallery; servants and the hoi polloi sat in the upper gallery for one shilling. An evening entertainment ran to about four hours. First there was an overture played by the orchestra, then the main play (a drama, musical, or opera), then an interlude (music or a dance), and then a shorter afterpiece, usually of a farcical kind. It was generally said that the main pieces were for the 'quality' and the afterpiece for the commoners. Certainly the upper galleries filled up halfway through the main performance, when punters could gain admission for half price at the end of the third act of a five-act play.

Garrick had transformed the theatrical profession. In 1762 he had banned the audience from sitting on the stage – previously drunken patrons occupying the stage seats had been known to molest actresses (on one infamous occasion a near rape took place in full view of the audience). He had also made major modernizations in lighting and scenery: he removed the great chandeliers from their traditional place above the stage and substituted them with oil lamps in the wings, which had tin reflectors attached and could be directed towards or away from the stage, giving a greater control over illumination. The waxing or waning of light at dusk or dawn could now be indicated. Garrick also employed the ingenious scene designer Philip de Loutherbourg, who specialized in stage illusions. He charmed his audiences by changing the tints of the scenery, throwing light through coloured silk screens that turned on pivots in the flies and wings. De Loutherbourg was thus able to conjure up moonlight, cloud and fire effects. House lights were not turned down, as the audience came to the theatre to look at each other as much as to look at the players.

When Mary made her debut, she was acting in the newly renovated theatre, recently remodelled by the celebrated Adam brothers. The ceiling had been raised 12 feet, improving the acoustic and giving a sense of space; it was designed in a sumptuous pattern of octagonal panels that rose from an exterior circular frame, diminishing towards the centre, giving the effect of a dome. The side boxes had also been heightened, with an improved view of the stage; they were decorated along the front with variegated borders inlaid with plaster festoons of flowers and medallions. The old square heavy pillars had been removed from each side of the stage and replaced with elegant slim pillars, inlaid with green and crimson plate glass, which supported the upper boxes and galleries. The boxes were lined with crimson spotted paper. New gilt branches with two candles each replaced the old chandeliers. The boxes in the upper tier – known as the 'green boxes', where prostitutes solicited rich patrons – were adorned with gilt busts, painted embellishments and gilt borders. There was crimson drapery edged with gold fringing over the stage.

The theatre was not, of course, decorated in any such way in the backstage space where Mary spent most of her time. This was a vast area – larger than the entire front of house – with a maze of stairs and passages, some of them sloped to take wheels and animals. There were twenty dressing rooms, with a dresser allocated to each room, though principal players usually had their own personal dressers. It was later rumoured that Elizabeth Armistead – actress, courtesan, and rival to Perdita – began her career as Mary's dresser. The dressing rooms, unlike the auditorium, had stoves to keep the actors warm. Some even had water closets. Other water closets were in the corridor adjacent to the stage area. The ladies' dressing rooms had a candle and a mirror for each actress, their space demarcated by chalk marks across the floor. A hairdresser would have prepared Mary's coiffure, but actresses put on their own make-up, a powder compounded with a liquid medium, which was often harmful to the skin and sometimes extremely dangerous, especially if white lead was used in its composition. White skin and rouged cheeks was the favoured image. In the green room, immediately to the side of the stage, actors, singers, and their invited friends mingled before the performance began.

The theatre was crowded on 10 December, the audience anxious to see Garrick's protégée who was now also Sheridan's new discovery. She had been advertised on the playbill as 'A Young Lady (1st appearance upon any stage)'. For Mary herself it was a frightening experience. She was exceedingly nervous, mindful of the critics in the pit and Garrick sitting there with his shrewd, intense stare. The fate of a play (and an actor) was sealed on the opening night even before the curtain fell on the concluding act.

Theatre audiences did not sit in darkness and silence as they do today. The atmosphere was boisterous, voluble and interactive; the lighted auditorium helped to establish a rapport between spectators and actors. Applause or hisses rang out throughout the performance, and it was the audience rather than the critics who determined whether there was to be a long run or a speedy closure. The audience in the lobby and auditorium put on a display of its own: the young men in the pit, who were probably the most attentive spectators, offered criticism and comment; cheers and jeers could be expected from the gods (the one-shilling galleries), accompanied by songs, laughter, and flying fruit. It was not only rotten fruit that was hurled at bad performers – broken glass tumblers, metal, and wood could also rain down onto the stage. Despite having a reputation for drunken and unruly behaviour, those in the cheap seats usually paid attention once the play had begun and they were satisfied all was well. Less attentive were the aristocracy and gentry in the boxes, where fashionable society peered at itself as if in a mirror. As Mr Lovel, the fop in Fanny Burney's contemporaneous novel *Evelina*, says, 'I seldom listen to the players: one has so much to do in looking at one's acquaintance, that, really, one has no time to mind the stage.'[5]

At last the huge curtain opened and Mary walked onto the stage clutching the arm of the nurse, almost fainting with anxiety.* Before she had even spoken a line, she was greeted with rapturous applause. The audience, who could be vicious and recalcitrant if they felt cheated or disappointed, could also be encouraging and kind. It helped that she was beautifully dressed: 'My dress was a pale pink satin, trimmed with crape, richly spangled with silver; my head was ornamented with white feathers.' In the final scene, when Juliet is in her tomb, she wore a white satin dress that was 'completely plain, excepting that I wore a veil of the most transparent gauze, which fell quite to my feet from the back of my head, and a string of beads round my waist, to which was suspended a cross appropriately fashioned'.[6] White satin was the customary dress for a tragic or mad scene.

* When first published, Mary's *Memoirs* filled two volumes: in a suitably dramatic touch, the first volume ends at this point in her story, as 'with trembling limbs, and fearful apprehension, I approached the audience'.

Playbills often advertised 'new dresses' – clothing was as important as scenery in making the theatre a place of spectacle. Fine robes and court dresses belonging to the aristocracy were sold to the theatres or given to favourite actresses, some of whom wore them irrespective of the role they were playing. There was much debate about consistency and historical accuracy of costumes in plays that mixed together 'Old English' style and contemporary dress. Newspapers often complained that the performers dressed according to their own whim and without the least regard for the consistency of the whole – a character might wear Turkish slippers together with a Grecian turban. Leading players could choose their own costumes, either from the stage wardrobe or made up by their own dressmakers. In the case of comedy, which was usually produced in contemporary dress, the female costumes were particularly elaborate, with hoops and high headdresses of plumed feathers. While performing, actresses prided themselves on dressing fashionably, regardless of the specific part they played. A chambermaid could look like a lady. The actress Sophia Baddeley, when encouraged to cut down her wardrobe expenses, reputedly answered, 'One may as well be dead as not in the fashion.'[7]

'The thundering applause that greeted me nearly overpowered all my faculties,' Mary remembered. 'I stood mute and bending with alarm, which did not subside till I had feebly articulated the few sentences of the first short scene, during the whole of which I never once ventured to look at the audience.' Her next scene was the masquerade. By now she had had time to collect herself. Being in an onstage crowd, she felt less self-conscious and dared to look out on the pit: 'I beheld a gradual ascent of heads: all eyes were fixed upon me; and the sensation they conveyed was awfully impressive: but the keen, the penetrating eyes of Mr Garrick, darting their lustre from the centre of the Orchestra, were, beyond all others, the objects most conspicuous.' The rest of the performance passed in a daze and ended with 'clamorous approbation' and compliments on all sides.[8]

Sheridan was pleased with her and paid her well. After only two performances as Juliet, she was given a much-needed £20.[9] Ten pounds per appearance was the top rate for an actress. But what she most desired was the approbation of Garrick. His praise sparked in her an intensity of feeling greater than she had ever known. She had gained the respect of 'one of the most fascinating men and most distinguished geniuses of the age'; she felt 'that emulation which the soul delights to encourage, where the attainment of fame will be pleasing to an esteemed object'.[10]

Mary's performance was well received. The prompter William Hopkins, who had seen all the greats and all the failures, was not an easy man to impress. 'Juliet by Mrs Robinson – a genteel Figure – a very tolerable first Appearance, and may do in time,' he noted laconically.[11] The writer of 'Theatrical Intelligence' in the leading newspaper, the *Morning Post*, saw considerable potential:

> A Lady, whose name is *Robinson*, made her first appearance last night at this theatre, in the character of *Juliet*; her person is genteel, her voice harmonious, and admitting of various modulations; and her features, when properly animated are striking, and expressive—
>
> At present she discovers a theatrical genius in the rough; which, however, in elocution, as well as action, seems to require considerable polishing, before it can be brought to perfection. In the scene with the Nurse, where she mistakes *Tibalt*'s murder, for that of her lover, *Romeo*, she gave an earnest of stage-abilities, which, if properly attended to, may prove a credit to herself and the Theatre. – We shall be able to speak of her powers at large when we find her become a little more familiar with the stage.[12]

A gentleman signing himself 'Fly Flap', writing in the same paper, found her 'love-inspired Juliet' most 'truly and naturally depicted'. Two days later, following a repeat performance, the *Morning Post* confirmed its favourable first impression: Mrs Robinson 'has a considerable share of untutored genius, and may, under proper instructions, become an acquisition to the stage'.[13]

A rival paper, the *General Advertiser* (where Garrick had good contacts), went much further: 'There has not been a lady on this, or any other stage, for some seasons, who promises to make so capital an actress . . . she has eloquence and beauty: the grace of her arms is singular . . . we may venture to pronounce her an acquisition and an ornament.' The *Gazetteer and New Daily Advertiser* said, 'the young lady who performed the part of Juliet last night was received with uncommon and universal applause'. The *Morning Chronicle* was also impressed, though it did sometimes think she 'substituted rant for passion, and dealt in whispers where she evidently meant to be pathetic'. 'Mrs Robinson,' the reporter added, had a 'genteel figure, with a handsome face, and a fine masking eye. She appeared to feel the character; and although there wanted a polish in her manner of speaking and more ease in her actions and attitudes, she gave the audience a better impression of her than we can remember them to have received from any new actress for some time past.'[14]

Mary played Juliet several more times over the following months. Her second role, in which she appeared on Monday, 17 February 1777, was as the exotic Statira in a tragedy called *Alexander the Great* by the verbose Restoration dramatist Nathaniel Lee. In the *Memoirs* she recollects her costume in great detail: 'My dress was white and blue, made after the Persian *costume*, and though it was then singular on the stage, I wore neither a hoop nor powder; my feet were bound by sandals richly ornamented; and the whole dress was picturesque and characteristic.'[15] Her willingness to defy the fashion of hoops and powder for the sake of dramatic verisimilitude, even though this was only her second role on the stage, was impressive. She also knew that her abandonment of contemporary attire for traditional costume would draw extra publicity.

A week after playing Statira she was Amanda in Sheridan's adaptation of Sir John Vanbrugh's venerable Restoration comedy *The Relapse*. The play was announced as a new piece under the title *A Trip to Scarborough*. The audience were furious when they realized that they had been duped and began hissing (ladies usually hissed through their fans). The leading actress, Mary Ann Yates, swept off the stage, leaving Mary to 'encounter the critical tempest' alone. The terrified Mary was rooted to the spot, but Sheridan – from the side wing – bade her to stay on the stage.

Then there was an intervention from the most prominent member of the audience. The King's younger brother, the Duke of Cumberland, was the black sheep of the royal family. He was a libertine, socialite, and avid theatregoer; his union to divorcée Anne Horton had been one of the causes of the Royal Marriage Act of 1772, which restricted the young royals' freedom to marry. He called out to Mary from his side box: 'It is not you, but the play, they hiss.' She curtsied in response and 'that curtsy seemed to electrify the whole house'. There was a thundering peal of applause and the play was allowed to continue. It ran for ten nights and remained a staple of the Drury Lane repertoire for many years to come.

As one contemporary noted, the great attraction of *A Trip to Scarborough* was that 'it gave an opportunity for producing, in one night, three most remarkable actresses, Mrs Abington, Miss Farren, and Mrs Robinson – the first at the very top of her profession for comic humour – the second of surpassing loveliness and elegance – and the third, one of the most beautiful women in London'.[16]

Mary's aplomb in response to the Duke of Cumberland had saved Sheridan's new show. The following morning's *Gazetteer and New Daily Advertiser* would have added to her delight: 'Mrs Robinson's acting had certainly a just claim to the encouragement of the audience . . . We will venture to affirm, that success cannot fail to attend her theatrical abilities.'[17]

Mary was at last gaining the financial independence that she had always wanted. In April she was given her first benefit. The benefit was the key to an actor's earnings. It was a special performance from which the financial proceeds, after deduction of expenses, were given to a member of the company, who was allowed to choose the play for the evening. Being nearly eight months pregnant by this time, Mary chose the role of the pregnant Fanny in *The Clandestine Marriage*, an exceptionally popular comedy of which Garrick was co-author. It was a brilliant choice, which at once fitted her figure, flattered Garrick and guaranteed a good box office return. The playbill announced that she was selling advance tickets herself, from 19 Southampton Street, Covent Garden. Receipts for the night amounted to a very satisfactory £189 (about £8,000 in today's terms). But her increasing size as she entered the final stages of pregnancy forced her to turn down Sheridan's offer of a role in his new play, *The School for Scandal*. It went to her school friend Priscilla Hopkins, who was also in the company. The play opened on 8 May and was an instant hit.

The Robinsons' new home in Southampton Street – where Garrick had lived for many years – was a stone's throw from Drury Lane. The area was full of actors and actresses. It was a hub of activity, with the Covent Garden Piazza, a cluster of market stalls in the centre, hotels, coffee houses, and shops, bathhouses, and taverns. The shops stayed open from seven in the morning till ten in the evening, lit by elegant double-branched street lamps. Unusually for eighteenth-century London, the streets were paved and clean. Nearby on the Strand the huge government office building

Somerset House was in the early stages of construction. To the west, new streets were being laid out – Bedford and Portman Squares and Portland Place, opening onto the fields of Marylebone. Money and the confidence of money were in the air. In Hyde Park the rich and elegant paraded on horseback or drove about in the latest carriages.

Mrs Robinson began to enjoy the fruits of her talent and popularity. She played light romantic roles, ingénues and virtuous wives – all parts that made the most of her beauty and fine figure. Sheridan lavished attention upon her, she received a handsome salary, the theatre boxes were full of people of rank and fashion. In her *Memoirs* she records the complete turnabout of her life: 'I looked forward with delight both to celebrity and to fortune.'[18]

She gave birth to another daughter, who was baptized Sophia on 24 May 1777. At the age of 6 weeks, the baby started having convulsions, as Maria Elizabeth had once done in Wales. This time the child did not survive. She died in her mother's arms. Sheridan called on Mary that very day. She would never forget his face as he entered the room and saw the dying baby on her lap. 'Beautiful little creature,' he said with 'a degree of sympathetic sorrow' that pierced Mary's heart. His sympathy was a harsh reminder of Robinson's lack of sensibility: 'Had I ever heard *such a sigh* from a husband's bosom?'[19] Throughout this period, Tom continued with his infidelities, but all she cared about now was that he could not even be discreet. With a disarming candour, she admits that her husband did not love her: 'I never was beloved by him . . . I do not condemn Mr Robinson; I but too well know that we cannot command our affections.'

Meanwhile, her friendship with Sheridan flourished. He gave Mary time and attention, despite all the demands of running Drury Lane – a company of 48 male actors, 37 actresses, 18 adult dancers, 2 child dancers, 30 dressers, and a whole panoply of box-keepers, porters, messengers, fruit-sellers, sweepers, carpenters, prompters, set-builders, and musicians. He was plagued with the business of the choice and casting of plays, but also more mundane matters such as the failure of performers to buy their own white silk stockings, dressers pinching leftover candles from the dressing rooms, late return of gloves and hats to wardrobe. Mr Sheridan and Mrs Robinson were kindred spirits, with their Irish blood, strong passions, high ambitions, and sharp sense of humour. They were both chameleons, players one moment and politicians the next. Perhaps they shared their thoughts on female education: Sheridan had written an essay sympathizing with the plight of impoverished gentlewomen and proposing the foundation of a new female university – just as Mary would do in her polemical *Letter to the Women of England* at the climax of her literary career twenty years later.

Sheridan's unremitting attentions initiated a whispering campaign. Up until now the press had been supportive, but the rumour mill was beginning to turn – though Mary always insisted that the relationship was merely a good friendship. When she was too weak and distressed to finish the season after the death of Sophia, Sheridan suggested convalescence in Bath. From there, she returned to nearby Bristol for the summer. In the autumn, she went back to London, to new lodgings in Leicester Square. Her second book of poetry – the volume dedicated to Georgiana, containing 'Captivity' and 'Celadon and Lydia' – was published at this time. The reviewers were kind. According to the *Monthly Review*, 'Two reasons preclude criticism here: the poems are the production of a lady, and that lady is unhappy.'[20]

For her second season, 1777–8, Mary opened in *Hamlet* at the end of September, taking the role of Ophelia, the commoner who is wooed and then rejected by a prince. According to one newspaper, 'Mrs Robinson looked Ophelia very beautifully, and for so young a theatrical adventurer, played it very pleasingly.'[21] A week later she played Lady Anne in *Richard III*, the widow wooed over the body of her father-in-law by the man who has killed her husband. Despite these successes in tragedy, Sheridan was keen that she try her hand at comedy. Her roles over the following weeks included Araminta in Congreve's popular Restoration comedy *The Old Bachelor* – the part is of a wealthy, witty, independent woman who runs rings round at least three male characters – and Emily, the ingénue in *The Runaway*, the first play of a woman dramatist who was beginning to make a name for herself, Hannah Cowley. She also took several roles of virtuous young women who refuse to give in to sexual temptation: the Lady in a version of Milton's *Comus*, Fanny in a dramatization of Henry Fielding's novel *Joseph Andrews*, and Octavia in *All for Love*, Dryden's reworking of Shakespeare's *Antony and Cleopatra*. Her abilities might have been better suited to the part of Cleopatra herself.

On Thursday, 30 April 1778, she played Lady Macbeth for her benefit (having originally been advertised as Cordelia). The afterpiece was a new musical farce called *The Lucky Escape*. Mary did not appear in it – but she was its author. It seems to have impressed the audience more than her performance as Shakespeare's 'fiend-like queen'. The *Morning Post* recorded that the operetta 'was well got up, and all the players acquitted themselves with credit. There is a *prettiness* and *sentiment* in the language strongly characteristic of the author.' The *Morning Chronicle* was more cynical: '*The Lucky Escape* is evidently one of those hasty escapes from the brain, which are from time to time served up at each theatre, during the course of the benefit season, with a view to engage the attention of the publick, on the score of novelty, but which, for want of solid merit, are rarely, if ever, heard of again.'[22] But even this churlish reviewer praised the music.

A few days later, there appeared on the London bookstalls ('printed for the author') *The Songs, Chorusses, etc. in The Lucky Escape, a Comic Opera as Performed at the Theatre-Royal, in Drury-Lane*. Mary was proving her versatility, moving with fleetness of foot from comic heroine to tragedy queen to composer of a musical. Her salary had risen to £2. 10*s*. a week, with the takings from the benefit night on top. She rounded off the season with a reprise of her Juliet.

It would be foolish to seek for biographical revelation in a light musical confection such as *The Lucky Escape*, but one cannot help wondering whether there is any significance in the fact that the heroine is called Maria (the name under which Mary had signed the dedication to her recent volume of poems). The heroine's father is called Steadfast – which is something that Nicholas Darby was not. Another character is Venture, 'a Sharper', who sings that the attractions of a 'comely lass of gay fifteen' (Mary's age when she married Tom Robinson) quickly pall in comparison to the allure of money:

The comely lass of gay fifteen,
　May make a silly lover languish,
But the pain that lurks unseen,
　Often fills the heart with anguish.
Beauty once the heart possessing,
　Charms the sense and drowns our reason;
Gold the spring of every blessing,
　Finds a friend in every season.[23]

Robinson answers rather well to Dr Johnson's dictionary definition of a 'Sharper' as 'a tricking fellow' or 'a rascal': in creating the character of Venture, Mary may well have smiled to herself and thought of her husband.

Mary's commitment to continue her writing career was of a piece with her decision not to follow the usual actor's pattern of undertaking a gruelling tour in the provinces when the major theatres were closed for the summer. She was determined to cut a figure in London rather than wear herself out in provincial obscurity. She accordingly remained in her London lodgings in the summer of 1778. Early in August, Sheridan called on her to relay the sad news of the death of his brother-in-law Thomas Linley, 21 years old and the most promising composer in the land, in a freak boating accident.

Around the same time, Sheridan called again with a proposal that she should accept an engagement to play the short summer season at the Little Theatre in the Haymarket. She agreed, on condition that she should have control over her casting. She wanted to maximize her impact by only playing a few choice roles. Top of her list was the part of Miss Nancy Lovel in a comedy called *The Suicide* by Garrick's friend George Colman. This was a cross-dressed 'breeches role', a daring opportunity for an actress to show off her legs. Mary received her copy of the part and waited for rehearsals to begin. But then she was startled to see a playbill advertising Miss Farren for the part. Elizabeth Farren was the beautiful low-born actress who would later marry into the aristocracy, becoming the Duchess of Derby. Mary wrote to the manager of the Haymarket demanding an explanation and was told that he had already promised the role to Farren and would not risk offending her. Mary responded that she must either be given the part as originally agreed or released from her contract. The manager refused to sign her off the books, she refused to play another role, and so an impasse was reached: 'the summer passed without my once performing, though my salary was paid weekly and regularly'.[24] It was a highly unusual occurrence for a player to be paid for not acting. Mrs Robinson was proving herself a determined manager of her own career.

She added several new roles to her repertoire during the following season at Drury Lane. Some were histrionic tragic performances dripping with sensibility. In *Mahomet* (an English version of a tragedy by Voltaire), reported the *Morning Post*, 'Mrs Robinson performed *Palmira* with spirit, and discovered stage powers that should be more frequently called forth by the managers.'[25] Others were lighter, among them Lady Plume in *The Camp*, a musical entertainment put together by Sheridan, and Miss Richly in *The Discovery*, a comedy by Sheridan's mother Frances, in which Mary engaged in a coquettish double act with Elizabeth Farren. For her benefit in April 1779 she was Cordelia in *Lear* – tickets were available from her new residence in the Great Piazza on the corner of Russell Street, Covent Garden. Receipts were £210, of which she received half, following the deduction of the theatre's 'charges' for expenses. By now she and Tom were leading separate lives, although he took her money. He was supporting two women in one house at Maiden Lane, which was also in Covent Garden. One was a figure dancer from the Drury Lane company, the other 'a woman of professed libertinism'. The bond creditors, meanwhile, 'became so clamorous' that the whole of Mary's benefit was 'appropriated to their demands'.[26]

On 10 May 1779, Sheridan presented Mary as Jacintha in *The Suspicious Husband* by Benjamin Hoadly, a comedy that had been premiered by Garrick thirty years before. It involved many exits and entrances through windows at night, and some risqué small talk. More to the point, it was her first cross-dressed role. 'Last Night,' the *Morning Post* informed its readers, 'Mrs Robinson *wore the breeches* for the first time (on the stage at least) in the character of *Jacintha* in the Suspicious Husband, and was allowed to make a *prettier fellow* than any of her female competitors.'[27] 'On the stage at least' seems to imply that Mary might have appeared in breeches off the stage some time before. That is certainly what she did two weeks later, when she attracted great attention by wearing Jacintha's breeches at a masquerade in Covent Garden. This created a stir in the fashionable world, though at considerable risk to her reputation. To appear cross-dressed on stage was one thing; to do so in society quite another.

Five days after playing Jacintha for the first time, Mary took on another breeches role, Fidelia in Isaac Bickerstaffe's reworking of William Wycherley's comedy *The Plain Dealer* – the part is in the tradition of Shakespeare's Viola, in which a young woman follows her beloved to sea dressed in man's clothes. But it is a darker play than *Twelfth Night*: in Wycherley's original Fidelia is almost raped on stage.[28] From this point on in Mary's career both on stage and in society, it is hard to avoid the subject of sex. Breeches roles were tremendously popular – they afforded male audiences their only public glimpse of the shape of a woman's leg – but they reinforced the old prejudice that women who disported themselves on stage were little better than prostitutes. Actresses were required to lead exemplary lives if they stood a chance of earning respectability, and very few did, exposed as they were to the temptations of the rich patrons who frequented the theatres looking for mistresses. One commentator compared the stage to the window of a toyshop through which actresses could be seen and purchased.[29] Actresses in the 1780s were seen as no different in kind, but only in degree, from the more obviously sexually available performers of the brothel. 'Drury Lane Ague' was slang for syphilis, 'Drury Lane Vestal' for a whore, 'Covent Garden Abbess' for a madam. Drury Lane and Covent Garden were in close physical proximity to bagnios and brothels; prostitutes sold their services in and around the theatre buildings.

Actresses were thrilling to look at, glamorous and mysterious. Because they were on public display, they broke all the conduct-book rules about feminine modesty. Periodically there were outcries against the immorality of the stage, and it was the actresses who usually bore the brunt of the the press's opprobrium. In private, too, even those who were closely connected to the theatre had their doubts. Sheridan forbade his wife to perform in public once they were married, earning the approbation of Dr Johnson. When his wife's sister Mary Linley was offered a contract by Garrick, he wrote a letter to her brother that positively bursts with invective: were she to accept Garrick's offer, she would become 'the unblushing Object of a Licentious gaping croud', the 'Creature of a mercenary Manager, The Servant of the Town, and a licens'd Mark for Libertinism . . . a Topick for illiberal News-Paper Criticism and Scandal'. 'It would be needless to add the circumstance of a Girl's making a Shew of herself in Breeches.'[30] He argued that no decent man ever married an actress and that nine out of every ten actresses ended up bitterly regretting going on the stage. He would rather see his sister-in-law dead than become an actress.

Furthermore, there was anxiety about actresses emulating aristocratic women so successfully that they could play the fine lady offstage as well as on it. Well-to-do women often sold their second-hand clothes to

By Command of their MAJESTIES.
The SIXTH TIME theſe TEN YEARS.
At the Theatre Royal in Drury-Lane,
This preſent Friday, December 3, 1779,
The WINTER's TALE.
(Altered by GARRICK from SHAKESPEARE.)
Leontes by Mr. SMITH,
Polixenes by Mr. BENSLEY,
Florizel by Mr. BRERETON,
Camillo Mr. AICKIN, Old Shepherd Mr. PACKER,
Autolicus by Mr. VERNON,
And the Clown by Mr. YATES.
Perdita by Mrs. ROBINSON,
Paulina by Mrs. HOPKINS,
And Hermione by Mrs. HARTLEY.
In Act II. a Sheep ſhearing Song by Miſs ABRAMS.
And a NEW DANCE, by
Sig. & Sig^a Zuchelli, Miſs Stageldoirs, Mr. Henry, & Sig^a Creſpi
After which (by Command) will be preſented (the 21ſt time) a new Dramatic Piece, in 3 Acts, call'd
The CRITIC;
Or, A TRAGEDY Rehears'd.
The PRINCIPAL CHARACTERS by
Mr. KING,
Mr. DODD, Mr. PALMER,
Mr. PARSONS, Mr. BADDELEY,
And Mrs. HOPKINS.
PRINCIPAL TRAGEDIANS,
Mr. FARREN, Mr. WALDRON, Mr. BURTON,
Mr. BANNISTER jun.
And Miſs POPE.
With a SEA FIGHT and PROCESSION.
The Prologue to be ſpoken by Mr. KING.
With NEW SCENES, DRESSES, and Decorations.
The Scenery deſigned by Mr. DE LOUTHERBOURG, and executed under his Direction.
The Doors to be opened at a Quarter after FIVE o'Clock, to begin at a Quarter after SIX.
To-morrow. (perform'd but once) a new Comedy call'd The TIMES.

Playbill for Mary Robinson as Perdita on the night of the royal command performance.

actresses. Actresses used their freedom in selecting their own apparel to associate themselves further with women of quality. By dressing fashionably both onstage and off, they reinforced the idea that there was little to separate them from their most established and wealthy patrons. Mary was careful to emphasize the continued patronage of the Duchess of Devonshire and the esteem in which she was held by several other 'respectable and distinguished females'. The prominence of ladies of quality in the theatre world was another bane of anti-theatrical pamphleteers. Actresses would often speak Prologues and Epilogues that appealed to the generosity of 'The Ladies' for applause and approval. Actresses increasingly aligned themselves with aristocratic women to defend themselves against the less flattering comparisons suggested in scurrilous biographies and the ever more scandalous paragraphs in the newspapers and periodicals. As Mary insisted, 'I had still the consolation of an unsullied name. I had the highest female patronage, a circle of the most respectable and partial friends.'[31]

Such patronage could not, however, shield her from family disapproval. When Mary's elder brother John visited England from Tuscany, where he had become a respectable merchant, he was horrified by his sister's choice of profession. She managed to persuade him to see her perform, but the moment he saw her entering the stage he 'started from his seat in the stage-box, and instantly quitted the theatre'. Hester, meanwhile, heartily disliked the idea of her daughter being on stage and, although she would go to the theatre to see her perform, she did not hesitate to show 'painful regret'.[32] Mary claims that fortunately her father remained abroad all this time, so never saw her act. But actually he came in and out of the country during these years. In 1779 he opened a subscription at the London Coffee House 'for fitting out a stout privateer'. So it is not beyond the bounds of possibility that one night Nicholas Darby may have slipped into Drury Lane and seen his daughter under the lights.

In Mary's 1796 novel, *Angelina*, the heroine's despotic father (who is a merchant like Nicholas Darby) condemns female stage players: 'my daughter an actress! why, I'd cut her legs off, if I thought she wished to disgrace herself by such an idea'. He would rather 'see her dead, than making such a moppet of herself, as to run about like a vagrant, play-acting'. Mary's own attitude comes across when one of her female characters voices an impassioned defence of the profession as a serious and respectable art:

> We have many females on the stage, who are ornaments to society, and in every respect worthy of imitation! For my part, I adore the Theatre, and think there is more morality to be found in one good tragedy, than in all the sermons that ever were printed. With regard

to acting; it is an act which demands no small portion of intellectual acquirements! It polishes the manners; enlightens the understanding, gives a finish to external grace, and calls forth all the powers of mental superiority![33]

CHAPTER 7

A Woman in Demand

> It has ever been a decided opinion in my mind, that the man who first seduces a woman from the paths of chastity is accessory to all the ills that may await her during the remaining hours of her existence.
>
> Mary Robinson, *Walsingham*

Mary's marriage had become a sham. Nevertheless, in the summer of 1779 she accompanied Tom to Tregunter once again. In all probability, he was seeking breathing space from his creditors and wanted to make another attempt to get money out of Harris.

Her reception at Tregunter House was much better than it had been the time when prison loomed: 'Mrs Robinson, the promising young actress, was a very different personage from Mrs Robinson who had been overwhelmed with sorrows, and came to ask an asylum under the roof of vulgar ostentation.' Elizabeth Robinson expressed her disapproval of Mary's profession, but the 'supposed immorality was . . . *tolerated*' as the labour was 'deemed *profitable*'.[1] The visit appeared to go well. Harris arranged parties and dinners to show her off. The well-to-do women of the locality treated her as 'the very oracle of fashion'. After two weeks in Wales, she returned to London to prepare for the new season. On the way home, a pause at Bath exposed her to the solicitations of the dangerous duellist, George Brereton, prominent amongst her husband's creditors. Tom had met him in the racing town of Newmarket some time before.

Mary's re-enactment of the story is one of the best scenes in the *Memoirs*. It reads like a true novel of sensibility. Brereton had married his cousin, the daughter of the Master of Ceremonies at Bath. Despite the Robinsons' financial difficulties, they stayed at the Three Tuns, one of the city's best inns. Brereton was initially friendly, but then his attentions turned to ardour: he made 'a violent and fervent declaration of love', which 'astonished and perplexed' Mary. She thought the best course of action was to leave town and go to Bristol. They checked into an inn there, in Temple Street. The next morning, just as they were going out to make a visit in Clifton, Tom was arrested at the suit of Brereton on the basis of a promissory note 'in magnitude beyond his power to pay'. A few minutes later, Mary was informed that a lady wished to see her in an upstairs room. Assuming it was one of her old acquaintances, she followed a waiter into another room, while her husband was detained by the sheriff. Brereton was waiting for her: he had got wind of their movements and followed them to Bristol. 'Well, Madam,' he said with a sarcastic smile, 'you have involved your husband in a pretty embarrassment! Had you not been severe towards me, not only this paltry debt would have been cancelled, but any sum that I could command would have been at his service. He has now either to pay me, to fight me, or to go to a prison; and all because you treat me with such unexampled rigour.'[2]

When she begged for mercy, he asked her to promise that she would return to Bath and 'behave more kindly' to him. She realized what he was asking and burst into tears. She accused him of inhumanity. He replied that she was the one being inhuman – for not giving in to him and for making him follow her to Bristol at a time when his own wife lay dangerously ill in Bath. He rang the bell and ordered the waiter to look for his carriage. Mary lost control of herself and screamed that she would expose him as a seducer and villain. Brereton changed colour and tried to calm her down, fearing an embarrassing incident in a public place. He tried to reason with her, asking why she chose to stay with a husband who treated her so badly. It would be an act of kindness to estrange her from such a man. His neglect of her would justify any action she took. Was it not 'a matter of universal astonishment' in society that a woman renowned for her 'becoming spirit' should 'tamely continue to bear such infidelities from a husband'? This hit a nerve with Mary, for

Brereton was echoing the view taken not only by the gossips in the theatre world but also by her closest circle of friends. At the same time, it was a line that libertines had tried on her before.

Brereton continued to taunt her as she paced the room in anguish. 'How little does such a husband deserve such a wife,' he said:

> 'How tasteless must he be, to leave such a woman for the very lowest and most degraded of the sex! Quit him, and fly with me. I am ready to make any sacrifice you demand. Shall I propose to Mr Robinson to let you go? Shall I offer him his liberty on condition that he allows you to separate yourself from him? By his conduct he proves that he does not love you; why then labour to support him?'[3]

Mary was almost frantic. 'Here, Madam,' continued Brereton, after pausing four or five minutes, 'here is your husband's release.' So saying, he threw a written paper on the table. 'Now,' he added, 'I rely on your generosity.' She trembled, unable to speak. Brereton told her to compose herself and to conceal her distress from the staff and guests at the inn. 'I will return to Bath,' he said, 'I shall there expect to see you.' He stormed out of the room, got into his chaise and drove away from the inn door. Mary hurried to show her husband the discharge. All the expenses of the arrest were settled shortly afterwards. They returned to Bath. Robinson did not ask too many questions. Mary warned him against placing his freedom in the hands of a gamester and his wife's virtue in the power of a libertine, but she knew he would not listen.

Back in Bath, they moved to a different inn, the White Lion. The next afternoon, a Sunday, Mary was astonished to look out of the window and see Brereton parading down the road 'with his wife and her no less lovely sister' – the story of the wife's dangerous illness was a lie. When the Robinsons sat down to dinner, Brereton was announced by the waiter. He 'coldly bowed' to Mary and then apologized to Tom, producing a story about how he had only taken action because he was himself being menaced for the money, that he had come to Bristol to prevent rather than to enforce the arrest, and that he had now paid off the demand. Perhaps he would have the honour of seeing the Robinsons later that evening? They did not wait around for him: immediately after dinner they set off for London. Mary dramatizes this story – like that of her meeting with her husband's first mistress, Harriet Wilmot – so as to emphasize that she was a wronged woman long before any scandalous liaison of her own, but the vivid details have the ring of truth.

Back in London, the Robinsons rented a spacious and elegant house from the actress Isabella Mattocks, in the heart of Covent Garden, near Drury Lane Theatre. They entertained with abandon: 'My house was thronged with visitors, and my morning levees were crowded so that I could scarcely find a quiet hour for study.'[4] Robinson had a lucky streak with the cards and they spent the money on horses, ponies and a new carriage.

Once again the gossip sheets whispered that the rising star Mary and the dashing theatre manager Sheridan were more than friends. A letter to the *Morning Post* signed 'Squib' said 'Mrs Robinson is to the full, as beautiful as Mrs Cuyler [another actress]; and Mrs Robinson has not been overlooked; the manager of Drury-Lane *has pushed her forward*.' Mary responded: 'Mrs Robinson presents her compliments to *Squib*, and desires that the next time he wishes to exercise his *wit*, it may not be at *her expense*. Conscious of the rectitude of her conduct, both in public and private, Mrs Robinson does not feel herself the least hurt, at the ill-natured sarcasms of an anonymous detractor.'[5] She was learning to play the press, an art for which she had good masters in Sheridan and Garrick.

Sheridan continued to pay her marked attention, but she claimed that – in contrast to the behaviour of the libertines – his attitude was always courteous and respectful. He was too good a friend and a man of too much honour to take advantage of her miserable marriage. 'The happiest moments I then knew, were passed in the society of this distinguished being. He saw me ill-bestowed on a man who neither loved nor valued me; he lamented my destiny, but with such delicate propriety, that it consoled while it revealed to me the unhappiness of my situation.' And yet she also writes more defensively: 'Situated as I was at this time, the effort was difficult to avoid the society of Mr Sheridan. He was manager of the theatre. I could not avoid seeing and conversing with him at rehearsals and behind the scenes, and his conversation was always such as to fascinate and charm me.'[6] Is there a hint of some impropriety here? In the original manuscript of the *Memoirs* a long paragraph immediately preceding this remark is heavily deleted – could Mary have confessed something and then thought better of it? On the other hand, it is striking that the author of the anonymous *Memoirs of Perdita*, who was for the most part eager to accuse her of having affairs with almost every important man she met, restrained himself in the case of Sheridan: 'Of the *nature* of their intimacy, though the tattle of the day may have spoke freely, no particulars have transpired; nor should tattle always be regarded.'[7]

At this time, Mary was increasingly subjected to the 'alluring temptations' of noblemen who wished to take her under their protection. Charles Manners, the fourth Duke of Rutland, offered her £600 a year for the privilege. She turned him down. She wanted the patronage of the theatregoing and poetry-reading public, not that of an aristocrat seeking a courtesan. In her *Memoirs*, Mary refused to name all the men who propositioned her, so as not to 'create some reproaches in many families of the fashionable world'.[8] But she let it be known that advances were made by a royal Duke, a lofty Marquis, and a city merchant of 'considerable fortune'. Many of these men conveyed their proposals via Mary's milliners and dressmakers. The scurrilous *Memoirs of Perdita*, published in 1784 for the purpose of discrediting her, gives graphic details of her purported sexual adventures with both the conceited dandy Lord Cholmondeley and an unnamed heavy-drinking importer of vintage wines. Though not to be trusted, this source provides incidental confirmation of the impression that men from both the established aristocracy and the world of new city money had designs on her.

One of the men who paid her most attention was Sir John Lade, the wealthy heir to a brewery fortune and former ward of Henry Thrale, friend of Dr Johnson. Soon after coming of age, Lade concentrated all his energies on the Robinson household in the Great Piazza. He gambled with Tom and paid court to Mary. Gossip columnists were soon sniffing round the ménage:

> A certain young Baronet, well known on the Turf, and famous for his high phaeton, had long laid siege to a pretty actress (a married woman) at one of our theatres; he sent her a number of letters, which after she had read (and perhaps did not like, as they might not speak to the purpose) she sent him back again; a kind of Bo-peep Play was kept up between them in the theatres, and from the Bedford

> Arms Tavern and her window. The Baronet is shame-faced, and could not address her in person, but by means of some good friend they were brought together, and on Sunday se'en-night set out in grand cavalcade for Epsom, to celebrate the very joyful occasion of their being acquainted. The Baronet went first, attended by a male friend, in his phaeton, and the lady with her husband in a post coach and four, with a footman behind it; the day was spent with the greatest jollity, and the night also, if we may believe report. Since that time they are seen together in public at the theatres and elsewhere, the husband always making one of the party, between whom and the Baronet there is always the greatest friendship.[9]

Lade, who later managed the Prince's racing stables, affected to dress and speak like a groom. He eventually married a girl called Letty, who had been a servant in a brothel. Lady Letty Lade went on to have affairs with both the Duke of York and a highwayman known as 'Sixteen-string Jack'.

As rumour spread that Lade had won the affections of the actress, every rake in London began seeking the acquaintance of the beautiful Mrs Robinson. Sheridan was worried that his star would be tempted away by one of the men who were paying court to her. He warned Mary about her expensive lifestyle and the company she kept. The image of her younger self that she presents in the *Memoirs* is, to say the least, wide-eyed: 'I had been then seen and known at all public places from the age of fifteen; yet I knew as little of the world's deceptions as though I had been educated in the deserts of Siberia. I believed every woman friendly, every man sincere, till I discovered proofs that their characters were deceptive.'[10] Given all that she had seen in both high society and low, she could not really have been that naive.

Despite the fact that she was treated as public property by the men who pursued her, Mary evoked this time as a golden age of theatre. Sheridan was at the peak of his reputation as a playwright and manager, following the success of his *School for Scandal*. He was beginning to turn his mind towards a political career and had recently met the young radical politician Charles James Fox. The green room was frequented by the nobility and 'men of genius' such as Fox and Lord Derby, who was to marry Elizabeth Farren: 'the stage was now enlightened by the very best critics, and embellished by the very highest talents'. Mary also remarked that one of the reasons for Drury Lane's popularity during this season of 1779–80 was that nearly all the principal women were under the age of twenty (a slight exaggeration). As well as herself and Farren, the lovely Charlotte Walpole and Priscilla Hopkins were on the payroll.

The public's appetite for news, gossip, and scandal about the stage was insatiable. One of the consequences of the system of stock companies was that the audience became familiar with a small group of actors, seeing them in a variety of different roles and plays of all types, coming to know not only their styles of acting, but the details of their private lives. The proliferation of stage-related literature meant that readers were able to discover the intimate details of actors' lives. A successful player could only have a public private life. Actors' journals and memoirs, biographies of playwrights and managers, histories and annals of the theatre, periodicals and magazines rolled off the press. Prints and caricatures of actresses could be bought cheaply. Theatre gossip could be picked up from the newspapers, together with instant accounts of the latest performances – this was the age when professional theatre reviewing grew to maturity.

Sheridan launched his new season on 18 September 1779 with Mary as Ophelia. 'Natural and affecting,' said the *Morning Chronicle*. 'Ophelia found a more than decent representative in Mrs Robinson,' judged the *Morning Post*, 'except in her singing, which was rather too discordant even for madness itself!' It also noted that 'the house, though not a very brilliant [i.e. aristocratic], was a crowded one, and both play and entertainment [the musical *Comus*] went off with considerable éclat'.[11] Mary was Lady Anne in *Richard III* a week later.

Next, she reprised her Fidelia in *The Plain Dealer*. Her costume drew attention, though the critic in the *Morning Post* tried to give the impression that he was only looking at it from the point of view of dramatic verisimilitude, not that of the shapely leg to which it clung:

> *Fidelia* was performed with great ease and feeling by Mrs Robinson, and is by far the best character she has hitherto attempted; but as propriety of stage dress should always be strictly attended to, particularly in the professional characters, it may not be improper to inform Mrs Robinson, that *Fidelia* as a *Volunteer* cannot wear a *Lieutenant's* uniform, without a violation of all dramatic consistency.[12]

She played fifty-five nights that season, adding to her repertoire Viola in *Twelfth Night*, Nancy in *The Camp*, Rosalind in *As You Like It*, Oriana in George Farquhar's *The Inconstant*, Widow Brady ('with an Epilogue Song') in Garrick's *The Irish Widow*, and Eliza Camply in *The Miniature Picture* by Lady Elizabeth Craven. As Oriana, she had to win over a reluctant lover by engaging in various schemes including dressing as a nun, feigning madness, and disguising herself as a page-boy. As the Irish Widow, she had to mimic a strong brogue, put down an assortment of men, talk about her clothes, claim that she despised money, and cross-dress as a sword-bearing officer called Lieutenant O'Neale. But it was the Shakespearean breeches roles of Viola and Rosalind that were her greatest triumph. She revealed a gift for both the expression of Shakespeare's language and the characters' emotional range – from pathos through wit to fortitude and command.

Admirers began to address her through the medium of the daily press. The *Morning Post* printed a long and not a little voyeuristic letter to her. 'Madam,' it began,

> Criticism is a *cold* exercise of the mind: but as I feel an inexpressive glow, while my imagination takes your fair hand in mine, I think I may venture to court your acceptance of two or three remarks, which are conveyed in a temperament of blood somewhat differing from the chill, and the *acid* of the critique. I am the veriest bigot to old Shakespeare. – The Genius himself could not have gazed upon you with more delight; nor have forerun your *motion*, *action*, and utterance, with more tremulous solicitude for your excellence in *Viola*, than I did. Shakespeare's principal substantives should never be *sunk*, nor *kept back*, as it were, from the attention, by an emphatic tone upon his epithets.
>
> In the manner of speaking the '*green and yellow melancholy*,' I would, sweet woman, that the *yellow tinge* appeared no more than equal to the *green*; and, that the *melancholy* so coloured should have a *principal* share of your voice to mark the subject.
>
> I have seen you too in *Fidelia*, and am apt to think, that the *tone*, *force*, and *manner* of tragedy make a kind of apparel, both too *magnificent*, and too *solemn*, for the sentimental part of comedy.
>
> BO-PEEP[13]

The author sounds as if he would very much like to pay a private visit to her dressing room in order to advise her upon her Shakespearean epithets.

She also played the female lead in *Florizel and Perdita*. This was Garrick's 1756 version of the final two acts of Shakespeare's *The Winter's Tale*. It was revived by Sheridan, after fourteen years' absence from the repertoire, on Saturday, 20 November 1779, in memory of Garrick, who had died earlier that year. It centred on the young lovers, Prince Florizel and Perdita, who is supposed to be a shepherd's daughter but is really a princess. It included a sheepshearing song, sung by Perdita, and a dance of shepherds and shepherdesses. Mary's performance was a success, though the *Morning Post* complained 'Mrs Robinson's *Perdita* would have been very decent, but for that strange kind of *niddle* to *noddle*, that she now throws into every character, comic, as well as tragic.'[14]

At the second presentation, the following Tuesday, she was honoured by the presence of such leaders of London society as the Duke and Duchess of Devonshire, Lord and Lady Melbourne, Lord and Lady Spencer, Lord and Lady Cranbourne, and Lord and Lady Onslow. After this performance the *Gazetteer and New Daily Advertiser* published a long criticism. It said that the piece 'is in general well cast and ably performed', but reservations were expressed about the costumes:

> The dresses on which much of the effect depends, were liable to very glaring objections. Shakespeare has been particularly attentive to the dress of Florizel and Perdita:
>
> Your high self you have obscur'd
> With a swain's wearing, and me poor lowly maid,
> Most goddess-like, prank'd up—
>
> To correspond with this description Florizel and Perdita have hitherto appeared in beautiful dresses, covered with flowers of both the same pattern, and she wore an ornamented sheep hook, instead of which Mrs Robinson appears in a common jacket, and wears the usual red ribbons of an ordinary milk-maid, and in this dress she also appears with the King to view the supposed statue of Hermione, after she is acknowledged his daughter.[15]

For most of the audience, though, the figure-hugging jacket and milkmaid's ribbons were exactly what they wanted to see. Takings were excellent and the show played again on the next Friday night and the Monday and Wednesday after that. Mary gained further public exposure when the *Morning Post* printed her poem 'Celadon and Lydia'.[16] Then on Friday, 3 December 1779 there was a royal command performance. A full house was assured. Mrs Robinson was about to become 'the famous Perdita'.

PART TWO

Celebrity

CHAPTER 8

Florizel and Perdita

> Her name is Robinson, on or off the stage for I have seen her both, she is I believe almost the greatest and most perfect beauty of her sex.
>
> George, Prince of Wales

King George and Queen Charlotte were ardent lovers of the stage, commanding over three hundred performances between 1776 and 1800. The King preferred modern comedies, calling Shakespeare 'sad stuff'. He also preferred the Theatre Royal in Covent Garden to its rival. Especially after Sheridan took over Drury Lane, and became more and more closely identified politically with the radical Whig faction of Charles James Fox, the two theatres – situated within a few hundred yards of each other – were seen as reflections of the political divisions within Parliament. Drury Lane was regarded as the Opposition's theatre, Covent Garden as the Government's. So the appearance of the royal family at Drury Lane on 3 December 1779 was a very special occasion.

They arrived at a door situated near the stage door. The royal box was next to the proscenium on the audience's left-hand side and always especially fitted up at command performances. The royals were met by one of the proprietors of the theatre. Equipped with a candelabrum, and walking backwards to face the King, he led them through a private corridor that gave direct access to the box. The King would pay £10 on every night that it was occupied. The royal party was presented with special playbills printed on satin. As the King came within sight of the audience, everybody stood up and applauded. The greeting was returned with a bow. The family would have had a very close view of the stage, and would even have been able to see the actors waiting in the wings.

Accompanying the King and Queen that night was 17-year-old George, soon to become Prince of Wales and eventually King George IV. He was dressed in blue velvet trimmed with gold and wore diamond buckles on his shoes. He would have sat in the Prince's box, which was adorned with his motif of three feathers and situated directly opposite the King's – and equally close to the stage.

The Prince at the age of 17 was not the fat, lecherous, dissipated hedonist of later years, depicted in so many satirical cartoons. When Mary first met him he was handsome, cultivated, and good-tempered. He was known as a man of enormous charm, intelligence, and taste. Mary was not exaggerating when she described him as 'the most admired and most accomplished Prince in Europe'.[1] He fenced and boxed, but also played the cello, drew and had a deep appreciation of painting. One of the members of the royal household, Mrs Papendiek, wrote in her journal, 'he was not so handsome as his brother, but his countenance was of a sweetness and intelligence quite irresistible. He had an elegant person, engaging and distinguished manners, added to an affectionate disposition and the cheerfulness of youth.'[2] In a letter to his first love, Mary Hamilton, written when he was 16, he described himself as follows:

> Your brother is now approaching the bloom of youth. He is rather above normal size, his limbs well proportioned, and upon the whole is well made, though he has rather too great a penchant to grow fat. The features of his countenance are strong and manly, though they carry too much of an air of hauteur. His forehead is well shaped, his eyes, though none of the best, and although grey are passable ... His sentiments and thoughts are open and generous. He is above doing anything that is mean (too susceptible, even to believing people his friends, and placing too much confidence in them, from not yet having obtained a sufficient knowledge of the world or of its practices), grateful and friendly to an excess where he finds a *real friend*. His heart is good and tender if it is allowed

> to show its emotions . . . Now for his vices, rather let us call them weaknesses. He is too subject to give vent to his passions of every kind, too subject to be in a passion, but he never bears malice or rancour in his heart. As for swearing, he has nearly cured himself of that vile habit. He is rather too fond of Wine and Women, to both which young men are apt to deliver themselves too much, but which he endeavours to check to the utmost of his power. But upon the whole, his Character is open, free and generous.[3]

His fondness for wine and women, even at such a young age, was a reaction against the restraint and rigid application to duty in which he had grown up. When he misbehaved as a child, he was beaten by the King in person. The royal household was based in secluded quarters at Kew and Windsor. The Prince and his brother, Frederick Duke of York, had their own apartments, where they were maintained under the watchful eye of an austere governor, the Earl of Holdernesse. Inevitably, the Prince sought more interesting company and developed a tendency to fall in with the wrong people. When he was 15, one of his tutors, a bishop, was asked his opinion of his pupil. 'I can hardly tell,' he replied. 'He will be either the most polished gentleman or the most accomplished blackguard in Europe, possibly an admixture of both.'[4]

Garrick's adaptation of *The Winter's Tale* omitted the first three acts of Shakespeare's original and began the action with a penitent Leontes washed up on the coast of Bohemia in company with his courtiers. Whereas Hermione is the most important female part in the original, the adaptation – which was published under the title *Florizel and Perdita* – concentrates more on the young lovers: the prince Florizel and the shepherdess who is really a princess. The name Perdita means 'the lost one', but, of course, she is found in the end and the Prince and the Princess are married. The outcome of the royal command performance that December night was, it might be said, the original 'scandal in Bohemia'.

By her own account, Mary was teased by the other players before the show began. William 'Gentleman' Smith, so called for his skill in playing genteel roles on the stage and for his manners and intelligence off it, was to be Leontes. 'By Jove, Mrs Robinson,' he said, 'you will make a conquest of the Prince; for to-night you look handsomer than ever.'[5]

PRICE SIX PENCE

FLORIZEL and PERDITA.

TUNE: *O Polly is a ſad Slut! &c.*

I'LL ſing a Song, a merry one,
To chear the doleful Times,
And ſhould you like a little Fun,
I'll tell it you in Rhimes.

A tender Prince, ah well-a-day!
Of Years not yet a Score,
Had late his poor Heart ſtol'n away,
By one of 's many more;

As many more (at leaſt) ſhe is,
And might have been the Mother,
(You'd ſay it, if you ſaw her Phiz)
Perhaps of ſuch an other,.

Her Cheeks were vermeil'd o'er with Red,
Her Breaſt enamell'd White,
And nodding Feathers deck'd her Head,
A Piece for Candle Light.

Sometimes ſhe'd play the Tragic Queen,
Sometimes the Peaſant poor,
Sometimes ſhe'd ſtep behind the Scenes,
And there ſhe'd play the W——.

Two Thouſand Pounds, a princely Sight!!
For doing juſt no more,
Than what is acted every Night,
By every Siſter W——,

She never play'd her Part ſo well,
In all her Life before,
Yet ſome, as well as Florizel,
Knows how ſhe plays the W——.

Her Huſband too, a puny Imp,
Will often guard the Door,
And humbly play Sir Peter Pimp,
While ſhe performs the W——.

'Florizel and Perdita': the earliest caricature of the Robinsons and the Prince.

Before she was due to go on, Mary chatted in the wings to Richard Ford (son of one of the proprietors of Drury Lane), who introduced her to his friend, George Capel, Viscount Malden, who was a politician and also a boon companion to the young Prince of Wales. Malden was 22, the same age as Mary. Known as a dandy, he was attired in his usual flamboyant dress – pink satin with silver trim and pink heels to match his coat. The Prince watched them from his box, as he conversed with his companions. He was of medium height, stocky with a rather florid complexion and powdered hair. Mary always remembered the especially clear view of him that she had as she waited in the wings.

Mary hurried through her first scene and as she stood directly below the Prince's box, she heard him making flattering remarks. She was conscious that he was staring at her so much that it drew everyone's attention. For Mary, there must have been a special frisson in speaking some of Perdita's lines in front of the real Prince:

I am all shame
And ignorance itself, how to put on
This novel garment of gentility . . .
. . . I shall learn,
I trust I shall with meekness, and an heart
Unalter'd to my Prince, my Florizel. [*leans on Florizel's bosom*][6]

On the final curtsy, the royal family returned a bow to the performers. Mary's eyes met the Prince's: 'with a look that I *never shall forget*, he gently inclined his head a second time; I felt the compliment, and blushed my gratitude'.[7]

Any doubt that he had been charmed by the lovely shepherdess in her simple dress and milkmaid's red ribbons was dispelled as Mary was leaving the theatre: she met the royal family crossing the stage and 'I was again honoured with a very marked and low bow from the Prince of Wales.' One cannot help wondering whether she timed her departure from the green room in order to give herself the chance of bumping into the Prince. Since she was not appearing in that night's afterpiece, Sheridan's *The Critic*, she could have left the theatre much earlier. Instead, she waited backstage, chatting to her charming and well-connected new acquaintance Lord Malden: 'He remarked the particular applause which the Prince had bestowed on my performance; said a thousand civil things; and detained me in conversation till the evening's performance was concluded.'[8] At home after the show, she threw a lavish supper party for her friends. It lasted far into the night and the handsome young Prince was the only topic of conversation.

During the previous six months, the Prince had regularly poured out his heart to Mary Hamilton, the sub-governess of his sisters the royal princesses. She was 23 to his 16 (he would always prefer older women). His letters to her, in which he called her Miranda and signed himself Palemon, survive in a private collection. Like a young man in a novel of sensibility, he threatened that he would commit suicide if she rejected him. She in turn threatened to resign her post if he did not stop pestering her, so he promised to address her 'by the endearing names of *friend and Sister*, and no longer with the impetuous passion of a Lover urging his Suit'.[9] But he still sent her gifts, such as a 'Ring set with Brilliants', which she returned on the very day of the command performance of *The Winter's Tale*. He immediately penned a response in his favoured language of extreme sensibility: 'I am astonished, I am surprised I am enchanted I am enchanted thou ever ever ever dearest, dearest, dearest cruel Creature, Oh believe me my Miranda that if ever I could love *you* more *than I do* this has done it. I am & ever shall be unto my last health Thy Palemon *toujours de même*.' He also told her that he was looking forward to going to the theatre: 'how happy should I be to see you there and agreeably entertained with me'.[10] So the Prince went to the theatre that night full of thoughts of Mary Hamilton. By the end of the evening, he was 'head in heels in love' with Mary Robinson.

The unpublished letters to Miss Hamilton written by the Prince in the following few days tell the extraordinary story of the beginning of the relationship between the Prince and the actress from his point of view. It is a very different account from that in the *Memoirs*.

It must have come as something of a shock to Mary Hamilton at ten o'clock on Sunday morning to receive a letter in which, twenty-four hours after professing his undying passion for her, 'Palemon' announced that he had fallen in love with someone else:

> I was delighted at the Play last Night, and was extremely moved by two scenes in it, especially as I was particularly interested in the

> appearance of the most beautiful Woman, that ever I beheld, who acted with such delicacy that she drew tears from my eyes, she perceived how much of my attention was taken up with her, not only during her acting but when she was behind the Scenes, and contrived every little innocent art to captivate a heart but too susceptible of receiving every impression she attempted to give it, and Alas my Miranda my friend, she did but too well succeed, consider what is almost impossible, and allow whate'r next to impossibility for the lively and strong and lively passions of a Young Man glowing with the utmost Warmth of desire, and yet feeling himself incapable of gratifying his darling. Her name is Robinson, on or off the stage for I have seen her both, she is I believe almost the greatest and most perfect beauty of her sex.[11]

Whereas Mary's account, written twenty years later, emphasizes the Prince's gaze upon her, George's, written the very next day, suggests that she was acting for him alone, both onstage and off, contriving 'every little innocent art to captivate' his heart. This letter also reveals the emotional power of her performance as Perdita: she was able to draw tears from the eyes of the young Prince.

The real surprise in this letter is the phrase 'on or off the stage for I have seen her both'. In Mary's account and in the subsequent myth of 'Florizel and Perdita', the command performance on 3 December 1779 was the first time the couple saw one another. But the Prince reveals here that he had seen her before, not only on the stage but also in society. Indeed, in the very next sentence he explains that 'this passion has laid dormant in my bosom for some time, but last night has kindled it agair to such a degree (for what can be more moving interesting, or aimiable [sic] than exquisite beauty in distress) that Heaven knows when it will be extinguished'. He had fallen for Mary Robinson some time before, but put her out of his mind until he saw her play the part of Perdita, the lost one, the 'exquisite beauty in distress'. Already accustomed to projecting himself into dramatic roles ('Palemon to Miranda'), George cannot help imagining himself as Prince Florizel.

'Pardon me, pity me, comfort me,' he writes to Miss Hamilton, 'my heart is already something easier by having imparted to you my friend what I have not another friend I can strictly call so to whom I could with implicit confidence impart it.' He knows that all his secrets will lie as secure in her bosom 'as in the silent grave', so she will 'hear every thing relating to this affair'. He implores her not to reveal anything to the King and Queen. The letter ends with a postscript: 'a[dieu] a[dieu] a[dieu] *toujours chère*. Oh! Mrs Robinson.'

Upon receiving this astonishing letter, Miss Hamilton sat down immediately to reply. Acknowledging that the subject embarrassed her, she endeavoured to express her sentiments:

> Now my dear friend with respect to the present object of your passion and fancy – I know not what to say – let me however take the liberty of pointing out that a female in that line has too much trick and art not to be a very dangerous object – I do not reprove you for having fix'd your affections – for you tell me – *beauty* is *amiable* as well as interesting – how was it possible then for my young friend to steel his heart against the united forces of *Beauty* and *innocence* – when under (even of mock) appearance of distress – and likewise when that beauty and innocence could for his sake and to attract *his* regard, *condescend* to use the common little arts of *her sex* and *profession* to *captivate* a heart so much worth her while to conquer.[12]

This Mary has no illusions about what the other Mary is up to: for her, an actress is synonymous with 'trick and art'. In response to the Prince's request for 'comfort', she says that he will not need it, since it will be a 'pleasing certainty that the lady returns your love'. As for his statement that Heaven knows when his passion will be extinguished, she remarks that Heaven has nothing to do with the affair.

On the Tuesday morning, the Prince wrote again, signing himself, 'Your unfortunate brother Palemon': 'I am in tolerably good health, tho' over head in ears in love, and so much so that I do not know to what lengths it will carry me.' The next day, he announced a plan of action:

> My dearest friend does not seem to apprehend that the passion I have formed is for an Actress so that I scarcely dare flatter myself that she feels the same love for me that I do for her, I am convinced that she understood the language of my eyes and of my actions,

> from her manner and the tender and bewitching glances she gave me and her eyes said more than words can express. Heavens, was you but to see her, even if the most envious of her sex was to see her, they must confess that she is almost the most perfect beauty that ever was seen. However no more of these enthusiastic confessions or else you will take me to be mad, I know her to be very galant, and yet I can not help adoring her, however in a day or two I will inform you what opinion she has conceived of my person and how she is content with it, for I have an excellent person to employ who is well acquainted with her, who will inform me of these particulars and you may depend on my informing you immediately.[13]

He had obviously been asking around on the subject of Mrs Robinson: 'galant' is code for her dubious reputation, but this has not put him off. He had established that she 'lives totally separated from her husband', which had the advantage that an affair would not disrupt 'family peace'. He is, of course, aware that it would disturb the peace of the royal family, but he professed himself 'blinded by passion'.

In response, Miss Hamilton warned him that it was already rumoured that he thought Mrs Robinson 'a Divinity' and that he should be wary of trusting anyone who would take on so infamous a role as that of a pander. Though the Prince did not reveal his go-between's identity to Miss Hamilton, it was Lord Malden who paid Mrs Robinson a morning visit on his behalf.

On arriving in her drawing room, Malden seemed embarrassed and uncomfortable, even agitated. By Mary's account, he 'attempted to speak – paused, hesitated, apologized'. He was, he said, in a peculiarly delicate situation; he had something to deliver that he hoped she would not mention to anyone else. Finally, he produced a letter addressed to Perdita. She smiled a little sarcastically and opened it, finding it was a love letter. It contained only a few words, but 'those expressive of more than common civility'. The signature was FLORIZEL. Mary continues the story in her favoured form of dramatic dialogue:

> 'Well, my Lord, and what does this mean?' said I, half angry.
> 'Can you not guess the writer?' said Lord Malden.
> 'Perhaps yourself, my Lord,' cried I, gravely.

'Upon my honour, no,' said the Viscount. 'I should not have dared so to address you on so short an acquaintance.'

I pressed him to tell me from whom the letter came. – He again hesitated; he seemed confused, and sorry that he had undertaken to deliver it. 'I hope that I shall not forfeit your good opinion,' said he, 'but—'

'But what, my Lord?'

'I could not refuse, – for the letter is from the Prince of Wales.'[14]

Astonished, agitated, and sceptical, Mary 'returned a formal and a doubtful answer'. Lord Malden then took his leave.

She read over the 'short but expressive letter' a thousand times. Malden returned the next evening to Mary's house, where she was entertaining a card party of six or seven. He praised in extravagant terms the mind, manners, and temper of the Prince, while Mary's 'heart beat with conscious pride' as she thought of 'the partial but delicately respectful letter' she had received the day before.

The Prince, meanwhile, was still keeping Miss Hamilton informed of developments. He told her that he was going to the theatre again, but this time to Covent Garden rather than Drury Lane – 'Oh Mrs Robinson, Mrs Robinson, Mrs Robinson,' he wailed.[15] During the performance at Covent Garden, George appeared tired. A wag remarked that he would not have seemed so had he been at Drury Lane.

In his next letter he shared the news, which would hardly have been a surprise to Miss Hamilton, that there was every sign that his passion was reciprocated:

> Know then my friend, that I am more than ever in love, and that the dear object of my passion, corresponds with my flame, and that our love is mutual, she was attacked the other [night] in the house for addressing every tender speech she ought to have addressed to Prince Florizel to me, you may see of what texture they are by reading them in Shakespeare.[16]

Mary has, it seems, had to endure the embarrassment of heckling audience members accusing her of addressing her lines to the real Prince in the side box instead of the player prince, William Brereton, in the role of

Florizel. (It is also worth remembering that Miss Hamilton would not have found all the lines in question in her Shakespeare, since some of Perdita's 'tender speeches' had actually been written by Garrick.)

The Prince's infatuation was the talk of the town. One night a friend of his sat next to Sir John Lade at Covent Garden. The Prince knew that Lade had 'had an intimate connection avec mon *aimable et chère séductrice*'. Lade said that he had heard a great deal of the Prince's attachment to Mrs Robinson and that he could give an assurance that she was as much pleased with him as he could be with her. The friend asked whether, in view of his own intimacy with Mrs Robinson, Lade felt 'not undermined by this gallant young rival'. To which he replied, 'By God I should be very glad of it for both their sakes as they seem so perfectly attached to each other.' Having reported this to Miss Hamilton, the Prince signs off by regaling his long-suffering correspondent with a description of his ecstatic 'metamorphosis' from despondent victim of unrequited love to 'gay galent Lothario'. 'Love, passion, and the most ardent flame,' he writes, are 'boiling altogether in my bosom'.

'For the love of Heaven, Stop, O stop my friend! and do not thus headlong plunge yourself into vice,' Miss Hamilton responded. 'Your last note and the preceding one made every nerve of me thrill with apprehension . . . You listen not to the voice of reason . . . I conjure you, strive to conquer this unhappy infatuation.'[17] The letter continues for several pages in this vein, imploring the Prince not to become one of the 'votaries of vice'. A fragmentary draft chides him for comparing himself to the archetypal rake – 'Ah! boast not the title of a *Lothario* lest you should end with his fate' – and also reveals that she has been doing her own research on Mrs Robinson:

> My friend, you have been deceived, Mrs Robinson lives with her Husband and they have *never* been separated, – the young Baronet [i.e. Lade] if, he *did boast*, – boasted falsely. Her husband is young, Idle, and extravagant; and they have experienced distress, but her present occupation, as an actress, enables them to live perfectly to *their taste*, and at their ease – They have a little Girl about 4 or 5 years old – I know their whole History, which I got at by mere chance, and from what I think, the most undoubted authority – You have been abused by some designing person – take care that you are not drawn into some snare.

Mary Hamilton waited two weeks before posting her final letter. It had no effect on the infatuated Prince, so she terminated their correspondence. He had penned seventy-eight letters at a rate of approximately one every three days, thus establishing a pattern which he would surpass when taking on the name of Florizel. The impassioned style of the 'letters from Palemon to Miranda' reveals how inflammatory those from 'Florizel to Perdita' must have been. In writing so many love letters the Prince was courting danger. His banished uncle, the Duke of Cumberland, had been embroiled in an embarrassment over salacious letters that he had sent to his mistress, Lady Grosvenor, whose husband had subsequently sued for £13,000.

In Mary's version of the beginning of the affair, Malden soon brought another letter. As proof that it was indeed from the Prince, she was bidden to attend the oratorio that was to be performed at Drury Lane that night. There he would find a means of communicating to her that he was indeed the author of the letters. Mary and her husband got seats in a balcony box. The Prince arrived in the royal box with his favourite brother Frederick. He saw her at once, held his playbill in front of his face, drew his hand across his forehead, and stared at her meaningfully. He then moved his hand across the edge of the box, miming the action of writing. And he nudged his brother, who also stared at her. When a gentleman-in-waiting brought a glass of water, the Prince looked at her again before raising it to his lips.

Mary claims that she was fearful of her husband noticing what was passing, but at the same time she was conscious that 'So marked was his Royal Highness's conduct that many of the audience observed it.' The spectators in the pit directed their gaze at her, more interested in the drama off stage than Handel's rendition of Dryden's 'Alexander's Feast' to which they were supposed to be attending. According to Mary, one of the newspapers remarked the following morning that the Prince had expressed particular interest in one passage of Dryden's ode, the lines 'Gazed on the fair / Who caused his care, / And sigh'd, and look'd, and sigh'd again.'[18]

As so often, Mary's recollection, written twenty years after the event, must be taken with a grain of salt. It seems that the encounter at the oratorio occurred not within a few days of the command performance of *The Winter's Tale*, as she claims, but two months later, in February

1780. And, according to the *Morning Post*, it was the actress rather than the Prince who was making eyes:

> A circumstance of rather an embarrassing nature happened at last night's Oratorio: – Mrs R—, deck'd out in all her paraphernalia, took care to post herself in one of the upper boxes immediately opposite the Princes, and by those wanton airs, peculiar to herself, contrived at last to *basilisk* a certain heir apparent, that his fixed attention to the amorous object above, became generally noticed, and soon after astonished their M[ajestie]s, who, not being able to discover the cause, seemed at a loss to account for the extraordinary effect. No sooner however were they properly informed, but a messenger was instantly sent aloft, desiring the *dart-dealing* actress to withdraw, which she complied with, tho' not without expressing the utmost chagrin at her mortifying removal. Poor *Perdita!* – '*Queen* it not an inch further, But milk thy ewes and weep!' The *Maids of Honour* were thrown into the utmost consternation on the above *alarming* occasion![19]

It would seem, then, that not only the theatregoing public but also the King and Queen were aware that something might be brewing between Perdita and Florizel. According to Mary, her correspondence with Florizel lasted for several months before she agreed to meet him in person. 'There was,' she says, 'a beautiful ingenuousness in his language, a warm and enthusiastic adoration, expressed in every letter, which interested and charmed me.'[20] His ardour was doubtless increased by her elusiveness.

Meanwhile her career flourished and Sheridan made the most of it. During the holiday season she opened the festivities with Viola, and then played almost constantly over the Christmas week as Viola and Juliet. She closed the year with Viola. In the new year, capitalizing on the buzz that surrounded her, Sheridan made sure that she played regularly, especially in her cross-dressed roles. She added Rosalind to her repertoire. The *Morning Chronicle* suggested that she was trying just a little too hard to impress:

> Mrs Robinson last night acquitted herself very respectably in the character of Rosalind in Shakespeare's beautiful comedy, *As You Like*

> *It*. Her figure was perfectly proper, and her deportment sufficiently graceful. She will, however, improve her performance of the part, if she in the future uses less labour in her oratory, and does not aim at the emphatic so much.[21]

A good many ladies and gentlemen in London society thought they knew exactly who she was aiming at – but the situation was becoming complicated.

The Prince went to the theatre to watch Mary whenever he could. On one occasion he sent a lock of his hair from his box to her dressing room in an envelope on which he had written 'To be redeemed'. Florizel's letters arrived almost daily, delivered by Malden. He brought a miniature portrait of the Prince by the artist Jeremiah Meyer, set in diamonds. 'This picture is now in my possession,' she writes in the *Memoirs*. Within the case was a small heart cut in paper, which she treasured all her life. On one side was written '*Je ne change qu'en mourant*' and on the other '*Unalterable to my Perdita through life*'. From that day on, she wore the miniature picture pinned onto her bosom whenever she went out in public.

As usual, there is an alternative account which is less flattering to Mary. According to Georgiana Duchess of Devonshire, the miniature was not an offering sent via Malden, but a prize brazenly claimed by Perdita herself:

> To describe how confin'd he was in the early part of this connection, when he wanted to give Mrs Robinson his picture, he sent for a painter in miniature whilst he was dressing, who on a card was to sketch the likeness he was afterwards to render in ivory.
>
> This the P. of Wales assur'd the painter was destin'd for a present to some German relation, but during the sitting a page was posted at the door to give the allarm [sic] in case of intrusion. The next day as the painter was finishing the picture, Mrs Robinson, anxious to claim her prize, came to see it.
>
> Some time after her disgrace, preserving it as a relick, she set it round with diamonds to £900 value, and an inscription round it of *gage de mon amour*, which the Prince had written on its back in pencil when he gave it her.[22]

Georgiana was gossipy and occasionally malicious, but she was nevertheless a friend of Perdita. If she is to be believed, Mary's doctoring of the evidence of her past extended beyond the text of the *Memoirs* to the very token of the Prince's affection.

According to Mary, the correspondence lasted throughout the spring of 1780, with the Prince constantly pressing for an interview. She wrote back, reminding him of his royal duty, of the need not to displease the King, the fact that she was married, and that if they were to have a 'public attachment' she would have to abandon her profession and would then be financially dependent on him (which would not be a good idea, since, not having come of age, he had limited financial resources). What would her fate be if she relented and then found herself cast off? He replied with 'repeated assurances of inviolable affection'.[23] Malden piled on the pressure, telling Mary that the Duke of Cumberland had come to warn him that the Prince was most wretched on her account, and that things must come to a head. Cumberland had met the Prince in Hyde Park and they had struck up a friendship, despite the King's abhorrence of his brother.

Malden was beginning to regret his own part in the business, as he had fallen in love with Mary himself. As Mary put it, 'he had himself conceived so violent a passion for me that he was the most miserable and unfortunate of mortals'.[24] Gossip was spreading that Perdita had, in fact, become Malden's mistress.

In April she attended a masquerade with him on one side and Tom on the other, fuelling scandalous rumours that her husband was happy to act as her pimp, as he had supposedly done with Sir John Lade. The *Morning Post* reported: 'Mrs R—n, with a pink jacket and coat, with a loose gauze thrown over it, appeared melancholy from the provoking inattention of the company, and after a few *pouting* parings round the room, retired with her *pliant* spouse on one side, and the *Malden* hero on the other, who sympathetically *sulked* with his *acknowledged half*.'[25] Two weeks later she was seen again with Malden during a fabulous ridotto at the Opera House where 700 masqueraders danced through the small hours of the morning – he sported a 'black domino' and she was 'transparently *veiled*, in the antique style' (a 'domino' was a loose cloak with a mask for the upper part of the face, worn to conceal the wearer's identity at masquerades). The event almost broke up at half past five in the morning when two officers started fighting and the guard was called in with fixed bayonets, but the ferment happily subsided 'and the diversions continued as usual with tea, country dances, headaches, and morning qualms'.[26] A few days after this, the gossip columnist of the *Morning Post* confirmed that Sir John Lade had been replaced in Mary's retinue by Malden (Lade was now in pursuit of another actress).

The manuscript of Mary's autobiography breaks off shortly before her first private meeting with the Prince. The published text of the *Memoirs* narrates the rest of her life in the form of a 'Continuation by a Friend', which was almost certainly written by Mary's daughter Maria Elizabeth. The latter refers to 'the constant devoirs of Lord Malden, whose attentions were as little understood as maliciously interpreted',[27] but there is a body of evidence that he and Mary were, indeed, lovers.

At the beginning of each month, new issues of an array of monthly magazines would appear in the booksellers. The *Town and Country Magazine* was always eagerly awaited. Many readers would turn first to its column 'Histories of the Tête-à-Tête annexed': this consisted of a pair of oval portraits of a man and a woman, accompanied by a 'history' of their sexual liaisons, usually concluding with a description of their current romantic relationship and an estimate of its likely duration. The combination of image and text gave 'Tête-à-Tête' a double meaning: the subjects are head to head in the pictures while the story concerns their intimate affairs. It is the nearest the eighteenth century comes to the modern juxtaposition of paparazzi snapshots and tabloid titbits of gossip. In Hannah Cowley's 1780 comedy *The Belle's Stratagem*, a character called Crowquil is introduced as an author of Tête-à-Têtes; a porter says to him, 'Oh, Oh, what! You are the fellow that has folks nose to nose in your sixpenny cuts, that never met anywhere else.' But the editors refuted the accusation of inventing liaisons that did not exist. Crowquil suggests a more likely scenario – servants revealing information about their employers in exchange for money.

On 1 June 1780, the Tête-à-Tête was subtitled 'Memoirs of the DOATING LOVER and the DRAMATIC ENCHANTRESS'. It was adorned with engravings of a very fetching Mary Robinson and a youthful-looking Malden. His Lordship is described as a handsome womanizer who got his young bed-maker pregnant while he was an Oxford undergraduate.

He then went on his continental tour where he slept with many women, until his purse and his constitution suffered. On returning to England he went through 'a variety of amours' before falling in love with Mrs Robinson.

The account of her is reasonably accurate. 'The daughter of an eminent tradesman, who, from a variety of unforeseen accidents and disappointments, was obliged to become a bankrupt', she had a 'genteel education' with 'the improvements of dancing, music, and similar accomplishments'. From an early age, her personal charms were 'almost irresistible'. There is a list of her roles at Drury Lane, praise of her talents as an actress, and a defence of her honour in the face of improper advances: 'She was disgusted with the persons and address' of the 'suitors of the first rank and fortune' who 'treated her with as little ceremony as if she had been a prostitute by profession'.

An account is given of how a 'lady-abbess' tried to procure her for a Lord upon the pretence of buying tickets for her benefit. The 'abbess' had been instructed by Lord B— to give Mary a hundred pounds 'for the pleasure of passing a few hours with her'; she laid down the money, 'thinking the temptation was irresistible'. To her surprise, 'Mrs R— desired her to retire and return her tickets, as she should be greatly mortified to have any money in her possession from a woman of her complexion.' She also had a call from a lady known as 'Vis-à-vis Townshend' (that is to say, a woman whose sexual favours had been bought in return for a fashionable new carriage). She told Mary that Sir William S— had given orders for a new chariot to be built for her at Hatchet's. It would have her cipher on it – the equivalent of a personalized numberplate – and he would call in a few days. However,

> Even this bait did not take; Mrs R—n listened, shook her head, and retired. Mrs T—d rang the bell, and when the servant entered, was so nettled at the reception she had met with, as to say, 'I think your mistress is the rudest woman I ever saw in my life.' 'No, madam,' replied she, 'I am bold enough to say, you are the rudest woman I ever heard in my life, for I overheard all your conversation.'[28]

Mary seems to have inspired remarkable loyalty in her servants. She treated people who worked for her with great respect. Some years later, when she was at the height of her fame, a labourer was accidentally killed while doing some building work at her house in Berkeley Square. She paid for the funeral, which began from her house, and gave the man's widow a cash sum and an annuity. She wanted her generosity to be kept quiet, but like almost everything else in her life the story leaked out.[29]

The Tête-à-Tête suggests that the Dramatic Enchantress 'was not so easy a conquest as many imagined'. It denies the supposed affair with Sir John Lade. But when Malden wrote her a polite billet enclosing a *carte blanche*, then followed up with a pair of valuable diamond earrings, 'she surrendered at discretion'.[30]

Two very different sources corroborate the affair. In September 1782, Georgiana Duchess of Devonshire scribbled a manuscript note to the effect that

> Mrs Robinson was a natural daughter of Lord Northington's, and had been driven to the stage to support an extravagant husband, who was willing likewise to share the fruits of her ill conduct. She then liv'd with Lord Malden, Lord Essex's son. Her *agaceries* were soon level'd at the young Prince, and she especially *lorgnee'd* him in the part of *Perdita*, which, as it was afterwards suppos'd to be the name by which he call'd her, she was distinguish'd by it in all the public prints and the P. of Wales by that of *Florizel*.[31]

By this account, Mary was already intimately acquainted with Malden prior to the famous night when she played Perdita before the Prince.

According to the anonymous *Memoirs of Perdita*, Malden was captivated by Mary's performance as Ophelia in *Hamlet*; he supposedly set her up in 'an elegant habitation' in Clarges Street and presented her with a handsome red and silver carriage that was 'the admiration of all the *charioteering* circles of St James's'.[32] The latter details actually belong to a subsequent phase of Mary's relationship with Malden, but there can be no doubt that there was a widespread belief that she was mistress to the Prince's man before the Prince himself. So it was that Malden came to be represented as 'Lord Pander' to his own mistress.

The Prince raised the stakes. He asked Mary to come to his private apartment disguised in the boy's clothes that she had worn on stage in the character of the Irish Widow. She 'decidedly objected' to the plan. But she was beginning to relent, not least because her husband was spending all his time with mistresses and whores. Even the servants were victims of Robinson's lechery. On one occasion, Mary returned from rehearsal and found her husband locked in the bedroom with a dirty, squat housemaid. A short man himself, perhaps he felt more comfortable with her than his tall and beautiful wife. Of course, we only have Mary's word for all this – the more she writes about her husband's grossness and infidelity, the less likely the reader of the *Memoirs* is to condemn her for finally agreeing to meet the Prince.

Mary was playing a cool game. Without granting an interview, she continued to write to the Prince, giving him sisterly advice rather as Mary Hamilton had done. The Prince's love letters were ardent and beautifully written, but he was also indiscreet about his family. He told her how he hated his life at Kew Palace, that he and his brothers were prisoners there. The King was unkind to him. He called his sister, the Princess Royal, who was in poor health, '*that bandy-legged b[itc]h*'.[33] Mary advised him to be patient until he became his own master at the age of 21, not to do anything premature that would incur the displeasure of the King, and to wait until he knew her better before engaging himself in a public attachment to her.

It was common practice for a man to make a formal financial offer to an actress or a courtesan he wanted to keep. Sometimes there was a proper legal document, sometimes a more casual arrangement. Mary's references to the position she would be placed in should she accept the Prince and then be rejected reveal that she was at some level negotiating the terms of the relationship as shrewdly as she had negotiated her acting contract at the Haymarket two years earlier.

The Prince had hoped to see Mary at the masked ridotto in Covent Garden, but he had been prevented from attending. So he sent her jewels from Grey's instead, and two days later the *Morning Post* was reporting that 'Mrs Robinson shone with unusual lustre, exhibiting a rich suit of diamonds beautifully contrasted with a ruby head'.[34] It was reckoned that they were worth a hundred guineas. She was not, however, a woman to be bought for such a sum.

It was a different matter when he enclosed in one of his letters 'a bond of the most solemn and binding nature, containing a promise of the sum of twenty thousand pounds, to be paid at the period of his Royal Highness's coming of age'. Twenty thousand pounds was an enormous sum – the modern equivalent would be around a million pounds or more than a million and a half American dollars. The paper was signed by the Prince and sealed with the royal arms. 'It was expressed in terms so liberal, so voluntary, so marked by true affection, that I had scarcely power to read it.'[35] When she did so – she told a friend in a letter written in 1783 and printed in the 'Continuation' of her *Memoirs* – her eyes filled with tears of conflicting emotion. The Prince had said that it wounded his dignity that she was forced to earn a living on the stage, and he was desperate for her to separate from her wretched husband. The bond was both a sign of her suitor's utter seriousness and a document that had the power to convert her into a courtesan. For nearly six months, she had held back, writing of virtue though hinting at the possibility of surrender. Now the gulf was before her.

She agreed to a meeting. Malden proposed his own house in Dean Street, Mayfair, but the Prince was being closely watched from within the royal household, so this was ruled out. There was talk of a visit to Buckingham House, but she thought this too dangerous. They finally agreed to meet at Kew, close to the residence of the Prince and his brother Frederick Duke of York.

Malden took her to the river and they were rowed out to Eel Pie Island, not far from Kew. They dined at the inn on the island. A signal had been arranged: when the Prince was ready, he would wave a white handkerchief and she would cross in the boat. They could only just make out the handkerchief through the dusk. She stepped into the boat with Malden and they were soon 'before the iron gates of old Kew palace'. The Prince and his brother were walking down an avenue towards them. He uttered a few barely audible words before they were startled by the noise of people approaching from the palace. The moon was rising and they were terrified of being seen. The Prince spoke a few words 'of the most affectionate nature' and they parted.

After this, there was no stopping them. They met many times at this 'romantic spot'. Mary claims that their respective chaperons, Lord Malden and Frederick Duke of York, were always present at these meetings. She no longer felt afraid of the Prince's royal stature: 'The rank of the Prince no longer chilled into awe that being, who now considered him as the lover and the friend.' It was his 'sweet smile' and 'melodious yet manly voice' that won her over. During their midnight rambles, dressed in a dark habit to conceal herself, she learned about his unhappy and secluded childhood. The men were dressed in greatcoats to disguise themselves, with the exception of Frederick who insisted upon wearing a buff coat – 'the most conspicuous colour he could have selected for an adventure of this nature'. The Prince would sing to her, his voice ringing out in the air of the warm summer nights. She was charmed by his polished manners and 'lamented the distance which destiny had placed between us'. 'How would my soul have idolized such a *husband*,' she wrote.[36]

In Mary's account, these meetings always take place in the romantic outdoors. According to a local tradition they also caroused in a house occupied by some of the royal family's servants: 'It was quite the usual thing to see the lights all over the house, and to hear sounds of revelry until three and four in the morning.' The place was nicknamed 'Hell House' – as in hell-raising – and was said to have had a private entrance at the back that allowed access from Kew Gardens.[37] The affair was almost certainly consummated either in this house or at the inn on Eel Pie Island. The Prince was approaching his eighteenth birthday, when he would receive a greater deal of freedom and independence (though nothing like the fortune that would be his when he turned 21): 'the apprehension that his attachment to a married woman might injure his Royal Highness in the opinion of the world, rendered the caution which we invariably observed of the utmost importance'.[38]

These meetings were in June and July 1780. Having received the assurance of the bond, Mary took the risk of retiring from the stage. She had told Sheridan that she would be giving up her acting career at the end of the season. He offered a 'considerable advance to her salary' in the event of her staying on, but she would not return a decisive answer. Sheridan was losing interest in the theatre himself, turning his mind towards a political career. On 24 May she played both leads in a double bill: Perdita and the cross-dressed role of Eliza Camply/Sir Harry Revel in a new comedy, *The Miniature Picture* by Lady Elizabeth Craven. There must have been palpable electricity in the house when Perdita spoke of splitting a son from his father – 'I have betray'd, / Unwittingly divorced a noble Prince / From a dear father's love' – and when Florizel swore undying loyalty to the prettiest low-born lass that ever walked upon the greensward.

The Miniature Picture was no doubt chosen not only to show off Mary's legs in breeches but also because she wore her own miniature of the Prince around her neck. The comedy revolved around the miniature portrait of Eliza Camply who, disguised as Sir Harry Revel, procures it from Miss Loveless who has been given the picture by Eliza's estranged lover, Belvil. At the climax there is a duel between the cross-dressed Eliza and Belvil – a kind of romantic variant on the comic duel between Viola/Cesario and Sir Andrew Aguecheek in *Twelfth Night*.

Mary earned great accolades for this performance, even from the usually lukewarm *Morning Chronicle*: 'Mrs Robinson's Eliza does her infinite credit: she displays a degree of acting merit in the breeches scenes of the character, infinitely superior to any sample of professional talent she has before shown, and stands eminently distinguished from the other performers.'[39] Horace Walpole, in private correspondence, was less complimentary: 'Mrs Robinson (who is thought to be the favourite of the Prince of Wales) thought on nothing but her own charms and him.'[40]

On Wednesday, 31 May, the evening that Drury Lane closed for the summer, she performed for the last time.[41] She played Eliza/Sir Harry Revel and Widow Brady in *The Irish Widow*. On entering the green room, she told her stage partner Mr Moody that this was to be her last night on the stage, and – trying to smile – she sang what she knew would be her last words in the theatre, the closing lines of her epilogue song, 'Oh joy to you all in full measure, / So wishes and prays Widow Brady!' But when she walked on stage, her feelings overwhelmed her and she burst into tears:

> My regret at recollecting that I was treading for the last time the boards where I had so often received the most gratifying testimonies of public approbation; where mental exertion had been emboldened by private worth; that I was flying from a happy certainty, perhaps to pursue the phantom disappointment, nearly overwhelmed my faculties, and for some time deprived me of the powers of articulation. Fortunately, the person on the stage with me had to begin the scene, which allowed me time to collect myself. I went, however, mechanically dull through the business of the evening, and, notwithstanding the cheering expressions and applause of the audience, I was several times near fainting.[42]

CHAPTER 9

A Very Public Affair

The Prince's attachment seemed to increase daily, and I considered myself as the most blest of human beings.

Memoirs of the Late Mrs Robinson, Written by Herself

Early June 1780 was a time of high tension in London. The fanatical Protestant Lord George Gordon was stirring up protests against legal rights for Catholics and so-called popish influence in public life. On 2 June, he led a mob to Westminster to demand the repeal of the Catholic Relief Act. After attacking Members of Parliament, they moved into the streets and began six days of plunder and arson. A mob burned down the King's Bench Prison, and stormed Newgate, releasing prisoners. Houses belonging to prominent Catholics were razed to the ground. The rioters, incited by drink and the fanaticism of their leader, targeted the houses of prominent Whigs, as they were well known for their support of religious tolerance. The Duchess of Devonshire feared an attack on Devonshire House and made plans to escape to Chiswick. For days she stood on her balcony and watched the orange skies of Piccadilly as buildings burned and gunfire filled the air. The violence lasted until the Army was called out, at the King's command. The dead and injured stood at more than four hundred. Gordon was imprisoned in the Tower and tried for high treason. He was finally acquitted, though twenty-one of his followers were executed. The riot constituted the most violent uprising of the Hanoverian period.

The King's birthday celebrations took place on 4 June despite the rioting, although some stayed away. The Duchess of Devonshire was sorry to have missed the ball and the chance to wear her beautiful new blue gown made for the occasion. She was comforted by the fact that the Prince wrote to say he was sorry not to have danced with her – they had met recently and struck up a friendship, no doubt intensified by her support of Mary when she was penniless and friendless in the Fleet Prison. Now it was Georgiana who stayed at home, whilst Mary attended the birthday celebrations.

Although the Prince dared to invite Mary to the King's birthday ball, he was not so bold as to dance with her. He ensconced her in the Chamberlain's box, along with Lord Lyttelton's mistress, and she watched as he opened the dancing with Lady Augusta Campbell. Mary was amazed by the 'fashionable coquetry' of Lady Augusta, who handed the Prince two rosebuds from her bouquet, 'emblematical of herself and him'. In response, the Prince beckoned the young Earl of Cholmondeley and gave him the flowers to deliver to Mary. She placed them in her bosom, proud of the power by which she had 'thus publicly mortified an exalted rival'.[1]

Sooner or later the affair was bound to attract comment in the press. The story broke in the *Morning Post* on 18 July:

> Mr Editor,
> And so the Theatrical *Perdita* of Drury-Lane is labouring night and day to insinuate to the world, that an *amour* has taken, or is to take place, between her and a certain young illustrious character. If such a report may, in the smallest degree contribute to the fair lady, in her other pursuits and designs, it would be a pity to contradict the report; but, otherwise, Mr Editor, it may be friendly in you to whisper into her ear, that if the young gentleman had really any *penchant* for her, which, however, is not the case, her present system of *vain boasting* must give his heart a very speedy *quietus*.
> Yours, Ovid. Windsor, July 14

Another article, published the same day, alluded to the incident at the oratorio back in February, and in so doing became the first published source to call the lovers Florizel and Perdita:

> Anecdote. – In the last solemn season of Lent, whenever *Florizel* was present at the Oratorio, *Perdita* never failed to testify her taste for sacred music, or something else, by being there also. It was her custom to seat herself as nearly opposite to *Florizel* as she could contrive. They were apt to exchange looks; and they were remarked. *Florizel*, in consequence, was admonished; and measures were taken, though ineffectual, to prevent *Perdita's* future admittance. When *Perdita* next presented herself at the door, she was given to understand, that a certain *liberty*, which, in common with some others, she had long enjoyed, was now denied her. *Perdita*, without the least discomposure, and with that bewitching indifference for which she is admired – turned to her husband, who always accompanies her to public places, and said – *pay your guinea*. *Perdita* ascended to her box; she did the usual execution; and when the entertainment was over, she placed herself at the back of the stage, in a situation where *Florizel must* view her as he passed to his chair. *Florizel* gazed, and he departed, in all the grandeur of regal pomp. *Perdita* calmly retired to the carriage of *a late American Plenipo*; to which she was carefully handed by the most obliging, the most convenient of husbands.[2]

Two days later the paper returned to the scandal: 'A certain *young actress* who leads the *Ton* [fashionable world] appeared in the side-box at the Haymarket theatre a few evenings since with all the grace and splendour of a Duchess, to the no small mortification of the female world, and astonishment of every spectator.' And two days after that: 'A correspondent who read the anecdote of *Florizel* and *Perdita* in this paper of Tuesday last, observes, that the writer has paid the highest compliment to the young lady in question, who could make a conquest in the heart of a young and illustrious personage, at the very moment when he was surrounded by all the beauties of the British Court, vieing [sic] with each other to captivate and ensnare him.'[3]

Mary was soon to become the most talked about woman of the day, vilified as the older woman who had seduced the innocent young Prince, aided and abetted by her pimping husband. In reality, as George himself admitted, he was already fond of women and had affairs at court before he set eyes on Mary Robinson. Though she protested, there were many who thought that she cultivated the publicity. People wanted to know what she was buying, what clothes she was wearing. Whenever she appeared in public, she was 'overwhelmed by the gazing of the multitude'.[4] She was sometimes forced to leave Ranelagh because the crowd pressing round her box had become a safety hazard. Frequently, when she went into a shop she had to stay there in a state of siege until the dispersal of the crowd that surrounded her carriage, waiting for a glimpse of her as she came out.

She described her own celebrity as a 'national absurdity': 'I am well assured, that were a being possessed of more than human endowments to visit this country, it would experience indifference, if not total neglect, while a less worthy mortal might be worshipped as the idol of its day, if whispered into notoriety by the comments of the multitude.'[5] It always irked her that she achieved her greatest fame not as an actress or woman of letters, but – the word was current then as well as now – as a celebrity. At the same time, she relished the idea of being consulted as 'the very oracle of fashion'. She had moved seamlessly from the boards of Drury Lane to the broader stage of London itself. In a magazine essay written many years later, she celebrated the city as a 'focus of dazzling light' and 'the centre of attraction for the full exercise of talents'.[6]

Mary herself was now a public spectacle: 'you shall see the famous Perdita of Drury-Lane, sitting at the play-house in the side box opposite the P— of W—. Look how wantonly she looks, thinking, Gracious Sir! please to bestow one —— upon a poor woman! Ho! ho! fine raree show!'[7] The Prince was no longer afraid to be seen with her. He appeared in her company not only at the theatre, the oratorio and other places of entertainment, but also at the King's hunt at Windsor and at military reviews in Hyde Park.

The King hated all the bad publicity. He read the papers and was familiar with the stories of Florizel and Perdita. On 14 August, two days after his son's eighteenth birthday, he wrote, 'your foibles have been less perceived than I could have expected; yet your love of dissipation has for some months been with enough ill nature trumpeted in the public papers, and there are those ready enough to wound me in the severest place by ripping up every error they may be able to find in you'.[8] The Prince wrote back to assure his father that 'it will be my principal object thro' life to merit . . . the parental attachment and kindness you profess towards me'.[9] In private, however, he had no intention of changing his ways.

With this new-found confidence in publicly acknowledging Mary came an even greater rebellion against his father. Realizing the King's worst fears, the Prince was beginning to be 'driven into Opposition'. He was being drawn into Whig circles partly through his disreputable uncle, the Duke of Cumberland, but also through his acquaintance with the Devonshire House faction, who had close links with both Sheridan at Drury Lane and Charles James Fox, the leading politician on the radical edge of the Whig alliance. Georgiana, hostess to the Devonshire set, recorded her impressions of the Prince as he was at this time:

> The Prince of Wales is rather tall and has a figure which though striking is not perfect. He is inclined to be too fat and looks too much like a woman in men's cloaths, but the gracefulness of his manner and his height certainly make him a pleasing figure. His face is very handsome and he is fond of dress even to a tawdry degree, which, young as he is, will soon wear off . . . He is good-natur'd and rather extravagant . . . But he certainly does not want for understanding, and his jokes sometimes have an appearance of wit. He appears to have an inclination to meddle with politicks, he loves being of consequence, and whether it is in intrigues of state or of gallantry he often thinks more is intended than really is.[10]

His 'inclination to meddle with politicks' was welcomed by the Whigs, who were well aware that when he reached his majority he would enter the House of Lords. They were keen to have his support, as it could absolve them of the charge of disloyalty towards the crown. But when the King heard that his son was keeping an actress, he blamed the Whigs for leading him astray.

The Countess of Derby, who had caused a scandal by deserting her husband and children for her lover the Duke of Dorset, wanted to sell her house in wealthy Cork Street. The Prince ensconced Mary there, living up to his promise to look after her once she renounced the theatre. It was furnished lavishly, and Mary was given the funds to buy paintings and books. It is unlikely that her mother and daughter would have lived with her here – they probably remained in the Robinsons' former apartments in Covent Garden. Mary's move to Cork Street, just off

Piccadilly and close to St James's, marked a decisive transition from the theatre district to the fashionable west end.

The Prince gave a grand ball for Mary at Weltje's, though in order to avoid an offence against aristocratic precedence he opened the dancing with the Duchess of Devonshire. Her sister, Lady Harriet Spencer, wrote to a friend, 'The thing which is most talk'd of at present is the Prince of Wales, who keeps Mrs Robinson *en maîtresse décloseé, c'est toute à fait un établissement*;* she wears his picture about her neck, and drives about with four nag tailed horses and two servants behind her.'[11] The biggest talking point of all was the cipher on her carriage, a basket of five rosebuds, surmounting a rose wreath around the initials MR. From a distance and when in motion, the design gave the illusion of a royal coronet. It was created for her by the artist John Keyes Sherwin, whose pupil, the Italian engraver Albanesi, had been a friend of the Robinsons in their prison days. Sherwin, the son of a Sussex carpenter who cut pegs for ships, had risen to become a popular society artist. He became very intimate with Mary.

On one occasion, she swept into his handsome apartments in St James's Street, singing and accompanied by her mother. She asked to see a drawing of herself that Sherwin had made. He was not at home, but his apprentice offered to fetch it. The teenage boy went upstairs, humming a line from a popular song, 'I'll reward you with a kiss'. 'There, you little rogue,' said Mary, when he came down with the drawing – and she kissed him.[12] The drawing was probably the original of an 'engraving from the life' by Sherwin, in which she has beautiful, half-exposed breasts and is holding a letter that we are to imagine is from the Prince. Mary's earliest surviving manuscript letter is a brief note to Sherwin regarding one of her sittings for the portrait.[13]

Laetitia Hawkins, daughter of one of Dr Johnson's early biographers, records that Mary frequented Sherwin's painting room at irregular hours and 'consulted him, not only on a portrait of herself, but on circumstances still less connected with the art of engraving'.[14] Hawkins also remembered that Sherwin dined out on a story about how he and Mary discussed the possibility of including her in one of his biblical subjects. He had aspirations to become a large-scale history painter – a genre in which it

* 'fully established as his cloistered mistress'.

was customary to include representations of real people (thus, Pharaoh's daughter in his *Finding of Moses* was the Princess Royal). After consideration, Mary asked to be Solomon's concubine 'kneeling at the feet of her master'. But who should be Solomon? Sherwin saw her drift, but realized that the idea of engaging the Prince to sit with her was inappropriate, so he suggested Malden. 'Kneel to *him*?' she said indignantly. 'I will die first.'[15]

Miss Hawkins also penned a lively sketch of Mary's appearance at this time: 'She was unquestionably very beautiful, but more so in face than figure; and as she proceeded in her course, she acquired a remarkable facility in adapting her deportment to her dress. When she was to be seen daily in St James's Street and Pall Mall, even in her chariot this variation was striking.' She entertained lavishly, particularly the male friends of the Prince – her status as a courtesan meant that ladies would not visit her. She bought the latest Parisian fashions and ran into debt with her home furnishings. She took a side box at the Opera House, an unheard-of presumption for a woman of her background. She could be seen driving round St James's and Hyde Park in a succession of coloured phaetons. At the theatre, she appeared 'with all the splendour of a Duchess'. Many people made the obvious comparison with King Charles II and his mistresses such as the actress Nell Gwynne. Was Perdita angling for a title? The Duchess of Devonshire thought so: 'Mrs Robinson depended on being a Duchess of Cleveland at least.'[16]

Though she was living dangerously, Mary was enjoying every minute of her celebrity. Her energy and generosity are revealed by an encounter with Sophia Baddeley, an actress and courtesan who had fallen into illness and pecuniary embarrassment. One day, probably in October 1780, there was a loud rap on Mrs Baddeley's door. Her companion, Miss Steele, went to the window and saw a lady in an elegant phaeton with four beautiful ponies and two small post-boys in blue and silver jackets. The servant announced a lady whose name was Robinson. She paid her respects and said that she came bearing ten guineas from the Duke of Cumberland, who had begged her to enquire into Mrs Baddeley's situation and to assure her that more money would be forthcoming if it were needed. 'She begged Mrs Baddeley's pardon for not waiting on her the day before, as she meant to do; had not the Prince of Wales, who was then at her house, prevented her.'[17]

When Mrs Baddeley explained the neglect into which she had fallen, Mrs Robinson cried out, 'Oh, the ingratitude of mankind!' She shed some tears and promised to intercede on her fellow actress's behalf not only with the Duke but also with the Prince. She then talked about her own life: how she was living apart from her husband, but still on friendly terms – save that 'he drew her purse-strings too often; but, that as he was her husband, she could not refuse him'. She explained that the Prince wanted her to stay away from her husband, but that Robinson was always seeking her out in public places in order to get money from her.

She also revealed that with the Prince she was the happiest of women, explaining that 'the poor dear boy' often got out of his bed when he was at Kew and came to her in the middle of the night, at the inn on Eel Pie Island. 'How do you mean?' asked Mrs Baddeley, 'got out of bed?' 'Yes,' replied Mrs Robinson, 'their Majesties always paid such attention to their children, as to go and see them every night, after they were in bed; and often has the dear Prince got up after this, dressed himself, and with the assistance of his brother, the Duke of York, climbed over the garden-wall, after mid-night, and come to me; staid some hours, and returned home over the wall again, before day-light; unknown to any one, but his brother.' She added that his affection for her was 'of no short duration'.[18]

The inevitable price of Mary's high profile around London and loose tongue with regard to the Prince's favours was bad publicity in the papers. Though Mary glossed over the fact in her recollections, her simultaneous affair with Lord Malden also came under constant scrutiny. One paper published a vicious poem addressed to Malden on the 'report of Perditta's being created a Countess'. The presence of her husband gave fuel to the scandalmongers.

In September a letter from 'Dramaticus', written from the Piazza Coffee-house, was published in the *Morning Post*:

> The audacity of Mrs R—, who was an actress last winter, and whose situation and character is certainly not *improved* since her resignation from the stage, is beyond example or excuse; and the Monsieur M—, her *nominal* husband, deserves the severest reprehension, in daring to seat himself in a part of the house allotted to people of character and fashion.

> I know of no rank of prostitution that can either lessen the crime or disgrace of it; and, however profligate the age may be, I believe that the greatest libertine of our sex would revolt at the idea of handing a wife, sister, or daughter, in to a box where they were certain of being surrounded by public prostitutes.
>
> The managers owe it to the public, they owe it to themselves, to preserve the side-boxes for the modest and reputable part of the other sex; or at least, it is their duty to refuse them to actresses, swindlers, wantons in high keeping, who have the presumption to ask for them. Mrs R— is unquestionably a pretty woman, and her beauty would lose nothing from being exhibited in the green boxes; but when she has the assurance to mix with women of character and distinction her charms should no longer protect her from the reprehension due to her temerity.[19]

But she also had her defenders. A poem in praise of her reputation and her talents as an actress was published in the same paper on 28 September. It paid tribute to her incomparable art as Ophelia, Cordelia, Sir Harry, Rosalind, Viola, and Palmira. She was admirable in both tragedy and comedy, but especially comedy. The poem was accompanied by a defence of her conduct and even of her husband.[20]

Then there was another note of support, this one from 'an admirer of Modest Women'. It suggested that her reputation was '*only suspected* by the envious and ill-natured part of her own sex' – a charge that Mary would make herself in the *Memoirs*. The correspondent for the defence said that 'No ill conduct has ever been proved against this Lady, neither has she ever been *censured* beyond the *ill-nature* of a newspaper paragraph.'[21] 'Dramaticus' fought back a few days later, claiming that Mrs Robinson had arrogated to herself 'the importance of a person of fashion' by having the 'audacity to place herself in a part of the theatre, hitherto reserved for the reception of people of rank'. There were also references to her 'ingenious tricks' and her husband's '*lucrative* complacency'.[22] Another outraged letter, signed 'No Flatterer', was printed a week after this, objecting to the poem of 28 September as 'the most fulsome panegyric which ever disgraced a newspaper – on that *most* virtuous, *most* innocent, *most* amiable, *most* poetic, and *most* beautiful of her sex, the *most* renowned *Perdita*'. In reality, it said, she was none of these things. She had a '*positive* prostitute character' and was no better than an 'orange woman – she should keep out of side-boxes'.[23]

Around the same time, she hit the papers again as a result of an embarrassing incident at Covent Garden Theatre when she caught her estranged husband making love to a '*fillette*' in one of the boxes. She flew into a jealous rage, ran to the box, seized her unhappy husband, dragged him by the hair into the lobby 'and there spent her violence in blows and reproaches to the complete entertainment of a numerous auditory'.[24] At length she bore him away in triumph to her house. The Prince was reportedly not amused by this incident: Mary was beginning to seem a liability and other women were catching his eye.

Rumours circulated of her estrangement from the Prince. She was taunted, accused of being a 'ripe mine of diseases'.[25] Contradictory reports kept appearing: did the constant attentions of Lord Malden mean that he was her lover? Or was 'the silver R. upon the *dark green chariot* . . . nothing less than a token of *royal* favour'?[26]

Mary complained that 'Tales of the most infamous and glaring falsehood were invented, and I was again assailed by pamphlets, by paragraphs, and caricatures, and all the artillery of slander.'[27] One of the first full-scale printed assaults came in a one-shilling pamphlet called *A Satire on the Present Times*, which particularly emphasized her 'pimping spouse':

> A noted beauty, (Perdita her name,
> No matter where brought up, or whence she came,)
> Though bless'd with charms above her narrow soul,
> Was curs'd with pride not reason could controul.
> Where'er she came contending suitors bow'd:
> (Enough to make the giddy strumpet proud:)
> One boasted wealth; – Florio, in guile less vers'd,
> Preach'd up his passion, – but she chose the *first*.
> Mark what ensues; – our Perdita is caught;
> And her *rich* husband proves not worth a groat.
> Reduc'd to poverty; 'twas now her aim
> To tread the path which leads to public fame:
> In plainer terms; – with G—ck to engage,

And sport away her talents on the stage.
The bait soon took; her ev'ry wish prevail'd;
And charms succeeded where her merit fail'd.
Lords sigh'd for her, and Perdita for them,
Nor dar'd her pimping spouse such arts condemn.
He, of each spark of honest pride bereft,
Held her right hand while M-ld-n kiss'd her left.
But now no more a tool to Drury-lane,
She eyes her old associates with disdain;
For silk-brocade puts off the vulgar chintz,
And struts the would-be mistress of a p—e.[28]

The clear implication here is that the affair with Malden preceded that with the Prince.

The first of the many caricatures lampooning Florizel and Perdita was published in November (see p. 108). It shows Mary flanked by the Prince on one side and her husband on the other. She is wearing a low-cut dress and a high Welsh hat over a long wig. Robinson bears the cuckold's horns and is holding a paper inscribed with the words Sir Peter Pimp. The Prince's coronet, decorated with two ostrich feathers and a leek, emblem of Wales, is falling from his head. Mary holds out to him a book entitled *Essay on Man*. He looks at her with his two hands raised, as if dazzled by her beauty. At Perdita's feet are boxes inscribed *Whitewash*, *Carmine*, *Dentrifice*, *Perfume* and *Pomatum*, together with a letter inscribed Florizel. Below the engraving there is a song to the tune of 'O Polly is a sad slut!' (Polly was Mary's family name):

Sometimes she'd play the Tragic Queen,
Sometimes the Peasant poor,
Sometimes she'd step behind the Scenes,
And there she'd play the W[hore].

Two thousand Pounds, a princely Sight
For doing just no more,
Than what is acted every Night,
By every Sister W[hore],

She never play'd her part so well,
In all her Life before,
Yet some, as well as Florizel,
Knows how she plays the W[hore].

Her husband too, a puny Imp,
Will often guard the Door,
And humbly play Sir Peter Pimp
While she performs the W[hore].

The strain of all this was beginning to tell. A friend of Mary's signing himself A.B. wrote to the *Morning Post* warning that if the London papers continued to persecute her with scandalous paragraphs they would have her 'blood to answer for'.[29] There was also a rumour that she was going to escape all the attention by fleeing to Germany. The very next day she appeared at a masquerade with Lord Malden, fetchingly dressed in a brown capuchin cloak and hood. This fuelled more rumours that she was reunited with Malden.

The *Morning Post* was generally hostile to Mary, so she was fortunate that in November 1780 a new daily paper was launched. Its editor was Henry Bate, well known for his contacts in high society and his willingness to risk libel actions. The original for the scandalmonger Snake in Sheridan's *School for Scandal*, he was the son of a preacher and had been educated at Cambridge and intended for the Church. Despite being a clergyman, he became one of the first editors of the *Morning Post*. He always wore black and was known as 'the Fighting Parson' due to his excitable temper, which often got him into trouble. Bate lost his job at the *Morning Post* after he was jailed for a year for libelling the Duke of Richmond and, when he discovered that his position had not been kept open, he retaliated by founding the *Morning Herald*. He had long been fascinated with the theatre, having started his career as a young curate to the Reverend James Townley, who was famed for his farce *High Life Below Stairs*. Henry had published plays himself and had staged a successful opera. He was married to Mary White, sister to a celebrated Shakespearean actress. Mrs Bate knew all the actresses of the west end, and it was her job to file gossip for the *Morning Herald*.

Mary and Henry Bate were, on the whole, supportive towards Mary

Robinson. This was partly out of sympathy for a fellow thespian, but principally because it made good journalistic sense to take the opposite line to that of the *Morning Post*. The Bates knew that the best way to sell papers was to follow every twist and turn of a scandal. In time-honoured fashion, Mary began leaking her side of the story to the Bates. Even the *Morning Post* was persuaded to print a denial of the rumours that there was an estrangement between Florizel and Perdita.[30]

The King was doing his best to terminate the relationship. Just before Christmas he proposed a 'new arrangement' whereby at the end of the year the Prince would leave Windsor for Buckingham House (now Buckingham Palace), where he would have his own establishment and a degree of independence. 'My inclination,' His Majesty wrote, 'is to grant you all the rational amusement I can, and keep you out of what is improper, and so to steer you, that when arrived at the full stage of manhood, you may thank me for having made you escape evils that ill become a young man of rank, but in your exalted situation are criminal.'[31] The Prince would be allowed to dine with his companions in his apartment twice a week. He could go to plays and the opera provided he gave notice to the King and was accompanied by his regular attendants. He would be expected to attend church on Sunday and Drawing Room at St James's when the King was present, as well as the Queen's Thursday Drawing Room. When the King rode out of a morning, the Prince would accompany him. The price of an independent establishment was that he should keep away from masquerades ('you already know my disapprobation of them in this country'), assemblies in private houses, and other such dubious congregations. Assemblies in private houses served as shorthand for visits to Perdita in Cork Street.

All was going well with the Prince, at least as far as Mary was concerned, when, out of nowhere, she received a curt note from him informing her that '*we must meet no more!*'[32] The affair that had begun with scores of eloquent love letters had seemingly ended without explanation or apology. Mary was bewildered. At a meeting only two days before, her lover had professed his undiminished affection. She always remained adamant that there was no reason why the Prince had so abruptly terminated the relationship and complained that she was never given a proper explanation: 'I again most SOLEMNLY REPEAT, that I was totally ignorant of any JUST CAUSE for so sudden an alteration.'[33]

If the Prince thought that Mary would accept his rejection without

'Florizel and Perdita': anonymous caricature of the Prince and Mrs Robinson, October 1783.

demur, he did not know his fiery lover. After all, this was the woman who, heavily pregnant, had confronted her husband's mistress with impunity. She wrote twice to George for an explanation, 'but received no elucidation of this most cruel and extraordinary mystery'.[34] In the face of his stony silence, she panicked and set off in her phaeton to Windsor. The long drive from Cork Street to Windsor was fraught. It was late and growing dark, and Mary travelled unaccompanied except for her postillion, a 9-year-old boy. The phaeton was a light, open four-wheeled carriage, usually drawn by a pair of ponies, though Mary's was small, with only one pony. It would have been an easy target for highwaymen, who were aware that this was a vehicle favoured by wealthy ladies. Though highwaymen had a reputation for being glamorous figures, especially since the success of John Gay's *Beggar's Opera*, in reality they were brutal in their treatment of victims, often raping women.

Mary must have been alarmed when she reached Hounslow Heath and was warned by an innkeeper that 'every carriage which had passed the heath for the last ten nights had been attacked and rifled'.[35] But with her mind on the Prince, she did not care for personal danger. If her lover had truly rejected her, the idea of death was inviting. When she reached the middle of the pitch-black heath, she was startled by the appearance of a 'footpad' (a highwayman on foot). The man snatched at the reins, but the young postillion spurred the pony just in time and galloped off at full speed. The footpad gave chase, but could not outrun the carriage, and they reached the Magpie, a small inn on the outskirts of the heath, in safety, without sustaining a serious atttack.

Mary was exhilarated by her escape. When writing up her account of the journey, she asserted bravely that the highwayman would have had to strangle her before she would relinquish the costly jewels she had about her. Her courage only failed her when she arrived at the Magpie and bumped into the beautiful Elizabeth Armistead and the Prince's servant Meynel. The Armistead (as the press insisted on calling her) was evidently on her way back from an assignation with the Prince: 'My foreboding soul instantly beheld a rival.'[36] Mary remembered that the Prince had frequently expressed a wish to know the lady in question.

Elizabeth Armistead was a courtesan, who had risen from humble beginnings. She was 30 when she became mistress to the Prince. An unsubstantiated rumour suggested that for a time she had been Perdita's dresser at Drury Lane. She had certainly been a model for a hairdresser before being taken up by one of the famous madams of London's exclusive brothels. Her beauty swiftly acquired her a succession of rich and aristocratic patrons, such as the Duke of Ancaster, the Duke of Dorset, and the Earl of Derby, Viscount Bolingbroke. At the time of her assignation with the Prince, she was mistress to the Duke of Devonshire's brother, Lord George Cavendish.*

The inevitable had happened: the Prince had a new mistress. When Mary arrived at Windsor, he refused to see her.

The chronology of the end of the affair is uncertain. After a period of

* Lord George discovered the princely liaison one night when he arrived late and drunk at the Armistead house and was refused admittance. He barged into her chamber, stretched out his arm with a candle in his hand and discovered the Prince of Wales hiding behind the door. Cavendish burst out laughing, made his Royal Highness a low bow, and retired.

estrangement, the Prince apparently wanted to be reconciled with Mary. He suggested a meeting at Malden's home in Clarges Street. After much hesitation – so she said – Mary agreed. The Prince apologized for his neglect of her, put his arms around her and protested his love, claiming that it was the efforts of her 'concealed enemies' that had undermined her position. Mary was triumphant, but her victory was short-lived: she thought that they were fully reconciled, but to her 'surprise and chagrin', on meeting his Royal Highness in Hyde Park the very next day, he turned his head to avoid seeing her and even affected not to know her. Neither would he respond to any of the desperate letters she sent him.[37]

Mary did not despair. She probed Lord Malden for details about the Prince's change of heart. He told her that she had enemies in high places. She knew that the Duke of Cumberland was her enemy, but she now learnt that the ladies at court had begun a vicious whispering campaign. It was said that Mary had slandered one of the Prince's friends in public, giving him an excuse to drop her; in reality, the charms of Elizabeth Armistead and the knowledge that Mary had been having an affair with his own best friend Malden were of more pressing significance. Furthermore, with the prospect of some degree of independence close at hand the Prince did not want to tie himself to one person. Many members of his intimate circle disliked her, and she was pressing him for a better establishment of her own. The Prince of Wales wanted out. The problem for the palace was that she was not going to go quietly.

CHAPTER 10

The Rivals

> If women are fond of *Scandal*, it is the men who make us so; the avidity with which it is sought after, and the industry with which it is propagated, leads us to believe that it is the only pleasant source of conversation; and while we find that it commands the multitude, can we be blamed for using it as the magnet of attraction.
>
> Mary Robinson, *The Widow*

For once the *Town and Country Magazine* was behind the times. In its January 1781 issue, Mary appeared again in 'Histories of the Tète-à-Tète', this time coupled with the Prince. Under the oval portraits were the titles 'The Fair Ophelia' and 'The Illustrious Heir'. The biographical account of the Prince was flattering: 'He rides, walks, dances and fences, with skill, ease and grace.' He cut 'a very handsome stately figure'. He was every young lady's dream and many had set out to entrap him. Mary was presented as a beauty of obscure origins: 'Her bewitching face, and delicately handsome person, very early attracted the notice of the nobility.' She was the victim of a father who disposed of her to an unworthy husband: 'The devil appeared to her in the shape of an attorney's clerk, all glittering with spangles, and bedaubed with lace.' The Prince was said to have fallen in love with her in the character of Ophelia – it was presumably considered too close to the mark to say Perdita. According to the piece, the lovers were still together: 'They continue to reciprocate the finest feelings of which human beings are susceptible.'[1]

The *Town and Country Magazine* had the tact not to reiterate its earlier linking of Mary with Malden. People in the innermost circle of high society had a shrewd idea that his involvement had played a large part in the end of the royal affair. Thus Georgiana Duchess of Devonshire: 'the P. of Wales, discovering her infidelity, was shock'd at the treachery he had gone thro', and his friend and mistress were equally disgraced'.[2] Mary lent credibility to the rumours by allowing herself to be escorted around town by Malden. She insisted that, though she had placed herself under his protection, it was not a 'pecuniary' arrangement. At that time, she claimed, he was 'even poorer than myself: the death of his Lordship's grandmother, Lady Frances Coningsby, had not then placed him above the penury of his small income'.[3] But when her ladyship did die, later in 1781, Malden was in the position to offer Mary financial support.

Rumours soon abounded that Florizel and Perdita were no longer together. Mary was growing desperate as her measures to win back the Prince were not working and she was deep in debt, which she saw no way of discharging: 'I had quitted both my husband and my profession: – the retrospect was dreadful!' (she presumably means 'prospect', not 'retrospect'). She was £7,000 in debt – well over a quarter of a million in today's money – and her creditors were either threatening prison or seeking sexual favours in lieu of payment. She wondered about returning to the stage, but her friends advised that the public 'would not suffer a reappearance'. This surprised her, since Sophia Baddeley had returned to the theatre after a period as a full-time courtesan. A story was planted in the press in order to test the water; it was even provocatively suggested that she might move from Drury Lane to Covent Garden – the King's favoured theatre – and make her debut in the role of Jane Shore, deserted royal mistress.[4] But Mary followed the advice of her immediate circle and was 'thus fatally induced to relinquish what would have proved an ample and honourable resource for myself and my child'.[5]

On the eve of the new year there had been newspaper reports of the Prince's new establishment and his first public outing in his new role: 'This evening, at the Opera, his Royal Highness the Prince of Wales is to make his first appearance in public, in the character of the Heir apparent. He will be surrounded by his new established household, and his suite will be as numerous as his Majesty's.'[6] It was tantalizing for Mary that she had lost him at the very time when he became formal heir to the throne. A few days later it was reported that 'A certain young illustrious personage is said to have promised that Mrs R—'s *establishment* should immediately succeed his own, which, however, remaining still unsettled, though the former arrangement is made, has occasioned some severe reproaches on the part of the now suspicious *Perdita*.'[7] There was, however, no possibility of a resumption of the relationship. Mary did not blame the Prince's character so much as his station in life, which had put him so out of touch with the world. She returned his jewels and gifts, keeping only his miniature portrait and lock of hair. And the bond for £20,000.

On 5 January there appeared a very well-sourced story in the *Morning Herald*, possibly fed to Henry Bate by Mary herself. It gave the first public hint that she would stop at nothing, even blackmail, to get her 'establishment':

> A certain *amour royal* is now totally at an end; a separation has taken place *a thoro* for more than three weeks, and a *settlement* worthy of such a *sultana* is the only thing now wanting to break off all intercourse whatever. Mrs Robinson thinking the adjustment of this part of the *divorce* too essential to be trifled with, has roundly written to her once *ardent lover*, 'that if the establishment is not duly arranged within the *space of* fourteen days from the commencement of the new year, his —— must not be surprised, if he sees a full publication of all of those *seductory epistles* which alone estranged her from *virtue*, and the *marriage vow*.'

It was also reported that 'A certain young personage and Lord M—n are not on those terms of intimacy which formerly made them appear more like brothers than prince and subject.' Malden was paying the price of taking Perdita to his own bed as well as his master's. Mary was considered so newsworthy that there was even a report of Nicholas Darby's whereabouts: 'The father of the celebrated Perdita has lately taken the command of a stout Privateer sitting out in the River, and just ready to sail.'[8] He was redeeming himself with a naval career that would eventually take him into the service of Catherine the Great, Empress of Russia. The

Prince, meanwhile, was becoming a regular visitor at Cumberland House, home of his disgraced uncle, who was no friend to Mary.

The prospect of letters being published set tongues wagging. In the middle of January the *Morning Herald* announced that 'The Poetic Epistle from Florizel to Perdita; with Perdita's answer will be published during the course of next week, notwithstanding the repeated offers of the most lucrative kind, which have been made to the Editor to suppress the publication.'[9] The poem was duly published a few days later. It sold out within a week and was immediately reprinted; a third edition followed soon after. The popularity of this pamphlet, which cost half a crown even though it was only forty pages long, may be gauged from an anecdote published in the *Morning Herald* in early April:

> A gentleman happening the other day to be in a bookseller's shop – the author of a pamphlet of *Lasting Peace to Europe*, came in, and ask'd the bookseller how the book sold? 'But slowly,' answered the bookseller, 'It would have sold better if it had been put at eighteen pence' – 'How!' exclaimed the author, 'Give the plan of a lasting peace to Europe for eighteen pence, while Perditta is sold for half a crown?' – 'Aye, aye,' replied the bookseller, tapping the author upon the hand, 'Write me a history of scandal, the more scandalous, and the more scurrilous the better, and bring it to me, and I'll give you a good price for it, and pay you before hand, for nothing but scandal will sell' – 'What,' replied the author, 'can be more striking than to expose the vices of Kings, and the troubles that their reign causes upon the earth?' – 'True,' said the bookseller, 'but that is soaring too high, that, does not amuse the ladies – alas! Such are the depravity of the times, and the taste of the nobility.'[10]

In fact, the poem itself was hardly calculated to set the pulses racing. 'Florizel' writes as a boyish innocent:

> Unknown to all your sex, a perfect boy
> Fledg'd but unvers'd in manhood's greatest joy,
> You taught me what it is to be a Man
> And baffled all my Father's plan.

The poetic response of 'Perdita' offers the assurance that she was not interested in teaching him the erotic arts, but merely in helping him 'To find the young emotions room to shoot.' A little more riskily, the poem ends by claiming that the Queen and Mary's mother had colluded in the affair:

> Our two mammas have courteously agreed
> If we're content the nation need not heed.
> Your royal Father winks at all, no doubt.

The real meat of the pamphlet was not the exchange of poems but the 'Preliminary Discourse upon the Education of Princes' that was published with it. This is strongly pro-Perdita. 'Bristol is the place of her nativity,' it says, 'a circumstance alone sufficient to rescue that city from the sarcasm of abounding with ugly women.' Her respectable family and good education in the establishment of the More sisters are emphasized. It is claimed that 'we see no sharpers, fidlers, singers nor even other courtezans in her train'. She is even attempting to shake off 'Lord Pandar' (Malden), 'the mediator of her promotion'. What has happened, though, is that a plan has been laid to disturb the Prince's felicity, 'raise suspicions in a mind which never before suspected', and 'plot the interposition of another Fair one' in the good grace of the Prince.[11] It gradually becomes clear that this is a political pamphlet more than a piece of scandalmongering: its argument is that Perdita's name has been blackened and she has been excluded from the Prince's company by the Cumberland House and Whig factions who are attempting to win him over for the Opposition. Perdita, by contrast, is held up as the very model of political orthodoxy:

> The politics of a great Prince's mistress are so far from being unworthy of attention that it is very certain the true cause of all the royal smiles, which Perdita is well known to receive during her attendance upon the chace, are no compliments to the beauty of her person but merely meant as an approbation of her political system, which is intirely ministerial.[12]

Perdita was thus represented as the 'ministerial' candidate and her rival the Armistead as the 'Opposition' one, or – in the words of a newspaper report – the '*factious* representative' of the '*blue* and *buff* Junto'.[13]

The rivalry between the two mistresses was played out in the newspapers over a period of several months. Mary's contact with the Bates ensured that the *Morning Herald* was hostile to the behaviour of Elizabeth Armistead: 'Mrs Arms— has taken care to have it pretty repeatedly intimated to the celebrated *Perdita*, that *a certain young personage's* absence from her, is owing to the *Superior influence of certain charms* in another quarter, at the altar of which he still continues to sacrifice . . . the cruel mode of proclaiming the triumph, has visibly affected the deserted fair one.' Perdita took a centre box at the opera, but to no avail: the Prince did not once look at her. Mrs Armistead, it was soon reported, 'has certainly been gratified at last in an amour with a certain young personage; and now flatters herself that *her* charms will not be so soon unrivetted, as were those of the once exalted and enviable *Perdita*'.[14]

There was a showdown at the Opera House on the evening of Saturday, 17 February. While Perdita sat in a box directly above the Prince, Elizabeth 'directed her *artillery*' from a much better position on the opposite side: 'His Highness, in surveying them round, met in an upward glance the eyes of Mrs R. They scarce exchanged a look, when his attention was riveted by Mrs A—d, who, during the momentary victory over her competitor, drew a glove from a beautiful hand, and seemed to hold it as a gauntlet to her R—l admirer.' Having published this on the Monday, the *Morning Herald* could not resist returning to the story the next morning, telling of how the princely personage was besieged 'by a strong detachment of the *amorous* phalanx' while 'the Pensive *Perdita* every now and then sent down an unavailing sigh'.[15]

Whilst the rivalry between the women was being acted out in the press, the Prince, heady with his new-found freedom and denied the companionship of his brother the Duke of York and his trusted companion Colonel Lake (they had both gone abroad), fell in with the Duke of Cumberland and two notorious rakes, Charles Wyndham and Colonel St Leger. They frittered away the early months of 1781 in drunkenness and debauchery. During one raucous night in Blackheath they were so intoxicated that a member of the party tried to tear the tongue out of a fierce house dog. The dog responded by savaging a footman's leg and Wyndham's arm. Their host fell down the stairs, and the Prince was so drunk he was incapable of driving home.

Furthermore, the Prince was openly criticizing the King in the 'grossest terms', 'even in his hearing', which so alarmed George III that he confided in the Duke of Gloucester his fears that his son would soon refuse to obey him. But then the Prince suffered the ill effects of his hard living; according to Georgiana Duchess of Devonshire, 'Drinking and living too freely brought on a violent fever . . . which soon however spent itself in a hideous humour in his face.'[16] For most of March, he was in the care of his physician, who at one time even feared for his life. The Prince wrote to his brother in Germany, 'I remained cooped up in my bedchamber an entire fortnight without ever tasting anything but barley water and some damned wishy washy stuff of that sort.'[17] His brother warned him that he would seriously damage himself and blamed the debauchery on wicked Uncle Cumberland. But the Prince did not listen: when he recovered he carried on womanizing. Mary had not quite given up on him, and was concerned for his health. The *Morning Post* noted that 'ever since the late indisposition of the heir apparent, Perdita's face has remained *unvarnished*; but as he is now recovered, it is hoped the *lilly* and *carnation* will again blossom in her countenance'.[18]

By April, the papers were saying that the 'implacable rivals' were close to having a catfight in the street. They drove around in their brimstone-yellow equipages looking daggers at each other:

> The *Armst—d* and the *Perdita*, are grown such implacable rivals, that the most serious consequences are to be apprehended from a personal meeting, which the partisans of either are anxious to avoid: for some time they contented themselves with exchanging looks of fiery indignation as their carriages passed each other; but now, their glasses are let down as soon as the enemy is seen approaching, and they mutually exchange repeated broadsides of *grinnings* and *spittings*, to the no small entertainment of the neighbourhood, where the *rencontre* happens: thitherto, they have engaged only upon different tacks, and nothing has proved decisive; the Armst—d however we hear, is now practising a *grin* of so powerful a nature, under the notorious *Grimaldi*, that if she is fortunate enough to bring it to bear full upon the enemy, it cannot fail to insure her a complete victory!

Perdita seems to have known she was defeated. She was conspicuous by her absence from a gathering of more than a thousand ladies of rank and fashion in Kensington Gardens, the kind of assembly she would never have missed in happier times. Her rival had triumphed: the Armistead was secure in the Prince's love, while the Perdita was left slowly stalking 'the joyless round of *Ranelagh's* dreary dome: no pleasing memory left; no sympathies of mutual love, all former scenes of dear delight for ever gone!'[19]

But Mary still had the letters. The threat to publish was her most powerful weapon. Reputations could be seriously damaged by the appearance of private correspondence in the public domain. She discovered this to her own cost in March, when an alarming advertisement appeared in the papers: 'On Saturday next will be published in Quarto, Price 2 Shillings, *Genuine Letters* from *PERDITA* to a *JEW*; with the Jew's answer. This pamphlet will through [sic] new light on the Art of Love, and furnish useful hints to Lovers of every Denomination. Specimens of the Original Letters are left with the publishers.'[20] The letters written to 'Jew' King the moneylender back in the earliest days of her marriage had returned to haunt her.

Letters from Perdita to a Certain Israelite began with a preface in which King (anonymously) justified his 'indelicate' publication of private letters on the grounds that Perdita herself had breached decorum by authorizing the appearance back in January of the *Poetical Epistle from Florizel to Perdita*. He claimed, indeed, on the basis of his acquaintance 'with both the prosaic and poetic Stile of Mrs R—' that Mary herself had actually been the author not only of both sides of the poetic correspondence but also of the 'Preliminary Discourse upon the Education of Princes' that so flattered her. He countered with his own, far less flattering biography, dwelling on the Robinsons' swindling, their time in debtors' prison, and Mary's affairs with a string of aristocratic paymasters.

As was seen in chapter 3, there must have been a considerable element of authenticity to the letters that followed this prefatory blast: King could not have known about the Robinsons' trip to Oxford, Bristol, and Wales unless he was much better acquainted with them than Mary herself ever revealed. Strong evidence for authenticity is provided by a report that appeared in the *Morning Post* within days of publication:

> The *noble paramour* of the celebrated *Perditta*, and the fair dame herself, on Monday evening made a bold push to recover *certain*

> *letters*, upon the originality of which a *certain book* has lately been published; but the attempt was abortive; the publisher would not surrender, but challenged the demandant to the *Chapter coffee-house*, there to decide his right. The *attic regions* of *Pater-noster Row* were in an uproar, but, the amorous pair were obliged to retreat without the objects of their wishes.[21]

The pamphlet was published on a Saturday and on the Monday Mary and Malden attempted to retrieve the original letters.

A book attacking King, published some time later, provides a fuller account of the affair. Its version of the sequence of events is probably exaggerated, but has the ring of truth. When the *Poetical Epistle from Florizel to Perdita* became a bestseller, King saw the opportunity to make some money from his old package of Mrs Robinson's letters. He went to her house and tried to sell them back to her for £400. She refused, so he upped the ante by demanding £2,000. If she did not pay, he would have anonymous letters sent to Lord Malden accusing her of infidelity to him, would plant malignant stories about her in the daily papers, and publish letters revealing that they had had an affair during the first year of her marriage. This blackmail attempt also failed, with the result that the letters were published. According to this account, some of them were genuine and others forged.[22]

This source also suggests that King and his publishers hoped to sell 10,000 copies, but the grubby nature of their dealings meant that they shifted scarcely a hundred. In a contest between Perdita and an Israelite, the press – especially Bate's *Morning Herald* – would always be on the side of the British beauty. Besides, the real prize was the correspondence with the Prince. Within a few days of King's shabby little publication there appeared a pocket-sized volume of just under a hundred pages, priced one shilling and sixpence: *The Budget of Love; or, Letters between Florizel and Perdita. To which are prefixed some interesting Anecdotes of the Fair Heroine*. The 'interesting Anecdotes' consist of a brief and largely accurate account of Mary's early life and some fairly detailed allegations about her relationship with Lord Lyttelton. The book was furnished with an address to the reader explaining that Perdita had been so proud of her letters from the Prince that she read them out to her favourite chambermaid and then entrusted them to the girl's care. Unfortunately, mistress and maid had a falling out, with the result that the letters passed into the hands of the latter's betrothed, who 'advised her to dispose of them, for the gratification of the public and her own emolument'.[23] This story sounds like a blatant fabrication, leading one to assume that the letters are outright forgeries.

Nevertheless, they were written by someone with both a reasonable knowledge of the course of events and a good ear for the kind of language the Prince and the actress would have used in their letters. Thus Florizel: 'Did you perceive one more arduous than the rest, pressing his hand upon his heart, and looking all desire, – one more elevated than the common race of men?' And Perdita: 'You will say that I write you out of patience; but I have such a pleasure in writing to you, that I cannot forbear it.'[24] All the letters are dated between 31 March and 18 April 1780, which is exactly the time when the Prince and Mary were in almost daily correspondence before their first private meeting. Whoever wrote the letters knew that Malden was the intermediary, that financial guarantees were offered before Mary agreed to meet, and that an assignation was eventually made for Kew. There are also some very entertaining novelistic touches:

> At length the wished-for hour is fixed, – in my opinion, at a most convenient place: – I wish that you may think so too: – it is at the S[tar]and G[arter], K[ew]B[ridge] – If you will bless me with your sight there to-morrow night at seven o'clock, you will make me the happiest of mortals. – I have thought of a stratagem how to steal away disguised from home, but you will be pleased, my Love, to be at the appointed place first, that I may ask for you in some fictitious name. – Let me know if that hour will be convenient, and what name I shall call you by. – When you address me, call me *Williamson*.[25]

The hour of seven seems implausibly early, but the broad outline is consistent with Mary's own story to Mrs Baddeley of how the Prince would escape from the palace during the night to meet her at the inn on Eel Pie Island.

The broad humour of such publications was a severe embarrassment to Mary: the comedy queen of Drury Lane was now dupe to the hacks of Paternoster Row. A form of consolation came a few weeks later when the Prince tired of Elizabeth Armistead. The *Morning Herald* reported the news with its customary military metaphors:

> A *coalition* is about to take place between those celebrated leaders of the *amorous Squadron*, the *Arms—d* and the *Perdita*, on the grounds of mutual disappointment: the former having now lost all those *regal hopes* which kept her towering so long above the rest of the *frail Sisterhood*, and that to the inexpressible chagrin of the hapless *Perdita*. A singularity of distress has, however, at last wrought a miracle unlooked for, in uniting those once *jarring elements*, though it is but by the *brittle cement* of female *friendship*![26]

The Prince had turned his attentions to a 'demi-rep' (woman of doubtful reputation) with aristocratic pretensions called Grace Dalrymple Eliot. She was popularly known as 'Dally the Tall'. It may also be that he shied away from a commitment to Elizabeth Armistead because he realized that Perdita was going to cost him dear and the prospect of payouts to two women would have been too much to bear. Mrs Robinson's threat to publish the letters was 'chocolate-house chat' all through the spring and early summer.[27]

The Prince wrote to his brother Frederick, who was still in Germany, lamenting that he had not been present to assist him with the Perdita business. He had been forced to rely instead on the Duke of Cumberland. The news would not have pleased Frederick, given that the King had repeatedly advised the young princes to stay away from their gambling libertine uncle. The Prince insisted however that the Duke was not 'rioting and raking' with him. On the contrary, 'he has acted as my firmest, staunchest and best friend . . . in an affair in which I wanted the advice of such a friend, which has lately happened, and which I hope will now be speedily put an end to. It originated from the old infernal cause Robinson.'[28] He knew he had to get the letters back because of what he had rashly said in them about other members of the royal family, including the King.

Mary, meanwhile, was keeping up appearances. The *Morning Post* reported that 'A Pony phaeton is now building in Long-Acre, for the *celebrated Perdita*, which is said to be the most complete carriage of its kind that has made its appearance for many years.'[29] It was probably paid for by Malden. She seems to have been determined to fight fire with fire. If 'Jew' King, the pamphleteers, and the gossipmongers were to abuse her name, she would use the newspapers to promote a more positive image. 'Puffing is now at such a height,' observed the *Morning Herald*, 'that even the *fair frails* practice it with success . . . Perdita and others now puff off their qualifications in the different newspapers.'[30] From this time on she was often portrayed as a manipulator of the press; when she was poor, the papers joked that she could no longer afford to pay for her own publicity machine.

The first issue of the gossipy periodical the *Rambler's Magazine* includes an imaginary dialogue between Perdita, Dally the Tall, and another courtesan known as the Bird of Paradise. They discuss their methods. The Bird of Paradise says that the important thing when you take a lover is not to mention money until the morning. Perdita considers this 'No bad scheme for fleecing a Fumbler, or a Flogging Cull; but I always endeavour to rivet the nail at once by a settlement, and I have invariably my attorney ready to draw the deeds.' The Bird then proposes an item for insertion in 'the list' (the next day's gossip column): 'We hear that *Perdita* has absolutely refused a settlement of a thousand a year from the D— of N—, so strongly is she attached to her devoted and almost adored Florizel.' Perdita replies: 'But middling – however it will rouze Florizel's feelings, and I shall hear from him in consequence of reading this article. Besides, I shall see him this night at the Opera, and I will place Lord M—n and him so directly opposite, and the Duke on an angle, that one nod, with a smile from me, will bring him home again.'[31] This is good satire because it hits upon a truth: a woman such as Perdita was not merely the victim of the press, she was also an arch-manipulator of her public image. If the papers used military language to describe her rivalry with Mrs Armistead, then she would dress up in military regalia for a masked ball. In early May she appeared at the Pantheon '*en militaire*, regimentally equipped from top to toe'.[32] The Prince and Malden were both there to see her.

When the papers complained that she was making a show of herself, she announced that she would henceforth be cutting back on her public engagements: 'The *Perdita*, is determined, in consequence of her various disappointments, to lead a life of *penitence* and *retirement*.'[33] She took a house in Old Windsor, 'where she proposes enjoying the rural sweets of retirement the ensuing summer, unalloyed by domestic jars, or jealous inquietude'.[34] Renting a property on the Prince's doorstep was also a way of making sure that the question of the letters was not forgotten.

The rural retreat did not last for long. Soon she was back in London, attending a masquerade at the Haymarket. Once again she sported a 'most becoming' military costume (scarlet faced with apple green), though she did not stay late.[35] She was escorted by her two most ardent supporters, Lord Malden and Earl Cholmondeley. She may have had a brief affair with the latter at this time (there were also unsubstantiated rumours of a liaison with the 'unusually handsome' Duke of Dorset).

She commuted at high speed between town and Old Windsor in her powder-blue carriage drawn by four chestnut ponies. Both the postillion and the servant on the back wore livery of blue and silver. Sometimes Perdita had a dress to match: 'The lady *dashed* into town through Hyde-Park turnpike, at four o'clock, dressed in a blue great coat prettily trimmed in silver; a plume of feather graced her hat, which even Alexander the Great might have prided himself in.' On this occasion, the Bird of Paradise was passing in her coach and positively '*drooped her wings* at the superior stile in which [Perdita] moved'.[36] It was becoming customary for fashionable new garments to be named after the aristocratic lady who wore them first. Uniquely among commoners, Mary took on this role as fashion pioneer. In the spring of 1781, the *Lady's Magazine* appointed its first fashion correspondent, Charlotte Stanley, and gave her a monthly column. Under 'Full Dress for June' she recommended 'The Perdita. A chip hat with a bow, and pink ribbons puff'd round the crown.'[37]

Fearing that her creditors would foreclose on her, Mary spent money while she could. Increasingly wild parties were held in Cork Street and she sat for a portrait by George Romney, one of London's foremost painters. Around this time, Thomas Robinson returned to her. Mary was surprised to find a letter from him, full of regrets and apologies. The *Morning Herald* reported the reunion:

> The *Perdita* is unquestionably in better *plight* than any of her *frail sisterhood* of whatever denomination. *Coach*, *Vis-à-vis*, *Chariot*, *Gig*, *Cabriole*, *Phaetons* of every *complexion* have alternately swelled her transient equipage! In the midst of all this *whirl* of dissipation, she

'The Adventure of Prince Pretty Man': caricature of Fox, the Prince, the Perdita, and the Armistead.

> is not unmindful of her marriage vow. – Her *accommodating* spouse *participates* in all, and yields *implicit* the *connubial bed*, or drives her *petit ponies* black or grey, just as the *moment* suits, without or murmur or regret.[38]

Although Perdita was no longer Florizel's beloved, she had a panache that none of her rivals could match. The only option for the courtesans was to join forces. But when they did, there would always be a crowd of supporters ready to come to Mary's aid. One evening at the Opera House, the Armistead and Dally the Tall 'formed so determined a line against the *pink-sterned Perdita*' that 'the lookers on with all that *generous interference* which is the characteristic of the country at such times, *rushed* into her *wake* and carried her off with *colours* flying against such shameful odds'.[39]

CHAPTER 11

Blackmail

If Once betray'd, I scarce forgive:
And though I pity All that live,
And mourn for ev'ry pain;
Yet never could I court the Great,
Or worship Fools, whate'er their state;
For falsehood I disdain!

Mary Robinson, 'Stanzas to a Friend,
who desired to have my Portrait'

Thomas and Mary Robinson continued to accumulate debts, borrowing money against the security of an eventual payoff from the Prince. Mary's initial asking price was £2,500, which might be considered modest, given that she had in her possession a signed and sealed bond promising her £20,000 from the royal coffers. But her creditors were losing patience:

> The *creditors* of a once admired *Sultana* of R—l fame, are become of late more *restive* and *impatient* than heretofore, from a discovery that certain arrangements which have been sedulously reported to be in agitation, are proved to be no more than the *fairy fancies* of the deluded fair one; in consequence of which, a whole train of *danglers* and *dependants* have withdrawn their *assiduities*, a circum-

stance that must convey an inexpressible mortification to any young woman less *aspiring* than the once elevated Perdita.[1]

Becoming desperate, she seems to have recalled the device she had used to persuade Robinson to tell his family about their marriage. Early in July 1781 the *Morning Herald* reported that '*Perdita* is said to have declared herself *pregnant*, and desired the great event to be announced to certain R—l ears in form. – Lord C—y is appointed *plenipo* extraordinary on this important embassy.'[2] 'Lord C—y' was the fourth Earl of Cholmondeley. A chamberlain to the Prince, he had – like the Prince and most of his male friends – had an affair with Dally the Tall, but he was now, like Malden, inseparable from Perdita. According to the *Memoirs of Perdita* he was 'long indefatigable in the pursuit of her'.[3]

A few days later, the *Morning Herald* mischievously suggested that, not to be outdone, Elizabeth Armistead was going to try a similar trick: 'The declared pregnancy of the *Perdita*, has alarmed the Ar—d beyond expression, who, being strenuous in opposition, is determined to leave no stone unturned to get in the same *good* way. It is said, she has engaged the celestial bed as a powerful resolvent in obstructions, and drinks the waters of the Islington Spa, to brave the lax fibres, and restore the ravages of time or accident.'[4] The celestial bed belonged to Dr James Graham, sex therapist to the stars, whose public lectures on erotic rejuvenation by means of 'magnetico-electrical fire' would later be attended by Mary, the Prince, and Charles James Fox.

Press speculation was reaching fever pitch. One morning the *Morning Herald* carried three separate stories about Mary. The most talked about of them reported that 'The young *German Baroness*, who is the present rival of the *Perditta*, has taken an house in *Corke-Street*, next door to her celebrated predecessor.' 'Young men of fashion' were gathering round Perdita herself like bees to a honey pot, while she was 'equally sedulous in her attentions to a *young Pole*, the object of her choice'.[5] There were so many fashionable carriages rolling up in Cork Street that it was hard to know who was visiting whom.

The German Baroness was the Countess von Hardenburg, wife of a Hanoverian aristocrat who had come to London in the hope of gaining an ambassadorial position. She had already tried to seduce the Prince's brother whilst in Germany. The Prince found her 'devinely pretty'; when he tried to teach her to play cards at Windsor, neither of them could keep their eyes off each other. He soon enjoyed what he called 'the pleasures of Elyssium' with her.[6] The affair was kept secret until the *Morning Herald* broke the story in its article about Mary. But the press report was a case of mistaken identity. The Prince wrote to his brother to explain:

> Thus did our connexion go forward in the most delightful manner that you can form any idea to yourself of, till an unfortunate article in the *Morning Herald* appeared, saying that the German Baroness who had been imported by the Queen, had taken a house next door to Perdita's in Cork Street, and that my carriage was seen constantly at her door. The confusion which caused this article is that a Polish Countess, Countess Raouska, has taken the house next to Mrs R's, and the Duke of Gloucester's carriage is very often, nay even every day seen at her door.[7]

So it was not the Prince visiting the German Baroness and Perdita charming the Polish Count, but the Prince's uncle having an affair with the Polish Countess.

But the report in the *Morning Herald* was enough to make the German Baron suspicious. He confronted his wife and extracted from her an exchange of love letters with the Prince, which led to an ugly scene, with the upshot that the Prince's 'little angel' was dispatched to Brussels. The Armistead and Dally the Tall also retreated to the Continent at this point, leaving Perdita centre stage. The tantalizing prospect of a theatrical comeback was floated once more: 'The quondam Princess *Perdita* having had her share of courts and courtly things, is about to quit the delusive scenes of mock royalty, to resume her *lamb-collecting* crook, and return once more to her *innocent flock* on the dramatic plains of Old Drury.'[8]

With the *Morning Herald* emphasizing her resilience in this way, it was time for the *Morning Post* to respond with some smears:

> *Perdita*, finding neither tears, puffs, paragraphs, or intreaties, can regain the affections of a certain H—r App—t, has now levelled all her forces against the Earl of D—y, if possible to *seduce* him from the *lovely F—n*, whose beauty and amiable qualities render

> all her endeavours vain and fruitless, and the *poor Perdita* remains sick in a fit of *envy* and *vexation*.[9]

The lovely F—n was Elizabeth Farren, an actress who actually succeeded in becoming a wife rather than a courtesan: she would eventually marry the Earl of Derby and be praised by one and all as a true lady. There is no evidence that Mary made a play for Farren's lover. The *Morning Post* then resorted to the low tactic of adding a decade to her age: 'Poor Perdita still pursues her favourite point with unremitting attention, and has the vanity, no doubt, to suppose, *though turn'd of thirty-four*, and may shortly be a grand-mother, that she shall be able to supplant the *beautiful F—n*.'[10] As in a game of Chinese whispers, the rumour that Perdita was pregnant is here converted into a rumour that her daughter is pregnant. Maria Elizabeth was 6 at the time.

One malicious story in the *Morning Post*, concerning Mary's imminent arrest for debt, was almost certainly true: '*Perdita's* carriage was stopped in the streets last Wednesday and the pretty bauble *touched* on an *execution*; but we are happy to hear that it was soon restored, through the *pecuniary* interest of a noble friend.'[11] This suggests that Malden was now in a better position to help out. He was reaping the financial benefit of his grandmother's recent death.

The time had come to settle the business with the Prince. It was to be a drawn-out process. Mary's position was desperate. She was thousands of pounds in debt and had a young daughter to consider. She had sacrificed everything for the Prince and she expected redress. The Prince's hopes for a clean break were over-optimistic, while the King wrote furious letters to his son about the scandal: 'I do not doubt that the last evening papers, or those of tomorrow morning will have the whole business fully stated in it. Indeed it is now certain that some unpleasant mention of you is daily to be found in the papers.'[12]

The Prince, at the request of the King, relied on the 'discreet' Colonel Hotham, his treasurer and the King's aide-de-camp. A month of delicate and tense negotiations can be traced in a batch of surviving letters between the parties.

Hotham had an initial meeting with Mary herself at the house in Cork Street. She made it clear that she was not selling the letters, but was returning them in exchange for the payment of debts. Her point of principle was that she had been a highly paid actress and had given this up for the Prince. Hotham then reported back to the court, and Mary gave responsibility for negotiations to Lord Malden.

The intermediaries had the unenviable task of reaching a conclusion satisfactory to both parties. On 26 July Colonel Hotham wrote to Malden from Windsor, arranging to meet him the following day at Cranford Bridge. The meeting took place and was followed up by Hotham, in a letter written four days later, confirming the Prince's initial offer of £5,000 for the return of the letters. Lest any misunderstanding should occur, he set out the Prince's position clearly. Mrs Robinson was to accept the money as 'a proper and sufficient reward . . . on a strict retrospect into every part of Mrs Robinson's conduct during the time the attachment subsisted'. Hotham stressed that this 'past connexion . . . never more can be renewed'.[13] If she asked for more money, she would get nothing. This was the final offer. His letter drips with contempt for 'this unpleasant subject'.

Mary was angry and humiliated by the tone of the letter. Malden met with the Prince himself on 3 August at Buckingham House and then at the London home of Lord Southampton, another of his closest courtiers. Mary wanted Malden to raise the issue of 'future bounty', which Hotham had curtly dismissed: Mary had not forgotten the Prince's promise of £20,000 upon his coming of age. The palace wanted the £5,000 payoff to end the business, but Mary fought hard for future provision. Five thousand pounds would scarcely cover her debts. At the meeting the Prince insisted that he was 'at present' unable to make specific promises relating to future bounty. Malden informed Mary of this, much to her dismay. She prevailed upon Malden to write directly to the Prince, relaying her grief and anxiety. Perhaps she took heart from the phrase 'at present'.

In a letter dated 4 August Malden informed the Prince that he had assured Mrs Robinson of the Prince's 'sincerity of intention'. He then restated her position: the Prince was accountable for her debts, which had been incurred on the 'repeated assurances' that he would honour her expenses and 'raise her above the frowns of fortune'. She had told Malden that she would never have incurred such debts had it not been for those assurances. 'The idea of falling from a state of splendor and independence (to which she always flattered herself she should be raised) to a level that must at least be degrading to her, impresses her with feelings that are hard to be forgone.'

Malden desperately tried to strike the right balance between expectation and compromise: 'she now consoles herself under the hope, that whenever your Royal Highness's situation shall enable you – you will not be forgetful of her'. He explained that it was 'under this hope that she has delivered in trust to me every letter that your Royal Highness condescended to write to her'. Malden emphasized that Mary's pride and honour were at stake. She was anxious that her motives should not be viewed as mercenary:

> She still declares she cannot bear the idea held within Colonel Hotham's letters, that the money therein mentioned is to be the consideration for the restitution of those papers and that she is to be precluded all hope of your R[oyal] H[ighness]'s future bounty. The idea she says shocks her, as it not only carries the strongest appearance of a price put upon her conduct to your R. H. during the time of your attachment to her, but gives her reason to fear that she will be left wholly destitute and without income hereafter, which she trusts your R. H. does not intend should be the case.[14]

She wanted it to be made clear to the Prince that her only inducement for giving up the letters was his peace of mind. She now required a written acknowledgement that the Prince believed that she was acting in good faith: 'It is for her satisfaction then, that I request your R. H. to allow Col. Hotham to signify by letter to me, that you are satisfied with her inducement for parting with the papers. Nothing she says can be more injurious to her feelings, nor will she bear the idea of having it supposed that she has *sold* papers so dear to her.'

The letter ended by reiterating the hope that when the time came, the Prince would do more for her, although she would not lay him under any obligation of 'doing for her hereafter, any thing further than what your R. H.'s honour and generosity would prompt you to'.[15] The clear thrust of the letter is that an annuity on the Prince's coming of age was non-negotiable. Hotham was equally intransigent: there was £5,000 on the table in return for the letters and that was that.[16]

Malden wrote back to the Prince, stating that it was unacceptable for Mrs Robinson to receive only £5,000, with no expectation of further assistance. The sum would not even be sufficient to clear her debts;

such a proposal was 'extremely circumscribed and inadequate'.[17] Colonel Hotham was having none of it: whatever the Prince might have said in conversation, it 'never was intended to give Mrs Robinson any Expectation or Hope, much less any Promise more than the Specifick sum' mentioned in the first letter.[18] Malden then bypassed Hotham and wrote to Lord Southampton for clarification of what the Prince had said when they had met in person. Southampton reminded him of the Prince's exact words 'I will not say, what I will, or will not do in future. I will make no promises, and will not bind myself. I owe it to the K[ing] not to do it.' Southampton said that the meaning of the words was that 'neither your Lordship, nor any other Person should have *a right* to form future pretensions, in consequence of it'.[19] He signed off, saying that he wanted nothing further to do with the business.

The press quickly got wind of the negotiations. The *Morning Post* did not take a favourable view. What had the laws of Britain come to, it asked, when the royal family had no defence against a blackmail threat from a mere commoner? Besides, the whole negotiation was ridiculous, because even if Perdita were given money in return for the original letters, she would be bound to have kept copies that were just as dangerous. 'It is certain had *Florizel* debauched *Perdita*, he ought to have made her an ample settlement for the loss of her honour; but as it is notorious that this was not the case, his family ought to treat her menaces with a silent contempt.'[20]

The *Morning Herald* responded on Mary's side: the report in the *Morning Post* was illiberal and groundless; what was at stake was the Prince's honour – he had made a vow to assist Mary financially and he surely had 'too much liberality to break any engagement he has really entered into, let the consideration be what it may'. Besides, it was entirely his fault that Mary had for many months past been exposed 'to every insult and injury'.[21]

Malden, meanwhile, was unable to stop Mary from sending a furious letter directly to the Prince, stating that she categorically refused his 'unacceptable proposal':

> I will quit England instantly but no earthly power shall make me ever receive the smallest support from you. Your indelicacy in insulting me by such a proposal was totally unaccepted I confess –

my conduct has been *towards you* irreproachable. I hope you will feel every degree of satisfaction in your own mind when you reflect how you have treated me. I have nothing further to say but you shall never be troubled by any further application from me neither will I receive the smallest favour from you.[22]

Malden tried to cool the emotional temperature and restart negotiations. On 14 August, he wrote two letters, one to the Prince of Wales by the desire of Mrs Robinson and the other to Hotham. He informed the Prince that Mary had authorized him to restore the letters, but still had not abandoned the hopes she had conceived based on the sentiments he had previously expressed and the 'liberal promises' he had made her.[23] The letter to Hotham asked for a time and place to be specified for the return of the letters, and referred to a list of Mary's debts that had been sent to the Colonel on the understanding that the Prince had agreed to discharge them in full.[24]

The same day, a story was leaked to Bate at the *Morning Herald*, announcing that the dispute over the letters was resolved: 'It is beyond dispute that *Perdita* has at length succeeded in her *amorous litigation* with her hitherto tardy Banker in *Wales*. Not less than *twenty thousand pounds* were the stipulated *doceur*, which sum she is to be put in immediate possession of, on condition of certain *manuscripts* being surrendered.' The Perdita, 'having completed the sum of her *worldly wishes* with the *Treasury Bench*', would be retiring to France.[25]

It is not beyond the bounds of possibility that Mary herself was the source of this leak: a public perception that she had been offered the full £20,000 could prove useful in negotiating an increase on the much lower sum that had actually been proposed. On the other hand, the *Morning Herald* may have been shooting in the dark: a further report two days later said that she had '*apparently* received the vivifying drops of *Treasury* distillation', which was certainly not the case at this point.[26]

The wrangling continued. The Prince in person met Lord Malden at Cranford Bridge and quarrelled over the issue of future provision. The Prince would not bind himself to the future without the King's consent; the letters were to be returned to Hotham. Hotham wrote to confirm that nothing more would be done for Mary than the payment of the sum originally proposed: 'I beg, if Mrs Robinson entertains the smallest

Hope or Expectation of more being done for her, either now, or hereafter, than the Payment of the £5,000, (which I am concern'd to find she yet appears to do,) that she may be compleatly undeceived, for I am commanded to say nothing ever can.'[27] He agreed to meet Malden at Berkeley Square, but Malden refused to hand over the letters until the money had been paid. When Hotham returned to Windsor after this meeting, the Prince was furious that he was not bearing the letters. Hotham wrote again to stress that it was '*absolutely necessary*' that Mrs Robinson should give sufficient security that the restitution of the letters would be bona fide complete, with no originals or copies retained, 'in order that not only no Publication of them, or any part of them, shall take place, but that no Eye, except that of the Writer or of the Person they were written to, should look into Papers, which certainly never were intended for the Inspection of any Third Person whatever'.[28]

The next day (29 August) Mary retorted with a passionate letter to Malden, denouncing the Prince. He forwarded it to Hotham. This is the closest she comes to a direct threat of blackmail. His 'ungenerous and illiberal' treatment was justification for 'any step my necessities may urge me to take':

> I have ever acted with the strictest honour and candour towards HRH – neither do I wish to do any thing I may hereafter have cause to repent. I do not know what answer may be thought sufficient, the only one I can, or *ever will be*, induced to give, is that I am willing to return every letter I have ever received from his R. H. bona fide. Had HRH honorably fulfilled *every* promise he has heretofore made me, I never could or would have made him ampler restitution, as I have ever valued those letters as dearly as my existence, and nothing but my distressed situation ever should have tempted me to give them up at all.[29]

The King, meanwhile, was put in the embarrassing position of applying to the Prime Minister, Lord North, for the money:

> My eldest son got last year into a very improper connection with an actress and woman of indifferent character through the friendly assistance of Lord Malden. He sent her letters and very foolish

> promises, which undoubtedly by her conduct she has cancelled ... a multitude of letters passed, which she has threatened to publish, unless he, in short, bought them of her ... £5,000 is an enormous sum, but I wish to get my son out of this shameful scrape.[30]

Lord North sympathized with the King and admired his 'paternal tenderness and wisdom', but he still enjoyed reading the letters when Hotham finally obtained them. They were, he would later remark to his son-in-law, 'remarkably well written'.[31] The King comforted himself with the thought that he was not personally engaged in the transaction.

Malden and Mary had to accept that the other side was implacable. The 'disagreeable business' was concluded on 5 September when Hotham wrote to say that the payment of £5,000 had been authorized and that he would come round to Berkeley Square on the following Monday to pick up the letters.[32] The question of 'future bounty' on the Prince's coming of age was not mentioned. It was not, however, explicitly ruled out.

In public, Mary later claimed never to have held the Prince responsible for the sordid turn of events. But other, more private letters tell a different story, of anger, humiliation, and regret: 'I, who sacrificed reputation, an advantageous profession, friends, patronage, the brilliant hours of youth, and the conscious delight of correct conduct, am condemned to the scanty pittance bestowed on every indifferent page who holds up his ermined train of ceremony.'[33]

It seemed that the palace had triumphed over the actress, and that her hopes of an annuity were blasted. But Mary was only temporarily defeated. In the same week that Hotham paid over the £5,000, she raised eyebrows by ordering the very latest carriage, a *Bove de Paris*, which 'bids fair to kick the poor *brimstone-coloured* equipages quite out of doors'.[34] She was also causing a stir in the art world. Two weeks after the Prince had called off the affair in December, she had begun sitting for Romney. His asking rate was twenty guineas for a half-length portrait, thus undercutting Gainsborough (thirty guineas) and Sir Joshua Reynolds (fifty guineas). He produced at least two – and maybe up to six – portraits of Mary, one of which was published as an engraving at the height of the letter negotiations on 25 August 1781.

The original portrait from which the engraving was taken remained with Romney and appeared in the artist's sale after his death. This suggests that, rather than being paid for, it would have been undertaken as a kind of mutual publicity deal: Mary would have the honour of sitting for her portrait in the true manner of an aristocrat, while Romney would get to hang the canvas in his studio as a revelation of his art. Wealthy ladies would be able to come in and say words to the effect of 'I'd like to commission you to paint me looking as beautiful as her.' The portrait now hangs in the Wallace Collection in London. Mary appears as a demure Quaker, which, according to her *Memoirs*, was one of her favourite images. Her hair, bosom, and hands are covered modestly. She is the very picture of innocence.

The very same day that the engraving was published, as the polite world was gossiping about her impending payoff, the *Morning Herald* announced that Mrs Robinson was sitting for Gainsborough. He was also painting her rival, Dally the Tall. The papers joked that for once they would be painted naturally as opposed to artificially with make-up. Surprisingly, given the ferocity of the private negotiations that were going on between Malden and Hotham, Gainsborough planned to exhibit his Perdita at the Royal Academy beside his recently completed three-quarter-length portrait of the Prince himself, 'dressed in the Windsor Uniform, green, with buff collar and sleeves'.[35]

The portrait of Mary was apparently commissioned by the Prince himself. This seems extraordinary, given that he was trying to expunge her from his life at this time, though it may have been that the commission had come much earlier in the year and that the August sittings were not the first. But there is no doubt that the 'fine whole length portrait of Mrs Robinson by Gainsborough' was eventually to be seen hanging in the Prince's gallery at Carlton House. Perhaps he regarded it as a souvenir of his first great love affair. After all, he would never again have so beautiful a mistress. He was billed 105 guineas for the portrait and made a first payment – over ten years late – to Gainsborough's widow in 1793.

Gainsborough also executed a bust-length oval-shaped close-up – with the same pose, dress, and black velvet choker – for Mary's own collection. We do not know whether this was a gift or whether she paid for it. A treasured possession, she kept it in pride of place on her wall, flanked by engravings of the Prince and Banastre Tarleton, until 1785, when her financial affairs became so hopeless that her possessions were auctioned off. It fetched thirty-two guineas and has now found its way to the Rothschild collection at Waddesdon Manor in Buckinghamshire. There was also a preliminary study in oils for the main portrait, which remained with Gainsborough's nephew and assistant, Gainsborough Dupont, until he died in 1797. Then there was another sale, and the Prince bought this to add to his collection, which is testimony to the endurance of his affection for Mary. He gave the full-length portrait away in 1818, but the study is still in the Royal Collection at Windsor Castle.

The big painting – now in the Wallace Collection beside the Romney – has a seated Mary looking pensive and guarded, but very lovely, dressed in a simple and elegant gown, whose lacy hem reveals the most delicate of slippers and just a hint of slender ankle. She is clasping the Prince's miniature in her hand. Tactfully, it is not rendered in sufficient detail to make his features visible, but a spectator at the time would have had no doubt in interpreting its significance. The portrait is a clear evocation of Mrs Robinson's abandonment: she is Perdita the lost one, the pensive and thoughtful shepherdess, alone in a melancholy romantic landscape that is painted dreamily and almost impressionistically. The setting is a sharp contrast to the usual Gainsborough landscape style of realistically representing the great estates of the aristocrats who gave him commissions. Mary is carefully posed with only the miniature and a loyal Pomeranian lapdog to comfort her.

Gainsborough, a friend of Henry Bate (whom he also painted), is clearly taking Mary's side. One senses that he is half in love with her himself. A modern critic has suggested what a provocation this must have been, given that the painting was commissioned by the Prince: 'Gainsborough dramatises her beauty, sensitivity, sexuality, expressing his own feelings about her and offering the prince visual evidence that he has made a mistake in casting her off. You idiot, Your Highness, is the painting's message.'[36] If that was the message, the Prince either failed to perceive it or regarded it with equanimity, considering the implied insult a price worth paying for the beauty of the piece.

Mary still had her beauty, her health, and her youth. Moreover, she had been successful in portraying herself as a victim of the corrupt court. The *Morning Herald* took the view that, despite her 'fracas with her *illustrious amorata*', Perdita had 'preserved a line of conduct so irreproachable and prudent, that even her most rancorous enemies cannot stigmatize her with the smallest reflection'.[37] It also praised her 'universal character for *humanity*'.[38] Her father, meanwhile, was reported commanding a ship called the *Resolution*, employed to convey stores for the relief of Gibraltar, which had been besieged by the Spanish when they entered the Anglo-French war on the French side.

In early October, there was a sighting that seems to confirm the story that the diamond encrustation of the Prince's miniature was only undertaken after the end of the affair: 'The *Perdita* constantly wears the portrait of the *Princely Florizel* richly ornamented with brilliants, set in a peculiar and elegant stile.'[39] A week later her dress sense seemed to let her down for once. She appeared in a gaudy French outfit rather than the simple dress in which she was seen to best advantage: 'The Corke-Street Enchantress has adopted the mistaken notion of *Frenchifying* herself, and now dresses after the Parisian mode. She should leave Gallic *art* to the *old* and *hagged*; and while possessed of *nature*, beauty and *elegance*, disdain the borrowed trappings, only necessary to declining age, and *wrinkled* deformity.'[40]

Her mind had indeed turned to France. In mid-October she left England for the first time, accompanied only by her little daughter and 'a necessary suite of domestics'.[41] She was heading for Paris, via Margate and Ostend. Grace Dalrymple threw a party to celebrate her departure: 'A Correspondent says that *Dally the Tall* gave a superb *fete* last night at her house near Tyburn Turnpike, in consequence of the *Perdita's* departure for the Continent, whose superior charms have long been the daily subject of *Dally's* envy and abuse.'[42] Ten days later there was a rumour that the Gainsborough portrait was going to follow her across the Channel, reversing the customary etiquette whereby a picture was sent 'by way of flattering preludio to the arrival of the fair original' – 'here it is reversed, from a conviction that the claims of *Perdita* are such as stand in no need of a *false impression*!'[43] She would be feted as a heroine in the country that was still engaged in military skirmishes with the British. The Prince may have thought that he had got rid of her, but safe in Mary's keeping was his bond for £20,000.

CHAPTER 12

Perdita and Marie Antoinette

> To desert her country, to fly like a wretched fugitive, or to become a victim to malice and swell the triumph of her enemies, were the only alternatives that seemed to present themselves. Flight was humiliating and dreadful; but to remain in England was impracticable. The terrors and struggles of her mind, became almost intolerable, and nearly deprived her of her reason.
>
> Maria Elizabeth Robinson, 'Continuation' of her mother's *Memoirs*

Mary crossed the English Channel with letters of introduction to various respectable French families and also to Sir John Lambert, the resident English banker in Paris. She planned to stay for two months. Sir John procured her an apartment, a rental carriage, and a box at the opera. Parties were held in her honour, she cut a figure at '*spectacles* and places of public entertainment', and 'a brilliant assemblage of illustrious visitors failed not to grace at the opera the box of *la belle Angloise*'.[1]

Lambert was notorious for combining the cordiality of the English character with the stylishness of the French. He introduced Mary to Philippe, Duke of Chartres, the future Duke of Orléans, a cousin of King Louis XVI. Reputedly the richest man in Europe, he was a politician, an Anglophile, and a rake who was said to have a harem of concubines. He was always beautifully dressed and was rated the best dancer at court, though he had a reputation for cowardice, having once left the scene of a battle in order to return to the opera in Paris. A few months thereafter, when ogling the beauties at a ball, he described one unfortunate lady as 'faded'. She overheard him and replied 'Like your reputation, Monseigneur.'[2]

The papers back in London kept Mary's fans abreast of her latest conquests: 'She was much admired at the French Opera, and never appeared there without drawing his Royal Highness the Duke of *Chartres*, and several other leading men of fashion into her box, who it seems had been previously introduced to her by Sir John Lambert, her banker.'[3] The Duke quickly let it be known that he was determined to have Mrs Robinson. She was resolute in her resistance, despite his elaborate attempts at seduction. Maria Elizabeth Robinson takes up the story in a section of her 'Continuation' to the *Memoirs* that was almost certainly based on an unpublished manuscript by Mary entitled 'Anecdotes of distinguished Personages and Observations on Society and Manners, during her Travels on the Continent and in England':

> The most enchanting *fêtes* were given at Mousseau, a villa belonging to the Duke of Orleans near Paris, at which Mrs Robinson invariably declined to appear. Brilliant races *à l'Angloise* were exhibited on the plains *des Sablons*, to captivate the attention of the inexorable *Angloise*. On the birthday of Mrs Robinson a new effort was made to subdue her aversion and to obtain her regard. A rural *fête* was appointed in the gardens of Mousseau, when this beautiful *Pandaemonium* of splendid profligacy was, at an unusual expense, decorated with boundless luxury.
>
> In the evening, amidst a magnificent illumination, every tree displayed the initials of *la belle Angloise*, composed of coloured lamps, interwoven with wreaths of artificial flowers. Politeness compelled Mrs Robinson to grace with her presence a *fête* instituted to her honour. She, however, took the precaution of selecting for her companion a German lady, then resident at Paris, while the venerable chevalier Lambert attended them as a *chaperon*.[4]

On her first outings in London society while still a teenager, Mary had gazed with wonder on the coloured lights spangling the trees of Vauxhall Gardens. Now the richest man in Europe was illuminating the trees in his vast and elaborate gardens with her own initials. And yet she did not give in to him. After her affair with the future King of England, it would take something other than aristocratic ostentation to impress her.

A few days after this extraordinary birthday tribute, Mary saw Marie Antoinette. The Queen had at last given birth to an heir (the Dauphin) just over a month before. Soon after Mary's birthday, the Queen was due to dine in public at Versailles for the first time since her confinement. The Duke of Chartres brought Mary a message announcing that the Queen wished *la belle Angloise* to be there.* Mary immediately began to plan her outfit for the occasion. She hired the services of the royal couturier Mademoiselle Rose Bertin, who had dressed the Queen for her coronation and ever since then was rumoured to have visited Marie Antoinette's private apartments twice every week (more often even than the hairdresser, who was only summoned once a week). Bertin was notorious for her arrogance, especially in her shop in the rue de Saint-Honoré, once she had become famous as the Queen's designer. One lady came from the provinces to ask for a dress for her presentation at court, Bertin looked her up and down and then turned to one of her helpers with the words, 'Show Madame my latest work for her Majesty.' Bertin was nicknamed the 'Minister of Fashion',[5] and specialized in gowns in the pale colours that the Queen loved, powder blue, green, and soft yellow; she also loved gauzy flowing fabrics. Mary Robinson, however, was not intimidated by her and ordered a dress of pale green silk with a tiffany petticoat, festooned with delicate lilacs. She wore a magnificent headdress of white feathers, and, in tribute to the Queen and the fashion of the court, she stained her cheeks with the deepest rouge.

The royal diners were protected from the public by a crimson cord drawn across an alcove in the palace. As soon as Mary arrived, the Duke of Chartres left the King's side (where he was then in waiting) and procured her a place where she could be seen by the Queen. 'The *grand couvert*, at which the King acquitted himself with more alacrity than grace, afforded a magnificent display of epicurean luxury,' observed Mary. His Majesty was notoriously greedy. The Queen, meanwhile, ate nothing.

* So it is claimed in the 'Continuation' of the *Memoirs*, though Mary's own 'Anecdotes of the Late Queen of France', published five months before her death, says more modestly that she was 'induced by curiosity to attend at one of the public dinners of Versailles' (*Monthly Magazine*, August 1800).

'The slender crimson cord, which drew a line of separation between the royal epicures and the gazing plebeians, was at the distance but of a few feet from the table. A small space divided the Queen from Mrs Robinson, whom the constant observation and loudly whispered encomiums of her Majesty most oppressively flattered.'[6] As the Queen moved to draw on her gloves, she noticed that Mary was looking with admiration at her 'white and polished arms', and she immediately uncovered them again and leaned for a moment on her hand, so that Mary could gaze on her at will. Mary noticed that Marie Antoinette was, in turn, looking with particular attention at her bosom, which bore the miniature of the Prince of Wales.

The very next day the Duke of Chartres arrived at Mary's apartment with a special commission from the Queen for a loan of the miniature. When the Duke returned the picture he gave Mary an exquisite netted purse, a gift from her Majesty. Many years later, after Marie Antoinette had been guillotined, Mary wrote a Monody 'on the Death of the Queen of France':

> Oh! I have seen her, like a sun, sublime,
> Diffusing glory on the wings of Time:
> And, as revolving seasons own his flight,
> Marking each brilliant minute with delight.[7]

According to the unpublished testimony of Jane Porter, a close friend of Mary, the French Queen developed an intimate relationship with *la belle Angloise*. Porter claims that during her residence in Paris, 'when her loveliness shone in its brightest perfection',

> instead of receiving the Nobles of the French Court, who all crowded to pay her homage, she secluded herself within her closet; and for hours, and days, and weeks, has remained there, studying how to become wiser and better. At this time, (and every Englishman who was then at Paris, must know it;) her society was sought by the first literary characters, male and female, in that country. Even Antoinette herself used to say, 'Send for the lovely Mrs Robinson. Let me look at her again, and hear her speak, before I go to sleep!'[8]

The Fleet Prison where Mary and her husband were imprisoned for debt when she was a teenage bride.

George IV as Prince of Wales: the miniature by Jeremiah Meyer that was copied for Mary and kept by her till her dying day.

David Garrick, who launched Mary's theatrical career.

Theatre Royal, Drury Lane, as seen from the stage where Mary made her debut in 1776.

Mary Robinson by George Romney, 1781

Mary Robinson by Thomas Gainsborough, 1782.

Mary Robinson by Sir Joshua Reynolds, 1782.

Marie Antoinette in a white muslin dress of the kind that Mary was the first to popularize in England.

Colonel Banastre Tarleton by Sir Joshua Reynolds, 1782.

'The Thunderer': caricature of Tarleton, in the pose of the Reynolds portrait, by James Gillray; Mary, in the pose of the Romney portrait, is impaled above the inn sign.

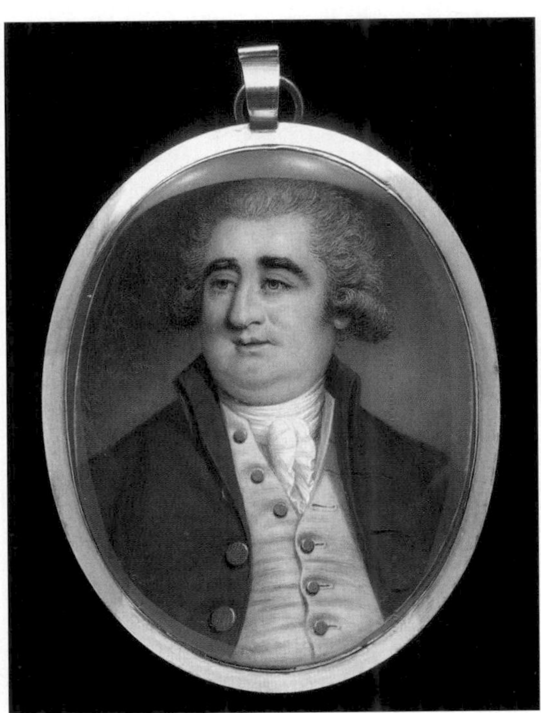

Charles James Fox:
politician, lover, friend.

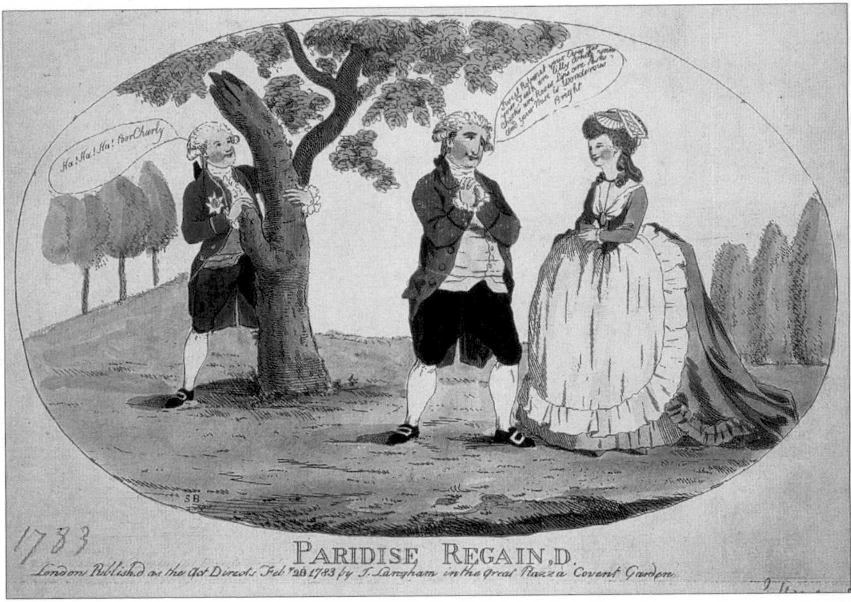
Ha! Ha! Ha! Poor Charly
Sweet Robinet your Eyes Jet
your Teeth are Lilly white your
Cheeks are Roses Lips are Ruby,
and your Nose is Wonderous
Bright
SB
1783
PARIDISE REGAIN,D.
London Publish,d as the Act Directs Feb 20 1783 by J. Langham in the Great Piazza Covent Garden

'Paridise Regain'd': caricature of Mrs Robinson, Fox and the Prince by James Gillray.

Mary Robinson by Sir Joshua Reynolds, second portrait, 1783.

Thomas Rowlandson, a fashionable gathering in Vauxhall Pleasure Gardens; Mary is flanked by the Prince of Wales and her (very short) husband Thomas Robinson.

John Hoppner's later portrait of Mary, circa 1796. There is some uncertainty over both attribution and sitter.

Here Mary is represented not only as a beautiful face but also as a cultivated mind and a mesmerizing voice. The impression is given that Marie Antoinette, who was well known for her extremely intense female friendships, has fallen half in love with her. The only problem with the story is that Mary returned to England about three weeks after her first meeting with Antoinette, so it is difficult to imagine that there was time for many nocturnal encounters.

Though Mary refused the Duke of Chartres, she was unable to resist his dashing friend the Duke of Lauzun. Armand Louis de Gontaut (later Biron) was a soldier and a philanderer. He had got into trouble over a misunderstanding with Marie Antoinette. She had admired his plume of white heron's feathers, and when he was told about her admiration he sent it to her with his compliments. As a courtesy, Antoinette wore it herself. Lauzun took this as an invitation to make a pass at her, but found himself rudely rebuffed. His memoirs suggested that the Queen was smitten with him, but they were generally regarded as a self-serving and unreliable source. Mary's *Memoirs* dismiss Lauzun as a disgrace to human nature on account of his vices, whilst at the same time acknowledging that 'the elegance of his manners rendered him a model to his contemporaries'.[9] Lauzun's memoirs, by contrast, claim that he had a brief affair with her:

> She was gay, lively, open, and a good creature; she did not speak French; I was an object to excite her fancy, a man who had brought home great tidings, who came from the war, who was returning there immediately; he had suffered greatly, he would suffer more still. She felt that she could not do too much for him; and so I enjoyed Perdita, and did not conceal my success from Madame de Coigny.[10]

The war to which he refers here was the American War of Independence. The tidings he had brought home were the news that a combined French and American army had defeated the British under Lord Cornwallis at Yorktown. Soon Mary would meet the most famous British soldier from that same campaign, a Colonel who had actually engaged in hand-to-hand combat with Lauzun (and later became friends with him).

Madame de Coigny was the woman with whom Lauzun was most

obsessed. His affair with Perdita caused a rift between him and three of his other mistresses, but he managed to remain on good terms with de Coigny despite the fact that his farewell to Mary caused him to miss a dinner engagement with her:

> Perdita left for England, and was so insistent that I should accompany her as far as Calais, that I could not refuse. It was a great sacrifice, for that very day I was engaged to dine at Madame de Gontaut's with Madame de Coigny; I wrote to Madame de Coigny to say that I was prevented from dining with her; and seized this singular occasion to assure her that I adored her, and should continue, whatever might befall, to adore her all my life.[11]

Mary made no mention of her noble companion on the road to Calais. There is no record of her feelings about being a mere distraction from Lauzun's true passion. She did, however, publish memoirs of both him and the Duke of Chartres in the last year of her life. Her account of Lauzun there was much more generous than that in the *Memoirs*.

'Perhaps in the pages of biography there never has appeared a more romantic or amiable character than that which was exhibited by this unfortunate nobleman,' she began her short life of Lauzun. She described how he was the idol of the women and the example for the men at the most polished court in Europe, how he was an Anglophile, a man of exquisite sensibility, an admirer of literature and fine arts. She recalled his residence in Pall Mall and his 'Platonic attachment' to a married lady, contrasting this to the marriage alliance into which he was forced by his family. She then told of his military triumphs in America – though without mentioning that he fought against her own lover Colonel Tarleton – and of how he was the man who was dispatched to Versailles with news of the triumph at Yorktown, at a time when she herself ('the writer of these pages') was in Paris. She fondly remembered his 'small villa at *Mont-rouge*' just outside the capital, fitted up in the English style and staffed with English domestics. She noted at this point that the Duke of Chartres' 'fairy palace of *Mouceau*', where she had been entertained so lavishly, was also 'inhabited by English domestics'.

Always acutely aware of reversals of fortune, Mary observed that Versailles was the temple of delight and Lauzun the hero of the day: 'His name was re-echoed by all ranks of people; and the surrender of York-Town was considered as the most promising event which had been recorded on the annals of the American war.' But the French people, particularly those who were blinded by courtly splendour, did not foresee that those 'who by their valour had contributed towards the establishment of liberty in America, would scarcely permit the ardent effects which it produced to lie dormant in their bosoms'.[12] The irony of history was that the Duke who had joined Lafayette in assisting the Americans in their revolution eventually became a victim of his own people's revolution: he took command of the Army in the Vendée during the anarchy of the early 1790s, where he 'hourly received accounts of massacres and horrors', but was then recalled to Paris, imprisoned, and executed by the Jacobins.

'Here let the sensible reader bestow a tear,' Mary concluded, 'while reflection shews the progress of [Lauzun's] fall from power to degradation; from the most splendid altitudes of fame and fortune, to the gloomy platform of the guillotine!' This was written at a time when she had undergone her own, albeit lesser, degradation from celebrity and temporary affluence to disability and neglect.

Her 'Anecdotes' of the Duke of Chartres ('by one who knew him intimately') emphasized the vicissitudes of his relationship with Marie Antoinette, his affair with Dally the Tall, and his path from 'the brilliant hemisphere' to the guillotine as 'the despotism of the French government' led to revolution, only for '*Egalité*'s revenge' to turn to bloody 'rancour'. For the mature Mary, Chartres epitomized the simultaneous allure and repulsion of the aristocracy. He had a fine figure, a constant smile, perfect manners, and great wit, yet 'under the specious semblance of a gay and fascinating exterior, he concealed an imagination at once bold, fertile, and ambitious'. Taken all in all, 'this extraordinary and daring personage presented, in his rapid descent from rank and fortune to the platform of a guillotine, perhaps the most singular compound of ambition and degradation, vanity and folly, courage and audacity, that ever marked the tablet of a chequered fortune'.[13]

News of Mary's Gallic triumph soon reached England. '*Dally the Tall*,' reported the *Morning Herald* with relish, 'is said to be dangerously ill; her indisposition is attributed to the *dreadful shocks* which convulsed her whole Frame, on hearing of the reception the *Perdita* met with among the Parisian nobility, who so cruelly disregarded *Dally*.'[14] The Prince was still intimate with Dally, but the *Morning Herald* took the view that she would not be able to withstand the reappearance of the lost one: 'The expected arrival of the *Perdita* from Paris has planted an agonizing thorn in the pillow of *Dally the Tall*, who has declared to her unsuccessful *Puff in Ordinary*, that she is determined upon quitting the Kingdom the moment she is assured of her rival's return.'[15] The advance word on Perdita was that she would be returning with 'such a train of first rate fashions that cannot fail to set the whole world "a madding"'.[16] Dally did, however, have a powerful retaliation: the day before Christmas it was revealed that she was pregnant. The Prince denied that he was the father, but when the baby was born the following March she was pointedly christened Georgiana.

Mary arrived back in London 'in perfect health and beauty' the day after Christmas.[17] On New Year's Day 1782 the *Morning Herald* reported that she had brought with her a silk in a hitherto unknown shade of grey and brown, which was 'at present kept a profound secret' but which 'promises soon to become the *rage!*'[18] She made her first public appearance early in the New Year, taking her place in a prominent box at the opera. The *Morning Herald* said that she was looking 'supremely beautiful' in a headdress that set the '*standard of taste*' – a cap of white and purple feathers entwined with flowers and fastened with diamond pins. Her gown was of white satin with purple breast bows, but it was the locket that drew most attention: 'Upon her breast she wore no *cross*, but the *image of a Royal Martyr*, over which *waved a brilliant plume*; and still above, far more refulgent, "*two lovely eyes* shot forth a lustre that seemed to give animation to the *picture*".' After the end of the performance 'she remained some time deliberating upon which box she should engage; and kept a considerable part of the audience in the house much beyond the usual time of departure'.[19]

The public were not disappointed by the clothes that Mary brought back from Paris. The fashionable world, as predicted by the *Morning Herald*, was indeed set 'a madding'. Mary now cemented her reputation as a highly prominent fashion icon; the details of her clothes were covered in loving and minute detail in the *bon ton* sections of the daily and monthly press: 'Perdita was now the envy of every female heart: her chariot, her phaeton, her dress, her every thing, was equally the subject of censure and imitation; and every new gown set the giddy circle in an uproar.'[20] She caused envy among the upper classes, while the lower classes were inspired to emulate her. In the words of one modern commentator, 'Robinson's glamorous appearance further initiated a new trend in fashion reporting in English periodicals: her dresses were reproduced with the loving care of a *couturier*. Every masquerade, party at Ranelagh or the Pantheon, or public occasion saw lengthy descriptions of Robinson's clothes, often to the exclusion of those of others, who were dismissed with a curt sentence or two.'[21]

Whereas many courtesans were discussed in terms of their looks alone, Mary was also praised for her brilliant wit. Even the scandalmongering author of the anonymous *Memoirs of Perdita* acknowledged her good judgement in the art of repartee: 'You, who doubtless have seen her person, know that her deportment is elegant, and to sprightliness of wit, she joins a share of levity, that attracts, rather than disgusts, because it is not carried to the excess that constitutes the affectation of wantonness.'[22] It was her verbal skills that placed her in a league apart from the 'Cyprian corps' and gave the opportunity to reinvent herself as a woman of letters after the accident that terminated her career as a fashionable beauty. Her sparkling tongue was matched by her sparkling eye, suggested the author of a *Morning Herald* article on wit: 'The *wit* of the *eye*. I have seen an eye full of rhetoric and elocution full of invitations and forbiddings. – I have spoken to a woman with an eye of such *wit* that has struck me *dumb* with a repartee flash, without the assistance of a single word. – Look at *Mrs Robinson's eyes!*'[23]

Mary continued to intrigue the press in the months after her return from Paris. In February she broke her shin and in March she suffered from the flu. In April her eyes were the talk of the town when her portrait was exhibited at the Royal Academy. So it was that, paradoxically, she reached the height of her celebrity and popularity after the affair with the Prince had ended. Far from being abashed and humiliated, she returned from France more resplendent than ever, given new glamour by the latest Paris fashions and renewed confidence as a result of Marie Antoinette's praises. But she was not the only celebrity in town. She had to share her fame with a dashing young dragoon who had just returned from the American wars.

* * *

Mary knew all about Colonel Banastre Tarleton and his reputation as a bold and fearless soldier. Tarleton's adventures in the American Revolution had been followed avidly by the newspapers. He was born in 1754 into a wealthy Liverpool merchant family who had made their fortune in sugar and slaves. He was intelligent, athletic, educated at Oxford, then trained for the law in the Middle Temple. He suspended his studies when his father died, leaving him an inheritance of £5,000. In less than a year he had spent the money, mostly at the Cocoa Tree, one of London's most popular gaming houses.

The military offered a way out for young men in such straits, and in April 1775 he persuaded his mother to buy him a commission in the King's Cavalry. Early the next year, he volunteered for service in America, where he soon attracted the attention of his superiors by his valour and enterprise. He was swiftly promoted to the rank of Lieutenant Colonel. His regiment was the newly-formed British Legion, which consisted mainly of American loyalists from New York and Pennsylvania. Their uniform was a dashing green jacket; it signified that they were a Tory regiment. Tarleton was a highly skilled horseman, auburn-haired, and of fiery temperament, stocky, muscular, and rather below middling height. A contemporary described him as 'a perfect model of manly strength and vigour': 'Without a particle of superfluous flesh, his rounded limbs and full broad chest seemed molded from iron, yet, at the same time, displaying all the elasticity which usually accompanies elegance of proportion.'[24] He loved to gamble, could tame a wild stallion, and was a well-known womanizer. His family frequently had to help him out of debt. He was a keen playgoer who took part in army theatricals to raise money for war widows.

Despite his arrogance, Tarleton was popular with his men. He believed that attack was the only form of defence, advocating rapid movement of the lines and full-frontal assault on the battlefield. Tactful coalition building with the resident loyalists of the Carolinas was not his strong point. He was the prime mover in the recovery of Charleston from the rebels in the early summer of 1780. He then pursued a regiment of Virginian Continentals to a settlement called the Waxhaws on the border of North and South Carolina. Though outnumbered two to one, Tarleton's dragoons went in so hard that the Americans soon raised a surrender flag. By Tarleton's own account, his horse was then shot and he was pinned beneath it. His men, assuming that their commander had been shot after the flag of truce had gone up, took revenge by hacking at the wounded survivors lying on the ground. The Patriot version of events was that Tarleton ordered a massacre because he could not be bothered to take prisoners. This encounter earned him his nicknames 'Bloody Tarleton' and 'Butcher Tarleton'. He became the figure most hated by the American patriots, who would rally to the cry 'Tarleton's Quarter' and use his example as justification for committing atrocities of their own.

His commander, Lord Cornwallis, never questioned his tactics and indeed used him and the British Legion as shock troops to demoralize Patriot resistance. During the ferociously fought Guilford Courthouse battle in March 1781, he lost two of his fingers when he took a bullet in his right hand. He often narrowly escaped death in battle and had serious bouts of malaria or yellow fever. When Cornwallis finally surrendered the entire British Army at Yorktown on 19 October 1781, the day after Mary set off from London for France, the Butcher was snubbed by French and American officers, and not invited to the post-war round of dinner parties. But as far as the British public back home were concerned, Tarleton was the one romantic figure in a drawn-out, dirty, disappointing war. When he returned to his native Liverpool in January 1782, he was given a hero's welcome. He then went down to London to bask in his glory. He was introduced to the Prince of Wales and Duke of Cumberland, and he embarked on a social whirl, with ladies swooning at the sight of his green tunic and mangled hand. His helmet, adorned with swan's feathers, took on the same notoriety as Mary Robinson's Parisian hats.

CHAPTER 13

A Meeting in the Studio

My Portrait you desire! and why?
Mary Robinson, 'Stanzas to a Friend, who desired to have my Portrait'

Some years ago arose this wondrous man,
From gaming tables, politics to scan . . .
Thus, in all politics, is he so winning!
An adept too in other modes of sinning;
Indiff'rently he taketh to his bed
Hackney'd Perdita, or old tough A—st—d!
'The Right Honourable C.J.F**' by a Moonraker[1]

In 1760, Joshua Reynolds bought the house in Leicester Fields (now Leicester Square) where he was to reside for the remainder of his life. Eight years later, the Royal Academy of Arts was founded and Reynolds elected its first President. He was knighted and for twenty years was the arbiter of artistic taste. Reynolds was to become one of Mary's most devoted and loyal friends. She regarded him as the greatest artist of the age and wrote in praise of him in her first major poem, *Ainsi va le Monde*:

Reynolds, 'tis thine with magic skill to trace
The perfect semblance of exterior grace;
Thy hand, by Nature guided, marks the line
That stamps perfection on the form divine.
'Tis thine to tint the lip with rosy die,
To paint the softness of the melting eye;
With auburn curls luxuriantly display'd,
The ivory shoulders polish'd fall to shade;
To deck the well-turn'd arm with matchless grace,
To mark the dimpled smile on Beauty's face:
The task is thine, with cunning hand to throw
The veil transparent on the breast of snow:
The Statesman's thought, the Infant's cherub mien,
The Poet's fire, the Matron's eye serene,
Alike with animated lustre shine
Beneath thy polish'd pencil's touch divine.
As Britain's Genius glories in thy Art,
Adores thy virtues, and reveres thy heart,
Nations unborn shall celebrate thy name,
And waft thy mem'ry on the wings of Fame.[2]

These lines are shaped by the memory of sitting for Sir Joshua: the tinted lip, melting eye, auburn curls, dimpled smile, and 'veil transparent on the breast of snow' are Robinson's own. Reynolds, who by the time of this poem was almost blind and rarely left his house, responded with a generous letter:

Dear Madam,
I am quite ashamed of not having returned my thanks before this time for the obliging notice which you have taken of me in your truly excellent poem: it was my intention to have done it in person, though I am not much in the habit of going out. I confess I am surprized at the wonderful facility (or *handling*, as we painters call it), which you have acquired in writing verse, which is generally the result of great practice. Were I to say all I think, even to yourself, it would, I fear, look like flattering; and perhaps to others, as proceeding from the high style in which I

have been bribed. I shall comfort myself therefore with saying, that I hope what you intend to publish will not be inferior to this specimen; if so, you will long remain without an antagonist in the field of poesy.

I am, with great respect,

DEAR MADAM,

Your most humble and most obedient servant,

J. Reynolds.

P.S. The picture is ready, whenever Mr Burke calls for it.[3]

The picture mentioned in the postscript was Reynolds's second major portrait of Mary, from which Thomas Burke took an engraving that formed the frontispiece to her *Poems* of 1791, and several subsequent volumes of her work.

For the first portrait, Reynolds's pocketbook records eleven appointments with Mary, beginning on 25 January 1782. He saw her three times before the end of the month and five times in February, then twice in March, once in April. On three successive appointments – 28 and 30 January, 1 February – another sitter was present in the studio: Lieutenant Colonel Tarleton.

This was a room in which the cream of society mingled. On moving into Leicester Fields Reynolds had built an extension in the form of an octagonal painting room that formed 'a splendid gallery for the exhibition of his works, and a commodious and elegant room for his sitters'.[4] Open house would be held for the viewing of new works and on sitting days three or four subjects were often present simultaneously – Mary also coincided with the chubby-cheeked 4-year-old George Brummell – Beau Brummell, as he was to become known. Perhaps it was his 'Infant's cherub mien' that Mary remembered in her lines on Sir Joshua. The centrepiece of the room, where Mary would have taken her place, was the sitter's chair or 'throne' raised 18 inches above the floor and on casters for ease of movement. Sir Joshua himself never sat when painting, but stood at his favourite mahogany easel. A screen covered in red and yellow reflected light on the sitter's face, while a mirror was arranged so that the sitter could observe him at work on the canvas. He had an extensive collection of clothes and props for his sitters, including a pet macaw that had the run of the house. Mary and Banastre brought along their own dashing

Colonel Tarleton.

trademark garments. There is always a peculiar intensity in the encounter between portrait painter and sitter. On the day that Mrs Robinson and Colonel Tarleton met, the atmosphere must have been electric.

In the Royal Academy show that April Reynolds exhibited them both: Mary as number 22, *Portrait of a Lady*, and Tarleton as number 139, *Portrait of an Officer*. The Colonel is portrayed wearing his trademark boots with overturns, tan trousers, and green coat with white edging, though the feathers in his cap are black instead of the customary white swan's. The stumps of the two fingers that he had lost in battle are clearly visible. He is posed as if in the midst of battle, coolly adjusting his sword and thereby – in a classical allusion typical of Reynolds – assuming an attitude reminiscent of an antique statue that was believed to represent the Roman warrior Cincinnatus. This may be a subtle gesture of defiance on Reynolds's part, since Tarleton's antagonist George Washington had become known as the Cincinnatus of the Americans. The head of the Colonel's horse is visible at the edge of the painting. The noble beast itself may have sat – or rather stood – for Sir Joshua on 11 April. The painting is now hung in the rotunda of the east wing of the National Gallery in London.

Romney's Mary Robinson, in her Quaker habit, retained some of the innocence of a girl. Gainsborough's, with the dog, portrayed a wronged woman. Reynolds for his part offers the *Portrait of a Lady*. She is in the pose of Rubens's wife, a prototype often employed by eighteenth-century British artists. Her dress is of dark blue silk with a low-cut neck and a wide embroidered collar. Her sweeping, wide-brimmed hat, with ostrich feathers, is set over powdered curls. Her blue eyes and dimples are prominent, and there is a thin black ribbon round her neck, setting off the whiteness of her neck and bosom.

The painting remained in Reynolds's studio until his death. This may mean that it was commissioned but not paid for (conceivably by Malden, which would have been ironic given that the meetings in the studio threw Mary into the arms of a new lover). An alternative possibility is that – like the Romney – this portrait was undertaken not as a commission but as a mutual publicity deal, with the intention that it should remain in the studio as a showpiece. Its presence there meant that it could readily be copied: it was engraved several times over and copies in oils were made by other artists, including John Hoppner, George Romney, and an anonymous miniaturist. Mary's image was a commodity in great demand: the Witt Library in London now holds photographs or descriptions of about seventy paintings of her. She was in all probability the most frequently painted female subject of the age. Her most celebrated sittings were for Reynolds, Gainsborough, and Romney, but there are also portraits of her by an array of lesser artists including Richard Cosway, John Downman, George Engleheart, and Jeremiah Meyer the miniaturists, in addition to William Grimaldi, Thomas Lawrence, William Owen, and many others.[5] Several of these artists were pupils of Sir Joshua and there is no doubt that the 1782 portrait that hung in his studio served as a template for many other images of Mary. The original portrait is now in the Rothschild Collection at Waddesdon Manor in Buckinghamshire.

When the Reynolds portrait was exhibited, a leading newspaper critic found 'the countenance grave and sensible, the likeness very strong, and the colouring correct'. The critic's only complaint was that the artist had 'not done so much on the score of beauty, as the Fair original has a claim to'.[6] This viewer was not alone in feeling that, for all the painting's force and elegance, it does not quite catch Mary's warmth and beauty. For James Northcote, Sir Joshua's pupil and first biographer, no artist could do justice to Mrs Robinson, not even his master. Talking to a fellow painter, after Reynolds's death, Northcote described Sir Joshua's two portraits of Mary as 'complete failures' because 'the extreme beauty' of the sitter was 'quite beyond [his] power[s]'. Northcote recalled Mrs Robinson, late in her life, when she was very ill and had to be borne upstairs by two men. 'Even then,' he said, 'I thought her remarkably beautiful. Now I think no man could have painted her.'[7] Northcote was a good friend to Mary in her final years; his own portrait of her is, unfortunately, lost.

Reynolds was acutely aware of the commercial potential that followed from the huge expansion of the market for engraved prints in the late eighteenth century. He sometimes painted famous beauties and actresses specifically with a view to the reproductions that would be made from them. It may not be by chance that his painting of Perdita employs a high proportion of black and white: this meant that it would translate well to the monochrome medium of engraving. A stipple engraving by William Dickinson, published in the summer of 1782, duly circulated in very large numbers. The very pose in which Mary sat became influential: Edward Burney copied it, in mirror image, for his portrait of his cousin, the novelist Fanny Burney.

Familiarity with Reynolds's portraits did not depend only on fine mezzotints; cheaper copies could be had for sixpence plain or one shilling coloured. A print seller's catalogue of 1784 noted that a variety of choice examples were always kept ready framed and glazed, available at the lowest prices. Reductions of Reynolds's images were also made for biographies and frontispiece portraits of authors. Prints after Reynolds were even available as household objects: his portrait of Tarleton appeared on a transfer-printed milk jug and some of his portraits of female figures were copied onto fans. His Kitty Fisher was miniaturized in a print to decorate a watchcase. There was, then, a fluid interchange between high art and low. Reynolds's originals were crowd pullers, both in his studio and at the annual Royal Academy exhibitions at Somerset House in the Strand. At the same time, shoppers could sift through a vast stock of engraved images in the print shops – and laugh at the caricatures displayed in the windows.

Portrait prints and caricatures catered in different ways for the public's avid interest in political faction, sexual scandal, and literary controversy. The reputation of a public man or woman might be enhanced by the idealization of a Reynolds portrait, but could equally fall victim to detraction and ridicule. In Robinson's second novel, *The Widow*, one of the dissipated fine ladies of fashion, Mrs Vernon, remarks to her friend, on the subject of her husband: 'leave him in the country, if you have any desire not to be caricatured in all the print-shops'.[8]

Caricatures frequently alluded knowingly to the postures of popular portraits. The images of Mary that began to appear in print-shop windows gave satirical illustrators every opportunity to capitalize on a ready market for images lampooning the current politicians, royals, and actresses. As will be seen, she received more than her fair share as she continued to scandalize with her colourful love life and mingled with controversial figures such as the politician Charles James Fox.

Perhaps the loveliest of the many portraits of Mary is by John Hoppner (who painted her several times). Hoppner was a figure to whom Mary would have felt very sympathetic. Reynolds, Gainsborough, and Romney were older men; Sir Joshua in particular became a father figure for Mary, just as Garrick had been. Hoppner, by contrast, was about the same age as her and, like her, he used his talents to gain access to a world far above his lowly status. A boy of German origins, he became a chorister in the royal chapel and showed such promise as an artist that the King paid for his training. Rather as Mary never denied the rumours that she was the illegitimate daughter of Lord Chancellor Northington, Hoppner encouraged the rumour that he was the illegitimate son of the King himself. He became known as the Prince of Wales's painter and his house off St James's Square, where he entertained with his American wife (who was also an artist), became a centre of fashionable society. He developed a well-deserved reputation for flattering his female sitters. The catalogue of his works reads like a register of the late Georgian beau monde, from the royal family downward.

The Hoppner portrait now at Chawton House in Hampshire was in the early twentieth century a trophy of William Randolph Hearst, the original for Orson Welles's Citizen Kane. It is not known when it was painted or by whom it was commissioned. It is half-length with Mary looking at the spectator. She wears a greyish low-cut dress (could it be the silk in a hitherto unknown shade which she brought back from Paris, initially 'kept a profound secret' and then made 'the *rage*'?). It is trimmed with white satin that highlights her creamy half-exposed breasts. She has white cuffs and a large white feather on her spectacular felt hat, which has a gorgeous diamond buckle in front. Her powdered hair falls over her neck; her luminous skin tones are set against a red curtain, a backdrop that may be influenced by the Reynolds portrait. Eighteenth-century art theory proposed that harmonious proportion was best achieved by imagining a triangle inside the rectangle of a portrait frame. At the apex of Hoppner's triangle, mesmerizing the spectator, are '*Mrs Robinson's eyes*'.

In the public eye, Mary was still associated with the Prince of Wales. It was reported that she had obtained a corner box at the opera 'from whence she *angularly* darts the artillery of her eyes against a certain *Royal breast-work*, and that with so much skill, that it is generally conceived she will be able to make *another breach* in it before the close of the season, and march in with all the *honors of love!*'[9] She was making herself highly visible in London society once again: on one occasion, she was spotted simply sitting in her stationary carriage in fashionable St James's, watching and being watched.

When Mary Robinson and Banastre Tarleton coincided in Sir Joshua Reynolds's studio on 28 January 1782, it may not have been their first meeting. The previous Thursday night there had been a brilliant midwinter masquerade at the King's Theatre. The auditorium was festooned with parti-coloured lamps and the upper tier of boxes was elaborately draped with garlands and bows. By half past midnight the place was crowded, though only a few were in fancy dress. The 'beautiful Perdita' was one of them. Dressed in a black domino, 'she did not unmask the whole evening; but there was just enough of her face seen, to make the rest wished for'. One of the few other people in fancy dress was Colonel Tarleton. He was also in a domino, but wore no visor. At one point in the evening, he was addressed by an unknown domino and replied: 'Sir, let me see your face. I fight in *open day*, and you attack me from a masked battery!'[10] Mary does not appear to have been cross-dressed that night, so this was probably not her, but since she and Tarleton were the most famous recently returned travellers in the theatre that night, it is highly likely that someone pointed them out to each other.

It is testimony to Mary's energy that, having danced through the night, she sat for Sir Joshua the next day. That was a Friday; it was on the following Monday that she and Tarleton were in the studio together for the first time. They were in the same place again in the evening, when there was another winter ball, this time at the Pantheon. Eight hundred members of the beau monde attended. Entertainment was provided by Signor Delphini the Italian dancer and John Bannister the comic actor. Supper was served at one in the morning: roast fowl, cold beef, and jellied tongue, with port, sherry, madeira, and Rhenish wine. The company danced until six. Colonel Tarleton was present, as were the Prince of Wales and his entourage, but as usual the press paid particular attention to Mary: 'The chief *constellation* of the *pleasurable sphere*, was the lovely *Perdita*, in a domino and mask that did not quite conceal her *dimples*.'[11] There was, however, a tense moment when 'a gentleman, a foreigner, as it is supposed, of some distinction, seeing the *Perdita* on a bench with Lord M—n, sat by her'. His exchange with Mary caused Malden to unmask and invite the gentleman to do likewise. This was the sort of incident that could provoke a duel, but on this occasion Mary succeeded in calming the situation.

It was a couple of months before she and the Colonel became lovers. Through the spring Mary continued to draw attention to her Parisian clothes. She created a new fashion in elaborate muffs:

> The *Cataract Muff* was no sooner exhibited on the arm of *Perdita* than a rivalship in that article of dress was planned. Numberless were the projects that miscarried. At length a genius of the superior order produced the *tablature muff*, whereon some little story of an amorous nature, is generally pencilled, and, like the *muff* itself, the painting is calculated to produce *a glow!* Some have improved on the above *muff*, by having several valves contrived, one under another, in the manner of Chinese looking-glasses, that, when one scene tires, by touching a spring another appears of a more *heightened* nature, by which means the *imagination* is gradually led on to *explore* every *recess* which the *muff* can contain![12]

The sexual connotations of the muff were well known. Even the genteel *Lady's Magazine* carried a story about the mythical origins of the garment.

It was a gift from Venus to keep Adonis warm, but he soon found 'a better application of it': 'In short, he cuddled, and moulded, and tossed and flirted, and branded the new instrument of amour, with so much regularity, and so just meaning, that it was not a month before, as the chronicles of those times relate, the language of the muff became as intelligible as that of the eyes.'[13]

An account of what Mrs Robinson wore became a fixed point in the newspaper reports of social gatherings. At the opera, her hair was 'ornamented with braided *wheat ears* fastened on with *diamond pins*'. On another occasion one of Mademoiselle Bertin's hats, imported especially from Paris, caused a sensation: 'The cap in which the beautiful Perdita has lately appeared is a *chef d'oeuvre* of elegance; it is ornamented with plumes of feathers and a wave of artificial roses, interspersed with various flowers, on a ground of sea green, and is fastened on with brilliant pins.' At another masquerade at the Pantheon (when she did not unmask) she wore a dress of white crape, decorated with festoons of white flowers, and 'was much admired for the elegant simplicity of her dress'.[14] Her carriages were equally prominent: 'The *Perdita* yesterday launched yet another new elegant coach, that far eclipses all the various equipages of the *bon ton*; it is a puce-coloured ground, lined with white satin, and curtains of the same, trimmed with broad silver fringe: the most invidious of her sex must allow, that she has displayed a supreme taste in the tout ensemble of this elegant vehicle.'[15] Sometimes the dress would be designed to match the carriage and sometimes vice versa.

In March 1782 it was announced that the forthcoming annual Royal Academy exhibition would include no fewer than four portraits of Perdita: full-lengths by Reynolds and Gainsborough, and two miniatures by Richard Cosway. Mary was painted several times by Cosway and his wife Maria, who had recently moved into the house next door to Gainsborough's studio on Pall Mall after its previous occupant, Dr James Graham (he of the celestial bed), had been forced to leave due to debt. The Cosways filled the house with paintings, held numerous society parties, and established a garden and greenhouse on the roof of the building.

The *Morning Herald* gushed that 'The ensuing exhibition at Somerset-house is likely to prove very *Splendid*, it will at least captivate the admirers of *beauty* and *elegance*, for the most distinguished pencils will exhibit the lovely *Perdita*!'[16] Gainsborough was to have six large canvases in the show, among them the Prince of Wales leaning against his horse and full-lengths of both Mrs Robinson and Colonel Tarleton. The *Public Advertiser* soon remarked upon Robinson's high public visibility: 'The *Perdita* has been particularly successful in the commerce of this Year. How immense must have been her *Imports* and *Exports* is cognisable from this one Circumstance: she has sate for her Picture four times, viz. twice to *Romney*, once to *Gainsborough*, and once to *Sir Joshua Reynolds*!'[17] Terms such as 'commerce' and 'exports and imports' are examples of what feminist critics call the commodification of women in the eighteenth century, but Mary Robinson was no passive victim in this regard: few women of the age had as great an understanding as she did of her own selling power. She knew how to manipulate her personal image and harness the insatiable public interest in her private life to her own advantage.

The *Public Advertiser* article went on to compare the different portraits of Mary. It regarded the Reynolds as the best, the Romney as 'second in Point of Merit' and the Gainsborough as 'one of his Few Failures' because it was not a good likeness. Stung by criticism of this kind, Gainsborough withdrew his Perdita from the Royal Academy show. When the annual exhibition opened on 29 April, it was Reynolds's portraits of Mary and Tarleton that were the talking point. The Robinson was widely praised, but the Tarleton drew a mixed response. The satirist John Wolcot, whose pseudonym was Peter Pindar and who later became a very close friend of Mary's, wrote in the first of his *Lyric Odes to Royal Academicians* of 1782 that he was not impressed with 'Tarleton dragging on his boot so tight!' and the distinctly Trojan – which is to say wooden – aspect of the horse.

Tarleton and Mary were observed together at several balls and masquerades in May, but she was officially still living with Lord Malden. They seem to have formed a fashionable threesome, who enjoyed playing pranks on less stylish characters who tried to enter their charmed circle. There is a story that a rake named Pugh, son of an alderman of the City of London, offered twenty guineas for 'ten minutes' conversation' with Mrs Robinson. She consented to grant him the favour he asked, for the sum stipulated. Pugh hurried to her house, anticipating speedy sexual gratification. But instead of being closeted privately with her, as he had expected, he was shown into a room where Mrs Robinson was sitting with Tarleton and

Malden. Mary took her watch from her side and put it on the table. She then turned away from her companions and addressed her conversation entirely to Pugh. For ten minutes. After which she picked up her watch, rang the bell, asked the servant to show out Mr Pugh, and relieved him of his twenty guineas, which on the following day was divided among her four favourite charitable institutions. Tarleton and Malden tittered throughout the ten-minute conversation.[18]

There is no surviving first-hand account of exactly how and when Mary transferred her affections from Malden to Tarleton. The former was her escort at the masquerade on 10 May but by the end of the month the *Morning Herald* was reporting that 'The *Perdita* was lately made *captive* by Lieutenant Colonel Tarleton, – on one of that officer's amorous reconnoitring parties: the consequence of which has proved very unfortunate to the fair one, her noble commander having refused to receive her back, at the hands of her new conqueror!' Her rivals in the demi-monde were said to have received the warmest congratulations on her 'impolitic lapse'.[19]

The scurrilous but well-sourced *Memoirs of Perdita* offered an account that drew upon the well-known fact that Tarleton, Malden, and their circle were all fanatical betting men. Malden had so strong a faith in Perdita's attachment to him that he would not believe that any man could possibly seduce her from his arms. He was always warm in her praise and boastful of her loyalty to him alone. One evening at the St Alban's tavern, in company with the Colonel and others, Malden 'offered to confirm this opinion, by a bet of a thousand guineas'. Tarleton instantly accepted the bet: he would not only win her from Malden, but also jilt her. So it was, claimed the *Memoirs of Perdita*, that, Othello-like, he seduced her with tales of 'the dangers he had undergone, the hair-breadth escapes he had ventured, the toilsome marches he had sustained, the wonders he had seen, and all the strange adventures which fill a soldier's life'. He took her to his bed, only to find that their amorous pleasures were constantly interrupted by callers, so they left London for Barrow-hedges, a small village not far from Epsom, where 'for a full fortnight they enjoyed themselves in an uninterrupted mutual possession, free from the impertinent cares and troubles of the world, strangers to its concerns, and totally occupied in the soft delights of communicating happiness: while every one of their acquaintance were totally ignorant whither they had flown'.[20]

Though there may be a grain of truth in all this, there are at least three problems with the story, quite apart from the way that it makes Mary into a passive agent, which she rarely was. For one thing, the man who wagers his lady's chastity among his male friends in a tavern is as traditional a literary figure as Othello wooing Desdemona – indeed, the plot of Shakespeare's *Cymbeline* turns on just such a bet. The author of the *Memoirs of Perdita* was as influenced by fictional convention as by historical fact. Secondly, the frequency with which the movements of Tarleton and Mrs Robinson were reported around this period was such that a two-week period of 'uninterrupted mutual possession' on the Epsom Downs is most unlikely to have gone unremarked by the newspapers. And, thirdly, the *Memoirs of Perdita* ends the story by saying that Malden paid his bet 'but totally renounced for ever his faithless mistress'. But he did not totally renounce her: he agreed to settle an annuity upon her, though he was very erratic in paying it.

There was fresh drama in early June. The *Morning Herald* reported news of a traffic accident in Hyde Park. A phaeton was driven into Mary's chariot with such violence that it overturned. In the fall she was so dangerously wounded that she was conveyed 'in a state of insensibility' to her house in Berkeley Square. It was noted that 'she was attended by Col. Tarleton when the above circumstance happened'.[21]

The house in Berkeley Square had been established for her by Malden. It was one of the most prestigious addresses in London: a generously laid out square with finely proportioned terraced houses fronted by elaborate wrought-iron railings. One of the properties had been fitted out in Oriental splendour by Clive of India, prior to his suicide in 1774; another was the family home of William Pitt the Younger; another, designed by William Kent, is regarded today as one of the finest Georgian terraced houses still standing anywhere in London.

A follow-up story published three days later claimed that when she was brought home unconscious Malden ensured that she was given the proper medical attention, but then left the house – presumably offended that she had been out driving with Tarleton. A different account was published the next day: far from having returned to her former lord, she was now 'divorced from him' and 'cohabits with her military seducer Col T— at his house in Hill Street'. Then two days after this, an article appeared, possibly at Mary's behest, denying rumours of 'the Perdita's having quitted her residence and attachment in Berkely Square'.[22] By late July, however, the *Morning Herald* was announcing unequivocally that 'The Perdita and her noble lover are now separated forever – it occasioned some convulsive pangs on either side, but at last *les noeuds d'amour* were torn asunder, never to be re-united!'[23] It is not known at what date Malden entered into the arrangement to pay her an annuity.

Some readers were disgusted by the amount of space that the papers devoted to the doings of Mary and other 'demireps'. Thus a letter signed 'Lover of Virtue':

> In what a degree of low scandal is a certain morning paper now held! Whole columns of it filled with Mrs Robinson's *green carriage.* It is of little consequence to the public whether an *impure*, as they are fashionably denominated, drives four ponies or two coach-horses; whether she paints her neck or her cheeks; whether she sports a phaeton or rides in a dung-cart; whether she is accompanied by a peer or a pimp; by a commoner or a bully . . . it sickens a modest woman, and creates belief that *girls of the town* are the whole entertainers of the polite circles in the metropolis. The papers have found out fine names for those prostitutes: they are called the *Cyprian Corps*, the *frail sisterhood*, the *nuns*, the *vestals*, the *impures*, and twenty other pretty names . . . meant as so many umbrellas to shade the infamy of their real appellation – the hired prostitution of the day.[24]

Within a few months of abandoning the aristocrat for the war hero, Mary also became involved with the most prominent and controversial politician in the land. Charles James Fox, the son of a politician, was eight years older than Mary. A drinker, a gambler, and a Member of Parliament since the age of 19, he had made a name for himself by opposing the Royal Marriage Bill and supporting the repeal of the tea duty that was so hated in the colonies across the Atlantic. His support for the American rebels provoked the King to write to the Prime Minister, Lord North, in 1774, 'That young man has so thoroughly cast off every principle of common honour and honesty, that he must become as contemptible as he is odious.'[25]

Over the next few years Fox became widely recognized as the leading figure on the more radical wing of the Whig party (the term 'party' denoted a broad alliance of interests, internally divided by different factions, rather than anything so strictly defined as a modern political party). He earned the title 'the man of the people' and became involved in prolonged infighting with Lord Shelburne, leader of the more moderate Whigs. In terms of public perception, Fox was regarded as the leader of the parliamentary opposition to Lord North's Tory administration. The King thoroughly approved of North, which inevitably threw the Prince into the arms of Fox. They became regular gaming companions at Brooks's Club in St James's. The politician became a kind of anti-father figure to the Prince: dozens of caricatures alluded to the relationship in the terms of Shakespeare's *Henry the Fourth*, representing Fox as Falstaff to the Prince's Hal. Though unshaven and slovenly, with grease spots on his coat, a paunch, a double chin, and beetling eyebrows, Fox was a figure of great charisma, principally because he was a brilliant orator and great wit. He had a reputation for taking a new mistress more frequently than he took a bath.

The loss of the American war precipitated the fall of North's Government in the spring of 1782. An uneasy alliance of Whigs took office, with the old rivals Fox and Shelburne as joint secretaries of state in charge of foreign affairs with responsibility for negotiating peace with America (Shelburne) and France (Fox). They quarrelled about priorities, could not agree, and in July Fox resigned in pique from the Government. He returned to the gaming tables and the company of the Prince of Wales and the Devonshire House set. He began an affair with Mary in July and persuaded her to drop Tarleton. The Colonel seems to have viewed this turn of events with equanimity, to judge from a letter to his brother Thomas (in which he also reveals that he and another of his brothers, John, had previously quarrelled over his relationship with Perdita): 'The seceded Secretary is now my rival with the Lady in whose cause and in defence of whose disinterested conduct John first took umbrage against me. The Fox will not be so fortunate in his association as I am fortunate in separation. I shall ever applaud the Perdita as the most generous woman on earth.'[26] That last sentence could be read in several different ways.

As only to be expected, the press made much of the affair. In the conservative *Morning Post* Fox was criticized for wasting his time and talents 'on the turf, in gaming houses, and sacrifices to the Cyprian

Goddess' while the rising Tory star William Pitt the Younger was studiously employed in qualifying himself for future ministerial greatness.[27] The more gossipy *Morning Herald* preferred to record sightings of Fox and Mary driving around together and to suggest that 'The present intimacy subsisting between the ex-minister and the *Perdita* is said to be perfectly *political* on the part of the lady' – she was supposedly anticipating the day when he would return to high office.[28] Fox reportedly claimed that the reason he was so often seen at Mrs Robinson's house in Berkeley Square was that it commanded a view of Lansdowne House, the residence of his rival Shelburne: 'You know, Sir, I have pledged myself to the *public* to have a strict eye on Lord S—'s motions; this is my sole motive for residing in Berkeley-square, and that you may tell my friends is the reason they have not seen me at *Brookes's*.'[29]

On 20 August a new caricature appeared in the window of Elizabeth D'Achery's print shop in St James's Street, a few doors from Brooks's Club and a few streets from both the home of Mary Robinson and the lodgings of Banastre Tarleton. Entitled 'The Thunderer', it was one of the earliest works of James Gillray, who would become the most brilliant and scabrous caricaturist in English history. The Thunderer is Tarleton: the caricature is a parody of Reynolds's portrait of him, with both posture and dress closely replicated. His crotch, however, is greatly enlarged, in order to suggest that he was physically much better endowed than the Prince.

The Colonel's facial expression has been changed from the alertness and ardour suggested by Reynolds into a contemptuous sneer. He is transposed from the American battlefield to a London tavern. The sign above the door, inscribed 'THE WHIRLIGIG *Alamode Beef, hot every Night*', takes the form of Mary Robinson impaled on a long pole, with legs spread wide apart and completely exposed breasts. A face on the bracket that holds the pole grins lasciviously at the sight of the exposed thighs above her stocking-tops and the delights above. From her mouth comes a speech-bubble saying 'This is the Lad'll kiss most Sweet / Who'd not love a Soldier?' The 'whirligig' was a large cage suspended on a pivot, in which army prostitutes were hoisted for punishment.

Gillray's satirical art relied on a combination of visual and verbal allusion. The posture of Tarleton is that of the Reynolds portrait, while the lines he speaks belong to the worthless adventurer Bobadill in Ben

Jonson's popular comedy *Every Man in his Humour*, who brags about his fictitious exploits in foreign wars and especially about his skill in sword-play. The thundering Tarleton/Bobadill stands beside the vain country gull Stephen, who represents the Prince of Wales, identifiable by the ostrich feathers (his insignia) that replace his head. 'Often in a mere frolic I have challeng'd Twenty of them, kill'd them,' says the Thunderer, 'Challeng'd Twenty more, kill'd them; – Twenty more, kill'd them too; and thus in a day have I kill'd Twenty Score; twenty score, that's two hundred, two hundred a day, five days a thousand; that's – a – Zounds, I can't number them half.' Tarleton was a notorious braggart. Horace Walpole said that he boasted of having butchered more men and lain with more women than anybody else in the Army. To which Sheridan acidly replied, '"Lain with" – what a weak expression! he should have said ravished. Rapes are the relaxation of murderers!'[30]

Gillray paid attention to minute details in his caricatures. Although modern scholars have not noticed the fact, the figure of the sexually impaled Mary reveals a clear allusion to the Romney portrait: the tilt of the head, the slightly hooked nose, the half-smile, the dimple beneath the lower lip, the strawberry blonde hair and the giveaway Quaker cap are all exact copies. As Reynolds's heroic Tarleton is subverted by the allusion to Bobadill, so Romney's chaste image of Perdita is transformed into a vicious representation of her as a prostitute selling her wares.

Even the *Morning Post*, which was usually unfavourably disposed towards Mary, felt that Gillray had gone too far. Just over a week after the publication of this caricature, it published a profile entitled '*Hasty Sketch of Perdita* By a Gentleman over Head and Ears in Love'. This was a very flattering portrait, describing her as a woman who embellished the *ton* naturally but instinctively shunned the bright lights of the fashionable world, seeing through its hollowness. An opening reference to her disdain for 'the whirl of life' may be intended specifically as a riposte to Gillray's 'whirligig':

> Formed by the hand of nature for almost every opposite pursuit to that in which the whirl of life has engaged her, Perdita but half enjoys her present situation; yet she gives to it every grace and embellishment of which it is susceptible . . . her soul turns unsatisfied away from whatever princes can bestow! Were her talents mean,

> her fancy less elevated, her heart less animated, her passions less vivid, she would derive a more constant pleasure from the gaieties which are now her occasional consolation. Her temper is by nature quick, impatient, excursive, and romantic; and makes her equal to every thing which is uncommon, adventurous, and unpremeditated. There is nothing enthusiastically *great* of which she is not capable, when she obeys the unresisted impulse of the moment: and love or generosity would carry her from pole to pole.

These traits – her passionate nature and quick temper, her generosity and impulsiveness – were all stressed by those who knew her, and were acknowledged in her own self-portraits. The author proceeds to represent her as a heroine of sensibility, sensitive to poetry and prone to melancholy like a character out of a novel in the tradition of Jean-Jacques Rousseau:

> Her love is the child of nature, nurs'd by the heart . . . She has taste and feeling which fit her for the retreats of life. Simplicity has charms for her. Attached to her, by nature, are the soft dejections of a pathetic spirit, a tender friendship with the Muse, and a soul that aches for the softness of unstraying love . . . it is to be deplored that she is not the happiest, because she has a heart to be the best; yet to her should be adjudged the highest praise, who in a difficult situation shows, by her sensibility, that she deserves a better.[31]

Gillray's caricature was, of course, rather behind the times. When it was published, Mary was Fox's lover rather than Tarleton's. The ex-minister and the ex-actress were to be seen driving around in her carriage, the ultimate symbol of luxury and conspicuous consumption:

> Now *Charles Fox* being dismissed from the Secretaryship of State returned again to Gaming and Dissipation. And he resumed his Pharoah Bank at *Brooke's* and sojourned with Mrs Rob—s—n, the Harlot of the Day, and he drived her about in a Phaeton. The rattling of the wheels filled the air of the streets, and the neighing, and trampling of the horses was heard afar off.
>
> And the people turned, and gazed upon him, and said, He driveth like *Jehu*, though not to the confusion of *Jezabel!*[32]

Fox's aunt, Lady Sarah Napier (one of the famous Lennox sisters, herself once beloved of George III), remarked in a letter dated 11 September:

> I hear Charles saunters about the streets and brags that he has not taken a pen in hand since he was out of place. *Pour se desennuyer* [to relieve his boredom], he *lives* with Mrs Robinson, goes to Sadler's Wells with her, and is all day figuring away with her. I long to tell him he does it all to show that he is superior to Alcibiades, for *his* courtesan forsook him when he was unfortunate, and Mrs Robinson takes *him* up.[33]

Several commentators considered that it was Fox who was acting the part of a kept man. Perdita was the one in the driving seat: 'In the late Phaetonic expedition of *Perdita* and the *eloquent patriot* it is to be distinguished that the lady gives the gentleman the airing, and not, as usual, the gentleman, the lady.'[34]

A caricature soon appeared with the title 'Perdito and Perdita – or – the Man and Woman of the People'. This alludes to a joke that was going the rounds in London society. Horace Walpole reported it in a letter: 'Charles Fox is languishing at the feet of Mrs Robinson. George Selwyn says, who should the man of the people live with, but the woman of the people?'[35] The latter phrase meant a prostitute, though when it was applied to both Mary Robinson and the Duchess of Devonshire during the Westminster election campaign a year and a half later it took on political connotations.

In the cartoon a resplendent Mary dressed in a strikingly tight masculine riding jacket and high-crowned feathered hat (resembling that in Reynolds's portrait) is driving Fox past the gateway of St James's Palace in her carriage, firmly holding the reins. Her famous cipher of roses entwined around her initials in the shape of a coronet is highly prominent. The fact that she is in the driving seat, flourishing a whip high above her head, is intended to show that she is keeping Fox, who looks characteristically shabby and unkempt with his unshaven face. He is clutching his stomach and looks disconsolate. On the upper margin of the print is engraved: 'I have now not fifty ducats in the World and yet I am in love.'

Again, though, the caricaturist had failed to keep up with the rapidity of events in Mary's love life. By the time this print was published, she had left Fox and was back with Tarleton. Like the Prince of Wales before him, Fox turned for consolation to Elizabeth Armistead – though, very much unlike the Prince, he would fall deeply in love with her, remain faithful to her, and eventually marry her.

There was talk of Mary attempting to win back the Prince, but struggling as a result of her recent amours: 'The Perdita has pitched upon the place where she is to erect her batteries next winter at the Opera-house; it is, as usual, pointed against the quarter of Florizel; but it is thought that her artillery is so weakened by constant use that it will not be able to do any great execution.'[36] A few days later, the military metaphor was replaced with a nautical one. In a paragraph of sustained and very obscene double entendre the Perdita's sexual exploits are described in the language of privateering on the high seas:

> Yesterday, a messenger arrived in town, with the very *interesting* and *pleasing* intelligence of the *Tarleton armed ship* having, after a chace of *some months*, captured the *Perdita frigate*, and brought her safe into *Egham* port. The *Perdita* is a prodigious fine *clean bottomed vessel*, and has taken many prizes during her cruize, particularly the *Florizel*, a most valuable ship belonging to the Crown, but which was immediately *released* after taking out the *cargo*. The *Perdita* was captured some time ago by the *Fox*, but was afterwards retaken by the *Malden*, and had a complete suit of *new rigging* when she fell in with the *Tarleton*. Her manoevering to escape was admirable: but the *Tarleton* fully determined to take her or perish, would not give up the chace; and at length, coming along side of the *Perdita*, fully determined to *board her sword in hand*, she instantly surrendered at *discretion*.[37]

The '*Tarleton armed ship*' and the 'prodigious fine *clean bottomed vessel*' Perdita were soon seen together in the environs of Windsor, Mary's favourite spot for amorous sojourns. They were said to have converted an inn called the Bush at Staines into 'the temple of the *Cyprian Goddess*'.[38] Fox appeared back in London, parading with a fashionable beauty on each arm, but lamenting that 'the *bird* in the *bush*' was 'worth two in the hand'.[39]

Rumour had it that Mary intended to remain in Windsor through the winter, but by mid-October she and the Colonel were back in town. She supposedly engaged in a lengthy wrangle with Dally the Tall for the best box at the opera from which to aim ocular artillery at the Prince. There were rumours that Mary was back in his favour and that he had named his favourite racehorse after her. A perusal of the racing news over the next few years reveals that 'Perdita' developed an excellent track record.

Whatever the success of the horse, as far as Henry Bate's *Morning Herald* was concerned, Dally offered no contest in the female stakes. Mrs Robinson was the queen of the side boxes, the undisputed beauty of the age:

> Whenever the beautiful *Perdita* puts in her claim for admiration, every heart must bestow its suffrage. Her late appearance at Covent-garden theatre justifies this remark, and shows that tho' other *Beauties* may dazzle for a time, yet like the mock suns of Greenland, they are totally lost and expire, whenever a superior *Splendour* approaches![40]

CHAPTER 14

The Priestess of Taste

> Delighted with the prospect of celebrity which opened to her view, she resolved seriously to invoke the supreme goddess, Fame!
>
> Mary Robinson, *Walsingham*

> To-day she was a *paysanne*, with her straw hat tied at the back of her head, looking as if too new to what she passed, to know what she looked at. Yesterday she, perhaps, had been the dressed *belle* of Hyde Park, trimmed, powdered, patched, painted to the utmost power of rouge and white lead; tomorrow she would be the cravatted Amazon of the riding house, but be she what she might, the hats of the fashionable promenaders swept the ground as she passed.
>
> Laetitia-Matilda Hawkins, *Memoirs*

On 30 October 1782 the *Morning Herald* reported that 'The Perdita has received a dress from *Paris*, which was introduced this Autumn by the Queen of France, and has caused no small anxiety in the fashionable circles. It is totally calculated for the Opera, where it is expected to make its *first appearance*.' The dress was a sensation and would revolutionize female fashion in England.

It was a simple white flowing shift that dispensed with bodice and hoops, panniers and trains. The resemblance to a nightgown or undergarment meant that the style became known as deshabille (undressed).

The dress was a copy of one first worn by Marie Antoinette, who had caused controversy by her adoption of a style of cool white muslin dress imported from the West Indies, where it was worn by Creole women. Unlike traditional dresses, which ladies stepped into, the *chemise de la Reine* was placed over the head and held with a drawstring at the neck or at the side. It was then tied at the waist by a silk sash, usually pale blue or striped, and often worn with a straw hat. Marie Antoinette's adoption of the style was immortalized in 1783 by the brush of her favourite painter, Madame Vigée-Lebrun. Thanks to the Queen of France at Versailles and Mrs Robinson in London, it became, in the words of the *Lady's Magazine*, 'the universal *rage*'.[1]

In France, the new dress carried dangerous political connotations, due to its disrespect for the supremacy of courtly tradition. The adoption of imported muslin also meant that the Queen was denounced by the French silk industry. Lebrun's beautiful portrait was criticized for being an irreverent and informal portrayal of royalty and was withdrawn from public display. The chemise seemed to epitomize Marie Antoinette's romantic ideal of a simplified life, an ideal that would have damaging and far-reaching consequences. In fact, Marie Antoinette was actually reflecting a trend that was emerging across Europe, whereby clothes and hairstyles were becoming more simplified on the model of ancient Greek statuary. This movement in fashion was of a piece with the gradual relaxation of feminine restraint that occurred in the course of the eighteenth century. There had been protests against the harm done to women by restrictive clothing, tight-lacing, and hoops. The new muslin tube was especially popular for pregnant women, for obvious reasons. Freedom of dress was a form of women's liberation and Mary Robinson would become an ardent subscriber to the theory that hoops and stays represented a kind of female imprisonment.

In the summer of 1784 Marie Antoinette sent samples of her new dress to some of her aristocratic admirers across the English Channel, such as the Duchess of Devonshire. After initially objecting to the garment's immodesty, Georgiana – always an arbiter of female taste – helped to popularize the style and has been credited by fashion historians with its introduction into England.[2] But it was Perdita who initiated the craze for the muslin chemise nearly two years before.

The dress, indeed, became known as 'the Perdita chemise'. 'An *amateur* of the Cyprian Corps,' the *Morning Herald* informed its readers, 'recommends to our fair countrywomen a total abolition of the *large hoop* and *long petticoat*, and to adopt the *PERDITA*, a system of elegant *simplicity* and *neatness*, which has ever so conspicuously marked the dress of that celebrated *leader* of the wantons of the age!'[3] This is a perceptive comment: even before her visit to France, Mary was always noted for her taste for simple lines of dress that showed off her figure to best advantage. Her adoption of the chemise was the natural conclusion of a style that was already her own.

The sexy loose muslin dress, which clung to the figure (especially when it rained), appealed to both men and women, and continued to occupy the minds of the beau monde. For three days running in November the *Morning Herald* gave news of the chemise's progress. 'Ladies of the first style adopt it, and gentlemen *patronize* it. The *Chemise de la Reine*, in which Mrs Robinson appeared at the Opera, is expected to become a favourite *undress* among the fashionable women, who are either by necessity or inclination put to their *shifts*, the ensuing winter!'[4]

The idea of a woman from the trading classes, and a member of the 'frail sisterhood' to boot, dressing in the style of the Queen of France prompted questions about propriety. A long article in the *Morning Herald* discussed the strife that the dress was causing between the factions of the 'impure' and the 'chaste' women:

> The *Chemise de la Reine*, promises to be the fashionable apparel for the ensuing season . . . It is supposed that the *female fashions* will this winter undergo various revolutions, as the Ladies of the *ton*, amongst the *chaste circles*, have determined never to appear in public in similar uniforms with the *Cyprian Corps*; a resolution which reflects credit on the lovely Duchess, who is said to have proposed it, and to keep which, will find full employ for the continual exertion of her Grace's elegant taste and decorative fancy.
>
> The *Perdita* is to lead the *fashionable Paphian Corps*, at the express desire of certain milliners, who have 'to be disposed of for ready money only' large quantities of *gauze trimmings*, which, like Edmund Burke's speeches, are *ready cut and dried* for immediate use![5]

The 'Duchess' mentioned here is Georgiana: it is ironic that posterity has given her credit for introducing a garment to which she was initially so publicly hostile. To begin with, aristocratic women tended only to wear the dress in the privacy of their homes, not daring to be seen in it in public. The *Rambler's Magazine* noted that a certain Lady B— 'made one of silver muslin to see her friends after her lying-in, but never appeared in it out of her own home'. As one modern critic wryly remarks, 'Robinson invaded aristocratic bedrooms in more ways than one.'[6]

Even the usually staid *Morning Chronicle*, which prided itself on not reproducing town gossip in the manner of the *Morning Herald* and the *Morning Post*, entered the debate about the new garment: 'The Queen's Chemise is the most unbecoming dress that was ever projected among the vagaries of fashion, except for those whom nature has distinguished with a slim and elegant form.' Unless the wearer had a figure like Perdita Robinson, she would 'look better in a linsey-woolsey nightgown'.[7] The fashion correspondent of the *Lady's Magazine*, meanwhile, charted the growing popularity of the 'Perdita chemise': by the spring of 1783 it was 'universally worn' and by the summer it was being imitated ('the *Waldegrave levette* . . . trimmed in the fashion of the *Perdita chemise*'). It was a new fashion that remained fashionable: five years after Perdita introduced it, the *Lady's Magazine* noted that 'all the Sex now, from 15 to 50 and upwards . . . appear in their white muslin frocks with broad sashes'.[8]

The trend endured over the next decades, with waists rising to the Empire line and dresses becoming more transparent and figure-hugging. A fashion that had begun with the French Queen became associated with liberation and the revolution that cost that Queen her head. One of Jane Austen's letters, written in 1801, notes that a Mrs Powlett 'was at once expensively and nakedly dressed; – we have had the satisfaction of estimating her Lace and her Muslin'.[9] The word 'nakedly' highlights how the Perdita chemise and its mutations drew attention to the body. Having made a name for herself through the cross-dressed comedy roles that revealed the shape of her legs, Mary found a way of continuing to celebrate her body after she left the theatre. In so doing, she freed her fellow women from restrictive dress for two generations. It was not until the beginning of the Victorian age that waistlines dropped, female bodies were cinched with tight boned stays, skirts were hooped again, and the freedom in dress which women had obtained over the last half century was gone.

Mary Robinson's status as a leader of fashion caused controversy because she was blurring the distinction between ladies of virtue and the 'impures'. As the newspapers pointed out, it was members of her own sex (and invariably highly born ones) who berated her for daring to steal the fashion mantle from them. A Mrs Robinson who was better dressed than a duchess raised troubling questions about class and status. For centuries, clothing had been a denominator of rank. When fashion was open to all, it became hard to identify people's social standing from their appearance. Mary Robinson later wrote of this phenomenon in an essay on London life that was one of her most astute pieces of writing:

> The public promenades, particularly on the sabbath, are thronged with pedestrians of all classes, and the different ranks of people are scarcely distinguishable either by their dress or their manners. The duchess, and her *femme de chambre*, are dressed exactly alike; the nobleman and his groom are equally ambitious of displaying the neat boot, the cropped head, and the external decorations, as well as the quaint language, of the stable-boy. The dapper milliner, and the sauntering female of slender reputation, imitate the woman of fashion, in their choice of their cloathes, and the tenour of their conversation.[10]

Mary's sense of how instability and topsy-turvy in rank and status were fuelled by sartorial innovation was of a piece with her background in the theatre: class confusion was a central motif of eighteenth-century comedy, and the basis of many a plot twist in several of the plays in which Mary achieved success, as well as such classic comedies as Oliver Goldsmith's *She Stoops to Conquer*, in which the gentleman-hero Marlow, who is terrified of high-born ladies, only falls in love with Kate Hardcastle because she dresses like a barmaid.

Mary Robinson developed a reputation as a fashion icon that was unique among non-aristocratic women. She was noted for her ability to wear strikingly different clothes. She would dress up, cross-dress, or wear gowns that were beautifully made but extremely simple in style. The greatest honour in the world of fashion was to give a name to a new design of gown or hat. The *Lady's Magazine* frequently listed the 'Fashionable Dresses' for the new season. A typical article was that for March 1784: it cited five members of the female nobility and their garments: 'the

Rutland Gown', the 'Westmoreland Sultan', the 'Stanhope Bonnet', the 'Spencer Cap', and the 'Waldegrave Hat'. But it gave pride of place to two items named for the only non-aristocratic woman on the list, the 'Robinson Vest' and the 'Robinson Hat'.

The first was lavishly described as the 'most beautiful half-dress that has been invented for many seasons'. It was 'either pale-blue, or straw-coloured satin for the petticoat, the sleeves and train white crape, edged with blond, worked with *chanelle*; the body fastened before with small buckles of diamonds or pearls'. The dress 'will serve as a spring suit, by changing the satin to a *demi-saison* silk'. The 'Robinson Hat' was just as innovative: 'plain black transparent crape, and ornamented with carmelite ribband; a curtain, which if up, serves as a band round the crown; but if down, as a veil, this is an excellent invention for the ensuing spring, and will be very excusable (notwithstanding its peculiar appearance), where beauty gives a sanction to taste'.[11] With creations such as these, Perdita outdid even such leaders of fashion as her patron Georgiana Duchess of Devonshire. The numerous paintings and engravings of her ensured that the image of her trademark hats – of chip and straw, large with broad sweeping brims bedecked with trailing ribbons and bows – circulated widely in polite society and beyond.

In the course of 1783, the *Lady's Magazine* detailed a luscious array of Robinsonian creations, among them the '*Perdita* Hood' ('made of Italian lawn . . . tied under the chin, in a large double bow'), the '*Robinson* hat for Ranelagh' ('a white chip, very large, trimmed with a wreath of white roses, and a panache of white feathers'), and the '*Robinson* hat' of white crape, transparent, 'bound at the edge with black velvet and a band of black velvet round the crown, edged with a broad flounce of crepe in small plaits and fastened in the front with a diamond buckle'. The Hoppner portrait shows a splendid example of a diamond buckle on a different Robinson hat. Other innovations were the '*Perdita* handkerchief' – worn like a ruff, but weather-dependent and 'will only suit a fine form' – and the '*Robinson* gown' ('universally worn, a chocolate coloured poplin, with plain cuffs of scarlet silk'). And it was thanks to Mary that in the summer of 1783 riding habits were 'much worn in the morning': 'the most fashionable are the Perdita's pearl colour, with jonquil yellow facings, and the dark brown with a scarlet waistcoat'.[12] As she said herself in her *Memoirs*, she set the fashion and others followed 'with flattering avidity'.

Late that same year, 'the amiable Duchess of Devonshire' was 'confined by the lovely duties of her nursery', while 'the beautiful Mrs Robinson' was indisposed. The result was that 'the *evening* dresses are as yet unknown'.[13] In the absence of Georgiana and Perdita no one knew what to wear. In terms of her influence on taste, the ex-royal mistress was as important as the celebrated Duchess. Perdita created an extremely awkward dilemma for well-to-do ladies: if they wanted to be fashionable they had to imitate her, but if they imitated her they were allowing a courtesan to establish the rules of taste.

In later years, when Mary remade herself as a serious poet who cared more for the beauty of the mind than that of the body, she wrote satirically of the obsession with fashion. Writing in the *Morning Post* under the nom de plume Tabitha Bramble, she enumerated the tasteless excesses of 'Modern Female Fashions':

Cravats, like towels thick and broad,
Long tippets made of bear skin;
Muffs, that a Russian might applaud,
And *rouge* to tint a fair skin.

Long petticoats, to hide the feet,
Silk hose, with clocks of scarlet;
A load of perfumes, sick'ning sweet,
Made by *Parisian* VARLET.

A bowl of straw to deck the head,
Like porringer, unmeaning;
A bunch of *poppies*, flaming red,
With tawdry ribbands, streaming.[14]

In a companion poem published a few days later she poked fun at male fashions:

Crops, like *Hedge hogs*, high-crown'd Hats,
Whiskers like *Jew* Moses;
Collars padded, thick Cravats,
And Cheeks as red as roses.

Faces painted deepest brown,
Waistcoats strip'd and gaudy:
Sleeves, thrice doubled, thick with down,
And Straps, to brace the body!

Short Great Coats, that reach the knees,
Boots like French *Postillion*;
Meant the *lofty race* to please,
But laugh'd at by the million.[15]

Tarleton was famous for his 'crop' (very short) hairstyle – it was affectionately mocked by Fox in a rhyme that is now preserved in the Tarleton family papers. Like his lover, the Colonel was an innovator in fashion, whose outfits were noted in the papers: 'The fashionable morning dress, introduced by Colonel Tarleton, is a horseman's coat, that looks, when on, very like a bed gown.'[16]

Mary's carriages caused as much of a sensation as her clothes. Like cars today, carriages were status symbols, the ultimate luxury item (in Jane Austen's class-ridden novel *Emma*, the upward mobility of the apothecary Mr Perry is signalled by the fact that he is considering buying a carriage). The papers reported the traffic jams in Hyde Park where the carriages brought the higher and the middling classes together. The park was a place of spectacle and theatre, especially for courtesans who would slide down the windows of their carriages and jostle elbows, or spit or sneer at their rivals. Mary was constantly associated with her carriages, in caricatures and newspaper accounts, though what started out as a symbol of her wealth and social status achieved a more practical significance later in her life after her accident. In a letter of 1794 she referred to her carriage as a 'necessary expense': it was necessary not because she was anxious to keep up appearances, but because her legs were not strong enough to allow her to walk any great distance.

In her heyday, though, each new carriage was a glorious luxury. In December 1782 newspaper readers learnt that 'Mrs Robinson now sports a carriage which is the admiration of all the *charioteering circles* in the vicinity of St James's.' Designed by the prestigious Mr Benwell of Long Acre, its chassis was in 'carmelite and silver, ornamented with a French mantle, and the cipher in a wreath of flowers'; the bodywork of the carriage was scarlet and silver, the seat-cloth richly ornamented with silver fringe. The Robinson livery was green, faced with yellow, and trimmed with broad silver lace; the elegantly finished harness was ornamented with silver stars; the interior was lined with white silk and embellished with scarlet trimmings. 'The *Perdita*,' concluded Henry Bate's *Morning Herald*, 'has set a very splendid example to her *impure sisters* in the *charioteering style*, which few of them will be able to follow!'[17]

The following day it was reported that 'Yesterday the *Perdita* sported her new carriage in various parts of town, accompanied by the gallant Tarleton. The *Perdita* seems determined to preserve her *Sovereignty* over the *female frails*; she has commenced her Winter campaign in a very *bold stile*, and her standard is already honoured by the presence of *would-be* ministers of state, martial heroes, amorous Lords etc. etc.'[18] The latter allusions are, of course, to Fox, Tarleton and Malden, though by this time Mary had broken with Malden and Fox was involved with Elizabeth Armistead. Knowing the fickleness of fashion, Mary ensured that her carriage remained in tiptop condition: only a few weeks after its first appearance, she returned it to Long Acre 'to be new gilt and painted'.[19]

Just before Christmas there was a false report, swiftly followed by a public denial, that Mary and Thomas Robinson were reconciled. It emerged that though a 'total *separation*' had long since taken place between the Robinsons, Thomas was in Italy, working for Mary's brother.[20] It was the Colonel, not the husband, who had been seen with Mary at the opera. They were now inseparable. They spent Christmas and New Year in Old Windsor, where they were spotted riding in the Great Park. The proximity to the royal residences inevitably fuelled rumours. One day Mary was returning from her morning ride when the Prince came through Old Windsor on his return from the chase. They met near the marketplace, both on horseback. The Prince stopped, pulled off his glove and shook her by the hand. As he did so, 'the blushing *Perdita*' held her other hand across her face. Was this a sign, the *Morning Herald* asked, in the eighteenth-century equivalent of a modern newspaper horoscope, that Venus was once again in transit over the *Georgium sidus*? A couple of days later the paper reported to the contrary that 'The once-admired *Perdita* seems now nearly approaching the horizon; whenever she sinks below, not even the *Man of the People* [i.e. Fox] can raise her again!'[21]

The question of whether her star was falling or still rising was picked up by one of Mary's defenders the next time the paper appeared: 'A Correspondent cannot help observing, that an article in the *Herald* of Saturday contains a very ill-natured remark on the lovely *Perdita* – So far from approaching the *horizon*, she may be said from her display in public scenes, her equipage, her stile of living, and undiminished beauty, to be in the very zenith of her power of making conquests!'[22] She continued to be celebrated for her risqué verbal brilliance as well as her physical beauty: 'The Perdita is allowed to have wit as well as beauty: She paid a fine turned compliment to her gallant Colonel a few days ago. The Colonel observed to her, that she looked divinely in a *riding-habit*; she assured him she would always wear that dress, provided he would always be in a *riding-habit* when he came to visit her.'[23]

Throughout that January, rumour and counter-rumour swirled in the press. She was reconciled with the Prince. She was not reconciled with the Prince. She was posturing arrogantly in her box at the opera. She was behaving with becoming dignity in her box at the opera, setting herself apart from the common courtesans of the day. There can be no doubt that, however far Mary was or was not attempting to orchestrate the press campaign herself, she read the papers with an eagle eye. In one issue of the *Morning Herald* a report about her appears in close proximity to the news that a woman called Ann Randall, possibly a prostitute, had been arrested for shoplifting. The name seems to have stuck in Mary's mind: sixteen years later she published her feminist treatise, *A Letter to the Women of England, on the Injustice of Mental Subordination*, under the pseudonym Anne Frances Randall.

Mary's own shopping expeditions – and even her airings in the park and the fashionable parts of town – had hazards of their own: 'Mrs *Robinson* drove two or three times up and down St James's street on Saturday, during the cavalcade at St James's. She attempted to stop once, or twice to view the procession, but her admirers crowding numerously round her, she was obliged to make a farewell bow, and drive home.'[24] The affair with Tarleton was now fully public and they were rapidly becoming London's leading celebrity couple. During the day they rode together in the park; in the evenings they were spotted strolling in the pleasure gardens, dancing at the masquerade, showing themselves in boxes at the theatre and the opera.

One day in March, the skirts of Mary's dress became caught as she dismounted from her horse in Hyde Park. Despite the best efforts of Tarleton, the watching crowd saw more than they should have done. The incident was duly reported, illustrated (Tarleton, a groom, and two fat gentlemen, one of them holding a perspective glass, are shown looking up her skirt), and dramatized in a sketch entitled 'The Discovery, a new comedy, acted in Hyde-Park; or, the downfall of Perdita and the uprise of her s—k [smock]:

> Alderman: 'I saw such a perspective which makes my mouth water.'
> Colonel T.: 'A fine view it must be owned; but there is no novelty in it to me.' . . .
> Colonel T.: 'Egad here is fine work, I shall have her covered, and before my face – what account shall I give to Florizel. Faith I may as well cover her myself.'[25]

'Cover her' is slang for have sex with her.

The Opera House was being rebuilt and the *ton* rushed to subscribe for the best seats. Mrs Robinson promptly put down her name for four seats, thus ensuring that she would have a whole box at her disposal. 'In regard to this circumstance,' observed the *Morning Herald*, 'though she appears *four times* over, we cannot have *too much of a pretty woman*! There is also a plan of the new Opera house with the names of the subscribers in each box. She is number 69, next to Lady Essex and Lady Maynard, and fairly close to the Prince of Wales.'[26] The name of Colonel Tarleton appeared beneath hers. Lady Essex was Malden's mother, which suggests that Mary's relations with him were still cordial.

Having subscribed for an entire box, Mary was entitled to fit it up in her own style. She chose pink satin chairs and wall-to-wall mirrors. Her detractors in the press and among the courtesans assumed that this was a monstrous act of vanity calculated to ensure that her reflected image would be visible to all parts of the house. It may have been Mary herself who fed the *Morning Herald* a response to this accusation: 'Mrs Robinson's box at the Opera has created universal envy and confusion among the frail sisterhood, who are *ignorant* that in Paris nothing is so common as a looking glass, which is placed *not* for the benefit of those in the box, but for the convenience of seeing the *stage* from every part of it.'[27] This is a brilliant piece of spin, which at once portrays her as a loyal woman of the theatre, interested in the stage and not the house, and a sophisticated innovator of the latest Paris fashion, leaving her provincial English sisters far behind.

The aura of Parisian sophistication that surrounded her was intensified by the arrival in town of the Duke of Chartres: 'one of his first visits will be to the fair *Perdita*; as during her residence of last year in Paris, there seldom passed a day in which he did not endeavour to pay court to her'.[28] A further sensation was caused by the Perdita's importation of French stockings embroidered with ornamental patterns (known as 'clocks') in golden silk: 'The *gold-clock'd* stockings, introduced by the lark-heeled *Perdita* occasions various disputes in the fashionable circles; the money-loving tribe reprobate so extravagant a fashion, while certain ladies of *solid understandings*, revile the fair inventor, with more than serpent tongues! If we may judge from her train of followers at the last masquerade.'[29]

Tarleton was on half-pay, awaiting a new military posting. He was gambling heavily, to the alarm of his family back in Liverpool. The papers, meanwhile, could not get enough of the glamorous couple. At each ball or masquerade, they paired off early in the evening. Their dress was always singled out as the most fashionable. Mary would wear a Quaker-style domino and go hatless in order to display a finished headdress, or she would set off pink and brown 'relieved and decorated with the greatest taste', as she 'reclined on the arm' of Tarleton while he strutted in the full regalia of a hussar. Blue jacket and waistcoat embroidered with silver (and small sugar-loaf silver buttons), buckskin breeches, boots of uncoloured leather reaching to the knee and fitted as tight as silk stockings, a buff belt over the jacket with a full-length scimitar hanging from it, a helmet on his head. Tempers flared late one evening: the *Morning Herald* revealed that there was an '*amorous fracas*' between the lovers, causing a piqued Perdita to take comfort on the arm of Mr John Townshend. 'The Prince of Wales was present,' the reporter pointedly added.[30]

Mary was in love. She blossomed: 'The *Perdita* is so much *improved* within these last two years, that she scarcely retains a resemblance of her *former self*; chiefly owing to her appearance being more en bon point, than she formerly did!' The Hoppner portrait, which probably belongs to this period, gives her breasts and cheeks a certain fullness that had not been apparent when Gainsborough painted her looking rather gaunt at the time of the stressful business of the Prince's letters. The *naturalness* of her beauty 'challenged universal admiration'; the favoured terms for newspaper descriptions of her dresses were 'neatness', 'delicacy', and 'decency'. When other women tried to ape her style, they failed miserably. So, for example, a courtesan known affectionately as 'Our Bridget': 'What was in the *Perdita* the result of a good natural taste, improved by Parisian refinement, is in poor *Bridget* intolerable affectation and as ill becomes her as a fine dress!' Bridget also made a terrible hash of her attempt to copy Mary's innovation of a mirrored opera box: 'The whole train of *inferior frails* are close copyists of the resplendent *Perdita*; viz. her Opera box copied by *Our Bridget*; her Carmelite Coach, by *old Friar Lawrence*; her phaeton and ponies by the mistress of *Sir Jacky Jehu*; her *starry harness*, by Mrs Byne, the *Swan*, etc. etc.; her mode of *dress* by the whole *corps*.' The Armistead alone had the taste 'to approach nearer the *Perditean* hemisphere, than any *other* in the *Paphian circles*'.[31]

There was news that once again Sir Joshua Reynolds was painting Perdita, in a manner totally different from formerly. Commentators waited eagerly to see what new image she would project.

Her celebrity reached its high-water mark. Inevitably the tide would soon turn against her. Despite the fact that her affairs with the Prince and Fox were over, she continued to be linked with them in the satirical press and began to receive seriously bad publicity. Charles Fox's increasing closeness to the Prince of Wales was a matter for great concern both in the conservative press and at court. Fox's political ambitions depended in part on the capacity of the Prince to bankroll him. He was, therefore, acutely conscious that in August the Prince would come of age, receive a substantial fortune – and be liable to pay the £20,000 bond that he had promised to Mary. As a former lover who remained on excellent terms with Mary, Fox took it upon himself to negotiate a deal that would satisfy her without damaging the Prince to the full extent of £20,000 (a sum, it should be remembered, that was the equivalent of nearly a million pounds in today's terms).

At the same time, Fox was engaged in a much bigger negotiation. In February 1783 the Government of the Earl of Shelburne fell, following defeat in debates on proposed peace treaties to end the American and

French wars. The loss of the colonies had to be acknowledged, but the terms of surrender were so humiliating that it was impossible for the Government to survive. The fall of Shelburne was precipitated by an unholy alliance of left and right: Fox and Lord North had formed an unlikely partnership in order to bring him down. It was a devastating blow to the King that his devoted lieutenant North should have entered into a coalition with Fox, the debauched radical, the misleader of the Prince. For six weeks, the King procrastinated, refusing to summon the Duke of Portland (who was to be the nominal head of the Fox–North coalition) to take office.

During this period of political vacuum, the press enlivened their coverage of the extraordinary political manoeuvring with reports of an equally unlikely alliance between those old rivals the Perdita and the Armistead: 'An *amorous coalition* is just formed between the *Perdita* and the *Armstead*, in consequence of which the former heroine has solemnly renounced all pretensions to the engaging person of Mr C— F-x and the latter to that of the H—r A—nt.'[32] In reality, Elizabeth Armistead was by this time well established as Fox's lover and Mary's only 'pretensions' to the Prince were of the financial kind. Fox was no doubt pleased with the opportunity to assist the ex-mistress who had relinquished him to his 'dearest Liz' without a fight, while at the same time helping the Prince of Wales out of a potential financial mire.

The first press reports that Mary was once again in negotiation with the Prince had surfaced back in January in a new monthly publication called the *Rambler's Magazine*, which followed Perdita's progress with avid attention. This journal's full title was *The Rambler's Magazine; or, The Annals of Gallantry, Glee, Pleasure, and the Bon Ton; calculated for the entertainment of the Polite World; and to furnish the Man of Pleasure with a most delicious banquet of Amorous, Bacchanalian, Whimsical, Humorous, Theatrical and Polite Entertainment*. It presented itself as a very different ramble through society than that of Dr Johnson: it was devoted exclusively to pleasure and amusement, free from 'dry Reasoning, Metaphysical conjectures, or Essays on Morality'. It promised accounts of female misbehaviour, graphically depicted in copperplate illustrations. The editor appealed to his readers to provide stories, in return for which they would receive a free copy. He was rewarded with such items as 'Mr Nisbett detects Captain Totty in bed with his wife' and 'Mrs H—n amusing herself with her black servant' (who is shown in an accompanying illustration lying on top of her with his hand on her naked breast).

Mary figures prominently in each issue throughout the year 1783. As her political engagement became more apparent, the treatment of her became conspicuously more scabrous. The first *Rambler's Magazine* began with 'An Eccentric Lecture on Procreation' and then proceeded to 'A singular lease of certain premises, from Perdita to Florizel, for a valuable consideration', accompanied by an engraving of 'Florizel granting Independence to Perdita'. This caricature makes its point by the traditional device of a picture within the picture: on the wall behind Perdita is an image of the mythological figure Danae (who is naked) receiving a shower of gold into her lap. The premises in the mock lease are 'Bushy-Grove, lying in between East-Ham and West-Ham', an allusion that simultaneously evokes a royal property (Bushy House) and Perdita's genital area. The Prince will get all the 'chambers, ways, paths, passages, shrubberies, water courses, cascades, ponds, rivers' thereon, together with everything else 'heretofore held, used, occupied, enjoyed by Charles Reynard [Fox], late occupier thereof'. He will have to keep the premises in good repair, and in return for his rent he can 'enter, and come into' her twice a week or oftener.[33]

This is innocuous stuff in comparison with some of the snippets about Mary published later in the year. A piece by one 'Tattle' told of how on one occasion before the affair with the Prince, Tom Robinson came in while Perdita was making love to someone else and merely said with sang-froid, 'I beg your pardon, I did not know you were engaged.' Her simultaneous affairs with the Prince and Malden were also dredged up: a report tells of how one evening at the Pantheon she was greeted overfamiliarly by a known whore: 'Pray,' asked Perdita, 'how long has the Pantheon been a thoroughfare to St Giles [the haunt of prostitutes]?' To which the other replied, 'Ever since the way to *Wales* was through *Malden*.'[34]

Fox's role as intermediary between the Prince and Perdita led to the perception among caricaturists that they were engaged in a sexual threesome. Gillray's 'Paridise [*sic*] Regain'd', published in February, shows Fox making his addresses to a demure mobcapped Perdita while the Prince looks on from behind a tree, saying, 'Ha! Ha! Ha! Poor Charley.' The main purpose of this caricature was to discredit Fox in the period when he was forging his alliance with North, but it had the inevitable side

'Scrub and Archer', caricature of Fox, Lord North, and Perdita. The picture on the wall shows Tarleton, as in the Reynolds portrait.

effect of undermining Mary's reputation. Unapologetic in her support for the new coalition, she began sporting the Fox and North colours of blue and buff in her dresses and on her coach, and lending ministers her house in Berkeley Square: 'From the number of meetings held by Mr Fox and his coadjutors, at the house of the *gentle Perdita*, the *apartment* where they resort may with the strictest justice be called the new *ministerial* cock-pit!'[35]

A spate of satirical caricatures played on these relationships. The new Government was established at the beginning of April, with North as Home Secretary and Fox as Foreign Minister. Within a few weeks, a caricature appeared under the title 'Scrub and Archer', an allusion to two characters in George Farquhar's popular Restoration comedy *The Beaux' Stratagem*. Portly Scrub is Fox and Archer – a gentleman playing the role of a gentleman's gentleman – is Lord North. The scene is one in the play where Scrub and Archer agree to become 'sworn brothers', a satire on the coalition between the two politicians and the way that Fox was the junior partner in terms of rank and experience, but the senior one in power and charisma. The maid who stands behind them is Perdita. Above her on the wall is a rendering of Reynolds's portrait of Tarleton. Archer/North says 'And this Col. I am afraid has converted the affection of your Perdita', to which Scrub/Fox replies, 'Converted, ay perverted my dear friend, for I am afraid he has made her a whore.'

It was unseasonably warm that May, so Perdita was constantly out in Hyde Park driving her carriage decorated with the blue- and buff-coloured cockades of Fox and North. Her new-found political prominence gave caricaturists and pamphleteers a fresh incentive to attack her.

One of the most damaging blows to her image was her connection with the sex therapist, Dr James Graham. His notorious Temple of Health and Hymen in Pall Mall (admission two guineas) was decked out with silver and crystal ornaments, gilded mirrors and lamps. Clients were sensualized with soft music and spices redolent of an Arabian seraglio. Graham delivered lectures, wearing doctoral robes; audience members would then receive an electric jolt from under their cushions. He claimed that his electrical charges were a cure for impotence, infertility, and lack of libido. The Temple's main attraction was the 'Celestial or Magnetico-electrico bed – the first and only ever in the world', an electrified bed on which jaded couples could lie beneath a mirrored canopy and rediscover their appetites with the assistance of 'magnetico-electrical fire' (hire charge: £50 per night). This contraption was fuelled by a combination of electricity and 15 hundredweight of compound magnets. Back in 1781 a satirical pamphlet called *The Celestial Beds* had suggested that Mary was using Graham's methods to become pregnant by the Prince:

And shall she not, his joy and pride,
Be for a pledge electrify'd?
Yes, Graham shall exert his art,
And give a bantling to her heart!
The Muses' darling it shall be,
The flow'r of royal progeny.[36]

'The Aerostatick Stage Balloon': caricature of James Graham, sexual therapist, and his fashionable clients. Mary is on the top tier.

Dr Graham's lectures, advertised almost daily in the *Morning Herald* and delivered with help from a scantily clad female assistant known as Vestina, attracted huge audiences – though many ladies veiled themselves in order to disguise their identities. The Prince of Wales, Charles Fox, Georgiana Duchess of Devonshire, and Mary Robinson were all patrons of the establishment, which gave satirists an opportunity to attack all four of them. In a caricature of February 1783 called 'The Doctor Himself

Pouring out His Whole Soul for 1 s[hilling]', Mary, together with Fox and her husband Thomas, is represented standing in the audience as Graham lectures on hygienic sex, the importance of bathing the genitalia and the fundament both before and after congress, and the evils of masturbation (which constituted the squandering of humankind's 'vivifying elementary fire').

Later in the year another caricature, entitled 'The Aerostatick Stage Balloon', engraved by the pseudonymous 'Hanibal Scratch', showed a balloon about to rise from the ground, carrying an array of fashionable passengers sitting in three tiers of galleries protected by railings. At the top are Perdita, Dally the Tall, and an adulterous aristocratic lady. Mary is clapping her hands with delight. In the middle are Fox and North, snuggled up in friendly coalition and holding a thread attached to the nose of the Duke of Portland, the nominal Prime Minister who was but their puppet. On the bottom row sit an assortment of quacks and other London characters, Dr Graham and his 'Vestina' among them. The caption numbers Perdita among the 'Fillies free', flashing her 'Lunar Vis à Vis'; it also alludes to North realizing his dreams and Fox pursuing 'his golden schemes'. The implication is that the Fox–North coalition is a piece of charlatanry, an effusion of hot air no better than Dr Graham's lectures and – by virtue of the presence of Perdita and her sisterhood – equally charged with sexual shenanigans. There were even rumours at this time that Mary was simultaneously having affairs with both Fox and North. Given North's rectitude and Fox's loyalty to Elizabeth Armistead, this is calumny, but it reveals how closely she was associated with the unlikely coalition.

James Graham eventually fell into debt, was imprisoned in Newgate, and descended into insanity. Mary later parodied him in her novel *Walsingham*, where he is Doctor Pimpernel, a jargon-spouting charlatan who is obsessed with beautiful young women. Walsingham is in a dangerous and delirious fever, which Pimpernel puts down to love:

> 'The foolish fellow, I tell you, is in love; I know his case – have often felt it – see it at this very moment on the tip of his nose – in his right eye – on his forehead; – damme, on the very point of his chin. Well, you must cure him, Amelia: the sublime essence of your odoriferous breath will do the business. Nothing like the

balsamic smile of a beautiful woman! More efficacious than all the drugs in Christendom; more skilful than all the bunglers of Warwick-lane. The breath of beauty would re-animate the heart of a dying anchoret! Nothing like it! I always recommend it in cases of extreme danger; seldom find it fail, where the patient is gifted with the true essence of sublime sensibility!'[37]

Like the real Graham, the fictional Pimpernel is a hypocrite, a shameless self-promoter, social climber, and sycophant:

'Cannot stay – must be at Highgate by nine, on a consultation. Overwhelmed with practice; – dine every day with the first men in the kingdom; – walk arm in arm with nothing but nobles; always take the wall, and shove the blockheads into the kennel: a pack of vagabonds all together: no matter for that; – they give sumptuous dinners! Recommend me to the divine creatures. Double profit. – Do a great deal of private business among women of fashion.'[38]

Both characterization and style uncannily anticipate Jane Austen's monstrous snob and show-off extraordinaire, Mrs Elton, in *Emma*.

Perhaps at some level Mary satirized Graham so severely in later years because she had been stung by the caricaturists' implicit comparison between the two of them: where the quack doctor was explicitly in the business of selling sex, Mary had developed a reputation for promoting herself by means of her sexual allure. The *Morning Herald* reported that 'the *Perdita* frequently seals her letters to her intimate friends with an *impression* of her own *bust*, which, being in wax, *hieroglyphically* conveys the idea of a *melting* fair, and is therefore kissed as the *symbol* of the beauty whom it represents'.[39] By this device, she becomes a symbol of her own desirability.

Despite her association with Fox, North, and the Prince, it was Tarleton who had captured her heart. But the bad press she was enduring did not endear her to his family. They attributed his debts to her bad influence and her extravagant spending, a charge he strenuously denied in letters home to Liverpool. Mary was certainly spending heavily – she had recently ordered a state-bed of pink satin embroidered with mythological scenes such as Venus and Mars in amorous dalliance, reputedly 'the most superb and elegant piece of furniture in Europe'[40] – but the real problem was that Tarleton was a gambling addict in a circle at Brooks's Club where huge sums changed hands in an instant. According to the press, he was quite capable of winning £30,000 from the Prince one night and losing all that and more to Fox another.

He found himself with no choice but to ask his family to bail him out. They agreed to help on the condition that he stop seeing Mary. His mother Jane had written a loving but firm letter pleading with him to give up his women and his gambling. On 5 May Tarleton wrote in desperation to his brother Thomas, pledging to break off his connection with Mary and flee from the gaming tables: 'Before I plunge deeper into play which may be my destruction, I make this earnest proposal: if my friends will lend me money to pay my debts, which amount to near three thousand pounds: I most solemnly pledge myself to them to quit London and my present connexion instantly, to come into the country till I embark for the E. Indies and never to play again for more than five pounds during my life.'[41]

When Tarleton informed Mary of this plan, she was prostrate with grief and became physically ill. This was a pattern frequently repeated when they fought. During her indisposition Fox called daily at her house in Berkeley Square; the Prince of Wales was also said to be distressed to hear that she was ill and to have made constant enquiry after her. But she soon recovered and relaunched herself into society in style: 'the envy of the *frail* world will soon be called forth by the launch of *Perdita's* new *vis-à-vis*, which certainly surpasses in style and decorative embellishments, all the equipages that have hitherto graced the *Cyprian circle!*'[42] According to the gossip, Fox was paying for this vehicle, which Benwell of Long Acre delivered to her at the end of May. An alternative story was that 'The *Perdita's* new *vis-à-vis* is said to be the aggregate of a few stakes laid at *Brooks's* which the competitors were not able to decide. Mr *Fox*, therefore, proposed that as it could not be better applied, than to the above purpose, that the *Perdita* should be presented with an elegant carriage. The ill-natured call it *Love's Last Stake* or *The Fools of Fashion*.'[43]

Love's Last Stake caused a great stir amongst the *ton*. Benwell was praised for his design of the matchless and superb equipage. It was by far the most splendid that Mary had ever owned. The bodywork was brown, richly bordered with a mosaic-painting of straw and silver. In the middle of the door panel there was a mantle of pink and silver, lined with ermine, enclosing an oval in which her cipher half appeared among the rays of a rising sun. Below was a representation of a lion couchant. The lining of the interior was straw-coloured silk, ornamented with a pink and silver fringe. The hammer-cloth was entirely composed of embroidered lace; the buckles, joints, and springs were silver. 'Mrs Robinson may now,' concluded the *Morning Post*, 'with infinite propriety, lay claim to a title she justly deserves, and without flattery, be proclaimed the *Priestess of Taste*.'[44]

Others were less enamoured of such show. A matter of days after the appearance of the new carriage, a satirical pamphlet was published under the title *The Vis-à-Vis of Berkley-Square. Or, A Wheel off Mrs W*t**n's Carriage. Inscribed to Florizel* (Mrs Watson and her sister were courtesans also renowned for their ostentatious vehicles). Here Perdita became 'Phryne', the name of a whore in a poem by Alexander Pope. The pamphlet was in verse. The following lines are typical:

The Carriages, the Streets, the Town,
The Prince, the Pickpocket, and Clown,
All stare at PHRYNE'S station!
The very stones look up, to see
Such very gorgeous Harlotry
Shaming a foolish Nation!

There were also footnotes, one of which expressed particular offence at the new cipher sported on the side of the carriage, with its juxtaposition of rising sun and lion couchant: 'if this was the Perdita's own fancy it might be pardoned, as the folly of a weak woman; but manners and decency should have whispered, that such puns as the *Rising Sun* and the *British Lion* humiliated under the curtain of a Courtezan's bed, were jokes unbecoming her fancy or her folly'.[45]

A newspaper report claimed that Mary threatened to sue the publisher of this pamphlet for libel:

> we hear, from unquestionable authority, that the Perdita has given orders to her solicitor to commence an immediate prosecution against the author of a late poetical publication, called *Vis-à-vis*, in

> behalf of herself, and such others, of the *sisterhood*, who have, as the author has asserted, dishonoured the sash or *cestus of Venus*. We are further informed, from the same authority, that a subscription is opened in the vicinity of Pall Mall and St James's-street for carrying on the prosecution.[46]

The case does not seem to have come to court. Perhaps Mary was just making the threat in an attempt to forestall further, more vicious satires.

Tarleton's debts had become public knowledge. A letter to his brother reveals his state of mind: 'I am at a loss what to do and what to say – Weltje [his principal creditor] is very importunate for his money and I can at present devise no way to satisfy him – it is lucky I returned when I did to this place for a report was prevalent (the P of Wales told it me) that I had shot myself – God forbid!'[47] He told his mother that he was contemplating selling his commission. She responded by telling him to give up his carriage, his 'boundless extravagance', his 'useless train of Men Servants', and his expensive house in St James's. In return, she would pay off his commercial creditors – but not his gambling debts. After a flurry of correspondence, and the intervention of Tarleton's old commanding officer Cornwallis, Mrs Tarleton wrote a long and impassioned letter laying out her position to the effect that she would not be able to assist him ever again and that he should leave immediately for the Continent. 'See your follies in their real light, and become a new man,' she wrote, before turning in her final paragraph to the person she held responsible for her beloved son's parlous condition: 'I must also add before I conclude this letter that it will give me real pleasure and satisfaction to hear that your connection with Mrs Robinson is at an end – without that necessary step all my endeavours to save you from impending destruction will be ineffectual.'[48]

Tarleton's reply made no mention of leaving England or of Mrs Robinson. Though his mother finally agreed – much against her better judgement – to pay his gaming debts, she continued to press him on the point: 'I am much surprised You have not yet made me acquainted with your view or intended destination on the Continent or taken the least notice of the paragraph in my last Letter in regard to Mrs Robinson – I must desire in Your next You will be more explicit on both these subjects.'[49]

It was July by this time. The public were surprised that Perdita was not seen parading *Love's Last Stake* in the charioteering circles of Hyde Park. Her secret reason was soon out. As usual, the *Morning Herald* was first to break the story: 'The Perdita is pregnant!'[50] At the same time, she could not escape the consequences of Tarleton's debts and she was desperate to keep him in London, despite his family's protestations that he should leave for the Continent forthwith. Her life was at a turning point. As Laetitia Hawkins put it, one moment 'the men of the day in Bond Street still *pirouetted* as her carriage passed them', but the next, the vehicle was reclaimed by its maker and Tarleton had fled.[51]

CHAPTER 15

The Ride to Dover

> In the [summer] of 1783 our poet was attacked with a violent and dangerous fever, occasioned by travelling all night in a damp post-chaise, to do an office of pecuniary friendship, for one who has since repaid her with neglect and ingratitude.
>
> Preface to *The Poetical Works of the Late Mrs Robinson*

Mary had word that Tarleton would be forced to leave the country unless he immediately paid off a debt of £800. She had no property on which she could instantly raise such a sum, so she sent a note to Fox requesting a loan. That evening she went to the opera with her French admirer (and ex-lover) the Duc de Biron and 'an English nobleman of the highest rank' – probably the Earl of Moira, who was always a good friend to both her and Biron. After the show, they returned to her house in Berkeley Square for supper. Whilst she had been at the opera a messenger from Fox had arrived with £300 and a note promising the remainder of the money in the morning.

She was anxious about Tarleton. He had promised to meet her at the opera, but had not joined her there. Nor did he come to her house. His own funds were reputedly diminished to a paltry £20. She sent servants to everywhere she could think of: his lodgings, his club, the homes of his friends and of Weltje. He was nowhere to be found and there was a rumour that he was already on the road to the Continent. Between one and two o'clock in the morning, without dressing herself for the night air or thinking of her pregnancy, she 'threw herself into a post-chaise to follow him'.[1]

What happened next will never be fully known. According to Maria Elizabeth Robinson's continuation of her mother's *Memoirs*, 'An imprudent exposure to the night air in travelling, when, exhausted by fatigue and mental anxiety, she slept in a chaise with the windows open, brought on a fever, which confined her to her bed during six months.'[2] An early biographical sketch, which has a fuller account of the incident than any other source, says that she let down the glass and fell asleep, then 'At the first stage, she was obliged to be carried into the inn, almost frozen.'[3] This sounds like hypothermia, which seems very unlikely on a July night in southern England.

The consequences of the ride to Dover were drastic. 'From that hour,' according to the early biographical sketch, she 'never recovered the entire use of her limbs. For a long time the joints of her fingers were contracted; but they were afterwards partially restored, and she could even write with facility. But from the time of that accident, she could never walk nor even stand; and was always carried from one room to another, and to and from her carriage.'[4] Whether her subsequent condition was always so severe is very much open to question, but there is no doubt that her health was never the same again.

The most trustworthy account is that of the daughter who stayed with her and nursed her for the rest of her life. She explains that after the long fever 'The disorder terminated, at the conclusion of that period [six months], *in a violent rheumatism, which progressively deprived her of the use of her limbs*.' At the age of just 25 the woman reputed to be the most beautiful in England was 'reduced to a state of more than infantine helplessness'.[5] A violent rheumatism does seem to be the correct diagnosis. That is certainly how her illness was described in later years by those who knew her best.

Acute rheumatic fever is now very rare in industrialized countries, but it remains common in the developing world and it was rife in eighteenth-century England. It is a disease that affects several parts of the body via the immune system, induced by streptococcal infection.[6] Females are more often affected than males and children than adults; infection rarely occurs beyond the age of 30. There is always a latent period between the infection and the development of acute rheumatic fever. This seems consistent with the timing implied by the preface to Mary's *Poetical Works*, which notes that 'The languor which remained on the abatement of the disease terminated in a rheumatic fever.'[7] Acute rheumatic fever most commonly affects the joints. It also weakens the heart: when Mary died at a relatively young age the diagnosis was 'dropsy', which means heart failure.

The chief manifestation of acute rheumatic fever is severe arthritis that migrates through the large joints. The knees and ankles are most commonly involved; only rarely are the small joints of the hands affected – Mary was fortunate in this at least, given that she remade herself as a prolific writer. At various times in later life, she suffered from especially bad swelling of the ankles. The fever and the long period of confinement to bed, leading to Mary's long-term problems with her legs, probably set in up to three or four weeks after the original infection. But what was the source of that infection and did the night-time carriage ride have anything to do with it?

When Mary set off for Dover she was pregnant. But she never had Tarleton's child – and, as far as we know, she never became pregnant again. Streptococcal infections are frequently located in the vagina. The most likely explanation of events is that she had a miscarriage in the post-chaise and an infection resulting from it was what led to the acute rheumatic fever. There is supporting evidence for this in some private gossip recorded at the time: Lord Pembroke wrote to a friend on 13 August to the effect that 'Her face is still pretty, but illness has brought on a disadvantageous additional scowl to it; and as to her body, she is quite défaite . . . She may possibly come about again, but she must not go any more to an Opera on the day of miscarriage.'[8]

Newspaper reports of the misadventure proposed various causes, several of them malicious. Thus the *Morning Herald* on 31 July: '*Mrs Robinson* lies dangerously ill at her house in Berkeley Square; the envious part of her own sex attribute her indisposition to chagrin at the declining influence of her charms; if that is really the case, the name of *Perdita* will soon be too truly applied to this once all-conquering impure.' 'Amorous and Bon Ton Intelligence' in the *Rambler's Magazine* for 26 August, claimed that '*Mrs Robinson* is not as bad as was reported; but is still very unwell. Her indisposition is said to be occasioned by her love of gaiety; and keeping her revels of midnight beyond her strength of constitution.'

* * *

Tarleton, meanwhile, had not gone to Dover, as Mary thought, but to Southampton. From there, he wrote to tell his mother that he had left town and was en route to France. He finally gave her the information that she had been waiting to hear: 'You desire me to write more fully about Mrs Robinson – The connection is closed. She is too proud to follow me and she has long been too generous, *always* I should have said, to encrease the poverty of any man – I most solemnly assure you she has not been the occasion of my bankruptcy – Play alone, which I abjure, has – I won't now complain of my bad fortune, it is too late.'[9] It was some time before he discovered that Mary had actually followed him, with the money he needed.

In the middle of August, Mary went down to Brighton, then called Brighthelmstone, which, like other seaside resorts of the time, was a favoured destination for convalescents. It was around this time, in close proximity to the Prince's twenty-first birthday, that her annuity was finally paid. Perhaps news of her ill health contributed towards the Prince's decision to resolve the question of the bond.

A caricature called 'The new Vis-à-vis, or Florizel driving Perdita' was published in the *Rambler's Magazine* that month. It shows the Prince driving Mary's splendid new carriage, drawn by two goats. A badly drawn Fox rides postillion, holding out a paper inscribed 'Grant of £60,000' – a reference to the sum bestowed on the Prince upon his coming of age for the purpose of forming an establishment. Lord North lies on the top of the carriage asleep, his arms folded; his head rests on a pillow inscribed *Royal Favor*. Perdita has three ostrich feathers in her hair, a sign of her link to the Prince. The caricature reveals that the negotiations between Perdita and the Prince, with Fox as intermediary, were very much in the public eye at this time. Through Fox's good offices, it was finally agreed that the Prince would pay Mary an annuity of £500 and that after her death her daughter would continue to receive half the sum. The settlement was presented as an equivalent to the bond of £20,000 that the Prince had given her back in 1780, to be paid on his establishment, 'as a consideration for the *resignation of a lucrative profession at the particular request of his Royal Highness*'.[10] Mary received her long-overdue reward for giving up her stage career at a time when illness was threatening to put an end to her public life altogether.

Surviving account books in the Royal Archives at Windsor reveal that over the years the Prince was irregular in his payment of the annuity. It was one of his largest regular outgoings, as is apparent from a list of pensions and annual donations made by his treasurer in 1787: £500 to Mrs Robinson is substantially more than the next highest payment (£300 for 'Musicians') and his largest donation (£105 to the Welsh Society). It is in an altogether different league from his more domestic disbursements, such as £31. 10*s.* for Humphreys the rat-catcher and £25. 4*s.* to a Mrs Duck for 'coach and necessaries'.[11]

Late in September, Tarleton wrote from Douai in France to his brother Thomas. The letter is an untidy, distracted, barely legible scrawl:

> My dear brother I have been rambling – I have been a vagabond and now do not know where to fix . . . Wisdom and Fortitude ought to teach Philosophy – I trust I shall attain it soon, for I have had adversity enough to chase away all passions.
>
> I reveal to you —— every thing. I reveal to you every thing. I have not forgot Mrs R— oh God such a conflict I hope never again to encounter. I hear she is dangerously ill – But no more. I shall grow distracted.[12]

He did not yet know that the catastrophe was in all probability precipitated by her night-time dash in pursuit of him.

Mary returned from Brighton, but remained virtually bedridden for the rest of the year. A newspaper report in October claimed that she had 'lost the use of one side of her frail and lovely tenement' as a result of a paralytic stroke, but a denial of this was published a few days later.[13] There was further cruel press comment the next month: 'The Perdita, who has been ill, mends but very slowly. She is said, from her shattered condition to be unfit for any further service. She is, however, in dock, and the colonel is emptying her cargo, and stopping her *leaks*.'[14] The Colonel was doing no such thing: he was far away in France, anxiously awaiting further news of her.

The caricaturists continued to harp on Florizel and Perdita. In a satirical engraving of October, she is the seducer of a naive, impressionable young man. George III laments his son's fall before the charms of the bare-breasted Perdita, while her husband, the King of Cuckolds, looks on, supporting her other lovers (North, Fox, and Tarleton) on his horns. She was still being branded a wanton long after she had been cast off by the Prince and Fox, even as her body was struck down with disease. Late in the year, the *Rambler's Magazine* published faked 'Letters from Florizel' of an obscene nature. In one he purportedly tells of how when she was visiting him at Colnbrook, he had her splayed out on the bed but then lost his erection: 'Her short and double breathings heaved her breast, her snowy, swelling breast; her hands that grasped me trembling as they closed, while she permitted mine unknown, unheeded to traverse all her beauties, till quite forgetting all, and abandoning my soul to joy, I rushed upon her, who lay all fainting beneath my useless weight; for on a sudden all my power was fled, swifter than lightning hurried through my enfeebled veins, and vanished all.'[15]

At the end of November there was a sighting of the vis-à-vis out and about in London, but the papers also reported that Mrs Robinson had given up her box at the opera and was rarely seen. It was lamented that her absence deprived the winter season of new dress designs: the *bon ton* had suffered a paralysis of its own as a result of the absence of its fashion leader. Mary's main occupation as she convalesced was her writing. Her daughter records that 'even under so severe a calamity, the powers of her mind, and the elasticity of her spirits, triumphed over the weakness of her frame. This check to the pleasures and vivacity of youth, by depriving her of external resource, led her to the more assiduous cultivation and development of her talents.'[16] Her return to writing was stimulated not only by her immobility but also by the fact that she was in financial difficulty. Creditors were reportedly knocking at her door. The £500 annuity was proving insufficient to clear her debts. The precious vis-à-vis was seized in execution for a debt, though recovered when Fox generously advanced the money. According to the *Morning Herald*, 'the grateful fair one' determined 'that the *Lion couchant* should be erased from the pannels, and a *Fox rampant* placed in his stead'.[17]

During December Sir Joshua Reynolds put the finishing touches to the painting on which he had been working all year. A reporter saw it in his studio:

> Sir Joshua Reynolds has lately finished another *portrait* of Mrs Robinson; in which she does not retain the composure given her in the character of a *beauty*, after the manner of Reubens, but

> appears the *dejected Charlotte* of Werter . . . Her aspect is *melancholy* itself; her hair is disordered; and her attire simple to a degree. The scene of landscape, and water, which is introduced, seems to illustrate the character, and give a portrait of a depressed state of mind.[18]

The impression given here is that the image reflects Mary's state of mind during her months of indisposition, but the decision to paint her in profile with a forlorn expression must have been made when she began sitting for the portrait back in the spring. This suggests that even before becoming immobilized she was planning a change of public image.

The second Reynolds portrait was widely circulated in the form of engravings in later years. In this form it was given various titles, including *Contemplation*. It appeared as frontispiece to Mary's *Poems* of 1791, her *Lyrical Tales* of 1800, and her posthumous *Poetical Works* of 1806. It was thus the authorized image of Mrs Robinson the author. Whereas Reynolds's first portrait had made her into 'the character of a *beauty*, after the manner of Reubens', in the second one the viewer is intended to concentrate upon her mood. She is the picture of thoughtfulness, introspection, wistfulness. This particular pose of the turned-away head was known technically as a lost profile: a fitting posture for Perdita, 'the lost one'.

The decision to place her in a bleak landscape of rock, sea, and overcast sky also turns the portrait into a history painting. The haunting background implies a narrative: Mary comes to resemble an abandoned woman filled with melancholy, gazing with sorrow on a tempestuous sea and a distant horizon. The article in the *Morning Herald* suggested a resemblance to the dejected Charlotte in the archetypal novel of sensibility, Goethe's *Sorrows of Young Werther*, but classically educated spectators would also have thought of Ariadne, deserted by her lover on a desolate rock on Naxos. Deserted females of classical mythology were associated with writing. Their stories reached the eighteenth century by way of Ovid's highly popular and influential epistolary poems the *Heroides*, love elegies written in the voices of figures such as Ariadne and Sappho. In this sense, the second Reynolds portrait prepares the way for Mary's later career as a writer who became known as the British Sappho. The portrait stayed with Reynolds until his death and is now in the Wallace Collection together with the Romney and the Gainsborough.

Mary's health began to improve in the New Year. In early January she was seen in the Prince of Wales's box at the opera, wearing a blue hat and looking very beautiful. Relations with her royal ex-lover must have remained cordial. But she was then 'confined to her chamber' for a further three weeks 'with a return of her rheumatic complaint'.[19] She was attended by a distinguished doctor called Sir John Elliott.

There was more bad publicity at this time. A scurrilous pamphlet seems to have been published under the title *The Amours of FLORIZEL, an entertaining narrative, by the highly esteemed Mrs R—n commonly called Perdita* (cost one shilling and sixpence). It apparently sold out in a matter of days: a press advertisement announced that 'Many Gentlemen having been disappointed of the above very entertaining production, have now an opportunity of being supplied with the second edition.'[20] Not a single copy of this pamphlet survives.

By the end of the month, Mary had her opera box back, 'cushioned with Rose-colored Sattin – like the Queen of France's'.[21] It was reported that news of her debts was false and that the rumour of them reflected badly on the Prince who had recently made her independent. The supposed state of her affairs, both personal and financial, was made public a few days later. Here there was even a mention of her estranged husband, who was still in town:

> It is asserted that Florizel has lately made Perdita a settlement of eight hundred pounds a year; she has likewise five hundred pounds a year, from Lord M—n, exclusive of her house, equipage, etc., which are provided for her. Renard, being now upon *half-pay*, cannot do any great matters for her in the pecuniary way. – When *he gets in again*, he proposes to make up all deficiencies.
>
> There has been a laudable pride in Mrs Robinson's preferring to withdraw herself from public diversions, rather than purchase *pleasure* at the expence of *delicacy*. She deserves applause for this conduct, in spite of all that envy or detraction can invent to condemn her; and, where incontrovertible facts appear to her honour and advantage, it would be unpardonable not to do her justice. – This lady's husband has got *apartments* in St George's Fields. *Quere*, as she enjoys all the *luxuries of life*, she should allow him, at least, the *necessaries of life*, such as *provision*, *pocket-money*, a *bed-fellow*, etc.[22]

The amount of the Prince's annuity is inflated here; the true value of Malden's is not known for sure.

On 31 January 1784 the *Morning Herald* celebrated Mary's full-scale re-emergence into the fashionable world: she had started 'appearing in all the attractions of beauty in the different streets of St James's to the great mortification of the female world' and 'notwithstanding the reports of her indisposition we never remember to have seen her look better'. Even the *Morning Post* was forced to admit that she had fully recovered from what it (inaccurately) called her 'palsy'. Each morning she drove a few hundred yards down to Piccadilly, took an airing down St James's Street, through Pall Mall, by the Prince's residence at Carlton House, and then back home to Berkeley Square again.

Tarleton was also planning a homecoming. The Fox–North Government had collapsed and he saw the opportunity to begin a political career of his own. He returned to town in March and moved straight in with Mary. Neither his mother nor his old commanding officer Cornwallis was best pleased. 'The gallant *Tarleton*,' the *Morning Post* revealed in a paragraph full of the double entendre that always surrounded the couple, 'is again on duty in Berkley-square. He is no longer Perditus but Restoratus. His skill is as great as ever and he can go through all the evolutions, from loading to firing, with the tattoo only.'[23] Whether or not the paralysis of Mary's legs affected the process of Tarleton's loading and firing in her bed during the later years of their relationship will never be known. Nevertheless, a full decade after being disabled she wrote in her 'Ode to Rapture' of 'Fierce Delight', 'The snowy Bosom, beating high', 'throbbing pulses', 'quiv'ring sighs', and an ecstasy 'Too Exquisite To Last'.[24] These may be phrases from the lexicon of sensibility, but they also suggest that erotic pleasure was by no means a distant memory.

CHAPTER 16

Politics

> I shall be rallied, condemned, – laughed at, and lampooned in all the diurnal prints. I shall be the hero of every magazine; the prominent figure in every caricature shop, for these six months to come!
>
> Mary Robinson, *Angelina*

Foreign affairs did not become easier, despite the end of the American war. With America gone, Britain's most important colony was India. For generations, it had been run indirectly: the East India Company was the de facto government. The state benefited from the colony through taxes and duties, without the expense of an administrative structure and an occupying army. The problem was that the head of the Company, Warren Hastings, was governing Bengal as if it were a personal fiefdom. Corruption was rife, security was unstable, and the Company was in debt. One thing that Fox and North could agree on was that the Indian situation must be taken in hand – North had previously introduced a Regulating Act and Fox was ready to take forward more radical reform. In November 1783 he introduced an India Bill in the House of Commons. Its intention was to oversee the East India Company much more rigorously than ever before: in effect, the Company would be run by a group of seven commissioners answerable to Parliament, rather in the manner of a modern quango. The commissioners would have the particular task of

'General Blackbeard Wounded at the Battle of Leadenhall', caricature of Fox and his followers, including Perdita – the only woman in the picture.

rooting out corruption and reining in the power of the governors in Bombay, Madras, and Calcutta.

The Bill was fiercely debated both inside and outside Parliament. Fox's enemies portrayed him as 'Carlo Khan', making his own bid for supreme power in the East. The House of Commons initially passed the Bill, but after the King wrote an open letter to the Lords stating that anyone voting for the Bill was not only not his friend but his personal enemy, the Bill failed at its second reading. Fox was furious: in his view, to have been beaten by the treachery of the King and the influence of the Lords called into question the constitutional settlement that had prevailed for most of the century. The King dissolved Parliament in mid-session, provoking a major constitutional crisis. He went ahead and appointed 24-year-old Tory William Pitt the Younger Chancellor of the Exchequer and First Lord of the Treasury (effectively Prime Minister). Fox was not to be a minister again for twenty-two years, and then only for a few months before his death.

The India Bill and its aftermath spawned many pamphlets and caricatures. In 'General Blackbeard Wounded at the Battle of Leadenhall' by John Boyne, Fox is shown lying on the ground, surrounded by his followers. Leadenhall Street was the location of the headquarters of the East India Company. The composition of the caricature is based on one of the most famous paintings of the age, Benjamin West's vast canvas of the death of General Wolfe at the Battle of Quebec. Immediately behind Fox stands Perdita, bending over him and administering a bottle of smelling salts to his nose. Her right arm is held out behind her to the Prince of Wales, who kneels, kissing her hand, which he holds clasped in his own. What is striking about this caricature is that Perdita is the only woman in it. Although Fox was really living with Armistead and the connection with the Prince was formally at an end, as far as the general public was concerned Mary remained the female face of the coalition.

The King's appointment of Pitt to the premiership meant that there was bound to be a general election early in the New Year. It was called in February and a vicious campaign began. The issue at stake effectively came down to a vote for or against the power of the King. Pitt triumphed in a contest that, in the words of Fox's authoritative biographer Lord John Russell, 'determined for more than forty years the question of the government of England'.[1]

Fox himself fought for the most prominent constituency in the land, that of Westminster itself. The voting system of the time was rather different from the modern system: two seats were available, for which there were three candidates, and the voting took place over a period of several weeks, with a running count of votes being announced each day. Nobody doubted that first past the post would be the war hero Admiral Hood, so the fight for the second seat was between Fox and Sir Cecil Wray.

The Prince of Wales canvassed the borough with Fox, which was a mixed blessing, but the aspect of the campaign that garnered most satirical attention was the prominence of Fox's female supporters – who, of course, did not have votes themselves. Georgiana Duchess of Devonshire campaigned tirelessly on behalf of the Whigs, sporting the blue and buff colours and wearing a fox-fur tippet and a foxtail in her hat. She was alleged to have shaken hands with a butcher and kissed a plumber to gain votes. Her sister Lady Duncannon and various other fine ladies assisted.

It was, however, not only the female aristocrats who canvassed, but also the 'frail sisterhood'. The *Morning Post*, which was vehemently anti-Fox, protested that his supporters were mere prostitutes: 'The modest women have now almost entirely deserted the *Fox-Corner*, Covent Garden, so that the "Man of the People" is at present supported by the *Women of the People*.'[2]

Mary always prided herself on not being a courtesan. She therefore sought to distance herself from Fox's less reputable supporters: '*Perdita* is so much offended with the *quondam* Man of the People for accepting the assistance of the *disciples of Sappho*, that she has withdrawn her support, declaring her interest shall alone be for a *Man for the Woman*.'[3] She was actually earmarked as the successor to Georgiana as leader of the female canvassers, as the *Morning Post* made clear in a striking report in the later stages of the campaign: 'The Duchess of Devonshire is so *jaded* by the fatigues of canvassing, that she must step down from the *niche* she has hitherto occupied among the BEVY OF BEAUTIES. *Perdita* is nominated for the succession by the *High Priest* of the Temple.'[4] Historians have made much of Georgiana's prominent role in the campaign, but wholly neglected Mary Robinson's equal prominence.

The pro-Fox *Morning Herald* celebrated her every public appearance during the month of April, when the canvassers were out daily, pulling in the voters: 'Mrs *Robinson's* equipage was yesterday exhibited in the environs of St James's, with the additional splendour of *new liveries*: in the room of the cockade *militaire*, a favor inscribed with *Fox and Freedom* struck the eye.'[5] The *Rambler's Magazine* also made a point of noting how her celebrated carriage was now sporting the motto 'Fox and Freedom'.

Soon after the end of the dramatic campaign a day-by-day account of its vicissitudes was published. It gives a fine sense of the highs and lows of Perdita's involvement. Thus one day: 'Henrietta-street is now become the resort of all the fashionable *reps*. *Perdita* attends constantly, and throws out Fox's colours. Query, How many voters may *Perdita's* fair face gain over to the cause?' Then another: 'Notwithstanding the assiduity of our modern Venus, in her canvass of yesterday, to her great disappointment, she could not secure a single *plumper*.'[6] And when the voting went badly: '*Perdita* seems to have *lost* her bloom as well as her spirits. Is the P— still *insensible*? Or does she lament the *decay* of the party?'[7]

Mary herself contributed not only with her presence on the streets but also with poems, squibs, and songs praising Fox and the Duchess of Devonshire and condemning Pitt and Sir Cecil Wray. The poems, published in the *Morning Herald*, are anonymous, but bear the hallmarks of her style. One of them, 'Stanzas in Season', is written in praise of Georgiana:

She saw, she conquer'd: *Wray* shrunk back;
Court mandates we no more obey;
Majorities no more they pack;
And *Fox* and *Freedom* win the day!

Who can deny when beauty sues?
And where's the tongue can blame her Grace?
Not timid slavery can refuse
Her life's as spotless as her face.

Let *Pitt* and *Wray* dislike the fair,
Decry our *DEVON*'S Matchless merit;
A braver, kinder soul we wear
And love her *beauty*, love her *spirit*.

Let distant times, and ages know,
When TEMPLE would have made us slaves,
'Tis thus we ward the fatal blow,
'Tis Fox that beats – 'tis DEVON saves![8]

Another witty little verse celebrates the fox's brush as a fashion adornment:

To adorn with its beauty, the hat of a beau,
Or when sew'd to a muff, it makes a fine show.
The brush of a Fox is the height of the taste,
And beautiful now, much as *rouge* or as paste;
Fair Devon and Portland, and Melbourne agree,
That the brush is by far the best branch of the tree.
So *Kepell's* and *Waldegrave's*, together unite,
And support with their interest, the *Fox* and his right.[9]

A more explicitly political song was set to the popular tune of 'Ballynamona Oro',

> Let liberty, mirth, and good humour abound,
> Let Fox, our brave Champion with laurels be crown'd.
> In bumpers of claret the toast shall go round,
> While a Man of the People is still to be found.[10]

The latter two songs, in which Mary puts her muse in the service of populist politics, were published on the final two days of the seven-week polling. Admiral Hood won, as expected, and Fox just squeezed into second place, only for there to be further controversy when instead of returning the two candidates highest on the poll the High Bailiff granted a 'scrutiny' (in modern parlance, a recount). It was confirmed that Fox had come in above Wray, and a jury in the Court of Common Pleas later fined the Bailiff £2,000 for his high-handed action in questioning the result. Fox was paraded through the streets on a chair and received in triumph at Devonshire House. He was back in Parliament, but facing long years on the Opposition benches.

Meanwhile, in Liverpool, Tarleton was narrowly defeated in his own election campaign. He returned to London to join in the celebrations on behalf of Fox. The Prince of Wales hosted a party at Carlton House with 600 guests, who overflowed into the gardens. Nine marquees were erected and refreshments consisted of the finest fruits of the season, confectionaries, ices, creams, and 'emblematical designs, ornamented with mottoes and other devices, in honor of the triumph which they were to celebrate'. Four bands of instruments were placed at different parts of the garden, and the company were 'entertained with various novelties of a comic kind'.[11] Tarleton was certainly there and, given her prominence in the campaign, Mary surely would have been, too.

Supporters of the Foxite cause had rallied behind Mary in the course of the campaign. The *Morning Herald* carried a serious defence of her probity:

> Nothing, says a correspondent, but female envy could give birth to the scandalous paragraphs frequently inserted in a certain morning paper [i.e. the *Morning Post*] respecting Mrs Robinson; there is a marked propriety in every part of her conduct that ought to disarm

> even malice itself; but the rancorous slanders of her own sex are not to be appeased. It is shameful to see this lovely and amiable woman ranked with notorious characters under the familiar appellation of *Perdita*. There is not, continues our correspondent, a woman in England so much talked of and so little known as Mrs Robinson, and while those who are acquainted with her private life admire and applaud her conduct, her good sense will teach them to despise the envious attacks of slander and malevolence.[12]

To call her 'Perdita', it is implied here, was to rank her among the courtesans, which was a gross injustice to her true status. In a sense, the transition from 'Perdita', actress and royal mistress, to 'Mary Robinson', woman of letters and political campaigner, began during the heat of the Westminster election.

She paid a heavy price for her personal and political commitment to Fox. Throughout the campaign she was pilloried mercilessly in caricatures, pamphlets, squibs, and newspaper paragraphs.

A caricature called 'The Goats Canter to Windsor or the Cuckold's Comfort' (14 March) shows her being driven by the Prince of Wales in a high gig drawn by six goats, one of them ridden by Fox. Three men on goats ride beside the gig: Thomas Robinson, wearing his customary cuckold's horns and facing backwards (which is to say that Mary has left him behind), Lord North (almost certainly not a lover, but perceived as such in the press), and Tarleton in military dress. A different caricature published the same day, showing Fox vomiting into a chamber pot, is captioned with some ribald verses that begin

> Mr Fox Mr Fox
> If you had the *** [pox]
> What a blessing t'would be to the nation;
> If Perdita Would
> For once do some good
> She'd Secure you a tight Salivation.

In another caricature, 'A Race For A Crown', published a few days later, Fox, North, and others ride a race mounted on lions, cheered on by the Prince and Mrs Robinson. The triangle of Fox, Prince, and Perdita is also the subject of 'The Adventure of Prince Pretty Man' (see p. 156), in which a Falstaffian Fox supports on his shoulders the Prince of Wales, who is stuffing the Great Seal of England into a burglar's swag bag. Perdita, wearing a trademark feathered hat and with her hands in one of her celebrated muffs, looks on, in the company of a bare-breasted Armistead. It is noteworthy that Perdita is the more decently dressed, not exposed in the manner of a whore.

In the course of the polling weeks there were many more caricatures of this kind, several of them associating Perdita with Georgiana, all linking her to Fox. So, for example, 'The Last Dying Words of Reynard the Fox' (early April, when Fox was behind in the poll) has him saying 'Perdition catch that *Wray!* I am lost for ever! . . . curse on all the World but my dear *Perditta*; oh! I am now nothing.' Mary's fame in *The Winter's Tale* merges nicely into the mesh of Shakespearean quotation.

Because Mary was so much more famous than Elizabeth Armistead and because she played such an active part in the campaign (Fox's 'dearest Liz' remained out of town at his country residence in Surrey), she was the one who was labelled 'The Woman of the People' and assumed to be Fox's mistress. Squibs on the Whigs would typically end with Fox saying that he was off to visit Perdita in Berkeley Square.

Sheridan was a close ally, so one satirical pamphlet took the form of a parody of his most famous play, entitled *The School for Scandal, A Comedy in Five Acts, As it is Performed by His Majesty's Servants, etc.* The title page mimics the typography of the authentic edition of the play so exactly that the British Library copy of the pamphlet is miscatalogued as Sheridan's own work. The characters are the usual crew: Boreas for North, Reynard for Fox, and so on. In the funniest scene – which was extracted and printed independently in the April issue of the *Rambler's Magazine* – Perdita enters alone and complains about how the affairs of state are depriving her of her Charley. The dialogue is full of references to his portly figure and hirsute features: 'With him I am in heaven – To gaze upon his patriarchal face, and lean upon his dear black bosom, is Elysium to me! – The covering of his breast resembles the downy plumage of the raven – The prickling of his manly beard, how grateful to my chin . . . the easy rotundity of his figure excels in excellence the well-turned nine-pin!' Reynard then enters and there is a discussion about Perdita's desirability.

'Do you know that princes have sighed for me, and sighed in vain!' she asks, to which he replies, 'That princes have sigh'd for you, is not at all improbable, but that they have *sigh'd in vain*, I cannot so readily admit.' Perdita then complains that her coach-maker is threatening her over unpaid bills. Reynard says that he cannot do anything until he is in 'place'. Perdita then makes her demand: 'Either produce me *the ready*, or you and I must be hereafter strangers to each other.' Reynard storms out and she confides in soliloquy that she is not really afraid of losing him because he cannot keep away from her above twenty hours at a time.

The satire here is innocuous enough. Far more damaging was a series of articles that began appearing in the *Rambler's Magazine*. They were advertised as extracts from a recently published book called *Annals of Gallantry*. The book itself, if it ever existed, has not survived, but the serialized extracts are identical to passages in the scurrilous *Memoirs of Perdita*: the account of her purported first love-tryst in the inn at Richmond, her encounter with the well-endowed sailor in the moving coach, the Prince in her bedroom, a gift of champagne from a wealthy merchant, the affair with Malden, an unsavoury incident involving a Jew at Margate. It can reasonably be assumed that the surviving *Memoirs of Perdita* is a reprint of the *Annals of Gallantry* with a new title page (still dated 1784). This strongly suggests that the first full-length 'biography' of Mary was written at the time of the Westminster election with the specific purpose of discrediting her because of her political activities on behalf of the Foxites. In this sense, her political commitment cost her dearly in respect of her long-term reputation.

The *Memoirs of Perdita* was published by a politically engaged bookseller named Lister. Around the same time, he also attacked Fox via his sex life in a very similar work entitled *The Amours of Carlo Khan*. Elizabeth Armistead is the main female interest here, but one chapter provides a fictionalized account of Fox's affair with Perdita, rendered in a style more comic than lascivious. Perdita spends most of her time complaining that she has failed to seduce Edmund Burke: 'though I admire the sublimity of his oratory, I neither look upon him as the man of business, nor the man of pleasure: for were I disposed to grant him the *last favour*, instead of coming to the *point*, he would read me a lecture upon the beautiful protuberance of my bosom, or the elegant *variations of the curves* in my limbs'.[13] As a helpful footnote indicates, the language parodied here is that of Burke's *Philosophical Enquiry into the Origin of our Ideas of the Sublime and the Beautiful.*

Lister also published *The Effusions of Love: being the Amorous Correspondence between the Amiable Florizel, and the Enchanting Perdita, in a series of letters, faithfully transcribed from the original Epistles and Billets-doux in Possession of the Editor.* Again, the satire is handled with a light touch. The epistles mock the language of sensibility which the original correspondence between the Prince and the actress unquestionably did use; 'Florizel' frequently drops into French, as the Prince indeed would have done; the opportunity is taken to mock Perdita for her succession of lovers from Sir John Lade to Fox to Tarleton, and for her extravagant taste, particularly in the matter of transportation; but the material never approaches the salaciousness of the *Memoirs of Perdita*. The purpose was to entertain male readers as much as to chip away at the credibility of the Foxites and the heir-apparent.

Mary was reputedly being maintained by a combination of the Prince's annuity and subventions from Fox, but in reality she was struggling financially. At the beginning of May it was reported that she had a sheriff instead of a prince in her house and that her thousand-guinea vis-à-vis was to be sold. The *Morning Herald* issued one of its denials, combined with some fresh double entendres: the carriage was still in the possession of the fair one, but she had dispensed with 'one of her flaunting footmen'. 'The *body*,' continued the report, 'still appears well hung, and the *wheels* run as free as ever.'[14]

Rumours of one sort and another continued to abound, for instance that she had designed a 'toilet' or dressing area of a circular form, contrived so that when she sat in the middle of it she could see all parts of her person at one view – she was supposed to be expecting 'a patent for the sale of it'.[15] Needless to say, this accusation of vanity was published in the *Morning Post*, where there was also an article saying that Mary was now so short of money she could neither afford to attend the masquerade nor to pay her tame editor for a newspaper puff concerning her appearance there. The pro-Pitt *Morning Post* simply could not forgive or forget Mary's public support for Fox in the streets of Westminster. Well over a month after the end of the campaign, it was reported that the white silk banner 'Sacred to female Patriotism' that had been sported in

Fox's victory procession to Whitehall was 'to be given to the *Perdita* for her memorable exertions in the service of the people!'[16] And again, two weeks later: 'The *Cyprian divinity* of Berkeley-square is said to be *on her last legs*. Thus the fate of the *Buff* and *Blue* extends through all their connexions; famine and disgrace bringing up the rear!'[17] The invective against 'the Perdita' as leader of 'the electioneering *petticoat squad*'[18] filled the pages of the *Morning Post* throughout the summer.

That phrase '*on her last legs*', an allusion at once to her illness and her financial embarrassment, inspired a particularly cruel caricature which served as frontispiece to the August issue of the *Rambler's Magazine*. Entitled 'Perdita upon her last legs', it shows her as a streetwalker, wearing a ragged low-cut dress. Her legs are thin and shrivelled. Posters advertising *Florizel and Perdita* and *Jane Shore* (the tragedy of a rejected royal mistress) are pinned on the wall as a reminder of the stage career in which those same legs had been so admired. She is begging from the Prince, who hands her a purse. An accompanying article, with the subtitle 'the lamentations of a Magdalen', has her complaining that she has been 'Forsaken by my P—, neglected by my c—l', that she is losing her looks to disease, and that her admired eyes are no longer shining so brightly.[19]

Tarleton and Mary spent the summer season in Brighton. It was not only fashionable – the Prince was there, with the Dukes of Chartres and Lauzun – but also afforded opportunities for treatment of the acute rheumatic fever, which had recurred. They stayed at the Ship Inn, from where a desperate Mary, knowing that the Prince was in town, appealed to him for help. His reply expressed his concern, but was cautious about any further financial assistance. He promised to visit her late in the evening. We do not know whether he made good on that assurance.

Mary kept the letter and treasured it for the rest of her life. Since she had been forced to return the 'Florizel' correspondence, this was the only letter of the Prince's that was hers to preserve. It is now bound together with the original manuscript of her *Memoirs*:

> Dear Mrs Robinson
> I have receiv'd your Letter, and it really quite overcomes me, the scene of distress you so pathetically paint. I will certainly wait upon you, but I am afraid it will be late before I can come to the Ship, as I have company with me. Should it be within *the*

> *compass of my means* to secure you from the abyss you apprehend that is before you, and for which you mention Mr Brent, I need not say that the temptation of gratifying others and at the same time, and by the same means, making one's self happy, is too alluring to be neglected a single moment; however you must allow me to be thus explicit and candid, that it must in great measure depend upon the extent of what will be necessary to be done for your service, and how far my funds may be adequate, as well as my powers equal to attain that object. In the mean time only rest assured of my good wishes and good intentions. I am dear Mrs Robinson, very sincerely yours George.[20]

'Mr Brent' was presumably one of the creditors beating on Mary's door. For all the tenderness expressed here, neither the Prince nor anyone else bailed her out this time: the abyss opened before her.

An execution on her property was placed by the Sheriff of Middlesex, and her belongings were auctioned off by Messrs Hutchins, Boulton, and Philips of King Street, Covent Garden. The famed vis-à-vis was finally disposed of; her Gainsborough painting went for just over thirty guineas. The sale also included other mementoes such as the Prince's lock of hair. Before starting the proceedings, the auctioneers stated that if anyone would pay or give security for £250 the goods would be returned to their owner. But no one came forward. The one valuable that Mary was able to hold back from the sale was the diamond-encrusted miniature portrait of the Prince that she had worn next to her bosom for so long.

The combination of bankrupty, ill repute, and degenerative disease was enough to drive her from the country. On 13 August 1784 it was announced that '*Mrs Robinson* has been obliged within these few days to leave England for the Continent for the recovery of her health. She has lost almost the use of her limbs, and upon her journey was lifted in and out of her carriage. Her disorder is a rheumatic gout of so obstinate a nature that her recovery is doubtful.'[21] When it came to the time for embarkation, she would have been carried into a rowing boat and then lifted onto the cross-Channel 'packet'.

Needless to say, a few days later the editor of the *Morning Post* found himself unable to resist a bout of moralizing on the news:

The example of the *Perdita*, which two or three years ago was of the most dangerous kind to the beautiful and the thoughtless of her sex, is now as salutary; a life of wanton dissipation has reduced her to penury and distress; poverty, with all its horrors, surrounds her; her constitution and the use of her limbs are gone; death stares her in the face, and no comfort is left but the recollection of such actions as contradicted the general tenor of her conduct. To view the Perdita *now*, would be a lesson indeed![22]

PART THREE

Woman of Letters

CHAPTER 17

Exile

> Mrs Robinson lived chiefly on the continent for nearly five years, and on her return home in 1788, she commenced her literary labours. We congratulate herself and the public that her mind took this more satisfactory turn; because it afforded not only an improved use of time, but has been the cause of engaging her attention to general delight.
>
> William Godwin, 'Character of Mary Robinson'

Wrapped in fur and fleecy hosiery, Mary huddled close to Tarleton on the deck of the Brighton–Dieppe packet boat. The Colonel and his lover, accompanied by her mother and young Maria Elizabeth, were setting off for the Continent in search of health cures and freedom from their creditors. They arrived in Paris with hardly any money and Mary in very poor health.

In October 1784, Tarleton's brother John crossed the English Channel and traced them to the Hôtel de Russie on the rue de Richelieu. He sent a report back to his mother:

> The Colonel and myself have met several times, and we seem to be on friendly terms – I have dined with him and he has returned the compliment. Mrs R. is in a bad state of health and cannot in my opinion survive the Winter, as she is most dreadfully afflicted with

the Rheumatism. I had the satisfaction of dining with him on Friday last, and was informed that she intended to reside here the whole season if her health would permit her.[1]

The newspapers back home still took an interest in them: there were paragraphs referring to Tarleton's boast that he had '*killed more men, and ruined more women, than any other man in Europe*' and to how 'the lovely, though ill-fated Mrs Robinson' was 'the now too verified *Perdita*' – in other words, she really was 'the lost one'. With the onset of winter, they seem to have headed south to the Côte d'Azur. The *Morning Post* reported that Perdita was 'in the South of France', wintering 'upon the scanty pittance gleaned from the Remnant of her amorous treasures'.[2] They apparently stayed for a few weeks in the resort of Villefranche, near Nice.

By mid-January they had returned to Paris. From there, Mary wrote one of her very few surviving letters to the Prince. It is, of course, about money:

Jan[uar]y 17th 1785, Hotel de Russie, rue de Richelieu, Paris

My dear Sir,
Colonel Hotham will perhaps inform your Royal Highness of my having apply'd for the last quarters annuity, if it is more convenient to you to pay it half yearly, I will with pleasure wait till that time, wishing in every respect to do what is most agreable [sic] to your Royal Highness.

I should not have made any application to Colonel Hotham, but being in want of money (on account of Lord Maldens neglecting to pay his annuity these *fifteen months* past,) – will I trust be deem'd a sufficient apology. –

As I fear I shall not dare return to England for some time, I shall be infinitely happy in executing any orders your Royal Highness will honor me with during my residence in Paris. I have the honor of subscribing myself

Your Royal Highness's affectionate and faithful servant
Mary Robinson[3]

It was a shrewd move to prick the Prince's conscience by telling him of Malden's failure to keep up with his annuity.

Another ex-lover, the Duke of Lauzun, came to Mary's assistance. In February she was reported to be at his chateau in the country, 'much invalided'.[4] All this travelling won Colonel Tarleton and Mrs Robinson a new nickname back home: 'The Wandering Lovers'.[5] They considered the possibility of wandering south to Italy, where Mary's merchant brothers lived. John, her elder brother, had offered to take her in; she seems to have seriously contemplated a permanent move to Leghorn, far from the 'calumny and persecution' of her life in England.

Despite her absence, Mary remained in the public eye in London for a few more months. That summer Thomas Rowlandson completed a watercolour panorama of the pleasure gardens at Vauxhall. It was engraved and widely circulated, becoming an iconic image of the fashionable world. It depicted an evening scene, with full orchestra and a famous soprano singing from a balcony. In the supper box beneath the orchestra sits Dr Johnson (who had actually died the previous year) with his friends James Boswell, Oliver Goldsmith (also dead), and Mrs Hester Thrale. In the foreground are the Duchess of Devonshire and her sister Lady Duncannon arm in arm. On the right stands the Prince of Wales, whispering to Mrs Robinson. Her arm is linked with that of her husband – unflatteringly shown as short and stooped, ugly and elderly. Mrs Robinson is beautifully dressed, wearing one of her trademark hats. She is imagined in her prime, slim and lovely, with no sign of her lameness.

Mary's doctor suggested that the spa town of Aix-la-Chapelle in Germany would be a more suitable destination than Italy. Now known as Aachen, it retains the status it had then as one of Europe's leading health resorts. Mary and Tarleton took up residence there and started on a joint literary work: an account of the Colonel's military campaigns in America. According to the testimony of 10-year-old Maria Elizabeth, who was with them, these were the most tranquil and in many respects happiest months of her mother's life. In their four years together, Mary's relationship with Tarleton had been beset with difficulties. As well as coping with the intense public interest in their lives, Mary was continually aware of the fact that Tarleton's family disapproved of the union. Other pressures were of their own making. The lovers were known for their fiery temperaments, both were flirtatious and attractive to the opposite sex, they were extravagant and struggled financially in keeping up with their aristocratic friends. Mary's accident and ensuing paralysis had forged a bond between them, but was it strong enough to withstand poverty and exile?

Love affairs between famous people can be severely put to the test when they are out of the public eye, but in this case Mary and Tarleton's relationship strengthened during their years abroad. Mary had her lover to herself, her health was improving, and they were working together, sharing each other's talents: as they pored over the source documents for the *History of the Campaigns* – pamphlets, order books, memoranda, letters from commanding officer Cornwallis – she became intimate for the first time with his military life, his courage and endurance, while he had the opportunity to share in her gift for writing.

For young Maria Elizabeth, time abroad provided an opportunity to learn foreign languages and read widely: she was tutored by a Frenchman, an 'excellent master' who was 'acquainted with all the modern languages' and who brought a certain frisson to the household by virtue of his claim to have been the tutor of the young woman who was the real-life original of Charlotte, the epitome of the sentimental heroine in Goethe's hugely influential novel *The Sorrows of Young Werther*.[6]

They did not devote themselves exclusively to the quiet life of the writer. There was plenty of new society in the fashionable spa town. The Duke and Duchess of Chatelet became particular friends. 'Balls, concerts, rural breakfasts, succeeded to each other in gay and attractive variety', not least in order to take Mary's mind off her physical pain: 'when compelled by severer paroxysms of her malady to seclude herself from their society, a thousand kind stratagems were planned and executed to relieve her sufferings, or soften the dejection to which they unavoidably gave rise'. The baths afforded the best available relief and they were made as inviting as possible: 'Sometimes, on entering her dark and melancholy bath', the gloom of which was increased by high grated windows, she beheld the surface of the water covered with rose-leaves, while the vapour baths were impregnated with aromatic odours.' The Duke and Duchess's nephews and niece did everything they could to cheer her spirits: when Mary could not sleep for pain, they stood beneath her window and sang her favourite songs to the accompaniment of a mandolin.

News of her literary endeavours filtered back to London. The *Morning Herald* announced that she had written a comic opera set in Villefranche, the principal character being 'a pretended experimental philosopher, who is visited by Ladies of all nations to learn the effect of animal magnetism'.[7] This would presumably have been a satire on James Graham and his Celestial Bed, though the setting suggests that she may have encountered some further fashionable eccentricities during her brief residence on the French Riviera. The work was never finished.

In December 1785, Mary's father, Nicholas Darby, who had become a Captain in the Russian Navy, died and was buried with full military honours. From the whale fisheries of Labrador via the assault on Gibraltar to the Navy of Catherine the Great: it had been a colourful life. He garnered some respectful obituaries, though Mary always resented the fact that he was accepted more fully into the Russian Navy than the British. She wrote a long and somewhat verbose elegy to his memory. On a foreign shore herself, she was acutely aware that her father had died an exile and that she might suffer the same fate herself. As far as is known, her mother Hester lived with her on the Continent – she would have looked after Maria Elizabeth when Mary was working – but there is no record of her reaction to the news of the death of her estranged husband.

During this time, Tarleton made periodic trips home in order to deal with his parlous financial affairs and pursue the possibility of new postings. Nothing came his way, but he no doubt returned with all the latest society gossip. The *ton* was agog with news of the Prince of Wales's affair with an older woman of the Roman Catholic faith, Maria Fitzherbert. Their clandestine marriage was an open secret in high society. The Prince's relationship with Mrs Fitzherbert provoked a new round of caricatures, in which Perdita frequently appeared in the role of a jilted lover.

On 14 July 1786 London society reacted with shock to the news of the sudden death of Mary Robinson in Paris, where she had been living in exile with her lover. The story was broken in a full-column report in the *Morning Post*: 'Mrs Robinson, the once famous *Perdita*, died a few days ago at Paris.'[8]

The obituary told of her rise from her obscure origins as an illegitimate child to her brief moment of fame as renowned actress and first mistress of the Prince of Wales. Courted by the rich and famous, she had enjoyed many love affairs before securing her place as a leader of the fashionable world and a dabbler in poetry. But once she retired to the Continent, the obituarist continued, her admirers lost interest in both her life and her poetry. She was abandoned by her lovers, sank into obscurity, and died in poverty.

The *Morning Post* described her as 'genteel in her manners, delicate in her person, and beautiful in her features'. It also acknowledged her literary abilities and her humanity, citing her kindness to her fellow actress Mrs Baddeley when she was at her lowest ebb. Had Perdita 'walked in the paths of virtue and peace' she 'would have been an ornament to her sex . . . but a strong propensity to dissipation and the *haut ton* overcame her virtue and her sense'. In mock-tribute to her reputation as a poet, the *Morning Post* added the following verse couplet 'as a good natured hint to the Cyprian multitude': 'Let coxcombs flatter, and let fools adore, / Here learn the lesson to be vain no more!'

But Mary Robinson had not died in Paris. She was alive and well in a spa town in Germany. Three weeks later the *Morning Post* printed her witty response to the obituary:

> Aux Bains de la Rose
> Aix-la-Chapelle, Germany, July 20, 1786
>
> SIR,
> With astonishment I read in a Morning Post, of the 14th instant, a long account of my *death*, and a variety of circumstances respecting my *life*, equally void of the smallest foundation.
>
> I have the satisfaction of informing you, that so far from being *dead*, I am in the most perfect state of health; except a trifling lameness, of which, by the use of the baths at this place, I have every reason to hope I shall recover in a month or six weeks. I propose passing my winter in London, having been near two years upon the continent, though not at Paris half the time.[9]

Mary had not lost her keen sense of the best way to handle the press and its readers. She had long been accustomed to dealing with scandal and gossip. The renewal of the old allegations about her sexual dissipation must have stung, yet the characteristically good-humoured opening sentences of her letter deflated the overblown vitriol of the *Morning Post*'s report. Having gained the readers' sympathy and support, she made no attempt to deny the cruel and lewd remarks levied against her. She simply corrected the erroneous facts regarding the circumstances of her birth, pointing out that she was not illegitimate but was the daughter of the recently deceased Captain Darby. Her mother was not an innkeeper, as the obituary had asserted, but was descended from a highly respectable family, the Seys of Boverton Castle in Glamorganshire. She was from the mercantile hub of Bristol, not, as had been suggested, the Somerset backwater of Ilminster ('a place to which I am a total stranger'). Her schooling, she reported, had been under the tutelage of the moralist and Evangelical writer, Hannah More.

Mary ended her letter with an appeal to the finer instincts of the editor: 'As a man of feeling, I request you to contradict the report, with candour, and all possible expedition. I have brothers in Italy, who will experience the greatest anxiety, should such a detail reach their ears.' She also stressed that her absence from home made her especially vulnerable: 'I am fully convinced, that your knowledge of the world, and liberal sentiments, will induce you to render justice to a person, whose absence requires an advocate.' The *Morning Post* made no apology or retraction, but at least it printed the letter.

In January 1787 Tarleton was back in London. He was spotted at a levee (morning party) and the papers reported that his '*History of the Campaigns in Virginia and the Neighboring Provinces* is well spoken of by those who have seen the manuscript'. The *Morning Herald* quipped: 'on this occasion we may say with Shakespeare "What, the sword and the pen, – do you study both, Mr Colonel?"'[10] It was widely assumed that Mrs Robinson's pen had done much of the work on her lover's behalf. The book was published in March and well reviewed. But the *History of the Campaigns* did not make Tarleton's fortune. He tried another course, becoming a professional gambler, with his own 'faro bank' (casino) at Daubigney's Tavern. Though he professed to despise affairs of honour, he also became involved in a duel, acting as second to the adventurer and man about town, Colonel Hanger.

Still struggling with her lameness, Mary decided to try the hot mud baths at St Amand les Eaux in Flanders (now near the border between France and Belgium). Though a smaller and less fashionable resort than Aix, it was prettily located on the edge of a forest and had the advantage of specializing – as it still does – in the treatment of rheumatism. Mary made several visits to the mud baths before she could be persuaded to enter the ditches. She was horrified by the experience of being immersed in mud and by the 'reptiles, unknown to other soils, which fasten on the bodies of those who bathe'.[11] But she eventually submitted herself to the treatment, encouraged by the reports of her fellow visitors on the 'wonderful efficacy' of the cure.

She rented 'a small but beautiful cottage near the springs' and passed the summer of 1787 there. Pasted into the original manuscript of her *Memoirs* there is a neat sepia sketch of the cottage, probably the work of her teenage daughter. It shows a long low building, with five windows at the front and four dormers above; two awnings are pulled down to provide shade; there is a picket fence, a grove of trees to the right, and a little arbour in front. The painting has the feel of Marie Antoinette playing the role of a shepherdess. Mary was always aware of the fleeting quality of things, whether fame or tranquillity. The cottage that had given her such a sense of peace and serenity subsequently became the headquarters of a republican French General during the revolutionary wars that swept across Europe in the 1790s: 'These peaceful vales and venerable woods were, at no distant period, destined to become the seat of war and devastation.'[12] Having completed her work on Tarleton's book, she had more time for her own poetry. A 'Sonnet to the Evening' that was 'written under a tree, in the Woods of St Amand, in Flanders' gives a sense of her mood at this time. It begins with pensive reflection in the 'sweet balmy hour' of dusk, but then turns in the sestet to a tone of melancholy:

> Oft do I seek thy shade, dear withering tree,
> Sad emblem of my own disastrous state!
> Doom'd in the spring of life, alas! like thee,
> To fade, and droop beneath the frowns of Fate;
> Like thee, may Heaven to me the meed bestow,
> To shelter sorrow's child, and soothe the tear of wo[e].[13]

By the autumn of 1787 her health was supposedly 'entirely recovered'.[14] She returned to Paris and stayed in the Hôtel d'Angleterre. Whilst there, she published some well-received poems in the French press. The New Year brought reports of her imminent return across the Channel, though now it was said that she was still in very poor health: 'The return of Mrs Robinson to England is an event that may be expected in a week or little better. She has appealed without success to every remedy on the continent for the restoration of her limbs, and has now the contemplation to try the Bath waters.'[15] Come the end of January, she was installed, together with mother and daughter, at 45 Clarges Street in Mayfair, very close to Devonshire House, the London home of Georgiana Duchess of Devonshire. Number 45 was at the end of the street closest to Piccadilly, just opposite the entrance to Green Park. Tarleton was lodging a few doors away at number 30. The *Morning Post* took a pessimistic view of her health, both physical and mental: 'Mrs Robinson, though better than when she left England, has returned in a very weakly situation, and appears deeply affected and oppressed in spirits.'[16]

She resumed some of her old habits, campaigning for the Foxite candidate Lord John Townshend in the Westminster election, mingling with the set that surrounded the dissipated royal princes, and sometimes appearing in public: 'The Perdita, notwithstanding her long indisposition, still keeps her good looks: she sports an elegant vis-à-vis, and her dress and liveries are in corresponding style.'[17] But physical and financial constrictions meant that she was a shadow of her former self. She also discovered on her return from the Continent that the mood of the times had changed. The public had, for the while, tired of the endless diet of gossip and scandal in the press. Commentators noted that the columns of the papers were no longer filled with the daily doings of the courtesans and fashion leaders:

> It was not without much indignation that I used to observe the paragraphs respecting our most elegant demi-reps with which the public prints abounded . . . Of late, however, I observe, that these articles are discontinued, and the publick are no more pestered with the names of *Perdita* and *the Bird of Paradise*, with the descriptions of their carriages, the colour of their liveries, and the names of their keepers.[18]

Even the *Rambler's Magazine* had taken a marked turn towards decency. The very absence of Perdita from the London scene may have been a contributory cause of this more general change. Shrewd as ever, Mary saw, perhaps with relief, that there would have been no point in trying to recapture past glories, even had it been physically possible to do so. Her own remaking of herself befitted the new world to which she had returned.

For Jane Porter, the novelist who later befriended Mrs Robinson, the years of exile and wandering on the Continent were the turning point in Mary's life. According to Porter's unpublished 'Character of the Late Mrs Robinson', she made a conscious decision at this time to spurn the great and the good in favour of the secluded literary life: 'She now dedicated all her time to the culture of her understanding.'[19] Maria Elizabeth's continuation of her mother's *Memoirs* also dated the commencement of her full-time literary career to this period. And a satirical poem of 1788, *The Promenade: or, Theatre of Beauty*, singled her out as something very unusual for the time: a beauty with brains.

> Next *R-b-ns-n* majestic swims along,
> And adds new beauties to the enchanting throng,
> Engaging Manners with a polish'd Mind,
> Give her distinction mid the most refin'd.[20]

It was the 'polish'd Mind' that would dominate her endeavours for the rest of her life.

On 11 June 1788, the King was seized with a bilious fever; he suffered from violent stomach spasms and bowel movements. After a couple of months' remission, his condition deteriorated rapidly in October and he began to exhibit alarming signs of mental derangement. We now know that he was suffering from a metabolic disorder, porphyria, but at the time it was believed that he had gone mad. His Majesty was locked up at Kew and a specialist doctor, Francis Willis, was called in. The King mouthed obscenities, behaved erratically, and often had to be secured with a straitjacket. A restraining chair, which the King called his 'Coronation chair', was installed at the palace. It was widely assumed that his indisposition would prove permanent, if not fatal, and that the Prince of Wales would have to take his place. On 15 December, Fox wrote to Elizabeth Armistead, 'At any rate the Prince must be Regent and of consequence the ministry must be changed . . . The King himself (notwithstanding the reports you may possibly hear) is certainly worse and perfectly mad.'[21] The Prime Minister, Pitt, tabled proposals for a restricted Regency, giving the Prince limited powers; after much debate, a Regency Bill was passed in February 1789. The Whigs were delighted that the Prince to whom they were so close was on the verge of becoming Regent, but their hopes were almost immediately dashed – with the Bill just days from becoming law, the King recovered.

Mary's thoughts on the prospect of her ex-lover becoming de facto monarch are not recorded. But in the public mind she remained a player in the Prince's drama. A satirical pamphlet entitled *The Death and Dissection, Funeral Procession and Will, of Mrs Regency* (with 'An Address to His Royal Highness the Prince of Wales') celebrated the end of the crisis and the dashing of Whig aspirations. It included amongst the mourners of 'Mrs Regency' the 'Cyprian Corps', processing 'two and two, dressed in weeds, and preceded by Mrs BENWELL and Mrs ARMISTEAD supporting poor PERDITA ROBINSON, in the last stage of an *incontinent* consumption'. 'Perdita' sings 'with a melancholy voice' the old song of 'When I was a young one, what girl was like me, / So wanton, so airy – so brisk as a bee.' This satire is truer than it knows: 'Perdita' may indeed be said to have expired contemporaneously with the first Regency crisis – her name was rarely seen again in the gossip columns of the newspapers. She would not, however, disappear from the public stage altogether, though she now planned a very different and difficult reinvention: Mrs Robinson would put the 'impure sisterhood' far behind her, restore her much-tarnished reputation, and remake herself as a woman of letters and of genius.

CHAPTER 18

Laura Maria

> She then took up new life in London, became literary, brought up her daughter literary, and expressed without qualification her rage when her works were not urged forward beyond all others.
>
> Laetitia-Matilda Hawkins, *Memoirs*

Tarleton resumed his old life of gambling and playing the man about town. The Prince of Wales was often seen at Tarleton's faro club or attending prize fights with him. Mary, meanwhile, concentrated on her poetry. Though she appeared less frequently in public, she still moved in the best circles. Her daughter recounts how the Prince himself resumed his friendship with her: 'Once more established in London, and surrounded by social and rational friends, Mrs Robinson began to experience comparative tranquillity. The Prince of Wales, with his brother the Duke of York, frequently honoured her residence with their presence.'[1]

Mary's work was interrupted when her beloved daughter fell ill with suspected consumption: 'Maternal solicitude for a beloved and only child now wholly engaged her attention: her assiduities were incessant and exemplary, for the restoration of a being to whom she had given life, and to whom she was fondly devoted.'[2] In the summer of 1788, Mary was recommended to go to the seaside resort of Brighton for the sake of her health. Sea-bathing was the latest vogue in healthcare. Tarleton had suffered a groin injury during a game of cricket, and Maria Elizabeth was still sick, so they all went to recuperate.

Mary devoted herself to the care of her daughter, feeling detached from her past life. According to Maria Elizabeth's continuation of the *Memoirs*, she 'beguiled her anxiety by contemplating the ocean, whose successive waves, breaking upon the shore, beat against the wall of their little garden'. Often she would spend the whole night at the window, looking out to sea and 'in deep meditation' contrasting 'the scenes of her former life' with her present circumstances.[3]

In this account, Mary is portrayed very much in the manner of the second Reynolds portrait: a woman of contemplation, gazing at the sea. There can be no doubt that she was a devoted mother, but it is questionable whether she spent all her days and nights at Brighton by her daughter's sickbed. After all, her own mother Hester was there to help (though she is barely mentioned in the latter part of the *Memoirs*), and for that matter Brighton was not so very different from 'the scenes of her former life': most of the fashionable world, including the Prince's secret wife Mrs Fitzherbert, had decamped there for the summer.

Contrary to Maria Elizabeth's image of her mother having been completely severed from her former life, Mary at this time is best described as semi-detached from the *ton*. The Prince was now her acquaintance rather than her lover and she did not wish to be considered solely as Tarleton's partner. She began to create a new circle of friendship for herself. It was developed not at social gatherings in the assembly rooms but on paper through poetic correspondence. Crutches were no impediment to a written self-image.

In 1785 a group of expatriate poets based in Tuscany had published an anthology called *The Florence Miscellany*. Their leader, Robert Merry, called himself 'Della Crusca'. The names of Merry and his colleagues such as William Parsons and Bertie Greatheed are now known only to a handful of literary historians, but in the late 1780s the 'Della Cruscan' style – flowery, effusive, artificial – was quite the rage. These poets were unashamedly concerned with style more than substance: 'Like theatrical dresses if tinsel'd enough, / The tinsel one stares at, nor thinks of the stuff' say the dedicatory lines to *The Florence Miscellany*. The Della Cruscans were mocked by the critics for their ornamental excess – their taste for words such as 'lawny', 'streamy', 'paly' and 'pearly' – but they were admired by readers for their fertility of invention. The Della Cruscans became characterized by their spontaneous, improvisatory quality: they would dash off lines to each other, responding at great speed supposedly in the white heat of pure inspiration.

William Wordsworth heartily disliked what he perceived as the strained artificiality of the Della Cruscans. Their flowery and ornate style could not have been further from his project to reinvigorate poetry by means of communion with sublime mountains and the sincere feelings of Lakeland shepherds. Della Cruscan verse had the same self-consciously theatrical quality that made Wordsworth uncomfortable in the streets of London. The language of Samuel Taylor Coleridge, by contrast, was strongly influenced by the Della Cruscans: when he writes in his early poems of 'dewy light', 'tear's ambrosial dew' and 'temples with Hymettian flow'rets wreathed', he could be a Della Cruscan himself.[4]

Robert Merry returned to England and published a poem under the pseudonym 'Della Crusca' in the newly launched newspaper, *The World*. Entitled 'Adieu and Recall to Love', it expressed his disillusionment with love and invited the public to assist him in finding Cupid again. A reply was soon published under the name 'Anna Matilda': 'O! seize again thy golden quill, / And with its point my bosom thrill.'[5] The poetry-reading public was captivated and the press began to speculate on the identity of the couple. Week by week, their poems to each other appeared, first mildly flirtatious, then notably erotic. It was over a year before they met. Some of Merry's poetic friends knew who 'Anna Matilda' really was: Hannah Cowley, successful comic dramatist, 45, married, respectable, with several children, overweight and showing her age. They kept this information from Merry, fearing that his Muse would dry up on the discovery that she was not in the first flush of youth and beauty. Only with the intervention of a third poetic lover, Mary Robinson, did the long-anticipated meeting between Della Crusca and Anna Matilda take place.

In the autumn of 1788, Mary, writing under the name Laura – the name, that is, of the love-object of Petrarch, father of the sonnet form – published in *The World* a lyric called 'To him who will understand it'.* The poem begins

* Later retitled 'Lines to him who will understand them'.

Thou art no more my bosom's Friend;
Here must the sweet delusion end,
That charm'd my senses many a year,
Thro' smiling summers, winters drear. –

'Laura' then threatens to leave England and take comfort in Italy, where she will find solace through poetry and philosophy:

Britain, Farewell! I quit thy shore,
My native Country charms no more;
No guide to mark the toilsome road;
No destin'd clime; no fix'd abode;
Alone and sad, ordain'd to trace
The vast expanse of endless space . . .
Sweet Poetry shall soothe my soul;
Philosophy each pang controul:
The Muse I'll seek, her lambent fire
My soul's quick senses shall inspire.

The poem appeared with a strong puff from John Bell, editor of *The World*: 'more fanciful and pathetic lines are scarcely to be understood in the whole body of English Literature'.[6]

The 'him who will understand it' was, of course, Tarleton. Mary had convinced herself that he was being unfaithful to her and that their relationship was near its end. But this was not information available to readers of the text published in the newspaper; they had no idea that 'Laura' was actually 'Perdita'. Robert Merry read the poem and assumed that it was a contribution to the ongoing poetic dialogue between 'Della Crusca' and 'Anna Matilda'. The 'him who will understand it' was surely himself! Now he had a second female poet swooning at his feet. He penned a reply 'To Laura', assuring her that all his 'soul was sympathy'.

'Anna Matilda' was not pleased. She was jealous and angry with this new flirtation in print: 'False *Lover!*' she wrote. 'Truest *Poet!* now farewell!' Mary as 'Laura' responded with a conciliatory poem in praise of 'Anna Matilda', and 'Della Crusca' proclaimed 'Heaven of my Heart! Again I hear / Thy long-lost voice.' 'Anna Matilda' was pacified. She published a tantalizing new poem – 'Ambiguous Nature form'd the *female heart*' –

that inspired Merry to go to his friends and demand the real name of his longstanding poetic correspondent.[7] As if walking on air, he hurried to Mrs Cowley's house in Cateaton Street – or Cateaton *Bowers* as he poetically insisted on calling it – only to be deflated by the middle-aged, distinctly unsylphlike figure of the distinguished female dramatist. He had obviously not paid enough attention to the references in her poems to her 'diminished beauty'.[8]

It quickly became public knowledge that Della Crusca was Merry and Anna Matilda Cowley. 'Laura' continued to publish widely admired lyrics in *The World*. They were quoted at fashionable gatherings, reprinted in provincial newspapers, in magazines, and in anthologies with titles such as *The Poetry of The World* (1788) and *The British Album* (1790). But it was some time before she revealed her identity. The *Morning Post* stirred up interest: 'Of all the Della Crusca school, of the *World*, the public is well acquainted with all the writers except the plaintive Laura . . . Mr Merry and Mrs Cowley exult in their poetic fame, while the elegant Laura continues to charm the town under a fictitious signature.'[9] Tribute poems were addressed to 'Laura', and even the Bluestocking Society of learned ladies, under the leadership of the formidable Elizabeth Montagu, 'ventured to admire, nay more, to recite her productions in their learned and critical *coterie*'.[10] They might not have done so had they known who 'Laura' really was.

After some months of such gratifying praise, Mary decided to test public reaction to the true identity of 'Laura' by sending her next poem to *The World* under her own name. She also claimed authorship of all the lines signed 'Laura'. John Bell, the publisher, replied that the poem was '*vastly pretty*', and that he was an admirer of the genius of Mrs Robinson, but that she could not have been the author of the 'Laura' poems because 'he was well acquainted with the author of the productions alluded to'. A 'little disgusted at this incredulity', Mary immediately sent for Bell, 'whom she found means to convince of her veracity, and of his own injustice'.[11]

Around this time, the two poetry editors who worked for Bell at *The World*, Captain Edward Topham and the Reverend Charles Este, had a quarrel as a result of which Este moved to a new paper, the *Oracle*, established by means of a takeover of the *Public Advertiser* and also published by Bell. Este, a Reader of the Chapel Royal in Whitehall, was the better connected of the two. He persuaded Mary to move with him to the *Oracle*. 'We are happy to introduce to Public View any Specimen of Classic Elegance, however short,' that paper announced. 'The following little *Sonnet*, RELISHES of the true Attic Taste; it breathes the tender Strain of *SAPPHO* with the soft pathetic Melancholy of *COLLINS*.'[12] 'Laura' – or rather 'Laura Maria' as she now signed herself, combining her own name with that of Petrarch's beloved – was thus praised for combining the qualities of Sappho, the most famous female poet of antiquity, with those of one of the most admired lyric poets of the later eighteenth century, William Collins. Later, Mary would earn the title 'the English Sappho'. The *Oracle* trumpeted its exclusive hold on her effusions: '*LAURA MARIA is received. It shall be our pride to pay the most respectful attention to her truly elegant Poetical Effusions. To the preference given us, we are by no means insensible; and we anxiously hope for the future communication of this Favourite of the Muses.*' And again, a few days later: 'LAURA MARIA has already acquired Fame, sufficient to excite curiosity and impatience whenever her Productions are announced – that Fame sprang from The ORACLE – To the ORACLE let her Productions, and the CONSEQUENT FAME, be confined.'[13]

Mary effectively became the house poet of the *Oracle*. The Della Cruscan triangle followed her there: Hannah Cowley, still smarting from the way in which 'Laura Maria' had replaced 'Anna Matilda' in the affections of 'Della Crusca', published 'a most malignant unwomanly attack on the *authenticity* of Mrs Robinson's productions', which inspired James Boaden, another poet in the *Oracle* group (and subsequently the paper's editor), to write verses in her defence under his signature 'Arno'. Mary herself responded with a somewhat inflated ode 'To the Muse of Poetry'.[14] Though her first loyalty was to the *Oracle*, Mary also published elsewhere. She cleverly used a variety of pen names, keeping Laura Maria for the *Oracle*. As 'Julia' she carried on a poetic correspondence with 'Arno' (James Boaden) in a number of papers; as 'Oberon' she wrote 'Fairy Rhymes'. On other occasions she was Daphne, Echo, and Louisa.

She later regretted her part in the Della Cruscan vogue: 'dazzled by the false metaphors and rhapsodical extravagance of some contemporary writers, she suffered her judgment to be misled and her taste to be perverted: an error of which she became afterwards sensible'.[15] So what drew her to the style in the first place? The answer seems to have been the poetic disguise, the possibility of experimenting with different voices. By clothing herself in a variety of new written dresses, she was able to put 'Perdita' behind her. At the same time, she was flattered to have male poets swooning at her feet in verse: literary love affairs became a substitute for the adoration of princes and politicians. She also liked the dash – the spontaneous, improvisatory quality – of the Della Cruscans. As she became a more experienced writer, she turned herself into one of the fastest pens in the business. This was a necessity if she was to make a living by means of her writing. Another factor was quite simply her desire to play for popularity: Della Cruscanism was flavour of the month, so she became a Della Cruscan.

Interestingly, Maria Elizabeth's continuation of the *Memoirs* tends to play down the importance of the Della Cruscan influence on Mary. It offers an account of the genesis of 'Lines to him who will understand them' and a number of other key poems that by-pass the story of Merry and Cowley. Here, the flowering of the poetic Muse is attributed not to participation in a literary vogue but to Mary's emotional state in Brighton in the summer of 1788, when she was caring for her sick daughter:

> In the intervals of more active exertion, the silence of a sick chamber proving favourable to the muse, Mrs Robinson poured forth those poetic effusions, which have done so much honour to her genius, and decked her tomb with unfading laurels. Conversing one evening with Mr Richard Burke – son of the celebrated Edmund Burke – respecting the facility with which modern poetry was composed, Mrs Robinson repeated nearly the whole of those beautiful lines, which were afterwards given to the public, addressed – '*To him who will understand them*'.[16]

Young Burke, says Maria Elizabeth, was astonished when Mary told him that the poem was an '*improvisatore*' and that this was the first time of its being repeated. In Maria Elizabeth's account, he asked her to commit the poem to writing and it was published in the *Annual Register* with a flattering encomium from the editor, the distinguished politician and man of letters Edmund Burke. The *Annual Register* did, indeed, print the poem, but not until 1791, three years after its first appearance in *The World*.

According to Maria Elizabeth, the melancholy and depression of spirits from which her mother suffered around this time inspired some of her best verses: 'Mrs Robinson continued to indulge in this solace for her dejected spirits, and in sonnets, elegies, and odes, displayed the powers and versatility of her mind.'[17] The extent to which Tarleton was the cause of her dejection of spirits is not made clear: Maria Elizabeth plays down his importance in her mother's life, confining his presence in the continuation of the *Memoirs* to a single footnote.

Maria Elizabeth preferred to continue her mother's story with some of the Gothic and romantic touches that had characterized the first part of the narrative, which Mary completed before her death. So it was that the continuation gave considerable space to a strange incident that happened during the summer in Brighton:

> On one of these nights of melancholy inspiration, she discovered from her window a small boat, struggling in the spray, which dashed against the wall of her garden. Presently two fishermen brought on shore in their arms a burthen, which, notwithstanding the distance, Mrs Robinson perceived to be a human body, which the fishermen, after covering with a sail from their boat, left on the land and disappeared. But a short time elapsed before the men returned, bringing with them fuel, with which they vainly endeavoured to reanimate their unfortunate charge. Struck with a circumstance so affecting, which the stillness of the night rendered yet more impressive, Mrs Robinson remained for some time at her window motionless with horror. At length, recovering her recollection, she alarmed the family; but before they could gain the beach, the men had again departed. The morning dawned, and day broke in upon the tragical scene. The bathers passed and repassed with little concern, while the corpse continued, extended on the shore, not twenty yards from the STEINE. During the course of the day, many persons came to look on the body, which still remained unclaimed and unknown.

The local Justice of the Peace and 'Lord of the Manor' refused to bury the body as the dead man '*did not belong to that parish*'. Mary was outraged by this injustice and tried to set up a subscription to bury the body, but without success. She gave her own contribution to the local fishermen without revealing her identity, sensitive as ever to the power of her name. The subscription scheme came to nothing and 'the body of the stranger, being dragged to the cliff, was covered by a heap of stone, without the tribute of a sigh or the ceremony of a prayer'.[18]

The incident of the abandoned corpse, never claimed by family or friend and left to rot on the beach, made a lasting impression on Mary. For many years after the event she could not repeat the tale without 'horror and indignation'. Just a few months before her death, she reworked the incident into one of her best poems, greatly admired by Coleridge, 'The Haunted Beach'. The incident also seems to have been one of the forces that conspired to take her in the direction of the Gothic novel, a form in which she started writing soon after this and with which she continued for the rest of her life – when she died, she left an unfinished novel called *Jasper*, which begins with a beach and a shipwreck. A drowned sailor, an exile whose identity is lost, an isolated death far from friends and family: the fate of her own father and fears for her own end undoubtedly played their part in the genesis of 'The Haunted Beach' and related works.

There was a period of estrangement from Tarleton, but in the summer of 1789 they were together again in Brighton. Mary's health continued to be erratic, but she seems to have found contentment by putting her energies into her literary career. The long hot summer by the sea passed with the *ton* oblivious to the consequences of events across the English Channel, where the Bastille was stormed on 14 July, heralding the French Revolution. Cricket – with heavy betting on the results – was the latest fashionable pursuit:

> Last Friday a match at Cricket was played, on the Flat near Brighton; the DUKE of YORK [the Prince of Wales's brother] on one side, and Colonel TARLETON on the other; who chose eleven each, one innings, which was not played out for want of time. The DUKE'S side fetched in their innings 292; Colonel TARLETON'S 70, having five wickets to go down. The same Gentlemen play again on Wednesday for 100 guineas; Colonel TARLETON to have Streeter the Miller.[19]

One day Tarleton and some other young blades were taking a turn on the cricket ground when they encountered 'Jew' King the moneylender. They hatched a plan to keelhaul him on a yacht, with Mary sitting on the deck watching, as if in revenge for his publication of the *Letters from Perdita to a Certain Israelite* so many years before. But King got wind of the plot and skipped town just in time.[20] Mary, meanwhile, was almost becoming her old self again: 'Mrs *Robinson* on Friday launched an elegant Phaeton, and four beautiful Grey Ponies. – She was attended by Colonel *Tarleton*, her constant and *cher ami*. Mrs Robinson is daily recovering from her long indisposition.'[21]

The following summer, Tarleton went to his home city of Liverpool to fight for a seat in Parliament. He set up headquarters in Bold Street and launched himself into a bitterly fought, violent campaign. The question of the slave trade was of pressing concern in the seaport that was the hub of traffic in human flesh. Nationally, the abolition movement was gaining ground, but for Tarleton's family and many of the Liverpool voters the slave trade was the basis of prosperity. Tarleton's association with Mary was used in the campaign against him: a procession, led by five local clergymen, marched through the streets in protest. Tarleton responded with some theatrical tricks that sound as if they were learnt from his partner's Shakespearean past: like Coriolanus (though without the reluctance) he held up his hand to show that he had given his fingers for king and country, rolled up his sleeve to show the scars where the enemy's sword had ripped his arm; then he transformed himself into Henry V and recited the Crispin's Day speech. He was victorious, and returned to London in triumph. It was widely assumed that Mary had written his speeches for him.

Mary's elder brother John died in Italy that year. Her thoughts, meanwhile, were turning to another kind of brotherhood: the universal *fraternité*, which, together with *liberté* and *égalité*, had been proclaimed by the revolutionaries in Paris. The Della Cruscans were liberal, cosmopolitan Europhiles, so they welcomed the French Revolution in its early days. Merry wrote a long poem called 'Laurel of Liberty', dedicated 'with every sentiment of admiration and respect' to the 'National Assembly of France, the true and Zealous representatives of a Free People'. He vowed to leave Cupid behind and instead devote his poetry to Freedom and Humanity, Reason and Truth.

On reading 'The Laurel of Liberty', Mary wrote an immediate response. It took her less than twelve hours to produce some 350 lines entitled *Ainsi va le Monde* ('thus goes the world'). Dedicated to Merry, it is an open avowal of revolutionary sympathies, complete with an attack on the *ancien régime* and an account of the storming of the Bastille. It ends with a rousing apostrophe to freedom:

Freedom – blithe goddess of the rainbow vest,
In dimpled smiles and radiant beauties drest,
I court thee from thy azure-spangled bed . . .
Hark! 'Freedom' echoes thro' the vaulted skies.
The Goddess speaks! O mark the blest decree, –
TYRANTS SHALL FALL – TRIUMPHANT MAN BE FREE![22]

John Bell published the poem as a sixteen-page pamphlet in June 1790, at exactly the time that Tarleton was campaigning against the freedom of slaves up in Liverpool – but political differences do not seem to have made Mary and Tarleton love each other any the less. *Ainsi va le Monde* went into a second edition and was translated into French – understandably, the English original 'acquired great popularity in Paris'.[23] In London, it was very well received by the critics: 'This poetic address to Mr Merry gives us a favourable opinion, in a general view, of the literary abilities of the fair writer, Mrs Robinson'; 'we think she is entitled to, and will obtain praise from a much more honourable cause [than praising Merry], her own merit. That her political talents are no way inferior to his; and her *patriotism*, or rather political sentiments, more just and rational, will appear from the lines quoted'; 'These verses, which the world owes to the pen of the celebrated Perdita, though the flash of a moment, are not a flash without fire. They discover a very refined sensibility, connected with considerable riches of fancy, and correctness of taste.'[24] Partly because of her skill in testing public opinion via the pen name Laura Maria, Mary had now succeeded in publishing a highly successful poem in her own name. The reviews were so good that it did not matter to her that one of them still referred to her as 'the celebrated Perdita'.

In the summer of 1790, when *Ainsi va le Monde* was written and published, opinion in Britain was still broadly supportive of the French Revolution. The storming of the Bastille seemed to have brought down a tyrannical regime and introduced into France the liberal and democratic principles on which the British had prided themselves for a hundred years. But the tide turned as blood was spilt in the prisons and streets of Paris. With the establishment of the Jacobin 'terror' one tyranny had replaced another. Inevitably, there was a political backlash against the Della Cruscan poets who had welcomed the revolution so warmly. William Gifford, subsequently editor of the influential right-wing *Quarterly Review*, attacked the movement in satirical poems called *The Baviad* (1794) and *The Maeviad* (1795). He lashed out at the female Della Cruscans, making a particularly cruel jibe about Mary's disability:

> See Cowley frisk it to one ding-dong chime,
> And weakly cuckold her poor spouse in rhyme . . .
> See Thrale's grey widow with a satchel roam,
> And bring, in pomp, her labour'd nothings home;
> See Robinson forget her state, and move,
> On crutches tow'rds the grave, to 'Light o' Love' . . .
> Some love the verse that like Maria's flows,
> No rubs to stagger, and no sense to pose;
> Which read, and read, you raise your eyes in doubt,
> And gravely wonder – what it is about.[25]

The 'Thrale' mentioned here was Dr Johnson's friend Hester Thrale, who was also a Della Cruscan poet. In sharp contrast to Gifford, she made a point of defending Mary, going out of her way to deny malicious rumours that Mrs Robinson's illness was caused by a sexually transmitted disease or somehow the result of her sexual promiscuity.[26] Gifford himself could not resist another twist of the knife even after Mary's death. He added a new footnote to his poem: 'This wretched woman, indeed, in the wane of her beauty fell into merited poverty, exchanged poetry for politics, and wrote abusive trash against the government at the rate of two guineas a week for the Morning Post.'[27] As Gifford's great enemy William Hazlitt said, such 'attacks on Mrs Robinson were unmanly'.[28]

Mary came to regret her involvement with the Della Cruscan movement for aesthetic reasons, not political ones. Her poetic style moved forward, but her politics of freedom remained consistent. Her rejection of Della

Cruscan tinsel is apparent from her novel *Walsingham* (1797), where she parodies Robert Merry as the melancholy poet Doleful, who writes:

The *silver* moon shall light the hills to dance,
The *golden* sun shall drink old ocean dry,
The *sapphire* mountains shrink to vallies low,
The day be *black*, the midnight *welkin* glow,
Ere truth and reason shall be hurl'd from France,
And *Liberty* in chains a *captive* lie.

This provokes an ecstatic literary critical commentary from 'Mr Optic' (an affectionate burlesque of another poetic friend, John Taylor, the royal oculist),

> 'There's fancy, variety, epithet, pathos, metaphor, allegory, and climax! Never talk of the old school mistress, the turner of couplets, or the inspired milk-woman – or Laura, or your Annas and Matildas, your Sapphos and Petrarchs – or your Maeviads and your Baeviads! – Doleful is the very cream of poetry – rich, pure, flowing, sweet! – the fountain of Helicon – the flowery top of the Parnassus!'[29]

Doleful is mocked for his mechanical adjectives and his florid metaphors. Looking back on the Della Cruscan movement Mary finds an implicit contradiction between their democratic sympathies and their refined poetic style, which appealed principally to an elite taste: '"That is the only reason why I admire the poetry of the present age," cried the Duke Heartwing: "I detest every thing that the multitude can partake of".'[30]

Building on the success of 'Laura Maria' in the *Oracle*, Mary prepared a collection of her poems for the press. Her home in Clarges Street became a meeting place for an array of literary figures. Among her regular visitors were editors – John Taylor, the former royal eye-doctor who had turned to journalism and become the editor of the *Morning Post*, and James Boaden, who took over as editor of the *Oracle* and exchanged many poems with Mary – and poets, notably the satirist John Wolcot (who wrote under the name Peter Pindar) and clergyman-turned-actor-turned-bookseller and all-round writer Samuel Jackson Pratt (who mostly published as 'Courtney Melmoth' and remained a close friend for the rest of Mary's life). She found a particular admirer in one of Tarleton's fellow officers, Lieutenant General 'Gentleman Johnny' Burgoyne, playwright, poet, and socialite. His tributary poem was typical of the verses that were constantly being laid at her feet:

Laura! when from thy beauteous eyes,
The tear of tender anguish flows;
Such magic in thy sorrow lies,
That ev'ry bosom shares thy woes.

When on thy lovely perfect face,
The sportive dimpled smile we see;
With eager hope the cause we trace,
And wish to share each bliss with thee.

For in thy highly gifted mind,
Superior charms so sweetly blend;
In each such gentle grace we find,
That Envy must thy worth commend.

Oh! who can gaze upon that lip,
That coral lip of brightest hue;
Nor wish the honied balm to sip,
More fresh, more sweet, than morning dew?

But when thy true poetic lays,
Pierce to the heart's remotest cell;
We feel the conscious innate praise,
Which feeble language fails to tell.[31]

Mary engaged John Bell to publish her new book of *Poems*. Not only was he the publisher of the newspapers where she had made her poetic name: he was also 'Bookseller to His Royal Highness the PRINCE of Wales'. In the light of her personal history, it must have given Mary a certain satisfaction to have this affiliation blazoned across her title page. The book was published by subscription. That is to say, production costs were defrayed by purchasers paying their money (one guinea – a substantial sum for a volume of poetry) in advance, in return for being listed in the book itself. An impressive 600 subscribers signed up.

The process of collecting names and putting the book through production took over a year. We know this because Mary kept the letter-wrappings in which subscribers sent in their names and used the backs of them many years later, when she was poor and short of paper, on which to write the manuscript of her *Memoirs*. On each letter-wrapping Mary wrote the correspondent's name and these names may be matched with those in the subscription list to the *Poems* of 1791. The earliest letters are postmarked March 1790. The volume was eventually published – on royal vellum paper and bound in boards (unlike most books, which were sold unbound) – on 3 May 1791. On that day the *Oracle* proudly reported that 'MRS ROBINSON this day presents the world with the long wished for, and admired Collection of Poems. The patronage MRS ROBINSON has received, does honour to this Nation.' The subscription list reads like a who's who of late Georgian high society. It is testimony to Mary's continuing prominence in the genteel world, despite her vicissitudes of fortune.

At the head of the list were His Royal Highness George, Prince of Wales; His Royal Highness Frederick, Duke of York; His Royal Highness William Henry, Duke of Clarence; His Royal Highness William, Duke of Gloucester (the Prince's three brothers); His Serene Highness the Duke of Orléans; His Serene Highness Prince Ferdinand, Duke of Württemberg. The patronage of both the Prince of Wales and the Duke of Orléans is a mark of her ability to remain on good terms with both ex-lovers and ex-suitors. The rest of the subscribers were listed alphabetically, with aristocrats preceding gentry under each letter (Dukes and Duchesses, then Earls and Countesses, then Lords and Ladies, then Baronets, Esquires, and the untitled). They included the Duke and Duchess of Devonshire, the Earl of Cholmondeley, Charles Fox, Sir Joshua Reynolds, Mr and Mrs Richard Sheridan, newspaper editor Henry Bate and his wife. There were friends from Tarleton's army circles, theatre people such as the actress Dora Jordan, literary figures such as Samuel Pratt and John Taylor, and ten copies for Tarleton and assorted family members, including his mother and his nephew who was a schoolboy at Eton. The family's hostility to Mary must have mellowed by this time. The list included clergymen, many Members of Parliament (mostly on the Whig side), and a large number of students and academics from Cambridge University.

An opening dedication explains that 'Many of the following poems having been honoured with public and repeated marks of attention from some of the most accomplished writers of the present age, when published in *The Oracle*, under the Signatures of LAURA, LAURA MARIA, OBERON etc. etc. the Author was induced to acknowledge, and arrange them in their present form.' 'MRS ROBINSON', the dedication continues,

> has the particular gratification of knowing that the efforts of her pen were warmly, and honourably patronized under FEIGNED Signatures: had she avowed them at an earlier period the pleasure she now feels would have been considerably diminished, in the idea that the partiality of friends had procured the sanction her Poems have been favoured with from the candid and enlightened – TO WHOM THEY ARE DEDICATED WITH THE MOST PROFOUND RESPECT.

The strategy of initial anonymous publication is thus revealed as a dazzling pre-emptive strike against critical carping to the effect that her poems might have been admired because she was a celebrity rather than because they were good.

Advertisements in the *Oracle* advised subscribers to pick up their copies from Mrs Robinson's home in Clarges Street or at Bell's British Library in the Strand. Vigorous puffing ensued upon publication: 'Mrs ROBINSON's Poems meet with such universal approbation, that the first edition is likely to be very soon disposed of.' And a few days later: 'Mrs ROBINSON's Poems, *so highly applauded in the Circles of Fashion and Taste, being now published, we are happy in the permission to announce for To-Morrow, one of the brightest gems in the Collection – The Monody to Poor CHATTERTON*.'[32] The Chatterton poem was a good choice to highlight in this way because he was a figure who served as an icon of neglected poetic genius (besides being a Bristolian, like Mary). Bell was skilfully using the paper to sell the book and vice versa.

Two weeks after publication, the *Oracle* published a large advertisement disguised as a review:

> Mrs ROBINSON'S POEMS
>
> The unavoidable attention to objects of great National importance, forbade us earlier to notice the elegance of this delightful Publication.
>
> The select Volume of this Lady's Compositions is, perhaps, as rich a banquet, as any FEMALE Votary of the Muses ever offered to the PUBLIC – Not a Poem in the collection but breathes the sweetest delicacy, and the high charm of polished cultivation.
>
> Many exquisite, and before unpublished originals, grace the collection, and our ORACLE of Wednesday gave, by permission, a very tender and finished Monody to the Memory of CHATTERTON. The Volume possesses many others of equal, and some we may say, of superior, merit . . .
>
> The author's PORTRAIT is in resemblance classically perfect, and the TYPOGRAPHICAL execution of the Work so beautiful, that we, who may be suspected of partiality, are constrained to say no more.[33]

By emphasizing the handsome typography and the frontispiece portrait engraving after Sir Joshua Reynolds, Bell is seeking to provide some justification for the high price of one guinea. The next day, it was reported that 'Mrs ROBINSON receives the most flattering Compliments upon the elegance of her late Publication – The Sale has been unexampled.'[34] There is no better way of creating demand than claiming that a product has nearly sold out. The reality seems to have been that the prohibitive price meant that few copies were sold above those that had already been subscribed for. Six hundred guineas from the subscribers would have left a reasonable profit after the deduction of production costs, but the book was in no sense a bestseller. Two years after publication, Mary wrote the following letter to a bookseller in Bristol:

> Sir
>
> In consequence of Mr Bell's bankruptcy, I have a few unsold Volumes of my Poems, in my possession. If you think proper to give them the chance of your shop, (with the customary profit on each Volume,) I will, without delay, send you a few copies. Your immediate answer will oblige.[35]

This request may be said to show her entrepreneurial flair in action, but the attempt to sell off remainders in her home town, presumably in the hope that there would be a market for the work of a local celebrity, suggests that demand for the *Poems* was never exceptionally high.

Within a few months of publication, Bell attempted to reach a broader market by licensing another publisher to produce *The Beauties of Mrs Robinson*, a fifty-page selection of the poems priced at a very reasonable one shilling and sixpence. There were some complaints from reviewers about the same poems appearing in two different volumes within such a short space of time.[36] The prefatory advertisement to *The Beauties* argued that a selection of the poems could only give a partial sense of Mrs Robinson's excellence as a poet, but that it might at least do enough to persuade those critics who regarded her as 'a mere WOMAN OF FASHION' rather than a 'SUBLIME GENIUS' to look into the original. Again, there was a defence of the cost of the subscription volume:

> The mode of publishing the original Poems by Subscription, and at so seemingly extravagant a price as a GUINEA for an Octavo Volume, has served to encourage these erroneous notions. Yet the Work is deservedly patronized by the FASHIONABLE WORLD, and is executed with an elegance and taste which abundantly apologize for the expence. The PORTRAIT is admirable! It is, indeed, a *chef d'oeuvre* of the arts.
>
> Should the Specimens thus rudely collected, not one of which is to be considered as a whole, induce the LEARNED WORLD to look into the ORIGINALS, and to speak of them as they merit, the first wish of the EDITOR will be accomplished: – They must obtain a speedy celebrity, without waiting the slow but sure plaudits of Posterity; and the POET, besides the emolument which she so well deserves, will receive a still higher gratification, to a mind of such exquisite sensibility and refinement, in the praises and esteem of the Wise and Good, for GENIUS which is not often equalled, and for SENTIMENT which dignifies human nature.[37]

This is an exceptionally interesting statement, revealing how Mary was now poised between the 'FASHIONABLE WORLD' and the 'LEARNED WORLD'. She wanted to be viewed by the fashionable world in the light of her mental abilities instead of her physical charms and at the same time she wanted to achieve 'a speedy celebrity' in the literary world.

The 'learned world' of monthly magazines treated her favourably. *Poems* garnered positive reviews in a majority of the principal monthlies. The *Analytical Review* praised its 'rich and beautiful imagery' and 'sweetly harmonious verse'; Mary would have been especially pleased with its emphasis on her mind above her beauty: 'the picture of the fair writer's mind pourtrayed [sic] in these poems, will long outlive the portrait of her person, though drawn by the pencil of a Reynolds'. The *Monthly Review* was extremely favourable: 'This ingenious and celebrated lady has attracted the attention of the public, both by her personal charms, and her mental accomplishments; and who can withstand the united powers of beauty and of wit.' The reviewer goes on to praise *Ainsi va le Monde* as a remarkable effusion of FREEDOM' and to say that those who enjoyed that poem

> will deem yet higher of our English SAPPHO, after the perusal of the present volume; in which are some pieces, equal, perhaps, to the best productions . . . of the *Lesbian Dame*, in point of tenderness, feeling, poetic imagery, warmth, elegance, and above all, DELICACY OF EXPRESSION, in which our ingenious countrywoman far excels all that we know of the works of the Grecian Sappho.[38]

The epithet 'English [or British] Sappho' would stick.

The *Critical Review* gave a more mixed verdict, condemning Della Cruscanism ('Rejecting the accustomed modes of description and phraseology, these fastidious writers seem fond of introducing uncommon terms and ideas, to provoke attention and to excite admiration') while offering somewhat condescending praise to Mrs Robinson ('It is certainly an elegant and original work, which coming from the pen of one person, and that person a woman, is entitled to singular approbation').[39] The *English Review* gave the most muted assessment:

> The poems now before us are the elegant effusions of a mind which seems to feel too much for its own peace . . . There is much pathos, sensibility, and poetry, in this publication; but we cannot help regret-

> ting that this fair writer has too often imitated the new school of poets, which has lately appeared among us, and which sacrifices nature, simplicity, and passion, to luxuriant and ill-placed description, and to a load of imagery and ornament of every kind. We are suffocated by the sweets of these poets, and dazzled by the glare of their tinsel.[40]

Many of the poems had been previously published in the newspapers, though others were appearing in print for the first time. The reviewers singled out 'Lines to Him Who Will Understand Them', two 'Odes to the Nightingale', and some 'Stanzas to Time' for particular praise. Disillusionment in love is a major theme throughout (it is notable that a passionate 'Adieu to Love' included here was excluded from the collected works which Maria Elizabeth put together after her mother's death). Readers and reviewers assumed that the poems contained a high degree of autobiographical content. The first 'Ode to the Nightingale', for instance, was written in the first person and outlined many of Mary's personal sorrows, her travels through foreign realms, her return to Britain, and her disappointment in love. A line such as 'And oft I've sought the HYGEIAN MAID' is a Della Cruscan way of saying 'I've been to many health resorts in search of a cure for my rheumatism' (Hygeia was the classical goddess of health, hence our 'hygiene'). 'Till forc'd with every HOPE to part, / Resistless Pain subdued my Heart' means 'but I'm still suffering'. Repeated phrases along the lines of 'And LOVE a false delusive flame' suggest that she often wrote poems at times when her relationship with Tarleton was going badly.

The collection has considerable formal variety; there are odes, sonnets, and ballads. Two poems about Georgiana Duchess of Devonshire are included, together with one to her sister Lady Duncannon. Many of the poems explore the transience of beauty and the folly of the fashionable world. There are elegies to Lady Middleton, who died in childbed, and to Richard Boyle, who died young despite the best efforts of a Dr Moseley (who would attend Tarleton when he was sick in 1793). A selection of light verses includes the charming and funny 'The Bee and the Butterfly'. A lovely sonnet 'To my Beloved Daughter' expresses the joy and comfort that Maria Elizabeth has brought to Mary's unhappy life, her ability to 'shed soft sunshine on my Wintry Hours'. An 'Ode to Valour' is inscribed to Tarleton. 'Intrepid Tarleton chas'd the foe,' wrote Mary, 'And smil'd in Death's grim face, and brav'd his with'ring blow.' The ode comes to a rousing climax in praise of him:

Tarleton, thy mind, above the Poet's praise
Asks not the labour'd task of flatt'ry lays! . . .
So shall the Muse spontaneous incense give!
Th' Historic page shall prove a lasting shrine,
Where Truth and Valour shall Thy laurels twine;
Where, with thy name, recording Fame shall blend
The Zealous Patriot, and the Faithful Friend![41]

Mary's own page did not 'prove a lasting shrine' to Tarleton: when she prepared the 'Ode to Valour' for inclusion in her *Poetical Works* at the end of her life, she excised all reference to him.

CHAPTER 19

Opium

Mentally perfect, her enlighten'd mind,
Superior to disease, springs unconfined.
James Boaden, 'To Mrs Robinson'

Alas, how little did I then know either the fatigue or the hazard of mental occupations! How little did I foresee that the day would come when my health would be impaired, my thoughts perpetually employed, in so destructive a pursuit! At the moment that I write this page I feel in every fibre of my brain the fatal conviction that it is a *destroying labour.*

Memoirs of the Late Mrs Robinson, Written by Herself

On 30 May 1791, the *Oracle* announced that Tarleton was in Bath, after a short visit to Liverpool. 'Mrs Robinson is also at Bath,' the report added, 'and extremely ill at her house in the North Parade. – The gout, with which she is troubled, has attacked her head so severely, that she is scarcely able to hold herself upright.' Her poetry was her comfort. In her daughter's words, 'The mind of Mrs Robinson, beguiled by these pursuits from preying upon itself, became gradually reconciled to the calamitous state of her health: the mournful certainty of total and incurable lameness, while yet in the bloom and summer of life, was alleviated by the consciousness of intellectual resource, and by the activity of a fertile fancy.'[1]

A sonnet in the *Oracle* by James Boaden writing as 'Arno' was entitled 'On Mrs Robinson's Visiting Bath'. Beneath a subtitle that hardly seems necessary – 'The Cause, BAD HEALTH' – it tells of how she has flown from the 'busy circle' and forsaken 'the scenes of her expanding fame' in order to 'renovate the anguish of her frame'. She is 'Mentally perfect' but 'keen pangs oppress her lovely face'. Her poetic Muse, meanwhile, 'Floats in the fragrance of the rubied rose'.[2] That last phrase hints that it was not only 'the consciousness of intellectual resource' that gave Mary relief from her physical pain: the fragrant rubied rose seems to be a euphemism for the opium poppy.

Maria Elizabeth records that her mother was prescribed a rest cure by her physician, who for a time forbade her from writing altogether: 'the perpetual exercise of the imagination and intellect, added to an uniform and sedentary life, affected the system of her nerves, and contributed to debilitate her frame'. The newspapers linked the 'pensive tendency' in her poetry to 'a depression of spirits, the consequence of long indisposition'.[3] It may have been at this point that she was first prescribed opium as a sedative; it would have been taken in solution with alcohol, in a tincture known as laudanum.

In July it was reported that she would soon be returning home to Clarges Street, 'greatly benefited by the Bath waters', but in early August she was still in Bath, 'getting better every day'. She had apparently not been taking her doctor's advice to stop writing. The *Oracle* teased its readers with the prospect of an exciting new publication: 'Her Muse is said to be now engaged on a work of so interesting a nature, that the world may look forward to a new source of elegant gratification.'[4]

Bath was the most fashionable resort town in England. Invalids, imaginary and real, flocked to the spa to drink the medicinal spring water and immerse themselves, fully clothed in special robes and headgear, in the steaming baths that had been first discovered by the ancient Romans. Summer in Bath was shaped by a highly structured social life, a round of assemblies, balls, teas, promenades, concerts, theatre visits, and excursions – a world familiar to readers of the novels of Fanny Burney and Jane Austen. Architecturally it was the most splendid and modern town in the land, with showpieces of design such as Queen Square, the North and South Parades, and the magnificent curved edifices of the Royal Crescent and Lansdown Crescent. Socially, the town offered a heady mix of aristocracy, gentry, and new money. Though Mary's indisposition prevented her from participating in the full range of social life, Bath was an ideal location to contemplate the fashionable world and brood upon the ways in which it might provide raw material for new literary production. The 'interesting' work on which she began to engage herself was a novel.

She also experimented with narrative poetry. One day, as she returned from the baths in her wheelchair, she saw an elderly man being chased by a mob, who pelted him with mud and stones. The man put up no resistance, and Mary, full of pity for his stoicism, enquired about his offences. She was told that the man was a maniac, known only by the name of 'Mad Jemmy'. As with the corpse on the beach at Brighton, which had so seized her imagination and inspired her compassion, Mary was deeply troubled by the beggar's plight. Perhaps the encounter also brought back memories of her traumatic meeting in a London street with her beloved teacher and mentor Meribah Lorrington, who had become an impoverished alcoholic. If the *Memoirs* are to be believed, Mary would wait for hours for the appearance of Mad Jemmy, and, whatever her occupation, the sound of his voice would draw her to the window: 'She would gaze upon his venerable but emaciated countenance with sensations of awe almost reverential, while the barbarous persecutions of the thoughtless crowd never failed to agonize her feelings.'[5]

One night after bathing, on a day when she had suffered even greater pain than usual, Mary swallowed nearly eighty drops of laudanum. She fell into a deep sleep but then awoke in a kind of reverie and called for her daughter to take up a pen and write down what she would dictate. Maria Elizabeth takes up the story herself:

> Miss Robinson, supposing that a request so unusual might proceed from the delirium excited by the opium, endeavoured in vain to dissuade her mother from her purpose. The spirit of inspiration was not to be subdued, and she repeated, throughout, the admirable poem of *The Maniac*, much faster than it could be committed to paper.
>
> She lay, while dictating, with her eyes closed, apparently in the stupor which opium frequently produces, repeating like a person talking in her sleep. This affecting performance, produced in circumstances so singular, does no less credit to the genius than to the heart of the author.

> On the ensuing morning, Mrs Robinson had only a confused idea of what had passed, nor could be convinced of the fact till the manuscript was produced. She declared, that she had been dreaming of mad Jemmy throughout the night, but was perfectly unconscious of having been awake while she composed the poem, or of the circumstances narrated by her daughter.[6]

This narrative anticipates by several years English literature's most famous story of drug-induced creativity: Samuel Taylor Coleridge's account of how he dreamed the poem of 'Kubla Khan' while under the influence of opium, but was only able to write down a fragment of it before being interrupted by the arrival of a 'person on business from Porlock'. Literary historians have endlessly debated the veracity of Coleridge's story of the poem's origins: was there ever a full-scale vision or was the story invented as an excuse to justify the fragmentary nature of 'Kubla Khan'? Who was the person from Porlock and how did he know that Coleridge was sheltering at a remote farmhouse in the Quantock hills? For that matter, did the person from Porlock really exist?

'Kubla Khan' seems to have been written in 1797, but it was not published until 1816. The earliest manuscript of the poem does not have the elaborate prefatory note concerning the person from Porlock. In 1800, Coleridge showed the unpublished 'Kubla Khan' to Mary. One of the last poems she wrote before her death was an ode to Coleridge that quoted several phrases from it. Mary's ode was, indeed, the first published reference to the existence of 'Kubla Khan' ('I'll mark thy *sunny dome*, and view / Thy *Caves of Ice*, thy fields of dew!').

Did Coleridge share this particular poem with Mary because he knew of her involvement with opium? His concern for her health is apparent from a letter he sent to William Godwin:

> Have you seen Mrs Robinson lately? How is she? – Remember me in the kindest and most respectful phrases to her . . . [Humphry] Davy has discovered a perfectly new Acid, by which he has restored the use of limbs to persons who had lost them for many years, (one woman 9 years) in cases of supposed Rheumatism. At all events, Davy says, it *can* do no harm, in Mrs Robinson's case – and if she will try it, he will make up a little parcel and write her a letter of *instructions* etc.[7]

The Minster House, Bristol, where Mary was born.

'The Dramatic Enchantress and The Doating Lover': Mary Robinson and Lord Malden, from the *Town and Country Magazine*, June 1780.

Mary Robinson cross-dressed.

Mary Robinson, engraved from the life by J. K. Sherwin, 1781.

Mary Robinson sitting for her picture, by Thomas Rowlandson. The date is uncertain: do the leering men suggest that it was when she was in her prime or does the way that she is lying suggest that it was after her paralysis?

Reverend Henry Bate, known as 'The Fighting Parson': journalist, editor, original of Sheridan's Mr Snake.

'Perdito and Perdita – or – the Man and Woman of the People': caricature of Fox and Mrs Robinson. She is in the driving seat.

'The new Vis-à-vis, or Florizel driving Perdita': caricature of the Prince, Mrs Robinson, Fox (in the footman's position behind) and Lord North (asleep on the roof).

'The Goats Canter to Windsor or the Cuckold's Comfort', caricature of Perdita and her lovers. The high-speed gig is driven by the Prince. Riding the goats are Fox, Tarleton, North and Robinson (backwards, with cuckold's horns).

'Perdita upon her last legs': caricature from the *Rambler's Magazine*, August 1784.

Mrs Robinson's cottage at St Amand les Eaux, ink drawing, probably by her daughter Maria, in the original manuscript of *Memoirs of the Late Mrs Robinson, Written by Herself.*

Mary Robinson in intellectual pose, by George Dance, 1793.

Portrait of Mary Robinson late in life, by John Chubb.
She has writing implements on the table,
but is holding the Prince's miniature.

William Godwin: philosopher and friend.

Mary Robinson's Grave in Old Windsor churchyard.

Samuel Taylor Coleridge around the time he met Mary Robinson.

It is highly probable that Coleridge and Robinson discussed the imaginative effects of opium when they met. The sense of unconscious composition, the inability of the writing pen to keep up with the dreaming mind, the vanishing of the vision once the poet awakes: in all these respects there is an uncanny resemblance between Robinson's account of the origin of her poem and Coleridge's of the origin of his. Could it then be that Coleridge made up the story about the person from Porlock in order to give his poem the same kind of authenticity as 'The Maniac'?[8]

Mary's poem about 'Mad Jemmy' was originally published as 'Insanity' in the *Oracle* in September 1791. As 'The Maniac' it appeared in her second volume of *Poems*. It has many references to what Coleridge, in another of his opium poems, called 'the pains of sleep'. One stanza contains images of watching eyes, of cold, and of petrification that are highly characteristic of the opium dreams of the age, such as those described by Coleridge's protégé Thomas De Quincey in his *Confessions of an English Opium-Eater*:

> Fix not thy steadfast gaze on me,
> Shrunk Atom of Mortality!
> Nor freeze my blood with thy distracted groan;
> Ah! Quickly turn those eyes away,
> They fill my soul with dire dismay!
> For dead and dark they seem, and almost chill'd to Stone!

De Quincey knew both the poem and the account of its origins in Mary's *Memoirs*.

In the final stanza of Mary's poem, the poet offers to share the pains of the maniac and calm him through her verses. Read in the context of daughter Maria Elizabeth's persistent references to the way in which the writing of poetry served as a kind of balm for her mother, Mad Jemmy in a sense becomes the suffering Mary herself and the poem becomes a self-referential piece about the healing effects of poetry:

> Oh! Tell Me, tell me all thy pain;
> Pour to mine ear thy frenzied strain,
> And I will share thy pangs, and soothe thy woes!
> Poor Maniac! I will dry thy tears,
> And bathe thy wounds, and calm thy fears,
> And with soft Pity's balm Enchant Thee To Repose.[9]

Opium references also crop up in a range of other Mary Robinson poems. So, for instance, her 'Ode to Health' (1791) has 'There I'll press from herbs and flow'rs / Juices bless'd with opiate pow'rs, / Whose magic potency can heal / The throb of agonizing pain' and an 'Invocation' in her 1793 *Poems* acknowledges that 'From the Poppy I have ta'en / Mortal's

Balm, and mortal's Bane!'[10] Keats famously wrote in his 'To a Nightingale' of feeling the sensation of having drunk some 'dull opiate'; Mary Robinson anticipated him by some twenty years in her 'Ode to Apathy':

> The poppy wreath shall bind my brows,
> Dead'ning the sense of pain;
> And while to thee I pay my vows,
> A chilling tide shall rush thro' ev'ry vein,
> Pervade my heart, and ev'ry care beguile,
> While my wan cheek shall bear the vacant smile.[11]

One of her last lyrics, 'The Poet's Garret', describes the drug's effect on the creative imagination in language that also foreshadows Keats in its mixture of archaism ('yclept') and yearning for poetic immortality:

> On a shelf,
> (Yclept a mantle-piece) a phial stands,
> Half fill'd with potent spirits! – spirits strong,
> Which sometimes haunt the poet's restless brain,
> And fill his mind with fancies whimsical.
> Poor poet! Happy art thou, thus remov'd
> From pride and folly! for in thy domain
> Thou canst command thy subjects; fill thy lines;
> Wield th' all-conquering weapon Heaven bestows
> On the grey goose's wing! which, towering high,
> Bears thy sick fancy to Immortal Fame![12]

The 'grey goose's wing' is, of course, the writer's quill.

Mary's novels as well as her poems reveal the influence of opium. In *Angelina*, published in 1796, the heroine is prescribed opium to help her sleep and calm her feverish imagination. There is a reference to 'the use of opiates, to tranquilize her irritated nerves, and, if possible, to deaden the powers of reflection' and, some pages later, 'again the powers of laudanum were called to our assistance; – by midnight they so far benumbed her faculties that she ceased to rave'. The effects of the drug are also compared to those of philosophical reflection:

> Years cannot heal the wound which sensibility receives, while the heart is warmly susceptible. – Philosophy may, like opium to the agonized, for a time deaden the acute torture of regret; but memory still survives the stupor which has benumbed the senses, and the fever returns with renovated fury; – we feel the malady with double force, because we are worn out with sorrow, weakened, and become less capable of encountering its poison.[13]

Though written in the voice of a character in an epistolary novel, these words are clearly composed by a woman who knows from hard personal experience that opium is at once balm and bane. An accidental overdose of opium also furnishes a key plot twist in a later novel, *Walsingham*. All this suggests that Mary Robinson, not Samuel Taylor Coleridge, may legitimately be claimed as the originator of the English Romantic tradition of opium-inspired writing.

Despite her ill health and depression, Mary kept a firm eye on public affairs. Like many of her Whig friends, she monitored events in France with alarm, as the Revolution they supported became increasingly militant. The King had been forced to reside in Paris, and was still head of state, but with the death of the moderate Comte de Mirabeau in April 1791, and the extremist Jacobins gaining ground, the prospect of a constitutional monarchy seemed increasingly unlikely. In June, the royal family fled Paris in the middle of the night in disguise but were arrested at Varennes and brought back to the capital, humiliated and defeated. The establishment of a republic was now a certainty.

In England, the Whigs were split over their views of the Revolution. Mary's friends Sheridan and Fox were on the side of the National Assembly, while Edmund Burke opposed it. In November 1790, Burke had published his *Reflections on the Revolution in France*, which condemned both the French insurgents and their British sympathizers. Burke, who had seen Marie Antoinette in Versailles a decade earlier, described her in the most eloquent terms: she was 'a delightful vision . . . glittering like the morning star, full of life and splendour and joy'. He condemned her fall from grace in a passionate denunciation: 'Little did I dream that I should have lived to see disasters fallen upon her in a nation of men of honour, and of cavaliers. I thought ten thousand swords must have leapt from their scabbards to avenge even a look that threatened her with insult. But the age of chivalry is gone.'[14]

Burke's *Reflections* immediately inspired refutations in the form of Thomas Paine's best-selling *The Rights of Man* and Mary Wollstonecraft's *Vindication of the Rights of Men*. In April 1791, soon after the death of Mirabeau, Fox, who had welcomed the fall of the Bastille as the greatest event in the history of the world, rekindled a furore in Parliament when he claimed that the Revolution was 'the most stupendous and glorious edifice of liberty which has ever been erected on the foundations of human integrity in any time or country'.[15] In August Mary's own contribution to the debate was published in the form of an anonymous pamphlet entitled *Impartial Reflections on the Present Situation of the Queen of France by a Friend to Humanity*.

Politically, Mary was torn between her sympathy for the Queen and her affiliation with the English supporters of the Revolution. She never forgot her encounter in 1781 with the Queen who had admired her so openly and approvingly. She had copied many of the Queen's fashions and brought them to England. And she felt a special affinity with a woman who was demonized in the press: like Mary herself, Marie Antoinette had been the subject of scabrous and sometimes pornographic pamphlets. The *Memoirs of Antonina* of 1791, for instance, was written as an exposé of the Queen's allegedly voracious sexual appetite, giving details of her lovers and her supposed lesbianism and drunkenness. Mary, remembering the *Memoirs of Perdita* with shame and anger, responded by portraying Marie Antoinette as a wronged wife and devoted mother.

Mary's pledge is to rescue Marie Antoinette from 'the absurd fabrications, the ridiculous inuendoes [sic], the cruel sarcasms and unprecedented reproaches thrown upon the conduct of an illustrious Character'. 'Though perpetually taunted with the barbarous insults of irritating malice; she has never, even for a moment, forgot that true, that innate dignity of character, which places the human soul far above the reach of sublunary calamity.' Marie Antoinette's beauty, intelligence, and innocence have made her the target of envious detractors: 'Had she been less lovely, less amiable, she might have escaped the arrows of insidious envy; but when the tide of patriotic reformation flowed with impetuous fury, every private enemy, every petty detractor, enjoyed the triumph of revenge, and exultingly heaped the load of recreant malevolence on the defenceless bosom of a fallen and unfortunate woman.'[16] This reads as if it were written as much about Mary herself as about Marie Antoinette.

For Robinson, a 'vacuity of mind, is the most dangerous calamity that can threaten humanity'. Marie Antoinette has intellectual and spiritual qualities, which ennoble her and render her worthy of compassion. In an impassioned plea, Mary asks:

> What has been the conduct of this august woman, since the memorable journey from Versailles? Has she not borne her sufferings, her humiliations, her anxieties, with the magnanimity of a Heroine, the philosophy of a Stoick? Has she not been loaded with reproaches, and branded with epithets, disgraceful to the enlightened humanity of a nation instinctively gifted with the most refined gallantry? Of what has she been accused, to authorise the virulence of rage, or the indecency of public insult? – NOTHING![17]

The rhetoric owes much to the treatment of the Queen in Burke's *Reflections*, but unlike Burke Mary does not use a defence of Marie Antoinette as a pretext for an attack on the Revolution. She describes the overthrow of the *ancien régime* as 'the most glorious achievement in the annals of Europe'. She also praises the members of the National Assembly who 'by their eloquent debates, and temperate proceedings, have done honour to the French nation'. And, in direct answer to Burke, she says that it is in the power of the Assembly to prove 'that *the Days of Chivalry* are not *at an end*; that as they have given innumerable testimonies of their patriotism and judgment, they also cherish the laudable and dignified sentiment of justice and humanity'.[18] She urges her readers to give the new French Government one more chance.

The more personal question on her mind at this time was whether or not to give Tarleton another chance. Not for the first time, he had been unfaithful to her. Late in 1791 he moved in with his 'low caprice', as Mary described his new woman. On 12 December, Mary published a poem in the *Oracle*, signed 'Julia' and addressed 'To ——', with an epigraph from Shakespeare reading 'I will instruct my sorrows to be proud.' To those in her circle, this was a public acknowledgement of her separation from Tarleton. 'My mind resists thy poison'd dart,' she wrote, 'And conscious pride sustains my heart.'

Tarleton had left her before and always soon returned. This time, he kept her waiting. Mary threw herself into her writing, believing as always that it was the best cure for heartache. She prepared to publish the novel which she had begun writing during her residence in Bath – the book that the *Oracle* had promised would provide the public with 'a new source of elegant gratification'.

Mary Robinson's first novel, *Vancenza; or, the Dangers of Credulity*, was published on 2 February 1792. It was a literary sensation. The entire print run sold out in one day and the book quickly went through five editions. Never before had a novel by a woman achieved the status of an instant bestseller in this way. A Gothic romance in the style of the novels of Ann Radcliffe, it had an ingredient that no other female writer of the day could offer: thinly veiled references, based on intimate personal experience, to the sexual character of the Prince of Wales.

Though nothing so crude as a work of coded autobiography, the novel draws on its author's own life. The heroine Elvira is 15 years old at the beginning of the story, Mary's age when she made her fateful marriage to Robinson. The novel's epigraph reads 'Be wary then: best safety lies in fear', which sounds like a warning from Mary to her teenage daughter Maria Elizabeth, advising her against making her mother's mistake of succumbing too soon to the allurements of love. Elvira is 'a finished model of perfection'. One reviewer picked out the following description of her and said that it was a portrait of Maria Elizabeth:

> Elvira had just attained her fifteenth year: her form was the animated portrait of her mind; truth, benignity, pure and unstudied delicacy, the meekness of sensibility and the dignity of innate virtue, claimed the esteem; while the exquisite beauty of her bewitching countenance captivated the heart of every beholder! She was tall, and finely proportioned! Her complexion was neither the insipid whiteness of the lily-bosomed Circassian, nor the masculine shade of the Gallic brunette; the freshness of health glowed upon her cheek, while the lustre of her dark blue eyes borrowed its splendour from the unsullied flame, that gave her mind the perfection of intellect! . . . She was every thing that fancy could picture, or conviction adore! – Perfection could go no further![19]

This was the kind of heroine whom Jane Austen hated: 'pictures of perfection make me sick and wicked'.[20] The novel as a whole is a typical 'romance', with improbable plot lines, elaborate poetic language ('novel slang', as Austen called it), and clichéd heroines and heroes. There is a locked casket containing secret papers, hidden behind a portrait in a secret chamber – just the sort of detail that was ripe for the parody of *Northanger Abbey*. But there is no gainsaying the popularity of this kind of mix of the Gothic and the sentimental among female readers. The fact that the novel sold out in a day is testimony to Mrs Robinson's gift of tapping into a lucrative market and bringing to it the added value of her celebrated name.

The hero, Prince Almanza, bears more than a passing resemblance to the handsome young Prince that Mary had once loved:

> Almanza had just arrived at the twenty-first year of his age; his person was graceful and majestic; his features manly, regular, and sedate; his countenance, though grave, bore not the smallest trait of severity. His eyes, beaming with sensibility, were overarched by brows as dark as ebony; his hair, which was glossy as the chesnut, hung in graceful ringlets on his finely-falling shoulders . . . on his cloak a brilliant star distinguished him from his companions . . . The Prince looked like a divinity; something more than mortal diffused animation over his face![21]

The resemblances to Mary's own story would have been readily recognizable to readers who had followed the press coverage of her affair with the Prince. There is, for instance, an attempted seduction of Elvira by the Prince's bosom friend Del Vero, echoing Mary's involvement with Lord Malden. Like Mary in her early years, Elvira is a naive in a world of sophistication and intrigue: 'She now perceived, that to *be*, and to *seem*, were very distinct things.'[22] The novel also confronts the issue of female reputation and, in particular, the perils that face a beautiful woman, a theme to which Mary would return in her feminist treatise some years later:

> There is nothing so difficult to preserve as female reputation; as it is rare, it creates universal envy: those who possess it, proud of the treasure, often become its detractors, merely because they cannot

> brook the presumption of a rival; while they practise, with insolent superiority, every vice that can contaminate the soul! How ridiculous is the woman that conceives a single perfection, which benefits no living creature but herself, sufficient to counterbalance the total want of every social virtue! – Small is the triumph of chastity that has never been assailed by the cunning of the seducer.[23]

Knowing so well the value of her own lost reputation, she could write eloquently on the vulnerability of a woman's position once she had forfeited her good name:

> She knew, that from the moment a woman places her reputation in the power of an undeserving object, she is no longer mistress of her own happiness; as perpetual dread of disgrace is worse than even the full conviction of the most atrocious crimes, she becomes the wretched and fearful dependant upon the mercy of her enemy at all time liable to the contempt and shame he may draw upon her: – he, on the other hand, holds himself the entire master of all her actions – a frown intimidates her; a sneer overwhelms her with apprehension – her good name is only maintained at his option, and if he proves a tyrant, she becomes his *slave*, if not his VICTIM.[24]

The Prince decides not to let Elvira's obscure birth and lowly rank prevent him from marrying her: 'her virtues place her above the trifling distinctions of rank or fortune'. This might suggest that the novel is a wish-fulfilment fantasy of Mary winning the hand of the accomplished young Prince – except that on the brink of their wedding, Elvira discovers that the Prince is really her brother! Upon which she falls into a delirium and dies.

Perhaps the most interesting feature of the novel is its revelation of the increasing radicalization of Mary's views on rank and power:

> Little and contracted minds are apt to envy the possessors of exalted titles and empty distinctions. IGNORANCE only descends to bestow admiration upon the *gew-gaw* appendages of what is commonly called RANK; it fancies it beholds a thousand dazzling graces, dignifying and embellishing the varnished front of artificial consequence. To the abject sycophant, who eats the bread of miserable

> obedience, poisoned by the breath of adulation, the *baubles* of greatness are objects of veneration; the imbecility of childhood is amused with every toy: – but the ENLIGHTENED MIND thinks for *itself*; explores the precepts of uncontaminated *truth*; weighs, in the even scale of unbiassed judgment, the rights and claims of *intellectual pre-eminence*; exults in the attributes of *reason*; and opposes, with dauntless intrepidity, every innovation that dares assail even the *least* of its prerogatives.[25]

Overt political commentary of this sort was unusual within the genre of the Gothic novel, which in the hands of writers such as Mrs Radcliffe displayed an inherent conservatism in its nostalgia for the feudal Middle Ages. As a broad generalization it may be said that sentimental fiction, as pioneered by Jean-Jacques Rousseau, was more amenable to radical thought: the sentimental novel offered a declaration of the universal rights of feeling, in which inequality of rank was no obstacle to spiritual union (typically, a well-born woman might fall in love with her impoverished tutor). Mary Robinson in many respects followed Mary Wollstonecraft's trajectory from sentimental fiction to radical feminism, but it is striking that this path is anticipated in her Gothic fiction.

The character in *Vancenza* who comes closest to representing Robinson's own authorial consciousness is the lively Carline, a feisty anti-heroine smuggled into an otherwise orthodox story line. She is the source of the novel's comic moments, principally by virtue of her semi-detachment from the sentimental convolutions of the plot: 'Elvira was overwhelmed with confusion – the Prince respectfully reserved – the Marchioness in high spirits; and Carline enjoying the general embarrassment.'[26]

The *Oracle* was quick to puff the new triumph of its most celebrated in-house author. James Boaden, now editor of the paper, wrote a sonnet on *Vancenza* and regular paragraphs were inserted with updates on the book's stunning sales figures: 'The rapid sale of Mrs *Robinson*'s novel of *Vancenza* has nearly taken all of the Second Edition already. This distinguished encouragement cannot but prove highly flattering to the Authoress, and will doubtless tempt her to pursue with unceasing and ardent zeal the paths of Literature.'[27]

For the third edition, prepared just three weeks after the publication of the first, Mary wrote a substantial new dedication: 'The sale of two Editions of *Vancenza*, within one month after its publication, is too unequivocal a proof of protection, to allow me a silent gratification, where my heart prompts me to acknowledge the gratitude of its feeling. I disclaim the title of a Writer of Novels; the species of composition generally known under that denomination, too often conveys a lesson I do not wish to inculcate.' Having detached herself from the run of the mill novelists of the day, she then concluded: 'TO THAT PUBLIC, by which my literary productions have been so warmly received, I embrace this occasion of expressing my sense of obligations, and of respectfully dedicating the volumes of VANCENZA. Clarges-Street, February 27, 1792.' This was a way of saying that she required no aristocratic or royal patron, but rather that she was a professional author whose patrons were her paying public.

If Mary expected Tarleton to return to her after the success of her first novel, she was to be disappointed. At the height of *Vancenza*'s success, she wrote a Valentine's Day poem full of love-melancholy and hinting at imminent death:

No more about my auburn hair
The sparkling gems shall proudly vie;
The cypress, emblem of despair,
Shall there a faded chaplet die.
Young dimpled Pleasure quits my breast
To seek some gaudier bower than mine,
Where low Caprice, by Fancy drest,
Enthrals my truant Valentine. . . .

Whene'er the icy hand of Death
Shall grasp this sensate frame of mine,
On my cold lip the fleeting breath,
Shall murmur still – 'Dear Valentine!'
Then o'er my grave, ah! drop one tear,
And sighing write this pensive line –
'A faithful heart lies mouldering here,
That well deserved its Valentine!'[28]

It is hard to judge whether this is an expression of heartfelt anguish or a bravura performance. Mary's poems came from her experience, but lyrics such as this were written in a heightened and self-dramatizing style designed to create a frisson of strong feeling in the readers of the *Oracle*. They should not necessarily be treated as 'raw' autobiography. That said, there is no doubt that she was capable of fierce jealousy. One can sense her venom towards the rival who has snared Tarleton's heart. *Vancenza* proposes that jealousy – which Mary carefully distinguishes from envy – is the inevitable concomitant of strong passion: 'There is a natural mistrustful timidity in the female heart, even though it possesses every exquisite and refined qualification, that makes it, if it *really loves*, throb at the very shadow of a rival: she, who has never experienced the truth of this observation, is either more or less than woman.'[29] This would be a recurring theme in her later novels.

The critical reception of Mary's first novel, like that of her poetry, was broadly favourable. 'An ancient Spanish record of domestic woe, extremely interesting and pathetic, has been decorated by the pen of our fair enchantress with peculiar taste, elegance and variety,' said the *European Magazine*.[30] The *Monthly Review* concentrated on the novel's heightened style:

> Vancenza, it is true, is not written in the simple style, but it is written, and in our opinion well-written, in the style of elegance peculiar to Mrs Robinson. The richness of fancy and of language, which the fair author had so successfully displayed in her poetical productions she has also transferred to prose narration; and has produced a tale, which, we venture to predict, will be much read and admired . . . the pleasing production of a fertile fancy, and a feeling heart.[31]

The *English Review* warmly commended the novel, though considered it somewhat below the high standard of her poetry. It was an 'elegant and affecting little tale' that would send readers 'weeping to their beds'. This might sound like lukewarm praise, but the reviewer still considered that Mrs Robinson was the greatest female author ever to have written in the English language:

> There have been so many elegant proofs of the poetical powers of Mrs ROBINSON, that the most churlish critic cannot refuse to

bear testimony in favour of her genius. Indeed, considering the number and the variety of her productions, we are disposed to think that she has more successfully climbed Parnassian heights than any female votary of the muses which this country has produced.[32]

There was inevitably a backlash against such high praise. In a damning article published some time later, the *Critical Review* objected to Robinson's ornate language – 'if you intended the language to be prose, it is too poetical; if to be poetry, it is very faulty' – together with her unrealistic details and inconsistencies of plot. The reviewer was clearly provoked by the excessive partiality of Mary's supporters:

Mrs Robinson's eager, partial, and injudicious friends, have misled and injured her; nor are we wholly free from the inconveniences which they have occasioned. The merits of Vancenza have so often met our eyes; it has so often been styled excellent, admirable; the world has been so frequently called on to confirm this suffrage with their plaudits, that we dare not *hint* a fault, or *hesitate* dislike. What we disapprove, we must speak of plainly, and if our *gallantry* is called into question, the blame will fall on those who have compelled us to be explicit. After this introduction, we need not say that we think this novel unworthy of the high reputation of its author, a reputation the source of which it is not our present business to examine . . . it is with reluctance that we have engaged in this disquisition; but whatever may be the splendor of a name, we have never scrupled offering our opinion. The public will ultimately decide, and to their supreme tribunal we leave the decision, scarcely apprehending that the judgement will be reversed.[33]

Though Mary's own public did decide in her favour, posterity has taken the opposite view: *Vancenza* was a product of the vogue for Gothic fiction and it now seems overblown to the point of absurdity. Its extraordinary commercial success and the way in which it established Mary's reputation as a novelist make it a fascinating historical document, but it is her later novels that are the ones still worth reading.

* * *

Mary's pleasure in the success of her first novel was marred by the death, on 23 February 1792, of her loyal friend Sir Joshua Reynolds. She published a poetic *Monody* in his memory. In early March her daughter Maria Elizabeth was ill as a result of her smallpox inoculation. Even a small domestic incident of this sort was reported in the *Oracle*: 'Mrs Robinson's literary pursuits are for the present interrupted by the claims of maternal affection. Her lovely and accomplished daughter is now under inoculation, and by the superior skill and attention of Dr MOSELEY, in fair way of doing well.'[34] A week later, Maria Elizabeth's return to health was celebrated in a poem published in the *Oracle* under the title 'Written on the Recovery of my Daughter from Inoculation'.

Although its sales were exceptionally strong, *Vancenza* made little money for Mary. The book was 'printed for the Authoress and sold by J. Bell'. This was a different arrangement from either subscription or the common practice of selling a limited copyright to the publisher for a fixed sum agreed in advance, in return for him taking the profit if a book succeeded or the loss if it failed. 'Printed for the Authoress' meant that Mary was standing the risk and should have reaped the profits: Bell would have charged for production costs and commission on sales, but Mary should have been entitled to substantial royalty earnings. She does not appear to have been given them, perhaps because Bell's business was in dire straits (he went bankrupt the following year). 'My mental labours have failed through the dishonest conduct of my publishers,' she later wrote. 'My works have sold handsomely, but the profits have been theirs.'[35]

So despite her literary success, Mary found herself deep in debt once again. She decided to leave England for the Continent. As she waited for her boat across the English Channel she wrote to Sheridan, begging for money and describing her miserable plight now that Tarleton had left her without his protection. It is the most raw and poignant of her surviving letters:

Dover, July 23 1792

My dear Sheridan

You will perhaps be surprized to hear that after an irreproachable connection of more than *ten years*, I am suffered to depart, an *Exile* from my country and all my hopes, for a few paltry debts. I sail this evening for *Calais* Alone – broken hearted, and without twenty pounds on the face of the Earth. My state of health is to[o] deplorable to bear description, totally lame and depressed in Spirits beyond what my strength can support. I conjure you not to mention this letter to anyone. I am sufficiently humbled by the base ingratitude of the world, without the additional mortification of public Exposure.

Since Colonel Tarleton has suffered me, to be thus driven a wanderer, upon the mercy of an unfeeling world, after having endured every insult from his present low associate, I am resolutely determined never to accept of any favour from him. – I shall in a few weeks be able to arrange my affairs – will you my dear Sheridan do me the kindness to lend me *one* hundred pounds? – I will pay you upon *my honour*; I know you will not refuse me; you will not suffer one whom you once honoured with your friendship, to endure every calamity, in a Country where she is without a friend to speak to. Indeed indeed my dear Sheridan I have not deserved what I Suffer – my Conduct has been Ever to[o] generous and too disinterested. I now feel the effect of my credulity.

When I arrive at Calais I shall not have five guineas – Send your letter under Cover carefully Seald, *to the care of Mrs Belsher City of London Inn, Dover.* She will forward it to me. Pray pray do not refuse me. I will – I will pay you upon my honour – I shall count the hours until I receive your answer – I have no other hope. Adieu.

Yours most truly
Mary Robinson

Pray don't tell Tarleton – he will triumph in my sorrows and delight in hearing me humbled. I am finishing an Opera in Three acts, which I mean to offer you – I think it will succeed – at least I hope so – Pray send me a line.[36]

The next evening, she and her mother and daughter left Dover. The journey must have been exceptionally difficult for the three women, especially as Mary would have needed assistance climbing aboard, moving around the boat, and disembarking – depending on the weather, the crossing could have taken up to twenty-four hours.

Her plan was to go to her brother George in Italy. On the passage to Calais, she wrote what she thought would be her final farewell to Tarleton. It was posted back to London and published in the *Oracle* under the pen name 'Julia' and with the title 'Stanzas Written between Dover and Calais, July 24th, 1792 Inscribed to ——':

Bounding billow, cease thy motion;
Bear me not so swiftly o'er!
Cease thy roaring, foamy ocean,
I will tempt thy rage no more.

Ah! within my bosom beating,
Varying passions wildly reign!
Love, with proud Resentment meeting;
Throbs by turn, of joy and pain.

Joy, that far from foes I wander,
Where their arts can reach no more;
Pain, that woman's heart grows fonder,
When the dream of bliss is o'er. . . .

Yet ere far from all I treasur'd,
********! ere I bid adieu,
Ere my days of pain are measur'd
Take the song that's still thy due!

Yet believe, no servile passions
Seek to charm thy wand'ring mind;
Well I know thy inclinations,
Wav'ring as the passing wind!

I have lov'd thee! Dearly lov'd thee!
Through an age of worldly woe!
How ungrateful I have prov'd thee,
Let my mournful exile show!

Ten long years of anxious sorrow,
Hour by hour, I counted o'er;
Looking forward till to morrow,
Every day I lov'd thee more!

Pow'r and Splendour could not charm me;
I no joy in Wealth could see;
Nor could threats or fears alarm me –
Save *the fear* of losing *thee*! . . .

Fare thee well, ungrateful Rover!
Welcome Gallia's hostile shore;
Now, the breezes waft me over;
Now we part – To Meet No More.[37]

This became one of Mary's most popular poems. It was set to music and, under the title 'Bounding Billow', became a well-known piece in the repertoire of drawing-room numbers to be sung around the piano.

Mary's tame paper the *Oracle* reported that she was only going to be on the Continent for the summer season; she would be returning in the autumn to bring out her newly composed opera at Drury Lane. Her daughter's account of this time abroad makes no mention of the break from Tarleton or Mary's debts, suggesting instead that she set off for Spa in search of help for her rheumatism. Like St Amand les Eaux, where Mary had taken her mud baths some years before, Spa was a health resort in Flanders. When the three women arrived in Calais, they were unsure whether or not to proceed there, since they had heard that the region was ablaze with revolutionary and counter-revolutionary violence. They decided to stay a while in Calais. According to Maria Elizabeth, Mary's time 'passed in listening to the complaints of the impoverished aristocrats, or in attending to the air-built projects of their triumphant adversaries. The arrival of travellers from England, or the return of those from Paris, alone diversified the scene, and afforded a resource to the curious and active inquirer.'[38] There was talk of the massacre in the Tuileries and the imprisonment of the royal family.

Maria Elizabeth was haunted by the sea, which sometimes swelled 'high as the white cliffs that mark the shores of Britain'. She was especially struck by a recently erected monument on the pier to some brave fishermen called Gavet and Mareschal who had perished in a terrible storm when they set out in their tiny vessel in a failed attempt to save an English ship that was going down. Shipwrecks are a recurring motif in her mother's writings and Maria Elizabeth wrote about this real-life tragedy in her one novel.[39]

To Mary's astonishment, Tom Robinson then turned up in Calais. His brother was in England on leave from India, where he had been building a career as distinguished as Tom's was ignominious. Tom had the idea that prosperous Uncle William could help Maria Elizabeth, so he crossed the Channel in order to bring her home and present her to him. Mary was torn between concern at parting from her beloved daughter and desire to further her interests. According to the *Memoirs*, mother and daughter had never been separated. Mary accordingly decided to return to England with her daughter. But she was unwell again: 'Mrs *Robinson* is detained on her route to England by extreme and alarming indisposition, and is now at Calais, where her Physician has ordered her to remain for a few days, till she is in a situation to cross the sea.'[40] On 2 September 1792 she was strong enough to make the crossing. It was the very day of the notorious September Massacres in Paris, when over a thousand royalist prisoners, including young children, were slaughtered. Tarleton was in Paris at the time – he may have been reconciled with Mary when he passed through Calais on the way there – and was swept into the mob. Within hours of the departure of the Robinson family on the Calais to Dover packet boat, an order was received in the French port to the effect that every British subject in France should be held under arrest.

Mary 'rejoiced in her escape, and anticipated with delight the idea of seeing her daughter placed in wealthy protection, the great passport in her own country to honour and esteem'. However, when they met with William Robinson he lost no time in telling them his condition for giving 'protection and favour' to Maria Elizabeth: she would have to renounce for ever '*the filial tie*, which united her to *both* parents'.[41] Maria Elizabeth turned down the offer: she would never abandon her mother.

At the end of September, Tarleton returned to London and was seen with Mrs Robinson and her party at the theatre. The lovers were together again. She presented him with a gold chain ring and an accompanying love poem. Her health was still poor and the laudanum was giving her nightmares. She published some 'Stanzas Written After Successive Nights of Melancholy Dreams': 'When, fev'rish with the throbs of pain, / And bath'd with many a trickling tear, / I close my cheated eyes again, / Despair's wild bands are hov'ring near.' She had a nightmare of being stabbed and then woke in a cold sweat. Death began to seem like a release.[42]

From a biographical point of view, the most revealing of the poems written around this time is one addressed to Tarleton entitled 'Stanzas to a Friend, who desired to have my Portrait'. It was thought by her friends to be very accurate. Published as the climax of her second volume of collected poems, it was a painfully honest self-estimate of her virtues and her foibles. It gives an insight into her ambition to be taken seriously as an author and to discard her image as a celebrated beauty. It is the 'laurel wreath' she desires, not titles or wealth. She begins by gently admonishing her 'friend' for wanting her portrait, with its fixed image and 'lips that *never* move', playfully suggesting that he desires a 'senseless frame' as it never answers back or reproaches him, but just smiles fixedly:

Perhaps, when silent, you will say,
Those lips no anger can betray;
But, fix'd, in smiles remain;
Those eyes, so gentle, can impart
No keen reproach to wound the heart,
No glance of cold disdain!

You'll say, this Form may quickly fade;
One hour in glowing health array'd,
The next, perchance, 'tis lost!
But, cherish'd by the Painter's skill,
An Age may see it blooming still,
As Evergreens in frost.

Mary then goes on to draw a different kind of picture from the one that Tarleton desires: 'Then take, my Friend, / The Lasting Sketch, which here I send, / The Picture of My Mind':

E'en from the early days of youth,
I've blessed the sacred voice of Truth;
And Candour is my pride;
I always Speak what I Believe;
I know not if I Can deceive;
Because I Never Try'd.

I'm often serious, sometimes gay;
Can laugh the fleeting hours away,
Or weep – for Others' woe;
I'm Proud! This fault You cannot blame,
Nor does it tinge my cheek with shame;
Your Friendship Made Me So!

I'm odd, eccentric, fond of ease;
Impatient; difficult to please:
Ambition fires my breast!
Yet not for wealth, or titles vain;
Let but the Laurel deck My strain,
And, dullness, take the rest.

In temper quick, in friendship nice;
I doat on Genius, shrink from vice,
And scorn the flatt'rer's art!
With penetrating skill can see,
Where, mask'd in sweet simplicity,
Lies hid the treach'rous heart.

If Once betray'd, I scarce forgive:
And though I pity All that live,
And mourn for ev'ry pain;
Yet never could I court the Great,
Or worship Fools, whate'er their state;
For falsehood I disdain!

I'm Jealous, for I fondly Love;
No feeble flame my heart can prove;
Caprice ne'er dimm'd its fires:
I blush, to see the human Mind,

For nobler, prouder claims design'd,
The slave of low desires!

Reserv'd in manner, where unknown;
A little Obstinate, I own,
And apt to form opinion:
Yet Envy never broke my rest,
Nor could Self-Int'rest bow my breast
To Folly's base dominion.

Having given her true portrait, she pleads with her lover to see her how she really is and to love her accordingly:

Such is my Portrait: now believe
My pencil never can deceive,
And know me what I paint:
Taught in Affliction's rigid school,
I act from Principle, not Rule,
No Sinner – yet No Saint.[43]

CHAPTER 20

Author

> Of all the occupations which industry can pursue, those of literary toil are the most fatiguing. That which seems to the vacant eye a mere playful amusement, is in reality an Herculean labour; and to compose a tolerable work is so difficult a task, that the fastidiously severe should make the trial before they presume to condemn even the humblest effort of imagination.
>
> Mary Robinson, *The Natural Daughter*

Mary still had the ear of the Prince, not least because of his friendship with Tarleton. In October 1792, she published a sonnet addressed 'To the Prince of Wales', under her pen name Julia:

> From Courtly Crowds and empty joys retir'd,
> Adorn'd with Heaven's best gift, a Lib'ral Mind!
> Still shall thy grac'd perfections be admir'd,
> Thy *polish'd Manners*, and thy sense refin'd . . .

The poem continued with the claim that the Prince was formed '*To prove* all trivial, empty Pleasures, Vain'; in return, the 'fond Muse' of Julia would offer him 'a Wreath Sublime'.[1] Politics was becoming ever more polarized in response to the increasing violence in France. The Prince had recently made his maiden speech in the House of Lords, aligning himself with the more moderate faction of the Whigs. By publishing a sonnet suggesting that the Prince was renouncing the 'empty joys' of the fashionable world and growing to political maturity, Mary was carefully positioning herself in the middle ground. The *Oracle* began to represent her as a moderate rather than an all-out 'Revolution Writer': 'Mrs ROBINSON's *Ode To Humanity*, which graced THE ORACLE some time since, is not so popular with the Revolution Writers as some of her former works. Sensible minds are always open to conviction, and ever swayed by the admonitions of Reason.'[2]

Pitt and the Tories were preparing for war. After the King of France was guillotined in the Place de la Révolution in Paris on 21 January 1793, Tarleton would have expected to rejoin the Army. But he was very ill throughout the early part of the year, suffering – ironically enough – from the same complaint that had plagued Mary ever since her night ride to Dover in pursuit of him: 'Colonel Tarleton has been confined for some days past, with a rheumatic fever, of which he still continues much indisposed.'[3] Mary nursed him and wrote poems for him. Mortality was on her mind. December had seen the death, after a short illness, of Louisa, musically accomplished daughter of novelist Mary Ann Hanway and Hanway Hanway, Tom Robinson's old friend who had been witness at their wedding. Mary had remained friends with the Hanways and would have been especially sensitive to the death of a beautiful and talented daughter. She wrote an elegy in Louisa's memory.[4] At the same time, the execution of Louis XVI inevitably made her contemplate the fate of Marie Antoinette. The Queen and her children were still in prison, waiting to hear whether they, too, would be guillotined. Mary wrote poems in the voice of Marie Antoinette: 'A Fragment, Supposed to be Written Near the Temple, at Paris, on the Night before the Murder of Louis XVI' and 'Marie Antoinette's Lamentation, in Her Prison of the Temple'. In the latter she emphasized Marie Antionette's role as devoted mother and wronged woman, as if she were a royal version of Mary herself.

She had completed the opera she had promised Sheridan. It was called *Kate of Aberdeen* and there were several announcements in the *Oracle* claiming that it was about to go into production. Dora Jordan, the most popular comic actress of the day, was hoping to appear in it.[5] The libretto had the 'approbation of the *best Authors* living' and it breathed 'that spirit of Loyalty' that would make it highly popular as the country was going to war, so why was the theatre management procrastinating? The probable reason was that the Theatre Royal Drury Lane was in the process of being rebuilt and the company, now managed by John Philip Kemble, was living from hand to mouth in borrowed premises. It was simply not a good time to stage a major new opera. The work was withdrawn; the *Oracle* promised to print it in full, but never did.[6]

Mary's supporters at the *Oracle* took the more jaundiced view that Kemble was prejudiced against her. There may be an element of truth in this: Kemble's greatest asset was his sister, Sarah Siddons, greatest tragedienne of the age. Siddons was almost single-handedly responsible for the changing attitudes towards actresses at the close of the eighteenth century, bringing to her profession a new respectability and dignity. Her reputation remained unblemished, but she knew the dangerous line she was treading, and to have been seen in the company of Perdita would have been an embarrassment. Kemble may not have wanted his new theatre tarnished by the living embodiment of the old image of the actress as mere courtesan – especially as this was the period when a great deal of publicity was being given to the affair between actress Dora Jordan and the Prince of Wales's brother, the Duke of Clarence.

Siddons herself was sorry that decency prevented her from ever making Mary's acquaintance. Mary sent her poems and tried to arrange an introduction, but to no avail. James Boaden, Mary's editor at the *Oracle*, later wrote the authorized biography of Siddons, in which he contrasted the probity of Sarah's personal life, in which she benefited from the protection of her brother, with the fate of Perdita, whose fall from purity he firmly blamed on her husband:

> Flattery soon withdrew the guards that reason had placed about beauty. He who should have commanded the garrison betrayed his trust, the husband made a sacrifice of his honour. Then establishments were soon seen, of which the *means* were invisible; the die was thrown that sealed the condition of the enchanting Maria, and she became in melancholy reality the PERDITA.[7]

'The charming and beautiful Mrs Robinson,' said Siddons, 'I pity her from the bottom of my soul.' On being invited to meet her, she wrote an exquisitely worded, regretful letter of refusal:

> I am very much obliged to Mrs Robinson for her polite attention in sending me her poems. Pray tell her so, with my compliments. I hope the poor, charming woman has quite recovered from her fall. If she is half as amiable as her writings, I shall long for the *possibility* of being acquainted with her. I say the *possibility*, because one's whole life is one continual sacrifice of inclinations, which to indulge, however laudable or innocent, would draw down the malice and reproach of those prudent people who never do ill.[8]

The mutual friend who sought to introduce Siddons and Robinson was John Taylor, royal oculist, sometime theatre critic and then editor of the *Morning Post*, man of letters, poet, and celebrity-chaser. He was the dedicatee of Mary's next book, a slim volume containing three poems, *Sight, The Cavern of Woe, and Solitude*. There she described Taylor as 'One whose friendship I am proud to enjoy, as proceeding from a penetrating and enlightened mind!'– though she added that she did not really like dedications, since they were 'too frequently calculated to feed the VANITY OF HIGH RANK'. She preferred the principle of the 'ARISTOCRACY OF GENIUS': as with the address to the reader inserted in the third edition of *Vancenza*, she was consciously positioning herself as an author in the marketplace, a meritocrat rather than a coterie writer relying on the patronage of the fashionable world. Taylor returned the tribute to Mary with the dedication to his own book of poems:

> To Mrs Robinson
>
> Dear Madam,
> It is not because you have paid so very flattering a tribute to my professional character, as to dedicate to me one of your most beautiful Poems, that I am induced to lay the following trifles at your feet. I am too sensible of the merit of that Poem, to make so inadequate a return. My object on this occasion, is at least to tender my thanks, and to indulge myself in the pleasure of boasting that I have for many years enjoyed the friendship of one of the most accomplished women of the present age.[9]

Mary was indeed becoming a celebrity poet – with the *Oracle* serving her as well as any modern public relations strategist. It puffed her to the skies: the publication of the slender volume of three poems was described as nothing less than the literary event of the century. The paper reported the ups and downs of her health and her relationship with Tarleton, the worldwide sales of her works (her poems were fetching three or four guineas a volume in India – 'if this is not gratifying to Literary emulation – what is?'), her movements in and out of town ('Mrs Robinson has been for some days in the neighbourhood of Windsor reposing in the most honourable of all gratifications, that of LITERARY FAME'), and the way in which her best pieces were being set to music as popular songs or recited on the London stage ('Mrs ROBINSON ought to be highly flattered, when her poetry is become the subject, for painters – musical composers, translators – public recitation – and theatrical remark. She must now expect all the shafts of ENVY to assail her, and arm herself against them accordingly').[10]

In early August, Mary's mother died. Though her brothers were wealthy, she had always refused their offers of financial assistance to help Hester: she alone was the one who cared for her mother from the day when Nicholas Darby walked out on her. According to Maria Elizabeth, Hester's death was a severe blow, which affected Mary's health for many months afterwards: 'even to the latest hour of her life, her grief appeared renewed, when any object presented itself connected with the memory of her departed mother'.[11] The three generations of women had, over the years, forged an extremely close bond. They had lived through public humiliation, exile, and physical disability, relying upon each other for comfort and support. A newspaper report telling of how Mary was badly injured when she fell from her crutches around this time brings home a sense of how difficult it must have been to care for her mother in her last days.

In the second half of 1793, Mary published two poems in very different styles: in her own name, a much-admired *Monody to the Memory of Marie Antoinette Queen of France*, in response to the execution of Marie Antoinette, and as 'Horace Juvenal', a satire in two cantos called *Modern Manners*, in which she lampooned such fashionable vices as gaming, gossip, and prizefighting (one of Tarleton's favourite pursuits). A passing reference to the 'magic force' of 'Fi-z—t's eyes' suggests that she was not without bitterness that it was Mrs Fitzherbert who commanded the Prince's heart. Mary's satire was said to have 'roused a nest of hornets' among the *ton*,[12] but critics admired the verve and dexterity of her rhyming couplets:

O, *Fashion*! delegate of taste and wit,
Oft do I see thee triumph in the pit;
When Hobart's critic fan, attention draws,
The airy signal of ill-judged applause!
When pale-faced misses sigh from side-box rows,
And *painted* matrons nod to *painted* beaux:
Where the lank lord, incircled in the throng,
Shews his white teeth, and hums a fav'rite song;
Who, spite of season, crowds it to the play,
Wrapp'd in six waistcoats – *in the month of May*;
Who, just at noon, has strength to rise from bed,
With empty pocket – and *more empty head*;
Who, scarce recover'd from the courtly dance,
Sees with disgust the vulgar day advance:
Anticipates the wax-illumin'd night,
Cassino's charms, and Faro's proud delight!
Who hates the broad intolerable sun,
That points his door to every gaping *dun*;
Who saunters all the morn, and reads the news,
'Midst clouds of odours and *Olympian dews*;
Till three o'clock proclaims the time to meet
On the throng'd pavement of St James's street;
Where various shops on various follies thrive,
'Beaux, banish beaux – and coaches, coaches drive:'
While to Hyde-park this titled tribe are flocking,
To *walk* in boots – or *ride* in silken stocking.[13]

'Could Horace and Juvenal have descanted thus eloquently, on Heroes and Bravoes and Buckskin, on box-lobbies, hops and shops?' asked one reviewer, while the *Morning Post* said that the poem was 'another striking proof of the versatile talents of this elegant and intelligent Author'.[14] When Mary wrote of the world she knew, and with a lightness of touch learned from Alexander Pope, she was at her best.

Mary and Tarleton were not living together by this time, but he was 'very often at her house in St James's Place'[15] – a compact little square that was just about as close as a commoner could live to the royal residence of St James's Palace (it also had the advantage of abutting onto St James's

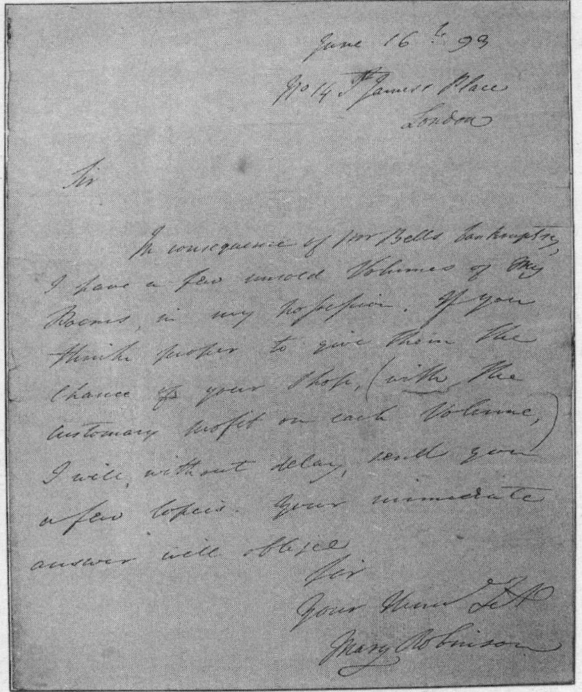

June 16th 93
No 14 St James's Place
London

Sir

In consequence of Mr Bells bankruptcy, I have a few unsold Volumes of my Poems, in my possession. If you think proper to give them the chance of your Shop, (with the customary profit on each Volume,) I will, without delay, send you a few copies. Your immediate answer will oblige

Sir
Your Hum^e Sert
Mary Robinson

A letter in Mary Robinson's hand, 1793.

Park, the most prestigious of the London parks, where one needed a royal warrant to drive one's carriage). In the public eye, Mary was now an independent woman of letters, not just the mistress of a famous man. She was sketched in profile by George Dance around this time, no longer looking like the woman of fashion, but very much the intellectual with her severe gaze, austere dress, and French Revolutionary headband.

A second volume of collected poems was published on 4 January 1794 (though with the previous year given on the title page). Entitled *Poems by Mrs M. Robinson Volume the Second*, it was designed typographically to make a set with the 1791 volume, though it came from a different publisher – John Bell having gone bankrupt – and it was not a subscription volume. Priced at twelve shillings in boards, it was aimed at the middle market, somewhere above the circulating libraries for which novels were published but below the elite audience that had characterized the subscription list of volume one. A prefatory advertisement informed the reader that 'Sight', 'The Cavern of Woe', and 'Solitude', the trio of poems published independently some months before, had been included 'in preference to printing a second Edition' of them; it was also made clear that many of the other poems in the volume had previously been published in the *Oracle* 'with the signatures of LAURA MARIA, OBERON, and JULIA'.

The volume includes many more personal poems than its predecessor had done, among them Mary's elegy for her father, many love poems for Tarleton, and a selection of lyrics written for her daughter, including some lines to Maria Elizabeth written on her nineteenth birthday (18 October 1793) that proclaim 'Whate'er my *chequer'd lot* has been, / No hour was *yet* so dear to me / As That Blest Hour which gave me Thee!'[16] Another glimpse of her life at this time is offered by 'Evening Meditations on St Anne's Hill, inscribed to The Right Hon. Charles James Fox'. Mary spent her summers in Old Windsor, not far from Fox's country home, where Elizabeth Armistead was in more or less permanent residence. Now that Mary was an author, she no longer considered the Armistead to be a rival. The poem ends by praising Fox's 'honest heart' and 'patriot bosom'. This was a way of defending her old protector's loyalty to king and country, despite his initial welcome of the French Revolution.

One reviewer objected to the fact that so many of the poems were personal: 'Many relate to incidents in her own connections, and are *proudly plaintive*.'[17] Another critic perceptively noted that the volume had 'the same beauties and the same faults' as the first one.[18] Perhaps Mary's greatest deficiency as a writer was the lack of a faculty of self-criticism: she was not good at discriminating between her own good work and bad, and she did not have editors who were strong enough to help her with this problem. Samuel Taylor Coleridge, the towering critical intelligence of the age, said some years later that her work was 'bad, good and indifferent, I grant you, but full, and overflowing'.[19] At this stage, much that was bad or indifferent about her poetry could be laid at the door of 'the gaudy trappings of the Della Crusca school'. She had some way to go before fully rooting out that influence. The *Oracle*, predictably, had no time for such reservations: 'we rarely, indeed, meet with elegance equal to the language of this work'.[20] Friends such as John Taylor also rallied round with tributes:

Impromptu to Mrs Robinson, on receiving her *Poems*

Then take, dearest Laura, the tribute sincere
From a friend who admired thee in life's early hour;
Who beheld in thy bloom, the sweet promise appear,
That time has matured to so lovely a flower.[21]

Sales figures for *Poems Volume the Second* do not survive. A new edition entitled simply *Poems* was published some time later at half the price of the original, which suggests an attempt to shift unsold stock.

After the success of *Vancenza*, Mary had been busy planning and writing her second novel, which was to be an exposé of 'modern times', an extended fictional equivalent of the poem *Modern Manners*. As usual, the *Oracle* furnished some pre-publication hype, this time to the effect that there would be 'striking resemblances' to certain well-known public characters. The day before publication, the *Morning Post* reported news of angry murmurings circulating amongst the *ton*: 'All the fashionable *Widows* are up in arms against Mrs Robinson and wonder how a woman without *rank*, dares take liberties with *great people*. – What adds to the crime, is her presuming to espouse the cause of the *Swinish Multitude*.'[22] The 'swinish multitude' was Burke's infamous term for the Parisian populus – it had constantly been thrown back at him by radicals such as Tom Paine and by caricaturists who mocked him as a turncoat. For the more conservative elements of the *ton*, it was outrageous that Mrs Robinson, sometime royal mistress, should now be mixing in radical circles and espousing the cause of the multitude. But on the principle that all publicity is good publicity, Mary would not have been unduly concerned about the pre-publication chatter.

The Widow, or a Picture of Modern Times was published on St Valentine's Day 1794. Dedicated 'To that Public and those Liberal Critics, who have so highly distinguished my former productions', it signalled a new departure for Mary's prose writing, in both style and content. It is an epistolary novel, centred upon a sentimental heroine called Julia St Lawrence, who, like the author, has an American merchant for a father and spends her time reading avidly and 'scribbling poetry'. She is an 'American beauty' with dark auburn hair and blue eyes. Julia elopes and marries and is believed to have perished at sea; her husband remarries and she lives incognito in the country, passing herself off as a widow. The other widow of the novel, who was clearly the cause of offence to the *ton*, is a vicious, unprincipled woman called Amelia Vernon. Utterly lacking in moral scruple, she wreaks havoc on all who come into contact with her. In a most undignified manner, she revels in her widowhood: '*Weeds* are delightfully becoming; I lamented the hour I left them off; and hope that, one day or other, I shall have the felicity of wearing them *again*.'[23]

Mrs Vernon's bosom friend Lady Seymour is the most convincing character in the book. She is neither too innocent like Julia nor too corrupt like Amelia; rather, she is a scheming but lively and charismatic anti-heroine who anticipates such figures as the Lady Susan of Jane Austen's juvenile epistolary novel, or for that matter Mary Crawford in *Mansfield Park*. Lady Seymour is exiled to the country, where she feels she is 'buried alive' and makes mischief amongst the locals to amuse herself. In contrast to the many characters in women's novels of the period who are victims of sensibility, she satirizes the foibles of sentimentalism, such as the love of nature:

> If I liked mountains and rivulets, and woods, and cascades, could I not have them painted and hung up in my house? They would appear quite as charming, and would have the additional merit of being the same at all seasons: for autumn is insupportable, it warns one of declining beauty! And winter, oh, winter! perpetually reminds me of Sir Charles! [her long-suffering husband] . . . I should expire, if any body thought me capable of obeying my husband.'[24]

As reviewers were quick to acknowledge, Mary drew the follies of fashionable society with a skilful hand. Writing vividly and candidly about the society she knew so well, she exposed the corruption of a world where extramarital affairs were commonplace, virtue ridiculed, and a self-satisfied sense of superiority endemic. 'My dear Lady Allford,' writes Lady Seymour, 'we must keep up an appearance of decorum, otherwise women of inferior rank, who boast only the *gothic* perfections of talents and sensibilities, would obtrude themselves into notice; and leave us of higher birth, quite in the mists of obscurity.' And Mrs Vernon: 'It is now too late to repent, you have *bought* a *titled* protection, and you may easily purchase happiness, for your rank places you above the low impertinence of censure.' People of lower rank but superior intellectual status are unjustly vilified by those who have power. As Julia St Lawrence is warned by her confidante, 'to be highly distinguished for *mental perfections*, is, in the eye of ignorance to be guilty of the *worst* of crimes; because, they are attributes *superior* to those of *birth*, are not to be acquired by rapacity, or robbed of their intrinsic value by the fluctuations of *fortune*'.[25]

The epistolary style freed Mary to experiment with different voices, ranging from the sharp satire of Lady Seymour to the cruel wit of Mrs Vernon and the egalitarian views of Lord Allford. Her novel became a forum for her increasingly radical views on education, revolution, reputation, and the iniquities of rank. 'Nothing shall persuade me, that *virtue* is not the natural inmate of the human breast; and I believe, that the vast difference of rank, and the vices of those favoured with the gifts of fortune, are entirely productive of all the ills that threaten humanity,' writes Lord Allford: the idea that humankind is innately virtuous and that inequalities of rank and wealth are the root of all evil comes straight from the thought of Jean-Jacques Rousseau and the other intellectual fathers of the French Revolution. Robinson is equally alert to the cycle of violence that is unleashed by the justifiable desire of the lower orders to liberate themselves from subjugation:

> The insolence of what is *called* the *higher* order of society, creates that sort of murmuring which awakens the slumbering mind; in those who are most enlightened, it produces a restlessness, which soon grows into contempt! contempt banishes respect, and produces *hatred*; the next idea is REVENGE! Reason then begins to ruminate on what are the real claims of superiority, and the powers of the intellect assert their right to pre-eminence; we shudder at the horrors of a civil war! We shrink when we behold a torrent of human blood, appeasing the thirst of an incensed multitude. But the ignorance in which the obscure order of the people are nursed, and the perpetual subjection in which they are educated, prevent the expansion of the

> mind, and make them only sensible of wrongs, and eager for redress. Take the tyger from his den, will he not seek for blood?[26]

As Mary wrote this, the Jacobin terror was about to be unleashed on the streets of Paris.

The novel was rightly praised for having an 'easier style' than *Vancenza* and for its truth to life: 'the principal merit of these volumes is their exhibiting a *picture of modern times*, in which the features of fashionable folly and depravity are drawn with a skilful hand'; 'her characters and manners are evidently drawn from an intimate acquaintance with the fashionable world'.[27] Engagingly, Mary was not averse to making jokes at her own expense: 'I tried to touch my pianoforte; the first song I opened in my music book was, *Adieu thou Dreary Pile*; I ventured to open a second, which presented that stupid old ditty, *Ye fair married Dames*; a third, *For Tenderness form'd*; and a fourth, *Mary's Lamentation*. This was too provoking!'[28] There is also a certain poignancy in the heroine's desire to be reconciled with her long-lost father and to live with him in America. For some readers, what was most powerful – especially in the light of Mary's past – was the book's defence of beautiful women who succumb to temptation:

> We are all subject to error, and the feeling, considerate mind readily embraces every occasion to commend, rather than to depreciate. Let those who censure examine their own hearts; let them before they condemn, prove themselves immaculate. The frailty of our sex depends on a thousand circumstances, and ought to claim the tenderest indulgence. A woman may be weak without being vicious; a variety of events may conspire to undermine the most powerful rectitude; and the severity frequently exercised by relations in the education of youth, gives an habitual discontent, which renders every scene of life dull and insipid. The mind so tinged with peevish indifference shrinks from the energies of virtue, and easily becomes a prey to the designing. There *are* women who have no opportunities to wander from the paths of propriety; peculiar deficiency in personal attractions will often shield the weakest heart from the attacks of the seducer; *others* are placed on such an eminence of delight, so surrounded by all the comforts, the luxuries of life, blessed with

the attentions of amiable kindred (while every wish is anticipated by the affections of a worthy husband) that to deviate from virtue would be unpardonable. But let the prejudiced observer turn to that woman, who, perhaps, tenderly educated in the bosom of affluence, with a mind exquisitely sensible, driven upon the mercy of an unfeeling world; young, beautiful, stricken with poverty, shrinking under oppression, assailed by flattery, and allured by splendor; surely the most obdurate heart must sigh for *such* a wanderer, and confess that, if any thing can palliate indiscretion, it is the combination of such circumstances. But, alas! How few will examine with candour, or judge with lenity! How few will look back upon past provocation, in order to extenuate present culpability![29]

Since Vancenza had been such a commercial success *The Widow* was printed, by Mary's personal request, in an edition of 1,500 copies, more than twice the usual print run for a novel. It sold briskly for the first few months, passing the break-even point (which would have been reached at about five hundred copies) and yielding Mary a first payment in July of £21, hardly the kind of money she required to maintain her establishment. Sporadic press comment on the book continued throughout the year. In May: 'The *Daughters of Pharoah* are highly offended at the liberties taken with their honourable employment by Mrs ROBINSON in her new Novel' – that is to say, the fashionable gambling ladies at their faro tables (a set that included Georgiana Duchess of Devonshire) had taken offence at the portrayal of their extravagant addiction. And in October, the *Morning Post* observed that whereas two years ago the multitude had worshipped Mrs Robinson's writings 'even to idolatry' and named her 'the English Sappho . . . whose literary fame would *outlive the Pencil of a Reynolds*', now she was 'the subject of abuse, because her Novel breathes the Spirit of *Democracy*!!'[30]

Mary was indisposed with 'a nervous fever' around the time of her book's publication. Her daughter, meanwhile, was beginning to appear in society. She attended a masquerade at Brandenburg House (the Prince of Wales and Sheridan were also present) wearing the costume of a nun. She was said to be, together with a Miss Jerningham and a Lady Asgill, one of the three 'prettiest women' in the room.[31]

Maria Elizabeth also made her literary debut. Her first novel was completed a few weeks after her mother's second one was published. Entitled *The Shrine of Bertha*, it was a Gothic romance written in epistolary form, with all the conventional elements of the genre: ancient ruins, secret caskets, corpses, and spectres. The heroines are Laura and Sophia. Laura – which was, of course, the best known of Maria Elizabeth's mother's pen names – has auburn hair and dark blue eyes (like Mary and several of her heroines). She has been educated at a convent in Lausanne, where much of the novel is set until the heroine travels to Germany. Laura's bosom friend Sophia resides in England and sends letters describing dissipated fashionable life. Laura is a disciple of 'the divine Rousseau', and is a much more typically sentimental and less feisty heroine than those of Mary. She is in love with her cousin, Henry Percival, who has gone abroad to escape his domineering mother. After many problems and obstacles, chiefly arising from mysterious details surrounding Laura's origins, they are united. The unexpected plot twist is that the suspected suicide Lady Bertha did not die by her own hand, but was accidentally given an overdose of opium – a misadventure that anticipates the climax of Mary's later novel, *Walsingham*, in which the hero nearly takes a potentially fatal dose of the drug.

Maria Elizabeth writes well about society and manners, offering some fascinating details, no doubt based on personal experience, of life abroad in France and Germany. There are, for instance, colourful descriptions of rural fetes, outdoor tables laden with eggs, cheese, breads, and wine, and of the national characteristics of German women: 'more like the English than any other nation. They are lively, sociable and unaffected; passionately fond of *dress* and *play*.'[32] The text is laced with quotations from Shakespeare and references to Homer and Virgil, demonstrating that Maria Elizabeth had received a superior and 'masculine' education rather than having merely been brought up for needlework and the piano. The book begins with a dedication to 'the best of mothers' from her 'most grateful and affectionate daughter'. Verses by both mother and daughter were woven into the narrative, the inclusion of new poetry by Mary serving as a *bonne bouche* for potential buyers.

A letter from Mary to her friend John Taylor reveals the excitement and apprehension mother and daughter felt in the days before publication:

7 o'Clock Wednesday evening –

Just returned completely drenched with an unceasing rain, from 2 o'Clock, to this moment –

Mary [i.e. Maria Elizabeth] trembles at the Idea of her hasty *Novel* letters appearing in public, – we shall see it tomorrow. *You are too kind, indeed Juan!* But we love you very *sincerely, purely, and disinterestedly.* –

Have you seen Whitehouse's Odes? I have received some very flattering letters from him, though personally unknown. You shall see them when I come to town. He has sent me his works, Splendidly bound. – I think his Odes Good – read them and give me your opinion.

Adieu Adieu
Yours very truly
M R

Mary will write to you by the next post – The General sends best Compts. with the little Bertha. My brother will be in town next month – when he hopes to meet with you often ~~and Mr H~~.[33]

The 'little Bertha' means a complimentary copy of the novel. The 'General' was Tarleton, who was promoted that year.* The full name of 'Mr H' is a mystery, though a paragraph in the *Oracle* reveals who he was: 'Mrs ROBINSON is to reside with her brother, Mr DARBY in Italy two years – From his house Mr H— will receive the hand of Miss R. with a fortune, generously suitable to her accomplishments.'[34] A possible candidate is the son of those old family friends, the Hanways. It is not known when Maria Elizabeth became engaged to 'Mr H' or when and why the engagement was broken off. She never married. The source of her 'fortune' is also a mystery: it is most probable that she was provided for by her uncle, George Darby, who had risen to become head of the British factory in

* There is a puzzle here, in that this letter was clearly written shortly before the publication of *The Shrine of Bertha*, but Tarleton was gazetted Major General some time later. The gazetting does seem to have been delayed, so perhaps Tarleton had heard about his prospects by this time. The alternative explanation is that the 'General' refers to another close mutual acquaintance of Mary Robinson and John Taylor, conceivably the Earl of Moira, who had been made a General by this time, and who seems to have been very intimate with Mary – the nature and extent of their relationship is one of the most intriguing mysteries of her later years.

Leghorn. The house in Englefield Green, by Windsor Great Park, in which Mary spent her last days was owned by the daughter not the mother; Maria Elizabeth remained there until her own death.

The Shrine of Bertha certainly did not bring Maria Elizabeth a great income. It was printed for her by William Lane at the Minerva Press, which churned out Gothic novels for the circulating libraries. Though there was a further edition in 1796, sales were by no means spectacular. There were a couple of reviews, one of them praising the book as 'on the whole, well-written'.[35]

Mary became involved with the theatre world again that summer. On 'the Glorious first of June', there was a major victory against the French Navy off the coast of Brittany. The occasion was marked a month later by a special evening at the new Drury Lane Theatre for the 'Benefit for the Relief of the Widows and Orphans of the Brave Men who fell in the Late Glorious Actions, under Earl Howe'. The event was under the patronage of the Prince of Wales and the Duke of Clarence. The main play was Garrick's ever-popular *The Country Girl*, after which the Duke of Clarence's mistress Dora Jordan spoke the original epilogue to Sheridan's *The Rivals*, and then there was a show, hastily put together by Sheridan, entitled *The Glorious First of June*. It included songs by various authors, among them Mary Robinson. The evening raised more than thirteen hundred guineas for the benefit fund.

Tarleton, meanwhile, was still gambling, even making a bet with Sheridan that he would not see active duty in Paris. It was rumoured that Mary's reason for writing was to pay his debts. So claimed a satirical pamphlet, *The Whig Club; or, a Sketch of Modern Patriotism:*

> If you will believe the Colonel, his exploits in love have at least equalled his achievements in war; it is his pleasure to relate how *often* and how *firmly* he has stood in the *imminent breach*. To this he could lately call Perdita to witness; but the once elegant frail one remains now only a melancholy ruin of her former beauty; and is reduced to beguile her hours, and prop the Colonel's tottering finances, by weaving novels, and fineering sonnets.[36]

This pamphlet was by Charles Pigott, a Shropshire gentleman who was a bon vivant, man of the turf, and unlikely Jacobinical radical. Regarding

Whigs such as Fox and Tarleton as no better than Tories such as Pitt, he wrote a series of scurrilous and best-selling satires that made radical capital out of the 'boudoir politics' of the aristocracy and the gentry who sat in Parliament.

Tarleton was further vilified in Pigott's *Female Jockey Club*, in which a biographical sketch of Mary was used as a pretext to attack princes, courts, and decadent aristocrats. There it was claimed that the Colonel had become estranged from Mary because he had made sexual advances to Maria Elizabeth: 'we have lately heard, with unfeigned sorrow, (so fugitive are lover's joys,) that there at present exists a serious difference between them, the *Liverpool hero* having betrayed certain symptoms of amorous fondness for Perdita's fair daughter'.[37] This was in the summer of 1794, when Mary went off to Windsor without Tarleton. As usual, a reunion soon followed: 'A certain *Literary Female* has good humouredly received a gallant Colonel into those habits of friendly attendance, so reciprocally gratifying, and which misconception alone could have broken off.'[38] But how many times could they go on breaking up and making up?

CHAPTER 21

Nobody

> Have I not reason to be disgusted when I see him, to whom I ought to look for better fortune, lavishing favours on unworthy objects, gratifying the *avarice* of *ignorance* and *dullness*; while I, who sacrificed reputation, an advantageous profession, friends, patronage, the brilliant hours of youth, and the conscious delight of correct conduct, am condemned to the scanty pittance bestowed on every indifferent page who holds up his ermined train of ceremony!
>
> Mary Robinson to John Taylor, 5 October 1794

In the autumn of 1794, Mary was lodging at Salt Hill, on the turnpike road out towards Windsor. She was waiting to hear from John Kemble at Drury Lane whether or not he intended to produce her comedy, *Nobody.* At this time she wrote several letters to one of her closest friends, John Taylor. They give an intimate insight into her struggles as her financial difficulties and feelings of isolation increased. Her fury with the Prince of Wales, whom she blamed for the onset of her misfortunes, exploded from her pen and she also unleashed her anger at being exploited by her (male) publishers and by Kemble.

Mary informed Taylor ('Juan') of a 'secret which must not be revealed'. Her brother George was urging her to leave England and retire to Tuscany: 'My dear and valuable brother, who is now in Lancashire, wishes to persuade me, and the unkindness of the *world* tends not a little to forward his hopes. I have no relations in England except my darling girl, and, I fear, few friends.' She was particularly grieved by what she considered to be the failure of her literary endeavours, those 'false prospects' that had led her 'into the vain expectation that fame would attend my labours, and my country be my pride'. She complained that her comedy had been in the manager's hands for two long years 'without a single hope that a trial would be granted'.

She also mentioned that both she and her daughter had received reviews from William Gifford, author of *The Baviad*. Her friend 'Peter Pindar' had told of an editor's intention to 'cut up' her work before even reading it. She felt especially indignant on her daughter's behalf: 'My poor little Mary, too – what had she done to injure those "Self-named monarchs of the laurelled crown, / Props of the press – and tutors of the town"' (the quotation is a couplet concerning critics from her *Modern Manners*). In reaction to all the recent bad press, she vowed to terminate her literary career: 'When I leave England – adieu to the *muse* for *ever!* – I will never publish another line while I exist, and even those manuscripts now finished I WILL DESTROY.' She could no longer see the point of working so hard when it was her publishers who reaped the financial reward.

Mary told Taylor that her annuity was barely enough to support her expenses, given that her lameness meant that she was unable to travel by foot: 'how can I subsist upon £500 a year when my carriage (a necessary expense) alone costs me £200.' Five hundred pounds was, of course, the amount of the Prince's annuity. It is here that she comes closest to confessing her remorse for taking that irreversible step so long ago when she agreed to become his mistress. The Prince had recently broken off his connection with Mrs Fitzherbert, much to the King's delight, and had agreed to marry Caroline of Brunswick. His debts were in excess of £600,000. Mary was 'disgusted' that the Prince was 'lavishing favours on unworthy objects', squandering his wealth while she who had 'sacrificed reputation, an advantageous profession, friends, patronage, the brilliant hours of youth, and the conscious delight of correct conduct' was condemned to poverty – and an annuity that was not paid when it should have been.[1]

Taylor responded with a kind and sympathetic letter. She wrote back the following week in a calmer state of mind:

In wretched spirits I wrote you last week a most melancholy letter. Your kind answer consoled me. The balsam of pure and disinterested friendship never fails to cure the mind's sickness, particularly when it proceeds from disgust at the ingratitude of the world.

As from the high and craggy peak,
Impetuous torrents rush below,
The peaceful valley's haunts to seek,
And midst its winding channels flow;
So wild affliction madd'ning flies,
For shelter to the feeling breast,
Where sympathy a balm supplies,
And friendship soothes the soul to rest.

So much for a simile. I am never happy but when I am *tagging* rhymes, and never pleased with them when they are finished.

What news is there in town? How do you like Miss Wallis? I saw her at Bath two years since in the character of Portia, and thought her *best* praise was the manner of a *gentlewoman*. But we shall wait long – very long – before we see anything like that *inspiration* which characterises a Siddons – that *soul* beaming through every veil of fiction, and making art more lovely than even nature in all its fairest adornments. For after all acting must be the perfection of *art*; nature, rude and spontaneous, would but ill describe the passions so as to produce effect in scenes of fictitious sorrow. Mrs Siddons, in my humble opinion, is the most perfect mistress of the character she undertakes to represent of any performer I ever beheld – Garrick not excepted. Her 'Was he alive?' in Lady Randolph [in John Home's popular tragedy *Douglas*], touched my feelings so acutely that I never wish again to give them so severe a trial. But whither is my pen rambling? Do not suppose I am pretending to the vanity of a critic. I am only humbly describing what I felt deeply and can only faintly express. One hour of rational gratification is worth an age of frivolous fashionable pastime. I never heard Miss Farren's *niminy piminy* but I instantly thought of Mrs Siddons's solemn 'remember twelve'; so natural it is for the mind to recur to the extreme of perfection on observing the insignificance of folly.

We shall return to town very soon. Adieu, etc.

The postman has released you from a stupid letter.[2]

Mary's admiration of Siddons knew no bounds, as this letter suggests. Her unflattering reference to Miss Farren's '*niminy piminy*' is wonderfully dismissive of her acting style, though Farren was supposedly to appear in *Nobody*. There could be no better revelation of Mary's mercurial nature than the shift from the bitterness and despair of the previous week's letter to the energy and cheerfulness of this one. Having threatened to stop writing altogether, she now claims that she is never happier than when '*tagging* rhymes'. Her mood swings were probably exacerbated by opium.

The very next day she wrote Taylor a mildly flirtatious letter. She mentioned Tarleton's promotion to 'Major General' and said that although she was 'no friend to new titles' his success was 'well earned and I rejoice in his acquiring it'. She enquired after mutual friends, such as 'Peter Pindar' the satirist, and shared theatre gossip. Elizabeth Farren had been to see her, with her 'constant little Earl'. Then she had a dig at Kemble – and indeed sketched into the letter a very funny profile of his head, with his famously large nose making him look very superior. In spite of his ill nature – and his postponement of her comedy – she 'cannot help *admiring*' him. She explained that she and her daughter had been busy with 'ramblings over the country', visiting notable sites such as the tomb of the poet Thomas Gray and 'Robin Hood's mansion'. She then turned to the Prince's new wife: 'I hear the Princess of Wales is handsome, and amiable, *tant mieux*; I hope she will be happy. I don't think the most Exalted situations promise the fairest prospects'. She wrote some lines of verse:

Heav'n knows, I never would repine,
Though fortune's fairest frowns were mine, –
If Fate would grant that o'er my tomb
One *little laurel wreath*, might bloom,
And Mem'ry, sometimes wander near,
To bid it live, – and drop a tear!

I never would, for all the Show
That tinsel Splendour can bestow
Or waste a thought, – or heave a sigh –
Too well I know, – 'tis pageantry!

At the end of the letter, she reiterated her desire to leave England for good:

> The many temptations to quit England, if you know *what a Brother* I have, you would think all others unnecessary. – Yet – I shall often think how
>
> The poor Captive, in some foreign realm
> Stands on the shore, and sends his wishes back
> To the *dear native spot* from whence he came.*

'What a long letter!' she concluded cheerily, 'pray scold me, and tell me, I am a troublesome Being: – Even *that*, will not do; – for I should be tempted to write *Volumes*, to make you think otherwise.' She sent love from the General and Maria Elizabeth, then signed herself off 'Mary Robinson, the poor Poetess'.[3]

Unlike Sheridan, Kemble had a poor reputation for man-management. As Mary's caricature suggests, he was lofty and aloof. His achievement was to restore discipline and order to the theatre and to see Drury Lane through the period of rebuilding, during which Sheridan was mainly concerning himself with politics. The new theatre was not easy to play. Its capacity was over three and a half thousand, with seats in four tiers, but the box tiers were too low and the sight lines were bad. The gallery was so far away from the stage that the actors could barely be heard. Sheridan had hoped it would become a 'Grand National Theatre', but it was plagued by difficulties from its opening. Prior to the official opening, with Sarah Siddons as Lady Macbeth, there had been a royal command performance, for which the marshalling of the pit doors was badly managed: the spectators crowded in, a man toppled on the stairs in the rush,

* She added a wittily self-deprecatory footnote, 'always wrong in a quotation'. She may be misquoting the opening of Coleridge's lovely sonnet 'To the River Otter': 'Dear native Brook!'

and fifteen people were crushed to death, with nineteen others seriously injured. The King was not told the news until he returned to the palace at the end of the evening.

At last Mary heard the news that her play was being submitted to the Lord Chamberlain for censorship and the actors were in rehearsal. She had written the comedy specifically as a vehicle for Dora Jordan – in her novel of 1799 *The False Friend* she would pay a warm tribute to the acting skills of this other royal mistress (she also set a hilarious scene in Drury Lane, with a country party watching Mrs Jordan and failing to appreciate her art, in the manner of the naive Partridge watching Garrick in Henry Fielding's *Tom Jones*). The illegitimate Dora Jordan had risen from her lowly and obscure origins to become the mistress of the King's third son, the Duke of Clarence. Both the Duke and the actress were subscribers to Mary's first volume of *Poems*. As Siddons was renowned as the Tragic Muse of the London stage, so Jordan was lauded as the Comic Muse. She was unparalleled in her comic gifts and the theatregoing public flocked to see her perform. Coleridge, Charles Lamb, Leigh Hunt, and Lord Byron all became admirers of her talents and expressed their admiration in flattering encomiums. To William Hazlitt she was 'the child of nature, whose voice was a cordial to the heart because it came from it . . . whose laugh was to drink nectar . . . whose singing was like the twang of Cupid's bow'. For the more prosaic theatre chronicler John Genest, 'she sported the best leg ever seen on the stage'.[4] Jordan was famous for her 'low' roles, playing chambermaids, romps, and hoydens to high acclaim.

Mary made a smart move when she decided to write a comedy to showcase Dora's talents. The part was Nelly Primrose, a 'west-country' girl (as Mary was herself). She is a naive chambermaid thrust into London high society with comic results. Mary's big mistake, however, was to target female gamesters for her theme. The part of Lady Languid was written with Elizabeth Farren in mind, but at the last minute she dropped out, alleging that the play ridiculed one of her friends. Given her own longstanding involvement with the Earl of Derby, Miss Farren had to be very careful not to offend the *ton*.

Nelly Primrose is the new maid to the widow Lady Languid, a compulsive gambler who runs the risk of alienating her lovers by her habit. The ladies in her circle are as corrupt as she, and are all avid players: 'we scarcely see the sun from November to February, we rise at noon, and go to bed at day-break'. Her Ladyship's reputation is almost ruined by huge losses at the table and by rumours that she has let a man into her closet, when in fact Nelly has inadvertently placed a pair of dirty 'Jack' (male) boots in there – one of her numerous blunders in attempting to obey her mistress's orders. Lady Languid mourns that 'Play! Destructive Play! Perpetual losses and no rest have destroyed me . . . This is it to be the Slave of Fashion! Our Equals laugh at us – Our inferiors don't understand us. In short now-a-days, we are *nobody*.'

The dialogue is fast, sharp, and witty. There are some 'in-jokes', as when Mary pokes fun at her own reputation for 'basilisking' the Prince: Lord Courtland says of Lady Languid at the opera, 'she was the figure in a Dutch-clock – perpetually turning her head from you to the stage, and from the stage to you thus'.

Mary has very specific costume requirements for her aristocratic characters: 'Lady Languid is dressed in a white chemise with *no waist* – a Turban with *one Feather of enormous Length*. Short sleeves much above the elbow – a *very large medallion* on her bosom.' The high-waisted chemise, exotic headdress, and medallion on the bosom were all famously associated with Perdita. The epilogue also refers to the politics of dress. There Mary praises the natural British maid, who 'depends on nobody, for fashion's aid'; nature is said to spurn women who dress like dolls in 'whalebone stays and hoops of stiff cane'. The play was written shortly after Mary Wollstonecraft complained in *A Vindication of the Rights of Woman* that uncomfortable clothes stiffened with whalebone stays were a means of both physically and mentally subduing women. The loose-fitting Perdita chemise was by this time a symbol of liberation.

The comedy is also about the hypocrisy of the rich and titled, who have affairs behind their husbands' backs and then on the slightest pretext condemn other women for adultery. The beautiful but dissolute Lady Languid is engaged to Sharpley, but is good friends with the banker Sir Henry Rightley, who is in love with her and tries to reform her morals: 'a beautiful hand never appears to such disadvantage as when it shakes a dice box'. Rightley succeeds in reclaiming her after she has proved the insincerity of her friends. The fashionable ladies in Languid's circle are selfish and catty, very much in the mould of the gossips in Sheridan's *School for Scandal*. When Lady Languid loses 9,000 guineas at play, and her reputation is at stake, her friends abandon her and delight in her downfall. Mary's ear for fashionable speech is at its sharpest in her writing for such characters: 'To see the fritting, frowning, beauteous circle! bending over pyramids of Rouleaus – To behold their delicious Agonies – their charming anxieties – their laughable vexations, and provoking triumphs! – And if we lose, to have the bliss of seeing others as wretched as ourselves! Where else can a Woman of Fashion be happy!'[5]

Mary knew she was in for trouble when both she and Dora Jordan received hate mail the day before the play opened. Dora's note read '*Nobody* should be damned!' and Mary was sent a 'scurrilous, indecent, and *ill-disguised* scrawl, signifying to her that the farce was already condemned'.[6] Dora, though intimidated, courageously vowed to go ahead and perform. Mary was nervous, as her prologue to the play suggests. Conventionally, prologues and epilogues – so important to an eighteenth-century audience – appealed to the patronage of the ladies. Mary's begged indulgence from 'the gentle race' to 'paint the living manners as they rise', claiming disingenuously that she condemned no one in particular: 'At Nobody we level Satire's thorn / We trust, such characters, are yet unborn.' She pleaded for mercy for the poor authoress, 'for if she's damn'd, this night will be her last'.[7]

The opening night was badly timed: it coincided with the beginning of the lady gamblers' faro season. *Nobody* went up as afterpiece at Drury Lane on Saturday, 29 November 1794. Takings for the evening were a respectable £334, but the reception of Mary's farce was a disaster. This is Maria Elizabeth's account of what happened:

> On the drawing up of the curtain, several persons in the galleries, whose *liveries* betrayed their *employers*, were heard to declare that they were sent to *do up Nobody*. Even women of distinguished rank hissed through their fans. Notwithstanding these manoeuvres and exertions, the more rational part of the audience seemed inclined to hear before they passed judgment, and, with a firmness that never fails to awe, demanded that the piece should proceed. The first act was accordingly suffered without interruption: a song in the second being unfortunately encored, the malcontents once more ventured to raise their voices, and the malignity that had been forcibly suppressed burst forth with redoubled violence.[8]

According to the notes of William Powell, the prompter at Drury Lane, the 'dissatisfaction to the Piece' was so great that Mrs Jordan 'was so much agitated as to be unable to repeat above one half of the Epilogue, which from the Opposition of Hisses and Applauses, not scarcely three lines of that could be distinctly heard'.[9] Dora had battled on bravely for her friend. On that terrible first night she sent her beloved Duke of Clarence a note telling him that the play had been '*damned* most unfairly . . . I send these few lines to anticipate the newspapers.'[10]

Dora was right to expect that the papers would be full of the controversy. To counteract the criticism, Mary, or one of her supporters, placed a puff in the *London Chronicle*, which emphasized the play's moral lessons:

> The object of this piece was to place in proper ridicule the follies and vices of fashionable Life; and the piece, though obviously intended as a mere dramatic sketch, was really a pleasant portrait of the manners of the higher ranks. – There was also another purpose in this drama, of more value in point of morals: for it was also intended to show how easily a reputation may be lost by the use to which mere *appearances* may be converted by the aid of *malice*.[11]

The latter was, of course, a favourite Robinson theme.

According to the *London Chronicle*'s version of events, the first act 'was very favourably received', but an air by Mrs Jordan, 'somewhat too long, being *encored*, the audience were thrown into ill humour, and the performers disconcerted. The piece then met with some opposition, but, however, was heard with applause and murmers [sic] to the end, when it was announced for Monday evening without any decisive objection or concurrence.' It also reported that the play was written by Mrs Robinson, 'to whom the literary world is indebted for so many beautiful effusions of poetry. The Prologue and Epilogue, which seemed to be spirited compositions, were both written by the fair author; but the agitated state of Mrs Jordan, on account of the opposition, obliged her, as we understand, to omit many lines.'[12]

The fact that there was applause as well as hisses shows that there were at least some supporters. But when the play was repeated on the Monday night – minus its epilogue – the papers quipped that *Nobody* was 'brought forward for the second time, and *Somebody* was found to applaud it, although *Nobody* appeared to be entertained' and that a better title might have been *St James's Square in an Uproar*.[13] The next Saturday a third attempt was made, with some alterations to the text (and again no epilogue). 'An entire new character' was introduced, but 'the audience still expressed so much dissatisfaction as to induce the author to withdraw it'.[14] Receipts were very poor for that third performance and the play was never seen again.

Despite her setback in the theatre, Mary continued to publish many poems. Early in 1795 she began contributing regularly to the *Morning Post*. Daniel Stuart, the editor, regarded her as the best-known poet of the day and she was the first person he hired to make regular poetic contributions to the paper. Under the pen name 'Portia', she wrote a sonnet 'To Liberty' and then a satirical poem on the current economic crisis and other topical matters such as the separation of George from Mrs Fitzherbert together with his impending marriage to Caroline of Brunswick. It was a bitterly cold winter of war, food shortages, and social inequality:

Pavement slip'ry; People sneezing;
Lords in ermine, beggars freezing;
Nobles, scarce the Wretched heeding;
Gallant soldiers – fighting – bleeding!

Lofty mansions, warm and spacious;
Courtiers, cringing and voracious:
Titled Gluttons, dainties carving;
Genius, in a garret, starving! . . .

Arts and Sciences bewailing;
Commerce drooping, Credit failing!
Placemen, mocking subjects loyal;
Separations; Weddings Royal! . . .

Poets, Painters, and Musicians;
Lawyers, Doctors, Politicians;
Pamphlets, Newspapers, and Odes,
Seeking Fame, by diff'rent roads.[15]

In addition to publishing 'public' poetry of this sort, she also wrote more intimately for her friends and acquaintances. So, for instance, the following letter to a Mrs Hankin accompanied an epitaph 'To the Memory of Thomas Hankin, Esq':

> If the small tribute I enclose is by you deemed acceptable, I shall feel the most sincere satisfaction. Believe me, it *came from the heart*, and but feebly speaks my regret for the loss of my esteemed friend, your worthy husband. I promised him when living that if he died before me I would write his epitaph. I lament that there was occasion for the melancholy task, and only wish I could perform it better.[16]

Her main task that year was a new novel, which was to be much longer than her previous efforts. She was so exhausted from writing it that she went to Bath to recover, once again taking rooms in North Parade. As usual, the *Oracle* gave information on her movements: 'Mrs Robinson has been at Bath, and thence round the country. She goes back again in a few days, and the latter end of October comes up to town. The purpose is to publish another Novel in three volumes, three *just* volumes, in the trade language – from which information and elegance will flow of course.'[17] In the autumn of 1795 she also finished a tragedy, *The Sicilian Lover*, which she intended for presentation at Drury Lane. According to Maria Elizabeth, it was left to languish in the prompter's closet for several months. It was never staged.

Whilst in Bath she also suffered a personal misadventure: 'Mrs ROBINSON has nearly fallen a sacrifice to the fury of an enraged mastiff, who lately assailed her on the Parade at Bath. General Tarleton was fortunately on the spot, and by the timely effort of great activity and strength, rescued her from a situation, which, in the helpless state of the lady, was perilous indeed.'[18]

The new novel, *Angelina*, was published in the first week of the New Year. Mary and her publishers learnt from their mistake of having printed too many copies of *The Widow*: this time the first edition was in a run of 750 copies, which sold out almost immediately. Mary instructed that a second edition should be rushed into print, but sales promptly stalled, leaving her to pick up the cost of printing, thus wiping out her profits on the first edition.

Angelina is 36, around the same age as Mary. She is the cast-off mistress of Lord Acreland. He proposes to marry Sophia Clarendon, the daughter of a West Indian merchant, but she is in love with a penniless orphan called Belmont – who, it finally transpires, is the son of Angelina and Lord Acreland. As the critics were quick to point out, some of the events in the novel 'outrage nature, probability, and common sense'. There are all the usual ingredients of the sentimental novel: duels, swoons, madness, Gothic horrors, secret chambers, improbable reconciliations and elopements (Sophia elopes four times in the course of the novel). A fainting heroine was a prerequisite for the novel of sensibility, but *Angelina* contains more fainting fits than half a dozen other novels put together.

What makes the novel interesting is the way in which Mary skilfully weaves her political concerns into its fabric, rather as the philosopher William Godwin had done in 1794 in his highly successful novel *Caleb Williams* and Mary Wollstonecraft was to do in her later *Maria, or the Wrongs of Woman*. *Angelina* was Mary Robinson's first genuinely radical novel. The plot may have been rambling and the dialogue sometimes overstretched, but there was a serious engagement with such questions as the iniquity of rank ('hereditary distinctions are more frequently the gifts of accident, than the rewards of virtue'), the neglect of genius ('The poverty, too often the companion of talents, in this country, is a national discredit'), female education, women sold into marriage by their parents, the marriage market as a form of 'legal prostitution' (a phrase Mary attributes to the dramatist Richard Cumberland), female reputation, slavery, and aristocratic hypocrisy. Mary also directs her satirical pen at the code of gallantry: one of the aristocratic characters describes it as 'an amusing pursuit, that neither fatigues the senses, or penetrates the heart: in short, it is—' upon which Sophia interrupts, 'A contemptible, destructive, and degrading avidity, to destroy the repose of every unprotected woman, whose perverse fate, renders her a fit object for pursuit . . . it is to profess, what you do not feel; to swear that which you never mean to perform; to flatter while you despise; to slander where you cannot triumph; and to desert the credulous fool, whom you have had the cunning to deceive.'[19]

For all its radical content, the novel is not a political tract masquerading as a story. It has some very strong, colourful characters and lively dialogue across the social spectrum from fine ladies of fashion to lowly characters such as the landlord of an inn. The *Oracle* puffed away in its usual manner: 'Mrs ROBINSON'S *Angelina* has the best praise – the praise of congenial talents.' But the reviews were generally lukewarm, or in some cases downright hostile, with comments such as 'the nonsensical jargon of mock sentiment and overstrained hyperbole'.[20] Critics honed in on autobiographical content as well as political opinions. The *Critical Review* reprinted the description of the beautiful and melancholy heroine, who, like Mary herself, is a fading beauty with large and mournful eyes:

> She was drest in white muslin; a narrow black zone served to fasten the drapery, which gave her the appearance of a Grecian statue: her head was unadorned, except by nature, which had bestowed a profusion of dark auburn hair, that waved about her shoulders, and partly shaded a white forehead; her eye-brows were nearly black; her eyes of the deepest blue, her nose beautifully formed, her cheek – O grief! What a banquet hadst thou there! It had lost the bloom of youth, of health, of sweet repose![21]

The *Monthly Mirror*, however, urged its young female readers to buy the book:

> Angelina, ladies, has long been out of her teens, but the magic of fancy has so enriched her autumnal suit, that she is an object of no small attraction. Her story is as romantic as you can wish, and there are among you so many lovers of tales of wonder about caverns, rocks, woods, lakes, castles, abbies, and manor-houses, that we make not the least doubt of your paying a visit to the pensive Angelina, in her RUIN, which is really well imagined, and the way to it prettily laid out.

It also drew attention to an allusion to Mary's merchant brother George: 'we think we know who is alluded to in the City Trader, who runs about the town to the hindrance of his business on the nights of his sister's new play' – presumably a reference to *Nobody*. 'Those tasks of brotherly love have ensured to him the approbation of all,' enthused the reviewer.[22]

In the novel the brother unashamedly collects friends to see his sister's new play: 'zealous to promote the fame of his sister, through a laudable pride, which taught him to consider her as the most distinguished ornament of a family whose name would be forgotten in another century, were it not immortalized by her literary labours!'[23]

Dedicated Perdita-watchers would have noted some further autobiographical touches. Angelina possesses 'a small picture, all done round with precious stones, which she will sit and cry over for whole hours without ceasing'. When George Fairford asks to see the painting, she says: 'it is true, I have a portrait: it has been painted many years. It once bore the strong resemblance of a beloved friend: but he is gone!'[24] There is also a memory of Nicholas Darby's hostility to Mary's becoming an actress: Sir Edward Clarendon would rather see his daughter Sophia 'dead' than on the stage. 'I'd cut her legs off, if I thought she wished to disgrace herself by such an idea.' Lady Selina, an acquaintance, responds with a defence of the profession:

> We have many females on the stage, who are ornaments to society, and in every respect worthy of imitation! For my part, I adore the Theatre, and think there is more morality to be found in one good tragedy, than in all the sermons that ever were printed. With regard to acting; it is an art which demands no small portion of intellectual acquirements! It polishes the manners; enlightens the understanding, gives finish to external grace, and calls forth all the powers of mental superiority![25]

A damning reference to a family making its money from the slave trade would have made interesting reading for Tarleton:

> Yet let me tell you, that though you have acquired wealth, in the barbarous traffic of your fellow creatures; though you have amassed treasures, sullied by the tears, if not the blood of persecuted slaves; you must not hope to sacrifice a daughter, without provoking the indignation, and exciting the contempt of those who are friends to the breathing race, and enemies to oppression . . . can the colour of a human creature authorize inhumanity?[26]

Mary's most enthusiastic reviewer was the radical and 'female' polemicist Mary Wollstonecraft. Mary knew her *Vindication of the Rights of Woman* and was soon to become acquainted with her. Wollstonecraft professed her admiration for the 'elegant pen' of Mrs Robinson and her 'well-earned reputation'. She considered that *Angelina*'s 'principal object' was 'to expose the folly and the iniquity of those parents who attempt to compel the inclinations of their children into whatever conjugal connections their mercenary spirit may choose to prescribe, and to hold forth to just detestation the cruelty of those who scruple not to barter a daughter's happiness, perhaps through life, for a sounding title or a glittering coronet'. For Wollstonecraft, 'the sentiments contained in these volumes are just, animated, and rational'.[27] From her point of view, there could be no higher praise than this.

Had she reviewed the novel at greater length, Wollstonecraft would doubtless also have praised Robinson's championing of female education – a major concern in her own *Vindication*. The young heroine Sophia has benefited from the educational beliefs of her aunt, Juliana Pengwynn, who is clearly in the mould of Mary Robinson's old tutor Meribah Lorrington. She is a scholarly, 'enlightened and intelligent' woman who has raised her niece as a woman of letters rather than giving her the traditional but useless female accomplishments. Sophia has travelled to Paris and Italy with her aunt, who is an expert on the ancients, a reader of Greek and Latin. She also writes sonnets in the style of Petrarch and is scorned for doing so. Sophia's brutal and ignorant father disapproves of education for women, seeing his daughter in terms of her market value as a 'piece of rich merchandise'. He takes the standard line against the dangerous influence of fiction on the minds of young girls: 'I suppose you are for love and a cottage: this comes of reading romances; – women have no business ever to read – or to write either.'[28]

The Sicilian Lover: a Tragedy went into print a few weeks after *Angelina*. Mary had heard that someone had pilfered one of its plot lines for a play of their own. She was annoyed that Drury Lane had let her down again: 'Disgusted with the delay, and universal negative which, for some unknown cause, she ever experienced from managers, she resolved to print the tragedy, and leave its merits and defects to the decision of the public.'[29] One man who admired it was the Duke of Leeds, a neighbour in St James's Square, whose wife had left him for Mad Jack Byron, father of the poet.

He sent Mary a poem describing her as 'the queen of song', together with an effusive letter:

> Madam,
> Permit me to thank you for the favour you conferred on me, by sending me your tragedy. I trust you will not deem me guilty of flattery when I assure you that few productions of the present poetical age have afforded me more pleasure, than the perusal of the second act; the scene between Honoria and her father is very well managed, and capable of much effect; as is the scene with the banditti in the third.
>
> I imagine many will unite with me in observing how much your continuing to persevere in this species of composition would increase your profit, and enhance your poetical reputation; which has already much signalized itself in the rich field of English literature.[30]

He could not have been more wrong: four months after publication, thirty-two copies had been sold. The net result was that, having earlier drawn some of her profits, Mary owed her publishers, Hookham and Carpenter, £133. 13*s*. 1*d*. She never paid the money back.[31]

Almost every poet of the age attempted the impossible task of writing a Shakespearean tragedy, usually with a Gothic setting involving castles, robbers, caves, and moonlight, all decked in pastiche Elizabethan language:

> Peace! Be silent. Heard you not the tempest
> That shook our lofty towers from their foundation?
> Saw you the black wing of the howling blast
> Sweeping our turrets, red with human gore?

Mary's effort has a similar theme to the much more successful *Angelina*: a father selling his daughter into the slavery of marriage.

> Relentless power may drag me to the altar;
> But the free soul shrinks from the tyrant's grasp,
> And lords it o'er oppression.[32]

Honoria's lover kills her father and she is finally reconciled with her mother, now a nun in a convent, before her own death. Some reviewers liked this sort of thing: 'he who can read its incidents without sympathy, and its imagery without delight, must have an unfeeling heart and a depraved taste. We congratulate Mrs Robinson that she has discovered the true bent of her talents; and we advise her to apply herself in the future to the improvement of them in the same walk.'[33] This judgement is far off the mark: it was as a novelist, satirist, and social commentator that Mary's true talents lay. Her European reputation witnessed to that: when a Leipzig publisher decided to launch some 'specimens of English Literature', Robinson's novels were the first to be chosen – 'very neatly printed, and embellished with engravings'.[34] Her first six novels were translated into both French and German, sometimes in competing versions. Six of the seven novels were also produced in Dublin editions for the Irish market.

Her rise to international success as an author was offset by a decline from the status of 'somebody' to that of 'nobody' in the fashionable world. Mary did still go to the opera and the theatre, but she no longer appeared in the prominent boxes. Laetitia Hawkins was coming out of the opera one night when she observed a woman of fashionable appearance, still beautiful but not 'in the bloom of beauty's pride'. The woman was sitting on a table in one of the waiting rooms, unnoticed, 'except by the eye of pity'. In a few minutes, two liveried servants came to her. They took from their pockets long white sleeves, which they drew on their arms. They lifted her up and conveyed her to her carriage. 'It was,' wrote Hawkins, 'the then helpless paralytic Perdita!'[35]

CHAPTER 22

Radical

> The limbs may languish, but the mind can't faint,
> Genius like freedom bows not to restraint;
> 'Down with all tyrants' strikes upon my ear!
> Alas! I've got a female Robespierre.
>
> Banastre Tarleton, manuscript verses to Mary Robinson

During these years, Mary met two men who were to become good and loyal friends. They were both to have an enormous impact on her work, as she was to influence them. One was the philosopher and radical William Godwin, the other the poet Samuel Taylor Coleridge. Godwin recorded the beginning of his friendship with Mary in one of his autobiographical sketches. Discussing the year 1796 he writes, 'I was also introduced about this time by Merry, the poet, to a most accomplished and delightful woman, the celebrated Mrs Robinson.'[1]

Godwin was interested in her because her social philosophy was similar to his own. Her long poem 'The Progress of Liberty', filled with denunciations of despotism and war, advances the Godwinian thesis that a new age of liberty and peace was arising from the workings of Reason:

> And Nature, towering mid the wrecks of war,
> Shall bless her British shores, which grandly lift

Their rocky bulwarks o'er the howling main,
Firm and invincible, as Britain's sons,
The sons of Reason! unappall'd and free![2]

The shy bachelor Godwin thought that Mary Robinson was not only intelligent and 'Rational', but also incomparably beautiful. His daughter Mary Shelley recorded that 'Among his acquaintances were several women, to whose society he was exceedingly partial, and who were all distinguished for personal attractions and talents. Among them may be mentioned the celebrated Mary Robinson, whom to the end of his life he considered as the most beautiful woman he had ever seen, but though he admired her so greatly, their acquaintance scarcely attained intimate friendship.'[3]

Godwin's friendship with Mary was more extensive and intimate than his daughter knew (or admitted). He was a friend and supporter of many literary women, such as Elizabeth Inchbald, Mary Hays, and Mary Wollstonecraft. Now he added another Mary to his circle of female intellectuals. He had recently been reintroduced to Mary Wollstonecraft after her time in France and Scandinavia, and her separation from her lover Gilbert Imlay, and was beginning to fall in love with her. He was also reading *Angelina* as Wollstonecraft was reviewing it.

Godwin's unpublished journal records his meetings with Mary Robinson. On 9 February he took 'tea with Mrs Robinson with Twiss and Tarleton'.[4] Francis Twiss was a contemporary of Mary's who hailed from Bath. A drama critic, he was married to Fanny Kemble, sister of Mrs Siddons, and was a close friend of Wollstonecraft's. The next day, Godwin took tea with his friend Elizabeth Inchbald, the novelist and dramatist, and then went on for supper with Mary and Tarleton. Merry, the Della Cruscan, was also there. Godwin had supper with Mary five times that month and also had tea and attended the theatre with her. At a performance of William Wycherley's *The Plain Dealer* they bumped into another literary man, C—, who – as was seen in a previous chapter – was also present at two of Mrs Robinson's supper parties at this time.

In March Godwin saw Mary and Maria Elizabeth at the Drury Lane dramatization of his novel *Caleb Williams*, renamed *The Iron Chest*. On a snowy day later the same month he finished his scrupulously slow reading of *Angelina*. Later in the year he turned his attention to young

Maria Elizabeth's *Shrine of Bertha.* He was regularly taking tea with Mary and Tarleton, and also meeting other literary folk, such as the novelist Eliza Parsons, at her supper table. In the summer, a party was made up consisting of Godwin and three of the most distinguished female writers of the age: Wollstonecraft, Inchbald, and Robinson.

As Mary became more closely involved with this circle of radical friends, she grew distant from Tarleton. Though he was perceived as a dangerous Jacobin sporting a revolutionary 'crop' haircut as he fought an election campaign in Liverpool against his own brother John, a dyed-in-the-wool Tory, he was in no position to support all his partner's radical causes. She was publishing powerful anti-slavery poems in the magazines and papers, while he was still compromised by his family interest in the traffic in human flesh.

In October 1796, a new volume of Mary's poetry was published: *Sappho and Phaon, a series of legitimate Sonnets, with Thoughts on Poetical Subjects, & Anecdotes of the Grecian Poetess.* It has been supposed that she wrote this sequence on being deserted by Tarleton, but Godwin's journal reveals that Tarleton was present at her supper parties and accompanied her on theatre visits throughout the months leading up to the book's publication. But she had been through the experience of separation from him, and from previous lovers, so she had no difficulty in writing from the point of view of the mother of ancient Greek lyric poetry, Sappho, who, according to Ovid and other sources, fell hopelessly in love with a handsome youth called Phaon and then committed suicide by throwing herself off a cliff when he deserted her.

The collection served as her poetic manifesto. Already known as 'the English Sappho' she now sought to detach herself from the Della Cruscans and the passing world of newspaper versification. In her preface to the sonnet sequence, she defended the 'legitimate' sonnet form of Petrarch (fourteen lines divided into an octave and a sestet) and condemned 'the non-descript ephemera from the heated brains of self-important poetasters' that filled the newspapers. She was setting herself up as a classical, intellectual poet. She complained that British poets were not given their due recognition ('It is at once a melancholy truth, and a national disgrace, that this Island, so profusely favored by nature, should be marked, of all enlightened countries, as the most neglectful of literary merit!') and she paid tribute to her 'illustrious country-women; who, unpatronized by the courts, and unprotected by the powerful, persevere in the paths of literature, and ennoble themselves by the unperishable lustre of MENTAL PRE-EMINENCE!'[5] 'Unpatronized by the courts' may well be a dig at the Prince.

Sappho was associated with passionate abandon and lyrical intensity. Mary's account of her reads like an idealized self-portrait: 'such a lively example of the human mind, enlightened by the most exquisite talents, yet yielding to the destructive controul of ungovernable passions'. She says that Sappho was the 'unrivalled poetess of the time: the envy she excited, the public honours she received, and the fatal passion which terminated her existence, will, I trust, create that sympathy in the mind of the susceptible reader, which may render the following poetical trifles not wholly uninteresting'.[6] Like most eighteenth-century accounts of Sappho, the brief biography that Mary includes in the prefatory material to her collection of poems only makes the briefest and most guarded reference to her presumed lesbianism: Sappho was regarded as a great love poet, a great technical innovator in poetical form, but – despite her origins on Lesbos – not primarily a 'sapphic' poet in the modern sense. There was much more emphasis on her being abandoned by men than on her love for women. Mary was called 'the English Sappho' as a compliment to her technical proficiency and her strong sensibility, not as a comment on her sexuality.

The collection consists of forty-four linked sonnets, telling the story of Sappho's passion for Phaon from its birth to her demise. Arguably the first narrative sonnet sequence since Elizabethan times, it did much – along with the sonnets of Charlotte Smith – to revive a poetic form that had fallen out of favour in the eighteenth century. Ever since Petrarch, the vast majority of sonnet sequences had been written from the male point of view. It was a refreshing change for the woman to be the gazer instead of the gazed upon: 'Why, when I gaze on Phaon's beauteous eyes, / Why does each thought in wild disorder stray?'[7] At the same time, Mary is acutely aware of how a woman makes herself desirable – for instance, by a dress that suggests but also conceals:

> Bring the thin robe, to fold about my breast,
> White as the downy swan; while round my waist

Let leaves of glossy myrtle bind the vest,
Not idly gay, but elegantly chaste!
Love scorns the nymph in wanton trappings dressed;
And charms the most concealed, are doubly grac'd.[8]

She also knows the contradictions of desire: 'Ah! why is rapture so allied to pain?' And, as the sequence comes to its climax, sustained imagery of stormy seas, the yawning ocean, and plunging waves serves to evoke the troubled mind of the deserted lover, while preparing the way for Sappho's death by water. The association of contemplation, desertion, and the sea may also allude to the second Reynolds portrait that had by this time, thanks to the frequency with which it was engraved and used as frontispiece to Mary's works, become the iconic image of her. It was also around this time that she returned to Hoppner's studio and was painted in a simple white 'Grecian' robe and a classical headdress, with the sea behind her.

The volume was generously reviewed. Meanwhile, the fashionable world was stunned by the news of a real-life separation: after an indecently short period of marriage, the Prince of Wales had deserted his wife Caroline. There was a wave of support for the Princess. Having been spurned by George herself, Mary knew where her sympathies lay. To judge from the attack on her in a pamphlet defending the Prince, she must have let her position be known in public:

> It cannot be supposed, that Mrs ROBINSON, or the *Perdita*, or the *lame Sappho*, or what you will, would, in the moment that she is receiving an annuity of five hundred pounds from the bounty of the PRINCE, unite in the interested cabal who labor to tarnish his good name; – she should have remained, at least, inactive during the crooked course of the floating falsehood. How lamentable it would be to admit, that the force of *any species of jealousy* can awaken impertinences, and connect *ideal events*, for the unwarrantable purpose of suppressing an unoffending individual whom we envy, but whom it was intended by Truth and Nature we should respect! – But it is not possible – Mrs ROBINSON'S morality cannot be so far unhinged.[9]

Mary's immensely productive year came to an end with the publication of her fourth novel, a Gothic extravaganza called *Hubert de Sevrac: A Romance of the Eighteenth Century*. De Sevrac is a French aristocratic émigré who becomes 'the convert of liberty'. Set in the turmoil of the French Revolution, Hubert and his family are dispossessed of their fortune and status. They have to disguise themselves as peasants to pass the gates of Paris. Hubert's daughter is Sabina, who empathizes with the peasants: 'Have not the poor, minds, as well as the rich.'[10] The family are imprisoned after Hubert fights a duel and there is a last-minute escape from the guillotine. The moral of the whole is the Godwinian idea that 'the vices of the rich produce the crimes of the poor'.[11]

Written in great haste as a money-spinner, this is probably her worst novel. Mary more or less admits as much in her next book, *Walsingham*, in which a character closely based on herself writes a romance 'of ghosts, ghouls, graves, blood-stained hands, daggers, caverns, velvet canopies and livid lightings' designed to 'frighten schoolgirls'.[12] Coleridge wrote a brief and judicious review:

> The character of Mrs Robinson's novels being generally known, it is perhaps sufficient to say, that *Hubert de Sevrac* is inferior to her former productions. It is an imitation of Mrs Radcliffe's romances, but without any resemblance that may not be attained by the common pen. There are detached parts, however, of which we may speak with approbation; and, during the prevalence of the present taste for romances, the whole may afford amusement to the supporters of circulating libraries. But it may be necessary to apprise novel-writers in general, that this taste is declining and that real life and manners will soon assert their claims.[13]

Wollstonecraft was also properly critical, suggesting that the problem was that the novel was written much too quickly:

> Mrs Robinson writes so rapidly that she scarcely allows herself to digest her story into a plot, or to allow those incidents gradually to grow out of it, which are the fruit of matured invention. She certainly possesses considerable abilities; but she seems to have fallen into an errour, common to people of lively fancy, and to think herself so

> happily gifted by nature, that her first thoughts will answer her purpose. The consequence is obvious; her sentences are often confused, entangled with superfluous words, half-expressed sentiments, and false ornaments. In writing the present romance Mrs Radcliffe appears to be her model; and she deserves to rank as one of her most successful imitators: still the characters are so imperfectly sketched, the changes of scene so frequent, that interest is seldom excited, and curiosity flags . . . She could write better, were she once convinced that the writing of a good book is no easy task.[14]

Mary herself later said that one of her regrets was that most of her works 'had been composed in too much haste'. It was good for her to have some proper critical reviews written by friends, in contrast to the puffs of the *Oracle*, which, needless to say, considered that 'the grateful terrors of the first volume are displayed with infinite address, and the greatest force of language'.[15]

This said, the novel is not without effective local details in its observations of morals and manners. Conservative reviewers preferred these to the novel's dangerous politics: 'there are interspersed through the whole many reflections on the conduct of human life, which shew the author to be an attentive observer of the manners of the world, and consequently better qualified to instruct it than most who undertake this species of composition. What we least approve of in this work is an evident partiality towards French Philosophy, and something too much of the cant of French Democracy.'[16]

All this time Mary was strengthening the circle of her literary acquaintance. Samuel Jackson Pratt, who wrote as 'Courtney Melmoth', was a regular visitor at her tea and supper parties, together with Godwin, Wollstonecraft, and Taylor, the literary oculist. The group visited the theatre together and lent each other books. Maria Elizabeth, now 22 and an author herself, was always present. One day she went to see Sarah Siddons at Drury Lane with Mary Wollstonecraft, who was suffering from a head cold: 'I increased my cold, or rather, cough, yesterday . . . Had not Miss R— promised to call for me, even Mrs Siddons would not have tempted me out to day.'[17] After the show Mary and Maria Elizabeth had Godwin and Wollstonecraft round to a family supper with Tarleton.

Wollstonecraft may have been a little jealous of Mary, to judge from the letter she wrote to Godwin the following day:

> I thought, after you left me, last night, that it was a *pity* we were obliged to part – just then. I was even vext with myself for staying to supper with Mrs R. But there is a manner of leaving a person free to follow their own will, that looks so like indifference, I do not like it. Your *tone* would have decided me – But, to tell you the truth, I thought, by your voice and manner, that you wished to remain in society – and pride made me *wish* to gratify you.[18]

But she appears to have got over her pique and the next morning was writing happily about a supper party that Mrs Robinson had planned for the three Marys, Robinson, Hays, and Wollstonecraft.

It was Wollstonecraft who introduced Mary to fellow novelist Mary Hays: 'I expect Mrs Robinson and daughter, to drink tea with me, on Thursday, will you come to meet them. She has read your novel,* and was *very much* pleased with the *main* story; but did not like the conclusion. She thinks the death of Augustus the end of the story and that the husband should have been suffered to die a natural death. Perhaps she is right.'[19] Hays accepted and Wollstonecraft wrote to Mrs Robinson:

> Dear Madam,
> I believe it is scarcely necessary to inform you that Miss Hays will accept of your invitation, and accompany me on Sunday next to dinner at your house.
>
> As you were so obliging as to offer to send the carriage for the little *Fannikin*, [Wollstonecraft's young daughter Fanny Imlay] I promised to call for her. In the evening, if one of your servants will put Marguerite [Fanny's nurse] in her way, she and Fanny may return at an early hour. You will smile at having so much of the womanish mother in me; but there is a little philosophy in it, *entre nous*; for I like to rouse her infant faculties by strong impressions.
>
> I write in haste, with kind remembrance to your Mary.[20]

* Mary Hays, *Memoirs of Emma Courtney*, 1796.

There is a strong sense here of a community of female friendship. Maria Elizabeth, having become a writer herself, would no doubt have held her own with the three distinguished female authors. The phrase 'one of your servants' suggests that the Robinson household was still reasonably well provided for at this time, however much Mary may have perceived herself as having declined into poverty.

The friends sometimes based fictional characters on each other. Hays actually used some of Godwin's letters for a philosopher in one of her novels and Godwin in his *Fleetwood* put something of Mary Robinson into a character called Mrs Gifford (could the name be a jibe at her old enemy William Gifford?):

> She was of exquisite beauty, tall, graceful, and captivating. Her tastes were expensive, and her manners gay. Her demeanour was spirited and impressive, her passions volatile, and her temper violent. With all this, she was by no means destitute of capacity. She was eloquent, witty, and sarcastic; exhibiting, when she pleased, the highest breeding, and delivering her remarks with inexpressible vivacity and grace. Thus endowed, she was surrounded, whenever she appeared, with a little army of suitors. Every youth of fashion, who had the courage to look up to her, became her professed admirer; and, among these admirers, it was pretty universally believed that all had not offered up their incense in vain . . . She had seen much of the high world, and she had eminently the talent of giving poignancy to her anecdotes and remarks.[21]

Mary's relationship with Tarleton was under great strain. His elder brother died at the end of 1796 and his mother was very ill. Godwin's diary records that Tarleton was still usually present at Mary's supper parties until the middle of March 1797. But he was conspicuously absent from a very large tea party she held on 2 April. Among her guests on this occasion were over a dozen writers, theatre people, and family friends (including the rising novelist and poet Amelia Opie, who a few years later would write *Adeline Mowbray*, a novel inspired by the life of Mary Wollstonecraft). Could it be that Mrs Robinson was gathering all her friends around her in order to receive support following another break-up with Tarleton?

This time their split was permanent. The *Oracle* was soon reporting that Tarleton's mother had died and that 'if we mistake not, this is not the only loss he has recently sustained, in that which comes nearest the heart, cherished by many years of social intercourse'.[22] After fifteen volatile years, their relationship was finally over. Mary was left many thousands of pounds in debt, not least because of Tarleton's losses at the faro table and via the betting book at his club. She was seriously ill that April. She and Maria Elizabeth set off for Bath, but a 'violent fever' kept her confined for several weeks in lodgings somewhere along the Bath road.[23] Whilst on her sickbed, she wrote a poem that may refer to the end of the affair:

Another night of feverish pain
Has slowly pass'd away!
I see the morning light again;
What does it bring? another day
Of hope – delusive – vain! . . .

I see Deceit in sainted guise
Of holy Friendship, smile;
I mark Oppression's eager eyes,
And tremble as the breath of Guile
Assumes Affection's sigh.[24]

Godwin was not available to comfort her. In March he married Wollstonecraft and stopped seeing Mary. He only resumed his regular visits several months after Wollstonecraft's death later that year as a result of septicaemia incurred during the birth of Mary Shelley. Wollstonecraft clearly made a huge and lasting impression on Mary: her subsequent novels are markedly more 'feminist' than the earlier ones and she began to create heroines who were based upon Wollstonecraft and professed themselves her disciples. She praised Wollstonecraft in her *Letter to the Women of England, on the Injustice of Mental Subordination* and came under attack in the anti-Jacobin press for her association with the so-called 'hyena in petticoats'.

In the autumn of 1797 the *Oracle* reported that 'The work which Mrs ROBINSON is now finishing will probably be her *last*. Her health declines rapidly. The sting of *ingratitude* wounds deeply in a sensible heart. Mrs ROBINSON'S works will live. They are translated into French and German, and are very popular in those languages.'[25] The work in question was a new novel, *Walsingham*, which was published in early December by Longman. She may have moved because of a financial dispute with her existing publisher, Hookham and Carpenter. The advantage of Longman was that they simply bought the copyright of a book for a flat fee in advance, instead of working on a complicated cost and royalty basis. They paid her £150 for *Walsingham*, which was printed in four volumes in a run of a thousand copies.

Mary was by now the most regular, prolific, and high-profile contributor of poetry to the *Morning Post*, so the press campaign to promote the novel had a second home in addition to the *Oracle*. The *Post* puffed that it had been many years since a novel had made so much notice in the literary and fashionable world. Coleridge, the paper's other poetry correspondent, chipped in with words of high praise. The *Morning Post* generated further interest by serializing extracts.

Walsingham was Mary's most controversial and radical novel to date. It remains one of her two strongest and most interesting books. The hero, Walsingham Ainsforth, is a figure who anticipates Emily Brontë's Heathcliff: described as gypsy-like, he is an outsider, swarthy, passionate, violent, and dangerous. He has been raised on Rousseau's principles, as a child of nature. He falls in love with Isabella, who – like Cathy in *Wuthering Heights* – was brought up with him as a sister and whom he loves 'much better than I love myself . . . Isabella was the companion of my studies, the play-fellow of my hours of recreation: in all my walks, in all my exercises, she was my associate: I loved her with a brother's fondness: I felt the irresistible power of female attraction, but I felt it unmixed with the destructive passions. I adored her, purely, tenderly. It was the idolatry of innocence; nothing sexual contaminated my bosom.'[26]

But – unlike Brontë's Cathy – Isabella does not return his affections. She falls in love with Walsingham's handsome and accomplished cousin Sir Sidney Aubrey. Walsingham is distraught when Isabella elopes with Sir Sidney, and vows to destroy him, even though he is drawn to his cousin's undeniable charm. He begins a picaresque journey, which takes him to London where he enters fashionable society and seduces a young woman whom he mistakenly believes to be a willing Isabella. Despite risking her reputation for Sir Sidney by her elopement, Isabella insists that she will never marry him and that she has preserved her virtue. Sir Sidney mentally torments Walsingham and prevents his marriage to other women until his secret is finally revealed: Sir Sidney, in order to gain his rightful inheritance, has been passed off as a man though she is in fact a woman. She is finally united in marriage with Walsingham.

Walsingham begins in epistolary form, but after a few letters are exchanged Walsingham sends his correspondent a packet containing an autobiographical narrative that 'unfolds the mystery of my misfortunes': the remainder of the novel is thus a first-person narrative written from Walsingham's point of view. This device of beginning with letters and then moving to first-person narrative was also used by Mary Shelley in *Frankenstein* twenty years later, with the added layer of further first-person narratives contained within that of Frankenstein. Given her parents' friendship with Robinson, there is a strong possibility that she learnt the technique from *Walsingham*. One of the two French translations of *Walsingham* was called *L'Enfant des montagnes* ('the child of the mountains') and the German version was *Das Naturkind* ('the child of nature'): Walsingham is given a Rousseauistic education and his favourite books are *La Nouvelle Héloïse* and *The Sorrows of Young Werther.* In all this, there is a marked anticipation of Mary Shelley's account of the natural education of Frankenstein's creature.

Walsingham explored many of Mary's favoured themes: personal merit versus the accidents of birth, the fate of the fallen woman, the dangers of excessive sensibility. But there is also a new (Wollstonecraft-inspired) interest in the question of a woman's right to inherit property. This is dramatized through the brilliant plot-twist – which some reviewers failed to notice – of the cross-dressed hero/ine Sir Sidney. Having established her name with Shakespearean and other comic cross-dressed parts in the theatre, Mary now gave a political spin to the motif in her novel: by impersonating a man, Sir Sidney is able to inherit the estate that would have been denied her as a woman. The transgendered upbringing also gave Mary a vehicle for one of her great passions: the right of a woman to receive a 'masculine education'.

Sidney is the perfect union of the sexes. S/he quivers with sensibility and sheds 'involuntary tears', but is also fit and strong: 'he fenced like a professor of the science; painted with the correctness of an artist; was expert at all manly exercises; a delightful poet; and a fascinating companion'.[27] S/he has benefited from a classical education and from vigorous physical exercise – both promoted by Wollstonecraft in her *Vindication* as necessary training for independent womanhood. He is adored by women, who are drawn to his irresistible combination of strength and gentleness, charm and intelligence. He is the perfect man because he is really a woman.

The novel maintains a sustained attack on aristocratic corruption. It was accordingly condemned by anti-Jacobin critics. *Walsingham* is among the radical books displayed in James Gillray's caricature 'New Morality', the age's most famous satire on the radical literati of the 1790s. The *Anti-Jacobin Review* complained of Mary that

> Her judgement is frequently distorted by very false notions of politics. Like Charlotte Smith, she has conceived a very high opinion of the wisdom of the French philosophers; and, like many other female writers, as well as superficial male writers, she considers the authority of those whom she admires as equivalent to argument . . . her peers or peeresses are all either weak or wicked . . . The miseries and vices of the *low* are uniformly deduced from the oppressions and the vices of the *high* . . . this representation is hurtful, because it tends to encourage the dislike for nobility, which, from the spirit of insubordination, and the fanciful notion of equality is already too prevalent . . . It is possible, and, indeed, very probable, that those persons of rank with whom Mrs Robinson has been in the habit of associating, may be as bad as she represents, but it is a very unfair and false assertion to say that all the nobility are profligate . . . *Her* experience, we think, must have taught her that, at least, equal profligacy obtains among *commoners* and *plebeians* . . . according to Mrs Robinson, Britain is the seat of ignorance, superstition, and tyranny, while other nations are enlightened; and the means of dispelling our ignorance, and delivering ourselves from superstition and tyranny, is the adoption of the principles of Voltaire and Rousseau!![28]

In a similar tone, Tory satirist T. J. Mathias complained that Robinson was a 'very ingenious' lady, but that her habit of '*whining* or *frisking* in novels' had the effect of making 'our girls' heads turn wild with impossible adventures' and that her fiction was 'tainted with democracy'.[29]

Another anti-Jacobin activist, Richard Polwhele, made a political distinction between Robinson's poems and her novels. In his satirical poem with notes called *The Unsex'd Females*, he linked the import of loose French garments to female interest in French radical ideas. Both developments were strongly associated with Mary. 'And ROBINSON to Gaul her Fancy gave,' he writes, 'And trac'd the picture of a Deist's grave!'[30] Deism was a watchword for French radicalism and Godwin's philosophy, otherwise known as 'Philosophism' – a new word that entered the English language in the early 1790s, specifically with reference to what was perceived as the atheistic and dangerously democratic philosophy of the French Encyclopedists. For Polwhele, Robinson's poems were wholesome, but her novels were beset with the French vice:

> In Mrs Robinson's Poetry, there is a peculiar delicacy: but her Novels, as literary compositions, have no great claim to approbation – As containing the doctrines of Philosophism, they merit the severest censure. Would that, for the sake of herself and her beautiful daughter (whose personal charms are only equalled by the elegance of her mind), would that, for the sake of the public morality, Mrs Robinson were persuaded to dismiss the gloomy phantom of annihilation; to think seriously of a future retribution; and to communicate to the world, a recantation of errors that originated in levity, and have been nursed by pleasure! I have seen her 'glittering like the morning star, full of life, and splendor and joy!' Such, and more glorious, may I meet her again, when the just 'shall shine forth as the brightness of the firmanent [sic] and as the stars for ever and ever!'[31]

For Polwhele, Mary's radicalism was a crime against her sex and a cause of potential damnation of her eternal soul. His worry about Mrs Robinson corrupting her fair daughter is especially striking.

Mary's strength had always been in exposing high society to the satirist's pen, but this time she courted extra publicity by the close parallels that she drew between real and fictional characters. Not only did she satirize the sex doctor James Graham as Dr Pimpernel and Robert Merry as

Mr Doleful, but she also included several characters based on her friends: the benevolent and trusty Mr Optic is John Taylor the eye doctor and the wild but amiable Lord Kencarth is Lord Barrymore, while Gnat the philosopher, critic, and writer is Godwin. Mary's close friend Samuel Jackson Pratt appears as himself as the writer of *Liberal Opinions* and *Family Secrets*, but under his alias Melmoth. One character wants to read *Family Secrets* to see if any of her friends are in it. The female gamesters that she parodies are all based on real people: this is what made the novel so scandalous in the fashionable world. There are easily recognizable portraits of the corpulent faro banker Albinia Hobart (later Countess of Buckinghamshire), of Lady Sarah Archer, of the duellist Lord Linbourne, and several others.

Mary had never been averse to using details of her own life for her creative works. Walsingham's opening letter is written from Aix-la-Chapelle, where Mary lived in the mid-1780s, and her travels on the Continent infuse her writing. She sets a scene in the Cocoa Tree, the famous coffee house on St James's Street that was a centre for gambling and one of Tarleton's favourite haunts. She includes characters that she knew would be compared with her own self. One such is a female author (who writes poems, novels, comedies, and verse tragedies), whose comedy is jettisoned by the women of rank who set out to destroy her reputation. They send both the author and the principal actress anonymous hate mail denouncing the play, as had happened with *Nobody*. This character is viewed as a 'petticoat pedant' and is subjected to malicious reviews by jealous critics: 'the most polished works suffer the severity of unjustifiable condemnation, merely to gratify the spleen of individuals [who] wield the pen with as little mercy as the sanguinary savage guides the blow of his death-inflicting tomahawk'. There is a passionate denunciation of a critic 'who wantonly destroys another's hopes, and takes from talents, industry and truth, the means of obtaining an honourable subsistence'.[32]

The *Telegraph* gave Mrs Mary Robinson a prominent place in a list of forty-two people who 'pay to have themselves puffed in the Newspapers'.[33] It could be argued that someone who indulged in such a practice had no right to complain about harsh treatment at the hands of critics and reviewers. But what is striking about the reception of *Walsingham* is that the criticism was motivated above all by politics. Perdita had remade herself as what the *Morning Post* rightly called a 'philosophical' author, and that was a very hard transformation for traditionalists to accept.

Late in the year 1797 Mary Robinson and Samuel Taylor Coleridge were formally engaged as 'poetical correspondents' of the *Morning Post*. This represented an extraordinary turnaround for Mary: in her early years of celebrity the *Morning Post* had dragged her through the mud. But now times and editors had changed. Her key supporter was a canny Scotsman called Daniel Stuart. Not everybody trusted him: the diarist Henry Crabb Robinson once asked Coleridge some 'awkward questions' about his association with Stuart, to which Coleridge replied, 'Why, if I'm pressed as to Dan's strict honesty, which I don't wish to be, I should say: Dan's a Scotchman who is content to get rid of the itch when he can afford to wear clean linen.'[34] But he was known for his good temper, and was a highly successful editor. He bought the *Oracle* in 1795 and kept its daily circulation near one thousand, whilst also taking over the *Morning Post* and turning around its fortunes: when he bought the paper's office and its copyright in the summer of 1795, circulation was at a meagre 350. By 1798 he had raised it to 2,000 and by 1803 to 4,500. No other daily paper sold more than 3,000.[35]

He had been editor of the paper before, when it was a pro-Pitt, anti-Prince paper in the 1780s. But when the *Morning Post* went public on the Prince's morganatic marriage to Mrs Fitzherbert – which was an open secret in society, but not to be mentioned in print – the Prince's faction promptly bought the paper in order to prevent further attacks. Stuart was fired from the editorship and John Taylor elevated from drama critic to editor (as well as being appointed oculist to the Prince of Wales). Given this history, Stuart must have taken a particular pleasure in the paper's decline and the opportunity to install himself as both proprietor and editor. This time he positioned its politics carefully: the *Morning Post* became, as Coleridge put it, '*un*ministerial, anti-opposition, anti-jacobin, anti-gallican'.[36] Not Tory, not Whig, not Jacobinical: independence was the editorial watchword.

This suited Mary, who by this time regarded herself as a fiercely independent writer, as sensitive to the horrors of radical extremism as she was satirical of the indulgence and corruption of the political establishment. And to have Mary on the books suited Stuart: he knew that her poems had for many years helped to sell the *Oracle* and he was eager to give the 'Poetical Department' a prominence it had not previously had in the *Morning Post*. The established talent of Mrs Robinson and the rising star of Mr Coleridge seemed to him to offer the ideal combination: 'The POETRY of the Morning Post will in future be critically select. None but first-rate compositions will be admitted to our columns; and we are promised the aid of several of the most distinguished writers of the present day.'[37] For three years, from December 1797 until her death, Mary regularly contributed between one and three poems per week to the paper – save in a period of severe illness in the winter of 1798–9. For this, she was paid at least a guinea a week.[38] At the end of 1799 she took over the role of poetry editor from Robert Southey, continuing to publish her own verses under a range of pseudonyms, including 'M. R.', 'Tabitha Bramble', 'Tabitha', 'T. B.', 'T.', 'Laura Maria', 'L. M.', 'Sappho', 'Bridget', 'Oberon', 'Julia', and 'Lesbia' (and sometimes no name at all).[39]

Her most provocative new poetic persona was 'Tabitha Bramble'. The name was taken from the character of a sex-starved spinster in Tobias Smollett's novel *Humphry Clinker*. Skinny, flat-chested, and still unmarried despite her best efforts, Smollett's Tabitha is 'a maiden of forty-five, exceedingly starched, vain and ridiculous'. There could hardly be a wittier pen name for the woman once described as the most beautiful woman in England, and the most sexually notorious. Maria Elizabeth Robinson called the Tabitha Bramble verses 'lighter compositions, considered by the author as unworthy of a place with her collected poems',[40] but Mary included six of them in the collection in which she took most pride, *Lyrical Tales*.

Tabitha Bramble made her first appearance in the *Morning Post* on 8 December 1797, in an ode in which she 'Visits the Metropolis'. Daniel Stuart heralded this new voice: 'We have received the first number of a series of Odes, by Tabitha Bramble. The elegance of the stile, and the richness of imagination displayed in this introductory Ode, will warrant our Readers in expecting much delight from the productions of this new Correspondent.'[41] Robinson's device was to satirize fashionable London life by squinting at the foibles of the *ton* through the eyes of an outsider. She was not averse to occasional recycling under Tabitha Bramble's name of poems that had been published in earlier years under different soubriquets.

Walsingham, meanwhile, was vigorously puffed in the *Morning Post*, where it was said to have established Mary's position 'in the front rank of Literature'.[42] The poems woven into the novel were especially admired. Signing himself 'Francini', Coleridge contributed his 'The Apotheosis, or the Snow-Drop', written 'immediately on the perusal of the beautiful poem, the Snow Drop':

Fear no more, thou timid flower!
Fear thou no more the Winter's might,
The whelming thaw; the ponderous shower;
The silence of the freezing night!
Since LAURA murmur'd o'er thy leaves
The potent sorceries of song,
To thee meek flow'ret! gentler gales
And cloudless skies belong.

On thee with feelings unreprov'd
Her eyes with tearful meanings fraught,
She gazed till all the body mov'd
Interpreting the spirit's thought:
Now trembled with thy trembling stem;
And, while thou drooped'st o'er thy bed,
With imitative sympathy
Inclin'd the drooping head.[43]

Coleridge here represents Robinson as a potent sorcerer of song who is in exquisite sympathy with the natural world – a worthy rival to his friend Wordsworth? 'The Snow Drop', written for *Walsingham* and reprinted in the *Morning Post*, is indeed one of Mary's best lyrics:

The snow-drop, Winter's timid child,
Awakes to life bedew'd with tears;
And flings around its fragrance mild,
And where no rival flowrets bloom,
Amidst the bare and chilling gloom,
A beauteous gem appears!

All weak and wan, with head inclin'd
Its parent breast, the drifted snow;

It trembles while the ruthless wind
Bends its slim form; the tempest lours,
Its em'rald eye drops crystal show'rs
On its cold bed below. . . .

Where'er I find thee, gentle flow'r,
Thou still art sweet, and dear to me!
For I have known the cheerless hour,
Have seen the sun-beams cold and pale,
Have felt the chilling wint'ry gale,
And wept, and shrunk like thee![44]

The snowdrop appears in the heavy dew of early spring before 'rival' flowers such as the 'gaudy crocus', and it does seem to incline its head: it is a fitting image for Mary herself, who bloomed early but soon came to droop with melancholy.

Daniel Stuart sent a complimentary copy of *Walsingham* down to Coleridge at Nether Stowey in Somerset, enclosing a letter from Mary expressing her gratitude at his response to her poem. A second set of the four volumes of *Walsingham* was enclosed in the same package with a request for Coleridge to pass it on to a Mr Chubb in nearby Bridgwater. This was John Chubb, an artist and merchant from Bristol, who was a family friend of the Darbys. He had painted a watercolour of Mary, sitting at her writing desk with quill and inkwell ready; she is shown gazing at her miniature portrait of the Prince, as if to imply that it was his rejection that turned her into a writer.

In the early days of 1798 Mary struggled with a 'nervous fever, attended by a depression of spirits, which all the attentions of her friends cannot alleviate'.[45] She began to write her memoirs, with a view to putting straight the record of her early years before she died. 'The vein of melancholy which pervades the pages of *Walsingham*,' remarked the *Oracle*, 'bespeaks an inquietude of *mind*, which in some measure proclaims the *cause* of her present indisposition.'[46]

The *Morning Post* informed its readers that 'The Publisher of "The Lives of Living Authors," has confirmed to Mrs ROBINSON the dignified title of *the English Sappho*: a title which was long since bestowed on her by the *literary tribunal* of the country.'[47] By the end of February, nursed as ever by her daughter, she was 'sufficiently recovered from her late illness, to resume her literary occupations'.[48] The *Morning Post* monitored her every movement, plugging her books, reporting on her health, and praising her daughter for beauty, correct manners, high accomplishment, and fetching outfits: 'The *gypsy hat* was first worn by MISS ROBINSON, who was also the first who introduced the Grecian head-dress, two winters ago.'[49] In addition to working on her memoirs, starting another novel, and churning out new verses for the *Morning Post* in an array of voices and styles, Mary also began to prepare a collected edition of her poems. The English Sappho merited nothing less: the plan was to publish 'three large volumes octavo *by subscription*'.[50]

The Duchess of Devonshire was said to be taking the lead in patronizing the edition,* but to judge from the urgency of the puffs in the *Oracle* and the *Morning Post* some weeks after this announcement, Mary may have had some difficulty in generating interest: 'Mrs ROBINSON confines her new Edition of Poetical Works to Subscribers only. And the commencement promises all the distinguished names in the kingdom, both for rank and talents'; 'Mrs ROBINSON, by reserving her new edition of poems for subscribers, has excited a desire to have copies, which promises to produce the most splendid and numerous list that ever graced a literary work. All party, ranks, and politics unite in patronizing a poetess, to whom the tribunal of letters has given the dignified appellation of the ENGLISH SAPPHO.'[51]

This sounds like the lady protesting too much that she has all the names she needs. A month later it was reported that 'MRS ROBINSON'S new List of Subscribers to her Poetical Works, goes on with brilliant success. She has the most splendid and flattering patronage that ever distinguished a literary production.'[52] It was stressed that, being subscription only, the volumes would not be available from circulating libraries; readers had to sign up (and pay up) for their own copies. The emphasis on aristocratic patronage is ironic given the way in which Mary had earlier trumpeted the fact that her true patrons were the members of the ordinary reading public. The problem was that readers of middling rank,

* Around this time Georgiana started writing poetry herself, heavily influenced by that of Mary.

especially women who did not have much disposable income of their own, were eager to read her poems in the papers and take out her novels from the circulating library, but this did not produce sufficient literary income to sustain Mary and her household. The collection of names seems to have stalled: the subscription edition did not appear. It was not until the sixth year after Mary's death that her daughter produced an edition of her *Poetical Works*.

In the light of Mary's excellent relationship with the editor of the *Oracle*, it is hardly likely to have been coincidental that her ex-lover came in for some very bad press in the paper around this time. Tarleton was criticized for his support for a new figure who had emerged in France: Napoleon Bonaparte. It was noted that his parliamentary speeches lacked style – were indeed 'somniferous' – now that Mary was no longer around to write them for him. The papers questioned how he could reconcile his pro-slavery stance with his professions of being the friend of 'universal freedom'. There were quips that there would not be any more works of military history under the name of Tarleton. Stuart's papers knew no bounds in their support for Mary, even complaining that her *Sicilian Lover* had not been acted despite being one of the 'best-written plays of the present century', which is a somewhat exaggerated claim for the work's quality.[53]

Mary was now making plans to retire to the country. 'Mrs ROBINSON, as soon as her new edition of Poems is published, means to reside wholly in the country. For this plan of retirement, a neat cottage is already preparing.'[54] She and Maria Elizabeth spent the summer in this cottage, which was at Englefield Green, on the edge of Windsor Great Park. Englefield Green was a newly fashionable destination for the gentry in summertime: sufficiently close to London for business, but pleasantly rural and with the prestige of being close to Windsor. New villas were being built around the green and in secluded sites that afforded excellent views of Runnymede, where Magna Carta had been signed, and Cooper's Hill, where in the seventeenth century Sir John Denham had written one of the founding poems of the tradition of English landscape poetry.

The rest of the year was devoted principally to work on her new novel, which was much her longest.

In December, it was announced that General Banastre Tarleton was to marry Susan Bertie, illegitimate daughter of the late Duke of Ancaster.

She was well educated, below middle height, in her early twenties, and worth about £20,000 a year. Tarleton was rewarded with a posting to Portugal and a ceremonial sword as a wedding present from the Prince of Wales. Tarleton christened it 'Sweet Lips' and it remains in the family to this day. Eighteen months after the end of his fifteen-year affair with Mary, he had succumbed to what in her novel *Angelina* she called 'the old expedient – a rich wife'.

CHAPTER 23

Feminist

Man is a despot by nature; he can bear no equal; he dreads the power of woman.

Mary Robinson, *A Letter to the Women of England, on the Injustice of Mental Subordination*

We have broke the destructive spell which manacled the mind; we are no longer the vassals of our imperious help-mates; we dare think; and we at length assert those rights which nature formed us to enjoy.

Mary Robinson, *The False Friend*

Two months after Tarleton's wedding, Mary's new novel was published. Back in 1791, her 'Ode to Valour' had ended by describing Tarleton as 'the Faithful Friend'. For anybody who knew her story and Tarleton's recent history, the title of the novel would have carried a strong hint: *The False Friend*. The *Morning Post*, having reported the fact that Tarleton and his bride had sailed for Lisbon, let it be known that in the novel Mary 'made her hero perish on his voyage to Lisbon' – poets are generally prophets, it added, 'and Mrs ROBINSON has, in more than one instance, been correct in her predictions'.[1]

In reality, the Tarletons did safely reach Portugal. The only storm was in the newspapers back home, where the coverage of Mary's novel focused on its supposed autobiographical content: 'The *sable* habit in which Mrs

ROBINSON has disguised her *False Friend* does not conceal the *glaring traits* of the character she means to delineate'; 'The character of Treville in Mrs Robinson's new novel is said to be drawn from an original. For the honour of human nature, we hope the anecdotes are not authentic.'[2] There was a general consensus that the book was shaped by the end of the long affair with Tarleton. 'A certain General would be entirely forgotten, but that a *false friend* will ever be remembered,' said the *Morning Post*, and in the monthly magazines reviewers sympathized with the author: 'as a domestic story, in which the author tells the tale of her own woes, it excites our sincerest sympathy'; 'We would gladly believe the sorrow that breathes through this production to be fictitious, but, in truth, it bears marks too affecting and characteristic. Cold must be the bosom in which it awakens no interest, and hard the nature that melts not in sympathy.'[3]

There can be no doubt that some passages were written out of anger and bitterness towards Tarleton:

> These are the despots who hold us in a state of bondage! who call themselves our idolaters, till the caprice of their natures prove their apostasy. Created to protect us, they expose us to every danger; endowed with strength to sustain our erring judgment, they are ever eager to mislead us . . . O man! thou pleasing, subtle, fawning, conquering foe! thou yielding tyrant! thou imperious slave! What language can describe thee?[4]

But in most respects the character of Treville is actually more a literary type than a portrait of Tarleton. He is a rake in the mould of Lovelace in Samuel Richardson's *Clarissa*. 'Too polite to be religious; too witty to be learned; too youthful to be serious; and too handsome to be discreet: in four words, a fashionable divine, divinely fashionable', he is 'a libertine of the most dangerous species; a dissembling sycophant; a being who hovered round the wealthy and the high-born . . . a coxcomb by education; a deceiver by practice; a flatterer by profession; and a profligate by nature'.[5]

A much more interesting character is the heroine, Gertrude St Leger. She is a self-professed disciple of Mary Wollstonecraft, whom she calls a 'champion of her sex'.[6] Like both Wollstonecraft and Mrs Robinson herself, Gertrude is a victim of excessively acute sensibility but also a free spirit, daring and unconventional. The *Monthly Mirror* astutely compared her to the protagonist of Godwin's *Caleb Williams*: 'She is a sort of female Williams, and, probably, Mrs Robinson was not unwilling to furnish a companion to Godwin's well-known hero.'[7]

As in so many of the novels of the 1790s, there is a whiff of incest to the plot. Gertrude is in love with Lord Denmore, who awakens dangerous passions in her before she finally discovers that he is really her father. If the novel is to be read as veiled autobiography, it might be said to reveal as much about Mary's conflicting feelings towards Nicholas Darby as it does about her pain and anger upon being deserted by Tarleton. Besides, Mary's motivation for writing was not personal pique but a desire to explore and express the nature of the passions. Gertrude subjects her own strong sensibility to a fierce interrogation:

> Lord Denmore has avowed his attachment to another; he is regardless of my sorrows; he insults my pride; he wounds my sensibility. There are moments when I experience an agitation of mind, which menaces my reason. I endeavour to methodize my feelings; I summons the resisting powers of pride and scorn; they do not calm my feverish brain; they agitate its fibres almost to frenzy . . . Oh, sensibility! thou curse to woman! thou bane of all our hopes, thou source of exultation to our tyrant man! How abject dost thou render even the most exalted minds; how decidedly dost thou fasten on the senses; how inevitably dost thou annihilate all that is dignified and noble . . . Are not even its raptures agonizing? Does not the tumult of excessive joy inflict a degree of agitation which amounts to pain? Will not an act of generosity experienced thrill through the brain, excite our tears, convulse the bosom, and convey through every fibre a sense of torturing ecstasy? . . . there is no soothing opiate for the mind but apathy: to feel is to be wretched.[8]

As in Mary's other novels, the man upon whom the woman lavishes her affections turns out to be unworthy. Gertrude reflects on man's dominion over woman: 'if we permit one object to influence every thought, to control every sentiment, to usurp an undivided dominion over our subjugated faculties . . . whether that object be the lover or the friend is of little importance; he holds the reins of government over our senses'; 'One hour I hate Lord Denmore . . . the next, my soul relapses into sadness, and the affections of the heart triumph over all the claims of reason . . . you will scarcely believe that it is possible to love and to hold in abhorrence the same object, and at the same moment.'[9]

The *Anti-Jacobin Review* was wrong in its contention that 'the author delights in presenting situations, in which passion, especially the passion of love, triumphs over virtue and reason'.[10] In her next novel, Mary would write a poem in which Love and Reason fight it out and Reason triumphs because he has Time on his side. As a novelist, Mary was more interested in the conflict between reason and passion than the resolution; her heroines are often found struggling between sense and sensibility. The *Anti-Jacobin Review* was right to say that *The False Friend* showed an interest in 'morbid sensibility', but failed to perceive the point that it is Gertrude's sensibility which destroys her, much as Mary Robinson presents herself in the *Memoirs* as a victim of 'too acute a sensibility'. For Mary, the problem was that, on the one hand, 'The heart must love, or it will be dead to every noble, every sublime propensity', but on the other, in order to survive in the world of men a woman had to learn to be a 'calmly thinking being, who can weigh the affections of the heart against the proprieties of Reason'.[11]

Treville taunts Gertrude on her political ideals: 'I make no doubt but you will shortly become a *he-she* philosopher; that you will pretend to inculcate new doctrines on the potency of feminine understanding, and the absurdity of sexual subordination . . . you will hope to equalize the authority of the sexes, and to prove that woman was formed to think, and to become the rational companion of man; though we all know that she was merely created for our amusement.' Gertrude replies that she is proud to be associated with Mary Wollstonecraft (who is praised by name in an authorial footnote):

> 'I shall preach, and I shall never fail to feel those precepts which have been inculcated by one who now sleeps in the grave . . . whose monument is built on the immortal basis which supports the rights of woman.'
>
> 'Preposterous!' exclaimed Mr Treville: 'woman is merely a domestic creature; take her from the humble avocations of life, and she becomes—

'Your equal!' interrupted I. 'If I speak individually at the present moment, I may add – your superior.'[12]

This was not Tarleton's attitude to women: he never attempted to confine Mary to the domestic sphere and always supported her writing. But perhaps in the end he did her a favour by leaving her: he showed her that she did not need a man. 'It is adversity alone that unfolds the page of knowledge,' she wrote in *The False Friend*. 'It is truth alone that can sustain the mind.' From this point forward, it was the mind alone – bolstered by the company of like-minded friends and a self-sacrificing daughter – that sustained Mary.

The end of the affair was the making of her as a feminist. *The False Friend* is in many ways more a response to the death of Mary Wollstonecraft than an outpouring of feelings about Tarleton. As a worried columnist in the *Gentleman's Magazine* would soon write, 'Mrs R. avows herself of the school of Wollstonecroft [sic]; and that is enough for all who have any regard to decency, order, or prudence, to avoid her company.'[13]

In January 1798, just four months after his wife's death, William Godwin had published a selection of Mary Wollstonecraft's *Posthumous Works* together with a biography of her called *Memoirs of the Author of A Vindication of the Rights of Woman*. It may have been the appearance of this book that gave Mary Robinson the idea of starting her own memoirs. The unworldly Godwin wanted to tell the truth about Wollstonecraft's life before anyone else sought to discredit her memory with a scandal-mongering biography. So he made public Wollstonecraft's love affairs, pregnancies, suicide attempts, and atheism. The book provoked a storm in the Tory press. Godwin was taunted as a pimp and Wollstonecraft branded a whore.

Mary almost certainly realized at this point that it would do her no good to publish her version of the affair with the Prince. She put her memoirs aside and concentrated on preparing her collected poems and writing *The False Friend* instead. She took on the mantle of Wollstonecraft, but initially voiced her feminist sentiments through the mouths of fictional characters, knowing that if she spoke in her own voice her scandalous past would be held against her. But by the spring of 1799 she was ready to publish a polemical feminist treatise. In order to avoid having her ideas discredited by means of personal attacks on her past conduct, she published under a pseudonym, Anne Frances Randall (perhaps a memory of Ann Randall, the supposed prostitute imprisoned for shoplifting whose story may have caught her eye in the *Morning Herald* sixteen years before).

The book was called *A Letter to the Women of England, on the Injustice of Mental Subordination*. It reproduces and develops many of the feminist sentiments that had been expressed in *The False Friend*. Mary attacks the law that gives a woman's property to her husband when she marries; she exposes the double standard that exists in attitudes to everything from money to sex and to physical exercise. Whereas a man may protect his honour in a duel, women are supposed to guard their virtue and 'possess an unsullied fame', yet if they are wrongly slandered they have no recourse to defend their honour (Sir Sidney in *Walsingham* can only defend her good name because she is disguised as a man). A promiscuous man is positively admired for his virility, whereas once a woman has lost her reputation she is no longer received in polite society. It is arguable whether this was strictly true in Mary's own case, given her ability to remain on amicable terms with her high-profile ex-lovers.

Women, Mary proposes, should be not 'the mere appendages of domestic life, but the partners, the equal associates of man'. 'Constrained obedience,' she writes, 'is the poison of domestic joy.' She argues directly from her own experience, asking her reader to think of a woman who has 'experienced every insult, every injury, that her vain-boasting, high-bearing associate, man can inflict; imagine her, driven from society; deserted by her kindred; scoffed at by the world; exposed to poverty; assailed by malice; and consigned to scorn; she has no remedy'.[14]

The respect with which she and her works had been treated in France and Germany led her to pay particular attention to the iniquities of the treatment of women in her own country:

> There is no country, at this epocha, on the habitable globe, which can produce so many exalted and illustrious women (I mean mentally) as England. And yet we see many of them living in obscurity; known only by their writings . . . we hear of no national honours, no public marks of popular applause, no rank, no title, no liberal and splendid recompense bestowed on British literary women! They

must fly to foreign countries for celebrity, where talents are admitted to be of no SEX.[15]

The unjust exclusion of women from Parliament was another of her principal themes: given her close involvement with Fox and the 1784 election campaign, she was especially well placed to comment on this issue. She also marshalled her art of observation to question the idea that men are superior to women because they are physically stronger:

> If woman be the *weaker* creature, why is she employed in laborious avocations? why compelled to endure the fatigue of household drudgery; to scrub, to scower, to labour, both late and early, while the powdered lacquey only waits at the chair, or behind the carriage of his employer? Why are women, in many parts of the kingdom, permitted to follow the plough; to perform the laborious business of the dairy; to work in our manufactories; to wash, to brew, and to bake, while men are employed in measuring lace and ribands; folding gauzes; composing artificial bouquets; fancying feathers, and mixing cosmetics for the preservation of beauty? I have seen, and every inhabitant of the metropolis may, during the summer season, behold strong Welsh girls carrying on their heads strawberries, and other fruits from the vicinity of London to Covent-Garden market, in heavy loads which they repeat three, four, and five times, daily, for a very small pittance; while the *male* domesticks of our nobility are revelling in luxury, to which even their lords are strangers. Are women thus compelled to labour, because they are of the WEAKER SEX?[16]

She was especially concerned to answer the accusation that woman was mentally inferior to man, citing a long list of female intellectuals and public servants. She argued that men despise and fear intellectual women:

> There are but three classes of women desirable associates in the eyes of men: handsome women; licentious women; and good sort of women. – The first for his vanity; the second for his amusement; and the last for the arrangement of his domestic drudgery. A thinking woman does not entertain him; a learned woman does not

> flatter his self-love, by confessing inferiority; and a woman of real genius, eclipses him by her brilliancy.[17]

Her own advantage over other female intellectuals such as Wollstonecraft was that she was the epitome of a handsome woman and a licentious woman as well as a thinking woman of real genius.

The boldest practical proposal in the *Letter to the Women of England* was that a 'UNIVERSITY FOR WOMEN' should be established. 'O my unenlightened country-women! read, and profit, by the admonition of Reason. Shake off the trifling, glittering shackles, which debase you,' wrote Mary, rousing herself to a pitch. 'Let your daughters be liberally, classically, philosophically, and usefully educated; let them speak and write their opinions freely; let them read and think like rational creatures; adapt their studies to the strength of their intellect; expand their minds.'[18] She also proposes the introduction of a meritocratic honours system in which women could be rewarded for their achievements with an 'ORDER OF LITERARY MERIT'. This is consistent with the theme that runs throughout her later writings of the need for the aristocratic class system to be replaced with an 'aristocracy of genius'.

At the end of the book, there is a 'List of British Female Literary Characters Living in the Eighteenth Century'. Thirty-nine women are named, including feminists such as Mary Wollstonecraft and Mary Hays, women of letters such as Charlotte Smith and Elizabeth Inchbald, 'Miss Robinson – Novelist', and, with more genres of writing to her credit than anyone else, 'Mrs Robinson – Poems, Romances, Novels, a Tragedy, Satires, etc. etc.'.[19]

The *Anti-Jacobin Review*, which had rapidly become the most influential right-wing magazine of the day, with a circulation in excess of three thousand, condemned Anne Frances Randall as one of the 'legion of Wollstonecrafts'.[20] The *Morning Post*, meanwhile, printed passages concerning the subjugation of women from *The False Friend*, which was selling well (it was soon to be reprinted). There was also news that Mary was at work on a long blank verse poem in celebration of the early years of the French Revolution entitled – in the spirit of Godwin – 'The Progress of Liberty'.

In the politically polarized Britain of the late 1790s, Mrs Robinson was regarded as a key literary figure. Fifteen years before, fictionalized 'memoirs' and 'letters' of Perdita had blackened her name. Now she was being damned as a Wollstonecraft by the *Anti-Jacobin Review* but praised in volumes with titles such as *Literary Memoirs of Living Authors*. Several of the more liberal monthly magazines printed biographical sketches that emphasized her respectability as an author, praising her monodies, the 'satirical vigour' of *Modern Manners*, her Sappho sonnets, and the progression of her novels away from sentimental and Gothic excess towards 'the style of common life', 'in which she exhibited great power of imagination, knowledge of human nature, acuteness of research, and skill in the delineation of character; as well as a vein of humour, in describing scenes of a whimsical and ludicrous kind'.[21]

Mary had resumed her friendship with Godwin and was regularly entertaining him for tea and supper together with a range of other writers, mostly women. By June 1799 another novel was finished. It was published by Longman and Rees at the end of August with the title *The Natural Daughter, with Portraits of the Leadenhead Family*. The *Morning Post* tried to create pre-publication interest by saying that 'expectation was on tip-toe' as to the identity of the real-life family on which the Leadenheads were based.[22]

In the twentieth century Tarleton's biographer suggested that the title was an allusion to the illegitimacy of Banastre's bride, Susan Bertie, but there is no contemporary evidence for this and no resemblance between her story and that of the illegitimate child in the book.[23] *The Natural Daughter* is Mary's most autobiographical novel, but it has very little to do with Tarleton.

It is written in the third person, not the epistolary first-person form that Mary habitually used. Though the novel was uniformly damned by the reviewers – disturbed by its Wollstonecraftian tendencies, they advised Mary to stick to poetry[24] – there is a real maturity and confidence in the style. The story is set in the year 1792 when the French Revolution was 'the great topic of conversation'. Unlike most women's novels, which were courtship stories, here the heroine Martha Morley is married off early to a wealthy man. He abandons her and in order to survive financially she pursues a career as an actress, poet, and novelist. In this, Martha is Mary's fictional double (in the Bible, the names Martha and Mary famously go together). *The Natural Daughter* predates by over fifty years Elizabeth Barrett Browning's epic poem *Aurora Leigh*, which literary historians usually describe as the first work in English by a woman writer in which the heroine is herself a professional author.[25]

The heroine sacrifices her reputation for the sake of an illegitimate child whom she befriends. The little girl Frances is conceived in a Paris prison (in real life Mary Wollstonecraft's illegitimate daughter Fanny Imlay was also conceived in France during the turmoil of the early revolutionary years). Martha's husband casts her off because he assumes the child is hers; at the end of the novel it is revealed that in fact the girl is his. Martha also has a sister Julia, who is her father's favoured daughter – but who imprisons her mother in a madhouse, poisons her own illegitimate daughter, and finally commits suicide in the bed of Robespierre. Julia behaves like the sentimental heroine of conventional romance, but is ostentatious and deceitful; Martha, with her 'face full of dimples', is noisy and robust, 'considered a mere masculine hoyden', but the true heroine of the story. Wrongly accused and spurned by her husband, she is a spirited independent woman in the Wollstonecraft mould. The title thus has a double meaning: little Frances is the 'natural daughter' in the sense of an illegitimate child, but Martha is the 'natural daughter' in the sense that she is rational and generous, in contrast to her financially favoured but morally unnatural sister.

Robinson is bold in her deployment of real historical figures. The revolutionary leader Jean-Paul Marat makes an appearance: he tries to seduce a tragic actress called Mrs Sedgley who is imagined as a 'juvenile Siddons'. Martha is a 'natural actress' who combines the 'easy elegance of a Farren' with the 'genuine playful graces of the queen of smiles – the attractive Jordan'.[26] Her experience of the acting profession reflects Mary's own: she at once becomes a figure of glamour and a woman regarded with suspicion in respectable society.

The Leadenhead family of the novel's subtitle are comic grotesques. They have made their fortunes from slavery, but want their son to win military honours. Rich and vulgar, they long for a title. Julia marries the son, but they soon separate. There may be a dig at the Tarleton family in all this.

Martha, meanwhile, is dismissed by her theatrical manager and turns to literature in order to support herself. She writes for 'fame and profit', and because there are so few opportunities for poor unprotected women. This sequence almost certainly reveals something of Mary's own novel-writing techniques: Martha sits down to plan what kind of novel would appeal in the light of contemporary fashion. When she has finished, 'The story was melancholy, the portraits drawn from living characters, and the title both interesting and attractive.' She finds it very difficult to get a publisher, but finally gets a deal with the dashing Mr Index. At this point there is some excellent satire on the publishing world, especially in the character of Index. 'We have our warehouses full of unsold sentimental novels already,' he says, 'they only sell for waste paper.' He encourages Martha to write a scandalous work instead: 'If your fertile pen can make a story out of some recent popular event . . . or anything from real life of equal celebrity or notoriety, your fortune is made; your works will sell, and you will either be admired or feared by the whole phalanx of fashionable readers.' Index also makes it clear that the author has to play a part in the promotion of a book: 'You should write a Dedication, full of fine words and laboured panegyric.'[27]

Mary was adept at shifting gear from satire to strong feeling. In one very moving passage, she reveals her own sense of isolation from the busy world. Martha looks out of the window of her west end apartment and contemplates life:

> From her window she observed the passing throngs, like the gaudy ephemera of a summer noon; the glittering atoms, which dazzle for an hour, and then shrink into nothing. There did she contemplate, with a philosophic smile, the motley idols of capricious fortune: the light gossomary visions of a day, borne on the gale and towering in the warm regions of a prosperous destiny; or shrinking from the cutting blasts of poverty, and creeping to oblivion.[28]

In the summer of 1799, just after the novel had been finished, the *Morning Post* carried similar reports of Mary herself: 'Mrs Robinson, from her temporary habitation in Piccadilly, looks down upon the *little great*, without envying their less permanent distinctions'; and, similarly, a week later, 'Mrs Robinson, from her Piccadilly window, has an opportunity of drawing characters from *life*; and her pen is equal to the variety of its subjects.'[29]

The description in the novel actually fits Mary herself – once the most sought-after woman about town, now confined by illness behind a window – better than it does Martha in the story:

> Often did she mark the cold retiring aspect of deserting friendship, the freezing half bend of distant civility, or the familiar nod of low presuming vanity ... It was then that she *really* knew many of those worldly associates who fly with the warm beams of a summer destiny; many who had obtrusively paid homage to her mind, and obsequiously courted her society, when she was above the necessity of seeking patronage, but who now, grown suddenly fastidious, scarcely condescended to recognize her.[30]

Mary becomes so caught up in the writing here that she forgets that her character never had people paying homage to her mind and obsequiously courting her society.

Martha's literary labours, like Mary's, threaten to destroy her health. All that her 'incessant industry could procure was insufficient for the purposes of gaining a permanent independence'.[31] A 'wealthy libertine' then offers to make her his mistress for £2,000 down payment and £300 per annum, but she is too proud to accept.

Martha goes to Spa in Belgium, where she meets the amiable Georgina Duchess of Chatsworth and makes a 'forcible impression on her' because of her 'easy modest grace'. Martha has been left without clothes, but Georgina lends her a wardrobe and asks her to stay:

> The Duchess of Chatsworth was not a being created in the common mould; she could hear and she could feel for the child of persecution: Mrs Morley's manners and her artless story were sure passports to a soul, sustained, inspired, and softened by the fine-wrought energies of virtue and benevolence: she knew that woman was an ill-fated being; that the world was ever ready to condemn, though tardy to investigate; she could discriminate betwixt the erring and the vicious; she could by soothing the compunctuous pangs of a too credulous bosom, reconcile it to that hope, that conscious pride, which would in future be its best and strongest safeguard.[32]

Snobbish and empty-headed Lady Penelope Pryer, meanwhile, 'could not conceive how the Duchess of Chatsworth, a woman of the most exemplary conduct, could receive a doubtful character, foster a stranger in a foreign country, and become the avowed patroness of one, who had nothing but talents to support her'. Now near the end of her literary career, Mary was paying retrospective tribute to Georgiana for her patronage at its beginning.

CHAPTER 24

Lyrical Tales

'Who, to see the lady they were now speaking to, could believe that she had once been called the *beautiful* Mrs Robinson?'

Memoirs of the Late Mrs Robinson, Written by Herself

I have also at Bristol (in the beautiful press of Biggs and Cottle) a volume of Lyrical Tales; my favourite offspring.

Mary Robinson to Jane Porter, August 1800

The strain of what the *Morning Post* called Mary's 'mental labours' led to a further period of indisposition. She remained at Englefield Cottage, dangerously ill and 'attended twice a day by a physician'. She had retrenched 'even her necessary expenses, and nearly secluded herself from society'.[1]

She was confined to her bed for over a month. One night her fever was so bad that her doctor expected imminent death, but she survived and in the morning fell into a peaceful sleep. Suddenly the door was forced open, shaking the whole cottage. Two men who looked like ruffians marched into Mary's bedroom. In a faint voice, she asked them who they were. One was an attorney and the other his client: they had come with a summons for her to appear as a witness in a lawsuit they were bringing against her brother. Refusing to leave the room, they persisted with a stream of personal questions. The client said sneeringly to his lawyer,

'Who, to see the lady they were now speaking to, could believe that she had once been called the *beautiful* Mrs Robinson?' After making more 'savage and brutal' observations, they threw a subpoena on the bed and left. Mary was so distressed that she suffered violent convulsions.[2]

As soon as she was well enough to hold a pen, she began writing again. The *Morning Post* reported that Mrs Robinson had once more resumed her nom de plume Laura Maria, 'a name by which her muse first obtained its increasing celebrity, and which will frequently appear in the poetry department of this paper'.[3] In September 1799 she republished her feminist treatise under her own name, with a slightly altered title: *Thoughts on the Condition of Women, and on the Injustice of Mental Subordination.* A preface explained that the first edition had been published back in February 'under the fictitious Signature of *Anne Frances Randall*', but that the recent publication in Paris of a work on a similar subject had induced Mrs Robinson 'to avow herself the Author of this Pamphlet'. A disadvantage of the acknowledgement of authorship was that the appearance of her name in the list of major female British authors at the back would have seemed egotistic, so the preface also explained that 'the mention of Mrs Robinson's works was merely inserted with a view to mislead the reader respecting the REAL AUTHOR of the Pamphlet'.[4]

At the end of the year, despite her poor health, she took over from Robert Southey as poetry editor of the *Morning Post.* Her poems were considered one of the 'principal embellishments and supports' of the paper. It was now her role not only to be chief contributor but also to select and edit submissions from other poets. She continued to write in a range of voices and styles: one day she would be 'Tabitha Bramble' discoursing wittily in verse on 'Modern Male Fashions' or 'The Ingredients which Compose Modern Love', the next she would be 'Laura Maria' composing a cautionary narrative poem about 'The Gamester' who loses everything as a result of his addiction, and a few days after that she would be 'M R' writing an ode 'To the New Type of the Morning Post' (designed to assure readers of the elegance of the paper's new layout).[5] Some of her older poems, meanwhile, took on a new life when they were set to music by the actress Dora Jordan.

Mary may also have been instrumental in introducing a fashion column to the *Morning Post* – here the public were informed that powder had gone out of fashion ('a *white head* was considered the height of *Gothic*

Absurdity') but that the simple white muslin dress, sometimes trimmed with velvet and satin ribbons, was still in vogue. There was also mention of the turban that Maria Elizabeth had made her trademark.[6]

On returning to London from Englefield Green, Mary took rooms at 66 South Audley Street, just off Grosvenor Square, a less prestigious address than Berkeley Square or Clarges Street but still within the fashionable Mayfair district, close to Hyde Park and St James's. Despite her new position at the *Morning Post*, she was very short of money. She wrote a round robin letter to various magazine publishers, seeking work:

> Sir
> Being at this period unoccupied in any literary pursuit, and wishing to employ my pen for the advantage of my finances, I would like to engage my services in the pages of any monthly publication. If you are the Conductor of a Magazine, I shall thank you to inform me, whether you can find me such employment, either in prose or Verse, and on what terms you could afford to treat with me?[7]

She signed herself 'Mary Robinson, author of Poems, Novels Etc. etc. etc. etc.' and added a postscript requesting a written answer.

Coleridge had come to London in late November 1799 so that he could take up a position on the *Morning Post*, providing articles on politics. On Christmas Eve, he went to supper with Mary and Maria Elizabeth. Godwin was also there. In the New Year, she frequently entertained Godwin, Coleridge, and her editor Daniel Stuart to tea or supper. Godwin's diary reveals that she also sometimes attended the theatre, despite her immobility.

Coleridge persuaded his friend Southey to include her poem 'Jasper' in the *Annual Anthology* of new poetry that he was editing:

> I have enclosed a Poem which Mrs Robinson gave me for your Anthology – She is a woman of undoubted Genius. There was a poem of hers in this Morning's paper which both in metre and matter pleased me much – She overloads every thing; but I never knew a human Being with so *full* a mind – bad, good, and indifferent, I grant you, but full, and overflowing. This poem I *asked* for

> you, because I thought the metre stimulating – and some of the Stanzas really *good* – The first line of the 12th would of itself redeem a worse Poem. – I think, you will agree with me; but should you not, yet still put it *in*, my dear fellow! for my sake, and out of respect to a Woman-poet's feeling.[8]

The line that Coleridge so admired was 'Pale moon! thou spectre of the sky!' He later quoted it in his tribute poem to Mary, 'A Stranger Minstrel'. Some weeks later he wrote again to Southey about another of her poems:

> In the Morning Post was a poem of fascinating Metre by Mary Robinson – 'twas on Wednesday, Feb 26. – and entitled the Haunted Beach. I was so struck with it that I sent to her to desire that [it] might be preserved in the Anthology – She was extremely flattered by the Idea of its being there, as she idolizes you and your Doings. So if it be not too late, I pray you, let it be in . . . the Images are new and very distinct – that 'silvery carpet' is so *just*, that it is unfortunate it should *seem* so bad – for it is *really* good – but the Metre – ay! that Woman has an Ear.[9]

'The Haunted Beach' does indeed have a powerful and original metre, not dissimilar to that of Coleridge's 'Ancient Mariner':

> The Spectre band, his messmates brave,
> Sunk in the yawning ocean,
> While to the mast he lash'd him fast
> And brav'd the storm's commotion.
> The winter moon, upon the sand
> A silv'ry carpet made,
> And mark'd the Sailor reach the land,
> And mark'd his murd'rer wash his hand
> Where the green billows play'd.[10]

As winter came to an end, Mary's health improved a little. She was seen taking airings in her carriage. This was not without hazard. One day she was involved in a serious traffic accident. Her carriage was 'shattered considerably' by a collision with another coach: 'fortunately Mrs ROBIN-

SON received no injury; on account of her lameness, the accident was particularly alarming'. On another occasion the *Morning Post* reported that Hyde Park 'was yesterday a scene of splendour; the *promenade* was crowded with beauty and fashion' – Mrs Robinson was duly listed among the notables observed. But she was an outsider now. Once she would have paraded the walks in her latest gown and hat, but now she could only watch from her carriage window. A few days later, as 'Oberon', she published a poignant poem called 'Stanzas written in Hyde Park on Sunday Last by Oberon reflecting on all the female beauties who parade in Hyde Park'.[11] Here she described the perambulating beauties as 'British Wonders'. Her comfort for no longer being numbered among the crowd was that she was now an acknowledged British Wonder among authors.

In order to maximize her literary earnings, she turned herself into a journalist as well as a poet. Between October 1799 and February 1800 she wrote a series of essays for the *Morning Post* under the heading 'The Sylphid'. Each piece took the form of a letter to the editor written in the voice of an invisible sylph. 'I am allowed the power of changing my form, as suits the observation of the moment,' she wrote in the first essay, 'I listen with equal scepticism to the Lover's vows and the Courtier's professions.' The role suited her mercurial personality.

The Sylphid essays return to several of her favoured themes. The neglect of literary talent: 'I repaired to the abode of neglected genius. I beheld the genuine sons and daughters of the Muses, pining in obscure poverty, and labouring incessantly for a scanty pittance.' The fickleness of fashion: 'Fashion is a Sylph of fantastic appearance, the illegitimate offspring of Caprice (for Fashion is of no sex) . . . Fashion is a distorted Sylph, decked with flowers, feathers, tinsel, jewels, beads, and all the garish profusion of degenerated fancy.' Demi-reps: 'A woman of *Demi-ton* is no less remarkable for her love of notoriety, than for the prominent figure she is ambitious of making, wherever she meets the eye of public observation.' When she describes a demi-rep as a woman who is conspicuous in her carriage, takes a prominent seat at the theatre, and is always outré in fashionable dress, she is gently mocking her own younger self, while when she writes an essay on the 'Male Coquet' who preens himself round the fashionable parts of London she is digging at Tarleton. The series ends with more of her habitual targets such as the 'WOU'D-BE MAN OF FASHION' and the pushy self-important 'Mrs Prominent', but along the way she takes on newly topical matters, for instance the courage of the 'British tar' in the naval war against the French.[12]

At the beginning of April, Coleridge said goodbye to Mary and headed north to the Lake District. He left the manuscript of his play *Osorio* with her, asking her to hand it on to Godwin when she had finished with it.

Mary had returned to the *Memoirs* that she had begun writing two years before, then put aside. The *Morning Post* whetted the public's appetite for their publication, but Mary broke off her narrative at the point of her affair with the Prince of Wales. When summer came, she drafted some materials regarding her later years under the title 'Anecdotes of Distinguished Personages and Observations on Society and Manners, during her Travels on the Continent and in England'. Some of the 'Anecdotes of Distinguished Personages' – brief biographies of Lauzun, the Duke of Chartres, and Marie Antoinette – were published by Richard Phillips in his *Monthly Magazine*. Phillips was Godwin's publisher; he was the man who called Mrs Robinson the most interesting woman in England.

Mary's four-part essay on the fashionable pursuits of the metropolis also appeared in Phillips's *Monthly Magazine*: it was probably a version of the 'Observations on Society and Manners' that she intended to include in her *Memoirs*. Phillips duly published the *Memoirs* in the year after Mary's death. The first part, told in her own voice and extending from her birth to the affair with the Prince, was based on her original manuscript, which survives in a private collection. The second part, or 'Continuation', was stitched together by Maria Elizabeth – and perhaps Phillips – from a combination of her own recollections and various fragmentary manuscripts by her mother that are now lost.

Mary Robinson's *Memoirs* is one of the earliest examples of an English writer's autobiography. Her intention was to undo the scandalous work of such purported biographies as the anonymous *Memoirs of Perdita*. At the same time, she wanted to trace the origins of her literary sensibility. Like William Wordsworth in his poetry, Dorothy Wordsworth in her journals, Samuel Taylor Coleridge in his notebooks, John Keats in his letters, and Leigh Hunt in his *Autobiography*, she considered her own life and feelings, her emotional and intellectual development, to be central to her writing.

Mary's *Memoirs* should, of course, be treated with a healthy degree of scepticism. It is difficult not to smile at the avowals of chastity from one of the most sexually talked-about women of her era. Notorious for her manipulation of the public, she was self-consciously pleading at the bar of public opinion in defence of her own reputation. Her memory was unreliable and her narrative contains many contradictions and improbabilities, leading at least one theatre historian to describe it as a 'work of fiction'.[13] Her mission was to present herself as a victim of both male duplicity and the passions of her own feeling heart, but also as a misunderstood genius. The book's frequent bouts of self-exculpation, together with its overwrought sentimental style and the unfortunate fact that the authorial narrative breaks off long before she began her career as a serious author, have damaged Robinson's reputation, encouraging romantic novelists of later years to portray her as 'Perdita' the royal mistress rather than 'Mrs Robinson' the distinguished writer. As late as 1994, the *Memoirs* was republished under the title *Perdita*.

Her other major literary task in the spring and summer of 1800 was the preparation of a new selection of her poems. She called it her 'favourite offspring'.[14] She had fallen under the spell of Wordsworth and Coleridge's *Lyrical Ballads* of 1798, so she decided to put together a volume of the same style, consisting mostly of narrative poems that she had published in the *Morning Post* or the monthly magazines. Such was her admiration for Wordsworth and Coleridge's book that she engaged the same London publisher (Longman and Rees) and the same Bristol printer (Biggs and Cottle). She chose *Lyrical Tales* as her title and even requested that the book should be printed in the same typeface as *Lyrical Ballads*.

Her admiration for Wordsworth was already apparent from an introductory paragraph that she composed when his poem 'The Mad Mother' appeared in the *Morning Post* during her literary editorship: 'We have been so much captivated with the following beautiful piece, which appears in a small volume LYRICAL BALLADS, that we are tempted to transgress the rule we have laid down for ourselves [of not printing previously published poems]. Indeed, the whole collection, with the exception of the first piece, which appears manifestly to be written by a different hand, is a tribute to genuine nature.'[15] The 'first piece' in *Lyrical Ballads*, manifestly written by a different hand, was Coleridge's 'Ancient Mariner'. Mary was not alone in finding it immensely powerful in itself, but disproportionately long and out of keeping with the rest of the volume: several reviewers of *Lyrical Ballads* had made the same point. Probably with this in mind, she placed her equivalent of 'The Ancient Mariner', a long Gothic narrative poem called 'Golfre', not at the front but at the back of *Lyrical Tales*, so that it would not be off-putting.

When Wordsworth heard that Mary Robinson was preparing a volume with the title *Lyrical Tales*, he was working on the second volume of *Lyrical Ballads*. He seriously considered changing his title, for fear that a book by the famous Mrs Robinson would steal his thunder. This was a sign of his insecurity: the anonymously published first volume of *Lyrical Ballads* had not sold well and had been given a very mixed critical reception. Because *Lyrical Ballads* is now among the two or three best-known volumes of poetry in the English language, it is easy to assume that by imitating it Mary was merely cashing in on a new fashion in poetry. But at the time she was a much more celebrated author than Wordsworth, so it would be truer to say that she was assisting his reputation by imitating him. Wordsworth's publishers must have been surprised and delighted to have received a letter from the renowned Mrs Robinson asking them whether they would be interested in publishing a new collection that 'will consist of Tales, serious and gay, on a variety of subjects in the manner of Wordsworth's Lyrical Ballads'.[16]

'Tales, serious and gay' is an excellent description. The collection juxtaposes stories of poverty and woe with humorous tales. The influence of *Lyrical Ballads* is apparent from the very first poem (which was actually the last to be written, inserted just before the book was printed). Entitled 'All Alone' it is about a boy who loiters in a graveyard, very much in the manner of Wordsworth's 'We are Seven', though with the difference that whereas in Wordsworth it is two siblings who lie beneath the earth, in Mary's poem it is a mother. Wordsworth's poem is about an adult's failure to understand the mind of a child: the poet-narrator does not comprehend that the girl still feels close enough to her dead siblings to say 'we are seven' even though only five of them are alive. Robinson's narrator, on the other hand, sympathizes with the orphaned boy, insisting that he is not 'all alone' while she is watching over him. Wordsworth was more interested in silences and the painful gaps between people, Robinson in the sympathetic power of 'sensibility' to instil fellow feeling.

The two poets resemble each other most in their choice of subject matter. Like Wordsworth, Mary makes it her business to bestow dignity upon ordinary people by writing tragic verse not about kings and heroes but about the poor and the dispossessed: the widow of a soldier who has been killed in the wars ('The Widow's House'), a priest who has fled from the Terror of revolutionary France ('The Fugitive'), a young female slave being shipped across the ocean ('The Negro Girl'), an old man who has lost his children ('The Deserted Cottage'), a suicidal girl whose lover is dead ('Poor Marguerite'). All this mournful matter is interspersed with lighter pieces, such as 'Deborah's Parrot: A Village Tale', most of which had been first published in the lively voice of Tabitha Bramble in the *Morning Post*.

The best poem in the collection is probably 'The Lascar', which tells of a persecuted East Indian sailor. His existence is a scar on the body politic of imperial Britain: 'Here, in this smiling land we find / Neglect and mis'ry sting our race.' Mary exposes how the prosperity of the fashionable world, with its luxury goods such as the silk garments she had once delighted in wearing, was achieved through the suffering of others:

> Was it for this, that on the main
> I met the tempest fierce and strong,
> And steering o'er the liquid plain,
> Still onward, press'd the waves among?
> Was it for this, the Lascar brave
> Toil'd, like a wretched Indian Slave;
> Preserv'd your treasures by his toil,
> And sigh'd to greet this fertile soil?
> Was it for this, to beg, to die,
> Where plenty smiles, and where the Sky
> Sheds cooling airs; while fev'rish pain,
> Maddens the famish'd Lascar's brain?[17]

Mary sympathized with the Lascar, together with the widows and orphans of her collection, because by this time she perceived herself as an outcast from high society, dying 'all alone' in poverty and pain. One of the poems is called 'The Poor, Singing Dame': it tells of an 'old dame' who lives in a 'neat little Hovel' just below the turrets of the wall that 'went round an old Castle' inhabited by a proud lord, who is irritated by her merry singing. Towards the end of the poem, the reader learns the woman's name: 'When poor singing Mary was laid in her grave.' As soon as she is dead, the lord is haunted by screech owls, which send him spiralling towards his own grave. Given that Mary spent many months during the last two years of her life in a tiny cottage on the edge of the Great Park that was dominated by Windsor Castle, it is hard to resist an autobiographical reading.

For Coleridge, Mary's excellence lay not in her narratives, which he often found weak, but in her poetic 'ear' and in particular her metrical skill. Though the blank verse poems in *Lyrical Tales* are generally written with less suppleness than their Wordsworthian equivalents in *Lyrical Ballads*, Mary's collection includes a remarkable range of metrical innovations and variations among its poems written in stanzaic and ballad form. It made a major contribution to the advance of English poetic metre: 'Tennyson's "Mariana" could not have been written without Mary Robinson's experiments to create a new lyric form in English verse,' writes one of the modern critics instrumental in the rediscovery of her poetry in the 1990s.[18]

In April 1800 Mary made one of her last public appearances, a trip to the opera 'attended by a NOBLE *cicisbeo* . . . though evidently labouring under the effects of indisposition'.[19] *Cicisbeo* was an alternative Italian term for a *cavaliere servante*, which meant either an acknowledged lover or a solicitous admirer. Given Mary's state of health, it seems most unlikely that she had any kind of romantic involvement with a nobleman this late in her life, so it must be assumed that this particular escort was motivated by courtesy and affection rather than desire. His identity is a mystery, though it is notable that at around this time in both an essay and a poem she expressed gratitude to the Earl of Moira for his habitual generosity.[20] A fellow officer of Tarleton, intimate with the Prince of Wales, and the closest English friend of Lauzun, this dashing Irishman, who would eventually become Governor General of India, might have helped her out financially and escorted her to the Opera House.

By a curious coincidence, another Mrs Robinson lived in Albemarle Street not far from Mary's home. She hosted society events that were reported in the newspapers. To Mary she must have seemed like a shadow of her own past self, a strange double in the world she had lost. Her own social life, by contrast, revolved around her circle of literary friends.

Having given a lavish description of the other Mrs Robinson's ball one day, the *Morning Post* noted a little dinner of Mary's the next: 'Mrs ROBINSON had a *conversatione*, on Sunday evening, at which many of the *literati* were present.'[21]

Two days later, the same paper reported that Mary was showing alarming symptoms of consumption. Though this was a false diagnosis, she was declining fast. Her doctor suggested that she should go west to try the waters at Bristol Wells. For Mary, this would also have been an opportunity to pay a last visit to her home city. She even thought that it would have been fitting to die there. But she did not have the money to make the journey. Reluctantly, she appealed to the wealthy men who had once supported her. Neither the Prince nor Lord Malden had been at all regular in paying his annuity. Mary seems to have written to them both. A copy of a letter on the subject has survived. It has been assumed that it was meant for the Prince, but the address 'My Lord' makes Malden the more likely candidate (Mary addressed the Prince as 'Your Royal Highness'):

> My Lord
> PRONOUNCED by my physicians to be in a rapid decline, I trust that your Lordship will have the goodness to assist me with a part of the sum for which you are indebted to me. Without your aid I cannot make trial of the Bristol waters, the *only* remedy that presents to me any hope of preserving my existence. I should be sorry to *die* at enmity with any person; and you may be assured, my dear Lord, that I bear none towards you. It would be useless to ask you to call on me; but, if you would do me that honour, I should be happy, *very happy*, to see you, being,
> My dear Lord,
> Yours truly,
> MARY ROBINSON.[22]

There was no reply from Malden. A similar letter to the Prince about the arrears in his annuity was graced with a reply – but not with any funds.

However bad the state of her health and her finances, Mary wanted to go on entertaining cultivated friends from the world of literature and painting. She wrote to Sir Joshua Reynolds's old pupil, the painter James Northcote:

> Dear Sir,
> I lament that confinement to my bed will prevent my having the pleasure to receive my friend, on Friday Evening, next. The very precarious state of my health forbids my naming the period, though I hope that it is not far distant, when I shall again have the pleasure of seeing you. Be assured that I shall embrace the earliest opportunity with great easiness.[23]

She was also still in touch with her artist friends the Cosways. Maria Cosway painted a series of scenes to illustrate her poem 'The Wintry Day'.

Still Mary went on turning out poems, not only for the *Morning Post* but also for the monthly magazines. In May the *Lady's Monthly Museum* published a good example of her gift for light-handed lyrical versification, this time under the name Bridget:

The Way to keep Him

A lover, when he first essays
A lady's heart to gain,
A thousand tender fears betrays,
And talks of jealous pain!
All day he sighs, and sighing swears,
That love, and hope, and anxious cares,
Destroy his peace, his nights molest,
And agonize his 'feeling breast!'

If not believ'd, he ardent pays
Obedient homage still!
And ev'ry gentle grace displays,
To gratify her will!
Where'er she goes, he follows true;
And if she flies him, he'll pursue;
And if she frowns – he'll still adore;
And if she scorns – he'll doat the more!

Let her another kindly treat,
He sighs in hopeless pain;
Let her his eyes with coldness meet,
And ev'ry glance disdain;
Let her avoid him, wayward prone,
To favour all, save him alone!
Let others see her always glad,
But let him find her – ever sad!

Thus would you keep a lover still,
Unkind and careless prove;
For man is humble – treated ill!
And coldness fosters love!
Spurn him with harshness, and he sighs;
Most servile, when most cross'd;
Reward with kindness – and he flies!
Adore him – and he's lost![24]

This is a mocking version of the advice promulgated in the popular eighteenth-century play, Arthur Murphy's *The Way to Keep Him*, which advocated submission and adoration as the way for a woman to keep her lover happy. Mary, writing from her long and bitter experience of men, suggests precisely the opposite: abuse him and he will love you for ever, adore him and you will lose him.

A few guineas received in return for a steady stream of poems such as this was not enough to clear her debts. An action was brought against her. She was arrested and held in custody. This must have been extraordinarily distressing, given her disability. It is not known where she was taken – possibly the sheriff's office – though a witty comment in a letter written at the time hints at the darkness of her surroundings: 'I hope that my health will not suffer by my present *obscurity*. I have seen so little Sun Shine, for some years past, that any thing short of total *oblivion* will now content me.'

She was in an exceptionally awkward dilemma, as she explained in a letter to her old friend William Godwin. Her good humour shines through even as she writes while under arrest: 'I assure you that my feelings are not wounded neither is my spirit dejected by the "cloud" you mention – and tho' I shall not dart through it like a Sun-beam, I shall warmly feel the attentions with which *you*, and my most valued friends have honoured me.' The dilemma was that because there was 'no kind of legal separation' between her and Robinson, she could, 'as a *married woman*', have had the action against her set aside and forced her husband to take on the debt. But she did not want to involve him. And she felt that it was beneath her dignity to borrow from her friends:

> I have had various proposals from many friends, to settle the business – but I am too proud to borrow, while the arrears *now due* on my annuity from the Prince of Wales would *doubly* pay the sum for which I am arrested – I have written to the Prince, and his answer is, that 'there is no money at Carlton House! That he is very sorry for my situation, but that his *own* is equally distressing!!' You will smile at such paltry excuses, *as I do!* But I am determined to persist in my demand, Half a years annuity being nearly *due*, which is Two Hundred and Fifty Pounds. And I am in custody for Sixty three Pounds Only! So Circumstanced I will neither *borrow, beg*, nor *Steal*. I owe very little in the world, and still less *to* the world, – and it is unimportant to me, where I pass my days. If I possess the Esteem and friendship of its best ornaments among which I consider *you* most *sincerely*—[25]

The £63 was paid – possibly by Godwin – and the shadow of an extended stay in debtors' prison was lifted.

In early July, she wrote to Robert Ker Porter, another artist friend whom she had known and admired for some time.[26] Porter, brother of Jane Porter the novelist, had achieved celebrity with his painting of the storming of Seringapatam in India by a small band of British Grenadiers in the spring of 1799 (the event that inspired the prologue to Wilkie Collins's novel *The Moonstone*). Mary had been commissioned to write a pen-portrait of Porter for another publication under the imprint of Richard Phillips, so she needed some biographical information:

> Dear Sir
> As Fame has a ladder which all must sooner or later ascend, who have *Genius* to guide them, and as you have made *long strides*

> towards the very top of its utmost altitude, I wish to hang upon your skirts, a biographical sketch of the *Painter of Seringapatam* for the octavo publication of *Lives of Celebrated Characters*. I shall thereby also have the field to scatter some flowers around the brows of your sweet and elegant Sisters: – the memoir will be anonymous, I shall therefore (if you are willing) thank you for a mere outline, which I will fill up to the best of my powers.[27]

She went on to reveal that the same volume would also contain 'a biographical sketch' of herself that is 'now writing by a very celebrated literary character'. The pen-portrait of Robert Porter, recognizably in Mary's style, was duly published at the end of the year in *Public Characters of 1800–1801*, an annual publication that consisted of biographical sketches of notable public figures. Mary's account of Porter gives a detailed and lively description of his famous painting and also refers to his 'two lovely, accomplished sisters, who have presented the world with many proofs of their taste for literature'.[28]

That year's edition of *Public Characters* included only two female subjects: the authors Charlotte Smith and Mary Robinson. Who, then, was the 'very celebrated literary character' responsible for the pen-portrait of Mrs Robinson? The opening of the essay gives the reader a strong indication:

> That this is the age of female British authors, and that the Lady who will be the subject of the following memoir, is of the number of those who have most eminently distinguished themselves amongst the numerous supporters of the female laurel, which is now confessedly one of the indisputable '*Rights of Women*,' we trust will be made manifest to all readers, who peruse with candour the various evidences of taste and genius, which we shall point out.[29]

The phrase '*Rights of Women*' suggests that it must have been Mary Wollstonecraft's husband William Godwin. He was writing regularly for Phillips at this time; there is a reference in his journal to a 'Character of Mrs Robinson'; and he was the most celebrated 'literary character' to spend time with her while she was writing her *Memoirs* that year.

The essay in *Public Characters* was the most detailed and accurate biographical account of her to appear prior to the posthumous publication of the *Memoirs*. It records, for instance, that her ancestor Richard Seys had a sister who married the Lord High Chancellor of Great Britain, that Mary was a collateral descendant of John Locke, that Lord Chancellor Northington was her godfather, that she was married at 15, that her relationship with the Prince of Wales lasted 'little longer than a year', that for twenty years she had benefited from the patronage of Georgiana Duchess of Devonshire, and that her works were warmly admired by Sir Joshua Reynolds, who painted her twice. The reader even learns that a copy of the first Reynolds portrait was requested by the Duke of Chaulne for the Empress of Russia. The second Reynolds and the full-length portrait by Gainsborough were in the possession of the Prince.

Other information included was that Mary's father had been buried with full military honours, his old friend Admiral Gregg in attendance; that her brother was a merchant of the highest respectability at Leghorn; and that Mr Robinson was still living, 'the only brother of Commodore William Robinson, the opulent East Indian'. At the time of writing, it was noted, Mrs Robinson enjoyed 'a respectable circle of society, among which some of the first literary characters, male and female, may be named'. Godwin, one of the towering intellects of the age, was at the centre of that circle, closely acquainted with Mary. He may well have seen the manuscript draft of the *Memoirs*.

The essay ends with a touching account of Mary's poor health and hard literary labour, describing how she 'has been afflicted with a rheumatic complaint upwards of eleven years, which has baffled the skill of the most eminent of the faculty, and which has been greatly increased by those close attentions to the labour of the pen, which a limited income, and helpless state of health, render absolutely necessary'. But more 'personal beauty' remained in her, Godwin adds, than most women possessed in the proudest May-time of their attractions: 'She is humane and hospitable to the poor and the unhappy; and entertains her chosen friends with great warmth of affection. Her conversation is enriched by sentiment and enlivened by wit, and her manners are distinguished by suavity and politeness.'[30]

These last months are the only period of Mary's life from which a substantial number of her letters survive. They give a powerful sense of her place among a small but loyal circle of friends, as in the following, to one of the Porter sisters:

On Tuesday, my charming and amiable friend, we will enjoy your society – I shall leave town soon after that day, for I do not find myself the better for the warm atmosphere of London; and I fear a relapse, – because I *know* that there *are Beings* whose society makes life desirable! If your lovely cheek does not wear a *conscious* smile – I am mistaken . . .

with united love to all your dear family I remain

sincerely yours Mary Robinson[31]

In another letter she asked the renowned sculptor John Flaxman 'if he could do her the Honor to arrange her Bust, as she is very earnestly requested, by many literary friends, to have one, completed'. She suggested that he could work from a mask of her face that she had modelled for him some years previously.[32]

At the end of July the *Morning Post* announced that 'Mrs ROBINSON means to pass the summer at her beautiful cottage in Surrey', adding that her *Lyrical Tales* had gone to press.[33] As for Tarleton, he was rapidly becoming a mere footnote in history. He had been dispatched to an obscure domestic posting in the Welsh mountains where, as the *Morning Post* derisively put it, 'he will *storm* the heights of hitherto inaccessible rocks, and pursue his *campaigns* among the peaceful peasantry'.[34]

LYRICAL TALES,

BY

MRS. MARY ROBINSON.

LONDON:

PRINTED FOR T. N. LONGMAN AND O. REES, PATERNOSTER-ROW,

BY BIGGS AND CO. BRISTOL.

1800.

Title page of Mary's last volume of poetry.

CHAPTER 25

'A Small but Brilliant Circle'

> Oh! Heavens! If a select society could be formed, – a little colony of mental powers, a world of talents, drawn into a small but brilliant circle, – what a splendid sunshine would it display!
>
> Mary Robinson to Jane Porter, September 1800

> I trust that a short period will effect a change in my mental system, which will be productive of repose: for the sorrows of sensibility, when they reach a certain climax, rise into fortitude, or soften into resignation.
>
> Mary Robinson, *The False Friend*

After finishing *Lyrical Tales*, Mary retired to the small cottage *ornée* near Windsor that belonged to her daughter. According to Maria Elizabeth, she was happy for a time: 'Rural occupation and amusement, quiet and pure air, appeared for a time to cheer her spirits, and renovate her shattered frame.'[1] Mary planned to translate one of the epic German poems of the age, Friedrich Klopstock's *Messiah*, intending to render it in blank verse, but her failing health persuaded her to abandon this idea.

On 5 August 1800 Mary wrote from Englefield Cottage to her friend the novelist Jane Porter: 'I should have done myself the pleasure of answering your letter before, had I not be [sic] very much indisposed. The warm weather has produced such languor in my spirits and constitution, that I am scarcely capable of holding my pen.' She went on to enquire after the health of mutual friends, and then turned to literary business: 'Tell your brother to read my first paper on "*Society and manners in the Metropolis of England*" page 35 of the Monthly Magazine, but desire him to substitute the word *gust* for *gusto* in column 5. page 37 – there are also some other *press errors*, which you will see.' Her work as poetry editor of the *Morning Post* was continuing unabated: 'I have transmitted your sweet lines on Mr Stocdale's Poems, to Stuart, and they will, unquestionably be inserted. They are very charming!' Then she concluded, 'You must pardon me for this short letter for I am half dead with a nervous head-ache.'[2]

The letter sets the tone for the final months of Mary's life: continuing literary productivity and professionalism despite a constant struggle against ill health and discomfort in the exceptionally hot weather that lasted through the summer. The series of essays on 'Society and Manners in the Metropolis of England' represents her prose writing at its very best, while the attention to detail (witnessed by her annoyance over press errors) and her encouragement of fellow writers are the marks of her excellence as an editor.

The letter to Miss Porter has a postscript: 'Maria writes in all good wishes – and Mrs Fenwick presents her Compliments.' Maria is, of course, her daughter, the constant companion who nursed her through her final months and who remained in the cottage at Englefield Green for many years after Mary's death. Mrs Fenwick is Eliza Fenwick, author of a highly successful novel called *Secrecy* and a large number of books for children. Her marriage was on the rocks in 1800 and she and her daughter stayed with the Robinsons for nearly the whole month of August, the first in a stream of visitors who over the coming weeks turned the cottage into a community of – mostly female – literary minds.

It is thanks to Eliza Fenwick that we have a vivid account of Englefield Cottage and its setting. She sent it to her friend, the feminist writer Mary Hays:

> Mrs Robinson's Cottage stands aloof from the grander dwellings of Lady Shuldam, Lord Uxbridge and Mrs Freemantle. Its front windows look over St Ann's Hill, the retreat of Mr Fox, and from the back we are sheltered by the tall trees of the forest. Mrs Robinson

> has displayed great taste in the fitting up of her cottage; the papers of the rooms in a particular degree are beautifully appropriated to the building and situation. The furniture is perhaps more ornamental than I should chuse for myself, but it is still elegant and quiet – nothing gaudy nor ill placed.[3]

Like everyone who knew Mary in her final years, Eliza Fenwick was full of praise for her hostess's intelligence and temperament: 'I may congratulate myself on being the guest of a woman whose powers of pleasing, ever varied and graceful, are united to quick feeling and generosity of temper.'

Windsor Great Park, where she had so often met the Prince, was immediately behind her cottage and Fox's rural estate visible from its front window, so Mary could hardly forget her past. In late August and early September, she wrote several very long and exceptionally revealing letters. The first of them, to Jane Porter, began by contrasting the female friendships of her later, literary years with her experience of society ladies in her years of fame:

> Indeed I have in my tedious journey through life found so few estimable women, (particularly where I beheld handsome ones) that I not only admire but value you, excessively. If I do not enter into the true spirit of Friendship for my own Sex, it is because I have almost universally found that Sex unkind and hostile towards *me*, I have seen the most miserable and degrading, the most contemptible *traits* of false delicacy, glaring through the thin veil of artificial virtue. I have found those women the most fastidiously severe, whose own lives have been marked by *private follies* and *assumed propriety.* The women whom I have most admired, have been the least prone to condemn, while they have been themselves the most *blameless.* – Of this distinguished class I consider you.[4]

She went on to say that she had spent the last few weeks confined with two unpleasant companions: one was a violently inflamed ankle that had given her considerable alarm ('which thank Heaven has disappeared for I should not admire a mutilated leg') and the other was a piece of literary hackwork – the task of translating a 200-page book from the German,

Joseph Hager's *Picture of Palermo*. She completed the job in ten days, testimony to her astonishing capacity for work despite her poor health. A happier writing task had been the completion of the *Lyrical Tales*.

Jane Porter and her mother were invited to stay, Eliza Fenwick having departed. Mary said that her 'intercourse with a few', such as the Porters, had helped her to overcome the dislike that she once entertained for the society of her own sex. The letter closes with an honest and moving insight into its author's condition:

> I find little benefit from the change of air. I work too hard, and too incessantly, at my pen, to recover rapidly: and, to say truly, I very little value life, therefore, perhaps, am neglectful of those attentions which are calculated to prolong it. My adored girl is an indefatigable nurse, – and *in her* I shall *live* – I trust, as I now exist *by her affectionate solicitudes.*

She cannot afford to stop writing, even though work is killing her. 'I am so accustomed to scribbling for Printers *Devils*, that I am now incapable of transcribing a single page for the perusals of *Angels*.' As so often, she describes her daughter – who was busy doing the '*Great Wash!!*' as Mary was writing the letter – as her only salvation.

Robinson's literary labours and her social life are brought further alive by a letter to fellow poet Samuel Jackson Pratt, written a few days later:

> My dear Friend
>
> I never wish to have any *introductions* to my own Poetry in the M[orning] P[ost]and therefore I thought of course that yours did not require it: the merit of *your* lines speaking for themselves . . . I continue my daily labours in the Post; all the Oberons, Tabithas, MRs and indeed most of the Poetry you see is mine.
>
> I remain secluded till November – will you come and pass a few days with us, this autumn? You must tell me what you think of my Lyrical Tales now printing by Longman and Reece. I am still tormented with ill health, but I have had my cottage perpetually full of visitors ever since I came to it; and some charming literary characters – *authoresses* – herein. I wish you would come and see us – I expect the Miss Porters, the beautiful

> sisters of the painter of the Seringapatam picture {with their mother}. I have had Mrs Fenwick, the elegant authoress of 'Secresy' and her daughter, here, this month past. Tomorrow I expect Godwin – and his philanthropic friend, Mr Marshall: they will only stay a day or two. . . .
>
> God bless you and farewell. Remember I have always a spare bed for my best friends, consequently *we* shall be delighted to see you. We have some thoughts of making an hasty journey to visit Coleridge, the Poet, and his amiable little wife, in Cumberland but *health* must decide this matter.[5]

Another 'authoress' with whom she was corresponding at this time was the successful novelist Elizabeth Gunning. On the same day that Mary wrote to Pratt, she penned a letter to her, sending condolences on a family bereavement, inviting her to stay in order to take her mind off her loss, and speaking encouragingly of 'your genius, your amiable and inestimable virtues'.[6]

She also told Pratt of her frustration – the perennial complaint of authors – at the slowness of her publisher in getting her new book into print. She was unsure whether *Lyrical Tales* would make it onto the autumn (Michaelmas) list, or whether it would have to wait for Christmas:

> The man of Books has kept me in waiting, to correct his and my own errors these apes – I am not now assured whether I am to appear at the criticks board in the form of a Michaelmas goose, or under go the minutest mortification of becoming *mince meat* at the Christmas revels of our literary executioners![7]

The *Lyrical Tales* finally made it into print just before Christmas. The three-volume edition of Mary's poetical works, with 'its brilliant list of subscribers', had been announced at the same time,[8] but it did not appear until long after her death (and without the subscription list).

The four-part essay in the *Monthly Magazine* on the 'Present State of the Manners, Society, etc. etc. of the Metropolis of England', mentioned in the letter to Jane Porter, reveals that Mary had genuine talent as an essayist, to add to her skills as poet, dramatist, and novelist. This extended essay, written in very poor health in the final months of her life, provides a valuable summation of many of her attitudes.

The argument of the essay is that as 'polished life' takes its impression from the example of those of 'exalted rank', so the community at large takes its lead from the pursuits and pleasures 'in the metropolis of a kingdom'. London is not only 'the great emporium of commerce' but also the 'centre of attraction for the full exercise of talents, and the liberal display of all that can embellish the arts and sciences'. At the same time, though, 'the very finest powers of intellect, and the proudest specimens of mental labour, have frequently appeared in the more contracted circles of provincial society. Bristol and Bath have each sent forth their sons and daughters of genius.' The county of Devon alone may 'boast the birth of Sir Joshua Reynolds; Coleridge, the exquisite poet; Wolcot, the unequalled satirist; Northcote, Cosway, Kendal, Tasker, Mrs Cowley, and many others of deserved celebrity'. Without dropping her own name, Mary thus placed herself amongst an extraordinary constellation of West Country talent (with all of whom she was personally acquainted).

She then turned her attention to the stage, again reflecting on the great talents she had witnessed in her lifetime. The theatres were 'the open schools of public manners, which exhibit at all times the touchstone of the public mind'. Dominating the age, as Garrick had dominated the previous generation, was 'the brilliant wit of a Sheridan', but at the same time 'the theatres have, frequently, exhibited the most sublime efforts of the dramatic art, with advantages that are scarcely to be paralleled. The astonishing powers of a Kemble and a Siddons, the magical fascination of a Jordan, have been a source of wonder and delight to the discriminating of all nations who have visited the metropolis.' The 'British stage', she rightly claimed, was at this time unparalleled anywhere in the world. She also observed that in time of war, the theatre was a valuable place of escape and national comfort.

For women, another kind of comfort had come from changes in fashion:

> Dress has also been considerably improved by our intercourse with foreign nations. The women of this country now adopt a species of decoration at once easy and grateful. Nature seems to resume her empire, while art is hourly decaying. The deformities of stiffened stays, high heels, powder, whalebone petticoats, and unmeaning

> flounces of many coloured frippery, now yield to the simple elegance of cambric and muslin drapery: thus health is preserved by an unconstrained motion of the body; and beauty is ascertained by the unequivocal testimonies of symmetry and nature.

Here Mary quietly took the credit she deserved for these innovations: 'The females of England are considerably indebted to our most celebrated actresses for the revolution in dress.'

She also suggested that she had lived through a golden age of painting (Reynolds above all, but also such rising stars as Flaxman and her friend Robert Ker Porter), of architecture, of improvements in public services ('The streets of London are better paved and better lighted than those of any metropolis in Europe'), and of female accomplishment: 'The women of England have, by their literary labours, reached an altitude of mental excellence, far above those of any other nation.' But they have failed to work together as a sisterhood. The great female writers are 'neglected, unsought, alienated from society', each pursuing her fame independently: 'How much is genius deceived when it seeks this single, this unconnected species of gratification! How powerful might such a phalanx become, were it to act in union of sentiment, and sympathy of feeling; and by a participation of public fame secure, to the end of time, the admiration of posterity.'

As in *A Letter to the Women of England*, Mary argued that public neglect of artistic talent was a peculiarly English vice. The great writers, actors, actresses, and painters were, she said, excluded from high society: 'these miserable discriminations are the offspring of the present age: the monsters of this island'. They ordered these things differently in France: 'even in the days of despotism . . . Versailles had its female constellations'. In all this, Mary was clearly generalizing from her own personal experience, but given the fullness and the vicissitudes of the life she had lived, she had a right to do so. The essays, like the private letters of her last months, were written out of a yearning for community, for the kind of sisterhood that she would have experienced had the nation adopted her proposal of establishing a university for women.[9]

She also began work on yet another novel. It survives only as a fragment entitled *Jasper*. It begins with a Madame de Stanheim perishing in a shipwreck. A sailor called Jasper rescues her 6-year-old son, struggles ashore and finds a hovel on a cliff top, in which there is a small packet of love letters and a lock of hair, with the words 'Shipwrecked on the 1st September 1766'. The letters are addressed to Henry, signed Cecile. She is an 18-year-old girl living in India; by order of her father, she has been separated from Henry and he has been sent back to England. Jasper the sailor, accompanied by Madame de Stanheim's child, returns to his native Cornwall, from where he has been exiled years before. When the child is feverish, he breaks into a party in a desperate bid to get the child a drink. He is promptly tied up in a stable, but a certain Lady Strickland shows pity and adopts the child. It turns out that she is Jasper's long-lost love, destined for a richer man with the result that he was forced to leave home. The parallels between the story of Henry and Cecile and that of Jasper and Lady Strickland, together with the orphaned and adopted child, suggest that the different plots would have been brought together through some device involving double lives or mistaken identity, but only about a hundred pages were written and nothing is known of Mary's larger intentions for the book. It is hard to see how the surviving fragment could have developed the political and feminist edge that characterized *The Natural Daughter*.

In early September, there was an unfortunate accident. Mary described how she had suffered 'a violent blow on the *head*, which very nearly put a period to my sensations, of every description'.[10] She showed a wonderful capacity to laugh at her own misfortune:

> Not a word, my dear Friend, to enquire after my poor head! which not only narrowly escaped destruction; but has been these ten days almost frantic with torture! On the day of your departure my coachman, probably mistaking me for a truss of Hay, in lifting me out of the slanting room where I slept, forgot the low roof, or rather penthouse; and threw me with considerable violence, so high in his arms, that the top of my head absolutely cracked the ceiling.

She joked that the fact that the ceiling was made of plaster probably saved her life:

> Had the adversary my *brain* encountered, been nearer of its own quality, (of *wood* or of *lead*,) I had never *lived* to write this letter,

> but *lath* and *plaster* were destined to be divided between us, and though I was stunned at the moment, I found my giddiness remain – during several succeeding days. But, to be serious, – I have really escaped a fractured skull; and though the application of Leeches considerably relieved me, my *head* is still – almost as tender as my *heart* – both I fear want strength – to bear the ills of life, *Philosophically.*[11]

Comic as it is, this letter is a sober reminder of the fact that she had to be carried everywhere, including in and out of bed.

Though for several days her 'poor head' suffered terribly from the effect of what she wittily called 'my late trial of its *thickness*', she still managed to pen a magnificent letter to Jane Porter contrasting the fickleness and malice of society – the world she had known in her youth – to the support network of 'a small but brilliant circle' of like-minded friends.

Coleridge was much on her mind at this time and it may be that her image of such a circle was inspired by his famous scheme to gather a small group of liberty-loving and literary-minded young men and women in a 'pantisocratic' commune on the banks of the Susquehanna River in the new world. For Mary, Englefield Cottage was just such a place, but much closer to home – on the banks of the Thames and a mere stone's throw from the world she had lost:

> I am grown a perfect misanthrope; and *almost* determined never again to mingle with the gay and busy world. After all, my lovely friend, the common routine of society is so full of thorns, and so bestowed with weeds, that the reflecting traveller finds only an augmentation of disgust, with his exercise of labour. Oh! Heavens! If a select society could be formed, – a little colony of mental powers, a world of talents, drawn into a small but brilliant circle, – what a splendid sunshine would it display; and how deeply in gloom around it throw all the uninteresting vapid scenery of human life! Visionary idea! It can never be! The malignant Spirit of Contention, – the Demons Envy Calumny, and Vanity, led on by the imp Caprice, and the phantom Imagination, would interrupt the harmony of souls; and, even while they enjoyed a fancied Heaven, would convince

> them, that their sphere was still terrestrial. Lovely and highly-gifted as you are, you will mix in the gay mazes of society, but for a time; for your soul is to [sic] finely organised, your head too sensitive, to enjoy for a long period the artificial Beings you will meet with, the Society which will present itself, – led by the ignis fatuus fashion, but no less fascinating than deceptive.[12]

Here Mary is projecting onto Jane Porter her own path from the fascinating but deceptive world of the 'gay mazes' of high society to the 'small but brilliant circle' of the 'little colony of mental powers' in which she now felt secure yet somehow confined.

From mid-September to mid-October, her health was so poor that she believed she would soon die. She wrote her last surviving letter to Jane Porter:

> Near a month confined to my bed, and every day expecting to prove that '*there is another, and a better world*' – I have scarcely strength to thank you for your kind enquiries. My illness has indeed been so perilous, that I believe little hopes were entertained of my recovery. When my daughter received your letter I was in a state too terrible to describe! – one blister on my shoulders, another on my head, – which with perpetual bleedings, with the lancet as well as with leeches, have so reduced me that I am a mere spectre. My disease lay cheifly [sic] on my head, – an intermitting fever on the brain, – attended with other symptoms of the most alarming nature . . .
>
> I write against the orders of my Physician. – But I could not resist my desire to thank you. I am still so feeble, that the smallest fatigue overwhelms me.
>
> God bless you, and bless all that are dear to you.
>
> yours most truly Mary Robinson
>
> P.S. I hope our friend Thomas is perfectly recovered.
> God knows when I shall be 'myself again', – I have but too much reason to believe, that my sojourn on this Earth, will shortly terminate. My daughter trusts that my illness will plead an apology for her silence.[13]

This letter was written six weeks before Mary's forty-third birthday. Sixteen years and thousands of pages of literary production after the vicious caricature following her accident, Perdita is now truly 'on her last legs'. Yet her good manners and her concern for others still shine through: her own physical disintegration does not stop her from enquiring after the health of 'our friend Thomas'.

The other person Mary was in correspondence with at this time was her friend William Godwin. They quarrelled and exchanged a batch of impassioned letters. Mary and Godwin, both known to be forthright and candid almost to a fault, tested the limits of their friendship over the last days in August, as her health deteriorated. They had probably always had a tempestuous relationship and were used to speaking their minds freely. Mary's letters to Godwin provide another close insight into her state of mind in those final months before her death. For Godwin, there is no mask of politeness, no jokey account of her bodily misadventures, only an uncompromising frankness and startling self-revelation.

It is impossible to recover the precise circumstances of the quarrel, but it seems to have originated with Godwin requiring some form of 'security' for a loan of money to Mary (possibly the £63 that got her out of custody). She objected to his tone in asking this: 'on the one hand you press your point with the utmost earnestness, as if it was of the last moment, and at the same time tell me that what you ask is of no consequence, a something that can not in the end signify'.[14] He also seems to have accused her of neglecting old friends for new.

Godwin replied with a letter accusing Mary of being 'capricious'. Though plagued with an 'excruciating head-ache', she retaliated with a long letter to her 'dear Philosopher' written 'in the warmth of feelings . . . [which] bespoke the language of my heart'. She began by recalling the joy she had felt on first meeting him four years before: 'I met you as a tutor of the *mind*, and I never expected to find you, an associate of the *soul*.' But she accused Godwin of taking pleasure in 'humbling her vanity' in company, of not esteeming her and her 'humble Talents'. She also accused him of hypocrisy: 'You love Sincerity, my dear Philosopher, and yet you are not pleased, when, even in womanish resentment, I have dared to be Sincere. Would you not despise a servile, fawning Hypocrite? . . . I am not capricious: new associates do *not* charm me from those that I have ever loved.'

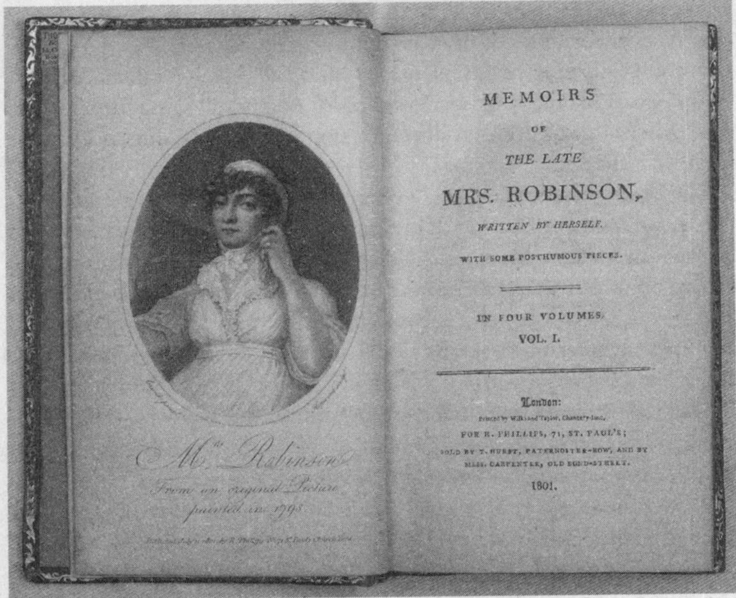

MEMOIRS

OF

THE LATE

MRS. ROBINSON,

WRITTEN BY HERSELF.

WITH SOME POSTHUMOUS PIECES.

IN FOUR VOLUMES.

VOL. I.

London:

Printed by Wilks and Taylor, Chancery-lane,

FOR R. PHILLIPS, 71, ST. PAUL'S;

SOLD BY T. HURST, PATERNOSTER-ROW, AND BY

MESS. CARPENTER, OLD BOND-STREET.

1801.

Title page of Mary's *Memoirs*, with frontispiece engraved from the portrait of Mary painted by James Crank in 1798.

The letter then becomes an essay on her own philosophy of life, a kind of personalized version of Godwin's theory of the perfectibility of society: 'I have been a wanderer in search of something, approaching to *my idea* of a perfect being.' But she has felt disappointed in this quest and badly let down by the important men in her life: 'If I am vain, – if I appear to be trifling, I have to thank the world for its foolish, fond indulgence; I have to reproach such men as Sheridan and Fox, for having professed, more than I had strength of mind to credit, without some little portion of self love.' Mary's problem, she tells Godwin, is her unflagging honesty: 'I cannot, I never could dissemble.' She knows that she wears her heart on her sleeve and this has proved fatal in some circumstances: 'Had I been an artificial creature – I might have been in wealth and vulgar estimation, a creature to be envied!'

This letter, in sharp contrast to the carefully crafted self-presentation of the *Memoirs*, reveals a woman who has delved into her own character and past, and has no illusions about herself: 'the impetuosity of my temper, the irritability of my feelings; – the proud energy of my soul, placed a barrier between me and Fortune, which has thrown a gloom on every hour of my existence'. She asks him to visit her in her 'hovel', though requesting him not to bring his little daughter (the future Mary Shelley), for fear of upsetting her shattered nerves: 'I am indeed too irritable, as well as too feeble, to bear the smallest fatigue, and I confess that my anxieties are so poignant, my fears are so easily awakened, my mind so bewildered by vexation, and my *heart* so oppressed by *sorrows*, that nothing which is not calm and soothing to the senses, – can delight me.' It may be that this admonition was the result of the strain of having had Eliza Fenwick and her young daughter staying for the previous weeks in the little cottage.

Mary tells Godwin that she is 'strongly impressed with a presentiment, that my days are nearly numbered', but that she is happier, 'more tranquil, more gay, than when I dreaded a long life of suffering'. She had a right to be irritable, given the depth of her ill health, but the letter still shows great charm and warmth. She thanks Godwin for introducing her to his friend James Marshall: 'To you, my dear *cross cross* Philosopher, I am indeed indebted for the introduction to this excellent mortal! – and I thank you, thank you, most sincerely. Come and accept the *olive branch* – if you think I ever acted, or felt, in any degree, with hostility towards you.'[15]

It seems, however, that Godwin wrote an angry and equally honest letter in return. He spoke of her 'alternate kindness and Indifference', her 'cold heart' and 'deceitful face', her inconstancy in friendship – a charge that she found particularly painful. 'How unjust, how severe are your reproaches!' she replied, reiterating that impetuosity and frankness were her hallmarks: 'I have ever been disposed to speak my sentiments, too freely. What I dislike, I condemn – what I love, I idolize.' She suggested that the accusation of inconstancy in friendship was hypocritical, given how he had taken her up but then neglected her after his marriage to Wollstonecraft. What appears to have caused her most distress was his accusation that she was unjustly discontented, despite possessing youth, beauty, and literary fame:

> You accuse me of cherishing a discontented Spirit! Alas! Had even your Philosophy been so tried – Had you been, in the spring and

> bloom of Youth frost-nipped by sickness and consigned to a premature old age, hurled from the most flattering prospect of delight and Fortune, to contemplate a long and dreary perspective, which only the Grave could terminate, would not your Spirit, like my own, be weary of its journey? You say that I have 'Youth and beauty', Ah! philosopher, how surely do I feel that both are vanished! You tell me that I have 'Literary Fame!' How comes it then that I am abused, neglected, – unhonoured, – unrewarded.
>
> Say no more that I am unjustly discontented. Tell me, no more, that I have the means of being Happy. Those, alone, who witnessed my early years of Hope, are capable of sympathizing in my present hours of pain and disappointment! You see me but a wreck, and the little love of life, which I now profess, is scarcely worth preserving. Adieu – my dear Philosopher, adieu.
>
> P.S. My adored and affectionate *secondself*, desires me to present her compliments. When will you honour our cottage with a visit?[16]

'*Secondself*' is a lovely phrase for her daughter and namesake. A few days later, Godwin went down to Englefield Green to make his peace. He stayed the night, though Mary was once again upset when he left in the morning before breakfast.

Mary wrote to him again, thanking him for the visit and apologizing for her refusal to receive his 'clever' friend John Philpot Curran. She told Godwin that her poverty and pride prevented her from inviting strangers into her cottage, and she was piqued by Curran's admission that he did not think it worth making a journey of 17 miles out from central London merely in order to visit Mary: 'I know that *I am* not of sufficient importance to command attention: – but I am too high-souled to *court it* . . . I cannot therefore condescend to receive, as *an honour*, that, which by my long intercourse with the first talents in the world, – in the society of the most enlightened men, I have been familiarized to enjoy.' She also expressed her chagrin at another social slight when one of Godwin's friends refused to be introduced to her on the roadside: 'I was placed in so *awkward* a situation Yesterday while *waiting* in the High road, and as he did not then *desire* to be presented *to me. I* now cannot suffer it.'[17]

The truth was that Mary was feeling highly insecure about strangers or even acquaintances seeing the miserable condition to which she had been reduced. Later in September, she confessed to James Marshall that she had scarcely enough money to put food on the table:

> I am hourly indulging a Misanthropic Spirit which takes from me the love of Society, and you will see that in a very short time, I shall seclude myself wholly – from the World, a solitary shadow of my former self. I am too poor to have [the] honour of receiving my friends hospitably; and I know by experience, that they will not chearfully partake of the scanty fare which fortune now affords me. I shall therefore resign myself to Solitary [Economy] and lament that the 'feast of Reason' will not always produce 'the flow of Soul'. I begin to hate the World! I feel no sensation but that of disgust – I enjoy no pleasure, but that of looking back on *past* felicity. I have outlived health, youth and happiness – then welcome Solitude, and 'musing melancholy'.[18]

She also admitted that her cherished 'small circle of society' was dwindling, and that she was faced with increasing loneliness and despair:

> I esteem you: – I esteem Mr Godwin. I *know* that you are my friend: – I *think* that he is, but I despair of finding the number, of *such friends*, multiplied; and therefore I am resolved to bid the busy scenes of life farewell for ever. Here, then, am I *friend*: – the solitary Recluse, the world-hating – thought cherishing – alien from everything worldly! If such a being can afford you pleasure by her society, Come – Come – as often as you have a day to throw away and pass it at our cottage. My head is so very bad that I can scarcely see the paper.

She thanked Marshall for the present of birds he had brought for their supper and also told him that an anonymous donor was leaving her baskets of apples and other fruits.

Godwin sent her a present in October, and she wrote thanking him, in a very feeble state and 'so depressed in spirit':

> The exertion of speaking almost destroys me; and I feel, still more strongly, the fatigue of *thinking*. I certainly cannot long resist the pressure of sickness exerted with the weight of never-ending sorrows! If you were to see me you would not, by any personal feature, know me: – but, if I know myself, my mind is unaltered, and my Esteem for you Undiminished. I dare not write any more – my head becomes giddy and my hand refuses the office of guiding my pen – God bless you – Dear Sir.[19]

She was still writing for the *Morning Post*, though the pressure to turn in regular copy weighed heavily upon her. Her relationship with Stuart suffered, as her daughter explained in the continuation of the *Memoirs*: 'She yet continued, though with difficulty, and many intervals, her literary avocations. When necessitated by pain and languor to limit her exertions, her unfeeling employers accused her of negligence. This inconsideration, though she seldom complained, affected her spirits, and preyed upon her heart.'

Maria Elizabeth also hinted rather mysteriously that her mother treated 'with just indignation those offers of service which required the sacrifice of her integrity'.[20] She was prolific as ever and wrote some of her best poems in these final months, including 'London Summer's Morning'* and 'Harvest Home', which reveals that, though primarily a city poet, she could also bring her political awareness to the pastoral tradition:

> On the plain
> The freckled gleaner gathers the scant sheaf,
> And looks, with many a sigh, on the tythe heap
> Of the proud, pamper'd pastor![21]

These provocative lines were censored out of the poem when it was later reprinted in the popular miscellany *The Every-Day Book*.[22]

The *Morning Post* provided Mary with subject matter as well as printing her poems. In October, it carried reports of the discovery of a feral child, the 'Wild Boy of Aveyron': 'He lived on potatoes, chestnuts and acorns . . . His features are regular, but without expression; every part of his

* Quoted in chapter 2.

body is covered with scars; these scars attest the cruelty of the persons by whom, it is presumed, he has been abandoned; or, perhaps, they are attributable only to the dangers of a solitary existence, at a tender age, and in a rude tract of country.'[23] The story of the wild child fed into the age's fascination with the return to nature and Rousseau's idea of the 'noble savage'. Mary promptly turned the newspaper reports into a narrative poem, written in a vigorous rhythm analogous to that of Coleridge's 'Kubla Khan'.

Mary's chronic ill health meant that she would never visit Coleridge in the Lake District. There was an exchange of poems instead.

Coleridge wrote to Daniel Stuart in early October: 'It grieves me to hear of poor Mrs Robinson's illness.' With the letter he enclosed 'Alcaeus to Sappho', a poem mostly written by Wordsworth but touched up by Coleridge. Published in the *Morning Post*, it described 'Sappho' – obviously Mary – as 'the fairest Face on Earth'.[24]

A poem by Wordsworth called 'The Solitude of Binnorie' was published in the *Morning Post* a week later, with a prefatory note explaining that it owed its metre to Mary's 'Haunted Beach', which had appeared some months before:

> Sir,
> It would be unpardonable in the author of the following lines, if he omitted to acknowledge that the metre (with the exception of the burthen) is borrowed from 'The Haunted Beach of Mrs ROBINSON;' a most exquisite Poem, first given to the public, if I recollect aright, in your paper, and since re-published in the second volume of Mr SOUTHEY'S Annual Anthology. This acknowledgement will not appear superfluous to those who have felt the bewitching effect of that absolutely original stanza in the original Poem, and who call to mind that the invention of a metre has so widely diffused the name of Sappho, and almost constitutes the present celebrity of Alcaeus.[25]

Mary probably assumed that the poem was by Coleridge. She would have been delighted at being praised by so technically accomplished a poet for inventing an entirely original metre. As was seen in the previous chapter, it was Coleridge who drew the attention of his fellow Lake Poets to 'The Haunted Beach'.

Unable to visit Coleridge, she wrote two poems for him instead. An 'Ode, Inscribed to the Infant Son of S. T. Coleridge' was written on hearing the news of the birth of his third child, Derwent. Coleridge must have told her of how the house where he was living, Greta Hall, nestled below the great curve of the mountain called Skiddaw. She imagines Derwent growing up as a 'babe of the mountain wild' and contrasts her own enclosure in Windsor Forest with his freedom among the hills:

> I sing to thee! On Skiddaw's heights upborne – . . .
>
> Ye Mountains! From whose crests sublime
> Imagination might to frenzy turn . . .
> Ye Cat'racts . . .
> Ye silent Lakes . . .
> And thou, meek Orb, that lift'st thy silver bow
> O'er frozen vallies, and o'er the hills of snow; –
> Ye all shall lend your wonders – all combine
> To greet the Babe, with energies divine! . . .
>
> Sweet Boy! accept a Stranger's Song,
> Who joys to sing of thee,
> Alone her forest haunts among,
> The haunts of wood-wild harmony![26]

Mary beautifully imagines Coleridge and his son hand in hand, treading 'In converse sweet, the mountain's head'. She hopes that one day Derwent will become a poet like his father – 'Shall sing the song thy father sung'. In thinking of Coleridge's son, she is also reflecting on the literary career of her own daughter.

Mary's ode for Derwent is full of deliberate allusions to 'Frost at Midnight', Coleridge's exquisite poem to his first son, Hartley. So, for example, 'Whether Skiddaw greets the dawn of light . . . Whether Lodore for thee its white wave flings' echoes the rhetorical structure of 'Whether the summer clothe the general earth . . . whether the eave-drops fall' in 'Frost at Midnight'. The key thought in Coleridge's poem was that he was reared 'in the great city', but he hopes that Hartley will 'wander like a breeze / By lakes and sandy shores, beneath the crags / Of ancient mountain'. Mary's response imagines Coleridge and Derwent wandering in just such a location.

The most interesting allusion is contained within the phrase 'accept a Stranger's Song'. 'Frost at Midnight' had included the mysterious lines

> How oft . . . have I gazed upon the bars,
> To watch that fluttering *stranger* . . .
> and still my heart leaped up,
> For still I hoped to see the *stranger's* face,
> Townsman, or aunt, or sister more beloved.[27]

Here the word *stranger* refers first to the fluttering film of soot on the grate of a fire and then to Coleridge's hope that he will soon be joined by a visitor. He explained the origin of the image in a footnote to the poem: 'In all parts of the kingdom these films are called *strangers* and supposed to portend the arrival of some absent friend.' In calling herself a stranger, Mary is not merely alluding to the fact that she has not met the baby Derwent, but also making herself into the *stranger* of 'Frost at Midnight', the 'absent friend', the 'sister' who because of her immobility cannot physically share in Coleridge's joy at the birth of his third son, but who can do so through her poem.

Around the same time, Mary sent Coleridge another poem, entitled simply 'To the Poet Coleridge'. Indeed, she may even have posted the two poems together. This one was published posthumously with her *Memoirs*, dated October 1800, and signed 'Sappho', then reprinted (with slight variants) in her *Poetical Works*. It was here that she quoted from 'Kubla Khan', which Coleridge had shown her in manuscript:

> I hear her voice! Thy *sunny dome*,
> Thy *caves of ice*, loud repeat,
> Vibrations, madd'ning sweet,
> Calling the visionary wand'rer home.
> She sings of Thee, O favour'd child
> *Of Minstrelsy*, Sublimely Wild!
> Of thee, whose soul can feel the tone
> Which gives to airy dreams a *magic* All Thy Own![28]

Coleridge wrote back with his poem 'A Stranger Minstrel'. This was also published in Mary's *Memoirs*, with the subtitle 'written to Mrs Robinson, a few weeks before her death'. The title is a clear response to the phrase 'accept a Stranger's Song' in the ode to Derwent. Here Coleridge poetically implores her to leave Windsor for Greta Hall. He imagines himself lying 'supine' halfway up the mountain of Skiddaw, thinking of Mrs Robinson and shedding 'the tear, slow travelling on its way'. 'I would, old Skiddaw! SHE were here!' he says, to which the mountain replies that she is here in spirit because 'her divinest melody' has freed her soul and 'She is where'er she wills to be / Unfetter'd by mortality!' He returns the compliment of quotation that she had paid him:

> Now to the 'haunted beach' can fly,
> Beside the threshold scourged with waves,
> Now where the maniac wildly raves,
> '*Pale moon, thou spectre of the sky!*'[29]

The last line was his favourite one from Robinson's 'The Maniac', the poem whose origin may have inspired 'Kubla Khan'.

Coleridge was one of the last friends Mary wrote to when she was on her deathbed. The letter is lost, but part of its content is preserved because Coleridge quoted it to his friend Tom Poole. He described it as a 'most affecting, heart-rending Letter' in which she expressed 'what she called her death bed affection and esteem for me'. 'The very last Lines of her Letter are indeed sublime,' he continued:

> My little Cottage is retired and comfortable. There I mean to remain (if indeed I live so long) till Christmas. But it is not surrounded with the romantic Scenery of your chosen retreat: it is not, my dear Sir! The nursery of sublime Thoughts – the abode of Peace – the solitude of Nature's Wonders. O! Skiddaw! – I think, if I could but once contemplate thy Summit, I should never quit the Prospect it would present till my eyes were closed for ever![30]

At the beginning of December she completed the arrangement of her *Poetical Works*. The *Lyrical Tales* were published two weeks later, with a sample poem ('All Alone') appearing in the *Morning Post*, prefaced with a generous tribute:

> Mrs ROBINSON'S volume of *Lyrical Tales* has just made its appearance; and in few recent publications have we discovered such a variety of pathetic and humorous pieces, written with great feeling and elegance; and abounding with rich and lively colouring, the effusion of real genius. We extract the following, one of the most affecting productions that has lately issued from the English Press.[31]

Her friend John Wolcot ('Peter Pindar') sent her a series of letters, with songs interspersed, addressing her as Sappho. In one of them he wrote, 'My dear friend, I have just heard that you have been exceedingly unwell: for God's sake do not be foolish enough to die yet, as you possess stamina for an hundred years, and a poetical mind that cannot be soon replaced.'[32]

Mary knew that she was dying, but she remained in good spirits for the sake of her daughter. Her mind was alert to the very end. 'As she hourly declined,' remembered her daughter, 'her mind seemed to acquire strength in proportion to the weakness of her frame':

> When no longer able to support the fatigue of being removed from her chamber, she retained a perfect composure of spirits, and, in the intervals of extreme bodily suffering, would listen, while her daughter read to her, with apparent interest and collectedness of thought, frequently making observations on what would probably take place when she passed that '*bourn*', whence no traveller returns.[33]

One of her final wishes was to see her remaining writings duly published. She placed her manuscript memoirs into the hands of her daughter 'with an *injunction* that the narrative should be made public; adding, "I should have continued it up to the present time, – but perhaps it is as well that I have been prevented. *Promise* me that you will print it!"'[34] Maria Elizabeth, of course, could not refuse such a request. She agreed, after which Mary became tranquil. Her daughter kept her word and saw the book into print within a matter of months.

Maria Elizabeth shared the nursing care with a companion, Elizabeth Weale, who lived with them in the cottage. One day when Maria Elizabeth was absent Mary took the opportunity to give Elizabeth instructions for her burial: 'I cannot talk to my poor girl on these sad subjects.' Then with an unruffled manner, and minute precision, she said that she wanted the simplest of burial services. '"Let me", said she with an impressive though almost inarticulate voice, "be buried in Old Windsor churchyard." For the selection of that spot she gave *a particular reason*.' The reason was, of course, its proximity to the place where she and the Prince had been lovers.

Almost penniless, she bequeathed a 'few trifling memorials' to friends. She desired that locks of her hair should be sent to '*two particular persons*', who must have been the Prince and Tarleton. Mary's final thoughts, though, were for her daughter, her 'adored and affectionate *secondself*'. When Maria Elizabeth and Elizabeth Weale tried to console her with hopes of recovery she shook her head, told them not to deceive themselves and then 'pressing to her heart her daughter, who knelt by her bed-side, she held her head for some minutes clasped against her bosom, which throbbed, as with some internal and agonizing conflict. – "*Poor heart!*" murmured she, in a deep and stifled tone, "*what will become of thee!*"'[35] She paused, stifled her sobs, and then asked if one of the young women could read to her.

That night, she seemed better, and even talked about her plans for composing 'a long work, upon which she would bestow great pains and time'. She spoke of her regret at writing too many of her books too quickly.

One of the symptoms of her final illness was water on the chest, which threatened suffocation. Maria Elizabeth and Elizabeth supported her in their arms, on pillows, to counteract this. She lasted in this state for fifteen days. On Christmas Eve, she asked how long it was until Christmas Day. On being told, she replied, '*Yet* I shall never see it.' Towards midnight she cried, 'Oh God, oh just and merciful God, help me to support this agony.' She lingered on through Christmas Day, enduring 'great anguish'. In the evening 'a kind of lethargic stupor came on'. Maria Elizabeth implored her mother to speak if she could. Her last words were '*My darling Mary!*'[36] After this, she fell into a coma. She died on 26 December 1800, just after noon.

The body was given an autopsy at the request of her physicians, Drs Pope and Chandler. She had died from '*a dropsy in the chest*' – heart failure. They also found six large gallstones in the gall bladder.

She was buried as she wished to be, in a corner of the churchyard at Old Windsor, just down the road from Englefield Green. Only two people came. Walking behind her coffin were her two literary friends, 'Peter Pindar' and William Godwin.

EPILOGUE

> Poor dear Mrs Robinson! you have heard of her Death . . . O Poole! That that Woman had but been married to a noble Being, what a noble Being she herself would have been. Latterly, she felt this with a poignant anguish. – Well! –
>
> O'er her pil'd grave the gale of evening sighs;
> And flowers will grow upon its grassy Slope.
> I wipe the dimming Water from mine eyes –
> Ev'n in the cold Grave dwells the Cherub Hope!
>
> Samuel Taylor Coleridge to Thomas Poole,
> February 1801

> As an AUTHORESS, few, if any, have risen higher in literary fame; or have maintained a more solid and permanent reputation than the distinguished PERDITA. Her talents were not limited, and the wide and extensive range she took in the field of literature, not only astonished the most acute; delighted the refined and elegant; but extorted approbation from the rigid and scrutinizing critic.
>
> Pierce Egan, *The Mistress of Royalty*, 1814

The *Morning Post*, Monday, 29 December 1800:

> The literary world have to regret the loss of Mrs Robinson, who died on Friday morning at eight o'clock, at her cottage on Englefield Green. She had been for several months in a declining state of health, which worldly troubles greatly aggravated. In her last moments, however, she was consoled by the tender attentions of her daughter and of many friends, who deeply lament that a woman

> of so much genius, of such an elegant taste, of so rich an imagination in poetry, should be cut off at a period when the mental faculties are in their prime. As the authoress of several popular novels and poetical pieces, many of them under the signature of LAURA MARIA, she was well known to the public, who would have been still further indebted to her pen, if she had been blessed with life and health.

The idea that she would eventually receive such an obituary would have been unimaginable back in 1786 when the *Morning Post* had erroneously reported that 'Mrs Robinson, the once famous *Perdita*, died a few days ago at Paris.' The transformation from royal mistress to one of the most admired authors of the age has never been achieved before or since.

In 1801, soon after Mary's death, the Prince confirmed that he would continue paying the annuity – at the reduced level of £200 – to her daughter. There was some correspondence between Maria Elizabeth and the palace with regard to arrears on the annual payments to her mother. Maria Elizabeth also kept in touch with Godwin. She wrote to thank him for attending her mother's funeral: 'If any *mortal* transaction, could soothe her dear spirit, it would be the knowledge of having been attended to her "long and lasting" repose, by so much worth, and genius, as yours.'[1] Maria Elizabeth also asked Godwin to return 'any letters from my darling Mother – to you – which *you think* would do her credit'.[2] This request was probably made in connection with her work completing her mother's *Memoirs*, but it is not impossible that she was considering writing a more ambitious 'life and letters'. In 1804, Maria Elizabeth was in possession of her mother's 'original MSS',[3] but all these papers have disappeared. To judge from the handful that have survived by chance, a collection of Mary's letters – not to mention those she received from her friends, lovers, and publishers – would have made fascinating reading.

In some circles, Mary's name remained tarnished. Jane Porter did not publish her memoir of her fellow novelist because she was warned that if her friendship with Mrs Robinson became public knowledge 'all the world would cut me'; another novelist, Mrs Crespigny, told her that 'she must drop me and that I should be shunned by all decent people'.[4]

Mary's life-story certainly remained in the public consciousness for some years. During the Regency crisis of 1808 the Prince was satirized by means of 'historical' novels that enacted the 'Florizel and Perdita' affair in medieval settings. The anonymous *The Royal Legend* included such readily recognizable characters as 'Colonel Carleton' and 'Lupo' (Fox). Its version of Mary was based on close acquaintance with the *Memoirs* and was not wholly unflattering:

> The youthful Perdita, which was the name of the female, gave early proofs of a sensibility of disposition very uncommon at her tender years: the gloomy ruins of the cloisters were her constant haunt during the day; and in their solitudes her mind received those intellectual rays which beamed so brightly in her more advanced years.[5]

Another similar novel, *The Private History of the Court of England*, introduced the pleasing fantasy that Perdita was especially attractive on stage when cross-dressed as Hamlet.

Public interest in the Prince ensured that Mary's name was kept alive throughout the Regency years. In 1814, the journalist Pierce Egan published *The Mistress of Royalty; or, the Loves of Florizel and Perdita, portrayed in the Amatory Epistles, between an Illustrious Personage, and a Distinguished Female.* This curiously hybrid book began by reprinting the 1784 *Effusions of Love*, without apparently realizing that its letters were fabrications, then proceeded to an extraordinary paean to Mrs Robinson's qualities: she was so beautiful that likenesses of her adorned the finest courts of Europe, as far away as Russia; she was always affable and courteous; she had the 'most refined and elegant conversation', together with a 'pregnant wit'; she showed enormous serenity of mind in her difficult last years; her novels 'abound with the most accurate delineations of human nature'; her pamphlet on Marie Antoinette was the product of a 'capacious, intelligent mind'; all in all, she had 'SUPERLATIVE TALENTS' and lacked only one thing – chastity.[6] The Prince finally became King George IV in 1820. Six years later, Mary's last publisher, Sir Richard Phillips, tried to sell back to the royal family the lock of the Prince's hair that she had kept all her life.

Phillips published the *Memoirs of the Late Mrs Robinson, Written by Herself* in 1801, in a four-volume set that also included some 'posthumous pieces', an elegy on her death by 'Peter Pindar', a full list of her published books, a list of the newspaper poems written in the last twelve months of her life, the 'Sylphid' essays, the fragmentary novel *Jasper*, 'The Savage of Aveyron', 'The Progress of Liberty', and 'The Haunted Beach'. There were also tributary poems and correspondence by Pindar, Pratt, Taylor, Merry, Boaden, Coleridge, Robert Ker Porter, Reynolds, and many more. Five years later, Phillips brought into print the long delayed three volumes of Mary's *Poetical Works*, prepared for the press by Maria Elizabeth.

After the *Memoirs* but before the *Poetical Works*, a brief selection of Mary's poems, together with others by a range of writers in her circle of acquaintance, was edited by Maria Elizabeth under the title *The Wild Wreath*. Publishing some of her mother's poems in this company was a way of honouring Mary's desire to be among 'a small but brilliant circle' of literary men and women. Maria Elizabeth includes some of her own poems in the anthology, but had no success in her attempts to publish another collection that consisted solely of her own work. Tarleton's wife Susan contributed some elegant engravings: she must have become friendly with her husband's ex-lover's daughter. Some of the poems in the volume, including one called 'To a False Friend', are by 'Susan': could it be that Tarleton had resumed his life of philandering and that his wife now found herself in the position Mary had endured for so long? If so, there was a reconciliation: the couple remained married, seemingly very happily in their later years, until Tarleton's death in January 1833. Susan lived on, an eccentric widow, well into her eighties.

Maria Elizabeth's request to Coleridge for a poem for *The Wild Wreath* elicited a long and tortuous reply. First he said that he had given up writing poetry and then he mingled his affectionate memories of Mary with a fit of moralizing:

> Your dear Mother is more present to my eyes, than the paper on which I am writing – which indeed swims before my sight – for I can not think of your Mother without Tears. Let not what I say offend you, – I conjure you, in the name of your dear Mother! let it not do so. Others flattered her – I admired her indeed, as deeply as others – but I likewise esteemed her *much*, and yearned from my inmost soul to esteem her *altogether*. Flowers, they say, smell sweetest at eve; it was my Hope, my heart-felt wish, my Prayer, my Faith, that the latter age of your Mother would be illustrious and redemptory –

> that to the Genius and generous Virtues of her youth she would add Judgement, and Thought – whatever was correct and dignified as a Poetess, and all that was matronly as Woman. Such, you best know, were her own aspirations – One of her poems written in sickness breathes them so well and so affectingly, that I never read it without a strange mixture of anguish and consolation. – In this Feeling I cultivated your Mother's acquaintance, thrice happy if I could have soothed her sorrows, or if the feeble Lamp of my friendship could have yielded her one ray of Hope and Guidance. Your Mother had indeed a good, a very good, heart – and in *my* eyes, and in *my* belief, was in her latter life a blameless Woman. – Her memoirs I have not seen – I understood that an excessively silly copy of Verses, which I had absolutely forgotten the very writing of, disgraced me and the volumes – this publication of a private Letter (an act so wholly unjustifiable, and in it's nature subversive of all social confidence) I attributed altogether to the Man, at whose Shop the Volumes were published –. I was sorry, no doubt, that so very silly a Poem had been published – for your mother's sake still more than for my own – yet I was not displeased to see my Name joined to your Mother's – I have said every where and aloud, that I thought highly both of her Talents and of her Heart, and that I *hoped* still more highly of both. I was not grieved at an occasion, which compelled me often to stand forth, as her Defender, Apologist, and Encomiast.[7]

The extraordinary mix of feelings expressed here reveals how difficult it was for a man such as Coleridge to reconcile the intensely fond emotions inspired by Mary's charm with the troubling associations of her reputation.

It transpired that Coleridge's real concern was the message that would be sent out by the appearance of his work between the same covers as authors such as the Gothic novelist 'Monk' Lewis, who had promised a poem. 'As to Peter Pindar,' he continued, 'By all the Love and Honor, I bear to your dear Parent's memory, by the anguish and the indignation at my inmost heart, I swear to you that my flesh creeps at his name!!' Did not Maria Elizabeth remember that Pindar had published a poem that described 'an infamous and mercenary Strumpet' as '*the Mrs Robinson of*

Greece'?[8] How could she associate her mother's memory with such a man? In the end, though, Coleridge relented and his Gothic poem 'The Mad Monk' duly appeared in *The Wild Wreath*.

Nothing is known of Maria Elizabeth's later years. She lived to a similar age as her mother, dying in 1818. At her own request, she was buried in Mary's tomb. According to local legend, her sad ghost walks the Old Windsor graveyard at dawn and dusk.[9] In her will she left everything to Elizabeth Weale, 'now residing with me'.[10] As has been seen, Miss Weale was nurse to Mary and companion to Maria Elizabeth at Englefield Cottage. It can only be presumed that the two unmarried women continued to live together there for the rest of Maria Elizabeth's life. Whether her mother's troubled history with men, together with the broken engagement to Mr H—, led Maria Elizabeth actively to prefer the companionship of a woman is not known.

The Prince's own marriage proved a disaster, reaching its low point when his consort arrived uninvited at his coronation in Westminster Abbey. Fox found great happiness with Elizabeth Armistead, though tucked away in some private papers there is a letter he wrote to a confidante admitting that Mrs Robinson was the true love of his life.[11] As for Lord Malden, he had a string of mistresses and an illegitimate daughter to whom he was devoted.[12] At the age of 81 he married his last mistress, a woman half his age, Catherine Stephens, who was admired during the Regency as the most beautiful actress on the London stage (she was especially renowned for her vocal skills in operatic roles such as Susanna in Mozart's *Marriage of Figaro*). He died a year after marrying her, but she lived on for another forty years as Countess of Essex. In raising an actress to the aristocracy was he finally atoning for his behaviour towards Mary? Perhaps he was haunted all through his later years by the letter she had written him a few months before her death in 1800.

The longevity of Wordsworth, coupled with the potent myths inspired by the premature deaths of Keats, Shelley, and Byron, meant that in the Victorian era Mary Robinson's poetry was forgotten, along with that of her talented female contemporaries such as Charlotte Smith. Gothic and sentimental fiction went out of fashion, so her novels also ceased to be read. Only in the 1990s, with the academic revival of interest in female authors (especially in America), did scholars begin to take her work seriously and to perceive her importance in the literary world of the 1790s.

The story of her affair with the Prince was sometimes retold in the twentieth century, in the purple prose of popular historical fiction. Jean Plaidy's *Perdita's Prince* (1969) is the best example: 'The Prince of Wales stalked up and down his apartments in the Dower Lodge on Kew Green and aired his grievances to his brother, Prince Frederick. "I tell you this, Fred," he declared, "I have had enough."' Or, as the blurb to G. P. Putnam's American edition put it: 'Their passionate affair was as star-crossed and amorous as any in the history of the English throne. *Perdita's Prince* is the haunting story of a sweeping love that threatened to divide politics and become a national scandal.'

The Gainsborough, Reynolds, and Romney portraits of her still turn heads in the Wallace Collection. The Hoppner portrait now hangs in the hall of Chawton House in Hampshire, the home of Jane Austen's wealthy relations, which has become a centre for the study of early women writers. It is the painting in the collection that visitors always ask about. Mary Robinson's time has come again in the early twenty-first century: she fashioned her own image, she knew how to manage the media, she lived in the world of celebrity, but she was also an acute and often comic analyst of that world.

The cottage at Englefield Green no longer exists. Close to where it probably stood there is now an exclusive residential community, its pastiche neo-classical architecture and decorative fountains enclosed behind high-security wrought-iron gates – a far cry from Mary's desire to gather a small but brilliant literary circle. She would, however, have been delighted that a few hundred yards down the road stands the huge Victorian Gothic edifice of Royal Holloway College, one of the first institutions in Britain to have fulfilled her demand that women should be allowed a university education.

Mary's grave is in the churchyard at Old Windsor. The ravages of time and weather have largely effaced the words on the original memorial stone, but it is still possible to read the poems on either side of the tomb. One is a sonnet by her friend Samuel Jackson Pratt:

> Of Beauty's Isle, her daughters must declare,
> She who sleeps here was fairest of the fair.

But ah! while Nature on her favourite smil'd,
And Genius claim'd his share in Beauty's child;
Ev'n as they wove a garland for her brow,
Sorrow prepar'd a willowy wreath of woe;
Mix'd luried nightshade with the buds of May,
And twin'd her darkest cypress with the bay:
In mildew tears steep'd every opening flow'r,
Prey'd on the sweets, and gave the canker pow'r:
Yet, O may Pity's angel, from the grave
This early victim of misfortune save!
And as she springs to everlasting morn,
May Glory's fadeless crown her soul adorn!

The other is an epitaph that Mary composed herself for inclusion in her best novel, *Walsingham*. Its last two stanzas read:

No wealth had she, nor power to sway;
Yet rich in worth, and learning's store:
She *wept her summer hours away*,
She heard the wintry storm no more.

Yet o'er this low and silent spot,
Full many a bud of Spring shall wave,
While she, by all, save ONE forgot,
SHALL SNATCH A WREATH BEYOND THE GRAVE![13]

I visited the grave on a sunny spring day. After walking away from it, I returned for one last look. Kneeling down at one end, I could just make out Mary's name and dates. I traced over them with my finger and then to my surprise discovered another name engraved just below: 'Perdita'. After all Mary's efforts to remake herself as Mrs Robinson the author, rather than Perdita the royal mistress, could her daughter really have allowed the infamous name to appear for posterity?

She probably did not: I subsequently learned from a local bookseller that the grave was restored in 1952 by Mary's great-great-niece, a descendant of her brother George Darby. It was probably she who added the name 'Perdita', but we cannot know for sure that she did not order the re-engraving of what was already there. Sadly, the grave is not the 'silent spot' of Mary's own epitaph. Old Windsor churchyard is only a few miles from Heathrow, directly below the flight path. Every few seconds a plane thunders low over her grave and almost shakes the ground with its noise.

APPENDIX:

The Mystery of Mrs Robinson's Age

Mary Robinson's gravestone and the published text of her *Memoirs* give her date of birth as 27 November 1758. All biographical and reference works in which she finds a place duly give the lifespan of Mary Robinson, née Darby, as 1758 to 1800. But the original parish register of the church of St Augustine the Less records that she was baptized on 19 July 1758. How could a child have been baptized in July and born the following November?

Was Mary exercising the traditional prerogative of the actress to lie about her age? Maybe it suited her self-image to pretend that she was younger than she was. Later in the *Memoirs* she represented herself as an innocent and, in particular, a child-bride: 'only three months before I became a wife,' she wrote, 'I had dressed a doll'.[1] Her friend Jane Porter said that Mary married 'at almost an infantine age'.[2] Furthermore, most of her readers would have known that she had a very public affair with the Prince of Wales in 1780, when he was just 17. Could it be that by giving her birth date as 1758 Mary made out that she was the 21-year-old lover of the teenage prince, when she was really a year or two older? Was she trying to represent herself as a mere ingénue being swept off her feet by the glamour of royalty when she was really more of a seductive 'older woman'? And here's to you, Mrs Robinson, one is tempted to add.

But there is another twist to the story. Tucked away in the library of one of the most closely guarded houses in England is a stout volume containing the original manuscript of the 'Memoirs of Mary Robinson written by Herself'. Halfway down its fourth page is the statement 'During a tempestuous night on the twenty seventh day of november, I first opened my eyes to this world of duplicity and sorrow.'[3] Mary did not mention the year of her birth. She never made the false claim that she was born in 1758. The date was added when the manuscript was printed after her death. If the misinformation was deliberate, the culprit was her daughter, who saw the *Memoirs* through the press. It is more likely that Maria Elizabeth Robinson, who was also responsible for the wording on the gravestone, misremembered or never knew the precise year of her mother's birth.

The manuscript provides proof that Mary did not deliberately lie about her age. So we probably should after all accept her statement later in the *Memoirs* that she was 15 when she married Thomas Robinson. Their wedding took place on 12 April 1773. By this account, she would have been born on 27 November *1757*.

When Mary was at the height of her fame, a letter appeared in the *Morning Herald* newspaper over the signature 'An invisible SPY'. 'Mr Editor,' it began, 'Many disputes having arisen, respecting the ages of our *celebrated Mistresses*, I have taken considerable pains to discover their *real* pretensions to youth, and leave you to judge by the following tabble [sic].' There followed a list of eight notorious women, among them, 'Mrs R-b-s-on. Born at Bristol 1757.' 'NB,' added the invisible spy, 'The above table may be depended on as authentic.'[4]

A further complication in the jigsaw puzzle of contradictory evidence suggests that she may actually have been born *two* years earlier than the date given on the gravestone: a scribbled note in the margin of the baptismal register of St Augustine the Less asserts that she was born on 27 November 1756. This, however, was not part of the official record (it was not copied into the Bishop's Transcript of the register), so it is not decisive evidence in itself. Error or confusion on the part of the parish clerk, or indeed Mary's parents, is a plausible explanation. The balance of the evidence favours the following year. In order to avoid constant reiteration of such phrases as 'when she was 15 or 16', I have assumed a birth date of 27 November 1757. Scrupulous readers may make a mental note of the possibility that one year should always be added! What can be said – on the basis of the baptismal record, the newspaper report and the original manuscript of the *Memoirs* – is that the 1758 birth date assumed by posterity is certainly wrong and that both Mrs Robinson herself and some of her public *believed* that she was born in 1757.

NOTES

PROLOGUE

1 See the list of her works at the beginning of the bibliography.

2 Jacqueline M. Labbe, 'Mary Robinson's Bicentennial', *Women's Writing*, 9:1 (2002), 'Special Number: Mary Robinson', p. 4.

3 Cynthia Campbell, *The Most Polished Gentleman: George IV and the Women in his Life* (London, 1995).

4 See especially the admirable work of Judith Pascoe, *Romantic Theatricality: Gender, Poetry, and Spectatorship* (Ithaca, NY, 1997) and *Mary Robinson: Selected Poems* (Peterborough, Ont., 2000).

5 Sir Richard Phillips (her last publisher), letter of 8 Jan. 1826, in *The Correspondence of George, Prince of Wales 1770–1812*, ed. Arthur Aspinall, 8 vols (London, 1963–71), iii, p. 135.

CHAPTER 1

1 Walpole, letter of 22 Oct. 1766; John Britton, *Bath and Bristol, with the Counties of Somerset and Gloucester* (1829), p. 5. I owe these references to Diego Saglia's excellent unpublished article 'Bristol Commerce and the Metropolitan Scene of Luxury in Mary Robinson's *Memoirs* and *The Progress of Liberty*'.

2 Bristol Record Office, FCP/St Aug/R/1 (f) 2. Spelt 'Polle' in the original register and 'Polly' in the Bishop's Transcript.

3 *Memoirs of the Late Mrs Robinson, Written by Herself* (1801). Quoted from the edition of M. J. Levy, *Perdita: The Memoirs of Mary Robinson* (London, 1994), pp. 17–18. For the convenience of the reader, all subsequent quotations are from this edition, but the text has been checked against the first edition.

4 According to the preface to *The Poetical Works of the Late Mrs Robinson, including many pieces never before published*, ed. Mary E. Robinson (1806), Mary's paternal grandfather married Benjamin's sister, Hester Franklin, but there was no Hester among Benjamin's many sisters.

5 *Memoirs*, p. 18.

6 Manuscript of *Memoirs*, fol. 4v, not in published text.

7 Mary writes that he was born two years after the marriage, but the baptismal record (9 June 1752) suggests three.

8 *Memoirs*, p. 21.

9 Anne Stott, *Hannah More: The First Victorian* (Oxford, 2003), p. 10.
10 Erased passage in manuscript of *Memoirs*, fol. 18.
11 See Richard Jenkins, *Memoirs of the Bristol Stage* (1826), p. 86.
12 *Memoirs*, p. 22.
13 Hannah More, *The Search after Happiness* (1774), quoted in Stott, *Hannah More*, p. 13.
14 *The Piozzi Letters: Correspondence of Hester Lynch Piozzi (formerly Mrs Thrale)*, ed. E. A. Bloom and L. D. Bloom, vol. iii (Newark, Del., 1993), p. 82.
15 *Memoirs*, p. 25.
16 *Memoirs*, p. 25.
17 *Memoirs*, p. 23.
18 *Memoirs*, p. 26.
19 *Memoirs*, p. 26. For historical verification, based on primary sources, see the entry on Nicholas Darby in the *Dictionary of Canadian Biography*, vol. iv (Toronto, 1979), pp. 194–5.
20 Manuscript of *Memoirs*, fol. 30v.
21 *Memoirs*, p. 28.
22 *Memoirs*, p. 29.
23 *Memoirs*, p. 29.
24 *The Memoirs of Perdita* (1784), p. iv.
25 *Memoirs of Perdita*, p. 11.
26 *Memoirs*, p. 30.
27 *Memoirs*, p. 31.
28 *Memoirs*, p. 33.
29 *Memoirs*, p. 34.
30 *Memoirs*, p. 34.
31 *Conversations of James Northcote R.A. with James Ward*, ed. E. Fletcher (London, 1901), p. 59.

CHAPTER 2

1 See James Walvin, *Fruits of Empire: Exotic Produce and British Taste 1660–1800* (London, 1997) and *The Birth of a Consumer Society: The Commercialization of Eighteenth-Century England*, ed. Neil McKendrick, John Brewer, and J. H. Plumb (London, 1982).
2 Wordsworth, *The Prelude*, book 7.
3 First published in *Morning Post*, Aug. 1800; in *Poetical Works* (1806) and *Selected Poems*, ed. Pascoe, p. 352.
4 *The Early Journals and Letters of Fanny Burney*, vol. i, 1768–1773, ed. Lars E. Troide (Oxford, 1988), p. 215.
5 *Memoirs*, p. 37.
6 Burney, *Early Journals*, vol. i, pp. 151, 322.
7 'Retaliation' (1774), in Oliver Goldsmith's *Collected Works*, vol. iv (Oxford, 1966).
8 *Memoirs*, p. 35.
9 *Memoirs*, p. 37.
10 *Memoirs*, p. 38.
11 *Memoirs*, p. 38.
12 *Memoirs*, p. 38.
13 *Memoirs*, p. 39.
14 *Memoirs*, p. 39.
15 [John King], *Letters from Perdita to a Certain Israelite* (1781), p. 7.
16 *Memoirs*, p. 41.
17 *Memoirs*, p. 42.
18 *Memoirs*, p. 42.
19 *Memoirs*, pp. 42–3.
20 *Memoirs*, p. 42.

CHAPTER 3

1 *Memoirs*, p. 43.
2 *Memoirs*, p. 45.
3 *Memoirs*, p. 45.
4 *Memoirs*, p. 46.
5 *Memoirs*, p. 46.
6 *Memoirs*, p. 47.
7 *Memoirs*, p. 48.
8 *Memoirs*, p. 48.
9 *Letters from Perdita to a Certain Israelite, and his Answers to them* (1781), quotations from the correspondence: pp. 17, 19, 22–3, 24–5, 26, 28–9, 32, 34, 35–6, 38–9, 40. The 'Answers' were probably embellished retrospectively for publication, just as Mary's letters may well have been doctored, but their consistency – in terms of dates and details – with Mary's side of the correspondence suggests that King had probably kept copies of his originals.
10 John Taylor, *Records of my Life*, 2 vols (1832), ii, p. 341.
11 *Memoirs*, p. 49.
12 *Memoirs*, p. 49.
13 *Memoirs*, p. 49.
14 *Memoirs*, p. 50.
15 *Memoirs*, p. 50.
16 *Memoirs*, p. 50.
17 *Memoirs*, p. 50.
18 *Memoirs*, p. 50.
19 *Memoirs*, p. 51.
20 *Memoirs*, p. 51.

CHAPTER 4

1 *Letters from Perdita to a Certain Israelite*, pp. 9–10.
2 *Memoirs*, p. 52.
3 Quoted John Brewer, *The Pleasures of the Imagination* (London, 1997), p. 62.
4 *Memoirs*, p. 52.
5 *Memoirs*, p. 52.
6 *London Magazine* (1774), quoted M. J. Levy, notes to *Memoirs*, p. 160.
7 *Memoirs*, p. 53.
8 *Memoirs*, p. 53.
9 *Memoirs*, p. 54.
10 *Memoirs*, p. 54.
11 *Memoirs*, pp. 54–5.
12 *Memoirs*, pp. 55–6.
13 *Memoirs*, p. 56.
14 *Memoirs*, p. 57.
15 *Memoirs*, p. 58.
16 *Memoirs*, p. 59.
17 *Memoirs*, p. 60.
18 *Memoirs*, p. 61.
19 *Memoirs*, p. 63.
20 *Letters from Perdita to a Certain Israelite*, pp. 10–11.
21 *Letters from Perdita to a Certain Israelite*, p. 11.
22 *Memoirs of Perdita* (1784), pp. 21–3.
23 *Memoirs*, p. 64.
24 *Memoirs*, p. 64. Italicized in published text, but not in manuscript.

CHAPTER 5

1 *Memoirs*, p. 67. As in the journals of contemporary novelist Fanny Burney, large chunks of dialogue are recorded verbatim in the *Memoirs*. Mary had a prodigious memory, but the *Memoirs* were written so long after the events of her early life that one may assume a degree of novelist's licence in the dramatization of memories into dialogue.

2 *Memoirs*, p. 68.
3 *Memoirs*, p. 69.
4 *Memoirs*, p. 71.
5 *Memoirs*, p. 72.
6 *Memoirs*, p. 76.
7 *Memoirs*, p. 77.
8 *Memoirs*, p. 78.
9 Laetitia-Matilda Hawkins, *Memoirs, Facts, and Opinions*, 2 vols (1824), ii, p. 25. Hawkins had this information on the authority of the man who took Robinson his weekly guinea.
10 *Memoirs*, pp. 79–80.
11 'The Nightingale, A Conversation Poem', in Samuel Taylor Coleridge, *Poems*, ed. John Beer (London, 1993), p. 196.
12 *Monthly Review*, Sept. 1775.
13 *Poems by Mrs Robinson* (1775), p. 48.
14 *Poems by Mrs Robinson* (1775), pp. 79–82.
15 *Memoirs*, p. 79.
16 *Letters from Perdita to a Certain Israelite*, p. 13.
17 *Captivity, a Poem; And Celadon and Lydia, a Tale* (1777), pp. 20–1.
18 *Memoirs*, p. 80.
19 *Memoirs*, p. 81.
20 *Memoirs*, p. 82.
21 *Memoirs*, p. 83.
22 *Memoirs*, pp. 84–5.

CHAPTER 6

1 *Memoirs*, p. 86.
2 *Memoirs*, p. 87.
3 *Poems* (1791), p. 72.
4 *Memoirs*, p. 87.
5 Fanny Burney, *Evelina* (1779), vol. i, letter 20.
6 *Memoirs*, pp. 87–8.
7 Elizabeth Steele, *Memoirs of Mrs Sophia Baddeley*, 3 vols (Dublin, 1878), ii, 114.
8 *Memoirs*, p. 88.
9 Drury Lane pay list, Folger Shakespeare Library manuscript W.b.319.
10 *Memoirs*, p. 89.
11 See *The London Stage 1660–1800. Part 5: 1776–1800*, vol. i, ed. C. B. Hogan (Carbondale, Ill., 1968), p. 43.
12 *Morning Post*, 11 Dec. 1779.
13 *Morning Post*, 13 Dec. 1779.
14 Quotations from newspapers of 11 Dec. 1779.
15 *Memoirs*, p. 89.
16 Quoted Madeleine Bingham, *Sheridan: The Track of a Comet* (London, 1972), p. 150.
17 *Gazetteer and New Daily Advertiser*, 25 Feb. 1777. The *Morning Post* was more half-hearted.
18 *Memoirs*, p. 90.
19 *Memoirs*, p. 91.
20 *Monthly Review*, Oct. 1777.
21 *Morning Chronicle*, 1 Oct. 1777.
22 *Morning Post*, 1 May 1778; *Morning Chronicle*, 2 May 1778.
23 *The Lucky Escape* (1778), p. 11.
24 *Memoirs*, p. 92.
25 *Morning Post*, 12 Nov. 1778.
26 *Memoirs*, p. 94.
27 *Morning Post*, 11 May 1779.
28 The savagery of the original was watered down in Bickerstaffe's adaptation.
29 *The Laureate. Or, the Right Side of Colley Cibber, Esq. Not Written by Himself* (1740), pp. 92–3.
30 *The Letters of R. B. Sheridan*, ed.

Cecil Price, 3 vols (Oxford, 1966), iii, pp. 296–7.
31 *Memoirs*, pp. 101, 93.
32 *Memoirs*, p. 99.
33 *Angelina, a Novel*, 3 vols (1796), ii, pp. 79–80.

CHAPTER 7

1 *Memoirs*, p. 94.
2 *Memoirs*, p. 96.
3 *Memoirs*, p. 97.
4 *Memoirs*, p. 100.
5 *Morning Post*, 25 and 27 Aug. 1779.
6 *Memoirs*, pp. 98, 100.
7 *Memoirs of Perdita*, p. 142.
8 *Memoirs*, p. 93.
9 *Gazetteer and New Daily Advertiser*, 9 Nov. 1779.
10 *Memoirs*, pp. 100–1.
11 *Morning Chronicle*, 19 Sept. 1779; *Morning Post*, 20 Sept. 1779.
12 *Morning Post*, 11 Oct. 1779.
13 *Morning Post*, 3 Nov. 1779.
14 *Morning Post*, 22 Nov. 1779.
15 *Gazetteer and New Daily Advertiser*, 24 Nov. 1779.
16 *Morning Post*, 25 Nov. 1779.

CHAPTER 8

1 *Memoirs*, p. 104.
2 *Court and Private Life in the Time of Queen Charlotte: Being the Journals of Mrs Papendiek*, ed. Delves Broughton and Mrs Vernon, 2 vols (1887), i, p. 132.
3 *Mary Hamilton at Court and at Home: From Letters and Diaries 1756–1816*, ed. Elizabeth and Florence Anson (London, 1925), pp. 83–4.
4 Quoted in Saul David's excellent biography *Prince of Pleasure: The Prince of Wales and the Making of the Regency* (London, 1998), p. 18.
5 *Memoirs*, p. 101.
6 *Florizel and Perdita. A Dramatic Pastoral, in Three Acts. Alter'd from The Winter's Tale of Shakespear. By David Garrick. As it is performed at the Theatre Royal in Drury-Lane* (1758), act three.
7 *Memoirs*, p. 102.
8 *Memoirs*, p. 102.
9 *Mary Hamilton*, pp. 75–6.
10 Anson Papers, folder 2, Prince of Wales to Mary Hamilton, letters 73, 72.
11 Anson Papers, Prince to Mary Hamilton, letter 74.
12 Anson Papers, Mary Hamilton to Prince, letter 30.
13 Prince to Mary Hamilton, letter 76.
14 *Memoirs*, p. 103.
15 Prince to Mary Hamilton, letter 77.
16 Prince to Mary Hamilton, letter 78.
17 Mary Hamilton to Prince, letter 34.
18 *Memoirs*, p. 104.
19 *Morning Post*, 12 Feb. 1780.
20 *Memoirs*, p. 105. The original manuscript has '~~attachment~~ adoration'.
21 *Morning Chronicle*, 28 Jan. 1780.
22 'Anecdotes concerning His Royal Highness the Prince of Wales by Georgiana Duchess of Devonshire', in *Georgiana: Extracts from the Correspondence of Georgiana, Duchess of*

Devonshire, ed. Earl of Bessborough (London, 1955), p. 290.
23 *Memoirs*, p. 105.
24 *Memoirs*, p. 106.
25 *Morning Post*, 5 Apr. 1780.
26 *Morning Post*, 19 Apr. 1780.
27 *Memoirs*, p. 109.
28 *Town and Country Magazine*, June 1780, p. 235.
29 *Rambler's Magazine*, Apr. 1783, pp. 159–60.
30 *Town and Country Magazine*, p. 236.
31 *Georgiana: Extracts from the Correspondence*, p. 290.
32 *Memoirs of Perdita*, p. 38.
33 Reported in *The Last Journals of Horace Walpole during the Reign of George III*, ed. A. Francis Steuart, 2 vols (London, 1910), ii, p. 361.
34 *Morning Post*, 3 May 1780.
35 *Memoirs*, p. 114.
36 Letter in 'Continuation' of *Memoirs*, p. 112.
37 Note by A. A. Barkas, Richmond librarian, quoted in M. J. Levy, *The Mistresses of King George IV* (London, 1996), p. 24.
38 *Memoirs*, p. 112.
39 *Morning Chronicle*, 27 May 1780. There was another rave review in the *London Courant*, 29 May 1780.
40 Letter of 28 May 1780, in *The Yale Edition of Horace Walpole's Correspondence*, ed. W. S. Lewis, vol. xxix (New Haven, 1955), p. 44.
41 Some sources, including the usually reliable *Biographical Dictionary of Actors, Actresses, Musicians, Dancers, Managers and Other Stage Personnel in London, 1660–1800*, ed. Philip H. Highfill Jr, K. A. Burnim, and E. A. Langhans, vol. xiii (Carbondale, Ill., 1991), incorrectly claim that Mary returned to the stage in 1783; this is because they confuse her with another actress named Mrs Robinson (who later became Mrs Taylor, the name under which her career is given in the *Biographical Dictionary*).
42 *Memoirs*, p. 113.

CHAPTER 9

1 Letter of 1783 in 'Continuation' of *Memoirs*, p. 116.
2 *Morning Post*, 18 July 1780.
3 *Morning Post*, 20, 22 July 1780.
4 *Memoirs*, p. 113.
5 *Memoirs*, pp. 113–14.
6 'Present State of the Manners, Society, etc. etc. of the Metropolis of England', *Monthly Magazine*, Aug. 1800, pp. 35, 37 (published anonymously but Mary claimed authorship in a letter to R. K. Porter, Pforzheimer Misc. MS 2290).
7 *Morning Post*, 9 Aug. 1780.
8 *The Correspondence of George, Prince of Wales 1770–1812*, ed. A. Aspinall, i, p. 34.
9 *Correspondence of George, Prince of Wales*, i, pp. 35–6.
10 'Anecdotes concerning His Royal Highness', in *Georgiana: Extracts from the Correspondence*, p. 289.
11 *Lady Bessborough and her Family Circle*, ed. Earl of Bessborough and A. Aspinall (London, 1940), p. 33.

12 Recorded by the apprentice, J. T. Smith, in *A Book for a Rainy Day* (1845), repr. in C. R. Leslie and T. Taylor, *The Life and Times of Sir Joshua Reynolds*, 2 vols (1865), ii, p. 346.
13 Now in the Harvard Theatre Collection.
14 Laetitia-Matilda Hawkins, *Memoirs, Facts, and Opinions*, ii, p. 30.
15 Hawkins, *Memoirs, Facts, and Opinions*, ii, p. 31.
16 *Georgiana: Extracts from the Correspondence*, p. 290.
17 Elizabeth Steele, *Memoirs of Mrs Sophia Baddeley*, 6 vols (1787), vi, p. 175.
18 *Memoirs of Mrs Sophia Baddeley*, vi, pp. 178–9.
19 *Morning Post*, 27 Sept. 1780.
20 *Morning Post*, 28 Sept. 1780.
21 *Morning Post*, 30 Sept. 1780.
22 *Morning Post*, 2 Oct. 1780.
23 *Morning Post*, 9 Oct. 1780.
24 *Morning Post*, 7 Oct. 1780.
25 *Morning Post*, 11 Nov. 1780.
26 *Morning Post*, 6 Nov. 1780.
27 *Memoirs*, p. 117.
28 *A Satire on the Present Times* (1780), pp. 11–12.
29 *Morning Post*, 16 Nov. 1780.
30 *Morning Post*, 16 Dec. 1780.
31 *Correspondence of George, Prince of Wales*, i, p. 37.
32 *Memoirs*, p. 115.
33 *Memoirs*, p. 117.
34 *Memoirs*, p. 115.
35 *Memoirs*, p. 115.
36 *Memoirs*, p. 116.
37 *Memoirs*, p. 119.

CHAPTER 10

1 *Town and Country Magazine*, Jan. 1781, pp. 8–11.
2 *Georgiana: Extracts from the Correspondence*, p. 290.
3 *Memoirs*, p. 118.
4 *Morning Herald*, 3, 4 Apr. 1781.
5 *Memoirs*, p. 118.
6 *Morning Herald*, 30 Dec. 1780.
7 *Morning Herald*, 4 Jan. 1781.
8 *Morning Herald*, 5 Jan. 1781.
9 *Morning Herald*, 17 Jan. 1781.
10 *Morning Herald*, 4 Apr. 1781.
11 *Poetical Epistle from Florizel to Perdita: with Perdita's Answer. And a Preliminary Discourse upon the Education of Princes* (1781), pp. 1–25.
12 *Poetical Epistle*, p. 17.
13 *Morning Herald*, 15 Feb. 1781.
14 *Morning Herald*, 22 Jan., 8 Feb. 1781.
15 *Morning Herald*, 19, 20 Feb. 1781.
16 *Georgiana: Extracts from the Correspondence*, p. 292.
17 *Correspondence of George, Prince of Wales*, i, p. 55.
18 *Morning Post*, 16 Mar. 1781.
19 *Morning Herald*, 16 Apr. 1781.
20 *Morning Herald*, 21 Mar. 1781.
21 *Morning Post*, 29 Mar. 1781.
22 *Authentic Memoirs, Memorandums, and Confessions. Taken from the Journal of his Predatorial Majesty, the King of the Swindlers* (n.d.), pp. 106–12.
23 *The Budget of Love; or, Letters between Florizel and Perdita* (1781), p. vi.
24 *Budget of Love*, pp. 18, 35.
25 *Budget of Love*, pp. 37–8.
26 *Morning Herald*, 18 Apr. 1781.

27 So described in *Town and Country Magazine*, Apr. 1781, p. 210.
28 *Correspondence of George, Prince of Wales*, i, p. 56.
29 *Morning Post*, 14 Apr. 1781.
30 *Morning Herald*, 3 May 1781.
31 *Rambler's Magazine*, Jan. 1783, pp. 17–19.
32 *Morning Herald*, 4 May 1781.
33 *Morning Herald*, 21 May 1781.
34 *Morning Herald*, 3 May 1781.
35 *Morning Herald*, 11 June 1781.
36 *Morning Herald*, 12 June 1781.
37 *Lady's Magazine*, June 1781, p. 287.
38 *Morning Herald*, 13 June 1781.
39 *Morning Herald*, 21 June 1781.

CHAPTER 11

1 *Morning Herald*, 21 June 1781.
2 *Morning Herald*, 2 July 1781.
3 *Memoirs of Perdita*, p. 165.
4 *Morning Herald*, 5 July 1781.
5 *Morning Herald*, 4 July 1781.
6 *Correspondence of George, Prince of Wales*, i, pp. 66–7.
7 Letter dated 17 July 1781.
8 *Morning Herald*, 12 July 1781.
9 *Morning Post*, 14 July 1781.
10 *Morning Post*, 18 July 1781.
11 *Morning Post*, 18 July 1781.
12 *Correspondence of George, Prince of Wales*, i, p. 60.
13 Colonel Hotham to Lord Malden, 31 July 1781, Capell Manuscript M274, Hertfordshire Archives and Local Studies.
14 Lord Malden to the Prince of Wales, 4 Aug. 1781, Capell M275.
15 Malden to the Prince of Wales, Capell M275.
16 Hotham to Malden, Capell M280.
17 Malden to Prince, Capell M277.
18 Hotham to Malden, Capell M282.
19 Southampton to Malden, Capell M289.
20 *Morning Post*, 4 Aug. 1781.
21 *Morning Herald*, 5 Aug. 1781.
22 Mary Robinson to the Prince of Wales, Capell M280.
23 Malden to Prince, Capell M284.
24 Malden to Hotham, Capell M285.
25 *Morning Herald*, 14 Aug. 1781.
26 *Morning Herald*, 16 Aug. 1781.
27 Hotham to Malden, 23 Aug. 1781, Capell M290.
28 Hotham to Malden, 28 Aug. 1781, Capell M294.
29 Mary Robinson to Lord Malden, 29 Aug. 1781, Capell M295.
30 *Correspondence of George III 1760–December 1783*, ed. Sir John Fortescue, 6 vols (London, 1927–8), v, pp. 269–70.
31 Lord Glenbervie's *Diaries*, quoted M. J. Levy, *The Mistresses of King George IV*, p. 38.
32 Hotham to Malden, Capell M295.
33 Mary Robinson to John Taylor, 5 Oct. 1794, first printed in *Catalogue of the Collection of Autograph Letters and Historical Documents formed between 1865 and 1882 by Alfred Morrison*, vol. v (1891), p. 286.
34 *Morning Herald*, 11 Sept. 1781.
35 *Morning Herald*, 25 Aug. 1781.
36 Jonathan Jones, 'The Hidden Story', *Guardian Weekend*, 19 Oct. 2002, p. 32, reviewing Tate Britain's Gainsborough exhibition (in which the portrait did not appear, since the Wallace Collection cannot lend its paintings).

37 *Morning Herald*, 11 Sept. 1781.
38 *Morning Herald*, 18 Sept. 1781.
39 *Morning Herald*, 2 Oct. 1781.
40 *Morning Herald*, 9 Oct. 1781.
41 *Morning Herald*, 19 Oct. 1781.
42 *Morning Herald*, 21 Oct. 1781.
43 *Morning Herald*, 31 Oct. 1781.

CHAPTER 12

1 *Memoirs*, p. 121.
2 See Antonia Fraser, *Marie Antoinette* (London, 2001), p. 153.
3 *Morning Herald*, 1 Dec. 1781.
4 *Memoirs*, p. 122.
5 See Fraser, *Marie Antoinette*, pp. 137–8.
6 *Memoirs*, p. 123.
7 *Monody to the Memory of Marie Antoinette Queen of France, written immediately after her Execution* (1793).
8 Jane Porter, 'Character of the Late Mrs Robinson', Pforzheimer Misc. MS 2296.
9 *Memoirs*, p. 121.
10 *Memoirs of the Duc de Lauzun*, trans. C. K. Scott Moncrieff (London, 1928), p. 211.
11 *Memoirs of Lauzun*, p. 211.
12 M. R., 'Memoirs of the late Duc de Biron', *Monthly Magazine*, Feb. 1800, p. 45.
13 'Additional Anecdotes of Philip Egalité late Duke of Orleans, by one who knew him intimately', *Monthly Magazine*, Aug. 1800, p. 39.
14 *Morning Herald*, 6 Dec. 1781.
15 *Morning Herald*, 12 Dec. 1781.
16 *Morning Herald*, 7 Dec. 1781.
17 Reported in *Morning Herald*, 29 Dec. 1781.
18 *Morning Herald*, 1 Jan. 1782.
19 *Morning Herald*, 9 Jan. 1782.
20 *Memoirs of Perdita*, p. 105.
21 Claire Brock, '"Then smile and know thyself supremely great": Mary Robinson and the "splendour of a name"', *Women's Writing*, 9 (2002), p. 112.
22 *Memoirs of Perdita*, p. 28.
23 *Morning Herald*, 18 Jan. 1781.
24 James Parton, *The Life of General Andrew Jackson* (1861), quoted Robert D. Bass, *The Green Dragoon* (New York, 1957, repr. Columbia, SC, 1973), p. 3.

CHAPTER 13

1 In *Brother Tom to Brother Peter*, satirical pamphlet of 1789, pp. 55–9.
2 *Ainsi va le Monde*, quoted from *Poems* (1791), pp. 200–1.
3 Letter of 18 Dec. 1790, printed in *Memoirs of the Late Mrs Robinson, Written by Herself, – with some posthumous pieces*, 4 vols (1801), iv, pp. 191–2.
4 James Northcote, *The Life of Sir Joshua Reynolds*, 2 vols (1818), i, p. 102. My account is heavily indebted to Nicholas Penny (ed.), *Reynolds* (Royal Academy exhibition catalogue, London, 1986).
5 There is a list of eighty-one images (including a handful of caricatures) at the end of the Mary Robinson entry in *A Biographical Dictionary of Actors, Actresses, Musicians, Dancers, Managers and Other Stage Personnel in London, 1660–1800*,

vol. xiii. It provides a useful starting point for study, but is incomplete and sometimes inaccurate. One especially interesting image is 'The British Sappho', attributed to the age's leading female artist, Angelica Kauffmann, reproduced in Joseph Grego, '"Perdita" and her Painters: Portraits of Mrs Mary Robinson', *The Connoisseur*, Feb. 1903, pp. 99–107, but the attribution is uncertain and it is not even clear that the sitter was Robinson.

6 *Public Advertiser*, 19 Apr. 1782.

7 *Conversations of James Northcote R.A. with James Ward*, ed. E. Fletcher (London, 1901), p. 59.

8 *The Widow* (1794), i, p. 158.

9 *Morning Herald*, 18 Jan. 1782.

10 *Morning Herald*, 25 Jan. 1782.

11 *Morning Herald*, 30 Jan. 1782.

12 *Morning Herald*, 4 Mar. 1782.

13 *Lady's Magazine*, July 1780, p. 363.

14 *Morning Herald*, 8 Mar., 9 Apr., 22 Apr. 1782.

15 *Morning Herald*, 20 Apr. 1782.

16 *Morning Herald*, 23 Mar. 1782.

17 *Public Advertiser*, 19 Apr. 1782.

18 Robert Huish, *Memoirs of George the Fourth*, 2 vols (1831), i, p. 74.

19 *Morning Herald*, 29, 30 May 1782.

20 *Memoirs of Perdita*, pp. 160–2.

21 *Morning Herald*, 4 June 1782.

22 *Morning Herald*, 7, 8, 10 June 1782.

23 *Morning Herald*, 23 July 1782.

24 *Morning Herald*, 31 July 1782.

25 John Clarke, *The Life and Times of George III* (London, 1972), p. 106.

26 Banastre Tarleton to Thomas Tarleton, Liverpool Record Office, 920 TAR 13 (11).

27 *Morning Post*, 7 Aug. 1782.

28 *Morning Herald*, 17 Aug. 1782.

29 *The Festival of Wit* (1783), p. 129.

30 *Last Journals of Horace Walpole*, ed. Steuart, i, p. 515.

31 *Morning Post*, 29 Aug. 1782.

32 *Morning Herald*, 3 Sept. 1782.

33 *Life and Letters of Lady Sarah Lennox*, ed. Countess of Ilchester, 2 vols (London, 1901), ii, pp. 25–6.

34 *Morning Herald*, 19 Sept. 1782.

35 *The Yale Edition of Horace Walpole's Correspondence*, ed. W. S. Lewis, vol. xxxv (New Haven, 1973), p. 523, letter of 7 Sept. 1782.

36 *Morning Herald*, 16 Sept. 1782.

37 *Morning Post*, 21 Sept. 1784.

38 *Morning Post*, 24 Sept. 1782.

39 *Morning Herald*, 30 Sept. 1782.

40 *Morning Herald*, 21 Oct. 1782.

CHAPTER 14

1 *Lady's Magazine*, Apr. 1782, p. 195.

2 See for example the usually reliable Aileen Ribeiro, *The Art of Dress: Fashion in England and France, 1780–1820* (New Haven, 1995), p. 71.

3 *Morning Herald*, 15 Oct. 1782.

4 *Morning Herald*, 20 Nov. 1782.

5 *Morning Herald*, 21 Nov. 1782.

6 Claire Brock, '"Then smile and know thyself supremely great": Mary Robinson and the "splendour of a name"', p. 114 (citing *Rambler's Magazine*, Jan. 1783).

7 *Morning Chronicle*, 28 Nov. 1782.

8 *Lady's Magazine*, Apr. 1783, p. 187; May 1783, p. 268; July 1787, p. 331.
9 *Jane Austen's Letters*, ed. Deirdre Le Faye (Oxford, 1995), p. 70.
10 *Monthly Magazine and British Register*, Sept. 1800, p. 138. See further, chapter 5 of Judith Pascoe's excellent *Romantic Theatricality: Gender, Poetry, and Spectatorship*.
11 *Lady's Magazine*, Mar. 1784, p. 154.
12 *Lady's Magazine*, Apr.–Dec. 1783, pp. 187, 268, 651.
13 *Lady's Magazine*, Dec. 1783, p. 650.
14 *Morning Post*, 28 Dec. 1799.
15 *Morning Post*, 3 Jan. 1800.
16 *Morning Post*, 23 Dec. 1782.
17 *Morning Herald*, 4 Dec. 1782.
18 *Morning Herald*, 5 Dec. 1782.
19 *Morning Herald*, 31 Dec. 1782.
20 *Morning Herald*, 23 Dec. 1782; *Morning Post*, 24 Dec. 1782.
21 *Morning Herald*, 2 Jan. 1783.
22 *Morning Herald*, 4 Jan. 1783.
23 'Amorous and Bon Ton Intelligence', 20 Jan. 1783, in *Rambler's Magazine*, Feb. 1783.
24 *Morning Herald*, 20 Jan. 1783.
25 *Rambler's Magazine*, May 1783.
26 *Morning Herald*, 5 Feb. 1783.
27 *Morning Herald*, 24 Feb. 1783.
28 *Morning Herald*, 2 Feb. 1783.
29 *Morning Herald*, 14 Mar. 1783.
30 *Morning Herald*, 5 Mar. 1783.
31 *Morning Herald*, 11 Mar. 1783.
32 *Morning Herald*, 25 Mar. 1783.
33 *Rambler's Magazine*, Jan. 1783, pp. 8–9.
34 *Rambler's Magazine*, Apr. 1783, p. 134.
35 *Morning Herald*, 21 May 1783.
36 *The Celestial Beds; Or, a Review of the Votaries of the Temple of Health, Adelphi, and the Temple of Hymen, Pall-Mall* (1781), p. 26. See further, Tim Fulford, 'The Electrifying Mrs Robinson', *Women's Writing*, 9 (2002), pp. 23–35.
37 *Walsingham; or, the Pupil of Nature*, ed. Julie Shaffer (Peterborough, Ont., 2003), p. 222.
38 *Walsingham*, p. 223.
39 *Morning Herald*, 24 May 1783.
40 *Rambler's Magazine*: 'Amorous and Bon Ton Intelligence', 18 Mar. 1783.
41 Tarleton Family Papers, Liverpool Record Office, 920 TAR 13 (12).
42 *Morning Herald*, 9 May 1783.
43 *Morning Herald*, 16 June 1783.
44 *Morning Post*, 29 May 1783.
45 *The Vis-à-Vis of Berkley-Square* (1783), dedication dated 14 June, pp. 19, 24n.
46 *Morning Herald*, 24 June 1783.
47 Tarleton Family Papers, Liverpool Record Office, 920 TAR 13 (9).
48 Tarleton Family Papers, Liverpool Record Office, 920 TAR 14 (18).
49 Tarleton Family Papers, Liverpool Record Office, 920 TAR 14 (19).
50 *Morning Herald*, 12 July 1783.
51 Hawkins, *Memoirs, Facts, and Opinions*, ii, p. 33.

CHAPTER 15

1 *Eccentric Biography; or, Memoirs of Remarkable Female Characters* (1803), p. 290.
2 *Memoirs*, p. 123.
3 *Eccentric Biography*, p. 290

(erroneously stating that the journey took place in winter).
4 *Eccentric Biography*, p. 290.
5 *Memoirs*, pp. 123–4.
6 I am most grateful to Dr Chris Clark for assistance with diagnosis and information from *Fundamentals of Surgical Practice*.
7 *Poetical Works* (1824 edn), p. 4.
8 *Pembroke Papers (1780–1794): Letters and Diaries of Henry, Tenth Earl of Pembroke and his Circle*, ed. Lord Herbert, 2 vols (London, 1950), i, p. 227.
9 Banastre Tarleton to Jane Tarleton, 25 July 1783, Liverpool Record Office, 920 TAR 13 (25).
10 *Memoirs*, p. 121.
11 *The Correspondence of George, Prince of Wales 1770–1812*, i, p. 305.
12 23 Sept. 1783, Liverpool Record Office, 920 TAR 13 (26).
13 *Morning Herald*, 22 Oct. 1783; 'Amorous and Bon Ton Intelligence', 30 Oct. 1783, in *Rambler's Magazine*.
14 'Amorous and Bon Ton Intelligence', Nov. 1783, in *Rambler's Magazine*.
15 *Rambler's Magazine*, Nov. 1783, p. 362.
16 *Memoirs*, p. 124.
17 *Morning Herald*, 21 Jan. 1784.
18 *Morning Herald*, 22 Dec. 1783.
19 *Morning Herald*, 26 Jan. 1784.
20 *Morning Herald*, 22 Jan. 1784.
21 *Morning Herald*, 27 Jan. 1784.
22 'Amorous and Bon Ton Intelligence', 4 Feb. 1784, in *Rambler's Magazine*.
23 *Morning Post*, 28 Mar. 1784.
24 *Oracle*, 30 Nov. 1793.

CHAPTER 16

1 *Memorials and Correspondence of Charles James Fox*, ed. Lord John Russell, 3 vols (1853–4), ii, p. 347.
2 *Morning Post*, 13 Apr. 1784.
3 *Morning Post*, 25 Apr. 1784.
4 *Morning Post*, 26 Apr. 1784.
5 *Morning Herald*, 15 Apr. 1784.
6 J. Hartley, *History of the Westminster Election, containing every material occurrence, from its commencement on the first of April, to the final close* (1784), p. 227.
7 Hartley, *History of the Westminster Election*, p. 231.
8 *Morning Herald*, 7 May 1784.
9 *Morning Herald*, 17 May 1784.
10 *Morning Herald*, 18 May 1784.
11 *London Chronicle*, 20 May 1784.
12 *Morning Herald*, 23 Apr. 1784.
13 *The Amours of Carlo Khan* (1784), pp. 162–3.
14 *Morning Herald*, 10 May 1784.
15 *Morning Post*, 10 June 1784.
16 *Morning Post*, 29 June 1784.
17 *Morning Post*, 13 July 1784.
18 *Morning Post*, 19 July 1784.
19 *Rambler's Magazine*, Aug. 1784, p. 281.
20 Letter bound with MS of *Memoirs* (private collection).
21 *Morning Post*, 13 Aug. 1784.
22 *Morning Post*, 16 Aug. 1784.

CHAPTER 17

1 Tarleton Family Papers, Liverpool Record Office, 920 TAR 14 (15).
2 *Morning Post*, 10 Nov. 1784.
3 Westminster Archives, Broadley Haymarket Collection, 3, p. 187.

4 *Morning Herald*, 11 Feb. 1785.
5 *Morning Herald*, 15 Feb. 1785.
6 Maria Elizabeth Robinson, *The Shrine of Bertha: A Novel*, 2 vols (1794), ii, pp. 127–8.
7 *Morning Herald*, 23 Nov. 1785.
8 *Morning Post*, 14 July 1786.
9 *Morning Post*, 4 Aug. 1786.
10 *Morning Herald*, 10 Jan. 1787.
11 *Memoirs*, p. 130.
12 *Memoirs*, pp. 130–1.
13 *Poetical Works* (1824 edn), p. 189.
14 *The World*, 30 Oct. 1787.
15 *Morning Herald*, 24 Jan. 1788.
16 *Morning Post*, 31 Jan. 1788.
17 *Morning Herald*, 19 Apr. 1788.
18 'The Moralist', in *The English Lyceum, or, Choice of pieces in prose and verse, selected from periodical papers, magazines, pamphlets*, vol. 1 (Hamburg, 1787), p. 376.
19 Pforzheimer Misc. MS 2296.
20 *The Promenade: or, Theatre of Beauty* (Dublin, 1788), p. 24.
21 *Memorials and Correspondence of Charles James Fox*, ii, pp. 299–300.

CHAPTER 18

1 *Memoirs*, p. 131.
2 *Memoirs*, p. 131.
3 *Memoirs*, p. 132.
4 See W. N. Hargreaves-Mawdsley, *The English Della Cruscans and their Time, 1783–1828* (The Hague, 1967), p. 57. This is the best account of the school.
5 July 1787; repr. in *The Poetry of The World*, 2 vols (1788), i, p. 3.
6 *The World*, 31 Oct. 1788.
7 This sequence of poems was repr. in *The British Album*, 2 vols (1790), ii, pp. 137–62.
8 For the meeting of Merry and Cowley, see *The Life and Times of Frederick Reynolds written by himself*, 2 vols (1826), ii, pp. 187–8.
9 *Morning Post*, 15 Apr. 1789.
10 *Memoirs*, pp. 136–7.
11 *Memoirs*, p. 137.
12 *Oracle*, 29 July 1789.
13 *Oracle*, 8, 13 Aug. 1789.
14 See Cowley, 'Armida to Rinaldo', *Oracle*, 5 Jan. 1791; Boaden, 'To Mrs Robinson' ('But Laura still shall dress the lay'), repr. among 'Tributary Poems' in Robinson's *Poetical Works* (1806); Robinson, 'To the Muse of Poetry' (included in *Poems*, 1791).
15 *Memoirs*, p. 136.
16 *Memoirs*, p. 132.
17 *Memoirs*, p. 135.
18 *Memoirs*, pp. 135–6.
19 *Morning Post*, 20 Aug. 1789.
20 *Authentic Memoirs, Memorandums, and Confessions. Taken from the Journal of his Predatorial Majesty, the King of the Swindlers*, pp. 215ff.
21 *Oracle*, 24 Aug. 1789.
22 *Ainsi va le Monde* (1790), p. 16.
23 *Oracle*, 19 July 1791.
24 *Monthly Review*, Apr. 1791, p. 223; *Critical Review*, Jan. 1791, pp. 73–5; *General Magazine*, 4 (1790), p. 548.
25 *The Baviad* (1794), quoted from combined repr. of *The Baviad and Maeviad* (1811), pp. 9–10, 30.
26 Thrale refers to a woman in her early thirties being suddenly struck with palsy: 'A horrible

Thing! And cannot be attributed as poor Lady Derby and the famous Courtesan Perdita's Paralytick Strokes have been, to Venereal Indulgences. I do not believe the Accusation even of them: it was Lord Deerhurst told me, and his veracity is not worth much': *Thraliana*, ed. K. C. Balderston, 2 vols (Oxford, 1951), ii, p. 830.

27 *Baviad and Maeviad*, p. 56n.
28 William Hazlitt, 'Mr Gifford', in *The Spirit of the Age* (1825; repr. Grasmere, 2004), p. 253.
29 *Walsingham*, ed. Shaffer, pp. 228–9.
30 *Walsingham*, ed. Shaffer, p. 230.
31 'To Mrs Robinson', dated 1 Feb. 1791, repr. as first of the 'Tributary Poems' in Robinson's posthumous *Poetical Works* (1806).
32 *Oracle*, 5, 9 May 1791.
33 *Oracle*, 16 May 1791.
34 *Oracle*, 17 May 1791.
35 16 June 1793, Bristol Central Library (uncatalogued manuscript).
36 *Critical Review*, 3 (1791), p. 353; *English Review*, 18 (1791), pp. 229–30.
37 *The Beauties of Mrs Robinson. Selected and Arranged from her Poetical Works* (1791), pp. iii–v.
38 *Analytical Review*, 10 (1791), pp. 279–83; *Monthly Review*, 6 (1791), pp. 448–50.
39 *Critical Review*, 2 (1791), pp. 109–14.
40 *English Review*, 19 (1792), pp. 42–6.
41 *Poems* (1791), p. 60.

CHAPTER 19

1 *Memoirs*, pp. 137–8.
2 *Oracle*, June 1791, repr. as 'Tributary Poem' in Robinson's *Poetical Works* (1806).
3 *Memoirs*, p. 138; *Oracle*, 12 July 1791.
4 *Oracle*, 12, 13 July, 9 Aug. 1791.
5 *Memoirs*, p. 138.
6 *Memoirs*, p. 139.
7 21 May 1800, *Collected Letters of Samuel Taylor Coleridge*, ed. E. L. Griggs, vol. i (Oxford, 1956), p. 589.
8 I am grateful to Adam Sisman for correcting an error at this point in the hardback edition (see *TLS* Letters 3 Dec, 2004).
9 Repr. in *Selected Poems*, ed. Pascoe, pp. 122–6.
10 *Poems* (1791), p. 14; *Poems* (1793), p. 52.
11 Keats, 'To a Nightingale' (1819); Robinson, 'Ode to Apathy', *Morning Post*, 1 July 1800.
12 *Morning Post*, 6 Sept. 1800. On Mary's opium poems, see further M. J. Levy, 'Coleridge, Mary Robinson and *Kubla Khan*', *Charles Lamb Bulletin*, 77 (1992), pp. 156–66.
13 *Angelina*, ii, pp. 270, 286, 107.
14 Edmund Burke, *Reflections on the Revolution in France*, ed. Conor Cruise O'Brien (Harmondsworth, 1968), pp. 169–70.
15 *Parliamentary History of England* (1806–20), xxix, p. 248.
16 *Impartial Reflections on the Present Situation of the Queen of France by a Friend to Humanity* (1791), pp. 6, 14, 24.

17 *Impartial Reflections*, pp. 17–18.
18 *Impartial Reflections*, pp. 19, 27.
19 *Vancenza; or, the Dangers of Credulity*, 2 vols (1792), i, pp. 17–18.
20 *Jane Austen's Letters*, p. 335.
21 *Vancenza*, i, pp. 41–2.
22 *Vancenza*, i, p. 70.
23 *Vancenza*, i, pp. 70–1.
24 *Vancenza*, ii, pp. 85–6.
25 *Vancenza*, ii, pp. 26–7.
26 *Vancenza*, ii, p. 96.
27 *Oracle*, 15 Feb. 1792.
28 'Stanzas written on the Fourteenth of February, 1792, to My Valentine', *Poems* (1793), pp. 138–9.
29 *Vancenza*, ii, p. 131.
30 *European Magazine*, 21 (1792), pp. 344–8. This was the review that also compared Elvira to Mrs Robinson's daughter.
31 *Monthly Review*, 7 (1792), pp. 298–303.
32 *English Review*, 20 (1792), pp. 111–13.
33 *Critical Review*, 4 (1792), pp. 268–72.
34 *Oracle*, 6 Mar. 1792.
35 Letter to John Taylor, 5 Oct. 1794, repr. in *Selected Poems*, ed. Pascoe, p. 366.
36 Widener Library, Harvard University (partially printed in Percy Fitzgerald, *The Lives of the Sheridans*, 2 vols (1886), i, p. 148n., but full text previously unpublished).
37 *Oracle*, 2 Aug. 1792, repr. *Poems* (1793), pp. 70–3.
38 *Memoirs*, p. 142.
39 Mary Elizabeth Robinson, *The Shrine of Bertha*, ii, pp. 107–10, with footnote attesting 'This anecdote is a fact.' The monument was later destroyed along with the wall of the old pier.
40 *Oracle*, 28 Aug. 1792.
41 *Memoirs*, p. 142.
42 *Oracle*, 30 Nov. 1792, repr. *Poems* (1793), pp. 62–4.
43 *Poems* (1793), pp. 221–6.

CHAPTER 20

1 *Oracle*, 20 Oct. 1792.
2 *Oracle*, 26 Jan. 1793.
3 *Oracle*, 26 Jan. 1793.
4 *An Ode to the Harp of the late accomplished and amiable Louisa Hanway*, published as a pamphlet (1793) and in *Oracle* on 15 Jan. 1793.
5 *Diary*, 19 Jan. 1793.
6 *Oracle*, 10 Jan., 23 Mar., 5 Apr., 30 Oct. 1793.
7 James Boaden, *Memoirs of Mrs Siddons*, 2 vols (1827), i, p. 79.
8 Letter from Sarah Siddons to John Taylor, spring 1800.
9 John Taylor, *Verses on Various Occasions* (1795).
10 *Oracle*, 16 July, 29 Mar., 23 July, 28 Nov. 1793.
11 *Memoirs*, p. 144.
12 *Oracle*, 9 Nov. 1793.
13 *Modern Manners: a Poem in two Cantos*, by Horace Juvenal (1793), pp. 15–16.
14 *Monthly Review*, Sept. 1794; *Morning Post*, 3 Aug. 1794.
15 Joseph Farington's diary, 1 Dec. 1793.

16 *Poems* (1793), p. 205.
17 *Critical Review*, 10 (1794), pp. 382–4.
18 *English Review*, 23 (1794), pp. 458–62.
19 Coleridge, *Collected Letters*, i, p. 562.
20 *Oracle*, 8 Jan. 1794.
21 Dated 9 Jan. 1794; among 'Tributary Poems' in Robinson's *Poetical Works*.
22 *Morning Post*, 13 Feb. 1794.
23 *The Widow, or a Picture of Modern Times: A Novel in a Series of Letters*, 2 vols (1794), i, p. 161.
24 *The Widow*, i, pp. 4–5.
25 *The Widow*, ii, p. 76; i, pp. 92, 168.
26 *The Widow*, ii, pp. 173–4.
27 *Monthly Review*, May 1794, p. 38; *Analytical Review*, 18 (1794), p. 453.
28 *The Widow*, i, p. 22.
29 *The Widow*, i, pp. 151–3.
30 *Oracle*, 2 May 1794; *Morning Post*, 14 Oct. 1794.
31 *Oracle*, 26 Feb. 1794.
32 Mary Elizabeth Robinson, *The Shrine of Bertha*, ii, p. 95.
33 Mary Robinson to John Taylor, summer 1794, private collection (Robert Woof).
34 *Oracle*, 22 Sept. 1794.
35 *Monthly Review*, Sept. 1794, p. 108.
36 Charles Pigott, *The Whig Club; or, a Sketch of Modern Patriotism* (1794), p. 208.
37 Charles Pigott, *The Female Jockey Club; or, a Sketch of the Manners of the Age* (1792), p. 84.
38 *Oracle*, 10 Sept. 1794.

CHAPTER 21

1 Robinson to Taylor, 5 Oct. 1794, in *Selected Poems*, ed. Pascoe, pp. 365–7.
2 Robinson to Taylor, 13 Oct. 1794, in *Catalogue of the Collection of Autograph Letters and Historical Documents formed between 1865 and 1882 by Alfred Morrison*, v, p. 287.
3 Robinson to Taylor, 14 Oct. 1794, Folger Shakespeare Library, W.b.112.
4 William Hazlitt, *Works*, ed. P. P. Howe, 21 vols (London, 1930–4), v, p. 252; John Genest, *Some Account of the English Stage 1660–1830*, 10 vols (Bath, 1832), viii, p. 431.
5 All *Nobody* quotations from Larpent manuscript, Huntington Library, San Marino, California.
6 *Memoirs*, p. 143.
7 Prologue and epilogue were published in the *London Chronicle*, 1 Dec. 1794.
8 *Memoirs*, p. 143.
9 *The London Stage 1660–1800, Part 5*, vol. iii, ed. C. B. Hogan (Carbondale, Ill., 1968), p. 1707.
10 Quoted Claire Tomalin, *Mrs Jordan's Profession* (London, 1994), p. 146.
11 *London Chronicle*, 1 Dec. 1794.
12 *London Chronicle*, 1 Dec. 1794.
13 *London Chronicle*, 2 Dec. 1794; *Morning Post*, 8 Dec. 1794.
14 *London Chronicle*, 9 Dec. 1794.
15 'January, 1795', *Morning Post*, 29 Jan. 1795.
16 Letter of 4 July 1795, in *Collection of Autograph Letters*, v, p. 288.
17 *Oracle*, 4 Sept. 1795.

18 *Oracle*, 16 Oct. 1795.
19 *Angelina*, i, pp. 55, 56, 155; ii, pp. 71–2.
20 *Oracle*, 23 Jan. 1796; *Critical Review*, 16 (1796), p. 397.
21 *Critical Review*, 16 (1796), p. 398.
22 *Monthly Mirror*, 1 (1795–6), p. 290.
23 *Angelina*, i, p. 86.
24 *Angelina*, i, pp. 204, 219.
25 *Angelina*, ii, pp. 79–80.
26 *Angelina*, ii, p. 49; iii, p. 102.
27 *Analytical Review*, 23 (1796), pp. 293–4.
28 *Angelina*, i, pp. 56, 84.
29 Preface to *Poetical Works* (1806).
30 Printed among 'Tributary Poems' in *Poetical Works* (1806).
31 See Jan Fergus and J. F. Thaddeus, 'Women, Publishers, and Money, 1790–1820', *Studies in Eighteenth-Century Culture*, 17 (1987), pp. 191–207.
32 *The Sicilian Lover: a Tragedy in Five Acts* (1796), 2. 3; 3. 1.
33 *Monthly Review*, 19 (1796), p. 312.
34 *Oracle*, 27 Aug. 1796. *The Widow* was reissued in Leipzig with the new title *Julia St Lawrence*.
35 Hawkins, *Memoirs*, ii, p. 34.

CHAPTER 22

1 C. Kegan Paul, *William Godwin: His Friends and Contemporaries*, 2 vols (London, 1876), i, p. 154.
2 End of Bk 2nd, *Poetical Works* (1824 reprint), p. 176. This was one of Mary's last poems, testimony to the endurance of her Godwinianism.
3 Paul, *Godwin*, i, p. 162.
4 Godwin's diary is now in the Abinger Deposit, Bodleian Library, Oxford.
5 Preface to *Sappho and Phaon, a series of legitimate Sonnets, with Thoughts on Poetical Subjects, & Anecdotes of the Grecian Poetess* (1796).
6 'To the Reader', in *Sappho and Phaon*.
7 Sonnet IV, in *Sappho and Phaon*.
8 Sonnet XIII, in *Sappho and Phaon*.
9 'Anthony Pasquin' (John Williams), *The New Brighton Guide* (London, 1796), p. 53.
10 *Hubert de Sevrac: A Romance of the Eighteenth Century*, 3 vols (1796), i, p. 14.
11 Mary Wollstonecraft's phrase, in her review of the novel.
12 *Walsingham*, ed. Shaffer, p. 218.
13 *Critical Review*, 23 (1798), p. 472.
14 *Analytical Review*, 25 (1797), p. 523.
15 *Oracle*, 12 Dec. 1796.
16 *Monthly Magazine*, 4 (1797), p. 121.
17 Wollstonecraft to Godwin, 12 Dec. 1796, *Collected Letters of Mary Wollstonecraft*, ed. Janet Todd (London, 2003), p. 383.
18 Wollstonecraft to Godwin, 13 Dec. 1796, *Letters*, pp. 383–4.
19 Wollstonecraft to Hays, Jan. 1797, *Letters*, p. 393.
20 Wollstonecraft, *Letters*, p. 387.
21 *Fleetwood* (1805), in *Collected Novels of William Godwin*, vol. v, ed. Pamela Clemit (London, 1992), pp. 220–1.
22 *Oracle*, 30 May 1797.
23 The *Oracle* records her departure from London on 6 April and has

her still confined on the Bath road on 8 May.
24 'Lines written on a sick-bed, 1797'.
25 *Oracle*, 17 Oct. 1797.
26 *Walsingham*, ed. Shaffer, p. 119.
27 *Walsingham*, ed. Shaffer, p. 129.
28 *Anti-Jacobin Review*, 1 (1798), pp. 160–4.
29 T. J. Mathias, *Pursuits of Literature* (9th edn, revised, Dublin, 1799), p. 58.
30 Richard Polwhele, *The Unsex'd Females: A Poem* (London, 1798), p. 16.
31 Polwhele, *Unsex'd Females*, p. 17n.
32 *Walsingham*, ed. Shaffer, p. 216.
33 *Telegraph*, 11 Feb. 1797.
34 Quoted *Essays on his Times in the Morning Post and the Courier*, ed. David V. Erdman, *The Collected Works of Samuel Taylor Coleridge*, 3 vols (Princeton and London, 1978), i, p. lxvii.
35 See obituary of Stuart, *Gentleman's Magazine*, NS 28 (1847), pp. 322–4.
36 Quoted Coleridge, *Essays on his Times*, i, p. lxxii.
37 *Morning Post*, 17 Apr. 1798.
38 This was Coleridge's retainer for weekly contributions of 'verses or political essays'. Given her greater prominence, Robinson may well have been in a position to hold out for more.
39 See Robert Woof, 'Wordsworth's Poetry and Stuart's Newspapers: 1797–1803', *Studies in Bibliography*, 15 (1962), pp. 149–89.
40 *Memoirs*, p. 146.
41 *Morning Post*, 7 Dec. 1797.
42 *Morning Post*, 9 Jan. 1798.
43 *Morning Post*, 3 Jan. 1798.
44 *Walsingham*, ed. Shaffer, pp. 59–60; *Morning Post*, 26 Dec. 1797.
45 *Morning Post*, 18 Jan. 1798.
46 *Oracle*, 25 Jan. 1798.
47 *Morning Post*, 20 Jan. 1798.
48 *Morning Post*, 28 Feb. 1798.
49 *Morning Post*, 19 May 1798.
50 *Morning Post*, 23 Apr. 1798.
51 *Oracle*, 22 May; *Morning Post*, 30 May 1798.
52 *Morning Post*, 21 June 1798.
53 *Oracle*, 7, 28 Apr.; *Morning Post*, 15 May 1798.
54 *Morning Post*, 2 May 1798.

CHAPTER 23

1 *Morning Post*, 18 Feb. 1799.
2 *Morning Post*, 22 Feb.; *Oracle*, 28 Feb. 1799.
3 *Monthly Magazine*, 7 (1799), p. 541; *Analytical Review*, NS 1 (1799), p. 209.
4 *The False Friend, a Domestic Story*, 4 vols (1799), i, p. 158.
5 *The False Friend*, i, p. 42; ii, p. 177.
6 *The False Friend*, ii, p. 78.
7 *Monthly Mirror*, 7 (1799), p. 166.
8 *The False Friend*, iv, pp. 91–2.
9 *The False Friend*, ii, p. 181; iii, p. 115.
10 *Anti-Jacobin Review*, 3 (1799), p. 39.
11 *The False Friend*, ii, pp. 284, 198.
12 *The False Friend*, ii, pp. 77–8.
13 *Gentleman's Magazine*, Apr. 1799, p. 311, reviewing *A Letter to the Women of England*.
14 *A Letter to the Women of England and The Natural Daughter*, ed.

Sharon Setzer (Peterborough, Ont., 2003), pp. 74, 72, 69–70.
15 *Letter to the Women*, p. 43.
16 *Letter to the Women*, pp. 48–9.
17 *Letter to the Women*, p. 65.
18 *Letter to the Women*, p. 83.
19 *Letter to the Women*, p. 87.
20 *Anti-Jacobin Review*, 3 (1799), pp. 144–5.
21 *Monthly Mirror*, Mar. 1799, p. 133.
22 *Morning Post*, 30 July 1799.
23 Bass, *The Green Dragoon*, p. 392. The claim is typical of Bass's absurdly Tarleton-centred account of everything about Mary.
24 'The heroine, a decidedly flippant female, apparently of the Wollstonecraft school': *British Critic*, 16 (1800), p. 327; 'We regret that the author will not confine her labours to poetry': *European Magazine*, 37 (1800), p. 138.
25 This point is made by Sharon Setzer in her excellent introduction to the novel, p. 28.
26 *Natural Daughter*, ed. Setzer, p. 180.
27 *Natural Daughter*, ed. Setzer, pp. 208–10.
28 *Natural Daughter*, ed. Setzer, p. 218.
29 *Morning Post*, 1, 7 June 1799.
30 *Natural Daughter*, ed. Setzer, pp. 218–19.
31 *Natural Daughter*, ed. Setzer, p. 221.
32 *Natural Daughter*, ed. Setzer, p. 255.

CHAPTER 24

1 *Morning Post*, 13 Dec. 1799; *Memoirs*, p. 144.
2 *Memoirs*, p. 145.
3 *Morning Post*, 7 Aug. 1799.
4 Preface to *Thoughts on the Condition of Women, and on the Injustice of Mental Subordination*, 2nd edn (1799).
5 All these examples from *Morning Post*, Jan. 1800.
6 *Morning Post*, 2 Jan. 1800.
7 To John Sewell, bookseller, Cornhill, British Library Add. MS 78689, fol. 9. An identical letter, to an unidentified publisher, survives in the Garrick Club Library.
8 To Southey, 25 Jan. 1800, *Collected Letters of Coleridge*, i, pp. 562–3.
9 28 Feb. 1800, *Collected Letters of Coleridge*, i, pp. 575–6.
10 *Morning Post*, 26 Feb. 1800.
11 *Morning Post*, 20 Mar., 3 Mar., 7 Mar. 1800.
12 Before her death Mary revised the Sylphid essays for publication in book form; Maria Elizabeth included them among the 'posthumous pieces' published in 1801 with the *Memoirs*. Quotations from pp. 4, 19, 22, 23–4, 36.
13 John Fyvie, *Comedy Queens of the Georgian Era* (London, 1906), p. 275.
14 Letter to Jane Porter, 27 Aug. 1800, Pforzheimer Misc. MS 2295.
15 *Morning Post*, 2 Apr. 1800.
16 Letter of 17 June 1800, Garrick Club Library.
17 'The Lascar', in *Selected Poems*,

ed. Pascoe, p. 198. This volume helpfully includes all the poems from *Lyrical Tales*.

18 Stuart Curran, in his important essay, 'Mary Robinson's Lyrical Tales in Context', in *Re-visioning Romanticism: British Women Writers, 1776–1837*, eds Carol Shiner Wilson and Joel Haefner (Philadelphia, 1994), pp. 17–35 (p. 22).

19 *Morning Post*, 15 Apr. 1800.

20 See her biographical sketch of Lauzun and 'Sappho – To the Earl of Moira', *Morning Post*, 3 July 1800.

21 *Morning Post*, 19 Apr. 1800.

22 23 Apr. 1800, printed in *Memoirs*, pp. 148–9.

23 Letter of Apr. 1800, Montagu MSS, Bodleian Library, Oxford.

24 Repr. in *The Wild Wreath* ed. Mary E. Robinson (1804), as 'A receipt [i.e. recipe] for modern love'.

25 Robinson to Godwin, 30 May 1800, Bodleian Library, Abinger Deposit, c. 810/2.

26 Back in April 1797 she had written to thank him for some verses and a picture, 'both of which she admires extremely', and rearranging a social call – 'Mrs Robinson would have called today had not the weather proved so unfavourable' (Pforzheimer Misc. MS 2289).

27 To R. K. Porter, 3 July 1800, Pforzheimer Misc. MS 2450.

28 *Public Characters of 1800–1801* (1801), p. 179.

29 *Public Characters of 1800–1801*, pp. 333–4. When the volume was reprinted some time later, after her death, the original eight-page essay on Mary was replaced by a twenty-page condensation of her *Memoirs*.

30 *Public Characters of 1800–1801*, pp. 336–41.

31 Probably to Jane Porter, Pforzheimer Misc. MS 2294.

32 Robinson to Flaxman, 18 July 1800, British Library Add. MS 39781, fol. 27.

33 *Morning Post*, 26 July 1800.

34 *Morning Post*, 2 Aug. 1800.

CHAPTER 25

1 *Memoirs*, p. 149.

2 Pforzheimer Misc. MS 2290.

3 Eliza Fenwick, *Fate of the Fenwicks: Letters to Mary Hays (1798–1828)*, ed. A. F. Wedd (London, 1927), p. 10.

4 27 Aug. 1800, Pforzheimer Misc. MS 2295.

5 31 Aug. 1800, Pforzheimer Misc. MS 2294.

6 31 Aug. 1800, Pforzheimer Misc. MS 2291.

7 Robinson to Pratt, MS in Harvard Theatre Collection, TS940.6, 1, p. 89.

8 *Monthly Magazine*, Aug. 1800, p. 48, announcing both collections as forthcoming in the winter; Dec. 1800, p. 450, announcing publication of *Lyrical Tales*. The November magazine announced publication of the Hager translation.

9 'Present State of the Manners, Society, etc. etc. of the Metropolis of England', *Monthly Magazine*,

10 (1800), pp. 35–8 (Aug.), 138–40 (Sept., signed MR), 218–22 (Oct.), 305–6 (Nov., signed MR).

10 11 Sept. 1800, Pforzheimer Misc. MS 2292.

11 Robinson to James Marshall, 10 Sept. 1800, Abinger Deposit, Bodleian Library, Oxford, b. 215/2.

12 Pforzheimer Misc. MS 2292.

13 To Jane Porter, 15 Oct. 1800, Pforzheimer Misc. MS 2293.

14 Robinson to Godwin, 16 Aug. 1800, Abinger Deposit, Bodleian Library, Oxford, c. 8101/2.

15 Robinson to Godwin, 24 Aug. 1800, Abinger Deposit, Bodleian Library, Oxford, b. 215/2.

16 Robinson to Godwin, 28 Aug. 1800, Abinger Deposit, Bodleian Library, Oxford, b. 215/2.

17 Robinson to Godwin, 2 Sept. 1800, Abinger Deposit, Bodleian Library, Oxford, c. 507.

18 Robinson to Marshall, 10 Sept. 1800, Abinger Deposit, Bodleian Library, Oxford, b. 215/2.

19 Robinson to Godwin, 10 Oct. 1800, Abinger Deposit, Bodleian Library, Oxford, c. 8101/2.

20 *Memoirs*, p. 149.

21 *Morning Post*, 30 Aug. 1800.

22 *Every-Day Book* (1827), pp. 1174–5.

23 *Morning Post*, 3 Oct. 1800.

24 Coleridge to Stuart, 7 Oct. 1800, *Collected Letters of Coleridge*, i, p. 629.

25 *Morning Post*, 14 Oct. 1800.

26 *Morning Post*, 17 Oct. 1800. A variant text was published in Mary's posthumous *Poetical Works*, including such lines as 'O hills! made sacred by thy parent's song!'

27 Samuel Taylor Coleridge, *Poems*, ed. John Beer (London, 1993), p. 189.

28 Quoted from text in 1806 *Poetical Works*. 1801 text repr. in Levy, 'Coleridge, Mary Robinson and *Kubla Khan*', pp. 165–6.

29 Coleridge, *Poems*, ed. Beer, p. 326.

30 Coleridge to Poole, *Collected Letters of Coleridge*, ii, p. 669.

31 *Morning Post*, 18 Dec. 1800.

32 18 Dec. 1800, repr. in *Memoirs, with posthumous pieces*, 4 vols (London, 1801), iv, p. 189.

33 *Memoirs*, p. 150.

34 *Memoirs*, p. 150.

35 *Memoirs*, p. 151.

36 *Memoirs*, p. 152. Maria Elizabeth may, of course, be indulging in a little literary embroidery of the deathbed sequence.

EPILOGUE

1 Maria Elizabeth Robinson to Godwin, 8 Jan. 1801, Abinger Deposit, Bodleian Library, Oxford, b.215/1.

2 Undated letter to Godwin, Abinger Deposit, Bodleian Library, Oxford, b.214/3.

3 Maria Elizabeth Robinson to Cadell and Davies, 11 June 1804 (private collection).

4 Jane Porter's Manuscript Diary, 1801, Folger Shakespeare Library, Mb. 15, fols. 2–3, referring to her memoir, 'Character of the Late Mrs Robinson, who is usually stiled the British Sappho, extracted from a letter to a lady'.

5 *The Royal Legend. A Tale* (1808), p. 34.

6 Pierce Egan, *The Mistress of Royalty; or, the Loves of Florizel and Perdita* (1814), pp. 124–42.

7 Coleridge to Maria Elizabeth Robinson, 27 Dec. 1802, *Collected Letters of Coleridge*, ii, p. 904.

8 *Collected Letters of Coleridge*, ii, pp. 905–6.

9 *Windsor, Slough and Eton Express*, 27 Aug. 1971.

10 See *Selected Poems*, ed. Pascoe, p. 35n.

11 Fox to Mary Benwell, preserved in Sheridan papers; see Walter Sichel, *Sheridan*, 2 vols (London, 1909), ii, p. 52.

12 His fascinating correspondence with her governess is preserved in the Surrey Records Office (3677/3/28–154).

13 In *Walsingham* as 'Penelope's Epitaph' (ed. Shaffer, p. 56). Both this poem and Pratt's were printed in the *Memoirs* (pp. 153–4).

APPENDIX

1 *Memoirs*, p. 42. A detail inserted in the manuscript of the *Memoirs* at a late stage.

2 Jane Porter, 'Character of the late Mrs Robinson', unpublished manuscript, Pforzheimer Misc. MS 2296.

3 Autograph manuscript of 'Memoirs', fol. 4, in a private collection.

4 *Morning Herald*, 29 June 1781.

BIBLIOGRAPHY

THE WORKS OF MARY ROBINSON

Poems by Mrs Robinson (London: C. Parker, 1775).

Captivity, a Poem; And Celadon and Lydia, a Tale (London: T. Becket, 1777).

The Songs, Chorusses, etc. in The Lucky Escape, a Comic Opera (London: printed for the Author, 1778), staged at Drury Lane, full text unpublished.

Ainsi va le Monde, a poem inscribed to Robert Merry, as Laura Maria (London: John Bell, 1790), 2nd edn, 1791.

Poems by Mrs Robinson, vol. i (London: J. Bell, 1791), vol. ii (London: printed by T. Spilsbury and sold by J. Evans, 1793; repr. as *Poems: A New Edition*, c. 1795).

The Beauties of Mrs Robinson. Selected and Arranged from her Poetical Works (London: H. D. Symonds, 1791).

Impartial Reflections on the Present Situation of the Queen of France by a Friend to Humanity (London: John Bell, 1791).

Vancenza; or, the Dangers of Credulity, 2 vols (London: printed for the Authoress and sold by J. Bell, 1792); 5 eds by 1794; also a Dublin edn in one vol., translated into French and German (1793).

Monody to the Memory of Sir Joshua Reynolds, Late President of the Royal Academy (London: J. Bell, 1792).

An Ode to the Harp of the late accomplished and amiable Louisa Hanway (London: J. Bell, 1793).

Sight, The Cavern of Woe, and Solitude (London: printed by T. Spilsbury and sold by J. Evans, 1793).

Modern Manners: a Poem in two Cantos, by Horace Juvenal (London: printed for the Author and sold by James Evans, 1793).

Monody to the Memory of Marie Antoinette Queen of France (London: printed by T. Spilsbury and sold by H. Evans, 1793).

The Widow, or a Picture of Modern Times: A Novel in a Series of Letters, 2 vols (London: Hookham and Carpenter, 1794); also a Dublin edn in one vol.; tr. into French and German (1795); repr. as *Julia St Lawrence* (Leipzig, 1797).

Nobody, staged at Drury Lane, 1794, unpublished.

Angelina, a Novel, 3 vols (London: printed for the Author and sold by Hookham and Carpenter, 1796); also a Dublin edn in two vols; tr. into French (undated) and German (1799–1800).

The Sicilian Lover: a Tragedy in Five Acts (London: printed for the Author by Hookham and Carpenter, 1796).

Hubert de Sevrac: A Romance of the Eighteenth Century, 3 vols (London: printed for the Author and sold by Hookham and Carpenter, 1796); also a Dublin edn in two vols (1797); tr. into French (1797) and German (1797–8).

Sappho and Phaon, a series of legitimate Sonnets, with Thoughts on Poetical Subjects, & Anecdotes of the Grecian Poetess (London: printed by S. Gosnell for the Author, and sold by Hookham and Carpenter, 1796).

Walsingham; or, the Pupil of Nature, a Domestic Story, 4 vols (London: Longman, 1797); Dublin edn in two vols (1798); tr. into French (twice) (1798–9) and German (1799).

The False Friend, a Domestic Story, 4 vols (London: Longman and Rees, 1799); 2nd edn, 1799; tr. into French (1799) and German (1800–1).

A Letter to the Women of England, on the Injustice of Mental Subordination. With Anecdotes, by Anne Frances Randall (London: Longman and Rees, 1799); reissued later same year under Robinson's own name with title *Thoughts on the Condition of Women, and on the Injustice of Mental Subordination.*

The Natural Daughter, with Portraits of the Leadenhead Family, a Novel, 2 vols (London: Longman and Rees, 1799); also a Dublin edn (1799).

Joseph Hager, *Picture of Palermo*, tr. from the German by Mary Robinson (London: Phillips, 1800).

Lyrical Tales (London: printed for Longman and Rees by Biggs & Cottle, Bristol, 1800).

The Mistletoe, a Christmas Tale, by Laura Maria (London: Laurie and Whittle, 1800).

Memoirs of the Late Mrs Robinson, Written by Herself, with some posthumous pieces in verse, ed. Mary Elizabeth Robinson, 4 vols (London: R. Phillips, 1801); New York and Philadelphia edns, 1802; tr. into French, 1802; vol. iii included essay series 'The Sylphid', novel-fragment *Jasper*, and poem 'The Savage of Aveyron'; vol. iv included two-book poem 'The Progress of Liberty', tributary poems and poetic correspondence, letters from 'Peter Pindar' (John Wolcot) and Sir Joshua Reynolds. *Memoirs* repr. without 'posthumous pieces', 1803, 1827.

The Wild Wreath, ed. Mary E. Robinson (London: Richard Phillips, 1804).

The Poetical Works of the Late Mrs Robinson, including many pieces never before published, ed. Mary E. Robinson, 3 vols (London: Phillips, 1806); repr. as *Poetical Works of the Late Mrs Robinson, including the pieces last published. The three volumes complete in one* (London: Jones, 1824).

Many individual poems and essays in newspapers and magazines remain uncollected, among them the series of articles on the 'Present State of the Manners, Society, etc. etc. of the Metropolis of England' and the 'Anecdotes' of Lauzun, Chartres, and Marie Antoinette, all published in the *Monthly Magazine* between Feb. and Nov. 1800.

MODERN EDITIONS

A Letter to the Women of England and The Natural Daughter, ed. Sharon Setzer (Peterborough, Ont., 2003); there is also a facsimile of *A Letter*, with intro. by Jonathan Wordsworth (Oxford, 1998).

Lyrical Tales, facsimile with intro. by Jonathan Wordsworth (Oxford, 1989).

Memoirs, ed. M. J. Levy, as *Perdita: The Memoirs of Mary Robinson* (London, 1994).

The Natural Daughter, see *A Letter*, above.

Poems, 1791, facsimile with intro. by Jonathan Wordsworth (Oxford, 1994).

Poetical Works of the late Mrs Robinson, facsimile with intro. by Caroline Franklin (London, 1996).

Sappho and Phaon, there are two facsimiles with intros by Jonathan Wordsworth (Oxford, 2000) and Terence Hoagwood and Rebecca Jackson (Delmar, 1995).

Selected Poems, ed. Judith Pascoe (Peterborough, Ont., 2000).

Walsingham; or, the Pupil of Nature, ed. Julie Shaffer (Peterborough, Ont., 2003); there is also a facsimile with intro. by Peter Garside (London, 1992).

Selected 'Laura Maria' poems are repr. in *British Satire 1785–1840*, vol. iv: *Gifford and the Della Cruscans*, ed. John Strachan (London, 2003).

INTERNET EDITIONS

1791 *Poems*:
http://digital.library.upenn.edu/women/robinson/1791/1791.html
A Letter to the Women of England:
http://www.rc.umd.edu/editions/contemps/robinson/cover.htm
Lyrical Tales:
http://www.lib.ucdavis.edu/English/BWRP/Works/RobiMLyric.htm
Sappho and Phaon:
http://etext.lib.virginia.edu/britpo/sappho/sappho.html
Memoirs:
http://digital.library.upenn.edu/women/robinson/memoirs/memoirs.html
The Wild Wreath:
http://www.lib.ucdavis.edu/English/BWRP/Works/RobiMWildW.htm

MANUSCRIPTS AND ARCHIVAL MATERIALS

A disappointingly small proportion of Mary Robinson's writings survive in her own hand. Among the manuscripts consulted in the writing of this biography were:

Anson Papers: correspondence of Prince of Wales and Mary Hamilton regarding Mrs Robinson, in the possession of Rear Admiral Sir Peter and Lady Elizabeth Anson.
Bodleian Library, Oxford: letters in Montagu manuscripts and Abinger Deposit; also references in William Godwin's manuscript diaries.
Bristol Central Library: letter.
British Library, London: letters; MS of songs etc. for *The Lucky Escape*; poems in a commonplace book.
British Museum, London: engravings and caricatures in Department of Prints and Drawings, some with manuscript annotations.
Folger Shakespeare Library, Washington DC: letter; poems in a commonplace book; also references in Jane Porter's manuscript diary.
Garrick Club, London: letters.
Harvard Theatre Collection: letters.
Hertfordshire Archives and Local Studies, County Hall, Hertford: correspondence of Mary Robinson, George Prince of Wales, Lord Malden, and Lord Southampton, pertaining to financial arrangements (Capell Collection).
Houghton Library, Harvard University: letter.
Huntington Library, San Marino, California: manuscripts of *The Lucky Escape* and *Nobody* in Larpent Collection of plays submitted to Lord Chamberlain's Office.
Liverpool Record Office: Tarleton family papers.
Pforzheimer Collection, New York Public Library: letters and other papers, including Jane Porter's 'Character of the late Mrs Robinson'.
Private Collections: letters in possession of two private collectors; manuscript of *Memoirs* and other papers, in a private collection.
Royal Archives, Windsor: account books and correspondence pertaining to annuity payable to Mary Robinson and subsequently her daughter.
Westminster Archives Centre: letter.

NEWSPAPERS AND MAGAZINES

Analytical Review
Annual Register
Annual Review
Anti-Jacobin Review
British Critic
Critical Review

Diary
English Review
European Magazine
Gazetteer and New Daily Advertiser
General Evening Post
General Magazine
Gentleman's Magazine
Lady's Magazine
Lady's Monthly Museum
London Chronicle
London Courant
London Gazette
London Magazine
Monthly Magazine and British Register
Monthly Mirror
Monthly Review
Morning Chronicle
Morning Herald
Morning Post
Morning Review
New Annual Register
Oracle
Poetical Register
Public Advertiser
Quarterly Review
Rambler's Magazine
Star
Sun
Telegraph
Town and Country Magazine
The World

OTHER BIOGRAPHICAL SOURCES

All pre-1900 books published in London, unless otherwise stated.

The Amours of Carlo Khan (1784).

Authentic Memoirs, Memorandums, and Confessions. Taken from the Journal of his Predatorial Majesty, the King of the Swindlers [John King] (n.d.)

Bass, Robert D., *The Green Dragoon: The Lives of Banastre Tarleton and Mary Robinson* (1957; repr. Columbia, SC, 1973)

A Biographical Dictionary of Actors, Actresses, Musicians, Dancers, Managers and Other Stage Personnel in London, 1660–1800, 16 vols (Carbondale, Ill., 1984–).

Biron, Armand Louis de Gontaut, Duc de Lauzun, *Memoirs of the Duc de Lauzun*, trans. C. K. Scott Moncrieff (London, 1928).

Boaden, James, *Memoirs of the Life of John Philip Kemble*, 2 vols (1825).

—— *Memoirs of Mrs Siddons*, 2 vols (1827).

The Budget of Love; or, Letters between Florizel and Perdita (1781).

Cameron, K. N., ed., *The Shelley Circle*, 2 vols (Cambridge, Mass., 1961).

Campbell, Thomas, *The Life of Mrs Siddons* (1832).

Coleridge, Samuel Taylor, *Collected Letters*, ed. E. L. Griggs, vols i–ii (Oxford, 1956).

——, *Poems*, ed. John Beer (London, 1993).

Court and Private Life in the Time of Queen Charlotte: Being the Journals of Mrs Papendiek, ed. Delves Broughton and Mrs Vernon, 2 vols (1887).

David, Saul, *Prince of Pleasure: The Prince of Wales and the Making of the Regency* (London, 1998).

Devonshire, Georgiana, Duchess of, *Georgiana: Extracts from the Correspondence of Georgiana, Duchess of Devonshire*, ed. Earl of Bessborough (London, 1955).

Douglas, D., *The Letters and Journals of Lady Mary Coke* (Edinburgh, 1888–9).

The Effusions of Love: being the Amorous Correspondence between the Amiable Florizel, and the Enchanting Perdita, in a series of letters, faithfully transcribed from the original Epistles and Billets-doux in Possession of the Editor (1784).

Egan, Pierce, *The Mistress of Royalty; or, the Loves of Florizel and Perdita* (1814).

Elliott, Grace Dalrymple, *Journal of my Life during the French Revolution* (1859).

Fenwick, Eliza, *Fate of the Fenwicks: Letters to Mary Hays (1798–1828)*, ed. A. F. Wedd (London, 1927).

Fergus, Jan and J. F. Thaddeus, 'Women, Publishers, and Money, 1790–1820', *Studies in Eighteenth-Century Culture*, 17 (1987), 191–207.

The Festival of Wit (15th edn, 1789).

Fitzgerald, Percy, *The Lives of the Sheridans*, 2 vols (1886).

Fyvie, John, *Comedy Queens of the Georgian Era* (London, 1906).

Garrick, David, *Florizel and Perdita. A Dramatic Pastoral, in Three Acts. Alter'd from The Winter's Tale of Shakespear* (1758).

Genest, John, *Some Account of the English Stage 1660–1830*, 10 vols (Bath, 1832).

George III, King, *Correspondence of George III 1760–December 1783*, ed. Sir John Fortescue, 6 vols (London, 1927–8).

——, *The Later Correspondence of George III*, ed. A. Aspinall, 5 vols (Cambridge, 1938).

George IV, King, *The Correspondence of George, Prince of Wales 1770–1812*, ed. A. Aspinall, 8 vols (London, 1963–71).

——, *The Letters of King George IV 1812–1830*, ed. A. Aspinall, 3 vols (Cambridge, 1938).

George, M. Dorothy, ed., *Catalogue of Political and Personal Satires Preserved in the Department of Prints and Drawings in the British Museum*, vols v–vii (London, 1938–42).

Grego, Joseph, '"Perdita" and her Painters: Portraits of Mrs Mary Robinson', *The Connoisseur*, February 1903, 99–107.

Griggs, Earl Leslie, 'Coleridge and Mrs Mary Robinson', *Modern Language Notes*, 45 (1930), 90–5.

Hamilton, Mary, *At Court and at Home: From Letters and Diaries 1756–1816*, ed. Elizabeth and Florence Anson (London, 1925).

Hanger, Colonel George, *The Life, Adventures and Opinions of Colonel George Hanger*, ed. W. Combe, 2 vols (1801).

Hargreaves-Mawdsley, W. N., *The English Della Cruscans and their Time, 1783–1828* (The Hague, 1967).
Hartley, J., *History of the Westminster Election, containing every material occurrence, from its commencement on the first of April, to the final close* (1784).
Hawkins, Laetitia-Matilda, *Memoirs, Facts, and Opinions*, 2 vols (1824).
Hibbert, Christopher, *George IV: Prince of Wales* (London, 1972).
Huish, Robert, *Memoirs of George the Fourth*, 2 vols (1831).
Ingamells, John, *Mrs Robinson and her Portraits* (London, 1978).
Leslie, C. R. and T. Taylor, *The Life and Times of Sir Joshua Reynolds*, 2 vols (1865).
Letters from Perdita to a Certain Israelite, and his Answers to them (1781).
Levy, M. J., 'Coleridge, Mary Robinson and *Kubla Khan*', *Charles Lamb Bulletin*, 77 (1992), 156–66.
——, 'Gainsborough's *Mrs Robinson*: A Portrait and its Context', *Apollo*, 136 (1992), 152–5.
——, *The Mistresses of King George IV* (London, 1996).
The London Stage 1660–1800, ed. William van Lennep, Emmett L. Avery, A. H. Scouten, G. W. Stone Jr, and C. B. Hogan, 12 vols (Carbondale, Ill., 1965–79).
The Memoirs of Perdita (1784).
Paul, C. Kegan, *William Godwin: His Friends and Contemporaries*, 2 vols (1876).
Pigott, Charles, *The Female Jockey Club; or, a Sketch of the Manners of the Age* (1792).
—— *The Whig Club; or, a Sketch of Modern Patriotism* (1794).
Poetical Epistle from Florizel to Perdita: with Perdita's Answer. And a Preliminary Discourse upon the Education of Princes (1781).
Polwhele, Richard, *The Unsex'd Females: A Poem* (1798).
Porter, Roy, *Quacks: Fakers and Charlatans in English Medicine* (Stroud, Glos, 2000).
Rivers, David, *Literary Memoirs of Living Authors of Great Britain*, 2 vols (1798).
Robinson, Mary Elizabeth, *The Shrine of Bertha: A Novel*, 2 vols (1794; 2nd edn, 1796).
Russell, Lord John, ed., *Memorials and Correspondence of Charles James Fox*, 3 vols (1853).
St Clair, William, *The Godwins and the Shelleys: The Biography of a Family* (London, 1989).
A Satire on the Present Times (1780).
The School for Scandal, A Comedy in Five Acts, As it is Performed by His Majesty's Servants, etc. [anonymous satire] (1784).
Sheridan, R. B., *Letters*, ed. Cecil Price, 3 vols (Oxford, 1966).

Steele, Elizabeth, *Memoirs of Mrs Sophia Baddeley*, 6 vols (1787); 3 vols (Dublin, 1878).
Taylor, John, *Records of my Life*, 2 vols (1832).
Thrale, Hester, *Thraliana*, ed. K. C. Balderston, 2 vols (Oxford, 1951).
Timbs, J., *Clubs and Club Life in London* (London, 1908).
*The Vis-à-Vis of Berkley-Square. Or, A Wheel off Mrs W*t**n's Carriage. Inscribed to Florizel* (1783).
Walpole, Horace, *Correspondence*, ed. W. S. Lewis, vols xxv–xxxv (New Haven, 1955–73).
——, *The Last Journals of Horace Walpole during the Reign of George III*, ed. A. Francis Steuart, 2 vols (London, 1910).
Waterhouse, E. K., 'A Gainsborough Bill for the Prince of Wales', *Burlington Magazine*, 88 (1946), 276.
Wollstonecraft, Mary, *Collected Letters*, ed. Janet Todd (London, 2003).
Woof, Robert, 'Wordsworth's Poetry and Stuart's Newspapers: 1797–1803', *Studies in Bibliography*, 15 (1962), 149–89.

MARY ROBINSON AS AUTHOR: SELECTED MODERN CRITICISM

Bolton, Betsy, 'Romancing the Stone: "Perdita" Robinson in Wordsworth's London', *ELH*, 64 (1997), 727–59.
Craciun, Adriana, 'Violence against Difference: Mary Wollstonecraft and Mary Robinson', *Bucknell Review*, 42 (1998), 111–41.
—— and Kari E. Lokke, eds, *Rebellious Hearts: British Women Writers and the French Revolution* (Albany, NY, 2001).
Cross, Ashley, 'From *Lyrical Ballads* to *Lyrical Tales*: Mary Robinson's Reputation and the Problem of Literary Debt', *Studies in Romanticism*, 40 (2001), 571–605.
Cullens, Chris, 'Mrs Robinson and the Masquerade of Womanliness', in Veronica Kelly and Dorothea von Mücke (eds), *Body and Text in the Eighteenth Century* (Stanford, 1994), pp. 266–89.
Curran, Stuart, 'The I Altered', in Anne K. Mellor (ed.), *Romanticism and Feminism* (Bloomington, Ind., 1988), pp. 185–207.
——, 'Mary Robinson's *Lyrical Tales* in Context', in Carol Shiner Wilson and Joel Haefner (eds), *Re-visioning Romanticism: British Women Writers, 1776–1837* (Philadelphia, 1994), pp. 17–35.
Ford, Susan Allen, '"A Name More Dear": Daughters, Fathers, and Desire in *A Simple Story. The False Friend*, and *Mathilda*', in Carol Shiner Wilson and Joel Haefner (eds), *Re-visioning Romanticism: British Women Writers, 1776–1837* (Philadelphia, 1994), pp. 51–71.
Fulford, Tim, 'Mary Robinson and the Abyssinian Maid: Coleridge's Muses and Feminist Criticism', *Romanticism on the Net*, 13 (Feb. 1999).

Kelly, Gary, *The English Jacobin Novel, 1780–1805* (Oxford, 1976).

Labbe, Jacqueline M., 'Selling One's Sorrows: Charlotte Smith, Mary Robinson and the Marketing of Poetry', *Wordsworth Circle*, 25 (1994), 68–71.

——, ed., *Women's Writing*, 9:1 (2002), 'Special Number: Mary Robinson'.

Lee, Debbie, '*The Wild Wreath*: Cultivating a Poetic Circle for Mary Robinson', *Studies in the Literary Imagination*, 30 (1997), 23–34.

Luther, Susan, 'A Stranger Minstrel: Coleridge's Mrs Robinson', *Studies in Romanticism*, 33 (1994), 391–409.

McGann, Jerome, *The Poetics of Sensibility: A Revolution in Literary Style* (Oxford, 1996), especially 'Mary Robinson and the Myth of Sappho', pp. 97–116.

Mellor, Anne K., 'British Romanticism, Gender and Three Women Artists', in Ann Bermingham and John Brewer (eds), *The Consumption of Culture 1600–1800* (New York, 1995), pp. 121–42.

——, 'Mary Robinson and the Scripts of Female Sexuality', in Patrick Coleman, Jayne Lewis, and Jill Kowalik (eds), *Representations of the Self from the Renaissance to Romanticism* (Cambridge, England, and New York, 2000).

Pascoe, Judith, *Romantic Theatricality: Gender, Poetry, and Spectatorship* (Ithaca, NY, 1997).

Perry, Gill, '"The British Sappho": Borrowed Identities and the Representation of Women Artists in late Eighteenth-Century British Art', *Oxford Art Journal*, 18 (1995), 44–57.

Peterson, Linda H., 'Becoming an Author: Mary Robinson's *Memoirs* and the Origins of the Woman Artist's Autobiography', in Carol Shiner Wilson and Joel Haefner (eds), *Re-visioning Romanticism: British Women Writers, 1776–1837* (Philadelphia, 1994), pp. 36–50.

Robinson, Daniel, 'From "Mingled Measure" to "Ecstatic Measures": Mary Robinson's Poetic Reading of "Kubla Khan"', *Wordsworth Circle*, 26 (1995), 4–7.

——, 'Reviving the Sonnet: Women Romantic Poets and the Sonnet Claim', *European Romantic Review*, 6 (1995), 98–127.

Setzer, Sharon, 'Mary Robinson's Sylphid Self: The End of Feminine Self-Fashioning', *Philological Quarterly*, 75 (1996), 501–20.

——, 'The Dying Game: Crossdressing in Mary Robinson's *Walsingham*', *Nineteenth-Century Contexts*, 22 (2000), 305–28.

Ty, Eleanor, *Empowering the Feminine: The Narratives of Mary Robinson, Jane West, and Amelia Opie, 1796–1812* (Toronto, 1998).

It should be noted that some of these modern critical accounts contain biographical inaccuracies both major and minor.

FICTIONAL TREATMENTS

Anon., *The Royal Legend: A Tale* (1808).
Barrington, E., *The Exquisite Perdita* (1926).
[Green, Sarah], *The Private History of the Court of England* (1808).
Makower, Stanley, *Perdita: A Romance in Biography* (1908).
Plaidy, Jean, *Perdita's Prince* (1969).
Steen, Marguerite, *The Lost One* (1937).

INDEX

Page numbers in *italics* denotes illustration

Abington, Fanny 51
actresses 88–90, 98
Aikin, Anna *see* Barbauld, Anna Laetitia
Ainsi va le Monde 182–4, 272, 280
Aix-la-chapelle (Aachen) 253
Albanesi, Angelina 71
Albanesi, Angelo 66, 69, 71, 132
Alexander the Great 81
'All Alone' 384
All for Love 84
American War of Independence 175, 177, 180–1
Amours of Carlo Khan, The 244
Analytical Review 280
'Anecdotes of Distinguished Personages' 382
Angelina 90–1, 290, 335–9
Annals of Gallantry 244
Anti-Jacobin Review 367, 371, 372
Armistead, Elizabeth 77, 160, 243, 315
  affair with Prince of Wales 141, 142, 150, 153
  and Fox 201, 216, 221, 424
  rivalry with Mary 147–8, 149
As You Like It 99, 117–18
Austen, Jane 206, 222, 294
Ayscough, Captain George 49–50, 63
Baddeley, Sophia 49, 79, 133–4, 144
Balack, Hanway *see* Hanway, Hanway
Bannister, John 190
Barbauld, Anna Laetitia 50, 66
Barrymore, Lord 356
Bate, Henry 18, 75, 138–9, 169
Bate, Mary 138–9
Bath 283–5
Beauties of Mrs Robinson, The 279
Beaux' Stratagem, The 218–19
Belgeioso, Count de 50, 71
Bell, John 265, 266, 272, 275, 278, 300, 314
Belle's Stratagem, The 120
Bertie, Susan 362–3, 372, 422
Bertin, Rose 173
Biron, Duc de 227
Bluestocking Society 266
Boaden, James 267, 274, 284, 297, 310
Boyle, Richard 281
Brereton, George 92–5
Brereton, William 51, 73–4, 75
Brighton 262–3
Bristol 7, 8
  theatre 11–12
British Legion 180
Broderip, Edmund 13
Browning, Elizabeth Barrett
  Aurora Leigh 372–3
Brummell, George 184

Budget of Love, or, Letters between Florizel and Perdita 151–2
Burgoyne, Lieutenant General 'Gentleman Johnny' 275
Burke, Edmund 268, 291
Reflections on the Revolution in France 291, 292
Burke, Richard 268
Burney, Edward 187
Burney, Fanny 24, 25, 187
Evelina 48, 78

Camp, The 87, 99
Campbell, Lady Augusta 128
Capel, George *see* Malden, Lord
Captivity, a Poem; And Celadon and Lydia, a Tale 69, 84
Caroline of Brunswick 326, 346
Carpenter, Lady Almeria 49
Cavendish, Lord George 141
Celestial Beds, The (pamphlet) 219
Charlotte, Queen 105
Chartres, Duke of 171–2, 173, 174, 175, 177, 214
Chatelet, Duke and Duchess of 254
Chatterton, Thomas 8, 277
chemise de la Reine 203–6
Cholmondeley, Earl of 155, 159
Chubb, John 360
Cibber, Susannah 24
Clandestine Marriage, The 34, 82
Clarence, Duke of 310, 323, 330, 333
Coleridge, Derwent 412
Coleridge, Samuel Taylor 3, 286–8, 315, 342, 357, 382, 411, 422–3
admiration of Mary's poetry 270, 379–80, 386
'Ancient Mariner' 380, 383–4
'The Apotheosis, or the Snow-Drop' 359
Bristol connections 8
concern for Mary's health 286–7
engaged with Mary as 'political corespondent' for *Morning Post* 357, 358, 379
'Frost at Midnight' 412–13
influence of Della Cruscans 264
'Kubla Khan' 286–7, 413, 414
letter written to by Mary whilst on deathbed 414
'The Mad Monk' 424
Mary's poem for son (Derwent) 66, 412
'The Nightingale' 65
and opium 287–8
poems written by Mary for 412–14
review of *Hubert de Sevrac* 347
'A Stranger Minstrel' 414
Colman, George 86
Comus 84
Coningsby, Lady Frances 144
Cornwallis, Lord 181, 225
Cosway, Maria 191, 388
Cosway, Richard 186, 191
Country Girl, The 323
Covent Garden theatre 75
Cowley, Hannah 25, 84, 264, 265–6, 267
Cox, Samuel 20, 21
Critical Review 280, 299, 337
Cumberland, Duke of 81, 116, 119, 131, 133, 142, 146, 148, 153
Curran, John Philpot 408

Dally the Tall (Grace Dalrymple Eliot) 153, 154, 160, 168, 170, 177–8, 202
Dance, George 314
Darby, Elizabeth (Mary's sister) 9

Darby, George (Mary's brother) 10, 14, 27–8, 39, 46, 322–3, 325–6
Darby, Hester (nee Vanacott) (Mary's mother) 255
background 9
death 312
marriage 9, 10, 14, 15–16
and Mary's acting career 20–1, 26, 90
relationship with Mary 13
and son-in-law 27–9, 33, 34–5
Darby, John (Mary's brother) 9, 14, 46, 90, 253, 271
Darby, Mary *see* Robinson, Mary
Darby, Nicholas (Mary's father) 7–8, 19–20, 21, 90, 145–6, 170
abandonment of family 15–16
death 255
lives openly with mistress 20
marriage 9, 10, 14, 15–16
scheme to establish whale fishery on Labrador 14–15, 16, 19
travelling and trading in Newfoundland 10, 13–14
Darby, William (Mary's brother) 14, 15
De Coigny, Madame 175–6
De Loutherbourg, Philip 76
De Quincey, Thomas *Confessions of an English Opium-Eater* 288
Death and Dissection, Funeral Procession and Will, of Mrs Regency, The 261
Della Cruscans 263–4, 267–8, 271, 273–4, 280, 315, 344
Delphini, Signor 190
Derby, Countess of 131
Derby, Earl of 97, 161, 330
Devonshire, Georgiana, Duchess of 118–19, 122, 127, 128, 281, 361, 392
and election campaign (1784) 238
and fashion 204, 205, 206
friendship with Mary 70
and Mary's acting career 75, 89
as Mary's literary patron 17, 69–70
view of Prince of Wales 131
Dickinson, William 187
Discovery, The 87
Dorset, Duke of 155
Downman, John 186
Drury Lane theatre 74, 75–7, 98, 310
backstage 77
design 76–7
rebuilding of by Kemble 329
seen as Opposition's theatre 105
Duncannon, Lady 281

East India Company 236, 238
Edwards, Molly 44
Effusions of Love 245
Egan, Pierce
The Mistress of Royalty 421
election (1784) 238–41
Eliot, Grace Dalrymple *see* Dally the Tall
Eliott, Sir John 234
Englefield Cottage 362, 396–7
Engleheart, George 186
English Review 280–1, 299
Essex, Lady 213
Este, Reverend Charles 266–7

False Friend, The 330, 364–8, 371
Farren, Elizabeth (later Duchess of Derby) 86, 87, 97, 161, 328, 330

fashion 27
Mary as icon of and innovator 27–8, 48, 155, 170, 178–9, 190–1, 203–9, 214, 378–9, 401
Female Jockey Club 324
Fenwick, Eliza 396, 397
Fitzgerald, George 51, 52, 54, 62–3
Fitzherbert, Mrs 255, 312
Flaxman, John 393
Fleet prison 63, 64
Florence Miscellany, The 263
Florizel and Perdita 100
royal command performance 1779) *89*, 101, 105–9, 110–11
Ford, Richard 109
Fox, Charles James 97, 105, 131, 188, 195–7, 223, 315
affair with Mary 2, 196–7, 9–200
and Armistead 201, 216, 221, 424
background 195
caricatures of *156*, 217–19, *218*, *237*, 238
coalition with North 215–16, 218, 219, 221
and election campaign (1784) 238, 240–1
as Foreign Minister 218
and French Revolution 291
and India Bill 236–7
and Prince of Wales 196, 215
role as intermediary between the Prince and Mary 215, 217, 230
Frederick, Duke of York 107, 124, 125, 148, 149, 153
French Revolution 270, 271, 272–3, 290–1, 292–3, 304, 309

Gainsborough, Thomas 2, 168–9, 186, 192
Garrick, David 1, 11, 21, 24–5, 33–4, 74–5, 76, 79–80, 100, 400
General Advertiser 80
Genest, John 330
George III, King 166–7, 196, 216
and India Bill 237
and political affairs 237, 238
rebellious behaviour towards by son 148–9
and son's relationship with Mary 130, 139, 166–7
suffering from porphyria 260–1
and theatre 105–6
Gifford, William 273, 326
Gillray, James 197, 198–9, 200, 217, 354
Godwin, William 3, 287, 350, 379, 420
biography of Wollstonecraft 368
Caleb Williams 226
correspondence with Mary in final years 405–8
Fleetwood 350
friendship with Mary 342–4, 372, 405
marriage to Wollstonecraft 351
pen-portrait of Mary for *Public Characters* 391–2
Goldsmith, Oliver 25
Gordon, Lord George 127
Graham, Dr James 159, 219–22, *220*, 355
Greatheed, Bertie 263
Grimaldi, William 186
Gunning, Elizabeth 399

Hamilton, Mary 110, 111–13, 115–16
Hamlet 84
Hanger, Colonel 257
Hanway, Hanway 32, 62, 309
Hanway, Louisa 309

Hanway, Mary Ann 309
Hardenburg, Countess von 159–60
Harris, Elizabeth 43, 44, 92
Harris, Howel 43
Harris, Thomas 27, 33, 36, 42, 43–5, 57, 58–9, 60
'Harvest Home' 410
Hastings, Warren 236
'Haunted Beach, The' 270, 380, 411, 412
Hawkins, Laetitia 64, 132, 226, 341
Haymarket theatre 86
Hays, Mary 250, 343, 349, 396
Hazlitt, William 273, 330
Henley, Robert *see* Northington, Lord
Herbert, Henry (Earl of Pembroke) 71
Hervey, Mrs 20
History of the Campaigns 253, 254, 257
Hoadly, Benjamin 87
Hood, Admiral 238, 241
Hopkins, Priscilla 12, 51, 73–4, 82, 98
Hopkins, William 80
Hoppner, John 2, 186, 188–9, 208, 214–15, 346, 425
Horton, Anne 81
Hotham, Colonel 161, 162, 163, 164, 165–6, 167
Hubert de Sevrac 347–8
Hull, Thomas 21

Imlay, Fanny 373
Inchbald, Elizabeth 343
Inconstant, The 99
India 236–7
Irish Widow, The 99, 126

'Jasper' (poem) 379–80
Jasper (novel) 270, 401–2
Johnson, Dr Samuel 21
Jordan, Dora 309, 310, 323, 330, 332, 333, 378
Joseph Andrews 84

Kate of Aberdeen 309–10
Keats, John 289
Kemble, Fanny 343
Kemble, John Philip 12, 310, 325, 328, 329
King, Charlotte (later Dacre) 42
King, John 53
  correspondence with Mary 37–42
  Letters from Perdita to a Certain Israelite 37–8, 55, 56, 68–9, 150–1, 271
  as man of culture 40–1
King Lear 87
Klopstock, Friedrich *Messiah* 395

Lade, Sir John 96–7, 115, 119, 120, 122
Lade, Lady Letty 97
Lady's Magazine 155, 206, 207–8
Lady's Monthly Museum 388
Lambert, Sir John 171–2
'Lascar, The' 385
'Laurel of Liberty' (Merry) 271–2
Lauzun, Duke of 175–7, 253
Lawrence, Thomas 186
Lebrun, Madame Vigée 204
Lee, Nathaniel 81
Leeds, Duke of 339–40
Leigh, Mrs 19
'Letter to a Friend on leaving Town' 67–8
Letter to the Women of England, A 16, 84, 212, 351, 369–71, 378
Letters from Perdita to a Certain Israelite (King) 37–8, 55, 56, 68–9, 150–1, 271
Lewis, 'Monk' 423

Licensing Act (1737) 75
Linley, Elizabeth 74
Linley, Mary 88
Linley, Thomas 86
Lister 244–5
London 22–3, 82–3
  Catholic uprisings (1780) 127
London Chronicle 333
'London's Summer Morning' 23
Lorrington Academy 16–17
Lorrington, Meribah 16, 17, 285
Louis XVI, King
  execution of 309
Lucky Escape, The 85
Lyrical Ballads 65, 383–4
Lyrical Tales 65, 358, 383, 384–6, *393*, 398, 399, 414–15
Lyttelton, Lord 50, 51, 52, 53–4, 55–6, 63

Mad Jemmy 285, 286, 288
Mahomet 86–7
Malden, Lord (George Capel) 109–10
  affair with Mary 37, 119, 120, 122, 134, 138, 142, 144, 145, 192, 193–4
  death 424
  ending of affair with Mary and annuity arrangement 194–5
  as go-between between Prince of Wales and Mary 113–14, 119, 124
  and negotiations over Prince's love letters 162–6
'Maniac, The' 285–6, 287, 288–9, 414
Manners, Charles (Duke of Rutland) 96
Manners, Frances (Countess of Tyrconnel) 49
Marie Antoinette 173–5, 204, 291–2, 309, 312
Marshall, James 409
Mathias, T.J. 354–5
Mattocks, Isabella 95
Memoirs of Antonina 291
Memoirs of the Late Mrs Robinson, Written by Herself 8, 13, 25, 30, 96, 382, *406*, 421–2
Memoirs of Perdita 18, 55, 96, 122, 159, 179, 193–4, 244, 382
Merry, Robert 263, 264, 265, 266, 343, 355–6
  'Laurel of Liberty' 271–2
Meyer, Jeremiah 186
Middleton, Lady 281
Miniature Picture, The 99, 125–6
Modern Manners 312–13
Moira, Earl of 227, 322, 386
Monody to the Memory of the late Queen of France 312
Montagu, Elizabeth 266
Montgomery, Anne (Marchioness Townshend) 49
Monthly Magazine 382, 399
Monthly Mirror 337
Monthly Review 280, 298
More, Hannah 11, 12, 17, 25, 257
Morning Chronicle 80, 117–18, 126, 206
Morning Herald 18, 138, 146, 148, 153, 154, 159, 164, 165, 169–70, 178, 202
Morning Post 80, 128, 134–5, 138, 160–1, 164, 239, 245–6, 334, 352, 357, 378, 419–20
Murphy, Arthur 389

Napier, Lady Sarah 200
Napoleon Bonaparte 362
Natural Daughter, The 372–6
Nobody 325, 328, 330–4
North, Lord 166–7, 196, 216, 218, 219, 221, 236
Northcote, James 21, 187, 388

Northington, Lord (Robert Henley) 20, 49, 51, 63, 188

O'Byrne, Captain 51, 63
'Ode, Inscribed to the Infant Son of S.T. Coleridge' 412
'Ode to Apathy' 289
'Ode to Health' 289
'Ode to the Nightingale' 281
'Ode to Rapture' 235
'Ode to Valour' 281–2, 364
Old Bachelor, The 84
Opera House 213
Opie, Amelia 350
Oracle 266–7, 274, 277–8, 297, 302–3, 309, 311–12, 357
Owen, William 186

Paine, Thomas
The Rights of Man 291
Pantheon (Oxford Street) 48–9
Parry, Catherine 51, 67
Parsons, William 263
'Perdita chemise' 203–6
Phillips, Sir Richard 382, 390, 421
Philosophism 355
Pigott, Charles 323–4
Pindar, Peter *see* Wolcot, John
Pitt the Younger, William 197, 237, 238
Plaidy, Jean
Perdita's Prince 425
Plain Dealer, The 87–8, 98
Poems by Mrs Robinson (1775) 66–8
Poems by Mrs Robinson (1791) 275–9, 280–2
Poems by Mrs Robinson (1793) 289, 305–7, 314–16
Poetical Epistle from Florizel to Perdita, The 146–7, 150, 151
Poetical Works 282, 361–2, 422
'Poet's Garret, The' 289–90
Polwhele, Richard 355
Poole, Tom 414
'Poor, Singing Dame, The' 385–6
Porter, Jane 174, 260, 390, 395, 397, 398, 403, 404, 420, 429
Porter, Robert Ker 390–1
Portland, Duke of 216
Powell, William 11–12, 333
Pratt, Samuel Jackson 274–5, 348, 356, 398, 425–6
'Progress of Liberty, The' 342–3, 371
Promenade: or, Theatre of Beauty, The 260
Public Advertiser 192
Public Characters of (1800–1801) 391

Quarterly Review 273

Radcliffe, Ann 293, 296
Rambler's Magazine 154, 206, 216–17, 232, 244, 246, 259
Randall, Ann 212, 369
Ranelagh pleasure gardens 47–8
Regency crisis (1789) 260–1
Regency crisis (1808) 420–1
Relapse, The 81
Reynolds, Sir Joshua 1–2, 182–3
death 300
Mary's poem on 182–4
popularity of paintings 187
portrait of Tarleton 184, 185–6, 192
portraits of Mary 21, 184, 186–7, 192, 232–3, 346, 392
Richard III 84
Richardson, Samuel
Sir Charles Grandison 54
'Robinson Hat' 208

Robinson, Henry Crabb 357
Robinson, Maria Elizabeth (daughter) 61, 65, 253, 254, 300, 304–5, 320, 348
  birth 59–60
  continuation of Prince's annuity to after mother's death 420
  later years and death 424
  literary career 321
  and mother's *Memoirs* 260, 268, 269, 415
  nursing of mother during final months 396
  publishing of mother's poems 422
  The Shrine of Bertha 321–2, 323
  suspected consumption 262–3
Robinson, Mary
  ACTING CAREER 1, 20–1
  benefits 82, 84–5, 87
  breeches roles 87–8
  debut role as Juliet at Drury Lane 75, 76–81
  decision to marry and relinquish early hopes of 30, 33
  family disapproval 90
  flourishing of 117
  last performance and retirement 126
  meeting with Garrick and tutoring of by 24, 25–6, 75
  patronage of by Duchess of Devonshire 75, 89
  Perdita role and royal command performance *89*, 100–1, 105–9
  reactivating of 73–4
  reviews 80–1, 82, 84, 87, 98, 100, 117–18, 126
  roles played at Drury Lane 81, 83, 84–5, 86–8, 98–101, 117–18, 125–6
  and Sheridan 95–6
  LITERARY CAREER 2, 16, 232, 254–5, 260
  'Anecdotes of Distinguished Personages' 382
  Angelina 90–1, 290, 335–9
  autobiographical details in works 356, 364–5
  bad press and feelings of failure at 326
  criticism of by anti-Jacobin critics 354–5
  earnings from 300, 320, 358
  essays on 'Society and Manners in the Metropolis of England' 396, 399–401
  The False Friend 330, 364–8, 371
  favourite themes in works 353
  Hubert de Sevrac 347–8
  influence of opium in novels 290
  influence of Wollstonecraft 351
  interest in conflict between reason and passion 367
  international success 341, 352
  Jasper 270, 401–2
  joint work with Tarleton (*History of the Campaigns*) 253, 254, 257
  A Letter to the Women of England 16, 84, 212, 351, 369–71, 378
  literary acquaintances 348–50
  Memoirs see Memoirs of the Late Mrs Robinson, Written by Herself
  The Natural Daughter 372–6
  Nobody 325, 328, 330–4
  and opera *Kate of Aberdeen* 309–10
  patronage of by Duchess of Devonshire 17, 69–70
  political commentary in novels 296

pseudonyms written under 2, 267, 358, 369, 378
radicalism of 344, 355
regarded as key literary figure 371–2
remaking of herself as 'philosophical' author 356–7
reviews 298–300, 337, 347–8
revival of interest in works of in 1990s 424–5
The Sicilian Lover 335, 339–41, 362
Sylphid essays 381–2
Vancenza; or, the Dangers of Credulity 293–7, 298–300, 320
Walsingham 221–2, 274, 290, 321, 347, 352–6, 358–9, 360, 369, 426
The Widow, or a Picture of Modern Times 188, 316–20
writing of *Memoirs* 3, 382–3
POETRY 2, 16, 50, 174
admiration of Wordsworth 383
Ainsi va le Monde 182–4, 272, 280
'All Alone' 384
Captivity, a Poem; And Celadon and Lydia, a Tale 69, 84
as a celebrity poet 312–13
contributions to monthly magazines 388–9
contributions to *Morning Post* 334, 352, 378, 410
and Della Cruscans 267–8, 273–4, 344
and emotional state whilst in Brighton 268–9
engaged with Coleridge as 'poetical correspondent' for *Morning Post* 357–8
as 'English Sappho' 280, 344, 345, 360–1
on fashion 209–10
'Harvest Home' 410
'The Haunted Beach' 270, 380, 411, 412
influence of opium 285–6, 288, 289–90
'Jasper' 379–80
'The Lascar' 385
'Letter to a Friend on leaving Town' 67–8
'London's Summer Morning' 23
Lyrical Tales 65, 358, 383, 384–6, 393, 398, 399, 414–15
'The Maniac' 285–6, 287, 288–9, 414
on Marie Antoinette 309, 312
Modern Manners 312–13
'Ode to Apathy' 289
'Ode to Health' 289
'Ode to the Nightingale' 281
'Ode to Rapture' 235
'Ode to Valour' 281–2, 364
and *Oracle* 267, 274, 311–12
Poems by Mrs Robinson (1775) 66–8
Poems by Mrs Robinson (1791) 275–9, 280–2
Poems by Mrs Robinson (1793) 289, 305–7, 314–16
poems for *Oracle* 300, 302–3
poems written for Coleridge 412–14
Poetical Works 282, 361–2, 422
poetry editor of *Morning Post* 278, 396
'The Poet's Garret' 289–90
'The Poor, Singing Dame' 385–6
'The Progress of Liberty' 342–3, 371

Robinson, Mary – *cont.*
POETRY – *cont.*
publishing of lyrics in *The World* under name of 'Laura' 264–5, 266
publishing of poems by daughter after death 422
reviews 272, 280–1, 313, 315–16
Sappho and Phaon 344–6
Sight, The Cavern of Woe, and Solitude 311
'The Snow Drop' 359–60
'Sonnet to the Evening' 258
sonnet to the Prince of Wales 308
'Stanzas in Season' 240
'Stanzas to a Friend, who desired to have my Portrait' 305–7
'Stanzas Written between Dover and Calais' 302–3
'Tabitha Bramble' poetic persona 358
Valentine's Day poem 297–8
written in final months 410
PERSONAL LIFE
and abandoned corpse incident 269–70, 285
admirers and suitors 26, 49–50, 52, 54, 92–5, 96–7, 172
affair with Fox 2, 196–7, 199–200
affair with Lauzun 175–6
affair with Malden 37, 119, 120, 122, 134, 138, 142, 144, 145, 192, 193–4
affair and relationship with Prince of Wales 1, 3, 110–13, 114–15, 117, 119, 122–3, 124–5, 131–2, 134, 136, 326, 392
affair and relationship with Tarleton 190, 193, 211, 212, 214, 222–3, 235, 251–2, 253–4, 270, 293, 297, 300, 305, 313, 324, 344, 350
ambivalence felt towards father 15
appearance 10, 17, 21, 133
arrest and held in custody due to debts 389–90
attacks on by caricaturists and pamphleteers *108*, 136–7, *140*, *156*, 188, 197, 198, 217–18, *218*, 219, 220–1, 224–5, 231–2, 234, 238, 242–5, 246, 261
attempt to seduce by Lyttelton 50, 51, 52, 54, 55–6
attempted abduction of by Fitzgerald 54
bankruptcy and auctioning of belongings 169, 247
in Bath 283–4, 285, 335
beauty and attributes 24, 34, 44, 187, 212, 215
birth 8–9, 429–30
birth of daughter 34, 59–60
birth and death of second daughter 83
caring for daughter when ill with suspected consumption 262–3
carriages 195, 210–11, 223–4
celebrity of 1–2, 129–30, 133, 179, 215
character 29, 199, 392
childhood and upbringing 10, 13, 20, 36
connection with Dr James Graham 219
correspondence with Godwin in final months 405–8
correspondence with King and publication of 37–42, 55, 56, 68–9, 150–1, 271

courtship with and engagement to Robinson 26–9
death and burial 229, 416–17
and death of father 255
and death of mother 312
in debtors' prison with husband 64–5, 68
devotion to daughter and upbringing of 62, 64, 65
dress and fashion innovator and icon 27–8, 48, 155, 170, 178–9, 190–1, 203–9, 214, 378–9, 401
education 11, 12–13, 16–17, 19, 20, 257
and education of women 339, 353, 371, 425
and election campaign (1784) 239–43, 245, 370
encounter with Brereton 92–5
ending of affair with Malden and annuity arrangement 194–5
ending of affair with Prince of Wales 139–42, 144–5
ending of relationship with Tarleton 350–1, 368
feminist sentiments 368–71
financial problems and debts 144, 158, 161, 169, 232, 245, 247, 300, 325, 326, 351, 389, 409
forged letters published between Prince and 151–2
in France 170, 171–8
and French Revolution 272, 291–2, 292–3
friendship with Godwin 342–3, 372, 405
grave 425–7
and husband's family 42–5, 58–9, 60
and husband's financial affairs and debts 37, 56–7
ill-health 351, 377, 387, 404, 411
influence on taste 209
lameness and immobility after 'accident' 232, 235, 247, 253–4, 257, 283, 326, 381
and Marie Antoinette 173–5, 291–2
marriage and relationship with Robinson 30–1, 32–3, 34–5, 41, 52–3, 83, 92, 136, 155–6, 211
negotiations over Prince's love letters and eventual payoff 161–7
negotiations with Prince over bond and payment of annuity 216, 230–1, 235, 326, 387, 390
obituary of in *Morning Post* 419–20
Opera House box 213–14, 215, 234
and opium 284, 285, 328
parental background 9, 257
pen-portrait of in *Public Characters* by Godwin 391–2
politics and political campaigner 2, 218, 219, 239–42, 259
portrait of by Hoppner 188–9, 208, 214–15, 346, 425
portraits of by Gainsborough 2, 168–9, 186, 192
portraits of by Reynolds 21, 184, 186–7, 192, 232–3, 346, 392
portraits of by Romney 167–8, 186, 192
press hostility towards 37, 134–5, 136–8, 154, 160–1
press interest and publicity surrounding affair with Prince of Wales 128–30

Robinson, Mary – *cont.*
PERSONAL LIFE – *cont.*
relationship with her servants 121–2
residences in London 46–7, 82, 131–2, 194, 313–14, 379
resides at Aix-la-Chapelle 253–4, 256
resides at St Amand les Eaux 257–8
retirement to Englefield Cottage and final months 395–7
return to Bristol and homecoming 35–6
rheumatic fever 228–9, 234, 246, 247, 254, 392
ride to Dover in pursuit of Tarleton and 'accident' 1, 227–30
rivalry with Armistead 147–8, 149
self-promotion 23, 192, 222
social life and circle in London 47–51, 62–3, 95
social philosophy 342–3
supporters of 135–6, 138–9
travels on Continent 251–9, 260, 302, 303–4
treatment of in *Rambler's Magazine* 217, 244
wit 179, 212
Robinson, Sophia (daughter) 83
Robinson, Thomas (husband) 36, 155–6, 304
arrest of and imprisonment 61–2, 63–4
courtship with Mary and engagement 26–9
in debtors prison and discharge 71, 72
financial affairs and debts 47, 52, 53, 56, 56–7, 60, 63, 73, 158
infidelities 52–3, 56, 71,, 87, 93–4, 123, 136
lies over origins and inheritance 33
living in London 47, 51
marriage to and relationship with Mary 30–1, 32, 33, 34–5, 35, 41
opposition to Mary's acting career 29–30
visits to father 42–5, 92
'Robinson Vest' 208
Robinson, William (brother of Thomas) 304–5
Romney, George 2, 155, 167–8, 186
Rousseau, Jean-Jacques 318
Rowlandson, Thomas 253
Royal Academy of Arts 182
exhibition (1782) 191–2
Royal Legend, The 421
Runaway, The 84

St Amand les Eaux (Flanders) 257–8
St Leger, Colonel 148
Sappho 344, 345
Sappho and Phaon 344–6
Satire on the Present Times, A (pamphlet) 136–7
Saunders, Dr Erasmus 30
School for Scandal, The (pamphlet) 243–4
School for Scandal, The (play) 82, 243
Search after Happiness, The 12
Seys, Richard 392
She Stoops to Conquer 207
Shelburne, Lord 196, 197, 215
Shelley, Mary 343, 351
Frankenstein 353

Sheridan, Richard Brinsley 243, 291, 400
friendship with Mary 83, 95–6
and Mary's acting career 79, 86
Mary's letter to begging for money 300–1
political career 97, 105, 125
running of Drury Lane 83
views of female education 84
Sherwin, John Keyes 132–3
Shrine of Bertha, The 321, 323
Sicilian Lover, The 335, 339–41, 362
Siddons, Sarah 12, 310–11, 327–8, 329
Sight, The Cavern of Woe, and Solitude 311
slave trade 271
smallpox 10
Smith, Charlotte 64, 345, 424
Smith, William 'Gentleman' 107
Smollett, Tobias *Humphry Clinker* 358
'Snow Drop, The' 359–60
Society of Merchant Venturers 7–8, 13
'Sonnet to the Evening' 258
Southampton, Lord 164
Southey, Robert 8, 358, 378, 379
Spa 303
Stanley, Charlotte 155
'Stanzas in Season' 240
'Stanzas to a Friend, who desired to have my Portrait' 305–7
'Stanzas Written between Dover and Calais' 302–3
Stephens, Catherine 424
Stuart, Daniel 334, 357–8, 360, 379, 410
Suicide, The 86
Suspicious Husband, The 87
Sylphid essays 381–2
Tarleton, Colonel Banastre 196, 394
affair and relationship with Mary 190, 193, 211, 212, 214, 222–3, 235, 251–2, 253–4, 270, 293, 297, 300, 305, 313, 324, 344, 350
and American War of Independence 180–1
appearance and physique 180
background 180
caricatures of 197–8
death 422
debts 222, 223, 225
ending of relationship with Mary 350–1, 368
as fashion innovator 210
and gambling 214, 223, 257, 262, 323, 351
History of the Campaigns 253, 254, 257
leaves England for France to escape debtors 1, 227, 230
marriage to Susan Bertie 362–3, 422
political career 271, 344
portrait of by Reynolds 184, 185–6, 192
press criticism of 362
promotion to Major General 322, 328
returns from France and resumes affair with Mary 235
rheumatic fever 309
vilified in pamphlets by Pigott 323–4
Tarleton, Jane (mother) 223, 225
Tarleton, John (brother) 251–2
Tate, Nahum 25
Taylor, John 40–1, 274, 311, 316, 325, 328, 356, 357
Temple of Health and Hymen 219

theatre 75–6
costumes 79
view of actresses 88–9
see also Drury Lane theatre
Theatre Royal (Covent Garden) 21, 105
Theatre Royal Drury Lane *see* Drury Lane theatre
Thrale, Hester 12, 273
'To the Poet Coleridge' 413–14
Topham, Captain Edward 266
Town and Country Magazine 120, 143–4
Townshend, Lord John 259
Trip to Scarborough, A 81–2
Twelfth Night 99
Twiss, Francis 343

Valentia, Lord 50–1
Vancenza; or, the Dangers of Credulity 293–7, 298–300, 320
Vauxhall pleasure gardens 253
Veigel, Eva Maria 24
Vis-à-Vis of Berkley-Square, The (pamphlet) 224–5

Wales, Prince of (later George IV) 106, 144–5, 246–7, 261, 424
affair with Elizabeth Armistead 141, 142, 150, 153
affair with Fitzherbert 255, 326
affair and relationship with Mary 1, 3, 110–13, 114–15, 117, 119, 122–3, 124–5, 131–2, 134, 136, 326, 392
agreement to marry Caroline of Brunswick 326
appearance and nature 106–7, 131
assures bond to Mary 123–4, 125, 215, 230
attends royal command performance of *Florizel and Perdita* and meets Mary 106, 107–10, 110–11
caricatures of *108*, 137–8, *140*, *156*, 217–18
correspondence with Mary Hamilton 110–11, 111–13, 114, 115–16
ending of affair with Mary 139–42, 144–5
and Fox 196, 215
health 149
love letters to Mary 1, 37, 113, 117, 118, 119, 123–4
Mary's sonnet to 308
negotiations with Mary over bond and payment of annuity 216, 230–1, 235, 326, 387, 390
negotiations over return of love letters 161–7
and politics 131, 308–9
press interest and publicity surrounding affair with Mary 128–30
rebellion against father 131, 148–9
relationship with Mary after ending of affair 262
separation from Caroline 346
Walpole, Charlotte 98
Walpole, Horace 7, 126, 200
Walsingham 221–2, 274, 290, 321, 347, 352–6, 358–9, 360, 369, 426
Way to Keep Him, The 389
Weale, Elizabeth 416, 424
Whig Club; or, a Sketch of Modern Patriotism (pamphlet) 323–4
Whigs 131, 195–6, 290–1
Widow, or a Picture of Modern Times, The 188, 316–20
Wild Wreath, The 422, 424

Willis, Francis 260
Wilmot, Harriet 52–3
Wolcot, John (Peter Pindar) 192, 274, 328, 415, 423
Wollstonecraft, Mary 3, 296, 339, 343, 348–9
  death 351, 368
  influence on Mary's writing 351
  Maria, or the Wrongs of Woman 336
  marriage to Godwin 351
  review of *Hubert de Sevrac* 347–8
  Vindication of the Rights of Woman 291, 339, 354
Wordsworth, William 23, 264, 383, 384–5, 411
  Lyrical Ballads 383, 384
  'The Mad Mother' 383
  The Prelude 23
  'The Solitude of Binnorie' 411
  'We are Seven' 384
World, The 264, 264–5, 266
Wray, Sir Cecil 238
Wyndham, Charles 148

Yates, Mary Ann 81
Yea, Lady Julia 51
York, Duke of *see* Frederick, Duke of York